Also by Russell Baker

Growing Up

The Good Times

The Rescue of Miss Yaskell

So This Is Depravity

There's a Country in My Cellar

The Norton Book of Light Verse (editor)

An American in Washington

No Cause for Panic

All Things Considered

Our Next President

Poor Russell's Almanac

Russell Baker's
book of
American Humor

Russell Baker's Book of American Humor

Edited by Russell Baker

W·W·Norton & Company·New York·London

Library of Congress Cataloging-in-Publication Data
Book of American humor
Russell Baker's book of American humor / edited by Russell Baker.
p. cm.
Includes bibliographical references and index.
1. American wit and humor. I. Baker, Russell, 1925–
II. Title.
PN6157.B66 1993
818'.02—dc20   93-22733

ISBN 0-393-03592-1
W.W. Norton & Company, Inc., 500 Fifth Avenue, New York, N.Y. 10110
W.W. Norton & Company Ltd., 10 Coptic Street, London WC1A 1PU
1 2 3 4 5 6 7 8 9 0

Contents*

*Selection titles appearing in quotation marks are the original titles; those without quotation marks have been devised by the editor for this volume.

SECTION THREE: THE HUMAN MUDDLE

SECTION FOUR: THIS SEX PROBLEM

SECTION FIVE: PARODY, BURLESQUE, CRITICISM, AND PAIN

SECTION SIX: FAMILY LIFE

SECTION SEVEN: GEOGRAPHICAL SNEERS

SECTION EIGHT: POLITICS AND PATRIOTS

SECTION NINE: MEDIA

SECTION TEN: FABLE, LORE, AND FANTASY

SECTION ELEVEN: LOOKING BACK

SECTION TWELVE: A GNASHING OF HUMORISTS

INTRODUCTION

I came to Mark Twain's *Tragedy of Pudd'nhead Wilson* late in life and raced through it in two days, which is rare speed for me. I was totally engrossed. It is late Twain. He is edging toward contempt for the universe, but he's not there yet. Hannibal, the town of glorious childhood, has become Dawson's Landing, where a man of wit and intelligence is cast out as a fool.

It's about slavery. The plot is jerry-built, creaky, and based on the old mixed-up-twins story. There are implausible Italian visitors, Luigi and Angelo, whom I took to be Italian rather than, say, Russian or Turkish, only because Mark Twain had probably traveled in Italy and fallen in love with it. They do, however, serve to make the silly dueling, which is essential to the plot, slightly plausible.

Implausibility and melodrama are rampant. There is a villain so despicable that he sells his own mother down the river. At the end Twain faces the exquisitely difficult problem of portraying the psychological and social adjustments that would have to be made by a man who has grown up as a black slave and suddenly learns that he is white and free. Twain deals with this problem by not dealing with it at all. He simply lets the whole matter slide, as though he can't wait to be finished with the damned book.

It is by many definitions a bad book, yet it is marvelous. A couldn't-put-it-down page turner. Mark Twain is the most readable of writers even when not in top form.

I set all this down with considerable amusement at my own presumption. It shows how wondrously a man's self-esteem may increase after he has been forty or fifty years out of school. Here am I, overly full of years and self, taking the liberty of criticizing Mark Twain as though he were human.

Still, it has done my mind a world of good. Scowling at the imperfections of *Pudd'nhead Wilson* made me realize how thoroughly *The New Yorker* magazine had shaped my notion of what constitutes quality in a humorist and encouraged me to reflect that perhaps I had become starchy, maybe even cranky, on the subject. I am speaking now of Harold Ross's *New Yorker,* the magazine of James Thurber, Robert Benchley, E. B. White, and S. J. Perelman with the elegant editing of Ross himself, Katharine S. White, and William Shawn. I thought that if Mark Twain had submitted *Pudd'nhead* to that *New Yorker,* he would have got back one of those polite notes in which editors say that while there is much to admire in your manuscript, they are afraid it's just not for them.

And there is the nub of the matter: Mark Twain was not for *The New Yorker* and not simply because the magazine didn't exist in Twain's time. Mark Twain was not for *The New Yorker* for the same reason that James Thurber was not for the *National Lampoon.*

Two very different strands run through American humor, and while I refuse to stoop to saying, "Never the twain shall meet," the truth is that they usually don't. Defining them to a graduate student's satisfaction would produce ten yards of academic prose ponderous enough to buckle a mule's knees, so I won't try it. The distinctions may be easier to grasp if we keep in mind why Mark Twain and *The New Yorker* would not have made a happy marriage.

Twain was western, *The New Yorker* eastern. Twain came out of nineteenth-century frontier culture, meaning a world with no memory older than last week. *The New Yorker,* though modern as skirts above the knee, represented an Atlantic seaboard culture with a memory that reached back to a time when Americans were colonials and considered themselves English. With a little streamlining, Benjamin Franklin's "Silence Dogood" humor columns of 1728 would have been right at home in *The New Yorker.* In the *Spectator* pieces of Joseph Addison and Richard Steele, Englishmen writing in the early 1700s, you see a couple of embryonic *New Yorker* staff writers.

I don't want to overstate the case. *The New Yorker* has conditioned me to eschew overstatement. If fancy easterners of post-Civil War America considered Twain a rustic vulgarian, the quality folk of Europe adored him. Oxford gave him a degree. Distinguished English writers like Robert Browning, Lewis Carroll, and Anthony Trollope wanted to be introduced when he came to Britain.

The trouble at home was America's long-cultivated sense of inferiority to everything European. In the overstuffed parlors of striving nineteenth-century America he was a potential embarrassment. You could never be sure he wouldn't say something to embarrass the whole family when you had the preacher in for Sunday dinner.

Twain's was the voice of the country's frontier newness, brashness, vigor, disdain for the polite and genteel. It was a voice that enjoyed shocking the squeamish, mocking the piously upright, and laughing at the earnest fraudulence so deeply embedded in American life. The problem, of course, was that America was painfully insecure about frontier vigor and newness. Even Abraham Lincoln's frontier humor seemed to embarrass more Americans than it entertained.

In a country that had started putting on fancy airs, unpolished humor seemed to menace hopes for creating a high culture. Henry James, yearning for the sublime, wrote, with an exquisitely delicate touch of contempt, "In the day of Mark Twain, there is no harm in being reminded that the absence of drollery may, at a stretch, be compensated by the presence of sublimity."

What stuffy nineteenth-century Americans deplored in Twain were the qualities that critics still deplore as "bad taste." "Bad taste" has been applied to the nightclub humor of Lenny Bruce, the television humor of "Saturday Night Live," the movie humor of comedians like Mae West and W. C. Fields, and the comic-strip humor of Garry Trudeau, among thousands of others.

"Rude," "coarse," and "vulgar" are the words commonly used to justify a "bad taste" verdict against humor, and they were often applicable to Mark Twain. "Rude" usually means nothing more shocking than "shows no respect for authority and convention," while "coarse" and "vulgar" mean pretty much the same thing with the added suggestion that the disrespectful party is also an untutored lout.

Mark Twain apparently felt so vulnerable to nice-Nelly criticism that he even let his wife occasionally purge his work of what she considered vulgarities. How the East's stiflingly insecure society must have weighed him down. Blessed with divine gifts, yet he so yearned for respectability that he took advice from wife and editor when they cautioned him not to let Huckleberry Finn utter that vulgar word "hell."

What would have happened had he fallen under the power of *The New Yorker*'s editors with their institutional contempt for the old lady from Dubuque? Hannibal, after all, is just a hundred miles or so downriver from Dubuque.

I mean *The New Yorker* no harm by suggesting it would never have got along with America's preeminent humorist. As the pieces in this book suggest, the magazine more or less defined American humor for a good third of the present century. It was the citified eastern voice of an America which, culturally, had begun to leave Europe behind. With *The New Yorker* American humor began to master the arts of understatement, to refine the crudities of old-fashioned burlesque into satire, to treasure subtlety and wit, things European humor seemed to have done forever. Very quickly, however, *The New Yorker* was doing them better.

For two generations after Harold Ross started his magazine in 1925 it was the home office of American humor. Every high school wit yearning for glory dreamed of being published there, and some of the funniest people who ever wrote the American language actually were. Ross changed the language of American humor as Ernest Hemingway, his contemporary, changed the language of American fiction. Both wanted a language rid of ornate fuss and fretwork, a more economical English in which every word counted, every sentence carried weight. The contagious idea that less is more was in the air, and Ross and Hemingway both seem to have caught it.

In *The New Yorker* this led to a humor of precision. It was vital to find the one word that was exactly right. Writers had to stay within the framework of their original conceit, which meant they no longer enjoyed the freedom to wander away from the subject and browse elsewhere as Mark Twain used to do, sometimes with great effect. In Robert Benchley, Ross was blessed with a humorist who always seemed to be wandering away for a browse far off the premises, and the astonishing brevity with which Benchley managed to make his ridiculous excursions not only upheld the principle of less-as-more but also seemed to satirize the woolgathering of oldfangled essayists.

Mind you, I do not insist that this is what Benchley was consciously up to. I don't know what Benchley was consciously up to, and maybe he didn't either, and it doesn't matter because the result was so totally and satisfyingly absurd.

Harold Ross's triumph encouraged American humorists to concentrate on producing small, highly polished gems. Though a few of the magazine's stars like Peter DeVries also wrote comic novels, what made it special were its short humor sketches, short stories in the style of James Thurber, the flawlessly casual essay style set by E. B. White, and S. J. Perelman's hilariously savage but always meticulously wrought assaults on the frauds of American life. The ultimate *New Yorker* product is Thurber's "The Secret Life of Walter Mitty." Because it comes as near perfection as it is possible to reach without poetry, I include it in this book, violating my policy decision to leave out everything you might find overly familiar. Even if you have read it before, you've probably forgotten how good it is. Try it again.

The New Yorker doesn't count for so much in the humor business these days. It is the children of the frontier, vulgar and insolent, shocking and rude, who seem to be in charge again. They live a million light-years from Thurber, White, Benchley, and Perelman. The totemic magazine of the new era has been *National Lampoon.* Writers who grew up working on it, or just loving it, now set the standards of what's funny, and what's funny nowadays would have got an even cooler reception than Mark Twain at the old *New Yorker.*

The wit is as subtle as a bladder slapped across the buttocks. The language is blue. The jokes are leers. Crude insult passes as satire. And often, as old *Lampoon* addicts and "Saturday Night Live" fans know, the ham-fisted assault of it all can be irresistibly funny.

You can propound dozens of explanations for the change. The courts have ended old taboos on crude language and expanded the public's right to abuse practically everybody. The collapse of public education was bound to end the demand for highly literate humor. There has been a breakdown in the American social contract. And so on. I prefer to think that there are cycles in American culture and that the old frontier tradition has simply come around again in humor, just as it has in gunplay. At its worst, today's humor makes you fearful about what may happen to the kiddies if you don't take them away from all this. At its best, it gives us most of the elements that produced Mark Twain. As those spoiled twerps in the beer commercial say, it doesn't get any better than that.

There is a minor third strand in American humor, which is neither frontier and rude nor citified and elegant. It is the territory of the professional joke-smiths. These are the writers who churn out laughs for the mass market. If once humor came naturally and easily to them, it does so no longer. They are toilers laboring in the funniness factory.

Working in platoons, they grind out the nightly supply of jokes with which your favorite late-night television "host" convulses you just before bedtime. They "doctor" troubled plays by adding laugh lines before Broadway openings. They invent yokkers for movies that star supposedly funny men who are often just glum neurotics. They play nightclubs using their own material, or maybe somebody else's at times. It's no fun being a jokesmith. It's hard labor, seven days a week, always struggling to keep the joke production line turning out an unbroken flow of mechanically engineered thigh slappers. The demand for laughs never lets up on them. They write newspaper columns. I think of them as poor wretches, though they are ridiculously overpaid.

The pieces collected here include samples of all three strands cited above, and quite a few hybrids. I leave it to you to classify them, if you are a classifying kind of person. If not, it doesn't matter. They don't exist to be classified, but only to make you laugh, or at least smile, or maybe just feel a little more interior warmth despite "the situation," which has been bleak ever since the cave dwellers organized things and shows no signs of improving. Humor is not supposed to make you forget that "the situation" is bleak, just to make the bleakness a little easier to tolerate.

It is entirely possible that you do not laugh or even smile at the same things I laugh and smile at and that what makes the world more tolerable for you would make me scream for mercy. A sense of humor is a highly idiosyncratic piece of equipment, like a taste for fast food. I am forever amazed that people can stomach the typical fast-food hamburger, yet I cannot get enough fast-food fried chicken soaked in well-aged grease and exuding the promise of a night rich in heartburn.

All I can say for these selections is that they are mine, and I like them all, and they wouldn't be here if I didn't. Some, let me hasten to add, I like better than others. One or two just barely made it on my faint-smile meter but got included anyhow for personal reasons. For instance? Well, Edgar Allan Poe's strong point is the crypt rather than the funny bone, so I couldn't resist "The Angel of the Odd." I was too delighted by the discovery that Poe had even tried his hand at humor. Best of all, if like me, you had grown up in Baltimore with tales about Poe's fatal election night of boozing, it was a story about a man far gone in wine. Irresistible!

A warning: Do not try reading this book from cover to cover. Except for computer manuals and high school operetta, there is nothing more deadening to the spirit than an uninterrupted diet of humor. I speak as an expert, having tried while assembling this book to read everything funny published in America since Captain John Smith said that people who don't work don't deserve to eat.

When you are creeping through the literary underbrush hoping to bag a piece of humor with your net, nothing seems funny. The thing works the other way around. Humor is funny when it sneaks up on you and takes you by surprise. When you stalk it through libraries and bookshops, reading, reading, reading, and always asking yourself, "Is this piece funny or not?" the effect is narcotic. At first you want never again to be faced with anything some writer thought funny. Then, after you have forced yourself to do it anyhow, your mind refuses to cooperate and a half hour later you wake up, chin on chest, drooling into your shirt.

Surprise and freshness are what make humor a delight. Many of the pieces here turned out to be ones I remembered having surprised and delighted me long ago. Many other pieces that once surprised and delighted are, sadly, not here. Humor is famous for its short shelf life. What convulsed Granddad is now mostly too quaint to read beyond the opening paragraph. A lot of the wit that was hilarious when Kennedy was president now just sits there mocking our youthful standards. Did we really think Vaughn Meader's mimicry of the Kennedy voice was funny?

I remember grown-ups laughing robustly at Will Rogers when I was a child. Touring his works as a grown-up myself left me baffled. What had been the secret of his success? The plain, mud-between-the-toes diction must have had something to do with it, but reading it now makes it seem dim, dated, and heavy going, as though you are in the hands of a country slicker doing his rube number on the gullible:

". . . there was nothing left to talk on."

"Now it ain't much of a speech. . . ."

"We got out of the state and we are so darn genrous that all we do is brag on the place where we are. . . ."

In the trade this is called cracker-barrel and used to be more popular than it is nowadays. Nowadays Americans seem to prefer everything, including humor, "in your face." I'm not sure what an American expects to have done "in your face" that is so entertaining, but I believe it is supposed to be something perfectly uncouth and therefore—such is the level of popular expectation here at the end of the century—exhilarating and delightful. Whatever it is, it's a long way from cracker-barrel.

Most humorists can anticipate ending up as sadly as Will Rogers, if sadness is simply a matter of having your work judged unfunny by the next generation. Rogers, of course, needs no tears. As a star of Broadway and Hollywood, he made millions, or the Depression equivalent thereof, which was even better because it was practically tax-free, and enjoyed the admiration of an entire generation.

Most humorists will have to settle for ending up more sadly than that. While putting this book together, I looked through E. B. and Katharine S. White's *A Subtreasury of American Humor*. It was published in 1941 and has ever since been considered a monument of the genre. Besides looking for something to filch, I was curious to see how many of their selections had survived time's brutal way with humorists. It was dispiriting. I judge that as many as half the eight hundred pages of humor that delighted America a mere half century ago would leave many readers today wondering what the Whites ever saw funny in them.

It is the other half, resistant to time's withering, that gradually gets taken up and admitted to the status of literature (Minor Works Division) and assigned as college reading, which is another form of death.

Several of the writers I have included here have reached this stage, and I urge the reader whose school experience may have poisoned his attitude toward these old-timers to give them at least a try. Senior among the group here are Benjamin Franklin and Washington Irving. Franklin's whimsical advice for getting rid of tiresome callers is modern newspaper humor-column stuff of a very high order. Irving's satire on a New York election seems as up-to-date now as it was two hundred years ago.

On balance, however, I have been ruthless with old-timers of literary stature if they seemed likely to put you to sleep. Many of them, working in the nineteenth century, wrote dialect humor, which is nearly impenetrable to a modern reader. Except for Finley Peter Dunne ("Mr. Dooley") and a couple of others whose Civil War satires seem as bitterly up-to-date as recent satires on the Vietnam War, the dialect crowd is not here. I take a particularly malicious delight in omitting James Russell Lowell's *Biglow Papers*. Encountering these in college many years ago, I swore to have my vengeance though it should take me a lifetime. I am pleased to do so now.

Henry Seidel Canby has tried to explain the nineteenth-century passion for dialect humor as a class phenomenon, and he is persuasive. This theory holds that Americans were not amused by social criticism from people who struck them as members of the elite. From somebody who talked like a hayseed, however, it registered as funny and was easy to take. In short, the dialect humorists were posing as hicks who were blessed with natural folk wisdom.

Disguised as a rustic Socrates who had flunked spelling and grammar, the dialect humorist could say a great deal that the public wouldn't have tolerated from a voice that sounded college-educated. This is something like the tradition of the king's fool, who was permitted to sass Majesty because he was presumed to be . . . well, a fool.

Even today the humorist with something controversial on his mind often puts it in the mouth of fictional fools invented to preserve his cover. H. L. Mencken, who preferred not to hide his highly interesting views under fool's cover, infuriated so many people with his forthright style that to this day Americans refuse to concede that he was a superb humorist. My prejudice in this matter explains Mencken's presence in this book as well as the absence of *The Biglow Papers.*

I have also omitted some extremely good pieces on grounds that they have been anthologized half to death. Though some of them, like Ring Lardner's baseball stories, are wonderful, I assume that you have already read them several times or, if not, that you are bound to stumble into them elsewhere before you get much older.

"Well," someone testy will say, "I notice you haven't bothered to omit yourself." In my defense, I'd like to point out that a humor collector who has spared the reader not only *The Biglow Papers* but also Sut Lovingood deserves to be forgiven for displaying just a little of his own work.

A book like this must necessarily omit a great many things you might like to find here. Cartoons are an art unto themselves and need their own fuller-size display case. Shrinking them to conventional book-page sizes simply destroys their impact.

I also omit almost all performance humor. If it can't exert its full charm on the printed page but needs an actor, a comedian, scenery, music, props, or film to make it work right, it's not here. This means you won't find your favorite television or radio comedian here, or that uproarious piece of business Bob Hope did in that wonderful movie with Bing Crosby, or those patter songs Danny Kaye used to reel off when he was on Broadway.

I love performance humor, but it is impossible to make it rise out of cold print and come to life without the help of the comedians who created it. A Jack Benny script without Jack Benny voice and pauses and timing loses everything—to wit, Jack Benny. Fred Allen's "Senator Claghorn" was terribly funny, but to work it needs a fraudulently bombastic voice suggestive of a Bible Belt snake-oil salesman, and this book, alas, lacks a sound system.

The Bob and Ray radio script included here succeeds as pure written humor because it does not need distinctive voices to enhance it. It sounds just as good to the eye as it must have sounded to the ear when Bob Elliott and Ray Goulding first did it on radio, whereas a piece of performance comedy that seemed hilarious when done by, say, W. C. Fields, loses its zip without Fields's voice to deliver it. In *My Little Chickadee,* for instance, there is a scene in which Fields is about to be lynched outside a western saloon. He is asked if he has a last request before being hanged.

Yes, says Fields, he'd like to see Paris before he dies. The mob, unamused, calls for the hangman to get on with it and string him up, and as the noose is tightened, Fields says, ''Philadelphia will do.''

That's my idea of funny, but if you can't hear Fields say it, it's not funny at all, is it?

Enough. Let's get on with trying to tolerate the bleakness.

SECTION ONE

COMICAL-TRAGICAL
TALES

*Here are some stories from the dark side of life. They are about greed,
arrogance, hatred, vengeance, and death. A marriage is doomed. Mr. Kaplan
suffers a humiliation. To the humorist this grim material is the stuff of
laughter, proving that whether you laugh or cry depends entirely on
perspective. Oscar Wilde said of one of Charles Dickens's famously sad death
scenes, it takes "a heart of stone to read the death of Little Nell without
laughing." Wilde's life was tragic, but his perspective humorous.*

*O. Henry's "Confessions of a Humorist" is included here as a warning to
all who think they might enjoy life in the humor trade. O. Henry wrote from
cruel experience. He began his career writing and publishing a humor weekly in
Texas. You will find some samples of that early work later in this book.*

*About the word "humorist": Reviewing a Ring Lardner book, Dorothy
Parker wrote that it demeaned the literary importance of a superb writer to call
Lardner a "humorist." Lardner didn't seem to agree. He once said that for a
writer to call himself "a humorist" betrayed a shameful lack of modesty, "like
a baseball player calling himself 'a great shortstop.'"*

NUNNALLY JOHNSON

"Clothes Make the Man"

When the creditors finally threw the Aragon into bankruptcy, the receivers appointed a man named Caldwell to operate the place until they could unravel its finances. This Caldwell was something. For one thing, he dressed much better than was necessary, even for a hotel manager. For another, he seriously thought of himself as an "efficiency engineer," and he had hardly got his hat off before he had the whole establishment completely demoralized with a whirlwind campaign of economizing on blotters, soap ends, slightly used lettuce leaves, last year's phone books, lost keys and bent coat hangers.

For still another, he decided that the entire character of the Aragon must be changed and its tone elevated. Years before, when it was first built, the Aragon had had a measure of class, but for a decade or more it had been one of Broadway's most contented flea bags—a bright and gilded rabbit warren inhabited by obsolete vaudeville performers, ancient song writers, one-client theatrical agents, nonproducing stage producers, and small-bore hustlers, of every age and police description. At seven o'clock of any evening, a good loud cry of "Thief!" would have emptied the lobby like a scene in Snow White and the Seven Dwarfs. Not that they were all guilty, of course—just nervous.

Every time Caldwell came out of his office and contemplated this motley crew of patrons, he shuddered. One and all, they must go, he decided, and be replaced with a clientele whose week's laundry might consist of something more than one shirt, one pair of socks and one change of underwear. What he had in mind was a good standard New York convention hotel, with a fair percentage of the guests wearing fezzes and smoking twenty-five-cent cigars. But it stood to reason that no delegation of nobles from North Attleboro was going to feel easy in a lobby peopled largely with men and women who looked like fugitives from an Edward G. Robinson picture.

The first step in this revolutionary program was not particularly difficult. Since 97¼ per cent of the Aragon's guests were anywhere from one week to ten months in arrears, and no prospects, they were chilled out in fairly short order; though, of course, at a cost. Those who, by some mad, fantastic freak of chance, were paid up had to be handled more delicately, but Caldwell had not majored in Hotel Offensiveness 2 in the School of Business, at Harvard, for nothing. No man is going to stand no towels in the bathroom indefinitely, and so, presently, the Aragon's new type of guest, from out of town, was managing to get through the lobby without figuring subconsciously on a good place to duck when the trouble started.

Such progress had been made, in fact, that Caldwell was beginning to fashion an opening for the third chapter of his autobiography: "Some critics of hotel administration have been kind enough to describe my conversion of the Aragon from a third-class tenderloin resort into the leading convention hostelry in America," and so on, when Mr. Enoch returned.

One way—the simplest—to account for the bloodcurdling distaste that Caldwell took for Mr. Enoch on sight would be to set it down as glandular—some poisonous secretion that welled up in him at the very thought of this gaudy gnome who beamed hopefully on one and all as he asked for his key and mail. Another would be to admit in all fairness that Mr. Enoch was, in appearance, a superb and flawless illustration of everything that Caldwell did not want to see in his hotel—or anywhere else, for that matter.

For, regarded squarely and without prejudice, Mr. Enoch was indeed a bit of a shocker. He looked like an oaf and was dressed like a Harlem hoofer. He wore a stiff-bosomed, horizontal-striped shirt and a voluminous cap of a pattern generally associated with the wallpaper in a small French hotel. His Miamian sports coat was belted, with a brass buckle—*très chic.* His overcoat was veritable polo straight out of Meadowbrook—unquestionably, by request—and four sizes too large. Mr. Enoch's face was round and bucolic, and his smile warm and simple and friendly, but what was that against a collection of haberdashery that would have staggered a Filipino?

The only coherent thought that came to Caldwell as, half stunned, he watched Mr. Enoch beam his way across the lobby and enter an elevator was that never in his life had he laid eyes on a man who reminded him less of Adolphe Menjou.

"This Enoch," he said to the bookkeeper that evening, "what about him?"

"Mr. Enoch?" The bookkeeper grinned. "A Number One. Oldest guest in the hotel—sixteen years—and pays right on the nose."

"What's he got?"

"Six-o-seven."

"How much?"

"Eighteen a week—one room."

"From now on, it's thirty," Caldwell said.

The bookkeeper stared. "That's quite a jump."

"All right," Caldwell said, "it's quite a jump."

"If you don't mind," the bookkeeper said presently, "I'd like to put you straight about Mr. Enoch. He isn't one of these Broadway turkeys. All the Broadway he ever sees is right here in this hotel, looking out of the window. He's a salesman—sells Smacko."

"Pardon?"

"Smacko," the bookkeeper repeated. "It's a candy bar, chocolate, full of nuts and raisins and something that looks and tastes like small lumps of coal. Most of the time he's on the road—keeps the room just the same—covering most of this side of the Mississippi. What I mean, he's quiet, keeps strictly in line at all times, tips a steady two bits, and if you had a whole hotel full of fellows like him, you'd never have another trouble in the world."

He paused, for at the thought of a whole hotel full of men dressed like Mr. Enoch, Boniface Caldwell had quivered like a boat struck by a torpedo.

"You see," the bookkeeper went on hurriedly, "He came to New York just about the time the Aragon opened, and because he was from a small town and didn't know there was any other part of New York but Broadway, nothing would do but he's got to get a room here, right in the heart of the bright lights."

"That cap he's wearing," Caldwell said coldly, "what's the idea of that?"

The bookkeeper chuckled. "We were kidding him about that getup once, me and the fellows at the desk, and afterward, over by the cigar counter, he kind of explained—funny as hell. The way he put it"—and the bookkeeper smiled reminiscently—"he said, 'You know what the truth is, Mr. Lawton?' I said, 'No. What?' He said, 'The fact of the case is, I like loud clothes! I like 'em and I don't care who knows it,' he said. 'They make me feel good. Give me a rich shirt or an outstanding suit of clothes or an overcoat that has character, and I am happy,' he said.

"I said, 'That's very interesting.' He said, 'I don't know about that, but you know why I like 'em?' I said, 'No. Why?' He said, 'The reason is that clothes like that give me confidence. They make me feel like somebody, and I need that feeling, Mr. Lawton, because naturally I just don't feel like anybody at all. That's the truth of the matter,' he said. 'If I was to be wearing a plain blue-serge suit, nobody in the world would pay the slightest bit of attention to me. Not that that would bother me, personally, because I never did mix much, but professionally, in my business, it's murder. Selling things, you have got to get their attention. I can't tell funny stories, I haven't got any accent, I never was able to rib, I can't do any of the things that the fellows usually do to jolly the account along, but the way I dress, that makes 'em notice.' And then he said, 'And besides, as I said before, I like clothes like these anyway.' "

The bookkeeper chuckled again, with sympathy and a kind of affectionate amusement.

"If you had sat down and calculated for a week," Caldwell said, "you couldn't have drawn me the portrait of a more unwinning character. From now on, the room's thirty-five."

The bookkeeper watched him until he was well out of earshot, and then he made a bubbling noise in his cheeks.

Thursday, the day Mr. Enoch's weekly bill was due, Caldwell made it his business to be conveniently near the cashier's window when his repulsive guest appeared, right on the nose, to get what he cheerfully described as the bad news. And bad it was, too, as the cashier regretfully admitted, for the new rate became effective immediately. He was still apologizing when Caldwell stepped up, steeling himself, for Mr. Enoch had exchanged his one-bushel cap for a little Tyrolean number, green, with a half-inch Manila-hemp band and a six-inch thistle to give it dash. Caldwell tried to keep his eyes away from it.

"Is there some difficulty?" he asked.

The cashier looked relieved. "This is Mr. Caldwell, our new manager, Mr. Enoch," and to Caldwell, "I was just explaining to Mr. Enoch the new rate—the—er—new conditions, I mean."

"Delighted to meet you, Mr. Caldwell."

"If Mr. Enoch is not satisfied with the terms we offer him—" Caldwell began coldly.

"Forget it!" Mr. Enoch cried affably, and Caldwell stiffened. "I'm one of the old-timers, Mr. Caldwell—one of the real old-timers. And if the old homestead's in a jam, we're the ones you can depend on to help pull her through—all for one and one for all, you know. The Aragon's stood by us; we'll stand by the Aragon."

"It may be that you'll find conditions changed," Caldwell tried again from another quarter. "In which case, if you wish to move—"

"Move!" Mr. Enoch stared at him in amazement. Then he smiled and shook his head slowly. "When you've lived in a place sixteen years, Mr. Caldwell, you don't just move out like that. You can't. Sixteen years is a long time. Sixteen years makes it your home, even if it's a hotel. The only home you've got, anyway. You don't run out on your home just when it's finding the going a little tough. You pitch in and help." He patted Caldwell encouragingly on the shoulder. "So don't you give it another thought. We'll stand by you, us old-timers."

"What did I say the new rate was?" Caldwell asked the cashier.

"Thirty-five."

"I made a mistake. It's forty."

Then he walked away. Mr. Enoch said nothing, but he looked after the manager soberly, thoughtfully. Then he crossed the lobby to the cigar counter, bought a fat, hairy-chested magazine full of hillbillies, pneumatic nudes and checked coats, and sat down to bone up on the new trend in lapels.

In his office Caldwell snapped three pencils in ruthless extravagance. It must have been glandular. Then, in a masochistic spasm, he went out to the desk and inspected Mr. Enoch again, across the lobby.

"Just look at that hat," he said.

"It's a diller," the clerk admitted.

Mr. Enoch said nothing after that for a long time. Nor did he smile. He got his key, he spoke politely but briefly to people, he tipped his steady two bits, he paid on the nose, and he continued to exercise his own taste in wardrobe.

So the following Monday the Big Push against Mr. Enoch got under way. At five A.M., the Zero Hour, he was awakened—by mistake. It wasn't a popular squeeze, nobody in the organization but Caldwell wanted to do it, but a job's a job, so what else are you going to do? The boss said give him the brush, didn't he?

With the well-oiled machinery of Aragon service operating strictly in reverse, Mr. Enoch began to get such a pushing around as has rarely been seen outside of Munich. The telephone switchboard, functioning with superb inefficiency, was presently giving him nothing but wrong calls, and if he'd been the Invisible Man the elevators could not have whizzed past him with less notice. Three times he was awakened from his lonely slumber by sharp orders from the house sleuth to get her out, and twice callers describing themselves as irresponsible stewpots banged him up at dawn to join them in some capers.

By the end of the week he had smuggled in his own soap, to take the place of the no soap he was getting, and it was not long until he was fairly resigned to drying himself on the shower curtain. Even when the dining room was otherwise completely empty, he was given a table only with the greatest reluctance, and on those rare occasions when he managed to snag a waiter long enough to place himself on the waiting list for a brace of eggs, he got chops.

It goes without saying that his weekly bill immediately became something that would have made Ripley whistle. Charged with all manner of odd purchases and services, from three gross of swizzle sticks to cash PD. OUT for the delivery of a buggy whip, Mr. Enoch regularly and quietly called the unhappy cashier's attention to the errors and, just as regularly and quietly, they were corrected. For no effort was being made to clip the Aragon's revolting little fashion plate. The errors were admonitory, not mercenary.

And finally, the throttle going all out, Mr. Enoch was moved. He was moved from 607 to 1146 to 1151 to 423 to 1896 to 605 to 901 to 555. He was moved so often and so unexpectedly that toward the end he was occasionally preparing to retire two rooms behind his luggage.

At what point in this institutional chill he became aware of the process, none can say, for a melancholy misanthropy soon settled down over him and he spoke only to one man, and to him but once. In an elevator on the occasion of his third move, he said to the operator, "What are they sore at me about?" to which the operator quoted himself as replying, "I don't get you." Thereafter, until the day he reported the disappearance of a new checked suit from his room of the moment, Mr. Enoch wasted never another word on the Aragon or its personnel.

It was on a Tuesday that he reported to the desk the disappearance of this suit, and in reply received Stock Promise 17b: A full investigation would be made immediately. On Wednesday he was presented with Standard Equipment Stall 11c: These things took time, but patience would unquestionably be rewarded with full and complete satisfaction. On Thursday his methodical inquiry evoked, somewhat mysteriously, a switcheroo in the shape of a spray of double-talk, and on Friday he was answered with downright incoherence. On Saturday Mr. Enoch asked quietly but firmly for the manager.

Now, in fairness to Caldwell, it must be explained that he knew no more about what had become of Mr. Enoch's raiment than Mr. Enoch himself. Such things happen in the best of hotels, which the Aragon certainly was not. But in this case the manager would have been the last man on earth to describe it as an unfortunate incident. On the contrary, to that inexplicable thief who had deliberately selected one of Mr. Enoch's choices in suits to pinch, Caldwell mentally broadcast his heartfelt gratitude for lining up a neat and sorely needed crisis.

So it was with cold satisfaction that Caldwell faced the issue.

Not one to whom words came easily, Mr. Enoch drove straight to the point. "How about that checked suit?" he asked.

"I beg your pardon?"

"That checked suit of mine—how about it?"

"I'm afraid—"

"I liked that suit. I liked it and I paid forty-five dollars for it. Brand-new." There was a simple but dogged determination in the way he clung to his one line of thought. "What I want to know now is how about it."

"The matter is receiving the fullest investigation," Caldwell stated formally, "and if it develops that any member of the Aragon's staff has been at fault, you may rest assured—"

"What's the use of talking like that?" Mr. Enoch asked fretfully. "What I want's my suit—either my suit or the money—forty-five dollars. Either give me my suit or give me the money, that's all I'm asking."

Caldwell sucked in his breath and counted, slowly, toward ten, for his thyroid, pituitary and adrenal glands had begun to pump like three Diesels.

"It was made to order for me, not a month ago, and I picked out the cloth myself," Mr. Enoch added morosely, "so how about it?"

"No about it!" Caldwell suddenly exploded. "No, no, no about it, you understand?'' Obviously, he felt that this was no time for either syntax or sense. ''I can tell you right now that I have no intention whatever of paying you one cent for those incredible hand-me-downs! Not one red cent! You understand?''

Mr. Enoch's eyes widened. ''Hand-me-downs!''

''Yes, hand-me-downs! And inferior hand-me-downs at that!'' The secretions were beginning to roar through his system like the torrents of spring. ''And furthermore''—Caldwell failed to hiss only because there were no *s*'s in the words—''if that clown suit of yours has indeed been stolen, it was unquestionably the noble work of some true friend of man laboring for the public good! For if ever I saw a more hideous caricature of civilized garments, it could only be that invitation to astigmatism you are wearing now! And the more I think of it—''

''That will do,'' Mr. Enoch said with dignity. ''I get the whole picture now.''

''What's that?''

''What's at the bottom of the whole thing,'' Mr. Enoch stated, ''is that you just don't like me personally.''

''Get out!'' Caldwell shouted. ''Get out and stay out! You can call the police, you can sue, you can do anything you please, but get out! Get out and never enter this hotel again as long as you live!''

He was breathing hard, every nerve raw and throbbing, and to a close observer it would have been clear that the veneer of civilization had fallen from him completely and he stood revealed to the world for what in truth he was—an outraged Beebe incarnate.

Mr. Enoch turned to the desk. ''My bill,'' he said evenly. But before paying he had a final word for his tormentor.

''Don't fool yourself that I haven't noticed everything,'' he said, and added darkly, ''and maybe—just maybe!—I'm not as dumb as you think I am.''

This time Caldwell ignored the absence of *s*'s. ''Get out!'' he hissed.

And so Mr. Enoch checked out of the Aragon after sixteen years of residence. Back in his office, Caldwell sank into his chair, exhausted. But it was a sweet exhaustion, the exhaustion of a fighter who has fought a long, hard battle, but successfully. He was not, at heart, an unfair man. He did not mean to take advantage of a weaker opponent. It was just that he was a heel and couldn't help it.

Time, as it will, marched on. The memory of Mr. Enoch and his gay raiment faded around the Aragon. Nor was there any reason why, two months later, the reservation clerk should have taken any particular note of a routine letter that came to his desk from Cleveland, Ohio. It was merely a request for the reservation of a room with bath for the night of April twenty-eighth, signed by one Ernest Ives. And he only smiled when, the following day, came another communication from Mr. Ives: "Please cancel my reservation. Last night in the lobby I was talking to a gentleman named Mr. Enoch, and he told me he had had a very unpleasant experience with you in regards to a nice checked suit. Sincerely yours," and so on. "That little rascal," the reservation clerk chuckled.

He still smiled the following week when, from Pittsburgh, Pennsylvania, came a similar cancellation. "Last night I was introduced to a gentleman in the lobby named Mr. Enoch," this one ran, "and the account he gave me of an incident concerning a checked suit, in which he got no satisfaction whatever, convinces me that I should go to the McAlpin instead." This cancellation was for a sitting room, bedroom and bath for a week.

The next one, from Detroit, was more violent. "That was certainly a hell of a way to treat Mr. Enoch, as nice a gentleman as I ever met in the lobby, and you can just cancel the whole business," this one declared, but since the signer, one Otis Myrick, had never made any reservation anyway, the incident, naturally, could be discounted.

The one from Chattanooga, Tennessee, was gently reproachful, and the one from Chicago, Illinois, downright abusive, while those from Dayton, Ohio; Paris, Kentucky; Indianapolis, Indiana; Kansas City, Missouri and Kansas; Jackson, Mississippi, and Atlanta, Georgia, rang other emotional changes on the same theme. One and all, the writers had met Mr. Enoch in the lobby the night before, and one and all, upon thinking it over, had decided to go instead to the Astor, the Taft, the McAlpin, the Commodore or the Alamac. By then the reservation clerk's smile had disappeared, and when, presently, seven of these messages arrived in one mail delivery, canceling all kinds of reservations from single rooms to housekeeping apartments, and all set down in various stages of indignation over the treatment accorded one Mr. Enoch in connection with the loss of a checked suit, he felt it was time to bring the matter to the attention of the manager.

Caldwell's first reaction was aloof impatience. "The whole thing is an absurd hoax," he declared, after running through the letters. "For example, four of these writers claim to have met the man the same night, in Louisville, Memphis, Baton Rouge and New Orleans—obviously a physical impossibility. Mrs. Roosevelt herself couldn't do it. It's a nuisance, to be sure, but no more than a nuisance. Don't bother me with it again."

"But how am I going to tell which reservation is a part of the hoax and which one is not?" the clerk remonstrated.

"Mr. Pembroke," Caldwell said, for that was the reservation clerk's moniker, "I am busy lining up accommodations for the Delta Psi Delta reunion and it stands to reason—"

"The Delta Psi Delta?" Pembroke said, puzzled. "But that's canceled too!"

"I beg your pardon?"

Pembroke got the letter. "The convention clerk received it last night," he explained, and as Caldwell read it his glands, weary though they were, began to pound like summer thunder in the distance. The secretary of the Delta Psi Deltas, it seemed, had run into a gentleman named Enoch in the lobby last night, and so on.

Presently, Caldwell lifted his head. "I get it now," he said. "He's using his friends," as one might say, "He has now resorted to dumdum bullets." "But leave it to me. Leave the whole thing in my hands. From now on, bring all reservation mail and telegrams to my desk. From now on, I will deal personally with the man."

Clearly, Mr. Enoch's friends covered the eastern half of the country like the dew, and to a man they were behind him. Reservations and cancellations poured in on the Aragon at the rate of ten and twelve a day; not a few of the cancellations arriving ahead of the reservations. And at the end of two weeks the whole world had begun to look to Caldwell like a nightmare in technicolor.

It was then that desperation and a mysterious buzzing at the base of his skull drove Caldwell to a foolish maneuver. He began to strike back. By then he had completely abandoned the rest of the hotel, which was functioning superbly without him, and was devoting the twenty-four hours of his day to the repercussions from Mr. Enoch's checked suit. He began to strike back because that strange buzzing finally persuaded him that he could detect the counterfeit reservations from the genuine.

Spotting a transparently spurious communication, he would call in a stenographer and freeze her blood with an answer that made his future residence, the Aragon or Leavenworth, merely the matter of a camera finish. These answers were never fewer than five pages long. In the course of another week this had two effects. It alienated a number of respectable Americans whose only fault was that they wrote like phonies, and it brought into the picture an elderly Philadelphian named Randolph Webster, who had been stunned to receive, in answer to a simple request for a reservation, six pages of what sounded to him like something written on the wall of a lunatic asylum. The only importance of Mr. Webster in this connection was that he was the trustee for the receivers who had employed Caldwell to build up friendship and good will for the Aragon.

"But what I can't see," he insisted to the perspiring manager in the latter's office the next day, "is how a letter like this is calculated to be of any benefit whatever to the hotel!"

Caldwell wiped his forehead. "It's not an easy thing to explain," he mumbled.

"I can well see that," Mr. Webster admitted.

"But it was this way," Caldwell began, groping for some comprehensible point of departure: "There was a man here who was terrible. He wore a large cap. He was quite small and he looked just awful. Well, he would sit around in the lobby with this cap on. He would sit around in the lobby day and night, night and day, with this cap on."

"You mean with just his cap on, nothing else?" Mr. Webster asked, startled.

"No, but his clothes were awful too. They were really hideous; checks and stripes and loud patterns. But there he was, with that cap and those horrible clothes, sitting around in the lobby all the time, just sitting and sitting, until it was just about driving me crazy!"

Mr. Webster jumped. "Good heavens!" he said.

"Then somebody stole his clothes," Caldwell went on morosely, "so he left. Then the next thing I knew, this man wrote from Cleveland, man named Ives, and canceled his reservation. And then a man from somewhere else. They all said Mr. Enoch put them up to it. Then it got worse. Nobody could tell anything. Next the Delta Psi Deltas called off their reunion, and this man Enoch was everywhere—Jacksonville, St. Louis, Chicago, Savannah, Memphis—"

He stopped. Horror swept over him, for Mr. Webster had shoved his chair back a good four feet and was regarding him in alarm and bewilderment.

"Go on, go on!" he cried, falsetto. "Go right on, but take it easy!"

"It was the man with the cap, don't you see?" Caldwell explained desperately. "He was behind the whole business—reserving and canceling, reserving and canceling, a dozen a day! And nobody could tell anything! I couldn't tell anything, the reservation clerk couldn't tell anything, the convention clerk couldn't tell anything! But it was Enoch all the time—the man with the cap! And that's why I wrote you that letter, don't you see?"

Holding his briefcase in easy position for quick defense, Mr. Webster was already at the door, his hand on the knob.

"I see, I see," he cooed soothingly. "There's nothing to be excited about. Just take it easy, that's all." He tested the door to see that it was not locked. "Meanwhile, get plenty of exercise, try not to smoke too much, and drink lots of water." He opened the door. "I'll explain the whole matter to the receivers and you'll hear from them in a day or two," and he leaped nimbly out of the room, slamming the door quickly behind him.

It was close on to eight o'clock when Cabot, the convention clerk, knocked at the manager's door. "Come in," a hollow voice called, and he entered.

The room was dark. "Pull that switch," the voice said wearily, and in the flood of light Cabot thought for a moment he had flushed a character from Outward Bound, or perhaps a white zombie.

"I was thinking," Caldwell explained dully.

"I'm sorry."

"It doesn't matter." He sighed. "What form of human woe have you come to burden me with now?"

Cabot smiled nervously. "Hardly that," he said. "Rather an embarrassment of riches. For the past two weeks I've been lining up a couple of convention dates, and it turns out now that they both want the grand ballroom for the same night. Both deals are practically set, all but that point, and I thought you might have a suggestion."

"Who are they?"

"One is the State Order of Bisons and the other is the International Treetop Trimmers of the World. I've been in communication—"

"Cabot," Caldwell interrupted gloomily, "would you say that I was unbalanced?"

"Pardon?"

"Would you say—" He stopped, suddenly frozen to the marrow. "What did you say the name of that second outfit was?"

"Why, the International Treetop Trimmers of the World, with headquarters in Boston."

"The International Treetop Trimmers of the World," Caldwell repeated slowly, his nerves beginning to hum. "The International—How far has it gone?"

"In the bag," Cabot reported with a certain satisfaction, "all but this banquet date. Five floors of rooms and suites, street banners and lobby decorations, small ballroom for business sessions, provisions for the ladies' auxiliary, everything. I've had a very agreeable correspondence with a Mr. Crampton, High Leaf of the order—"

"High Leaf," Caldwell murmured in awe. "High Leaf of the International Treetop Trimmers of the World." Then he was silent. Finally: "Bring me the correspondence."

It was flawless—letterheads, text and signature. The first two or three communications broke the ice. Then Mr. Crampton got down to cases. Patently he knew what he wanted and was not to be satisfied until he got it. He wanted street plans for the parade. He wanted the distances across streets, for the flying of Welcome banners. He wanted estimates on busses, for tours of sight-seeing for the ladies. For the annual banquet—one thousand plates—he wanted not only a price per plate, including potables, but also top entertainment, for which $2500 was available. He wanted at least one stage star, preferably female.

"I've got him three," Cabot explained with quiet pride, "two girls and a comedian."

"Already signed for?"

"Signed and sealed."

"Play or pay?"

"Naturally."

Caldwell's eyes, as he looked up at Cabot, were those of a collie that had been struck by Albert Payson Terhune, but he said nothing.

What was there to say? He himself might have been taken in, so guilelessly had the whole affair been conducted. There was not a false note in the entire structure, Caldwell reflected, except in the obviously implausible name of the organization.

It was while he was reading the last of the letters, received only that afternoon and concerned with a contract to cover the specifications, that suddenly something clicked in his mind. He became aware that the buzzing at the base of his skull had ceased. Out of the murk, in a flash, had come Eureka.

"You say they're already signed?" he asked.

"The actors? Why, yes," Cabot replied. "That's customary."

"And we have to pay 'em, whatever happens?"

"That's the only way you can get names," Cabot explained.

"Then we've got him!"

Cabot stared. "Got who?"

But Caldwell was already on his feet, a new man. There was the glint of triumph in his eyes and the old strength was in his bones and sinews again. In time's nick, as was proper, an American gunboat had appeared on the horizon. The United States cavalry was galloping over the crest of the hill. The serum had arrived.

"Enoch!" he cried. "We've got him by the throat at last! By the throat, I tell you! He's as good as in jail this very moment!"

Cabot was bewildered. "I don't get it," he said.

"Listen," Caldwell exulted. "The minute Mr. Enoch tricked you into signing those actors, play or pay, he outsmarted himself right smack into the middle of as beautiful an open-and-shut charge of using the United States mails to defraud as I have ever seen in my life!"

That midnight three men representing Mr. Whiskers, acting on a signed complaint from the manager of the Aragon, entered an apartment in Boston and arrested an indignant but perfectly innocent man named Crampton who turned out to be High Leaf in a perfectly innocent if somewhat idiotic fraternal order called the International Treetop Trimmers of the World.

By eight o'clock the following morning Mr. Crampton's cell was crowded with a battery of delighted lawyers drawing up a suit of practically textbook purity against the Aragon and Caldwell, as well as their heirs and assigns, charging them with false arrest and defamation of character, and suggesting $100,000 as fit and proper damages.

The human ferrets engaged for the purpose by Mr. Webster located Mr. Enoch three days later, in Albany, in the company of an old friend of his, the secretary of the State Order of Bisons, who, as chance would have it, had just taken his pen in hand to drop a letter to Caldwell, *in re* the convention arrangements. He was canceling them.

"What do you want?" Mr. Webster asked as soon as he could get there. "Whatever you want, just name it!"

"All I want's my suit," Mr. Enoch explained patiently, as he might to a case of arrested development; "either my suit or the money—forty-five dollars. That's all I want."

In a single blinding movement, miraculous in a man of his age, Mr. Webster had whipped out a fountain pen and was racing through a check.

"I was wondering," Mr. Enoch added shyly—"just wondering if it would be possible to have Mr. Caldwell hand me the money."

"Mr. Caldwell," Mr. Webster stated as if the very name itself dripped, "is no longer with us."

Mr. Enoch regarded him solemnly for a moment. "That's too bad," he said.

GARRISON KEILLOR

"Jack Schmidt, Arts Administrator"

It was one of those sweltering days toward the end of the fiscal year when Minneapolis smells of melting asphalt and foundation money is as tight as a rusted nut. Ninety-six, the radio said on the way in from the airport, and back at my office in the Acme Building I was trying to fan the memory of ocean breezes in Hawaii, where I had just spent two days attending a conference on midwestern regionalism.

It wasn't working. I was sitting down, jacket off, feet up, looking at the business end of an air conditioner, and a numb spot was forming around my left ear to which I was holding a telephone and listening to Bobby Jo, my secretary at the Twin Cities Arts Mall, four blocks away, reading little red numerals off a sheet of paper. We had only two days before the books snapped shut, and our administrative budget had sprung a deficit big enough to drive a car through—a car full of accountants. I could feel a dark sweat stain spreading across the back of my best blue shirt.

"Listen," I sputtered, "I still got some loose bucks in the publicity budget. Let's transfer that to administration."

"J.S.," she sighed, "I just got done telling you. Those loose bucks are as spent as an octogenarian after an all-night bender. Right now we're using more red ink than the funny papers, and yesterday we bounced three checks right off the bottom of the account. That budget is so unbalanced, it's liable to go out and shoot somebody."

You could've knocked me over with a rock.

"Sweetheart," I lied quietly, hoping she couldn't hear my heavy breathing, "don't worry about it. Old Jack has been around the block once or twice. I'll straighten it out."

"Payday is tomorrow," she sniffed sharply. "Twelve noon."

The Arts Mall is just one of thirty-seven arts organizations I administer, a chain that stretches from the Anaheim Puppet Theatre to the Title IX Poetry Center in Bangor, and I could have let it go down the tubes, but hell, I kind of like the joint. It's an old Henny Penny supermarket that we renovated in 1976 when Bicentennial money was wandering around like helpless buffalo, and it houses seventeen little shops—mainly pottery and macrame, plus a dulcimer-maker, a printmaker, a spatter painter, two sculptors, and a watering hole called The Barre. This is one of those quiet little bistros where you aren't driven crazy by the constant ringing of cash registers. A nice place to drink but you wouldn't want to own it.

I hung up the phone and sat for a few minutes eyeballing an old nine-by-twelve glossy of myself, trying to get inspired. It's not a bad likeness. Blue pin-striped suit, a headful of hair, and I'm looking straight into 1965 like I owned it, and as for my line of work at the time, anyone who has read *The Blonde in 204, Close Before Striking, The Big Tipper,* and *The Mark of a Heel* knows that I wasn't big on ballet.

I wasn't real smart at spotting trends, either. The private-eye business was getting thinner than sliced beef at the deli. I spent my days supporting a bookie and my nights tailing guys who weren't going anywhere anyway. My old pals in Homicide were trading in their wing tips and porkpie hats for Frye boots and Greek fisherman caps and growing big puffs of hair around their ears. Mine was the only suit that looked slept in. I felt like writing to the Famous Shamus School and asking what was I doing wrong.

"It's escapism, Mr. Schmidt," quavered Ollie, the elevator boy, one morning when I complained that nobody needed a snoop anymore. "I was reading in the *Gazette* this morning where they say this is an age of anti-intellectualism. A sleuth like yourself, now, you represent the spirit of inquiry, the scientific mind, eighteenth-century enlightenment, but heck, people don't care about knowing the truth anymore. They just want to have *experiences.*"

"Thanks for the tip, Ollie," I smiled, flipping him a quarter. "And keep your eyes open."

I was having an experience myself at the time and her name was Trixie, an auburn-haired beauty who moved grown men to lie down in her path and wave their arms and legs. I was no stronger than the rest, and when she let it be known one day that the acting studio where she studied nights was low on cash and might have to close and thus frustrate her career, I didn't ask her to type it in triplicate. I got the dough. I learned then and there that true artists are sensitive about money. Trixie took the bundle and the next day she moved in with a sandalmaker. She said I wasn't her type. Too materialistic.

Evidently I was just the type that every art studio, mime troupe, print gallery, folk-ballet company, and wind ensemble in town was looking for, though, and the word got around fast: Jack Schmidt knows how to dial a telephone and make big checks arrive in the mail. Pretty soon my outer office was full of people with long delicate fingers, waiting to tell me what marvelous, marvelous things they could do if only they had ten thousand dollars (minus my percentage). It didn't take me long to learn the rules—about twenty minutes. First rule: ten thousand is peanuts. Pocket money. Any arts group that doesn't need a hundred grand and need it *now* just isn't thinking hard enough.

My first big hit was a National Endowment for the Arts grant for a walk-up tap school run by a dishwater blonde named Bonnie Marie Beebe. She also taught baton, but we stressed tap on the application. We called the school The American Conservatory of Jazz Dance. A hundred and fifty thousand clams. "Send money" they called it, but it was good crisp lettuce to me.

I got the Guild of Younger Poets fifty thousand from the Teamsters to produce some odes to the open road, and another fifteen from a lumber tycoon with a yen for haiku. I got a yearlong folk-arts residency for a guy who told Scandinavian jokes, and I found wealthy backers for a play called *Struck by Lightning,* by a non-literalist playwright who didn't write a script but only spoke with the director a few times on the phone.

Nobody was too weird for Jack Schmidt. In every case, I had met weirder on the street. The Minnesota Anti-Dance Ensemble, for example, is a bunch of sweet kids. They simply don't believe in performance. They say that "audience" is a passive concept, and they spend a lot of time picketing large corporations in protest against the money that has been given to them, which they say comes from illicit profits. It doesn't make my life easier, but heck, I was young once, too. Give me a choice, I'll take a radical dance group over a Renaissance-music ensemble any day. Your average shawm or sackbut player thinks the world owes him a goddamn living.

So I was off the pavement and into the arts, and one day Bobby Jo walked in, fresh out of St. Cloud State Normal and looking for money to teach interior decorating to minority kids, and she saw I needed her more. She threw out my electric fan and the file cabinet with the half-empty fifth in the third drawer and brought in some Mondrian prints and a glass-topped desk and about forty potted plants. She took away my .38 and made me switch to filter cigarettes and had stationery printed up that looks like it's recycled from beaten eggs. "Arts Consultant," it says, but what I sell is the same old hustle and muscle, which was a new commodity on the arts scene then.

"What your arts organizations need is a guy who can ask people for large amounts without blushing and twisting his hankie," I told her one day, en route to Las Palmas for a three-day seminar on the role of the arts in rural America. "Your typical general manager of an arts organization today is nothing but a bagman. He figures all he has to do is pass the hat at the board meeting and the Throttlebottoms will pick up the deficit. The rest of the time he just stands around at lawn parties and says witty things. But the arts are changing, Bobby Jo. Nowadays, everybody wants arts, not just the rich. It's big business. Operating budgets are going right through the ceiling. All of a sudden, Mr. Arts Guy finds the game has changed. Now he has to work for the money and hit up corporations and think box office and dive in and fight for a slice of the government pie, and it scares him right out of his silk jammies. That's when he calls for Schmidt."

She slipped her hand into mine. I didn't take her pulse or anything, but I could tell she was excited by the way her breath came in quick little gasps.

"Now anyone who can spell 'innovative' can apply for a grant, government or otherwise," I went on, "but that doesn't mean that the bozo who reads the application is necessarily going to bust into tears and run right down to Western Union. He needs some extra incentive. He needs to know that this is no idle request for funds typed up by somebody who happened to find a blank application form at the post office. He needs to know that you are counting on the cash, that you fully expect to get it, and that if you are denied you are capable of putting his fingers in a toaster. The arts are growing, Bobby Jo, and you and me are going to make it happen."

"You are a visionary, J.S.," she murmured. "You have a tremendous overall concept but you need a hand when it comes to the day-to-day."

"Speaking of ideas," I muttered hoarsely, and I pulled the lap blanket up over our heads. She whispered my initials over and over in a litany of passion. I grabbed her so hard her ribs squeaked.

It was a rough morning. After Bobby Jo's phone call, I got another from the Lawston Foundry, informing me that Stan Lewandowski's sculpture, *Oppresso,* would not be cast in time for the opening of the Minot Performing Arts Center. The foundry workers, after hearing what Lewandowski was being paid for creating what looked to them like a large gerbil cage, went out on strike, bringing the sculpture to a standstill. I wasted fifteen minutes trying to make a lunch date with Hugo Groveland, the mining heir, to discuss the Arts Mall. He was going away for a while, Groveland said, and didn't know when he'd be back, if ever. He hinted at dark personal tragedies that were haunting him and suggested I call his mother. "She's more your type," he said, "plus she's about to kick off, if you know what I mean."

On top of it, I got a call from the director of our dinner theatre in upstate Indiana. He had been irked at me for weeks since I put the kibosh on *Hedda Gabler.* He had been plumping for a repertory theatre. "Fine," I said. "As long as you make it *Fiddler on the Roof, The Sunshine Boys,* and *Man of La Mancha.*" Now he was accusing us of lacking a commitment to new writers. He said I was in the business of exploiting talent, not developing it.

"Listen, pal," I snarled. "As a director, you'd have a hard time getting people to act normal. So don't worry about me exploiting your talent. Just make sure you have as many people in the cast as there are parts. And tell your kitchen to slice the roast beef thin."

So he quit. I wished I could, too. I had a headache that wouldn't. And an Arts Mall with twenty-four hours to live.

"It's a whole trend called the New Naiveté," offered Ollie when I asked him why artists seemed to hate me, on the way down to lunch. "I was reading in the *Gazette* where they say people nowadays think simplicity is a prime virtue. They want to eliminate the middleman. That's you, Mr. Schmidt. Traditionally, your role has been that of a buffer between the individual and a cruel world. But now people think the world is kind and good, if only they could deal with it directly. They think if they got rid of the middleman—the bureaucracy, whatever you call it—then everything would be hunky-dory."

"Thanks, Ollie," I said as the elevator doors opened. "Let's have lunch sometime."

It reminded me of something Bobby Jo had said in a taxicab in Rio, where we were attending a five-day conference on the need for a comprehensive system of evaluating arts information. "It's simple, J.S.," she said. "The problem is overhead. Your fat cats will give millions to build an arts center, but nobody wants to donate to pay the light bill because you can't put a plaque on it. They'll pay for Chippewa junk sculpture, but who wants to endow the janitor?"

"Speaking of endowments," I whispered hoarsely, and I leaned over and pressed my lips hungrily against hers. I could feel her earlobes trembling helplessly.

The mining heir's mother lived out on Mississippi Drive in a stone pile the size of the Lincoln Monument and about as cheerful. The carpet in the hall was so deep it was like walking through a swamp. The woman who opened the door eyeballed me carefully for infectious diseases, then led me to a sitting room on the second floor that could've gone straight into the Cooper-Hewitt Museum. Mrs. Groveland sat in a wing chair by the fireplace. She looked pretty good for a woman who was about to make the far turn.

"Mr. Smith, how good of you to come," she tooted, offering me a tiny hand. I didn't correct her on the name. For a few grand, I'm willing to be called a lot worse. "Sit down and tell me about your arts center," she continued. "I'm all ears."

So were the two Dobermans who sat on either side of her chair. They looked as if they were trained to rip your throat if you used the wrong fork.

Usually, my pitch begins with a description of the long lines of art-starved inner-city children bused in daily to the Arts Mall to be broadened. But the hounds made me nervous—they maintained the most intense eye contact I had ever seen from floor level—so I skipped ahead to the money part. I dropped the figure of fifty thousand dollars.

She didn't blink, so I started talking about the Mall's long-range needs. I mentioned a hundred thou. She smiled as if I had asked for a drink of water.

I crossed my legs and forged straight ahead. "Mrs. Groveland," I radiated. "I hope you won't mind if I bring up the subject of estate planning."

"Of course not," she radiated right back. "The bulk of my estate, aside from the family bequests and a lump-sum gift to the Audubon Society, is going for the care of Luke and Mona here." At the word "estate," the Dobermans seemed to lick their chops.

I had to think fast. I wasn't about to bad-mouth our feathered friends of the forest, or Mrs. Groveland's family, either, but I thought I just might shake loose some of the dog trust. I told her about our Founders Club for contributors of fifty thousand or more. Perhaps she could obtain *two* Founderships— one for each Doberman. "Perhaps it would take a load off your mind if you would let us provide for Luke and Mona," I said. "We could act as their trustees. We just happen to have this lovely Founders Club Kennel, way out in the country, where—"

At the mention of a kennel, the beasts lowered their heads and growled. Their eyes never left my face.

"Hush, hush," Mrs. Groveland scolded gently. "Don't worry," she assured me, "they don't bite."

They may not bite, I thought, but they can sue.

Then Mona barked. Instantly, I was on my feet, but the dogs beat me to it.

The sounds that came from their throats were noises that predated the Lascaux Cave paintings. They were the cries of ancient Doberman souls trying to break through the thin crust of domestication, and they expressed a need that was far deeper than that of the Arts Mall, the arts in general, or any individual artist whom I would care to know. The next sound I heard was the slam of a paneled oak door closing. I was out in the hallway and I could hear Mrs. Groveland on the other side saying, *"Bad* Luke, *naughty* Mona!" The woman who had let me in let me out. "They're quite protective," she informed me, chuckling. If a jury had been there to see her face, I'd have altered it.

When I got back to the office, I gathered up every piece of correspondence in our National Arts Endowment file and threw it out the window. From above, it looked like a motorcade was due any minute. I was about to follow up with some of the potted plants when the phone rang. It rang sixteen times before I picked it up. Before Bobby Jo could identify herself, I'd used up all the best words I know. "I'm *out,*" I added. "Through. Done. Kaput. Fini. The End. Cue the creditors. I've had it."

"J.S.," she began, but I was having none of it.

"I've had a noseful of beating money out of bushes so a bunch of sniveling wimps can try the patience of tiny audiences of their pals and moms with subsidized garbage that nobody in his right mind would pay Monopoly money to see," I snapped. "I'm sick of people calling themselves artists who make pots that cut your fingers when you pick them up and wobble when you set them on a table. I'm tired of poets who dribble out little teensy poems in lower-case letters and I'm sick of painters who can't even draw an outline of their own hand and I'm finished with the mumblers and stumblers who tell you that if you don't understand them it's *your* fault."

I added a few more categories to my list, plus a couple dozen persons by name, several organizations, and a breed of dog.

"You all done, J.S.?" she asked. "Because I've got great news. The Highways Department is taking the Arts Mall for an interchange. They're ready to pay top dollar, plus—you won't believe this—to sweeten the deal, they're throwing in six point two miles of Interstate 594."

"Miles of what?" Then it clicked. "You mean that unfinished leg of 594?" I choked.

"It's been sitting there for years. There are so many community groups opposed to it that the Highways Department doesn't dare cut the grass that's growing on it. They want us to take them off the hook. And if we make it an arts space, they figure it'll fulfill their beautification quota for the next three years."

"We'll call it The ArtsTrip!" I exclaimed. "Or The ArtStrip! The median as medium! Eight-lane environmental art! Big, big sculptures! Action painting! Wayside dance areas! Living poetry plaques! Milestones in American music!

Arts parks and Arts lots! A drive-in film series! The customized car as American genre! The customized van as Artsmobile! People can have an arts experience without even pulling over onto the shoulder. They can get quality enrichment and still make good time!''

''Speaking of making time—'' Her voice broke. She shuddered like a turned-on furnace. Her breath came in sudden little sobs.

I don't know what's next for Jack Schmidt after the Arts Highway is finished, but, whatever it is, it's going to have Jack Schmidt's name on it. No more Mr. Anonymous for me. No more Gray Eminence trips for yours truly. A couple of days ago, I was sitting at my desk and I began fooling around with an ink pad. I started making thumbprints on a sheet of yellow paper and then I sort of smooshed them around a little, and one thing led to another, and when I got done with it I liked what I saw. It wasn't necessarily something I'd hang on a burlap wall with a baby ceiling-spot aimed at it, but it had a certain *definite* quality that art could use a lot more of. I wouldn't be too surprised if in my next adventure I'm in a loft in SoHo solving something strictly visual while Bobby Jo throws me smoldering looks from her loom in the corner. In the meantime, good luck and stay out of dark alleys.

RING LARDNER

"Ex Parte"

Most always when a man leaves his wife, there's no excuse in the world for him. She may have made whoop-whoop-whoopee with the whole ten commandments, but if he shows his disapproval to the extent of walking out on her, he will thereafter be a total stranger to all his friends excepting the two or three bums who will tour the night clubs with him so long as he sticks to his habits of paying for everything.

When a woman leaves her husband, she must have good and sufficient reasons. He drinks all the time, or he runs around, or he doesn't give her any money, or he uses her as the heavy bag in his home gymnasium work. No more is he invited to his former playmates' houses for dinner and bridge. He is an outcast just the same as if he had done the deserting. Whichever way it happens, it's his fault. He can state his side of the case if he wants to, but there is nobody around listening.

Now I claim to have a little chivalry in me, as well as a little pride. So in spite of the fact that Florence has broadcast her grievances over the red and blue network both, I intend to keep mine to myself till death do me part.

But after I'm gone, I want some of my old pals to know that this thing wasn't as lopsided as she has made out, so I will write the true story, put it in an envelope with my will and appoint Ed Osborne executor. He used to be my best friend and would be yet if his wife would let him. He'll have to read all my papers, including this, and he'll tell everybody else about it and maybe they'll be a little sorry that they treated me like an open manhole.

(Ed, please don't consider this an attempt to be literary. You know I haven't written for publication since our days on "The Crimson and White," and I wasn't so hot then. Just look on it as a statement of facts. If I were still alive, I'd take a bible oath that nothing herein is exaggerated. And whatever else may have been my imperfections, I never lied save to shield a woman or myself.)

Well, a year ago last May I had to go to New York. I called up Joe Paxton and he asked me out to dinner. I went, and met Florence. She and Marjorie Paxton had been at school together and she was there for a visit. We fell in love with each other and got engaged. I stopped off in Chicago on the way home, to see her people. They liked me all right, but they hated to have Florence marry a man who lived so far away. They wanted to postpone her leaving home as long as possible and they made us wait till April this year.

I had a room at the Belden and Florence and I agreed that when we were married, we would stay there awhile and take our time about picking out a house. But the last day of March, two weeks before the date of our wedding, I ran into Jeff Cooper and he told me his news, that the Standard Oil was sending him to China in some big job that looked permanent.

"I'm perfectly willing to go," he said. "So is Bess. It's a lot more money and we think it will be an interesting experience. But here I am with a brand-new place on my hands that cost me $45,000, including the furniture, and no chance to sell it in a hurry except at a loss. We were just beginning to feel settled. Otherwise we would have no regrets about leaving this town. Bess hasn't any real friends here and you're the only one I can claim."

"How much would you take for your house, furniture and all?" I asked him.

"I'd take a loss of $5,000," he said. "I'd take $40,000 with the buyer assuming my mortgage of $15,000, held by the Phillips Trust and Mortgage Company in Seattle."

I asked him if he would show me the place. They had only been living there a month and I hadn't had time to call. He said, what did I want to look at it for and I told him I would buy it if it looked o. k. Then I confessed that I was going to be married; you know I had kept it a secret around here.

Well, he took me home with him and he and Bess showed me everything, all new and shiny and a bargain if you ever saw one. In the first place, there's the location, on the best residential street in town, handy to my office and yet with a whole acre of ground, and a bed of cannas coming up in the front yard that Bess had planted when they bought the property last fall. As for the house, I always liked stucco, and this one is *built*! You could depend on old Jeff to see to that.

But the furniture was what decided me. Jeff had done the smart thing and ordered the whole works from Wolfe Brothers, taking their advice on most of the stuff, as neither he nor Bess knew much about it. Their total bill, furnishing the entire place, rugs, beds, tables, chairs, everything, was only $8,500, including a mahogany upright player-piano that they ordered from Seattle. I had my mother's old mahogany piano in storage and I kind of hoped Jeff wouldn't want me to buy this, but it was all or nothing, and with a bargain like that staring me in the face, I didn't stop to argue, not when I looked over the rest of the furniture and saw what I was getting.

The living-room had, and still has, three big easy chairs and a couch, all over-stuffed, as they call it, to say nothing of an Oriental rug that alone had cost $500. There was a long mahogany table behind the couch, with lamps at both ends in case you wanted to lie down and read. The dining-room set was solid mahogany—a table and eight chairs that had separated Jeff from $1,000.

The floors downstairs were all oak parquet. Also he had blown himself to an oak mantelpiece and oak woodwork that must have run into heavy dough. Jeff told me what it cost him extra, but I don't recall the amount.

The Coopers were strong for mahogany and wanted another set for their bedroom, but Jake Wolfe told them it would get monotonous if there was too much of it. So he sold them five pieces—a bed, two chairs, a chiffonier and a dresser—of some kind of wood tinted green, with flowers painted on it. This was $1,000 more, but it certainly was worth it. You never saw anything prettier than that bed when the lace spreads were on.

Well, we closed the deal and at first I thought I wouldn't tell Florence, but would let her believe we were going to live at the Belden and then give her a surprise by taking her right from the train to our own home. When I got to Chicago, though, I couldn't keep my mouth shut. I gave it away and it was I, not she, that had the surprise.

Instead of acting tickled to death, as I figured she would, she just looked kind of funny and said she hoped I had as good taste in houses as I had in clothes. She tried to make me describe the house and the furniture to her, but I wouldn't do it. To appreciate a layout like that, you have to see it for yourself.

We were married and stopped in Yellowstone for a week on our way here. That was the only really happy week we had together. From the minute we arrived home till she left for good, she was a different woman than the one I thought I knew. She never smiled and several times I caught her crying. She wouldn't tell me what ailed her and when I asked if she was just homesick, she said no and choked up and cried some more.

You can imagine that things were not as I expected they would be. In New York and in Chicago and Yellowstone, she had had more *life* than any girl I ever met. Now she acted all the while as if she were playing the title rôle at a funeral.

One night late in May the telephone rang. It was Mrs. Dwan and she wanted Florence. If I had known what this was going to mean, I would have slapped the receiver back on the hook and let her keep on wanting.

I had met Dwan a couple of times and had heard about their place out on the Turnpike. But I had never seen it or his wife either.

Well, it developed that Mildred Dwan had gone to school with Florence and Marjorie Paxton, and she had just learned from Marjorie that Florence was my wife and living here. She said she and her husband would be in town and call on us the next Sunday afternoon.

Florence didn't seem to like the idea and kind of discouraged it. She said we would drive out and call on them instead. Mrs. Dwan said no, that Florence was the newcomer and it was her (Mrs. Dwan's) first move. So Florence gave in.

They came and they hadn't been in the house more than a minute when Florence began to cry. Mrs. Dwan cried, too, and Dwan and I stood there first on one foot and then the other, trying to pretend we didn't know the girls were crying. Finally, to relieve the tension, I invited him to come and see the rest of the place. I showed him all over and he was quite enthusiastic. When we returned to the living-room, the girls had dried their eyes and were back in school together.

Florence accepted an invitation for one-o'clock dinner a week from that day. I told her, after they had left, that I would go along only on condition that she and our hostess would both control their tear-ducts. I was so accustomed to solo sobbing that I didn't mind it any more, but I couldn't stand a duet of it either in harmony or unison.

Well, when we got out there and had driven down their private lane through the trees and caught a glimpse of their house, which people around town had been talking about as something wonderful, I laughed harder than any time since I was single. It looked just like what it was, a reorganized barn. Florence asked me what was funny, and when I told her, she pulled even a longer face than usual.

"I think it's beautiful," she said.

Tie that!

I insisted on her going up the steps alone. I was afraid if the two of us stood on the porch at once, we'd fall through and maybe founder before help came. I warned her not to smack the knocker too hard or the door might crash in and frighten the horses.

"If you make jokes like that in front of the Dwans," she said, "I'll never speak to you again."

"I'd forgotten you ever did," said I.

I was expecting a hostler to let us in, but Mrs. Dwan came in person.

"Are we late?" said Florence.

"A little," said Mrs. Dwan, "but so is dinner. Helga didn't get home from church till half past twelve."

"I'm glad of it," said Florence. "I want you to take me all through this beautiful, beautiful house right this minute."

Mrs. Dwan called her husband and insisted that he stop in the middle of mixing a cocktail so he could join us in a tour of the beautiful, beautiful house.

"You wouldn't guess it," said Mrs. Dwan, "but it used to be a barn."

I was going to say I had guessed it. Florence gave me a look that changed my mind.

"When Jim and I first came here," said Mrs. Dwan, "we lived in an ugly little rented house on Oliver Street. It was only temporary, of course; we were just waiting till we found what we really wanted. We used to drive around the country Saturday afternoons and Sundays, hoping we would run across the right sort of thing. It was in the late fall when we first saw this place. The leaves were off the trees and it was visible from the Turnpike.

" 'Oh, Jim!' I exclaimed. 'Look at that simply gorgeous old barn! With those wide shingles! And I'll bet you it's got hand-hewn beams in that middle, main section.' Jim bet me I was wrong, so we left the car, walked up the driveway, found the door open and came brazenly in. I won my bet as you can see."

She pointed to some dirty old rotten beams that ran across the living-room ceiling and looked as if five or six generations of rats had used them for gnawing practise.

"They're beautiful!" said Florence.

"The instant I saw them," said Mrs. Dwan, "I knew this was going to be our home!"

"I can imagine!" said Florence.

"We made inquiries and learned that the place belonged to a family named Taylor," said Mrs. Dwan. "The house had burned down and they had moved away. It was suspected that they had started the fire themselves, as they were terribly hard up and it was insured. Jim wrote to old Mr. Taylor in Seattle and asked him to set a price on the barn and the land, which is about four acres.

They exchanged several letters and finally Mr. Taylor accepted Jim's offer. We got it for a song.''

"Wonderful!" said Florence.

"And then, of course," Mrs. Dwan continued, "we engaged a house-wrecking company to tear down the other four sections of the barn—the stalls, the cow-shed, the tool-shed, and so forth—and take them away, leaving us just this one room. We had a man from Seattle come and put in these old pine walls and the flooring, and plaster the ceiling. He was recommended by a friend of Jim's and he certainly knew his business."

"I can see he did," said Florence.

"He made the hay-loft over for us, too, and we got the wings built by day-labor, with Jim and me supervising. It was so much fun that I was honestly sorry when it was finished."

"I can imagine!" said Florence.

Well, I am not very well up in Early American, which was the name they had for pretty nearly everything in the place, but for the benefit of those who are not on terms with the Dwans I will try and describe from memory the *objets d'art* they bragged of the most and which brought forth the loudest squeals from Florence.

The living-room walls were brown bare boards without a picture or scrap of wall-paper. On the floor were two or three "hooked rugs," whatever that means, but they needed five or six more of them, or one big carpet, to cover up all the knots in the wood. There was a maple "low-boy"; a "dough-trough" table they didn't have space for in the kitchen; a pine "stretcher" table with sticks connecting the four legs near the bottom so you couldn't put your feet anywhere; a "Dutch" chest that looked as if it had been ordered from the undertaker by one of Singer's Midgets, but he got well; and some "Windsor" chairs in which the only position you could get comfortable was to stand up behind them and lean your elbows on their back.

Not one piece that matched another, and not one piece of mahogany any-where. And the ceiling, between the beams, had apparently been plastered by a workman who was that way, too.

"Some day soon I hope to have a piano," said Mrs. Dwan. "I can't live much longer without one. But so far I haven't been able to find one that would fit in."

"Listen," I said. "I've got a piano in storage that belonged to my mother. It's a mahogany upright and not so big that it wouldn't fit in this room, especially when you get that 'trough' table out. It isn't doing me any good and I'll sell it to you for $250. Mother paid $1,250 for it new."

"Oh, I couldn't think of taking it!" said Mrs. Dwan.

"I'll make it $200 even just because you're a friend of Florence's," I said.

"Really, I couldn't!" said Mrs. Dwan.

"You wouldn't have to pay for it all at once," I said.

"Don't you see," said Florence, "that a mahogany upright piano would be a perfect horror in here? Mildred wouldn't have it as a gift, let alone buy it. It isn't in the period."

"She could get it tuned," I said.

The answer to this was, "I'll show you the up-stairs now and we can look at the dining-room later on."

We were led to the guest-chamber. The bed was a maple four-poster, with pineapple posts, and a "tester" running from pillar to post. You would think a "tester" might be a man that went around trying out beds, but it's really a kind of frame that holds a canopy over the bed in case it rains and the roof leaks. There was a quilt made by Mrs. Dwan's great-grandmother, Mrs. Anthony Adams, in 1859, at Lowell, Mass. How is that for a memory?"

"This used to be the hay-loft," said Mrs. Dwan.

"You ought to have left some of the hay so the guests could hit it," I said.

The dressers, or chests of drawers, and the chairs were all made of maple. And the same in the Dwans' own room; everything maple.

"If you had maple in one room and mahogany in the other," I said, "people wouldn't get confused when you told them that so and so was up in Maple's room."

Dwan laughed, but the women didn't.

The maid hollered up that dinner was ready.

"The cocktails aren't ready," said Dwan.

"You will have to go without them," said Mrs. Dwan. "The soup will be cold."

This put me in a great mood to admire the "sawbuck" table and the "slat back" chairs, which were evidently the *chef-d'œuvre* and the *pièce de résistance* of the *chez Dwan*.

"It came all the way from Pennsylvania," said Mildred, when Florence's outcries, brought on by her first look at the table, had died down. "Mother picked it up at a little place near Stroudsburg and sent it to me. It only cost $550, and the chairs were $45 apiece."

"How reasonable!" exclaimed Florence.

That was before she had sat in one of them. Only one thing was more unreasonable than the chairs, and that was the table itself, consisting of big planks nailed together and laid onto a railroad tie, supported underneath by a whole forest of cross-pieces and beams. The surface was as smooth on top as the trip to Catalina Island and all around the edges, great big divots had been taken out with some blunt instrument, probably a bayonet. There were stains and scorch marks that Florence fairly crowed over, but when I tried to add to the general ensemble by laying a lighted cigaret right down beside my soup-plate, she and both the Dwans yelled murder and made me take it off.

They planted me in an end seat, a location just right for a man who had stretched himself across a railway track and had both legs cut off at the abdomen. Not being that kind of man, I had to sit so far back that very few of my comestibles carried more than half-way to their target.

After dinner I was all ready to go home and get something to eat, but it had been darkening up outdoors for half an hour and now such a storm broke that I knew it was useless trying to persuade Florence to make a start.

"We'll play some bridge," said Dwan, and to my surprise he produced a card-table that was nowhere near "in the period."

At my house there was a big center chandelier that lighted up a bridge game no matter in what part of the room the table was put. But here we had to waste forty minutes moving lamps and wires and stands and when they were all fixed, you could tell a red suit from a black suit, but not a spade from a club. Aside from that and the granite-bottomed "Windsor" chairs and the fact that we played "families" for a cent a point and Florence and I won $12 and didn't get paid, it was one of the pleasantest afternoons I ever spent gambling.

The rain stopped at five o'clock and as we splashed through the puddles of Dwan's driveway, I remarked to Florence that I had never known she was such a kidder.

"What do you mean?" she asked me.

"Why, your pretending to admire all that junk," I said.

"Junk!" said Florence. "That is one of the most beautifully furnished homes I have ever seen!"

And so far as I can recall, that was her last utterance in my presence for six nights and five days.

At lunch on Saturday I said: "You know I like the silent drama one evening a week, but not twenty-four hours a day every day. What's the matter with you? If it's laryngitis, you might write me notes."

"I'll tell you what's the matter!" she burst out. "I hate this house and everything in it! It's too new! Everything shines! I loathe new things! I want a home like Mildred's, with things in it that I can look at without blushing for shame. I can't invite anyone here. It's too hideous. And I'll never be happy here a single minute as long as I live!"

Well, I don't mind telling that this kind of got under my skin. As if I hadn't intended to give her a pleasant surprise! As if Wolfe Brothers, in business thirty years, didn't know how to furnish a home complete! I was pretty badly hurt, but I choked it down and said, as calmly as I could:

"If you'll be a little patient, I'll try to sell this house and its contents for what I paid for it and them. It oughtn't to be much trouble; there are plenty of people around who know a bargain. But it's too bad you didn't confess your barn complex to me long ago. Only last February, old Ken Garrett had to sell his establishment and the men who bought it turned it into a garage. It was a livery-stable which I could have got for the introduction of a song, or maybe just the vamp. And we wouldn't have had to spend a nickel to make it as nice and comfortable and homey as your friend Mildred's dump.''

Florence was on her way upstairs before I had finished my speech.

I went down to Earl Benham's to see if my new suit was ready. It was and I put it on and left the old one to be cleaned and pressed.

On the street I met Harry Cross.

''Come up to my office,'' he said. ''There's something in my desk that may interest you.''

I accepted his invitation and from three different drawers he pulled out three different quart bottles of Early American rye.

Just before six o'clock I dropped in Kane's store and bought myself a pair of shears, a blow torch and an ax. I started home, but stopped among the trees inside my front gate and cut big holes in my coat and trousers. Alongside the path to the house was a sizable mud puddle. I waded in it. And I bathed my gray felt hat.

Florence was sitting on the floor of the living-room, reading. She seemed a little upset by my appearance.

''Good heavens! What's happened?''

''Nothing much,'' said I. ''I just didn't want to look too new.''

''What are those things you're carrying?''

''Just a pair of shears, a blow torch and an ax. I'm going to try and antique this place and I think I'll begin on the dining-room table.''

Florence went into her scream, dashed upstairs and locked herself in. I went about my work and had the dinner-table looking pretty Early when the maid smelled fire and rushed in. She rushed out again and came back with a pitcher of water. But using my vest as a snuffer, I had had the flames under control all the while and there was nothing for her to do.

''I'll just nick it up a little with this ax,'' I told her, ''and by the time I'm through, dinner ought to be ready.''

''It will never be ready as far as I'm concerned,'' she said. ''I'm leaving just as soon as I can pack.''

And Florence had the same idea—vindicating the old adage about great minds.

I heard the front door slam and the back door slam, and I felt kind of tired and sleepy, so I knocked off work and went up to bed.

That's my side of the story, Eddie, and it's true so help me my bootlegger. Which reminds me that the man who sold Harry the rye makes this town once a week, or did when this was written. He's at the Belden every Tuesday from nine to six and his name is Mike Farrell.

O . HENRY

"Confessions of a Humorist"

There was a painless stage of incubation that lasted twenty-five years, and then it broke out on me, and people said I was It.

But they called it humor instead of measles.

The employees in the store bought a silver inkstand for the senior partner on his fiftieth birthday. We crowded into his private office to present it.

I had been selected for spokesman, and I made a little speech that I had been preparing for a week.

It made a hit. It was full of puns and epigrams and funny twists that brought down the house (which was a very solid one in the wholesale hardware line). Old Marlowe himself actually grinned, and the employees took their cue and roared.

My reputation as a humorist dates from half-past nine o'clock on that morning.

For weeks afterward my fellow clerks fanned the flame of my self-esteem. One by one they came to me, saying what an awfully clever speech that was, old man, and carefully explained to me the point of each one of my jokes.

Gradually I found that I was expected to keep it up. Others might speak sanely on business matters and the day's topics, but from me something gamesome and airy was required.

I was expected to crack jokes about the crockery and lighten up the granite ware with *persiflage*. I was second bookkeeper, and if I failed to show up a balance-sheet without something comic about the footings or could find no cause for laughter in an invoice of plows, the other clerks were disappointed.

By degrees my fame spread, and I became a local "character." Our town was small enough to make this possible. The daily newspaper often quoted my sayings. At social gatherings I was indispensable.

I believe I did possess considerable wit and a facility for quick and spontaneous repartee. This gift I cultivated and improved by practice. And the nature of it was kindly and genial, not running to sarcasm or offending others. People began to smile when they saw me coming, and by the time we had met I generally had the word ready to broaden the smile into a laugh.

I had married early. We had a charming boy of three and a girl of five. Naturally, we lived in a vine-covered cottage, and were happy. My salary as bookkeeper in the hardware concern kept at a distance those ills attendant upon superfluous wealth.

At sundry times I had written out a few jokes and conceits that I considered peculiarly happy, and had sent them to certain periodicals that print such things. All of them had been instantly accepted. Several of the editors had written to request further contributions.

One day I received a letter from the editor of a famous weekly publication. He suggested that I submit to him a humorous composition to fill a column of space; hinting that he would make it a regular feature of each issue if the work proved satisfactory. I did so, and at the end of two weeks he offered to make a contract with me for a year at a figure that was considerably higher than the amount paid me by the hardware firm.

I was filled with delight. My wife already crowned me in her mind with the imperishable evergreens of literary success. We had lobster croquettes and a bottle of blackberry wine for supper that night. Here was the chance to liberate myself from drudgery. I talked over the matter very seriously with Louisa. We agreed that I must resign my place at the store and devote myself to humor.

I resigned. My fellow clerks gave me a farewell banquet. The speech I made there coruscated. It was printed in full by the *Gazette*. The next morning I awoke and looked at the clock.

"Late, by George!" I exclaimed, and grabbed for my clothes. Louisa reminded me that I was no longer a slave to hardware and contractors' supplies. I was now a professional humorist.

After breakfast she proudly led me to the little room off the kitchen. Dear girl! There was my table and chair, writing pad, ink and pipe tray. And all the author's trappings—the celery stand full of fresh roses and honeysuckle, last year's calendar on the wall, the dictionary, and a little bag of chocolates to nibble between inspirations. Dear girl!

I sat me to work. The wall paper is patterned with arabesques or odalisks or—perhaps—it is trapezoids. Upon one of the figures I fixed my eyes. I bethought me of humor.

A voice startled me—Louisa's voice.

"If you aren't too busy, dear," it said, "come to dinner."

I looked at my watch. Yes, five hours had been gathered in by the grim scytheman. I went to dinner.

"You mustn't work too hard at first," said Louisa. "Goethe—or was it Napoleon?—said five hours a day is enough for mental labor. Couldn't you take me and the children to the woods this afternoon?''

"I *am* a little tired," I admitted. So we went to the woods.

But I soon got the swing of it. Within a month I was turning out copy as regular as shipments of hardware.

And I had success. My column in the weekly made some stir, and I was referred to in a gossipy way by the critics as something fresh in the line of humorists. I augmented my income considerably by contributing to other publications.

I picked up the tricks of the trade. I could take a funny idea and make a two-line joke of it, earning a dollar. With false whiskers on, it would serve up cold as a quatrain, doubling its producing value. By turning the skirt and adding a ruffle of rhyme you would hardly recognize it as *vers de société* with neatly shod feet and a fashion plate illustration.

I began to save up money, and we had new carpets and a parlor organ. My townspeople began to look upon me as a citizen of some consequence instead of the merry trifler I had been when I clerked in the hardware store.

After five or six months the spontaneity seemed to depart from my humor. Quips and droll sayings no longer fell carelessly from my lips. I was sometimes hard run for material. I found myself listening to catch available ideas from the conversation of my friends. Sometimes I chewed my pencil and gazed at the wall paper for hours trying to build up some gay little bubble of unstudied fun.

And then I became a harpy, a Moloch, a Jonah, a vampire to my acquaintances. Anxious, haggard, greedy, I stood among them like a veritable killjoy. Let a bright saying, a witty comparison, a piquant phrase fall from their lips and I was after it like a hound springing upon a bone. I dared not trust my memory; but, turning aside guiltily and meanly, I would make a note of it in my ever-present memorandum book or upon my cuff for my own future use.

My friends regarded me in sorrow and wonder. I was not the same man. Where once I had furnished them entertainment and jollity, I now preyed upon them. No jests from me ever bid for their smiles now. They were too precious. I could not afford to dispense gratuitously the means of my livelihood.

I was a lugubrious fox praising the singing of my friends, the crows, that they might drop from their beaks the morsels of wit that I coveted.

Nearly every one began to avoid me. I even forgot how to smile, not even paying that much for the sayings I appropriated.

No persons, places, times or subjects were exempt from my plundering in search of material. Even in church my demoralized fancy went hunting among the solemn aisles and pillars for spoil.

Did the minister give out the longmeter doxology, at once I began: "Doxology—sockdology—sockdolager—meter—meet her."

The sermon ran through my mental sieve, its precepts filtering unheeded, could I but glean a suggestion of a pun or a *bon mot*. The solemnest anthems of the choir were but an accompaniment to my thoughts as I conceived new changes to ring upon the ancient comicalities concerning the jealousies of soprano, tenor and basso.

My own home became a hunting ground. My wife is a singularly feminine creature, candid, sympathetic and impulsive. Once her conversation was my delight, and her ideas a source of unfailing pleasure. Now I worked her. She was a gold mine of those amusing but lovable inconsistencies that distinguish the female mind.

I began to market those pearls of unwisdom and humor that should have enriched only the sacred precincts of home. With devilish cunning I encouraged her to talk. Unsuspecting, she laid her heart bare. Upon the cold, conspicuous, common, printed page I offered it to the public gaze.

A literary Judas, I kissed her and betrayed her. For pieces of silver I dressed her sweet confidences in the pantalettes and frills of folly and made them dance in the market place.

Dear Louisa! Of nights I have bent over her, cruel as a wolf above a tender lamb, hearkening even to her soft words murmured in sleep, hoping to catch an idea for my next day's grind. There is worse to come.

God help me! Next my fangs were buried deep in the neck of the fugitive sayings of my little children.

Guy and Viola were two bright fountains of childish, quaint thoughts and speeches. I found a ready sale for this kind of humor, and was furnishing a regular department in a magazine with "Funny Fancies of Childhood." I began to stalk them as an Indian stalks the antelope. I would hide behind sofas and doors, or crawl on my hands and knees among the bushes in the yard to eavesdrop while they were at play. I had all the qualities of a harpy except remorse.

Once, when I was barren of ideas, and my copy must leave in the next mail, I covered myself in a pile of autumn leaves in the yard, where I knew they intended to come to play. I cannot bring myself to believe that Guy was aware of my hiding place, but even if he was I would be loathe to blame him for his setting fire to the leaves, causing the destruction of my new suit of clothes, and nearly cremating a parent.

Soon my own children began to shun me as a pest. Often, when I was creeping upon them like a melancholy ghoul, I would hear them say to each other: "Here comes papa," and they would gather their toys and scurry away to some safer hiding place. Miserable wretch that I was!

And yet I was doing well financially. Before the first year had passed I had saved a thousand dollars, and we had lived in comfort.

But at what a cost! I am not quite clear as to what a Pariah is, but I was everything that it sounds like. I had no friends, no amusements, no enjoyment of life. The happiness of my family had been sacrificed. I was a bee, sucking sordid honey from life's fairest flowers, dreaded and shunned on account of my sting.

One day a man spoke to me, with a pleasant and friendly smile. Not in months had the thing happened. I was passing the undertaking establishment of Peter Heffelbower. Peter stood in the door and saluted me. I stopped, strangely wrung in my heart by his greeting. He asked me inside.

The day was chill and rainy. We went into the back room, where a fire burned in a little stove. A customer came, and Peter left me alone for a while. Presently I felt a new feeling stealing over me—a sense of beautiful calm and content. I looked around the place. There were rows of shining rosewood caskets, black palls, trestles, hearse plumes, mourning streamers and all the paraphernalia of the solemn trade. Here was peace, order, silence, the abode of grave and dignified reflections. Here, on the brink of life, was a little niche pervaded by the spirit of eternal rest.

When I entered it the follies of the world abandoned me at the door. I felt no inclination to wrest a humorous idea from those somber and stately trappings. My mind seemed to stretch itself to grateful repose upon a couch draped with gentle thoughts.

A quarter of an hour ago I was an abandoned humorist. Now I was a philosopher, full of serenity and ease. I had found a *refuge* from humor, from the hot chase of the shy quip, from the degrading pursuit of the panting joke, from the restless reach after the nimble repartee.

I had not known Heffelbower well. When he came back I let him talk, fearful that he might prove to be a jarring note in the sweet, dirge-like harmony of his establishment.

But, no. He chimed truly. I gave a long sigh of happiness. Never have I known a man's talk to be as magnificently dull as Peter's was. Compared with it the Dead Sea is a geyser. Never a sparkle or a glimmer of wit marred his words. Commonplaces as trite and as plentiful as blackberries flowed from his lips no more stirring in quality than a last week's tape running from a ticker. Quaking a little I tried upon him one of my best pointed jokes. It fell back ineffectual, with the point broken. I loved that man from then on.

Two or three evenings each week I would steal down to Heffelbower's and revel in his back room. That was my only joy. I began to rise early and hurry through my work, that I might spend more time in my haven. In no other place could I throw off my habit of extracting humorous ideas from my surroundings. Peter's talk left me no openings had I besieged it ever so hard.

Under this influence I began to improve in spirits. It was the recreation from one's labor which every man needs. I surprised one or two of my former friends by throwing them a smile and a cheery word as I passed them on the streets. Several times I dumfounded my family by relaxing long enough to make a jocose remark in their presence.

I had so long been ridden by the incubus of humor that I seized my hours of holiday with a schoolboy's zest.

My work began to suffer. It was not the pain and burden to me that it had been. I often whistled at my desk, and wrote with far more fluency than before. I accomplished my tasks impatiently, as anxious to be off to my helpful retreat as a drunkard is to get to his tavern.

My wife had some anxious hours in conjecturing where I spent my afternoons. I thought it best not to tell her; women do not understand these things. Poor girl!—she had one shock out of it.

One day I brought home a silver coffin handle for a paper weight and a fine, fluffy hearse plume to dust my papers with.

I loved to see them on my desk, and think of the beloved back room down at Heffelbower's. But Louisa found them, and she shrieked with horror. I had to console her with some lame excuse for having them there, but I saw in her eyes that the prejudice was not removed. I had to remove the articles, though, at double-quick time.

One day Peter Heffelbower laid before me a temptation that swept me off my feet. In his sensible, uninspired way he showed me his books, and explained that his profits and his business were increasing rapidly. He had thought of taking in a partner with some cash. He would rather have me than any one he knew. When I left his place that afternoon Peter had my check for the thousand dollars I had in the bank, and I was a partner in his undertaking business.

I went home with feelings of delirious joy, mingled with a certain amount of doubt. I was dreading to tell my wife about it. But I walked on air. To give up the writing of humorous stuff, once more to enjoy the apples of life, instead of squeezing them to a pulp for a few drops of hard cider to make the public feel funny—what a boon that would be!

At the supper table Louisa handed me some letters that had come during my absence. Several of them contained rejected manuscript. Ever since I first began going to Heffelbower's my stuff had been coming back with alarming frequency. Lately I had been dashing off my jokes and articles with the greatest fluency. Previously I had labored like a bricklayer, slowly and with agony.

Presently I opened a letter from the editor of the weekly with which I had a regular contract. The checks for that weekly article were still our main dependence. The letter ran thus:

> DEAR SIR: As you are aware, our contract for the year expires with the present month. While regretting the necessity for so doing, we must say that we do not

care to renew same for the coming year. We were quite pleased with your style of humor, which seems to have delighted quite a large proportion of our readers. But for the past two months we have noticed a decided falling off in its quality.

Your earlier work showed a spontaneous, easy, natural flow of fun and wit. Of late it is labored, studied and unconvincing, giving painful evidence of hard toil and drudging mechanism.

Again regretting that we do not consider your contributions available any longer, we are, yours sincerely.

THE EDITOR

I handed this letter to my wife. After she had read it her face grew extremely long, and there were tears in her eyes.

"The mean old thing!" she exclaimed, indignantly. "I'm sure your pieces are just as good as they ever were. And it doesn't take you half as long to write them as it did." And then, I suppose, Louisa thought of the checks that would cease coming. "Oh, John," she wailed, "what will you do now?"

For an answer I got up and began to do a polka step around the supper table. I am sure Louisa thought the trouble had driven me mad; and I think the children hoped it had, for they tore after me, yelling with glee and emulating my steps. I was now something like their old playmate as of yore.

"The theatre for us to-night!" I shouted, "nothing less. And a late, wild, disreputable supper for all of us at the Palace Restaurant. Lumty-diddle-de-dee-de-dum!"

And then I explained my glee by declaring that I was now a partner in a prosperous undertaking establishment, and that written jokes might go hide their heads in sackcloth and ashes for all me.

With the editor's letter in her hand to justify the deed I had done, my wife could advance no objections save a few mild ones based on the feminine inability to appreciate a good thing such as the little back room of Peter Hef—no, of Heffelbower & Co.'s undertaking establishment.

In conclusion, I will say that to-day you will find no man in our town as well liked, as jovial and full of merry sayings as I. My jokes are again noised about and quoted; once more I take pleasure in my wife's confidential chatter without a mercenary thought, while Guy and Viola play at my feet distributing gems of childish humor without fear of the ghastly tormentor who used to dog their steps, notebook in hand.

Our business has prospered finely. I keep the books and look after the shop, while Peter attends to outside matters. He says that my levity and high spirits would simply turn any funeral into a regular Irish wake.

BRUCE JAY FRIEDMAN

"The Mourner"

One day, Martin Gans found himself driving out to the Long Island funeral of Norbert Mandel, a total stranger. A habit of his was to take a quick check of the orbit section in the New York *Times* each day, concentrating on the important deaths, then scanning the medium-famous ones and some of the also-rans. The listing that caught his eye on this particular day was that of Norbert Mandel, although Gans did not have the faintest idea why he should be interested in the passing of this obscure fellow. The item said that Mandel, of Syosset, Long Island, had died of a heart attack at the age of seventy-three, leaving behind two sisters, Rose and Sylvia, also one son, a Brooklyn optometrist named Phillip. It said, additionally, that Mandel had served on an East Coast real-estate board and many years back had been in the Coast Guard. An ordinary life, God knows, with nothing flashy about it, at least on the surface. Gans read the item in a vacant, mindless way, but suddenly found his interest stirred, a fire breaking out with no apparent source. Was it the sheer innocuousness of the item? Of Mandel's life? He traveled on to other sections of the paper, sports and even maritime, but the Mandel story now began to prick at him in a way that he could not ignore; he turned back to the modest paragraph and read it again and again, until he knew it by heart and felt a sweeping compulsion to race out to Mandel's funeral, which was being held in a memorial chapel on the south shore of Long Island.

If this had happened at some idle point in his life, it might have made some sense. But Gans was busier than ever, involved in moving his ceramics plant to a new location on Lower Fifth Avenue, after twenty years of being in the same place. It was aggravating work; even after the move, it would take six months before Gans really settled in to the new quarters. Yet you could hardly call Mandel's funeral a diversion. A trip to Puerto Rico would have been that. Nor was Gans the type of fellow who particularly enjoyed funerals. His mother and father were still living. No one terribly close to him had died up to now, just some aunts and uncles and a couple of nice friends whose deaths annoyed rather than grieved him. Gans had probably contributed to one aunt's death, come to think of it. A woman in the hospital bed next to Aunt Edna had attacked a book the visiting Gans held under his arm. Gans struck back, defending the volume, and a debate began over poor Aunt Edna's head, as she fought a tattered intravenous battle for life.

The day of Mandel's funeral, Gans took a slow drive to the memorial chapel, allowing an extra half hour for possible traffic problems and the chance that he might lose his way on the south shore, which had always been tricky going for him. On the way, he thought a little about Mandel. He pictured him in an overcoat, also with a beard, although a totally nonrakish one. Mandel struck him as being a tea drinker and someone who dressed carefully against the cold, owning a good stock of mufflers and galoshes. Gans did not particularly like Mandel's association with the East Coast real-estate board, but at the same time, he saw him as a small property owner, not really that much at home with the big boys and actually a decent fellow who was a soft touch. He liked the sound of Mandel's two sisters, Rose and Sylvia, envisioning them as buxom, good-natured, wonderful cooks, enjoying a good pinch on the ass, provided it remained on the hearty and nonerotic side. Phillip, the optometrist, struck Gans as being a momma's boy, into a bit of a ball-breaking marriage, but not too bad a fellow; the Army, Gans felt, had probably toughened him up a bit. There was a chance, of course, that Gans was completely wide of the mark, but these were his speculations as he breezed out to the chapel to get in on the funeral of Norbert Mandel, a fellow he didn't know from Adam.

The chapel was part of an emporium that lay just outside a shopping center and was used as well for bar mitzvahs and catered affairs of all kinds. An attendant in a chauffeur's uniform took his car, saying, "No sweat, I'll see it don't get wet." Inside the carpeted chapel, a funeral-parlor employee asked him if he were there, perchance, for Benjamin Siegal. "No, Norbert Mandel," said Gans. The attendant said they had Mandel on the second floor. Before climbing the stairs, Gans stopped to relieve himself in the chapel john and realized he always did that before going in to watch funeral services. Did this have some significance, he wondered, a quick expulsion of guilt, a swift return to a pure state? Or was it just the long drives?

There was only a small turnout for Mandel. Those on hand had not even bothered to spread out and make the place seem a little busier. Mandel's friends and relatives were all gathered together in the first half dozen rows, giving the chapel the look of an off-Broadway show that had opened to generally poor notices. Gans estimated that he was about fifteen minutes early, but he had the feeling that few additional mourners were going to turn up and he was right about that. Somehow he had sensed that Mandel was not going to draw much of a crowd. Was that why he had come? To help the box office?

Come to think of it, funeral attendance had been on his mind for some time. He had been particularly worried, for example, that his father, once the old man went under, would draw only a meager crowd. His father kept to himself, had only a sprinkling of friends. If Gans had to make up a list of mourners for his dad, he was sure he would not be able to go beyond a dozen the old man could count on to turn up, rain or shine. This was troubling to Gans: in addition, he wondered what there was a rabbi could actually say about his dad. That he was a nice man, kept his nose clean? First of all, he wasn't that nice. People see an old grandmother crossing a street and assume she's a saint. She might have been a triple ax murderer as a young girl in Poland and gotten away with it, thanks to lax Polish law enforcement. Who said old was automatically good and kind? Who said old and short meant gentle and well meaning? Gans' own funeral was an entirely different story. He wasn't worried much about that one. At least not about the turnout. He had a million friends and they would be sure to pack the place. His mother, too, could be counted on to fill at least three quarters of any house: if you got a good rabbi, who knew something about her, who could really get her essence, there wouldn't be much of a problem in coming up with send-off anecdotes. She didn't belong to any organizations, but she had handed out plenty of laughs in her time. It would be a tremendous shame if she were handled by some rabbi who didn't know the first thing about her. He had often thought of doing his mother's eulogy himself; but wouldn't that be like a playwright composing his own notices?

Gans felt a little conspicuous, sitting in the back by himself, and didn't relax until three middle-aged ladies came in and took seats a row in front of him. He had them figured for cousins from out of town who had taken a train in from Philadelphia. They did not seem deeply pained by the loss of Mandel and might have been preparing to see a Wednesday matinee on Broadway. Their combined mood seemed to range from aloof to bitter, and Gans guessed they were on the outs with the family, probably over some long-standing quarrel involving the disposition of family jewelry and china. Gans had little difficulty picking out Rose and Sylvia, Norbert's sisters, who were seated in the front row, wearing black veils and black fur coats. They wept and blew their noses and seemed deeply troubled by Mandel's death, which had come out of the blue. Phillip, the only son, was a complete surprise to Gans. Gans assumed he was the one who was wedged between Rose and Sylvia in the front row. He was certainly no momma's boy. He was every bit of six-three and you could see beneath his clothes that he was a bodybuilder. His jaw was tight, his features absolutely perfect, and you simply wouldn't want to mess with him. Let a woman get smart with this optometrist and she'd wind up with her head in the next county. What woman would want to get smart with him? Jump through a few hoops is what a girl would prefer doing for this customer.

The rabbi came out at a little trot, a slender fellow with brown disappearing hair and rimless glasses—ideal, Gans felt, for a career in crime investigation, since he was totally inconspicuous. Gans did not know much about rabbis, but when this fellow began to speak, he could see that his was the "new style"; that is, totally unflamboyant, low-pressure, very modest, very Nixon Administration in his approach to the pulpit. As he spoke, one of the sisters, either Rose or Sylvia, cried in the background, the bursts of tears and pity coming at random, not really coinciding with any particularly poignant sections in the rabbi's address. "I regret to say that I did not know the departed one very well," he began. "However, those close to him assure me that this was, indeed, my great loss. The late Norbert Mandel, whom we are here to send to his well-earned rest this day, was, by all accounts, a decent, fair, kind, generous, charitable man who led a totally exemplary life." He went on to say that death, sorrowful as it must seem to those left behind in the valley of the living, was not a tragedy when one looked upon it as a life-filled baton being passed from one generation to another or, perhaps, as the satisfying final act of a lifetime drama, fully and truly lived. "And who can say this was not the case with the beloved Norbert Mandel, from his early service to his country in the Coast Guard, right along to his unstinting labors on behalf of the East Coast real-estate board; a life in which the unselfish social gesture was always a natural reflex, rather than something that had to be painfully extracted from him."

"Hold it right there," said Gans, rising to his feet in the rear of the chapel.

"Shame," said one of the Philadelphia women.

"What's up?" asked the rabbi.

"You didn't even know this man," said Gans.

"I recall making that point quite early in my remarks," said the rabbi.

"How can you just toss him into the ground?" said Gans. "You haven't told anything about him. That was a man there. He cut himself a lot shaving. He had pains in his stomach. Why don't you try to tell them how he felt when he lost a job? The hollowness of it. Why don't you go into things like his feelings when someone said kike to him the first time? What about all the time he clocked worrying about cancer? And then didn't even die from it. How did he feel when he had the kid, the boy who's sitting over there? What about the curious mixture of feelings toward his sisters, the tenderness on one hand and, on the other hand, the feelings he couldn't exercise, because you're not allowed to in this society? How about some of that stuff, rabbi?"

"And they're just letting him talk," said one of the Philadelphia women.

"They're not throwing him out," said another. But Rose and Sylvia kept sobbing bitterly, so awash in sorrow the sisters appeared not to have even realized that Gans had taken over from the rabbi. Gans was concerned about only one person, the well-built son Phillip; but, to his surprise, the handsome optometrist only buried his head in his hands, as though he were a ballplayer being scolded at half time by an angry coach. The rabbi was silent, concerned, as though the new style was determined to be moderate and conciliatory, no matter what went on in the chapel. It's a big religion, the rabbi seemed to be saying by his thoughtful silence, with plenty of room for the excessive.

Up until now, it had been a kind of exercise for Gans, but the heat of his own words began to excite him. "Can you really say you're doing justice to this man?" he asked. "Or are you insulting him? Do you know how he felt? Do you know anything about his disappointments? How he wanted to be taller? To you, he's Norbert Mandel, who led an exemplary life. What about the women he longed for and couldn't get? How he spent half his life sunk in grief over things like that. And the other half picking his nose and worrying about getting caught at it. Do you know the way he felt about yellow-haired girls and how he went deaf, dumb and blind when one he liked came near him? Shouldn't some of that be brought out? He wanted blondes right into his seventies; but did he ever get a taste of them? Not on your life. It was Mediterranean types all the way. Shouldn't you take a minute of your time to get into how he felt about his son, the pride when the kid filled out around the shoulders and became tougher than Norbie would ever be, and the jealousy, too, that made him so ashamed and guilty? Do you have any idea what he went through, playing the kid a game, beating him and then wanting to cut off his arm for it? Then letting the kid win a game and that was no good, either. You act as though you've scratched the surface. Don't make me laugh, will you please. You know about his vomiting when he drank too much? On the highway. How do you think that felt? What about a little something else you're leaving out? Those last moments when he knew something was up and he had to look death right in the face. What was that for him, a picnic? I'll tell you, rabbi, you ought to pull him right out of the coffin and take a look at him and find out a little bit about who you're talking about."

"There was a time," said Phillip, the sole surviving son, as though he had received a cue, "when he left the family for a month or so. He was around, but he wasn't with us. He got very gray and solemn and didn't eat. We found out it was because an insurance doctor told him he had a terrible heart and couldn't have life insurance. He called him an 'uninsurable.' That was something, having an uninsurable for a dad. It was a mistake—his heart was healthy at the time—but it was the longest month of my life. The other time that comes to mind is when he shut someone up on the el when we were going out to Coney Island. Shut him up like you never saw anyone shut up. Guy twice his size."

"Very touching," said the rabbi. "Now may I ask how you knew the deceased?"

"I used to see him around," said Gans.

"Fine," said the rabbi. "Well, I don't see why we can't have this once in a while. And all be a little richer for it. If the family doesn't object. Do you have anything else?"

"Nothing I can think of," said Gans. "Unless some of the other members of the family would like to sound off a bit."

"He had a heart of solid gold," said one of the sisters.

"He was some man," said the other.

"Sounds like he was quite a fellow," said the rabbi.

Gans had no plan to do so originally but decided now to go out to the burial grounds, using his own car instead of accepting the offered ride in one of the rented limousines. After Mandel had been put into the ground, Gans accepted an offer from one of the sisters, whom he now knew to be Rose, to come back and eat with the family in a Queens delicatessen. Gans' own mother had always been contemptuous of that particular ritual, mocking families who were able to wolf down delicatessen sandwiches half an hour after a sup- posedly beloved uncle or cousin had been tossed into the earth. "They're very grief-stricken," she would say, "you can tell by their appetites." Gans, as a result, had developed a slight prejudice against the custom, although the logical part of him said why not eat if you're hungry and not eat if you're not. There seemed to be a larger crowd at the delicatessen than had been at the funeral. And it wasn't delicatessen food they were eating, either; it was Rose's cooking. Evidently, the family had merely taken over the restaurant for the afternoon, but Rose had brought in her own food. Gans had some difficulty meeting young Phillip's eyes and Phillip seemed equally ill at ease with him. Gans could not get over how wrong he had been about the boy. He had had an entirely different feeling about what a Brooklyn optometrist should look like. This fellow was central casting for the dark-haired hero in Hollywood West- erns. Even the right gait, slow and sensual; Gans wondered if he had ever thought seriously about a career in show business. Gans ate a hearty meal, and there was something in his attack on the food that seemed to indicate he had earned it. He sat at the same table as Phillip, who ate dreamily, speculatively and seemed, gradually, to get comfortable with the mysterious visitor who had taken over the funeral service.

"You know," said Phillip, "a lot of people never realized this, but he was one hell of an athlete. He had two trophies for handball, and if you know the Brooklyn playground league, you know they don't fool around. And a guy once offered him a tryout with the Boston Bees." The boy paused then, as if he expected a nostalgic anecdote in return from Gans.

Instead, Gans took a deep breath, tilted his chair back slightly and said, "I have to come clean, I never met the man in my life."

"What do you mean?" said Phillip, hunching his big shoulders a bit, although he seemed more puzzled than annoyed. "I don't understand."

Gans hesitated a moment, looking around at the sisters, Rose and Sylvia, at the cousins from Philly, who seemed much more convivial, now that they were eating, at the rabbi, who had come over for a little snack, and at the other mourners. He complimented himself on how easily he had fitted into the group, and it occurred to him that most families, give or take a cousin or two, are remarkably similar, the various members are more or less interchangeable.

"I don't know," he said, finally, to the blindingly handsome optometrist, sole surviving offspring of the freshly buried Norbert Mandel. "I read about your dad in the paper and I had the feeling they were just going to throw him into the ground, and that would be the end of him. Bam, kaput, just like he never lived. So I showed up."

"Now that I think of it," he said, reaching for a slice of Rose's *mohn* cake and anticipating the crunch of poppy seeds in his mouth, "I guess I just didn't think enough of a fuss was being made."

LEO ROSTEN

"The Death of Julius Caesar"

It was Miss Higby's idea. (At least, Mr. Parkhill reflected, it had all started that way.) One night in the faculty lounge, Miss Higby remarked how unfortunate it was that students came to her class wholly unaware of the *finer* side of English, of its beauty and grandeur, of (as she put it) "the glorious heritage of our literature." "There is no reason on earth," Miss Higby had blurted, "why the beginners' grade might not be introduced to a *taste,* at least, of Longfellow or Tennyson or—even Shakespeare!"

Mr. Parkhill could not deny that there was much to be said for Miss Higby's point of view. His pupils *were* adults, after all; they had come to our shores from lands renowned for poets and scholars and men of letters; and many a fledgling in English referred, on occasion, to some classic of European literature. Mr. Matsoukas, for all his cryptic grunts and saturnine moods, sometimes tossed off names from the *Iliad* with considerable fervor. Miss Tarnova (who could wring lurid overtones from a telephone number) rarely let slip by a chance to extol Tolstoy or Gogol or Lermontov. Wolfgang Schmitt, who had gone halfway through a *gymnasium* in Ulm, once delivered an impassioned testimonial to great Thomas Mann. (''Who said he vas a voman?'' Mr. Kaplan had scoffed.) And any number of others in the beginners' grade had seen one or another production, in their native tongue, of *Hamlet* or *The Cherry Orchard, Cyrano de Bergerac* or *A Doll's House* (whose author had unfortunately been identified by Nathan P. Nathan as ''Henry Gibson'').

Apart from Miss Higby's effusive recommendation, Mr. Parkhill realized that his students had been studying English for some time now; they had added *hundreds* of words and phrases to their vocabularies; they had reached a level of familiarity with their new tongue which few teachers would have thought possible when the term began.

''Poetry will alert your class to more precise enunciation,'' Miss Higby had gone on to say, ''and may even attune their ears to the subtleties of English inflection!'' (Miss Higby, whose master's thesis was on Coventry Patmore, *loved* poetry.)

Mr. Parkhill had remarked, ''I just wonder whether my beginners may not feel a bit beyond their depth—''

''Nonsense!'' Miss Higby promptly retorted. ''As Plaut and Samish dis-*tinct*ly state in their final chapter. . . .''

That was the crowning argument. No one teaching English to foreigners could fault a fiat from the magisterial opus of Plaut and Samish.

So it was that when he faced the class the next Tuesday night, a beautiful night, soft and smelling of spring, Mr. Parkhill produced his portable Shake-speare. The love Miss Higby felt for poetry in general was nothing compared to the love Mr. Parkhill bore for Shakespeare in particular. (How many years was it since he had played Polonius at Amherst?)

''Tonight, class,'' Mr. Parkhill smiled, ''I am going to try a little—experiment.''

Thirty heads swung upward. Sixty eyes turned guarded. The beginners' grade had learned to regard Mr. Parkhill's innovations with foreboding.

''We shall take a little excursion into poetry—great poetry—from the greatest master English has ever known. . . .'' Mr. Parkhill delivered a little sermon on the special beauty of poetry, its charm and precision and economy, its revelation of the loftiest thoughts and emotions of mankind. ''I think this will be a welcome relief, to all of us, from our—er—run-of-the-mill exercises!'' The approving nods and murmurs heartened Mr. Parkhill no end. ''So . . . I shall write a famous passage on the board. I shall read it for you. Then, as our Recitation and Speech exercise, you will give short addresses, using the passage as the—springboard, as it were, for your own interpretation: your own thoughts and ideas and reactions.''

He could not remember the last time an announcement had so roused the rows before him.

"Bravo!" sang Carmen Caravello.

"How my mohther did lof Heinrich Heine," sighed Mr. Finsterwald.

Miss Mitnick blushed, mingling pride and wonder. Mr. Bloom clucked—but rather cagily. Mrs. Rodriguez wrinkled her nose: *her* last foray into loftiness was a speech praising Brooklyn Bridge. And Hyman Kaplan, the smile on his face more salubrious than ever, showered Mr. Parkhill with expressions of admiration, whispering: "Poyetry. Now is poyetry! My! Must be som progriss ve makink!"

"The passage," said Mr. Parkhill, "is from Shakespeare."

A bolt of lightning could not have electrified the room more than did the magic of that name.

"*Shakes*peare?!" echoed Mr. Perez. "Eee-ai-ee!"

"The greatest poet from English?" gasped Miss Ziev.

"Imachine!" murmured Mr. Kaplan. "Villiam Jakesbeer!"

" '*Shakes*peare,' Mr. Kaplan, not '*Jakes*beer'!"

Mr. Parkhill took a fresh stick of chalk to write the passage on the board in large, crystal-clear letters:

> Tomorrow, and tomorrow, and tomorrow
> Creeps in this petty pace from day to day,
> To the last syllable of recorded time;
> And all our yesterdays have lighted fools
> The way to dusty death.

"Be*au*riful!" glowed Mr. Kaplan.

> Out, out, brief candle!
> Life's but a walking shadow, a poor player
> That struts and frets his hour upon the stage,
> And then is heard no more; it is a tale
> Told by an idiot—

"True; sod, but true," moaned Olga Tarnova.

> —full of sound and fury,
> Signifying nothing.

The hush of consecration muffled that mundane chamber. Open mouths and suspended breaths, gulps of awe and gapes of reverence edified the eyes that drank in the deathless phrases of the immortal bard. Even Nathan P. Nathan sat solemn.

Mr. Parkhill cleared his throat. "I shall read the passage aloud. Please listen carefully; let Shakespeare's words—I know some are difficult—sink into your minds . . . 'Tomorrow, and tomorrow and tomorrow . . .' '' Mr. Parkhill read very well; and this night he endowed each word with an eloquence even Miss Higby would have admired. " 'Out, out, brief candle!' '' Miss Mitnick's face was bathed in wonderment. " 'Life's but a walking shadow . . .' '' The brow of Gus Matsoukas furrowed. " 'It is a tale told by an idiot . . .' '' Mr. Kaplan's cheeks were incandescent. " '. . . full of sound and fury . . .' '' Mr. Trabish's eyes were shut. (Mr. Parkhill could not tell whether Mr. Trabish had surrendered to the spell of Shakespeare or the arms of Morpheus.) " '. . . signifying nothing!' '' Miss Goldberg fumbled for a jellybean.

"I—shall read the passage once more." Mr. Parkhill's voice was so loud and clear that it roused Mr. Trabish from his coma. " 'Tomorrow, and tomorrow, and tomorrow . . .' ''

After Mr. Parkhill completed that incomparable passage, he surveyed his congregation gravely. "I am sure there are words, here and there, which some of you may find—uh—difficult. Before I call upon you to recite, please feel free to ask—"

Freedom of inquiry erupted within the instant. Mrs. Tomasic asked if "petty" was the diminutive of "pet." (Mr. Parkhill could scarcely blame her for asking if it could be used for her neighbor's "small white rabbi.") Wolfgang Schmitt asked why "frets" lacked a capital "f." (The meticulous butcher thought "frets" was the Americanized form of "Fritz.") Mrs. Shimmelfarb wondered whether "creeps" was a variation of "creaks." Miss Gidwitz, who was exceedingly clothes-conscious, asked if "fury" was the "old-fashion" way of spelling "furry" (her new coat was a beautiful "tweet" with "a furry collar").

Each of these queries Mr. Parkhill explained with patience. " 'Petty' means trivial, mean, or—not worthy, as in 'Jealous people tend to be petty.' . . . 'Frets,' Mr. Schmitt, means to be impatient, showing discontent, as in 'She frets because her train is late!' . . . 'Creeps,' Mrs. Shimmelfarb, means to move slowly, *very* slowly; for instance, 'A turtle *creeps* through the grass.' . . . And 'fury,' Miss Gidwitz, denotes a powerful emotion, not an animal's— er—hide. . . . Anyone else?"

Up stabbed the finger of Casimir Scymczak. "Why," he mumbled, "is no 'l' in word 'pace'? Wrong spalled?!" Mr. Parkhill saw in a flash that Mr. Scymczak was confusing motion with location. "The spelling is entirely correct: you see, *'pace'* is in no way related to *'place.'* '' Mr. Parkhill found, to his surprise, that he was beginning to perspire. " 'Pace' means the rate or speed of movement, as 'The soldiers marched at a brisk pace,' or 'The cars moved in slow, respectful pace to the cemetery.' ''

This saddened Mr. Scymczak.

"Are we ready now, class?"

"No!" came from sultry Miss Tarnova. "Did Shakespeare steal that whole idea from Dostoevsky?!"

Before Mr. Parkhill could nip this delusion in the bud, Mr. Kaplan wheeled around. "Are you *crazy?* You talkink about *Jakes*beer!"

"*Shakes*peare, Mr.—"

"I'm sick an' tiret hearing soch chipp remocks. Lat's begin recitink!"

Mr. Parkhill wiped his palms. (He felt rather grateful to Mr. Kaplan.) "Very well, class . . . Miss Caravello."

Miss Caravello lunged to the podium. "Da poem isa gooda!" she proclaimed. "Itsa have beautiful wordsa, *bella,* lak great musica anda deepa, deepa philosophy. Shakespeare isa lak Alighieri Dante, da greatest Italiano—"

"Vhat?!" bristled Mr. Kaplan. "Shakesbeer you compare mit Dante? *Shakesbeer?!* Ha!"

"Mr. Kaplan, Miss Caravello is merely expressing her opinion."

"Dat's not an opinion, it's a crime! How ken she compare a ginius like Shakesbeer mit a dantist like Dante?!"

"Dante wasa no dentist!" fumed Miss Caravello. "He—"

"He didn't iven stody *teet?*" purred Mr. Kaplan.

Miss Caravello blazed an execration from her homeland and shot back to her seat, gibbering calumnies worthy of Juvenal. Mrs. Shimmelfarb soothed her with sympathy. Miss Goldberg offered her a sourball.

Mr. Parkhill felt dizzy.

"Corrections, anyone?"

Aside from Mr. Trabish's sleepy remark anent Miss Caravello's tendency to add the vowel "a" to any word in sight, and a gritty observation from Mr. Perez that *"bella"* was a foreign word "and we supposed dzhust to talk English!" criticism expired.

The next speaker, Mrs. Yanoff, began, "This pome is full high meanings." Her eyes, however, were fixed on the floor. "Is hard for a person who is not so good in English to catch all. But I like."

" 'Like'?!" flared Mr. Kaplan. "Batter *love,* Yanoff! Mit Shakesbeer must be *love!*"

"*Mr.* Kaplan . . ."

Mrs. Yanoff staggered through several skittish comments and stumbled back to safety.

Next came Norman Bloom. Mr. Kaplan groaned. Mr. Bloom was as brisk, bald, and emphatic as ever. Only his peroration was unexpected: "But Shakespeare's *ideas* are too passimistical. I am an optimist. Life should be with hope and happy! . . . So, remember—this is only a poem, by a man full of gloomy! I say, 'Mr. Shakespeare, why don't you look for a silver lining on the sonny side of each street?' "

"Bloooom!" bawled anguished Kaplan. "You forgat how *honist* is Shakesbeer! He is a passimist because *life* is a passimist also!"

"Not *my* life!" sneered Mr. Bloom.

"You not dad yat," observed Mr. Kaplan, not without regret.

Nathan P. Nathan caterwauled.

"Gentlemen!" Mr. Parkhill was growing quite alarmed. It was clear that Mr. Kaplan had so identified himself with Shakespeare that he would not tolerate the slightest disparagement of his alter ego. How harness so irate a champion? How dampen such flames of grandeur? Perhaps the best course (Mr. Parkhill stifled many misgivings) was to call on Mr. Kaplan at once.

After pointing out several flaws in Mr. Bloom's syntax, and the thoroughly improper use of "gloomy" as a noun, Mr. Parkhill said, "Mr. Kaplan, you—er—seem to be bubbling with so many ideas, perhaps you—would prefer to recite?"

The smile that spread across Mr. Kaplan's countenance rivaled a rainbow. *"Me* next?" The innocent blink of surprise, the fluttering lashes of unworthiness—rarely was modesty so fraudulent.

"Yes."

"Now comes the circus!" announced laughing Nathan. "Rose, get ready all your penecils and all your paper!"

"Go, Keplen!" grinned Mr. Pinsky.

"Trobble, trobble," moaned Olga Tarnova.

"For God's sek, talk *briff*!" growled Mr. Blattberg.

"Give him a *chence*!" snapped "Cookie" Kipnis.

"Oyyy," forecast Mrs. Moskowitz.

Mr. Kaplan rose with dignity, slowly, affecting the manner of one lost in unutterable profundities. In stately stride he mounted the platform. He clutched his lapels à la Daniel Webster. Never had the plump figure appeared so lordly, or displayed such consciousness of a rendezvous with history. He surveyed the ranks before him, thoughtful, silent, deliberating how to clothe majesty in words fit for commoners.

"Omi*god*!" blared Mr. Blattberg.

"So *talk*!" glowered Mr. Matsoukas.

"You are waiting for *bugles*?" taunted Miss Valuskas.

Mr. Kaplan ignored the carping crowd. "Fallow lovers of fine literature. Edmirers of immortable poyetry."

" 'Immor*tal*,' " Mr. Parkhill put in. (He would not have been surprised if Mr. Kaplan had launched into "Friends, Romans, countrymen . . .") "And it's '*po*-etry,' not '*poy*-etry.' If you will try to speak more slowly, Mr. Kaplan, I'm sure you will make fewer mistakes."

Mr. Kaplan inclined his head graciously. "So I'll begin over . . . Ladies an' gantlemen . . . Ve hoid fine spitches by odder members of de cless abot dese vunderful voi—*words* from Shakesbeer. Vell, are you sarisfite?''

'' 'Satisfied'!''

''Not me. I am ebsolutcly not satisfite. Because to me dos movvelous *words* on de blackboard are not *words!* Dey are jools! Poils! Diamonds!''

''Psssh!'' crowed Mr. Pinsky.

''T'ink abot it, cless. T'ink *bilow* an' *arond* dose ectual phrases Shakesbeer put in de mot of—of who? Dat's de important point! *Who is talkink?* A man mit a tarrible problem lookink him in de face. Try to remamber how dat man, Julius Scissor, himsalf falt—''

''*Mr.* Kaplan! It was *not* Julius—''

The eulogist heard him not. ''—on dat historical night! Because in dose movvelous *words* on dis simple bleckboard''—he flung out his right arm, as if from under a toga, pointing to the fateful passage—''Julius Scissor is sayink—''

''Mr. *Kap*lan! That passage is from *Macbeth!*''

Hyman Kaplan stopped in his tracks. He stared at his master as if at his executioner. *''Not* from *Julius Scissor?!''*

''No, no!''

Mr. Kaplan gulped. ''I vas sure—''

''The passage is from *Macbeth,* Mr. Kaplan. And it's not Julius 'Scissor'— but Julius C*ae*sar!''

Woe drowned the once lofty countenance. ''Excuse me. But isn't a 'see-zor' vhat you cottink somt'ink op mit?''

''That,'' said Mr. Parkhill, ''is *'scis*sor.' You have used 'Caesar' for 'scissor' and 'scissor' for 'Caesar'!''

''My!'' Mr. Kaplan was marveling at his virtuosity.

Mr. Parkhill stood shaken. He blamed himself for not having announced at the very beginning that the passage was from *Macbeth.* ''Mr. Kaplan, may I ask what on earth made you think that the passage is from *Julius Caesar?*''

''Because I see it all before mine two ice! De whole scinn—just like a movie. Ve are in Julius's tant. It's de night bafore dey making him Kink fromm Rome. So he is axcited, netcheral, an' he ken't slip—''

'' 'Sleep.' ''

''—so he's layink in his bad, t'inking: 'Tomorrow an' tomorrow an' to-morrow. How slow dey movink. De practically cripp. Soch a pity de pace!' ''

Before Mr. Parkhill could protest that ''petty pace'' did not mean ''Soch a pity de pace!'' Mr. Kaplan, batteries recharged, had swept ahead: ''An' he t'inks: 'Oh, how de time goes slow, fromm day to day, like leetle tsyllables on phonograph racords of time.' ''

''Mr. Kap—''

'' 'An' vhat abot yastidday?' esks Julius Scissor. Ha!'' Mr. Kaplan's eyes blazed. '' 'All our yastiddays are only a light for fools to die in de dost!' ''

" 'Dusty death' does not mean—" But no dam could block that mighty flood.

"An' Julius Scissor is so tiret, an' vants to slip, so he hollers, mit fillink, 'Go ot, go ot, short candle!' "

Mr. Parkhill sank into a chair.

"So de candle goes ot." Mr. Kaplan's voice dropped to a whisper. "Still, pracious slip von't come to Julius. Now is bodderink him de whole idea fromm Life. 'Vhat is Life altogadder?' t'inks Julius Scissor. An' he gives his own soch an enswer!—de pot of dat pessitch I like bast!"

" '*Passage*,' " groped Mr. Parkhill.

" 'Life is like a bum actor, strottink an' hollerink arond de stage for vun hour bafore he's kicked ot! *Life*? Ha! It's a pail full of idjots—' "

"No, *no!* A '*tale*' not a '*pail*'—"

" '—full of funny sonds an' phooey!' "

" '*Sound* and *fury*!' " cried the frantic tutor.

" 'Life is monkey business! It don't minn a t'ing! It singleflies nottink!' . . . Den Julius closes his ice fest"—Mr. Kaplan demonstrated Caesar's exact ocular process by closing his own "ice"—"an' drops dad!"

Silence throbbed its threnody in that hall of learning. Even Miss Tarnova, Mr. Blattberg, flighty Miss Gidwitz sat magnetized by such eloquence. Nathan P. Nathan was holding Miss Mitnick's hand. Miss Goldberg sucked a mint.

Mr. Kaplan nodded philosophically. "Yas, Scissor, great Scissor, dropped dad, forever!" He left the hallowed podium. But just before he took his seat, Mr. Kaplan added this postscript: "Dat vas mine idea. But ufcawss it's all wronk, because Mr. Pockheel axplained how it's not abot Julius Scissor altogadder." A sigh. "It's about an Irishman by de name MacBat!"

It seemed an age before Mr. Parkhill reached his desk, and another before he could bring himself to concentrate on Mr. Kaplan's memorial. For Mr. Parkhill found it hard to wrench his mind back to the cold world of grammar and syntax. Like his students, he was still trying to tear himself away from that historic tent outside Rome, where "Julius Scissor," cursed with insomnia, had pondered time and life, and philosophized himself to a strange and sudden death.

Mr. Parkhill felt distinctly annoyed with Miss Higby.

DAMON RUNYON

"Broadway Complex"

It is along toward four o'clock in the morning, and I am sitting in Mindy's restaurant on Broadway with Ambrose Hammer, the newspaper scribe, enjoying a sturgeon sandwich, which is wonderful brain food, and listening to Ambrose tell me what is wrong with the world, and I am somewhat discouraged by what he tells me, for Ambrose is such a guy as is always very pessimistic about everything.

He is especially very pessimistic about the show business, as Ambrose is what is called a dramatic critic, and he has to go around nearly every night and look at the new plays that people are always putting in the theaters, and I judge from what Ambrose says that this is a very great hardship, and that he seldom gets much pleasure out of life.

Furthermore, I judge from what Ambrose tells me that there is no little danger in being a dramatic critic, because it seems that only a short time before this he goes to a play that is called Never-Never, and Ambrose says it is a very bad play, indeed, and he so states in his newspaper, and in fact Ambrose states in his newspaper that the play smells in nine different keys, and that so does the acting of the leading man, a guy by the name of Fergus Appleton.

Well, the next day Ambrose runs into this Fergus Appleton in front of the Hotel Astor, and what does Fergus Appleton do but haul off and belt Ambrose over the noggin with a cane, and ruin a nice new fall derby for Ambrose, and when Ambrose puts in an expense account to his newspaper for this kady they refuse to pay it, so Ambrose is out four bobs.

And anyway, Ambrose says, the theatergoing public never appreciates what a dramatic critic does for it, because it seems that even though he tips the public off that Never-Never is strictly a turkey, it is a great success, and, moreover, Fergus Appleton is now going around with a doll who is nobody but Miss Florentine Fayette, the daughter of old Hannibal Fayette.

And anybody will tell you that old Hannibal Fayette is very, very, very rich, and has a piece of many different propositions, including the newspaper that

Ambrose Hammer works for, although of course at the time Ambrose speaks of Fergus Appleton's acting, he has no idea Fergus is going to wind up going around with Miss Florentine Fayette.

So Ambrose says the chances are his newspaper will give him the heave-o as soon as Fergus Appleton gets the opportunity to drop the zing in on him, but Ambrose says he does not care a cuss as he is writing a play himself that will show the theatergoing public what a real play is.

Well, Ambrose is writing this play ever since I know him, which is a matter of several years, and he tells me about it so often that I can play any part in it myself with a little practice, and he is just getting around to going over his first act with me again when in comes a guy by the name of Cecil Earl, who is what is called a master of ceremonies at the Golden Slipper night club.

Personally, I never see Cecil Earl but once or twice before in my life, and he always strikes me as a very quiet and modest young guy, for a master of ceremonies, and I am greatly surprised at the way he comes in, as he is acting very bold and aggressive toward one and all, and is speaking out loud in a harsh, disagreeable tone of voice, and in general is acting like a guy who is looking for trouble, which is certainly no way for a master of ceremonies to act.

But of course if a guy is looking for trouble on Broadway along toward four o'clock in the morning, anybody will tell you that the right address is nowhere else but Mindy's, because at such an hour many citizens are gathered there, and are commencing to get a little cross wondering where they are going to make a scratch for the morrow's operations, such as playing the horses.

It is a sure thing that any citizen who makes his scratch before four o'clock in the morning is at home getting his rest, so he will arise fully refreshed for whatever the day may bring forth, and also to avoid the bite he is apt to encounter in Mindy's from citizens who do not make a scratch.

However, the citizens who are present the morning I am speaking of do not pay much attention to Cecil Earl when he comes in, as he is nothing but a tall, skinny young guy, with slick black hair, such as you are apt to see anywhere along Broadway at any time, especially standing in front of theatrical booking offices. In fact, to look at Cecil you will bet he is maybe a saxophone player, as there is something about him that makes you think of a saxophone player right away and, to tell the truth, Cecil can tootle a pretty fair sax, at that, if the play happens to come up.

Well, Cecil sits down at a table where several influential citizens are sitting, including Nathan Detroit, who runs the crap game, and Big Nig, the crap shooter, and Regret, the horse player, and Upstate Red, who is one of the best faro bank players in the world whenever he can find a faro bank and something to play it with, and these citizens are discussing some very serious matters, when out of a clear sky Cecil ups and speaks to them as follows:

"Listen," Cecil says, "if youse guys do not stop making so much noise, I may cool you all off."

Well, naturally, this is most repulsive language to use to such influential citizens, and furthermore it is very illiterate to say youse, so without changing the subject Nathan Detroit reaches out and picks up an order of ham and eggs, Southern style, that Charley, the waiter, just puts in front of Upstate Red, and taps Cecil on the onion with same.

It is unfortunate for Cecil that Nathan Detroit does not remove the ham and eggs, Southern style, from the platter before tapping Cecil with the order, because it is a very hard platter, and Cecil is knocked as stiff as a plank, and maybe stiffer, and it becomes necessary to summon old Doctor Moggs to bring him back to life.

Well, of course none of us know that Cecil is at the moment Jack Legs Diamond, or Mad Dog Coll, or some other very tough gorill, and in fact this does not come out until Ambrose Hammer later starts investigating the strange actions of Cecil Earl, and then Nathan Detroit apologizes to Cecil, and also to the chef in Mindy's for treating an order of ham and eggs, Southern style, so disrespectfully.

It comes out that Cecil is subject to spells of being somebody else besides Cecil Earl, and Ambrose Hammer gives us a very long explanation of this situation, only Ambrose finally becomes so scientific that nobody can keep cases on him. But we gather in a general way from what Ambrose says that Cecil Earl is very susceptible to suggestion from anything he reads, or is told.

In fact, Ambrose says he is the most susceptible guy of this kind he ever meets up with in his life, and it seems that when he is going to Harvard College, which is before he starts in being a dramatic critic, Ambrose makes quite a study of these matters.

Personally, I always claim that Cecil Earl is a little screwy, or if he is not screwy that he will do very well as a pinch-hitter until a screwy guy comes to bat, but Ambrose Hammer says no. Ambrose says it is true that Cecil may be bobbing a trifle, but that he is by no means entirely off his nut. Ambrose says that Cecil only has delusions of grandeur, and complexes, and I do not know what all else, but Ambrose says it is 9 to 10 and take your pick whether Cecil is a genius or a daffydill.

Ambrose says that Cecil is like an actor playing a different part every now and then, only Cecil tries to live every part he plays, and Ambrose claims that if we have actors with as much sense as Cecil in playing parts, the show business will be a lot better off. But of course Ambrose cares very little for actors since Fergus Appleton ruins his kady.

Well, the next time I see Cecil he comes in Mindy's again, and this time it seems he is Jack Dempsey, and while ordinarily nobody will mind him being Jack Dempsey, or even Gene Tunney, although he is not the type for Gene

Tunney, Cecil takes to throwing left hooks at citizens' chins, so finally Sam the Singer gets up and lets a right hand go inside a left hook, and once more Cecil folds up like an old accordion.

When I speak of this to Ambrose Hammer, he says that being Jack Dempsey is entirely a false complex for Cecil, brought on mainly by Cecil taking a few belts at the Golden Slipper liquor during the evening. In fact, Ambrose says this particular complex does not count. But I notice that after this Cecil is never anybody very brash when he is around Mindy's.

Sometimes he is somebody else besides Cecil Earl for as long as a week at a stretch, and in fact once he is Napoleon for two whole weeks, but Ambrose Hammer says this is nothing. Ambrose says he personally knows guys who are Napoleon all their lives. But of course Ambrose means that these guys are only Napoleon in their own minds. He says that the only difference between Cecil and them is that Cecil's complex breaks out on him in public, while the other guys are Napoleons only in their own bedrooms.

Personally, I think such guys are entitled to be locked up in spots with high walls around and about, but Ambrose seems to make nothing much of it, and anyway this Cecil Earl is as harmless as a bag of marshmellows, no matter who he is being.

One thing I must say for Cecil Earl, he is nearly always an interesting guy to talk to, because he nearly always has a different personality, and in fact the only time he is uninteresting is when he is being nobody but Cecil Earl. Then he is a very quiet guy with a sad face and he is so bashful and retiring that you will scarcely believe he is the same guy who goes around all one week being Mussolini in his own mind.

Now I wish to say that Cecil Earl does not often go around making any public display of these spells of his, except when the character calls for a display, such as the time he is George Bernard Shaw, and in fact unless you know him personally you may sometimes figure him just a guy sitting back in a corner somewhere with nothing whatever on his mind, and you will never even suspect that you are in the presence of J. Pierpont Morgan studying out a way to make us all rich.

It gets so that nobody resents Cecil being anything he pleases, except once when he is Senator Huey Long, and once when he is Hitler, and makes the mistake of wandering down on the lower East Side and saying so. In fact, it gets so everybody along Broadway puts in with him and helps him be whoever he is, as much as possible, although I always claim he has a bad influence on some citizens, for instance Regret, the horse player.

It seems that Regret catches a complex off of Cecil Earl one day, and for twenty-four hours he is Pittsburgh Phil, the race track plunger, and goes overboard with every bookie down at Belmont Park and has to hide out for some time before he can get himself straightened out.

Now Cecil Earl is a good master of ceremonies in a night club, if you care for masters of ceremonies, a master of ceremonies in a night club being a guy who is supposed to make cute cracks, and to introduce any celebrities who happen to be sitting around the joint, such as actors and prominent merchants, so the other customers can give them a big hand, and this is by no means an easy job, as sometimes a master of ceremonies may overlook a celebrity, and the celebrity becomes terribly insulted.

But it seems that Cecil Earl is smart enough to introduce all the people in the Golden Slipper every night and call for a big hand for them, no matter who they are, so nobody can get insulted, although one night he introduces a new head waiter, thinking he is nothing but a customer, and the head waiter is somewhat insulted, at that, and threatens to quit, because he claims being introduced in a night club is no boost for him.

Anyway, Cecil gets a nice piece of money for being master of ceremonies at the Golden Slipper, and when he is working there his complexes do not seem to bother him very much, and he is never anybody more serious than Harry Richman or Mort Downey. And it is at the Golden Slipper that he meets this guy, Fergus Appleton, and Miss Florentine Fayette.

Now Miss Florentine Fayette is a tall, slim, black-haired doll, and so beautiful she is practically untrue, but she has a kisser that never seems to relax, and furthermore she never seems much interested in anything whatever. In fact, if Miss Florentine Fayette's papa does not have so many cucumbers, I will say she is slightly dumb, but for all I know it may be against the law to say a doll whose papa has all these cucumbers is dumb. So I will only say that she does not strike me as right bright.

She is a great hand for going around night clubs and sitting there practically unconscious for hours at a time, and always this Fergus Appleton is with her, and before long it gets around that Fergus Appleton wishes to make Miss Florentine Fayette his ever-loving wife, and everybody admits that it will be a very nice score, indeed, for an actor.

Personally, I see nothing wrong with this situation because, to tell you the truth, I will just naturally love to make Miss Florentine Fayette my own ever-loving wife if her papa's cucumbers go with it, but of course Ambrose Hammer does not approve of the idea of her becoming Fergus Appleton's wife, because Ambrose can see how it may work out to his disadvantage.

This Fergus Appleton is a fine-looking guy of maybe forty, with iron-gray hair that makes him appear very romantic, and he is always well dressed in spats and one thing and another, and he smokes cigarettes in a holder nearly a foot long, and wears a watch on one wrist and a slave bracelet on the other, and a big ring on each hand, and sometimes a monocle in one eye, although Ambrose Hammer claims that this is strictly the old ackamarackuss.

There is no doubt that Fergus Appleton is a very chesty guy, and likes to pose around in public places, but I see maybe a million guys like him in my time on Broadway, and not all of them are actors, so I do not hate him for his posing, or for his slave bracelet, or the monocle either, although naturally I consider him out of line in busting my friend Ambrose Hammer's new derby, and I promise Ambrose that the first time Fergus Appleton shows up in a new derby, or even an old one, I will see that somebody busts it, if I have to do it myself.

The only thing wrong I see about Fergus Appleton is that he is a smart-Alecky guy, and when he first finds out about Cecil Earl's complexes he starts working on them to amuse the guys and dolls who hang out around the Golden Slipper with him and Miss Florentine Fayette.

Moreover, it seems that somehow Cecil Earl is very susceptible, indeed, to Fergus Appleton's suggestions, and for a while Fergus Appleton makes quite a sucker of Cecil Earl.

Then all of a sudden Fergus Appleton stops making a sucker of Cecil, and the next thing anybody knows Fergus Appleton is becoming quite pally with Cecil, and I see them around Mindy's, and other late spots after the Golden Slipper closes, and sometimes Miss Florentine Fayette is with them, although Cecil Earl is such a guy as does not care much for the society of dolls, and in fact is very much embarrassed when they are around, which is most surprising conduct for a master of ceremonies in a night club, as such characters are usually pretty fresh with dolls.

But of course even the freshest master of ceremonies is apt to be a little bashful when such a doll as Miss Florentine Fayette is around, on account of her papa having so many cucumbers, and when she is present Cecil Earl seldom opens his trap, but just sits looking at her and letting Fergus Appleton do all the gabbing, which suits Fergus Appleton fine, as he does not mind hearing himself gab, and in fact loves it.

Sometimes I run into just Cecil Earl and Fergus Appleton, and generally they have their heads close together, and are talking low and serious, like two business guys with a large deal coming up between them.

Furthermore, I can see that Cecil Earl is looking very mysterious and solemn himself, so I figure that maybe they are doping out a new play together and that Cecil is acting one of the parts, and whatever it is they are doing I consider it quite big-hearted of Fergus Appleton to take such a friendly interest in Cecil.

But somehow Ambrose Hammer does not like it. In fact, Ambrose Hammer speaks of the matter at some length to me, and says to me like this:

"It is unnatural," he says. "It is unnatural for a guy like Fergus Appleton, who is such a guy as never has a thought in the world for anybody but himself, to be playing the warm for a guy like Cecil Earl. There is something wrong in this business, and," Ambrose says, "I am going to find out what it is."

Well, personally I do not see where it is any of Ambrose Hammer's put-in even if there is something wrong, but Ambrose is always poking his beezer into other people's business, and he starts watching Cecil and Fergus Appleton with great interest whenever he happens to run into them.

Finally it comes an early Sunday morning, and Ambrose Hammer and I are in Mindy's as usual, when in comes Cecil Earl all alone, with a book under one arm. He sits down at a table in a corner booth all by himself and orders a western sandwich and starts in to read his book, and nothing will do Ambrose Hammer but for us to go over and talk to Cecil.

When he sees us coming, he closes his book and drops it in his lap and gives us a very weak hello. It is the first time we see him alone in quite a spell, and finally Ambrose Hammer asks where is Fergus Appleton, although Ambrose really does not care where he is, unless it happens to turn out that he is in a pesthouse suffering from smallpox.

Cecil says Fergus Appleton has to go over to Philadelphia on business over the week-end, and then Ambrose asks Cecil where Miss Florentine Fayette is, and Cecil says he does not know but supposes she is home.

"Well," Ambrose Hammer says, "Miss Florentine Fayette is certainly a beautiful doll, even if she does look a little bit colder than I like them, but," he says, "what she sees in such a pish-tush as Fergus Appleton I do not know."

Now at this Cecil Earl busts right out crying, and naturally Ambrose Hammer and I are greatly astonished at such an exhibition, because we do not see any occasion for tears, and personally I am figuring on taking it on the Dan O'Leary away from there before somebody gets to thinking we do Cecil some great wrong, when Cecil speaks as follows:

"I love her," Cecil says. "I love her with all my heart and soul. But she belongs to my best friend. For two cents I will take this dagger that Fergus gives me and end it all, because life is not worth living without Miss Florentine Fayette."

And with this Cecil Earl outs with a big long stabber, which is a spectacle that is most disquieting to me as I know such articles are against the law in this man's town. So I make Cecil put it right back in his pocket and while I am doing this Ambrose Hammer reaches down beside Cecil and grabs the book Cecil is reading, and while Cecil is still sobbing Ambrose looks this volume over.

It turns out to be a book called The Hundred-Per-Cent-Perfect Crime, but what interests Ambrose Hammer more than anything else is a lead-pencil drawing on one of the blank pages in the front part of the book. Afterwards Ambrose sketches this drawing out for me as near as he can remember it on the back of one of Mindy's menu cards, and it looks to me like the drawing of the ground floor of a small house, with a line on one side on which is written the word Menahan, and Ambrose says he figures this means a street.

But in the meantime Ambrose tries to soothe Cecil Earl and to get him to stop crying, and when Cecil finally does dry up he sees Ambrose has his book, and he makes a grab for it and creates quite a scene until he gets it back.

Personally, I cannot make head or tail of the sketch that Ambrose draws for me, and I cannot see that there is anything to it anyway, but Ambrose seems to regard it as of some importance.

Well, I do not see Ambrose Hammer for several days, but I am hearing strange stories of him being seen with Cecil Earl in the afternoons when Fergus Appleton is playing matinees in Never-Never, and early in the evenings when Fergus Appleton is doing his night performances, and I also hear that Ambrose always seems to be talking very earnestly to Cecil Earl, and sometimes throwing his arms about in a most excited manner.

Then one morning Ambrose Hammer looks me up again in Mindy's, and he is smiling a very large smile, as if he is greatly pleased with something, which is quite surprising as Ambrose Hammer is seldom pleased with anything. Finally he says to me like this:

"Well," Ambrose says, "I learn the meaning of the drawing in Cecil Earl's book. It is the plan of a house on Menahan Street, away over in Brooklyn. And the way I learn this is very, very clever, indeed," Ambrose says. "I stake a chambermaid to let me into Fergus Appleton's joint in the Dazzy apartments, and what do I find there just as I expect but a letter from a certain number on this street?"

"Why," I say to Ambrose Hammer, "I am greatly horrified by your statement. You are nothing but a burglar, and if Fergus Appleton finds this out he will turn you over to the officers of the law, and you will lose your job and everything else."

"No," Ambrose says, "I will not lose my job, because old Hannibal Fayette is around the office yesterday raising an awful row about his daughter wishing to marry an actor, and saying he will give he does not know what if anybody can bust this romance up. The chances are," Ambrose says, "he will make me editor in chief of the paper, and then I will can a lot of guys I do not like. Fergus Appleton is to meet Cecil Earl here this morning, and in the meantime I will relate the story to you."

But before Ambrose can tell me the story, in comes Fergus Appleton, and Miss Florentine Fayette is with him, and they sit down at a table not far from us, and Fergus Appleton looks around and sees Ambrose and gives him a terrible scowl. Furthermore, he says something to Miss Florentine Fayette, and she looks at Ambrose, too, but she does not scowl or anything else, but only looks very dead-pan.

Fergus Appleton is in evening clothes and has on his monocle, and Miss Florentine Fayette is wearing such a gown that anybody can see how beautiful she is, no matter if her face does not have much expression. They are sitting there without much conversation passing between them, when all of a sudden in walks Cecil Earl, full of speed and much excited.

He comes in with such a rush that he almost flattens Regret, the horse player, who is on his way out, and Regret is about to call him a dirty name when he sees a spectacle that will always be remembered in Mindy's, for Cecil Earl walks right over to Miss Florentine Fayette as she is sitting there beside Fergus Appleton, and without saying as much as boo to Fergus Appleton, Cecil grabs Miss Florentine Fayette up in his arms with surprising strength and gives her a big sizzling kiss, and says to her like this:

"Florentine," he says, "I love you."

Then he squeezes her to his bosom so tight that it looks as if he is about to squeeze her right out through the top of her gown like squeezing toothpaste out of a tube, and says to her again, as follows:

"I love you. Oh, how I love you."

Well, at first Fergus Appleton is so astonished at this proposition that he can scarcely stir, and the chances are he cannot believe his eyes. Furthermore, many other citizens who are present partaking of their Bismarck herring, and one thing and another, are also astonished, and they are commencing to think that maybe Cecil Earl is having a complex about being King Kong, when Fergus Appleton finally gets to his feet and speaks in a loud tone of voice as follows:

"Why," Fergus Appleton says, "you are nothing but a scurvy fellow, and unless you unhand my fiancée, the chances are I will annihilate you."

Naturally, Fergus Appleton is somewhat excited, and in fact he is so excited that he drops his monocle to the floor, and it breaks into several pieces. At first he seems to have some idea of dropping a big right hand on Cecil Earl somewhere, but Cecil is pretty well covered by Miss Florentine Fayette, so Fergus Appleton can see that if he lets a right hand go he is bound to strike Miss Florentine Fayette right where she lives.

So he only grabs hold of Miss Florentine Fayette, and tries to pull her loose from Cecil Earl, and Cecil Earl not only holds her tighter, but Miss Florentine Fayette seems to be doing some holding to Cecil herself, so Fergus Appleton cannot peel her off, although he gets one stocking and a piece of elastic strap from somewhere. Then one and all are greatly surprised to hear Miss Florentine Fayette speak to Fergus Appleton like this:

"Go away, you old porous plaster," Miss Florentine Fayette says. "I love only my Cecil. Hold me tighter, Cecil, you great big bear," Miss Florentine Fayette says, although of course Cecil looks about as much like a bear as Ambrose Hammer looks like a porcupine.

Well, of course, there is great commotion in Mindy's, because Cecil Earl is putting on a love scene such as makes many citizens very homesick, and Fergus Appleton does not seem to know what to do, when Ambrose Hammer gets to him and whispers a few words in his ear, and all of a sudden Fergus Appleton turns and walks out of Mindy's and disappears, and furthermore nobody ever sees him in these parts again.

By and by Mindy himself comes up and tells Cecil Earl and Miss Florentine Fayette that the chef is complaining because he cannot seem to make ice in his refrigerator while they are in the joint, and will they please go away. So Cecil Earl and Miss Florentine Fayette go, and then Ambrose Hammer comes back to me and finishes his story.

"Well," Ambrose says, "I go over to the certain number on Menahan Street and what do I find there but a crippled-up middle-aged doll who is nobody but Fergus Appleton's ever-loving wife, and furthermore she is such for over twenty years. She tells me that Fergus is the meanest guy that ever breathes the breath of life, and that he is persecuting her for a long time in every way he can think of because she will not give him a divorce.

"And," Ambrose says, "the reason she will not give him a divorce is because he knocks her downstairs a long time ago, and makes her a cripple for life, and leaves her to the care of her own people. But of course I do not tell her," Ambrose says, "that she narrowly escapes being murdered through him, for the meaning of the floor plan of the house in Cecil's book, and the meaning of the book itself, and of the dagger, is that Fergus Appleton is working on Cecil Earl until he has him believing that he can be the super-murderer of the age."

"Why," I say to Ambrose Hammer, "I am greatly shocked by these revelations. Why, Fergus Appleton is nothing but a fellow."

"Well," Ambrose says, "he is pretty cute, at that. He has Cecil thinking that it will be a wonderful thing to be the guy who commits the hundred-per-cent-perfect crime, and furthermore Fergus promises to make Cecil rich after he marries Miss Florentine Fayette."

"But," I say, "what I do not understand is what makes Cecil become such a violent lover all of a sudden."

"Why," Ambrose Hammer says, "when Cecil lets it out that he loves Miss Florentine Fayette, it gives me a nice clue to the whole situation. I take Cecil in hand and give him a little coaching and, furthermore, I make him a present of a book myself. He finds it more interesting than anything Fergus Appleton gives him. In fact," Ambrose says, "I recommend it to you. When Cecil comes in here this morning, he is not Cecil Earl, the potential Perfect Murderer. He is nobody but the world's champion heavy lover, old Don Juan."

Well, Ambrose does not get to be editor in chief of his newspaper. In fact, he just misses getting the outdoors, because Cecil Earl and Miss Florentine Fayette elope, and get married, and go out to Hollywood on a honeymoon, and never return, and old Hannibal Fayette claims it is just as bad for his daughter to marry a movie actor as a guy on the stage, even though Cecil turns out to be the greatest drawing card on the screen because he can heat up love scenes so good.

But I always say that Cecil Earl is quite an ingrate, because he refuses a part in Ambrose Hammer's play when Ambrose finally gets it written, and makes his biggest hit in a screen version of Never-Never.

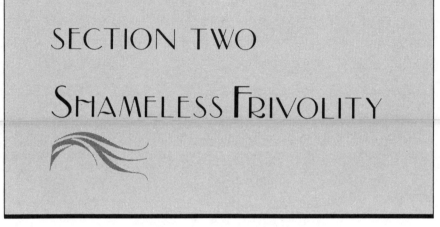

SECTION TWO

SHAMELESS FRIVOLITY

The pieces in this section have no higher or deeper meaning. No serious messages are hidden within. They point to no moral, preach no lesson, deplore no vice, assault no tyrant. They may even strike you as childishly frivolous nonsense. If so, it simply reflects how seriously we take our humor here at the end of the century, when the fires of moral and social uplift burn with unusual passion, threatening to purify America of sass and vinegar.

Some of the most magical humor springs from a joy in playfulness which is natural to children. The pieces that follow seem to have been written by people who never lost childhood's delight in play for the pure joy of play.

The charm of their work may suggest they were written by blessedly carefree innocents. Not so. Most of those represented here have also written humor that is decidedly bleak. Even Robert Benchley, with that feather-light touch of the playful child, could not conceal his loathing for childhood's favorite festival when writing about Christmas.

ROBERT BENCHLEY

"Contributors to This Issue"

Unfortunately the current issue of our magazine has had to be abandoned because of low visibility and an epidemic of printers' nausea, but we felt that our readers would still want to know a little something of the private lives of our contributors. At any rate, here we go:

ELWOOD M. CRINGE, who contributed the article *Is Europe?* is a graduate of Moffard College and, since graduation, has specialized in high tension rope. He is thirty-two years old, wears a collar, and his hobbies are golf, bobbing for apples, and junket.

HAL GARMISCH, author of *How It Feels to Be Underslung,* writes: "I am young, good-looking and would like to meet a girl about my own age who likes to run. I have no hobbies, but I am crazy about kitties."

MEDFORD LAZENBY probably knows more about people, as such, than anyone in the country, unless it is people themselves. He has been all over the world in a balloon-rigged ketch and has a fascinating story to tell. *China Through a Strainer,* in this issue, is not it.

ELIZABETH FEDELLER, after graduation from Ruby College for Near-Sighted Girls, had a good time for herself among the deserted towns of Montana and writes of her experiences in a style which has been compared unfavorably with that of Ernest Hemingway. She is rather unattractive looking.

On our request for information, GIRLIE TENNAFLY wrote us that he is unable to furnish any, owing to a short memory. He contributed the article on *Flanges: Open and Shut,* which is not appearing in this issue.

We will let ESTHER RUBRIC tell about herself: "Strange as it may seem," writes Miss Rubric, "I am not a 'high-brow,' although I write on what are known as 'high-brow' subjects. I am really quite a good sport, and love to play tennis (or 'play at' tennis, as I call it), and am always ready for a good romp. My mother and father were missionaries in Boston, and I was brought up in a strictly family way. We children used to be thought strange by all the other 'kids' in Boston because my brothers had beards and I fell down a lot. But, as far as I can see, we all grew up to be respectable citizens, in a pig's eye. When your magazine accepted my article on *How to Decorate a Mergenthaler Linotype Machine,* I was in the 'seventh heaven.' I copied it, word for word, from Kipling.''

DARG GAMM is too well known to our readers to call for an introduction. He is now at work on his next-but-one novel and is in hiding with the Class of 1915 of Zanzer College, who are preparing for their twentieth reunion in June.

We couldn't get IRVIN S. COBB or CLARENCE BUDINGTON KELLAND to answer our request for manuscripts.

ROY BLOUNT, JR.

"Hymn to Ham"

Though Ham was one of Noah's sons
(Like Japheth), I can't see
That Ham meant any more to him
Than ham has meant to me.

On Christmas Eve
I said, ''Yes ma'am,
I do believe
I'll have more ham.''

I said, ''Yes ma'am,
I do believe
I'll have more ham.''

I said, ''Yes ma'am,
I do believe
I'll have more ham.''

And then after dinner my uncle said he
Was predominantly English but part Cherokee.
"As near as I can figure," I said, "I am
An eighth Scotch-Irish and seven-eighths ham."

Ham.
My soul.
I took a big hot roll,
I put in some jam,
And butter that melted down in with the jam,
Which was blackberry jam,
And a big old folded-over oozy slice of HAM . . .
And my head swam.

Ham!
Hit me with a hammah,
Wham bam bam!
What good ammah
Without mah ham?

Ham's substantial, ham is fat,
Ham is firm and sound.
Ham's what God was getting at
When he made pigs so round.

Aunt Fay's as big as she can be—
She weighs one hundred, she must weigh three.
But Fay says, "Ham! Oh Lord, praise be,
Ham has never hampered me!"

Next to Mama and Daddy and Gram,
We all love the family ham.

So let's program
A hymn to ham.
To appetizing, filling ham.
(I knew a girl named Willingham.)
And after that we'll all go cram
Ourselves from teeth to diaphragm
Full of ham.

Roy Blount, Jr.

"Song to Bacon"

Consumer groups have gone and taken
Some of the savor out of bacon.
Protein-per-penny in bacon, they say,
Equals needles-per-square-inch of hay.
Well, I know, after cooking all
That's left to eat is mighty small
   (You also get a lot of lossage
   In life, romance and country sausage),
And I will vote for making it cheaper,
Wider, longer, leaner, deeper,
But let's not throw the baby, please,
Out with the (visual rhyme here) grease.
There's nothing crumbles like bacon still,
And I don't think there ever will
Be anything, whate'er you use
For meat, that chews like bacon chews.
Also, I'd like these groups to tell
Me whether they factored in the smell.
The smell of it cooking's worth $2.10 a pound.
And howbout the *sound*?

ROY BLOUNT, JR.

"Song to Grease"

I feel that I will never cease
To hold in admiration grease.
It's grease makes frying things so crackly,
During and after. Think how slackly
Bacon lies before its grease
Effusively secures release.
Then that same grease protects the eggs
From hard burnt ruin. Grease! It begs
Comparison to that old stone
That turned base metals gold. The on-
Ly thing that grease won't do with food

Is make it evanesce once chewed.
In fact grease lends a certain weight
That makes it clear that you just ate
Something solid. Something thick.
Something like *das Ding an sich.*
This firm substantiation is al-
Lied directly with the sizzle.

Oh when our joints refuse to function,
When we stand in need of unction,
Bring us two pork chops apiece,
A skillet, lots of room and grease.

Though Batter's great and Fire is too,
And so, if you can Fry, are You,
What lubricates and crisps at once—
That's Grease—makes all the difference.

WOODY ALLEN

"A Look at Organized Crime"

It is no secret that organized crime in America takes in over forty billion dollars a year. This is quite a profitable sum, especially when one considers that the Mafia spends very little for office supplies. Reliable sources indicate that the Cosa Nostra laid out no more than six thousand dollars last year for personalized stationery, and even less for staples. Furthermore, they have one secretary who does all the typing, and only three small rooms for headquarters, which they share with the Fred Persky Dance Studio.

Last year, organized crime was directly responsible for more than one hundred murders, and *mafiosi* participated indirectly in several hundred more, either by lending the killers carfare or by holding their coats. Other illicit activities engaged in by Cosa Nostra members included gambling, narcotics, prostitution, hijacking, loansharking, and the transportation of a large whitefish across the state line for immoral purposes. The tentacles of this corrupt empire even reach into the government itself. Only a few months ago, two gang lords under federal indictment spent the night at the White House, and the President slept on the sofa.

HISTORY OF ORGANIZED CRIME IN THE UNITED STATES

In 1921, Thomas (The Butcher) Covello and Ciro (The Tailor) Santucci attempted to organize disparate ethnic groups of the underworld and thus take over Chicago. This was foiled when Albert (The Logical Positivist) Corillo assassinated Kid Lipsky by locking him in a closet and sucking all the air out through a straw. Lipsky's brother Mendy (alias Mendy Lewis, alias Mendy Larsen, alias Mendy Alias) avenged Lipsky's murder by abducting Santucci's brother Gaetano (also known as Little Tony, or Rabbi Henry Sharpstein) and returning him several weeks later in twenty-seven separate mason jars. This signalled the beginning of a bloodbath.

Dominick (The Herpetologist) Mione shot Lucky Lorenzo (so nicknamed when a bomb that went off in his hat failed to kill him) outside a bar in Chicago. In return, Corillo and his men traced Mione to Newark and made his head into a wind instrument. At this point, the Vitale gang, run by Giuseppe Vitale (real name Quincy Baedeker), made their move to take over all bootlegging in Harlem from Irish Larry Doyle—a racketeer so suspicious that he refused to let anybody in New York ever get behind him, and walked down the street constantly pirouetting and spinning around. Doyle was killed when the Squillante Construction Company decided to erect their new offices on the bridge of his nose. Doyle's lieutenant, Little Petey (Big Petey) Ross, now took command; he resisted the Vitale takeover and lured Vitale to an empty midtown garage on the pretext that a costume party was being held there. Unsuspecting, Vitale walked into the garage dressed as a giant mouse, and was instantly riddled with machine-gun bullets. Out of loyalty to their slain chief, Vitale's men immediately defected to Ross. So did Vitale's fiancée, Bea Moretti, a showgirl and star of the hit Broadway musical *Say Kaddish,* who wound up marrying Ross, although she later sued him for divorce, charging that he once spread an unpleasant ointment on her.

Fearing federal intervention, Vincent Columbraro, the Buttered Toast King, called for a truce. (Columbraro has such tight control over all buttered toast moving in and out of New Jersey that one word from him could ruin breakfast for two-thirds of the nation.) All members of the underworld were summoned to a diner in Perth Amboy, where Columbraro told them that internal warfare must stop and that from then on they had to dress decently and stop slinking around. Letters formerly signed with a black hand would in the future be signed "Best Wishes," and all territory would be divided equally, with New Jersey going to Columbraro's mother. Thus the Mafia, or Cosa Nostra (literally, "my toothpaste" or "our toothpaste"), was born. Two days later, Columbraro got into a nice hot tub to take a bath and has been missing for the past forty-six years.

Mob Structure

The Cosa Nostra is structured like any government or large corporation—or group of gangsters, for that matter. At the top is the *capo di tutti capi,* or boss of all bosses. Meetings are held at his house, and he is responsible for supplying cold cuts and ice cubes. Failure to do so means instant death. (Death, incidentally, is one of the worst things that can happen to a Cosa Nostra member, and many prefer simply to pay a fine.) Under the boss of bosses are his lieutenants, each of whom runs one section of town with his "family." Mafia families do not consist of a wife and children who always go to places like the circus or on picnics. They are actually groups of rather serious men, whose main joy in life comes from seeing how long certain people can stay under the East River before they start gurgling.

Initiation into the Mafia is quite complicated. A proposed member is blind-folded and led into a dark room. Pieces of Cranshaw melon are placed in his pockets, and he is required to hop around on one foot and cry out, "Toodles! Toodles!" Next, his lower lip is pulled out and snapped back by all the members of the board, or *commissione*; some may even wish to do it twice. Following this, some oats are put on his head. If he complains, he is disquali-fied. If, however, he says, "Good, I like oats on my head," he is welcomed into the brotherhood. This is done by kissing him on the cheek and shaking his hand. From that moment on, he is not permitted to eat chutney, to amuse his friends by imitating a hen, or to kill anybody named Vito.

CONCLUSIONS

Organized crime is a blight on our nation. While many young Americans are lured into a career of crime by its promise of an easy life, most criminals actually must work long hours, frequently in buildings without air-condition-ing. Identifying criminals is up to each of us. Usually they can be recognized by their large cufflinks and their failure to stop eating when the man sitting next to them is hit by a falling anvil. The best methods of combatting organized crime are:

1. Telling the criminals you are not at home.
2. Calling the police whenever an unusual number of men from the Sicilian Laundry Company begin singing in your foyer.
3. Wiretapping.

Wiretapping cannot be employed indiscriminately, but its effectiveness is illustrated by this transcript of a conversation between two gang bosses in the New York area whose phones had been tapped by the F.B.I.

ANTHONY: Hello? Rico?
RICO: Hello?
ANTHONY: Rico?
RICO: Hello.
ANTHONY: Rico?
RICO: I can't hear you.
ANTHONY: Is that you, Rico? I can't hear you.
RICO: What?
ANTHONY: Can you hear me?

RICO: Hello?

ANTHONY: Rico?

RICO: We have a bad connection.

ANTHONY: Can you hear me?

RICO: Hello?

ANTHONY: Rico?

RICO: Hello?

ANTHONY: Operator, we have a bad connection.

OPERATOR: Hang up and dial again, sir.

RICO: Hello?

Because of this evidence, Anthony (The Fish) Rotunno and Rico Panzini were convicted and are currently serving fifteen years in Sing Sing for illegal possession of Bensonhurst.

CHESTER HIMES

"There Ain't No Justice"

When I am in this joint ten years and have been flopped many times, I figure the parole board won't release me, so I try another avenue. Then suddenly after eleven years the parole board lets me go.

I am so excited I am on the train before I realize my oversight. Right away I go back.

I approach the hack on the gate and say, "I have left some possessions here; I would like to get them if you have no objections."

"No ex-con can come back without they have a pass from the governor," the hack declares. "However, I will take you to the warden."

"No. I do not wish this matter to go beyond you and me," I say, pressing fifty bucks into his palm.

"Since you have put it this way," he says, "tell me where you have left your possessions and I will gladly get them."

"They are in a hole in the floor underneath the commode in cell No. 8 on range 3 in Stone City," I say. "If you pull the commode forward you will see the hole."

In an hour the hack comes back. "I have found the hole all right, but I have not found anything in it. Did you say cell 8 on range 3 in Stone City?"

"That is where I left them, I know," I say, "because daily for two years after the parole board flopped me I took them out and employed them more or less."

"Well, I am sorry about your possessions," the hack sympathizes. "However, I noticed the hole is considerably larger than is required for a convict's possessions. In fact, it is almost large enough to go through."

I see no point in this small talk. "Let us forget we even mentioned this," I say over my shoulder.

However, I am not convinced that he has looked carefully. So that night I borrow a ladder a painter has left beside a house, and also some rope. I put the ladder against the wall and climb up on top and let myself down into the yard by means of the rope. The wall guard flashes his spot on me, and yells, "Where do you think you are going?"

"I am the electrician," I say.

"Why didn't you say so?" he says.

"I am saying so now," I state.

He lights me on across the yard and I reach cell No. 8 on range 3 in Stone City without another tip. It is empty, though I see someone has been there. When I try to pull the commode forward it will not budge because the hole is filled with concrete.

While I am thus engaged the guard shift changes and the night hack begins to take count. Not wishing to be discovered in such a predicament, I jump into the bottom bunk and cover myself with a blanket. When the hack passes the cell he sees me, says, "Thirty-one," and then goes on counting.

In a few minutes there are signs of confusion down at the lower end of the range where the hack is turning in his count to the night captain. I look up and see that both hack and the night captain are taking the count again. When they get to the end of the range the confusion increases, and there are signs of what might be a rumpus.

I hear old man Potts, the night captain, beefing, "I have took count in this stir for thirty years and sometimes the count has been short; but this is the first time I have known the count to be long."

Now hacks from all over the institution are coming down the range taking count. Finally, I hear the warden tell the hacks to open each cell and take out each convict and identify him so as to find the stowaway.

When they open my cell I simply say, "It is me, Oscar Harrison, warden. You remember me."

"I remember you well," he glares. "I remember it was only day before yesterday that you left here. How did you get back?"

"Well," I say, "I was informed I could not be permitted to come and seek some possessions I left behind, excepting I had a pass from the governor. I do not wish to disturb the governor when I only need some rope and a ladder.''

"I have your possessions,'' he states. "In fact I was just about to mention them to the parole board, since they consist of a hammer and a chisel.''

"But,'' I argue, "I have made my parole and do not wish to get mixed up in any jail breaking, I only came back to take them from harm's way. I hope you are not mad about me paying you this little visit.''

"I do not object to your choice of entrance,'' he declares. "What alarmed me for the moment was the matter of the tools. But you know, there is a penalty of five years for jail breaking, and the law don't designate whether it's breaking out, or breaking in.''

"What kinda law is it that works two ways?'' I protest.

But they gave me five years anyway.

BOB ELLIOTT AND RAY GOULDING

"Wally Ballou Visits Sturdley House"

From the 1950s to the 1980s, while broadcast humor was going down the tube of television situation comedy, Bob Elliott and Ray Goulding were using radio to produce the funniest satire ever done on broadcasting itself. The characters populating their sketches included Biff Burns, David Chetley, Harold the Baboon, the Murchfields, Nurse Rudehouse, King Zog, Jasper Witherspoon, Tippy the Wonder Dog, and Wally Ballou. Wally, whose character owed a lot to local TV news reporters, was a roving correspondent whose deadpan interviews plumbed the depths of utter pointlessness.

RAY

This is the birthday of Fabian Sturdley, born in 1868 in Kenosha, Wisconsin . . . and our correspondent, Wally Ballou, is standing by with a report on what's happening at the birthplace of this famous American. He's at Sturdley House out there. It's a great tourist attraction, we're told, so . . . come in please, Wally Ballou . . .

BALLOU

——ly Ballou at "Driftwood," the stately old mansion where Fabian Sturdley was born, and I'm talking with his grandson, Van Tassel Sturdley, who manages this museum.

STURDLEY

Thanks, Mr. Ballou.

BALLOU

Is it true that the house has been restored to the original run-down condition it was in old Mr. Sturdley's time?

STURDLEY

Yes. They were going to tear down this grand old saltbox to make way for a combination car wash and bowling alley, but a group of public-spirited relatives banded together and have managed to save it, and have it declared a public shrine—with no taxes to pay!

BALLOU

Now, I know, of course, about Fabian Sturdley, but there may be some— especially children—who don't. Could you tell us something about your grandfather?

STURDLEY

Well, I'd say the big thing about him was eccentricity. For instance, he had electric lights in this house as far back as 1912—but because the neighbors laughed at him, he had them all taken out.

BALLOU

Replacing them with kerosene lamps, as the story goes. He took part in the Spanish-American War, I believe?

STURDLEY

Yes.

BALLOU

And upon his return he opened a puttee shop here?

STURDLEY

He was so impressed with the usefulness of puttees—convinced that civilians would want them for walking in tall grass—that he put all his money into his shop here, calling it "House of Puttees."

BALLOU

And it was in this very room that he held his famous meeting with Henry Ford in 1899.

STURDLEY

Mr. Ford came all the way out from Detroit to offer half interest in his company for ten thousand dollars. Of course, Grandpa realized that the automobile would never be more than a plaything for the wealthy . . . and he turned the offer down.

BALLOU

I was noticing a couple of other things visitors will see when they come here to fabulous Sturdley House . . . Here's a pillow that says, "Greetings from San Juan Hill."

STURDLEY

Yes, it's filled with balsam needles. It smelled nice for a while.

BALLOU

. . . An ash tray from Franconia Notch, New Hampshire . . . And what's the significance of that hole in the wall with a frame around it?

STURDLEY

That was when Grandfather shot at a traveling tinker and missed. He was moody that day because the bottom had fallen out of puttees. And there was a tight money situation, too.

BALLOU

Now, there's a kitchen out that way . . . and through this door a small den. I can see a pile of *National Geographics* and a picture of a blank Mount Rushmore. Not many of those around, I bet.

STURDLEY

It's a rare, valuable possession, yes.

BALLOU

Upstairs, there are two bedrooms and a bath.

STURDLEY

Yes, but they're roped off with a red velvet rope. That's where we live.

BALLOU

Do visitors get to see the attic?

STURDLEY

Yes. There are more *Geographics* up there—and about eleven cartons of puttees.

BALLOU

How about the basement?

STURDLEY

Down there they'll see our cat . . . and our trash cans . . . and several hundred cartons of puttees.

BALLOU

And outside, there's a small parking area.

STURDLEY

They can park on the street, too, as long as they don't block the Henshaws' driveway next door. The Henshaws don't like that!

BALLOU

Well, I'd like to thank you . . .

STURDLEY

Let me say that a visit to Sturdley House should be a must in anyone's vacation plans. We're open from nine to five. Admission is five dollars for adults, two dollars for children, and eighty-five cents for pets.

BALLOU

And if one were planning to stop here . . . how much time should they set aside to be sure to see everything?

STURDLEY

Including the vegetable garden out back?

BALLOU

Yes, and allowing about fifteen or twenty seconds to look at the bullet hole.

STURDLEY

I'd say . . . about . . . four and a half minutes.

BALLOU

Okay then, and thank you, Van Tassel Sturdley, grandson of Fabian Sturdley. Incidentally, when did he pass on?

STURDLEY

Grandpa?

BALLOU

Yes.

STURDLEY

Who said he died? He's downtown—getting a haircut!

BALLOU

Wally Ballou, then, at Sturdley House in Kenosha, Wisconsin, returning it to Bob and Ray!

ROBERT BENCHLEY

"Exam Time"

What ought to be the last word in our national craze for examinations and tests is found in the announcement of an aged man in North Carolina that he is ready to take the "Charlie Ross Test."

"The Charlie Ross Test" seems to have for its object the examination of the candidate to see whether or not he is the Charlie Ross who was kidnaped, as a little boy, from his home in Germantown, Pa., in 1873. The successful candidate is to receive an embossed certificate with the name "Charlie Ross" in Old English type at the top. He is also allowed to say, "I am Charlie Ross," when introducing himself to people.

Candidates in the Charlie Ross Test are given two hours in which to complete the examination, and a choice of seven questions out of ten. Question No. 4, however ("Are you white or black?"), must be answered, as the Charlie Ross who was kidnaped was known to have been white.

Mr. Julius Dellinger, the present contestant, has been cramming for the test for over six months, and feels fairly confident that he will pass with flying colors. A question of ruling came up last week, when it was discovered that Mr. Dellinger had been tutoring on the side with a man supposed to have been the original Charlie Ross's uncle, but it was decided to allow this provided that the candidate does not take notes into the examination-room with him.

"What will you do if you win?" Mr. Dellinger was asked.

"I will be just the happiest man in the world," was the reply. "First of all, I will have stationery made with 'C. R.' on it, and then I will look up all my new relatives in the Ross family and perhaps visit them for a while."

"When you have passed the Charlie Ross Test, do you expect to take the Ambrose Bierce Test?" the reporter asked.

"I looked into the Ambrose Bierce Test before I decided on the Charlie Ross one," Mr. Dellinger said, "but as Bierce was quite well on in years when he disappeared in Mexico, it would be rather a tough examination to take. So many people knew what Bierce looked like, and then, too, there would always be the possibility that I might *not* be Bierce after all. It would be very humiliating to get up before the Board of Regents and discover that you were Charlie Ross when you were taking the Ambrose Bierce examination, or vice versa."

"Had you ever thought that perhaps you might be the Man with the Iron Mask?" Mr. Dellinger was asked.

"Well, that would hardly be possible," he said with a smile, "as the Man with the Iron Mask lived in the seventeenth century and spoke French. I speak no French. Still," he added with a touch of wistfulness, "I might learn."

"Aside from the language," the reporter suggested, "it ought to be an easier test than either the Ross or Bierce one, for no one knows what the Man with the Iron Mask looked like."

Mr. Dellinger thought for a minute. Then a look of determination came into his eyes. "I'll send for a set of last year's examination papers tomorrow," he said. And into his bearing there crept something of the grand manner, a slightly imperious gesture with the hand, a courtly toss to the head. For the Man with the Iron Mask was said by some to have been the son of Cardinal Mazarin and Anne of Austria.

With a low bow the reporter withdrew.

BILL VAUGHAN

"Reader's Digest *Threatened* . . ."

Let me tell you, folks, this is a world of sadness. It isn't all roses and riots. There is the darkness as well as the sunlight. In the midst of life we may receive the word which clutches at our heart with icy fingers. It was a plain envelope in the mail, and it seems odd that the postman could have brought it, blithely, whistling as he walked, blissfully ignorant of its dread contents.

Tears blurred my eyes as I read:

"Dear Subscriber: Your address above is made with the little metal stamp which has brought you the *Reader's Digest* every month.

"But your subscription has *expired*.

"It seems a shame to remove your stencil from the good company it is now keeping. In the same file with it are the stencils of General Douglas MacArthur, Helen Hayes, Henry J. Kaiser, Sinclair Lewis, Admiral Ernest J. King, Walt Disney, and thousands of other distinguished persons. . . .

"We don't believe that you want us to destroy this little stencil—the last link between you and the continued visits of the stimulating, significant, and enduring articles gleaned from the world of current literature."

It is quite dark now; I am sitting alone in the living room. Soddenly I gaze at the empty bottle in my hand. With a curse I throw it into the fireplace. That is not the solution. This thing must be faced. It is not for myself that I am afraid. But the little home, the little family. The ones who trust and love me. How long will it be before the neighbors know? And the children, in their thoughtless cruelty—will they be whispering behind my child's back: "His father's little stencil is no longer keeping good company"?

How could I have been such a blind fool? To let my subscription expire! To desert that little metal stamp which has done so much for me.

My face is buried in my hands. Where to turn? What hope can there be for the future? There is no hope.

I am resigned, however. I wait here quite calmly now in the silent room, the dark room. They will be coming soon. I don't know what it will be like, but I can imagine.

The public humiliation. As I stand by, head bowed, my little metal stencil is removed from the files and tossed into a pot of molten metal. Walt Disney turns his back. Admiral Ernest J. King stands rigidly at attention, but the telltale whiteness around the lips bespeaks the iron control he is forced to exert to repress a sob.

A last look at these old companions, a half wave which they ignore, and I turn and trudge away.

Why don't they come? I am ready for the final degradation. Somewhere the little family can find another home under an assumed name, while I wander the earth alone, homeless, reading copies of *Playboy* at drugstore magazine racks, sinking lower and lower, the old familiar path—*True Stories, TV Guide,* down, down. But on snowy Christmas eves I will stand outside the bright, modern-type home of my ex-loved ones and look in through the holly-decked windows at the scene within. The brightly lighted tree, the mother slowly turning the pages of *Reader's Digest,* reading aloud the stimulating, significant, and enduring articles.

Will they ever, between "Life in These United States" and "The Most Unforgettable Character I've Met," pause to think of one who loved and failed them long ago?

DONALD BARTHELME

"Captain Blood"

When Captain Blood goes to sea, he locks the doors and windows of his house on Cow Island personally. One never knows what sort of person might chance by, while one is away.

When Captain Blood, at sea, paces the deck, he usually paces the foredeck rather than the afterdeck—a matter of personal preference. He keeps marmalade and a spider monkey in his cabin, and four perukes on stands.

When Captain Blood, at sea, discovers that he is pursued by the Dutch Admiral Van Tromp, he considers throwing the women overboard. So that they will drift, like so many giant lotuses in their green, lavender, purple, and blue gowns, across Van Tromp's path, and he will have to stop and pick them up. Blood will have the women fitted with life jackets under their dresses. They will hardly be in much danger at all. But what about the jaws of sea turtles? No, the women cannot be thrown overboard. Vile, vile! What an idiotic idea! What could he have been thinking of? Of the patterns they would have made floating on the surface of the water, in the moonlight, a cerise gown, a silver gown . . .

Captain Blood presents a façade of steely imperturbability.

He is poring over his charts, promising everyone that things will get better. There has not been one bit of booty in the last eight months. Should he try another course? Another ocean? The men have been quite decent about the situation. Nothing has been said. Still, it's nerve-wracking.

When Captain Blood retires for the night (leaving orders that he be called instantly if something comes up) he reads, usually. Or smokes, thinking calmly of last things.

His hideous reputation should not, strictly speaking, be painted in the horrible colors customarily employed. Many a man walks the streets of Panama City, or Port Royal, or San Lorenzo, alive and well, who would have been stuck through the gizzard with a rapier, or smashed in the brain with a boarding pike, had it not been for Blood's swift, cheerful intervention. Of course, there are times when severe measures are unavoidable. At these times he does not flinch, but takes appropriate action with admirable steadiness. There are no two ways about it: when one looses a seventy-four-gun broadside against the fragile hull of another vessel, one gets carnage.

Blood at dawn, a solitary figure pacing the foredeck.

No other sail in sight. He reaches into the pocket of his blue velvet jacket trimmed with silver lace. His hand closes over three round, white objects: mothballs. In disgust, he throws them over the side. One *makes* one's luck, he thinks. Reaching into another pocket, he withdraws a folded parchment tied with ribbon. Unwrapping the little packet, he finds that it is a memo that he wrote to himself ten months earlier. *"Dolphin,* Captain Darbraunce, 120 tons, cargo silver, paprika, bananas, sailing Mar. 10 Havana. *Be there!"* Chuckling, Blood goes off to seek his mate, Oglethorpe—that laughing blond giant of a man.

Who will be aboard this vessel which is now within cannon-shot? wonders Captain Blood. Rich people, I hope, with pretty gold and silver things aplenty.

"Short John, where is Mr. Oglethorpe?"

"I am not Short John, sir. I am John-of-Orkney."

"Sorry, John. Has Mr. Oglethorpe carried out my instructions?"

"Yes, sir. He is forward, crouching over the bombard, lit cheroot in hand, ready to fire."

"Well, fire then."

"Fire!"

BAM!

"The other captain doesn't understand what is happening to him!"

"He's not heaving to!"

"He's ignoring us!"

"The dolt!"

"Fire again!"

BAM!

"That did it!"

"He's turning into the wind!"

"He's dropped anchor!"

"He's lowering sail!"

"Very well, Mr. Oglethorpe. You may prepare to board."

"Very well, Peter."

"And Jeremy—"

"Yes, Peter?"

"I know we've had rather a thin time of it these last few months."

"Well, it hasn't been so bad, Peter. A little slow, perhaps—"

"Well, before we board, I'd like you to convey to the men my appreciation for their patience. Patience and, I may say, tact."

"We knew you'd turn up something, Peter."

"Just tell them for me, will you?"

Always a wonderful moment, thinks Captain Blood. Preparing to board. Pistol in one hand, naked cutlass in the other. Dropping lightly to the deck of the engrappled vessel, backed by one's grinning, leering, disorderly, rapacious crew who are nevertheless under the strictest buccaneer discipline. There to confront the little band of fear-crazed victims shrinking from the entirely possible carnage. Among them, several beautiful women, but one really spectacular beautiful woman who stands a bit apart from her sisters, clutching a machete with which she intends, against all reason, to—

When Captain Blood celebrates the acquisition of a rich prize, he goes down to the galley himself and cooks *tallarínes a la catalána* (noodles, spare ribs, almonds, pine nuts) for all hands. The name of the captured vessel is entered in a little book along with the names of all the others he has captured in a long career. Here are some of them: the *Oxford*, the *Luis*, the *Fortune*, the *Lambe*, the *Jamaica Merchant*, the *Betty*, the *Prosperous*, the *Endeavor*, the *Falcon*, the *Bonadventure*, the *Constant Thomas*, the *Marquesa*, the *Señora del Carmen*, the *Recovery*, the *María Gloriosa*, the *Virgin Queen*, the *Esmeralda*, the *Havana*, the *San Felipe*, the *Steadfast* . . .

The true buccaneer is not persuaded that God is not on his side, too— especially if, as is often the case, he turned pirate after some monstrously unjust thing was done to him, such as being press-ganged into one or another of the Royal Navies when he was merely innocently having a drink at a waterfront tavern, or having been confined to the stinking dungeons of the Inquisition just for making some idle, thoughtless, light remark. Therefore, Blood feels himself to be devout *in his own way,* and has endowed candles burning in churches in most of the great cities of the New World. Although not under his own name.

Captain Blood roams ceaselessly, making daring raids. The average raid yields something like 20,000 pieces-of-eight, which is apportioned fairly among the crew, with wounded men getting more according to the gravity of their wounds. A cut ear is worth two pieces, a cut-*off* ear worth ten to twelve. The scale of payments for injuries is posted in the forecastle.

When he is on land, Blood is confused and troubled by the life of cities, where every passing stranger may, for no reason, assault him, if the stranger so chooses. And indeed, the stranger's mere presence, multiplied many times over, is a kind of assault. Merely having to *take into account* all these hurrying others is a blistering occupation. This does not happen on a ship, or on a sea.

An amusing incident: Captain Blood has overhauled a naval vessel, has caused her to drop anchor (on this particular voyage he is sailing with three other ships under his command and a total enlistment of nearly one thousand men), and is now interviewing the arrested captain in his cabin full of marmalade jars and new perukes.

"And what may your name be, sir? If I may ask?"

"Jones, sir."

"What kind of a name is that? English, I take it?"

"No, it's American, sir."

"American? What is an American?"

"America is a new nation among the nations of the world."

"I've not heard of it. Where is it?"

"North of here, north and west. It's a very small nation, at present, and has only been a nation for about two years."

"But the name of your ship is French."

"Yes it is. It is named in honor of Benjamin Franklin, one of our American heroes."

"*Bon Home Richard?* What has that to do with Benjamin or Franklin?"

"Well it's an allusion to an almanac Dr. Franklin published called—"

"You weary me, sir. You are captured, American or no, so tell me—do you surrender, with all your men, fittings, cargo, and whatever?"

"Sir, I have not yet begun to fight."

"Captain, this is madness. We have you completely surrounded. Furthermore there is a great hole in your hull below the waterline where our warning shot, which was slightly miscalculated, bashed in your timbers. You are taking water at a fearsome rate. And still you wish to fight?''

"It is the pluck of us Americans, sir. We are just that way. Our tiny nation has to be pluckier than most if it is to survive among the bigger, older nations of the world.''

"Well, bless my soul, Jones, you are the damnedest goatsucker I ever did see. Stab me if I am not tempted to let you go scot-free, just because of your amazing pluck.''

"No, sir, I insist on fighting. As founder of the American naval tradition, I must set a good example.''

"Jones, return to your vessel and be off.''

"No, sir, I will fight to the last shred of canvas, for the honor of America.''

"Jones, even in America, wherever it is, you must have encountered the word 'ninny.' ''

"Oh. I see. Well then. I think we'll be weighing anchor, Captain, with your permission.''

"Choose your occasions, Captain. And God be with you.''

Blood, at dawn, a solitary figure pacing the foredeck. The world of piracy is wide, and at the same time, narrow. One can be gallant all day long, and still end up with a spider monkey for a wife. And what does his mother think of him?

The favorite dance of Captain Blood is the grave and haunting Catalonian *sardana,* in which the participants join hands facing each other to form a ring which gradually becomes larger, then smaller, then larger again. It is danced without smiling, for the most part. He frequently dances this with his men, in the middle of the ocean, after lunch, to the music of a single silver trumpet.

E. B. WHITE

"The Retort Transcendental"

In May of the year 1927 I bought a World's Classics edition of "Walden" for, I think, ninety cents and slipped it in my pocket for convenient reading. Since then I have carried it about with me on the cars and in buses and boats, as it is the most amusing detective story I possess. There is, however, a danger in rereading a book, or rather in dipping frequently into the same book: the trouble is you begin to learn some of the lines. In my case, with "Walden," I have recently found that when someone asks me a simple question I reply with a direct quote.

I go into a restaurant, we'll say, at the lunch hour, and the headwaiter approaches me, accusingly.

"All alone?" he asks.

"I feel it wholesome to be alone the greater part of the time," I reply. "To be in company, even with the best, is soon wearisome and dissipating. I love to be alone." Then I glare triumphantly at the waiter and snatch the napkin from the plate.

Or I am walking along the street and meet an acquaintance—someone I haven't seen in a long time and don't care if I never see again.

"Where y'been all this time?" he demands.

"If a man does not keep pace with his companions," I retort, "perhaps it is because he hears a different drummer."

Actually, I suppose, I don't say that at all; yet it often seems to me as though I were saying it. More and more I find it difficult to distinguish clearly between what I am saying and what I might easily be saying. Maybe it's the times. At any rate, Thoreau answers a surprisingly large number of the commonest questions that get thrown at me these days. He is a Johnny-on-the-spot for all ordinary occasions and situations.

I enter a room.

"Won't you sit down?" asks my hostess, indicating a vacancy.

"I would rather sit on a pumpkin and have it all to myself," I reply, accepting the velvet cushion with weary resignation.

"What would you like to drink?" she continues.

"Let me have a draught of undiluted morning air," I snarl. "If men will not drink of this at the fountainhead of the day, why, then, we must even bottle up some and sell it in the shops, for the benefit of those who have lost their subscription ticket to morning time in the world." Then I slump into my cushion and wait for the clear amber liquor and the residual olive.

"Know any good books?" my partner asks at dinner. Slowly I swing my head around, bruising my chin on the hard, rough wing of my collar, my eyes glazed with the strain of evening. I place my lips to her ear.

"Much is published," I whisper, cryptically, "but little printed. We are in danger of forgetting the language which all things and events speak without metaphor, which alone is copious and standard."

Or I am at home, getting ready, perhaps, to escort my wife to a soirée.

"What's it like out tonight?" she asks, glancing anxiously at her rubbers in the corner of the closet.

"This is a delicious evening," I hear my voice saying, "when the whole body is one sense, and imbibes delight through every pore."

Next morning, seeing my suit lying rumpled and mussed on the chair beside the bed, she will inquire, "You got anything to go to the presser's?"

"No, my dear," I reply. "Every day our garments become more assimilated to ourselves, receiving the impress of the wearer's character. If you have any enterprise before you, try it in your old clothes." (I am glad to say my wife doesn't mind Thoreau any more and simply calls the presser.)

The situations are endless, the answers inexhaustible. I recall that one of my angriest and boldest retorts was made on a day when a couple of silly, giggling girls arrived at our house and began effervescing.

"Isn't this an attractive place?" they squealed.

"On the contrary," I snapped, "I sometimes dream of a larger and more populous house, standing in a golden age, of enduring materials, and without gingerbread work, which shall consist of only one room, a vast, rude, substantial primitive hall, without ceiling or plastering, with bare rafters and purlins supporting a sort of lower heaven over one's head—useful to keep off rain and snow; where the king and queen posts stand out to receive your homage, when you have done reverence to the prostrate Saturn of an older dynasty on stepping over the sill; a cavernous house, wherein you must reach up a torch upon a pole to see the roof . . . a house whose inside is as open and manifest as a bird's nest."

The girls sobered up instantly and were quiet and tractable the rest of their visit. But I don't know—I'm afraid I shall have to put "Walden" away and buy another book to travel with. Or possibly a link puzzle. One doesn't remember anything much from long association with a link puzzle.

ROBERT BENCHLEY

"More Songs for Meller"

As Señorita Raquel Meller sings entirely in Spanish, it is again explained, the management prints little synopses of the songs on the program, telling what each is all about and why she is behaving the way she is. They make delightful reading during those periods when Señorita Meller is changing mantillas, and, in case she should run out of songs before she runs out of mantillas, we offer a few new synopses for her repertoire.

(1) ¿Voy Bien?
(Am I Going in the Right Direction)

When the acorns begin dropping in Spain there is an old legend that for every acorn which drops there is a baby born in Valencia. This is so silly that no one pays any attention to it now, not even the gamekeeper's daughter, who would pay attention to anything. She goes from house to house, ringing doorbells and then running away. She hopes that some day she will ring the right doorbell and will trip and fall, so that Prince Charming will catch her. So far, no one has even come to the door. Poor Pepita! if that is her name.

(2) Camisetas de Flanela
(Flannel Vests)

Princess Rosamonda goes nightly to the Puerta del Sol to see if the early morning edition of the papers is out yet. If it isn't she hangs around humming to herself. If it is, she hangs around humming just the same. One night she encounters a young matador who is returning from dancing school. The finches are singing and there is Love in the air. Princess Rosamonda ends up in the Police Station.

(3) La Guia
(The Time-table)

It is the day of the bull fight in Madrid. Everyone is cockeyed. The bull has slipped out by the back entrance to the arena and has gone home, disgusted. Nobody notices that the bull has gone except Nina, a peasant girl who has come to town that day to sell her father. She looks with horror at the place in the Royal Box where the bull ought to be sitting, and sees there instead her algebra teacher, whom she had told that she was staying at home on account of a sick headache. You can imagine her feelings!

(4) No Puedo Comer Eso
(I Can Not Eat That!)

A merry song of the Alhambra—of the Alhambra in the moonlight—of a girl who danced over the wall and sprained her ankle. Lititia is the ward of grouchy old Pampino, President of the First National Banco. She has never been allowed further away than the edge of the piazza because she teases people so. Her lover has come to see her and finds that she is fast asleep. He considers that for once he has the breaks, and tiptoes away without waking her up. Along about eleven o'clock she awakes, and is sore as all get-out.

(5) La Lavandera
(The Laundryman)

A coquette, pretending to be very angry, bites off the hand of her lover up to the wrist. Ah, naughty Cirinda! Such antics! However does she think she can do her lessons if she gives up all her time to love-making? But Cirinda does not care. Heedless, heedless Cirinda!

(6) Abra Vd. Esa Ventana
(Open That Window)

The lament of a mother whose oldest son is too young to vote. She walks the streets singing "My son can not vote! My son is not old enough!" There seems to be nothing that can be done about it.

O. Henry

"A Strange Story"

In the northern part of Austin there once dwelt an honest family by the name of Smothers. The family consisted of John Smothers, his wife, himself, their little daughter, five years of age and her parents, making six people toward the population of the city when counted for a special write-up, but only three by actual count.

One night after supper the little girl was seized with a severe colic, and John Smothers hurried downtown to get some medicine.

He never came back.

The little girl recovered and in time grew up to womanhood.

The mother grieved very much over her husband's disappearance, and it was nearly three months before she married again, and moved to San Antonio.

The little girl also married in time, and after a few years had rolled around, she also had a little girl five years of age.

She still lived in the same house where they dwelt when her father had left and never returned.

One night by a remarkable coincidence her little girl was taken with cramp colic on the anniversary of the disappearance of John Smothers, who would now have been her grandfather if he had been alive and had a steady job.

"I will go downtown and get some medicine for her," said John Smith (for it was none other than he whom she had married).

"No, no, dear John," cried his wife. "You, too, might disappear forever, and then forget to come back."

So John Smith did not go, and together they sat by the bedside of little Pansy (for that was Pansy's name).

After a little Pansy seemed to grow worse, and John Smith again attempted to go for medicine, but his wife would not let him.

Suddenly the door opened, and an old man, stooped and bent, with long white hair, entered the room.

"Hello, here is grandpa," said Pansy. She had recognized him before any of the others.

The old man drew a bottle of medicine from his pocket and gave Pansy a spoonful.

She got well immediately.

"I was a little late," said John Smothers, "as I waited for a street car."

O. HENRY

"The Prisoner of Zembla"

So the king fell into a furious rage, so that none durst go near him for fear, and he gave out that since the Princess Ostla had disobeyed him there would be a great tourney, and to the knight who should prove himself of the greatest valor he would give the hand of the princess.

And he sent forth a herald to proclaim that he would do this.

And the herald went about the country making his desire known, blowing a great tin horn and riding a noble steed that pranced and gambolled; and the villagers gazed upon him and said: "Lo, that is one of them tin-horn gamblers concerning which the chroniclers have told us."

And when the day came, the king sat in the grandstand, holding the gage of battle in his hand, and by his side sat the Princess Ostla, looking very pale and beautiful, but with mournful eyes from which she scarce could keep the tears. And the knights which came to the tourney gazed upon the princess in wonder at her beauty, and each swore to win so that he could marry her and board with the king. Suddenly the heart of the princess gave a great bound, for she saw among the knights one of the poor students with whom she had been in love.

The knights mounted and rode in a line past the grandstand, and the king stopped the poor student, who had the worst horse and the poorest caparisons of any of the knights and said:

"Sir knight, prithee tell me of what that marvellous shacky and rusty-looking armor of thine is made?"

"Oh, king," said the young knight, "seeing that we are about to engage in a big fight, I would call it scrap iron, wouldn't you?"

"Ods Bodkins!" said the king. "The youth hath a pretty wit."

About this time the Princess Ostla, who began to feel better at the sight of her lover, slipped a piece of gum into her mouth and closed her teeth upon it, and even smiled a little and showed the beautiful pearls with which her mouth was set. Whereupon, as soon as the knights perceived this, 217 of them went over to the king's treasurer and settled for their horse feed and went home.

"It seems very hard," said the princess, "that I cannot marry when I chews."

But two of the knights were left, one of them being the princess's lover.

"Here's enough for a fight, anyhow," said the king. "Come hither, O knights, will ye joust for the hand of this fair lady?"

"We joust will," said the knights.

The two knights fought for two hours, and at length the princess's lover prevailed and stretched the other upon the ground. The victorious knight made his horse caracole before the king and bowed low in his saddle.

On the Princess Ostla's cheeks was a rosy flush; in her eyes the light of excitement vied with the soft glow of love; her lips were parted, her lovely hair unbound, and she grasped the arms of her chair and leaned forward with heaving bosom and happy smile to hear the words of her lover.

"You have foughten well, sir knight," said the king. "And if there is any boon you crave you have but to name it."

"Then," said the knight, "I will ask you this: I have bought the patent rights in your kingdom for Schneider's celebrated monkey wrench, and I want a letter from you endorsing it.''

''You shall have it,'' said the king, ''but I must tell you that there is not a monkey in my kingdom.''

With a yell of rage the victorious knight threw himself on his horse and rode away at a furious gallop.

The king was about to speak, when a horrible suspicion flashed upon him and he fell dead upon the grandstand.

''My God!'' he cried. ''He has forgotten to take the princess with him!''

MARK TWAIN

The Horace Greeley Story

Here is a passage from Chapter Twenty of Roughing It, *Mark Twain's account of his adventures in Nevada and California. The book is not to be taken as gospel in its entirety. When he had to choose between dull fact and a good story, Twain went for the story. He insists there is a grain of truth in this one. Maybe so.*

. . . Just after we left Julesburg, on the Platte, I was sitting with the driver, and he said:

''I can tell you a most laughable thing indeed, if you would like to listen to it. Horace Greeley went over this road once. When he was leaving Carson City he told the driver, Hank Monk, that he had an engagement to lecture at Placerville and was very anxious to go through quick. Hank Monk cracked his whip and started off at an awful pace. The coach bounced up and down in such a terrific way that it jolted the buttons all off of Horace's coat, and finally shot his head clean through the roof of the stage, and then he yelled at Hank Monk and begged him to go easier—said he warn't in as much of a hurry as he was awhile ago. But Hank Monk said, 'Keep your seat, Horace, and I'll get you there on time'—and you bet you he did, too, what was left of him!''

A day or two after that we picked up a Denver man at the cross roads, and he told us a good deal about the country and the Gregory Diggings. He seemed a very entertaining person and a man well posted in the affairs of Colorado. By and by he remarked:

''I can tell you a most laughable thing indeed, if you would like to listen to it. Horace Greeley went over this road once. When he was leaving Carson City he told the driver, Hank Monk, that he had an engagement to lecture at Placerville and was very anxious to go through quick. Hank Monk cracked his whip and started off at an awful pace. The coach bounced up and down in such a terrific way that it jolted the buttons all off of Horace's coat, and finally shot his head clean through the roof of the stage, and then he yelled at Hank Monk and begged him to go easier—said he warn't in as much of a hurry as he was awhile ago. But Hank Monk said, 'Keep your seat, Horace, and I'll get you there on time!'—and you bet you he did, too, what was left of him!''

At Fort Bridger, some days after this, we took on board a cavalry sergeant, a very proper and soldierly person indeed. From no other man during the whole journey, did we gather such a store of concise and well-arranged military information. It was surprising to find in the desolate wilds of our country a man so thoroughly acquainted with everything useful to know in his line of life, and yet of such inferior rank and unpretentious bearing. For as much as three hours we listened to him with unabated interest. Finally he got upon the subject of trans-continental travel, and presently said:

"I can tell you a very laughable thing indeed, if you would like to listen to it. Horace Greeley went over this road once. When he was leaving Carson City he told the driver, Hank Monk, that he had an engagement to lecture at Placerville and was very anxious to go through quick. Hank Monk cracked his whip and started off at an awful pace. The coach bounced up and down in such a terrific way that it jolted the buttons all off of Horace's coat, and finally shot his head clean through the roof of the stage, and then he yelled at Hank Monk and begged him to go easier—said he warn't in as much of a hurry as he was awhile ago. But Hank Monk said, 'Keep your seat, Horace, and I'll get you there on time!'—and you bet you he did, too, what was left of him!''

When we were eight hours out from Salt Lake City a Mormon preacher got in with us at a way station—a gentle, soft-spoken, kindly man, and one whom any stranger would warm to at first sight. I can never forget the pathos that was in his voice as he told, in simple language, the story of his people's wanderings and unpitied sufferings. No pulpit eloquence was ever so moving and so beautiful as this outcast's picture of the first Mormon pilgrimage across the plains, struggling sorrowfully onward to the land of its banishment and marking its desolate way with graves and watering it with tears. His words so wrought upon us that it was a relief to us all when the conversation drifted into a more cheerful channel and the natural features of the curious country we were in came under treatment. One matter after another was pleasantly discussed, and at length the stranger said:

"I can tell you a most laughable thing indeed, if you would like to listen to it. Horace Greeley went over this road once. When he was leaving Carson City he told the driver, Hank Monk, that he had an engagement to lecture in

Placerville, and was very anxious to go through quick. Hank Monk cracked his whip and started off at an awful pace. The coach bounced up and down in such a terrific way that it jolted the buttons all off of Horace's coat, and finally shot his head clean through the roof of the stage, and then he yelled at Hank Monk and begged him to go easier—said he warn't in as much of a hurry as he was awhile ago. But Hank Monk said, 'Keep your seat, Horace, and I'll get you there on time!'—and you bet you he did, too, what was left of him!''

Ten miles out of Ragtown we found a poor wanderer who had lain down to die. He had walked as long as he could, but his limbs had failed him at last. Hunger and fatigue had conquered him. It would have been inhuman to leave him there. We paid his fare to Carson and lifted him into the coach. It was some little time before he showed any very decided signs of life; but by dint of chafing him and pouring brandy between his lips we finally brought him to a languid consciousness. Then we fed him a little, and by and by he seemed to comprehend the situation and a grateful light softened his eye. We made his mail-sack bed as comfortable as possible, and constructed a pillow for him with our coats. He seemed very thankful. Then he looked up in our faces, and said in a feeble voice that had a tremble of honest emotion in it:

"Gentlemen, I know not who you are, but you have saved my life; and although I can never be able to repay you for it, I feel that I can at least make one hour of your long journey lighter. I take it you are strangers to this great thoroughfare, but I am entirely familiar with it. In this connection I can tell you a most laughable thing indeed, if you would like to listen to it. Horace Greeley—''

I said, impressively:

"Suffering stranger, proceed at your peril. You see in me the melancholy wreck of a once stalwart and magnificent manhood. What has brought me to this? That thing which you are about to tell. Gradually but surely, that tiresome old anecdote has sapped my strength, undermined my constitution, withered my life. Pity my helplessness. Spare me only just this once, and tell me about young George Washington and his little hatchet for a change.''

We were saved. But not so the invalid. In trying to retain the anecdote in his system he strained himself and died in our arms.

I am aware, now, that I ought not to have asked of the sturdiest citizen of all that region, what I asked of that mere shadow of a man; for, after seven years' residence on the Pacific coast, I know that no passenger or driver on the Overland ever corked that anecdote in, when a stranger was by, and survived. Within a period of six years I crossed and recrossed the Sierras between Nevada and California thirteen times by stage and listened to that deathless incident four hundred and eighty-one or eighty-two times. I have the list somewhere. Drivers always told it, conductors told it, landlords told it, chance passengers told it, the very Chinamen and vagrant Indians recounted it.

I have had the same driver tell it to me two or three times in the same afternoon. It has come to me in all the multitude of tongues that Babel bequeathed to earth, and flavored with whiskey, brandy, beer, cologne, sozodont, tobacco, garlic, onions, grasshoppers—everything that has a fragrance to it through all the long list of things that are gorged or guzzled by the sons of men. I never have smelt any anecdote as often as I have smelt that one; never have smelt any anecdote that smelt so variegated as that one. And you never could learn to know it by its smell, because every time you thought you had learned the smell of it, it would turn up with a different smell. Bayard Taylor has written about this hoary anecdote, Richardson has published it; so have Jones, Smith, Johnson, Ross Browne, and every other correspondence-inditing being that ever set his foot upon the great overland road anywhere between Julesburg and San Francisco; and I have heard that it is in the Talmud. I have seen it in print in nine different foreign languages; I have been told that it is employed in the inquisition in Rome; and I now learn with regret that it is going to be set to music. I do not think that such things are right.

Stage-coaching on the Overland is no more, and stage drivers are a race defunct. I wonder if they bequeathed that bald-headed anecdote to their successors, the railroad brakemen and conductors, and if these latter still persecute the helpless passenger with it until he concludes, as did many a tourist of other days, that the real grandeurs of the Pacific coast are not Yo Semite and the Big Trees, but Hank Monk and his adventure with Horace Greeley.*

*And what makes that worn anecdote the more aggravating, is, that the adventure it celebrates *never occurred*. If it were a good anecdote, that seeming demerit would be its chiefest virtue, for creative power belongs to greatness; but what ought to be done to a man who would wantonly contrive so flat a one as this? If *I* were to suggest what ought to be done to him, I should be called extravagant— but what does the thirteenth chapter of Daniel say? Aha!

ROBERT BENCHLEY

"Maxims from the Chinese"

Three crows are there, if only there were three crows. . . . Oh, well, anyway—!

The wise man moves fast, yet a great many times it is hard to catch him. This is because he has no soul. This is because he lives up there with all those radicals.

It is rather to be chosen than great riches, unless I have omitted something from the quotation.

One day Lee Fee was walking along the countryside, with his hands on his elbows. He was thinking, thinking, thinking. So far he has failed to interest us as a character.

"I am wondering," said Lee Fee aloud, in case anyone was asking him. "I am wondering what comes after 'W.' " And, as he wondered, Lee Fee walked, and, as he walked, he wondered, and pretty soon he didn't know *what* he was doing.

Soon he came to Lee Fee, walking in the opposite direction. This put a stop to his monkey-business. He was good and scared. But he said: "Well, easy come, easy go!" and tried to brush by himself. But that is no easier than it seems.

"We are getting nowhere," said the east-bound Lee Fee to the west-bound Lee Fee. "Let's see if we can't come to some compromise. We are both sensible men, and there is a saying of Confucius that the sensible man goes but a short distance with himself before taking his own temperature. It is also said that eggs do not roll sideways. There is also an old saying—"

But when Lee Fee looked up, Lee Fee was gone. He just couldn't take it. Too much wisdom gets on the wise man's nerves.

It is often difficult to tell whether a maxim means something, or something means maxim.

Three women were keeping house. It was too rainy. The First Old Woman said: "What wouldn't I give for three wishes at this very minute!"

"Well, what *wouldn't* you give?" asked the Second Old Woman.

"I wouldn't give my new silk coat, and I wouldn't give the roast pigeon in my oven, and I wouldn't give *that,*" replied the First Old Woman, snapping her fingers.

"And why wouldn't you give any of these things for three wishes?" asked the Third Old Lady, who had heard nothing of what was going on.

"Because, even if I had three wishes," replied the First Old Woman, dying, "what chance would there be of their being granted?"

A wish without the giver is bare.

The wise man thinks once before he speaks twice.

SECTION THREE

THE HUMAN MUDDLE

The human race, or at least that part of it occupying the so-called civilized world, spends its life struggling against what Albert Camus called "the benign indifference of the universe," and losing. Its problem is its stubborn refusal to submit peaceably to the universe's preference for quixotic happenstance. We insist on order and reason. In an absurd world, striving to live orderly, reasoned lives leads to ever more absurd situations.

Humorists thrive on the foolishness that comes of trying to run a neatly ordered life in a cosmic fun house, or, as the cliché has it, of trying to cope with life's vicissitudes.

Inevitable defeat is everywhere in these pieces. Thomas Meehan tells how he beat a terrible addiction but leaves us in no doubt that we will find him tonight hunkered down shamelessly with Victor McLaglen and Boris Karloff in The Lost Patrol.

Benjamin Franklin, noting that man will contrive a thousand ways to avoid saying he is "drunk," shows us how our trick of using language as a shield against reality becomes a trick for deceiving ourselves about ourselves. The Duke and the Dauphin, Mark Twain's outrageous confidence men, fancying themselves masters of fraud, are too inept to deceive even an unschooled country boy.

Briefly Speaking

Whin I think what this gob iv arth is like that we live on f'r a few hours, spinnin' around f'r no sinsible raison in th' same foolish, lobsided circle, an' comin' back to th' same place ivry year, without thought or care iv th' poor crathers hangin' onto it, I'm inclined to think a betther race wud be wasted on it. We may be bad, but we're plenty good enough f'r what we get fr'm th' wurruld.

—Finley Peter Dunne

Mr. Dooley was the creation of Finley Peter Dunne, a Chicago newspaperman sensitive to the ways in which immigration was changing the meaning of what it meant to be American. Mr. Dooley was the original philosopher-bartender. His foil was Hennessy, whose bafflement about America, politics, and human nature gave Mr. Dooley a constant invitation to entertain us all. If the Irish dialect looks forbidding at first, try speaking it aloud and see how easily it flows. There is more Mr. Dooley to come in these pages. It would be a pity to miss any of it.

Langston Hughes

"Tain't So"

Miss Lucy Cannon was a right nice old white woman, so Uncle Joe always stated, except that she really did *not* like colored folks, not even after she come out West to California. She could never get over certain little Southern ways she had, and long as she knowed my Uncle Joe, who hauled her ashes for her, she never would call him *Mister*—nor any other colored man *Mister* neither for that matter, not even the minister of the Baptist Church who was a graduate of San Jose State College. Miss Lucy Cannon just wouldn't call

131

colored folks *Mister* nor *Missus,* no matter who they was, neither in Alabama nor in California.

She was always ailing around, too, sick with first one thing and then another. Delicate, and ever so often she would have a fainting spell, like all good Southern white ladies. Looks like the older she got, the more she would be sick and couldn't hardly get around—that is, until she went to a healer and got cured.

And that is one of the funniest stories Uncle Joe ever told me, how old Miss Cannon got cured of her heart and hip in just one cure at the healer's.

Seems like for three years or more she could scarcely walk—even with a cane—had a terrible bad pain in her right leg from her knee up. And on her left side, her heart was always just about to give out. She was in bad shape, that old Southern lady, to be as spry as she was, always giving teas and dinners and working her colored help to death.

Well, Uncle Joe says, one New Year's Day in Pasadena a friend of hers, a Northern lady who was kinda old and retired also and had come out to California to spend her last days, too, and get rid of some parts of her big bank full of money—this old lady told Miss Cannon, "Darling, you just seem to suffer so all the time, and you say you've tried all the doctors, and all kinds of baths and medicines. Why don't you try my way of overcoming? Why don't you try faith?"

"Faith, honey?" says old Miss Lucy Cannon, sipping her jasmine tea.

"Yes, my dear," says the Northern white lady. "Faith! I have one of the best faith-healers in the world."

"Who is he?" asked Miss Lucy Cannon.

"She's a woman, dear," said old Miss Northern white lady. "And she heals by power. She lives in Hollywood."

"Give me her address," said Miss Lucy, "and I'll go to see her. How much do her treatments cost?"

Miss Lucy warn't so rich as some folks thought she was.

"Only Ten Dollars, dearest," said the other lady. "Ten Dollars a treatment. Go, and you'll come away cured."

"I have never believed in such things," said Miss Lucy, "nor disbelieved, either. But I will go and see." And before she could learn any more about the healer, some other friends came in and interrupted the conversation.

A few days later, however, Miss Lucy took herself all the way from Pasadena to Hollywood, put up for the week end with a friend of hers, and thought she would go to see the healer, which she did, come Monday morning early.

Using her customary cane and hobbling on her left leg, feeling a bit bad around the heart, and suffering terribly in her mind, she managed to walk slowly but with dignity a half-dozen blocks through the sunshine to the rather humble street in which was located the office and home of the healer.

In spite of the bright morning air and the good breakfast she had had, Miss Lucy (according to herself) felt pretty bad, racked with pains and crippled to the use of a cane.

When she got to the house she was seeking, a large frame dwelling, newly painted, she saw a sign thereon:

MISS PAULINE JONES

"So that's her name," thought Miss Lucy. "Pauline Jones, Miss Jones."

Ring And Enter said a little card above the bell. So Miss Lucy entered. But the first thing that set her back a bit was that nobody received her, so she just sat down to await Miss Jones, the healer who had, she heard, an enormous following in Hollywood. In fact, that's why she had come early, so she wouldn't have to wait long. Now, it was only nine o'clock. The office was open—but empty. So Miss Lucy simply waited. Ten minutes passed. Fifteen. Twenty. Finally she became all nervous and fluttery. Heart and limb! Pain, pain, pain! Not even a magazine to read.

"Oh, me!" she said impatiently. "What is this? Why, I never!"

There was a sign on the wall that read:

BELIEVE

"I will wait just ten minutes more," said Miss Lucy, glancing at her watch of platinum and pearls.

But before the ten minutes were up, another woman entered the front door and sat down. To Miss Lucy's horror, she was a colored woman! In fact, a big black colored woman!

Said Miss Lucy to herself, "I'll never in the world get used to the North. Now here's a great—my friend says great faith-healer, treating darkies! Why, down in Alabama, a Negro patient wouldn't dare come in here and sit down with white people like this!"

But, womanlike, (and having still five minutes to wait) Miss Lucy couldn't keep her mouth shut that long. She just had to talk, albeit to a Negro, so she began on her favorite subject—herself.

"I certainly feel bad this morning," she said to the colored woman, condescending to open the conversation.

"Tain't so," answered the Negro woman placidly—which sort of took Miss Lucy back a bit. She lifted her chin.

"Indeed, it is so," said she indignantly. "My heart is just about to give out. My breath is short."

"Tain't so a-tall," said the Negro calmly.

"Why!" gasped Miss Lucy, "such impudence! I tell you *it is so*! I could hardly get down here this morning."

"Tain't so," said the Negro calmly.

"Besides my heart," went on Miss Lucy, "my right hip pains me so I can hardly sit here."

"I say, tain't so."

"I tell you it *is* so," screamed Miss Lucy. "Where is the healer? I won't sit here and suffer this—this impudence. I can't! It'll kill me! It's outrageous."

"Tain't so," said the large black woman serenely, whereupon Miss Lucy rose. Her pale face flushed a violent red.

"Where is the healer?" she cried, looking around the room.

"Right here," said the colored woman.

"What?" cried Miss Lucy. "You're the—why—you?"

"I'm Miss Jones."

"Why, I never heard the like," gasped Miss Lucy. "A *colored* woman as famous as you? Why, you must be lying!"

"Tain't so," said the woman calmly.

"Well, I shan't stay another minute," cried Miss Lucy.

"Ten Dollars, then," said the colored woman. "You've had your treatment, anyhow."

"Ten Dollars! That's entirely too much!"

"Tain't so."

Angrily Miss Lucy opened her pocketbook, threw a Ten Dollar bill on the table, took a deep breath, and bounced out. She went three blocks up Sunset Boulevard walking like the wind, conversing with herself.

" 'Tain't so,' " she muttered. " 'Tain't so!' I tell her I'm sick and she says, 'Tain't so!' "

On she went at a rapid gait, stepping like a young girl—so mad she had forgotten all about her infirmities, even her heart—when suddenly she cried, "Lord, have mercy, my cane! For the first time in three years, I'm *without* a cane!"

Then she realized that her breath was giving her no trouble at all. Neither was her leg. Her temper mellowed. The sunshine was sweet and warm. She felt good.

"Colored folks do have some funny kind of supernatural conjuring powers, I reckon," she said smiling to herself. Immediately her face went grim again. "But the impudence of 'em! Soon's they get up North—calling herself *Miss* Pauline Jones. The idea! Putting on airs and charging me Ten Dollars for a handful of *Tain't so's*!"

In her mind she clearly heard, "Tain't so!"

BENJAMIN FRANKLIN

"The Busy-Body, No. 4"

Nequid nimis.

At the age of seventeen, Benjamin Franklin created Silence Dogood, the Busy-Body, in a series of fourteen articles published in the New-England Courant. Mistress Dogood's counterparts thrive today in every newspaper columnist who advises inquiring readers how to deal with troubles ranging from romance to plumbing repair. Franklin's intent was satirical rather than educational, so he also wrote the letters asking Mistress Dogood to share her wisdom. His fourth article dealt with a delicate problem of etiquette.

TO THE BUSY-BODY.

Sir,

"You having set your self up for a *Censuror Morum* (as I think you call it) which is said to mean a *Reformer of Manners*, I know no Person more proper to be apply'd to for Redress in all the Grievances we suffer from *Want of Manners* in some People. You must know I am a single Woman, and keep a Shop in this Town for a Livelyhood. There is a certain Neighbour of mine, who is really agreeable Company enough, and with whom I have had an Intimacy of some Time standing; But of late she makes her Visits so excessively often, and stays so very long every Visit, that I am tir'd out of all Patience. I have no Manner of Time at all to my self; and you, who seem to be a wise Man, must needs be sensible that every Person has little Secrets and Privacies that are not proper to be expos'd even to the nearest Friend. Now I cannot do the least Thing in the World, but she must know all about it; and it is a Wonder I have found an Opportunity to write you this Letter. My Misfortune is, that I respect her very well, and know not how to disoblige her so much as to tell her I should be glad to have less of her Company; for if I should once hint such a Thing, I am afraid she would resent it so as never to darken my Door again.——But, alas, Sir, I have not yet told you half my Afflictions. She has two Children that are just big enough to run about and do pretty Mischief: These are continually along with *Mamma,* either in my Room or Shop, if I have never so many Customers or

People with me about Business. Sometimes they pull the Goods off my low Shelves down to the Ground, and perhaps where one of them has just been making Water; My Friend takes up the Stuff, and cries, *Eh! thou little wicked mischievous Rogue!*—But however, it has done no great Damage; *'tis only wet a little;* and so puts it up upon the Shelf again. Sometimes they get to my Cask of Nails behind the Counter, and divert themselves, to my great Vexation, with mixing my Ten-penny and Eight-penny and Four-penny together. I Endeavour to conceal my Uneasiness as much as possible, and with a grave Look go to Sorting them out. She cries, *Don't thee trouble thy self, Neighbour: Let them play a little; I'll put all to rights my self before I go.* But Things are never so put to rights but that I find a great deal of Work to do after they are gone. Thus, Sir, I have all the Trouble and Pesterment of Children, without the Pleasure of—calling them my own; and they are now so us'd to being here that they will be content no where else. If she would have been so kind as to have moderated her Visits to ten times a Day, and stay'd but half an hour at a Time, I should have been contented, and I believe never have given you this Trouble: But this very Morning they have so tormented me that I could bear no longer; For while the Mother was asking me twenty impertinent Questions, the youngest got to my Nails, and with great Delight rattled them by handfuls all over the Floor; and the other at the same Time made such a terrible Din upon my Counter with a Hammer, that I grew half distracted. I was just then about to make my self a new Suit of Pinners, but in the Fret and Confusion I cut it quite out of all Manner of Shape, and utterly spoil'd a Piece of the first Muslin. Pray, Sir, tell me what I shall do. And talk a little against such unreasonable Visiting in your next Paper: Tho' I would not have her affronted with me for a great Deal, for sincerely I love her and her Children as well I think, as a Neighbour can, and she buys a great many Things in a Year at my Shop. But I would beg her to consider that she uses me unmercifully; Tho' I believe it is only for want of Thought.—But I have twenty Things more to tell you besides all this; There is a handsome Gentleman that has a Mind (I don't question) to make love to me, but he can't get the least Opportunity to—: O dear, here she comes again;—I must conclude

Yours, &c.
Patience."

Indeed, 'tis well enough, as it happens, that *she is come,* to shorten this Complaint which I think is full long enough already, and probably would otherwise have been as long again. However, I must confess I cannot help pitying my Correspondent's Case, and in her Behalf exhort the Visitor to remember and consider the Words of the Wise Man, *Withdraw thy Foot from the House of thy Neighbour least he grow weary of thee, and so hate thee.* It is, I believe, a nice thing and very difficult, to regulate our Visits in such a Manner, as never to give Offence by coming too seldom, or too often, or departing too abruptly, or staying too long. However, in my Opinion, it is safest for most

People, in a general way, who are unwilling to disoblige, to visit seldom, and tarry but a little while in a Place; notwithstanding pressing Invitations, which are many times insincere. And tho' more of your Company should be really desir'd; yet in this Case, too much Reservedness is a Fault more easily excus'd than the Contrary.

Men are subjected to various Inconveniences meerly through lack of a small Share of Courage, which is a Quality very necessary in the common Occurrences of Life, as well as in a Battle. How many Impertinences do we daily suffer with great Uneasiness, because we have not Courage enough to discover our Dislike? And why may not a Man use the Boldness and Freedom of telling his Friends that their long Visits sometimes incommode him?—On this Occasion, it may be entertaining to some of my Readers, if I acquaint them with the *Turkish* Manner of entertaining Visitors, which I have from an Author of unquestionable Veracity; who assures us, that even the Turks are not so ignorant of Civility, and the Arts of Endearment, but that they can practice them with as much Exactness as any other Nation, whenever they have a Mind to shew themselves obliging.

"When you visit a Person of Quality, (says he) and have talk'd over your Business, or the Complements, or whatever Concern brought you thither, he makes a Sign to have Things serv'd in for the Entertainment, which is generally, a little Sweetmeat, a Dish of Sherbet, and another of Coffee; all which are immediately brought in by the Servants, and tender'd to all the Guests in Order, with the greatest Care and Awfulness imaginable. At last comes the finishing Part of your Entertainment, which is, Perfuming the Beards of the Company; a Ceremony which is perform'd in this Manner. They have for the Purpose a small Silver Chaffing-Dish, cover'd with a Lid full of Holes, and fixed upon a handsome Plate. In this they put some fresh Coals, and upon them a piece of *Lignum Aloes,* and shutting it up, the Smoak immediately ascends with a grateful Odour thro' the Holes of the Cover. This Smoak is held under every one's Chin, and offer'd as it were a Sacrifice to his Beard. The bristly Idol soon receives the Reverence done to it, and so greedily takes in and incorporates the gummy Steam, that it retains the Savour of it, and may serve for a Nosegay a good while after.

"This Ceremony may perhaps seem ridiculous at first hearing; but it passes among the *Turks* for an high Gratification. And I will say this in its Vindication, that it's Design is very wise and useful. For it is understood to give a civil Dismission to the Visitants; intimating to them, that the Master of the House has Business to do, or some other Avocation, that permits them to go away as soon as they please; and the sooner after this Ceremony the better. By this Means you may, at any Time, without Offence, deliver your self from being detain'd from your Affairs by tedious and unseasonable Visits; and from being constrain'd to use that Piece of Hypocrisy so common in the World, of pressing those to stay longer with you, whom perhaps in your Heart you wish a great Way off for having troubled you so long already.''

Thus far my Author. For my own Part, I have taken such a Fancy to this Turkish Custom, that for the future I shall put something like it in Practice. I have provided a Bottle of right French Brandy for the Men, and Citron-Water for the Ladies. After I have treated with a Dram, and presented a Pinch of my best Snuff, I expect all Company will retire, and leave me to pursue my Studies for the Good of the Publick.

BENJAMIN FRANKLIN

"The Drinker's Dictionary"

Nothing more like a Fool than a drunken Man.
                                        Poor Richard.

'Tis an old Remark, that Vice always endeavours to assume the Appearance of Virtue: Thus Covetousness calls itself *Prudence; Prodigality* would be thought *Generosity;* and so of others. This perhaps arises hence, that Mankind naturally and universally approve Virtue in their Hearts, and detest Vice; and therefore, whenever thro' Temptation they fall into a Practice of the latter, they would if possible conceal it from themselves as well as others, under some other Name than that which properly belongs to it.

But DRUNKENNESS is a very unfortunate Vice in this respect. It bears no kind of Similitude with any sort of Virtue, from which it might possibly borrow a Name; and is therefore reduc'd to the wretched Necessity of being express'd by distant round-about Phrases, and of perpetually varying those Phrases, as often as they come to be well understood to signify plainly that A MAN IS DRUNK.

Tho' every one may possibly recollect a Dozen at least of the Expressions us'd on this Occasion, yet I think no one who has not much frequented Taverns would imagine the number of them so great as it really is. It may therefore surprize as well as divert the sober Reader, to have the Sight of a new Piece, lately communicated to me, entitled

THE DRINKERS DICTIONARY.

A
He is Addled,
He's casting up his Accounts,
He's Afflicted,
He's in his Airs.

B
He's Biggy,
  Bewitch'd,
  Block and Block,
  Boozy,
  Bowz'd,
  Been at Barbadoes,
  Piss'd in the Brook,
  Drunk as a Wheel-Barrow,
  Burdock'd,
  Buskey,
  Buzzey,
Has Stole a Manchet out of the
    Brewer's Basket,
His Head is full of Bees,
Has been in the Bibbing Plot,
Has drank more than he has bled,
He's Bungey,
  As Drunk as a Beggar,
He sees the Bears,
He's kiss'd black Betty,
He's had a Thump over the
  Head with Sampson's
  Jawbone,
He's Bridgey.

C
He's Cat,
  Cagrin'd,
  Capable,
  Cramp'd,
  Cherubimical,
  Cherry Merry,

Wamble Crop'd,
  Crack'd,
  Concern'd,
  Half Way to Concord,
Has taken a Chirriping-Glass,
  Got Corns in his Head,
  A Cup to much,
  Coguy,
  Copey,
He's heat his Copper,
He's Crocus,
  Catch'd,
He cuts his Capers,
He's been in the Cellar,
He's in his Cups,
  Non Compos,
  Cock'd,
  Curv'd,
  Cut,
  Chipper,
  Chickery,
  Loaded his Cart,
He's been too free with the
    Creature,
Sir Richard has taken off his
    Considering Cap,
He's Chap-fallen,

D
He's Disguiz'd,
He's got a Dish,
  Kill'd his Dog,
  Took his Drops,
It is a Dark Day with him,
He's a Dead Man,
Has Dipp'd his Bill,
He's Dagg'd,
He's seen the Devil,

E
He's Prince Eugene,
   Enter'd,
   Wet both Eyes,
   Cock Ey'd,
   Got the Pole Evil,
   Got a brass Eye,
   Made an Example,
He's Eat a Toad & half for
     Breakfast.
In his Element,

F
He's Fishey,
   Fox'd,
   Fuddled,
   Sore Footed,
   Frozen,
   Well in for't,
   Owes no Man a Farthing,
   Fears no Man,
   Crump Footed,
   Been to France,
   Flush'd,
   Froze his Mouth,
   Fetter'd,
   Been to a Funeral,
   His Flag is out,
   Fuzl'd,
   Spoke with his Friend,
   Been at an Indian Feast.

G
He's Glad,
   Groatable,
   Gold-headed,
   Glaiz'd,
   Generous,
   Booz'd the Gage,
   As Dizzy as a Goose,
   Been before George,

Got the Gout,
Had a Kick in the Guts,
Been with Sir John Goa,
Been at Geneva,
Globular,
Got the Glanders.

H
Half and Half,
Hardy,
Top Heavy,
Got by the Head,
Hiddey,
Got on his little Hat,
Hammerish,
Loose in the Hilts,
Knows not the way Home,
Got the Hornson,
Haunted with Evil Spirits,
Has Taken Hippocrates grand
     Elixir,

I
He's Intoxicated,
   Jolly,
   Jagg'd,
   Jambled,
   Going to Jerusalem,
   Jocular,
   Been to Jerico,
   Juicy.

K
He's a King,
   Clips the King's English,
   Seen the French King,
   The King is his Cousin,
   Got Kib'd Heels,
   Knapt,
   Het his Kettle.

L
He's in Liquor,
  Lordly,
  He makes Indentures with his
    Leggs,
  Well to Live,
  Light,
  Lappy,
  Limber,

M
He sees two Moons,
  Merry,
  Middling,
  Moon-Ey'd,
  Muddled,
  Seen a Flock of Moons,
  Maudlin,
  Mountous,
  Muddy,
  Rais'd his Monuments,
  Mellow,

N
He's eat the Cocoa Nut
  Nimptopsical,
  Got the Night Mare,

O
He's Oil'd,
  Eat Opium,
  Smelt of an Onion,
  Oxycrocium,
  Overset,

P
He drank till he gave up his
    Half-Penny,
  Pidgeon ey'd,
  Pungey,
  Priddy,
  As good conditioned as a Puppy,

Has scalt his Head Pan,
  Been among the Philistines,
  In his Prosperity,
He's been among the Philippians,
He's contending with Pharaoh,
  Wasted his Paunch,
He's Polite,
  Eat a Pudding Bagg,

Q
He's Quarrelsome,

R
He's Rocky,
  Raddled,
  Rich,
  Religious,
  Lost his Rudder,
  Ragged,
  Rais'd,
Been too free with Sir Richard,
Like a Rat in Trouble.

S
He's Stitch'd,
  Seafaring,
  In the Sudds,
  Strong,
  Been in the Sun,
  As Drunk as David's Sow,
  Swampt,
His Skin is Full,
He's Steady,
He's Stiff,
He's burnt his Shoulder,
He's got his Top Gallant Sails out,
  Seen the yellow Star,
  As Stiff as a Ring-bolt,
  Half Seas over,
  His Shoe pinches him,
  Staggerish,
  It is Star-light with him,

He carries too much Sail,
Stew'd
Stubb'd,
Soak'd,
Soft,
Been too free with Sir John
    Strawberry,
He's right before the Wind
    with all his Studding
    Sails out,
Has Sold his Senses.

T
He's Top'd,
    Tongue-ty'd,
    Tann'd,
    Tipium Grove,
    Double Tongu'd,
    Topsy Turvey,

    Tipsey,
Has Swallow'd a Tavern Token,
He's Thaw'd,
He's in a Trance,
He's Trammel'd,

V
He makes Virginia Fence, Valiant,
    Got the Indian Vapours,

W
The Malt is above the Water,
He's Wise,
He's Wet,
He's been to the Salt Water,
He's Water-soaken,
He's very Weary,
    Out of the Way.

The Phrases in this Dictionary are not (like most of our Terms of Art) borrow'd from Foreign Languages, neither are they collected from the Writings of the Learned in our own, but gather'd wholly from the modern Tavern-Conversation of Tiplers. I do not doubt but that there are many more in use; and I was even tempted to add a new one my self under the Letter B, to wit, *Brutify'd:* But upon Consideration, I fear'd being guilty of Injustice to the Brute Creation, if I represented Drunkenness as a beastly Vice, since, 'tis well-known, that the Brutes are in general a very sober sort of People.

THOMAS MEEHAN

"Add Hot Water; Serves Fourteen Million"

Until about one-fifteen of a recent weekday morning, when I found a cure for my long torment, I was abysmally hooked, an addict. Erratic, perpetually exhausted, filled with self-loathing, and vilely short-tempered, I was in danger of losing my job, my friends, even my marriage. "Either you say goodbye to the habit or you can say goodbye to *me!*" my wife cried one night. I started to plead with her, but at that moment my bloodshot eyes strayed to our bedroom clock and I saw that it was That Time again. I shrugged and scuttled into the living room and turned on. I was, to admit the ugly truth, a late-night television-movie addict.

In my case, at least, the addiction was localized—I went only for Hollywood movies of the late nineteen-thirties. It is to this circumstance that I can attribute the suddenness with which I was able to kick the habit. Others, hooked on everything from *Hell's Angels* to *Platinum High School,* may, I'm afraid, have a more difficult time with their cold turkey, but, if my case is any indication, there's hope for them too.

Like a drug addict who will sniff only cocaine, I was interested in the pure pre-1940 stuff, but careful conning of newspaper TV listings and some deft channel-switching enabled me to get all of the junk I needed to feed my habit. Four or five evenings each week, I would awaken at dawn from a confused dream involving Richard Arlen, Kay Francis, and Bonita Granville, to find myself sprawled, still fully clothed, in my living-room chair, with a heap of cigarette butts and apple cores before me and only the taunting eye of the empty screen to witness my shame and degradation.

I had no warning that an escape from my torture was at hand. On the night in question, I had already taken in a Deanna Durbin musical and had just settled down miserably to a 1938 Warner Brothers gangster movie called *Angels with Dirty Faces.* Then it happened. Midway through the first reel, one of the supporting players snarled, "Them rotten coppers will never get Rocky

Sullivan—he's too smart for them,'' and at that instant I knew, as if by magic, everything that was going to take place during the rest of the movie, right down to that final scene when Rocky Sullivan would be dragged screaming to the electric chair. I rose at once, strode to the television set and snapped it off, and went straight to bed.

Not until I awoke in the morning, refreshed by the longest sleep I'd had in months, did I fully understand the liberating significance of that scrap of dialogue. Thinking about *Angels with Dirty Faces,* and about the vast, tawdry repertory of thirties films that I knew so well, it suddenly dawned on me that the early scenes of virtually every Hollywood movie of that era contained a similar moment of précis—a brief exchange of dialogue, or in some instances merely one line, that gave away the entire film and made further viewing unnecessary. This scrap of dramaturgy, I realized, was the distilled essence, the Nescafé, of the film, and once the experienced viewer extracted this essence he could switch off his set and go to bed, where simply by adding a generous amount of mental hot water he could turn it into a full-length feature, creating what I've lately come to think of as the Instant Movie, a potion that can be consumed in two or three fast gulps just before sleep.

Now that I've kicked the habit, I feel that the very least I can do is to help pry the monkey off the backs of my erstwhile fellow-addicts, and I have therefore cooked up the makings of a handful of Instant Movies. As an example, consider a 1938 horse-racing picture. In this imaginary film, the quintessential line of dialogue comes early in the second reel, in a scene that takes place outside a rustic stable. A freckle-faced eleven-year-old tomboy named Cindy (Marcia Mae Jones) is looking pleadingly up into the moist blue eyes of an old white-haired Southern gent (Walter Brennan).

CINDY: They won't have to shoot Firefly, will they, Gramps?

Now, adding hot water to this line, we immediately have a ninety-seven-minute feature entitled *Kentucky Sunshine.* And who among us, viewing *Kentucky Sunshine,* would be able to blink back the tears when Gramps experiences a painless but garrulous death halfway through the sixth reel, or, indeed, would be able to repress a grin at the endearing high junks of Jazzbo (Stepin Fetchit), the good-natured but bumbling Negro stable hand? What's more, would we not all feel a sudden warm glow (something akin to heartburn) when, in the closing moments of the film, Peggy (Ann Rutherford), Cindy's wind-blown older sister, at last gets together with Jim Crankshaw (Dick Foran), the idealistic young veterinarian from down the road, as Cindy and Jazzbo chuckle on the back porch and, in the final fadeout, Firefly sticks his head out of his stall and whinnies playfully? Which reminds me. No, Cindy, they won't have to shoot Firefly. In fact, in the last reel, in the running-of-the-

Derby sequence, guess which 95–1 shot is going to win the race by a nose?

I suppose the addicts in the audience have got the idea by now, but as a further guide toward their salvation I have cooked up ten other prototypical Instant Movies, all from the powerful 1938 crop, of which I shall pass along only the Nescafé; for these flickers, the reader will have to supply his own hot water.

1. THE INSTANT 1938 HIGH-CLASS MUSICAL BIOGRAPHY MOVIE.

SCENE: *A candle-lit garret in a squalid corner of Vienna in 1843. On a narrow cot, a pale, lovely, dying young woman* (Anita Louise) *is whispering huskily to a sensitive-looking young man* (Richard Greene), *whose hair is even longer than hers.*

DYING YOUNG WOMAN *(in a heavy Vienna accent):* You must forget me, Franz. The vorld is vaiting for your beaudiful melodies.

2. THE INSTANT 1938 SPOILED DEBUTANTE MOVIE.

SCENE: *An outsize white-on-white bedroom in a North Shore Long Island mansion. Midge* (Jane Bryan), *a wide-eyed, saccharine young thing, is talking with Cynthia Marlowe* (Bette Davis), *a chain-smoking, hyperthyroid, but madly attractive heiress of twenty-four.*

MIDGE: But gee whiz, Cynthia, Polly is your own identical twin sister!

CYNTHIA: Polly is a sentimental little fool. Gordon Hughes is the most fascinating man I've ever met, and I'm going to have him.

MIDGE: But Gordon is taking Polly to the Harbor Club dance tonight.

CYNTHIA: That's what he thinks. Aunt Agatha's had another one of her attacks, and Polly left unexpectedly this morning for California to be at her bedside. Isn't that *sweet* of Polly? Gordon will never know the difference.

MIDGE: But, Cynthia, you wouldn't . . .

3. THE INSTANT 1938 NAVAL ACADEMY MOVIE.

SCENE: *A dormitory room at Annapolis on the Friday evening before the crucial annual weekend maneuvers. A veteran chief petty officer* (Wallace Beery) *is addressing a handsome but insolent young midshipman* (Robert Taylor), *who is lounging on his cot with an infuriating half smile on his lips.*

CHIEF PETTY OFFICER *(angrily):* Look, playboy, this isn't a country club, it's the *U*-nited States Navy. Your dad stood for something at this Academy, and I'm not going to let you ruin his good name.

MIDSHIPMAN: If you're quite through with the hearts and flowers, Clancy, I still have that date with Brenda at the Kit Kat Club in half an hour, and Flotilla

C won't lose the Academy flag unless you decide to turn me in. So actually it's up to you, isn't it?

4. THE INSTANT 1938 NEWSPAPERMAN MOVIE.

SCENE: *The cluttered City Room of the New York* Daily Chronicle. *The managing editor* (William Frawley) *is having a heated argument with his star reporter* (Edmund Lowe).

MANAGING EDITOR: Listen, O'Brien, you've spent enough of the paper's time on that wild-goose chase. Drop that story or consider yourself fired!

STAR REPORTER: O.K., Chief, I admit it—all the evidence says no. But somehow I think that poor guy in the death house, Stragella, is telling the truth. Give me just three hours more. I've got a hunch.

5. THE INSTANT 1938 COLLEGE FOOTBALL MOVIE.

SCENE: *The campus of Cantwell College, somewhere in the Middle West. A coed* (Patsy Kelly) *is talking excitedly with the captain of the football team* (Jack Oakie).

COED: Gee whiz, Windy, if Blinky Walinkowitz can't play on Saturday we haven't got a chance against State. And he'll never pass Professor Gottsegen's botany exam.

FOOTBALL CAPTAIN: I wouldn't be so sure of that, Glenda. Remember how Blinky was able to remember, for exactly twenty-four hours, every single word of the songs you sang when we were all riding the merry-go-round at the student carnival last week?

COED: Yes, but what's that got to do with—

FOOTBALL CAPTAIN: Plenty. The exam is tomorrow morning, and you're a straight-A student in botany. Right? Now, here's my plan. You bring Blinky here after lights-out, and I'll get my sax, and we'll . . .

6. THE INSTANT 1938 AFRICAN SAFARI MOVIE.

SCENE: *A clearing in a notably phony-looking bit of back-lot jungle. Captain Jack Clifton* (Bruce Cabot), *a world-famous African explorer, and Bob Thayer* (John Payne), *an earnest young anthropologist, are questioning a frightened native messenger* (Sam Jaffe).

NATIVE MESSENGER: Uga wamba bonga tonga. Wamba munga tbaga kwumba sbimba mboga.

BOB: What is he saying?

CAPTAIN JACK: He says that it is still two days' march to the Valley of the Lost Elephants, through Umphalombi Swamp and over Jackal's Tooth Range.

Sleeping sickness has decimated the bearers we hoped to meet at the watering hole. And he says between here and the Valley there is a fierce tribe of headhunters that is holding prisoner a bearded old man and a beautiful young blond woman.

BOB: Gosh, then . . .

CAPTAIN JACK: Yes, Bob, I'm afraid it's just as we feared. The Ugwambas have captured Janet and Professor Bartelstone.

7. THE INSTANT 1938 MYSTERIOUS FATAL DISEASE MOVIE.

SCENE: *The office of James Hartwell, M.D. Dr. Hartwell* (Henry O'Neill), *a silver-haired gentleman, is talking privately with Sally Forsythe* (Loretta Young), *a beautiful young wife and mother, who has lately been having the most painful headaches.*

DR. HARTWELL *(gravely):* I'd say six months, Sally . . . if you're careful.

SALLY: I see. Dr. Jim, promise you won't say a word about this to Jeff. He's been working so hard these last six years on his arthritis experiments. This trip to Sweden for the Nobel Prize was to have been our second honeymoon.

8. THE INSTANT 1938 LOWER EAST SIDE MOVIE.

SCENE: *The roof of a tenement on an oppressively hot and humid New York summer's night. A moody young slum dweller* (John Garfield) *is looking out on the lights of the city, as his best girl* (Priscilla Lane) *stands adoringly at his side.*

YOUNG SLUM DWELLER: You wait and see, Lois, I'm going to do just like Ma wanted me to. I'm going to write a symphony of the city. And there's gonna be everything in it—the lights, the rattle of the subways at night, the taxicabs honking, Mrs. Callaghan yelling at her kids.

BEST GIRL: Gee, that's swell, Danny. Then you're . . . you're going to give up boxing for good?

9. THE INSTANT 1938 SOPHISTICATED ROMANCE MOVIE.

SCENE: *The private New York office of Chris Baxter, the president of Amalgamated, Inc. Tim Roderick* (Melvyn Douglas), *a handsome corporation lawyer in his mid-thirties, has just burst unannounced into the room and is speaking angrily to a trim, beautiful young woman* (Rosalind Russell), *who is seated behind an enormous mahogany desk.*

TIM: All right, Miss whatever your name is, I want to see your boss, Chris Baxter, right away. Right away, you hear?

YOUNG WOMAN: If you'll please calm down, perhaps you can tell me what it is you want. I'm Chris Baxter.

TIM: You're Chris Baxter? But you're . . . you're a woman.
YOUNG WOMAN *(coolly lighting a cigarette):* And is there anything so unusual
about that?

1 0. THE INSTANT 1 9 3 8 BIG HOUSE MOVIE.

SCENE: *A cellblock at State Penitentiary. A soft-spoken Irish-American priest* (Pat O'-
Brien) *is reasoning quietly with an escaping convict* (James Cagney), *who is wildly
waving a loaded revolver.*

PRIEST: Hand over that gun, my son.
CONVICT: Stand back, Father Jerry, or I'll drill you! I swear I'll drill you!
(Click!)

No, that wasn't the revolver misfiring—it was me turning off my television
set. Good night.

O. HENRY

"*A Comedy in Rubber*"

One may hope, in spite of the metaphorists, to avoid the breath of the
deadly upas tree; one may, by great good fortune, succeed in blacking the eye
of the basilisk; one might even dodge the attentions of Cerberus and Argus,
but no man, alive or dead, can escape the gaze of the Rubberer.

New York is the Caoutchouc City. There are many, of course, who go their
ways, making money, without turning to the right or the left, but there is a
tribe abroad wonderfully composed, like the Martians, solely of eyes and
means of locomotion.

These devotees of curiosity swarm, like flies, in a moment in a struggling,
breathless circle about the scene of an unusual occurrence. If a workman opens
a manhole, if a street car runs over a man from North Tarrytown, if a little boy
drops an egg on his way home from the grocery, if a casual house or two drops
into the subway, if a lady loses a nickel through a hole in the lisle thread, if the
police drag a telephone and a racing chart forth from an Ibsen Society reading-

room, if Senator Depew or Mr. Chuck Connors walks out to take the air—if any of these incidents or accidents takes place, you will see the mad, irresistible rush of the "rubber" tribe to the spot.

The importance of the event does not count. They gaze with equal interest and absorption at a chorus girl or at a man painting a liver pill sign. They will form as deep a cordon around a man with a club-foot as they will around a balked automobile. They have the furor rubberendi. They are optical gluttons, feasting and fattening on the misfortunes of their fellow beings. They gloat and pore and glare and squint and stare with their fishy eyes like goggle-eyed perch at the hook baited with calamity.

It will seem that Cupid would find these ocular vampires too cold game for his calorific shafts, but have we not yet to discover an immune even among the Protozoa? Yes, beautiful Romance descended upon two of this tribe, and love came into their hearts as they crowded about the prostrate form of a man who had been run over by a brewery wagon.

William Pry was the first on the spot. He was an expert at such gatherings. With an expression of intense happiness on his features, he stood over the victim of the accident, listening to his groans as if to the sweetest music. When the crowd of spectators had swelled to a closely packed circle William saw a violent commotion in the crowd opposite him. Men were hurled aside like ninepins by the impact of some moving body that clove them like the rush of a tornado. With elbows, umbrella, hat-pin, tongue, and fingernails doing their duty, Violet Seymour forced her way through the mob of onlookers to the first row. Strong men who even had been able to secure a seat on the 5:30 Harlem express staggered back like children as she bucked centre. Two large lady spectators who had seen the Duke of Roxburgh married and had often blocked traffic on Twenty-third Street fell back into the second row with ripped shirt-waists when Violet had finished with them. William Pry loved her at first sight.

The ambulance removed the unconscious agent of Cupid. William and Violet remained after the crowd had dispersed. They were true Rubberers. People who leave the scene of an accident with the ambulance have not genuine caoutchouc in the cosmogony of their necks. The delicate, fine flavor of the affair is to be had only in the after-taste—in gloating over the spot, in gazing fixedly at the houses opposite, in hovering there in a dream more exquisite than the opium-eater's ecstasy. William Pry and Violet Seymour were connoisseurs in casualties. They knew how to extract full enjoyment from every incident.

Presently they looked at each other. Violet had a brown birthmark on her neck as large as a silver half-dollar. William fixed his eyes upon it. William Pry had inordinately bowed legs. Violet allowed her gaze to linger unswervingly upon them. Face to face they stood thus for moments, each staring at the other. Etiquette would not allow them to speak; but in the Caoutchouc City it is permitted to gaze without stint at the trees in the parks and at the physical blemishes of a fellow creature.

At length with a sigh they parted. But Cupid had been the driver of the brewery wagon, and the wheel that broke a leg united two fond hearts.

The next meeting of the hero and heroine was in front of a board fence near Broadway. The day had been a disappointing one. There had been no fights on the street, children had kept from under the wheels of the street cars, cripples and fat men in negligée shirts were scarce; nobody seemed to be inclined to slip on banana peels or fall down with heart disease. Even the sport from Kokomo, Ind., who claims to be a cousin of ex-Mayor Low and scatters nickels from a cab window, had not put in his appearance. There was nothing to stare at, and William Pry had premonitions of ennui.

But he saw a large crowd scrambling and pushing excitedly in front of a billboard. Sprinting for it, he knocked down an old woman and a child carrying a bottle of milk, and fought his way like a demon into the mass of spectators. Already in the inner line stood Violet Seymour with one sleeve and two gold fillings gone, a corset steel puncture and a sprained wrist, but happy. She was looking at what there was to see. A man was painting upon the fence: "Eat Bricklets—They Fill Your Face."

Violet blushed when she saw William Pry. William jabbed a lady in a black silk raglan in the ribs, kicked a boy in the shin, hit an old gentleman on the left ear and managed to crowd nearer to Violet. They stood for an hour looking at the man paint the letters. Then William's love could be repressed no longer. He touched her on the arm.

"Come with me," he said. "I know where there is a bootblack without an Adam's apple."

She looked up at him shyly, yet with unmistakable love transfiguring her countenance.

"And you have saved it for me?" she asked, trembling with the first dim ecstasy of a woman beloved.

Together they hurried to the bootblack's stand. An hour they spent there gazing at the malformed youth.

A window-cleaner fell from the fifth story to the sidewalk beside them. As the ambulance came clanging up William pressed her hand joyously. "Four ribs at least and a compound fracture," he whispered, swiftly. "You are not sorry that you met me, are you, dearest?"

"Me?" said Violet, returning the pressure. "Sure not. I could stand all day rubbering with you."

The climax of the romance occurred a few days later. Perhaps the reader will remember the intense excitement into which the city was thrown when Eliza Jane, a colored woman, was served with a subpoena. The Rubber Tribe encamped on the spot. With his own hands William Pry placed a board upon two beer kegs in the street opposite Eliza Jane's residence. He and Violet sat there for three days and nights. Then it occurred to a detective to open the door and serve the subpoena. He sent for a kinetoscope and did so.

Two souls with such congenial tastes could not long remain apart. As a policeman drove them away with his night stick that evening they plighted their troth. The seeds of love had been well sown, and had grown up, hardy and vigorous, into a—let us call it a rubber plant.

The wedding of William Pry and Violet Seymour was set for June 10. The Big Church in the Middle of the Block was banked high with flowers. The populous tribe of Rubberers the world over is rampant over weddings. They are the pessimists of the pews. They are the guyers of the groom and the banterers of the bride. They come to laugh at your marriage, and should you escape from Hymen's tower on the back of death's pale steed they will come to the funeral and sit in the same pew and cry over your luck. Rubber will stretch.

The church was lighted. A grosgrain carpet lay over the asphalt to the edge of the sidewalk. Bridesmaids were patting one another's sashes awry and speaking of the bride's freckles. Coachmen tied white ribbons on their whips and bewailed the space of time between drinks. The minister was musing over his possible fee, essaying conjecture whether it would suffice to purchase a new broadcloth suit for himself and a photograph of Laura Jane Libbey for his wife. Yea, Cupid was in the air.

And outside the church, oh, my brothers, surged and heaved the rank and file of the tribe of Rubberers. In two bodies they were, with the grosgrain carpet and cops with clubs between. They crowded like cattle, they fought, they pressed and surged and swayed and trampled one another to see a bit of a girl in a white veil acquire license to go through a man's pockets while he sleeps.

But the hour for the wedding came and went, and the bride and bridegroom came not. And impatience gave way to alarm and alarm brought about search, and they were not found. And then two big policemen took a hand and dragged out of the furious mob of onlookers a crushed and trampled thing, with a wedding ring in its vest pocket and a shredded and hysterical woman beating her way to the carpet's edge, ragged, bruised and obstreperous.

William Pry and Violet Seymour, creatures of habit, had joined in the seething game of the spectators, unable to resist the overwhelming desire to gaze upon themselves entering, as bride and bridegroom, the rose-decked church.

Rubber will out.

JAMES THURBER

"How to Tell a Fine Old Wine"

In spite of all that has been written about wines, the confusion in the minds of some lay drinkers is just as foggy as it was—in the case of some minds, even foggier. The main trouble, I think, is that the average wine connoisseur has suddenly become rather more the writing man than the sipping man without possessing that fine precision in expository composition which comes only from long years of writing, rewriting, cutting down, and, most especially, throwing away. It is my hope in this article, somehow or other, to clear up a few of the more involved problems of nomenclature and of geographical (or viticultural) distribution, for I believe I know what the wine experts have been trying to say and I believe I can say it perhaps a little more clearly.

France, then, is divided into ninety different *Départements,* all but four of them ending in *"et-Oise"* (and-Oise) and twenty-seven of them having towns named Châlons. Fortunately, in only three of the Châlons *communes* are there *girondes* where any of the great wines of France are grown. We can safely confine ourselves to the Bordeaux region and the Burgundy region, respectively the *Côte-d'Or* and the *Côte de Châlons,* or as the French trainmen say, *"L'autre côté!"* The great wines of France are divided into only three classifications with which we need to be concerned: the *grands vins,* the *petits vins,* and the *vins fins.* And it is with the last that we shall be most particularly concerned. *Vins fins* means, simply enough, "finished wines," that is, wines which did not turn out as well as might have been expected. It is these wines and none others which America is getting today and which America is going to continue to get. Just what causes this I don't exactly know, but something.

In the old days of the great *châteauxiers,* there was never any question about what to do with a *vin* when it turned out to be *fin.* The *châteauxiers* simply referred to it philosophically as *"fin de siècle"* (finished for good) and threw it out. They would have nothing to do with a wine that wasn't noble, distinguished, dignified, courageous, high-souled, and austere. Nowadays it is different. The *vins fins* are filtered through to the American public in a thousand different disguises, all spurious—not a genuine disguise among them. It is virtually impossible for the layman, when he picks up a bottle labelled "St. Julien-Clos Vougeot-Grandes Veuves, 1465A21, *mise du château,* Perdolio, Premier Cru, Marchanderie: Carton et Cie., 1924," to know whether he is getting, as should be the case with this label, a truly noble St. Estèphe or, as is more likely to be the case, a Benicarló that has been blended with Heaven only knows what, perhaps even a white Margelaise! Well then, how *is* he to know?

Let us say that a bottle has come into our hands labelled as above. "St. Julien" is simply the name of the *commune* and "Clos Vougeot" the name of the château around which the grapes are grown. "Grandes Veuves" is either an added distinguishing flourish put on the noble old label years and years ago by some *grandes veuves* (large widows) or it is a meaningless addition placed thereon since repeal by those French *flâneurs* who hope to inveigle the American public into buying cheap and tawdry wines under elaborate and impressive-sounding labels. So much for the name of the wine itself.

The number, 1465A21, is nothing to be bewildered by. It is simply the official *estampe française de la douane* and it can be checked against the authentic "serial-running" of the official French revenue stamping machine by applying to somebody in the French Embassy here, or the French Consulate, and asking him to get in touch with the man in charge of the registered files of the French revenue stamping department. If the letter used (in this case "A") proves to be the actual letter employed in 1924 by the revenue stampers, the vintage date on the bottle is authentic, providing, of course, that the identifying letter was, in that year, inserted between the fourth and fifth figures of the serial number and that 146521 fell among the *estampages* allocated to the St. Julien *commune* in that year. It is, of course, unfortunate that the Stavisky affair in France threw all the numbers in that country into the wildest sort of confusion, so that it is hardly likely that any stamp numbers can be certified with confidence by anybody for the next six months or so. But the wine will be all the better after six months and France may by then have its records in order once more, if she can find them.

The phrase *"mise du château"* is extremely simple, and it is astonishing how many Americans are puzzled by it. It means nothing more than "mice in the château," just as it says. The expression goes back to the days, some twenty years ago, when certain French manufacturers of popular "tonic wines" made fortunes almost overnight and in many cases bought up old châteaux, tore them down, and built lavish new ones in the rococo manner. These new châteaux were, of course, clean and well kept, but so garish and ugly that a disdainful expression grew up among the French peasantry in regard to them: *"Ils n'ont jamais de mise du château là-bas"* ("They never have any mice in that château over there"). The grand old *châteauxiers* thereupon began to add to their labels, *"mise du château"*—in other words, "There are mice in *this* château," a proud if slightly incongruous legend for a bottle of noble old wine.

The label symbol "Perdolio" on our bottle might equally well have been "Manfreda," "Variola," "Muscatel," "Amontillado," "Sauternes," "Katerina," or any one of a couple of hundred others. The idea of this name originated with the old Spanish *vinteriosos,* especially those of Casanovia and Valencia, and indicated simply a desire on the part of a given merchant to place the name of a favorite daughter, son, mistress, or wine on the bottles he merchandised.

"Premier Cru," which we come to next in looking back at our St. Julien label, means "first growth," that is, wine that was grown first. And "Marchanderie: Carton et Cie." is the name of the shipper. In some cases the name of the captain of the ship transporting the wine is also added to the label, some such name as Graves or Médoc, and one need not take alarm at this, but one should be instantly suspicious of any marks, names, numbers, or symbols other than those I have gone into here. Bottles which bear such legends as "George H. Kansas City, '24" or "C. M. & Bessie B., '18" or "Mrs. P. P. Bliss, Ashtabula, O., '84" or "I Love My Wife But Oh You Kid (1908)" may be put down as having fallen into the hands of American tourists somewhere between the bottling and the shipping. They are doubtlessly refills containing a colored sugar water, if anything at all.

The vintage year is, of course, always branded into the cork of the bottle and is the only kind of bottle-cork date mark to go by. Dates laid in with mother-of-pearl or anything of the sort are simply impressive and invidious attempts to force high prices from the pockets of gullible Americans. So also are French wine labels bearing the American flag or portraits of Washington or such inscriptions, no matter how beautifully engraved or colored, as "Columbia, the Gem of the Ocean" and "When Lilacs Last in the Dooryard Bloom'd."

In summing up, it is perhaps advisable to say a few words about the vineyards themselves. Some vineyards, facing north, get the morning sun just under the right side of the leaf; others, facing south, get the sun on the other side. Many vineyards slope and many others do not. Once in a while one straggles into a graveyard or climbs up on a porch. In each case a difference may or may not be found in the quality of the wine. When a town has been built on the place where a vineyard formerly was, the vineyard is what the French call "out" (a word adopted from our English tennis term). There may be a few vines still producing in gutters and backyards of the town, but the quality of their output will be ignoble. The "out" taste is easily discernible to both the connoisseur and the layman just as is the faint flavor of saddle polish in certain brands of sparkling Burgundy. In the main, it is safe to go by one's taste. Don't let anybody tell you it is one-tenth as hard to tell the taste of a good wine from the taste of a bad wine or even of a so-so wine as some of the *connaisseurs écrivants* would have us believe.

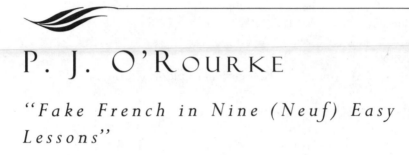

P. J. O'ROURKE

"Fake French in Nine (Neuf) Easy Lessons"

One way to say nothing while impressing people who aren't listening is to speak Fake French. Fake French lends you all the cachet of speaking French without tedious memorization or stupid Berlitz records lying around the house. Besides, no one learns real French anymore because Americans already have a language they can't understand and don't speak well—English.

Lesson Un: Articles

Use *"le"* or *"la"* in place of "the," "a," and "an" to make *anything* you say sound sophisticated.

Examples:
"Pass le coleslaw."
"Open la door."

Lesson Deux: Prepositions

All English prepositions can be replaced with the French prepositions *"à"* and *"de"* which mean "at," "of," "with," "on," and anything else you want them to mean because we're not really trying to speak French, so who cares?

Example:
   "I'll have le cheeseburger à la french fries."
   Throw in *"chez," "sur," "dans,"* and *"voilà,"* too, if you feel like it.

Example:
   "I'll have sur le cheeseburger chez dans à la french fries voilà."

Lesson Trois: Pronouns

   "I" is *"je"* when it's the subject of the sentence and *"moi"* when you're being silly. "You" is *"Vous."* "We" is *"nous."*

Example:
   "Moi loves vous."—Fake French in its ultimate form.

Lesson Quatre: Nouns

   Use as many as you can recall from high school French, whether you remember the correct translation or not.

Examples:
   "Soir of the living dead."
   "Drinks on the maison!"
   "No use crying over spilt au lait."

Lesson Cinq: Modifiers

   All French adjectives and adverbs mean "lots of," e.g., *"très" "plus" "beaucoup,"* et cetera. Use them everywhere.

Example:
   "I've très de had too much plus to drink beaucoup."

Lesson Six (Say "Sees"): Verbs

   There's only one French verb of any note, *"faire,"* meaning "make," "do," "be," "become," "create," and so on and so forth. The construction "faire de ———" turns any English word into a French verb.

Examples:
   "Je faire de whoopee."
   "Vous faire de hell out of here."

Any English word can also be turned into a French verb by adding *"-ez vous"* to the end of it.

Examples:
  "Je buyez vous le drink?"
  "Mais non?"
  "Screwez vous, too."

Lesson Sept: Negation

"No" is said in French by forming the construction *"Ne* [verb] *pas."*

Example:
  "Ne run vous hand up moi jamb pas or je smackez vous plus dans le mouth beaucoup." (Note garbled word order to aid in "foreign" sound.)

Lesson Huit: Advanced Fake French

To give the impression of a really thoroughgoing fluency, translate all your favorite English phrases into literal French with a pocket dictionary.

Examples:
  "frapper la rue"
  "droit sur"
  "donnez moi une fracture"
  "hors de vue"
  "Qu'est-ce que votre signe?"
  "Pas merde"

Lesson Neuf: Fake French in Action

Below is the translation of an answering machine message from Babs Muddleprep, a sophomore at Bennington, to her older sister, Puffy, in Santa Barbara. The first version is given in English. The second version is in Fake French. Notice how much more, well, *je ne sais quoi* the second version is:

Message from Babs to Puffy, translated into English:
  "I had a long talk with mother last night. There's good news and bad news. She's not drinking as much lately, but she's still really cheesed about the mess we left in her apartment. Did I tell you about the dress I found in Bendel's? It's *so cool.* But I couldn't afford it at all so I charged it to Mummy. Now she'll be pissed to the max. Have to hit the books now—French final is tomorrow and

must do well because the professor is to die over. Also, I flunked the midterm. Love you bunches. See you in Sun Valley.''

Message from Babs to Puffy in its original Fake French:
''Je faire le beaucoup chatez avec la Mother last soir. There est le news bien and le news mal. She's ne drinking pas as beaucoup lately mais she's still plus de fromaged about le mess we left dans le apartment hers. Did I tellez vous about le chemise je trouvez at le Bendel's? C'est *très froid*. Mais je ne affordez pas it at all so je chargez à Mama. Now she'll be pissoired à la maximum. Have to frapper les libres now—examination terminal de la français is demain and must faire bon because le professor est to mort sur. Aussi, je flunked le term-midi. Je t'aime beaucoup. See vous dan le Valle du Soleil.

Briefly Speaking

It must be a good thing to be good or ivrybody wudden't be pretendin' he was. But I don't think they'se anny such thing as hypocrisy in th' wurruld. They can't be. If ye'd turn on th' gas in th' darkest heart ye'd find it had a good raison for th' worst things it done, a good varchous raison, like needin' th' money or punishin' th' wicked or tachin' people a lesson to be more careful, or protectin' th' liberties iv mankind, or needin' the money.

—FINLEY PETER DUNNE

RUSSELL BAKER

"Bye-Bye, Silver Bullets"

The Lone Ranger is through. Washed up. He stands in a Los Angeles law office. Oriental rugs under foot. A Kandinsky on the wall. The desk rich and sleek, covered with writs, injunctions, habeas corpus, mandamus, certiorari, nolo contendere, duces tecum, bills of attainder.

The lawyer has handled people like the Lone Ranger before. The world is full of them if you are a lawyer. People who go around the country drawing down Big Jack by passing themselves off as the Lone Ranger, Popeye the Sailor Man, Boob McNutt, Secret Agent X-9, the Green Hornet.

"You're all washed up, Popeye," he tells them. Or, "O.K., Hornet, one more rendering of 'The Flight of the Bumble Bee,' and we're going to slap you with so many injunctions you'll have to hawk your Orphan Annie decoder and Cocomalt shaker to pay your court costs."

The Lone Ranger is easier meat than most. He is getting old. He is 64 now. It shows. His mask is deeply wrinkled. Tonto urged him five years ago to see a plastic surgeon about having tucks taken in the eye slits, but the Lone Ranger refused. He is old-fashioned about too many things.

"I'll give it to you straight from the shoulder, Ranger," the lawyer says. "You're washed up. Over the hill."

The Lone Ranger's reflexes are slow. He would like to leap aboard his fiery horse with the speed of light and gallop away with a hearty "Heigh-ho, Silver!" He cannot. The lawyer's receptionist made him leave Silver outside on account of the oriental rugs. The Lone Ranger can read the secrets of a cold campfire, but he is no match for the guile of receptionists.

The lawyer urges the Lone Ranger to look at himself. A wrinkled man in a world whose heart goes out only to smooth men.

"I don't smoke or drink," says the Ranger. "I work out every morning to keep my body trim."

The lawyer has heard it all before. These old crocks are all alike. "I still eats my spinach three times a day and avoids all heavy lifting to keep my upper arms skinnier than Slim Summerville," Popeye once told him.

"I'm not talking two-for-a-penny Mary Janes, Ranger," says the lawyer. "I'm talking big law. Now come across with that mask."

The Lone Ranger recoils. They always recoil at this stage of the interview. The lawyer remembers how the Phantom recoiled when ordered to come across with both his mask and his form-fitting rubber suit, remembers how ridiculous the Phantom looked when it had been peeled off him. His entire body wrinkled like hands left too long in hot dish water.

The lawyer is not a cruel man. He remembers the years he sat by his television set, thumb in mouth, marveling at the Lone Ranger. Once, he wanted to grow up to be the Lone Ranger's sidekick and gallop behind him on a small gray stallion named Zirconium.

Life for the lawyer has been a series of disappointments, except for the oriental rugs and the Kandinsky and the cunning receptionist. In law school he had wanted to grow up to be Perry Mason and save the innocent from the noose and be admired afterwards by Paul Drake and Della for refusing to take a fee.

Instead, here he was, pushing around heroes for getting long in the tooth. He hoped the Lone Ranger wouldn't cry. He couldn't stand it when they cried. He remembered the Katzenjammer Kids, doddering octogenarians, weeping like babies when he told them it was time for the nursing home.

"Ranger," he says, "promise me you won't cry and I'll try to explain."

"I feel like crying," the Lone Ranger says. "It's the worst I've ever felt in my life. But I won't cry. The Lone Ranger doesn't cry."

The lawyer explains that his client owns the rights to the Lone Ranger and means to make a bundle from them. There was going to be a young, new Lone Ranger, a smooth man. Having a dilapidated old Lone Ranger galloping the plains is bad for the young, new, smooth-man Lone Ranger image necessary for the making of bundles.

"You're trying to tell me I'm not the Lone Ranger any more?"

They always asked that. "You mean to tell me I'm not Flash Gordon any more?" Flash had asked when ordered to hand over Emperor Ming and the Planet Mongo. And the lawyer had said, "That's right—you're just Buster Crabbe now."

It was the only legal answer. To the Ranger he says, "From now on, you're just Clayton Moore. Your revels now are ended. Turn in your mask and your silver bullets, your white hat and your faithful Tonto and your fiery steed with the speed of light."

"What will I do for a living from now on?" the ex-Lone Ranger asks. The lawyer explains that this is a question nobody has been able to answer satisfactorily to retirees. Many of them, he says, find shuffleboard fulfilling.

When the Ranger leaves, the lawyer considers calling in his receptionist and Paul Drake and telling them he refuses to take a fee for this case. Instead he pushes the intercom button.

"You can send Buck Rogers in now," he says.

MARK TWAIN

Duke and Dauphin Excerpt from The Adventures of Huckleberry Finn

In Chapter Nineteen of The Adventures of Huckleberry Finn *the raft has been floating peacefully down the Mississippi, "wherever the current wanted her to." In that calm, Huck and Jim, the runaway slave, lit their pipes "and dangled our legs in the water and talked about all kinds of things." This peace was soon to be broken by two of the great rascals of all literature.*

Sometimes we'd have that whole river all to ourselves for the longest time. Yonder was the banks and the islands, across the water; and maybe a spark—which was a candle in a cabin window—and sometimes on the water you could see a spark or two—on a raft or a scow, you know; and maybe you could hear a fiddle or a song coming over from one of them crafts. It's lovely to live on a raft. We had the sky, up there, all speckled with stars, and we used to lay on our backs and look up at them, and discuss about whether they was made, or only just happened—Jim he allowed they was made, but I allowed they happened; I judged it would have took too long to *make* so many. Jim said the moon could a *laid* them; well, that looked kind of reasonable, so I didn't say nothing against it, because I've seen a frog lay most as many, so of course it could be done. We used to watch the stars that fell, too, and see them streak down. Jim allowed they'd got spoiled and was hove out of the nest.

Once or twice of a night we would see a steamboat slipping along in the dark, and now and then she would belch a whole world of sparks up out of her chimbleys, and they would rain down in the river and look awful pretty; then she would turn a corner and her lights would wink out and her pow-wow shut off and leave the river still again; and by-and-by her waves would get to us, a long time after she was gone, and joggle the raft a bit, and after that you wouldn't hear nothing for you couldn't tell how long, except maybe frogs or something.

After midnight the people on shore went to bed, and then for two or three hours the shores was black—no more sparks in the cabin windows. These sparks was our clock—the first one that showed again meant morning was coming, so we hunted a place to hide and tie up, right away.

One morning about day-break, I found a canoe and crossed over a chute to the main shore—it was only two hundred yards—and paddled about a mile up a crick amongst the cypress woods, to see if I couldn't get some berries. Just as I was passing a place where a kind of a cow-path crossed the crick, here comes a couple of men tearing up the path as tight as they could foot it. I thought I was a goner, for whenever anybody was after anybody I judged it was *me*—or maybe Jim. I was about to dig out from there in a hurry, but they was pretty close to me then, and sung out and begged me to save their lives—said they hadn't been doing nothing, and was being chased for it—said there was men and dogs a-coming. They wanted to jump right in, but I says—

"Don't you do it. I don't hear the dogs and horses yet; you've got time to crowd through the brush and get up the crick a little ways; then you take to the water and wade down to me and get in—that'll throw the dogs off the scent."

They done it, and soon as they was aboard I lit out for our tow-head, and in about five or ten minutes we heard the dogs and the men away off, shouting. We heard them come along towards the crick, but couldn't see them; they seemed to stop and fool around a while; then, as we got further and further away all the time, we couldn't hardly hear them at all; by the time we had left a mile of woods behind us and struck the river, everything was quiet, and we paddled over to the tow-head and hid in the cotton-woods and was safe.

One of these fellows was about seventy, or upwards, and had a bald head and very gray whiskers. He had an old battered-up slouch hat on, and a greasy blue woolen shirt, and ragged old blue jeans britches stuffed into his boot tops, and home-knit galluses—no, he only had one. He had an old long-tailed blue jeans coat with slick brass buttons, flung over his arm, and both of them had big fat ratty-looking carpetbags.

The other fellow was about thirty and dressed about as ornery. After breakfast we all laid off and talked, and the first thing that come out was that these chaps didn't know one another.

"What got you into trouble?" says the baldhead to t'other chap.

"Well, I'd been selling an article to take the tartar off the teeth—and it does take it off, too, and generly the enamel along with it—but I staid about one night longer than I ought to, and was just in the act of sliding out when I ran across you on the trail this side of town, and you told me they were coming, and begged me to help you to get off. So I told you I was expecting trouble myself and would scatter out *with* you. That's the whole yarn—what's yourn?"

"Well, I'd ben a-runnin' a little temperance revival thar, 'bout a week, and was the pet of the women-folks, big and little, for I was makin' it mighty warm for the rummies, I *tell* you, and takin' as much as five or six dollars a night—ten cents a head, children and niggers free—and business a growin' all the time; when somehow or another a little report got around, last night, that I had a way of puttin' in my time with a private jug, on the sly. A nigger rousted me out this mornin', and told me the people was getherin' on the quiet, with their dogs and horses, and they'd be along pretty soon and give me 'bout half an hour's start, and then run me down, if they could; and if they got me they'd tar and feather me and ride me on a rail, sure. I didn't wait for no breakfast—I warn't hungry."

"Old man," says the young one, "I reckon we might double-team it together; what do you think?"

"I ain't undisposed. What's your line—mainly?"

"Jour printer, by trade; do a little in patent medicines; theatre-actor—tragedy, you know; take a turn at mesmerism and phrenology when there's a chance; teach singing-geography school for a change; sling a lecture, sometimes—oh, I do lots of things—most anything that comes handy, so it ain't work. What's your lay?"

"I've done considerble in the doctoring way in my time. Layin' on o'hands is my best holt—for cancer, and paralysis, and sich things; and I k'n tell a fortune pretty good, when I've got somebody along to find out the facts for me. Preachin's my line, too; and workin' camp-meetin's; and missionaryin' around."

Nobody never said anything for a while; then the young man hove a sigh and says—

"Alas!"

"What 're you alassin' about?" says the baldhead.

"To think I should have lived to be leading such a life, and be degraded down into such company." And he begun to wipe the corner of his eye with a rag.

"Dern your skin, ain't the company good enough for you?" says the baldhead, pretty pert and uppish.

"Yes, it *is* good enough for me; it's as good as I deserve; for who fetched me so low, when I was so high? *I* did myself. I don't blame *you,* gentlemen—far from it; I don't blame anybody. I deserve it all. Let the cold world do its worst; one thing I know—there's a grave somewhere for me. The world may go on just as it's always done, and take everything from me—loved ones, property, everything—but it can't take that. Some day I'll lie down in it and forget it all, and my poor broken heart will be at rest." He went on a-wiping.

"Drot your pore broken heart," says the baldhead; "what are you heaving your pore broken heart at *us* f'r? *We* hain't done nothing."

"No, I know you haven't. I ain't blaming you, gentlemen. I brought myself down—yes, I did it myself. It's right I should suffer—perfectly right—I don't make any moan.''

''Brought you down from whar? Whar was you brought down from?''

''Ah, you would not believe me; the world never believes—let it pass—'tis no matter. The secret of my birth—''

''The secret of your birth? Do you mean to say—''

''Gentlemen,'' says the young man, very solemn, ''I will reveal it to you, for I feel I may have confidence in you. By rights I am a duke!''

Jim's eyes bugged out when he heard that; and I reckon mine did, too. Then the baldhead says: ''No! you can't mean it?''

''Yes. My great-grandfather, eldest son of the Duke of Bridgewater, fled to this country about the end of the last century, to breathe the pure air of freedom; married here, and died, leaving a son, his own father dying about the same time. The second son of the late duke seized the title and estates—the infant real duke was ignored. I am the lineal descendant of that infant—I am the rightful Duke of Bridgewater; and here am I, forlorn, torn from my high estate, hunted of men, despised by the cold world, ragged, worn, heart-broken, and degraded to the companionship of felons on a raft!''

Jim pitied him ever so much, and so did I. We tried to comfort him, but he said it warn't much use, he couldn't be much comforted; said if we was a mind to acknowledge him, that would do him more good than most anything else; so we said we would, if he would tell us how. He said we ought to bow, when we spoke to him, and say ''Your Grace,'' or ''My Lord,'' or ''Your Lord-ship''—and he wouldn't mind it if we called him plain ''Bridgewater,'' which he said was a title, anyway, and not a name; and one of us ought to wait on him at dinner, and do any little thing for him he wanted done.

Well, that was all easy, so we done it. All through dinner Jim stood around and waited on him, and says, ''Will yo' Grace have some o' dis, or some o' dat?'' and so on, and a body could see it was mighty pleasing to him.

But the old man got pretty silent, by-and-by—didn't have much to say, and didn't look pretty comfortable over all that petting that was going on around that duke. He seemed to have something on his mind. So, along in the after-noon, he says:

''Looky here, Bilgewater,'' he says, ''I'm nation sorry for you, but you ain't the only person that's had troubles like that.''

''No?''

''No, you ain't. You ain't the only person that's ben snaked down wrong-fully out'n a high place.''

''Alas!''

''No, you ain't the only person that's had a secret of his birth.'' And by jings, *he* begins to cry.

"Hold! What do you mean?"

"Bilgewater, kin I trust you?" says the old man, still sort of sobbing.

"To the bitter death!" He took the old man by the hand and squeezed it, and says, "The secret of your being: speak!"

"Bilgewater, I am the late Dauphin!"

You bet you Jim and me stared, this time. Then the duke says:

"You are what?"

"Yes, my friend, it is too true—your eyes is lookin' at this very moment on the pore disappeared Dauphin, Looy the Seventeen, son of Looy the Sixteen and Marry Antonette."

"You! At your age! No! You mean you're the late Charlemagne; you must be six or seven hundred years old, at the very least."

"Trouble has done it, Bilgewater, trouble has done it; trouble has brung these gray hairs and this premature balditude. Yes, gentlemen, you see before you, in blue jeans and misery, the wanderin', exiled, trampled-on and sufferin' rightful King of France."

Well, he cried and took on so, that me and Jim didn't know hardly what to do, we was so sorry—and so glad and proud we'd got him with us, too. So we set in, like we done before with the duke, and tried to comfort *him.* But he said it warn't no use, nothing but to be dead and done with it all could do him any good; though he said it often made him feel easier and better for a while if people treated him according to his rights, and got down on one knee to speak to him, and always called him "Your Majesty," and waited on him first at meals, and didn't set down in his presence till he asked them. So Jim and me set to majestying him, and doing this and that and t'other for him, and standing up till he told us we might set down. This done him heaps of good, and so he got cheerful and comfortable. But the duke kind of soured on him, and didn't look a bit satisfied with the way things was going; still, the king acted real friendly towards him, and said the duke's great-grandfather and all the other Dukes of Bilgewater was a good deal thought of by *his* father and was allowed to come to the palace considerable; but the duke staid huffy a good while, till by-and-by the king says:

"Like as not we got to be together a blamed long time, on this h-yer raft, Bilgewater, and so what's the use o' your bein' sour? It'll only make things oncomfortable. It ain't my fault I warn't born a duke, it ain't your fault you warn't born a king—so what's the use to worry? Make the best o' things the way you find 'em, says I—that's my motto. This ain't no bad thing that we've struck here—plenty grub and an easy life—come, give us your hand, Duke, and less all be friends."

The duke done it, and Jim and me was pretty glad to see it. It took away all the uncomfortableness, and we felt mighty good over it, because it would a been a miserable business to have any unfriendliness on the raft; for what you want, above all things, on a raft, is for everybody to be satisfied, and feel right and kind towards the others.

MARK TWAIN

Emmeline Excerpt from The Adventures of Huckleberry Finn

In Chapter Seventeen of The Adventures of Huckleberry Finn, *Jim and Huck have become separated and Huck has been taken in by the Grangerfords. Aside from pursuing a murderous feud, the Grangerfords are a genial, civilized family who used to have a remarkable daughter.*

It was a mighty nice family, and a mighty nice house, too. I hadn't seen no house out in the country before that was so nice and had so much style. It didn't have an iron latch on the front door, nor a wooden one with a buckskin string, but a brass knob to turn, the same as houses in a town. There warn't no bed in the parlor, not a sign of a bed; but heaps of parlors in towns has beds in them. There was a big fireplace that was bricked on the bottom, and the bricks was kept clean and red by pouring water on them and scrubbing them with another brick; sometimes they washed them over with red water-paint that they call Spanish-brown, same as they do in town. They had big brass dog-irons that could hold up a saw-log. There was a clock on the middle of the mantel-piece, with a picture of a town painted on the bottom half of the glass front, and a round place in the middle of it for the sun, and you could see the pendulum swing behind it. It was beautiful to hear that clock tick; and sometimes when one of these peddlers had been along and scoured her up and got her in good shape, she would start in and strike a hundred and fifty before she got tuckered out. They wouldn't took any money for her.

Well, there was a big outlandish parrot on each side of the clock, made out of something like chalk, and painted up gaudy. By one of the parrots was a cat made of crockery, and a crockery dog by the other; and when you pressed down on them they squeaked, but didn't open their mouths nor look different nor interested. They squeaked through underneath. There was a couple of big wild-turkey-wing fans spread out behind those things. On a table in the middle of the room was a kind of a lovely crockery basket that had apples and oranges and peaches and grapes piled up in it which was much redder and yellower and prettier than real ones is, but they warn't real because you could see where pieces had got chipped off and showed the white chalk or whatever it was, underneath.

This table had a cover made out of beautiful oil-cloth, with a red and blue spread-eagle painted on it, and a painted border all around. It come all the way from Philadelphia, they said. There was some books too, piled up perfectly exact, on each corner of the table. One was a big family Bible, full of pictures. One was "Pilgrim's Progress," about a man that left his family it didn't say why. I read considerable in it now and then. The statements was interesting, but tough. Another was "Friendship's Offering," full of beautiful stuff and poetry; but I didn't read the poetry. Another was Henry Clay's Speeches, and another was Dr. Gunn's Family Medicine, which told you all about what to do if a body was sick or dead. There was a Hymn Book, and a lot of other books. And there was nice split-bottom chairs, and perfectly sound, too—not bagged down in the middle and busted, like an old basket.

They had pictures hung on the walls—mainly Washingtons and Lafayettes, and battles, and Highland Marys, and one called "Signing the Declaration." There was some that they called crayons, which one of the daughters which was dead made her own self when she was only fifteen years old. They was different from any pictures I ever see before; blacker, mostly, than is common. One was a woman in a slim black dress, belted small under the arm-pits, with bulges like a cabbage in the middle of the sleeves, and a large black scoop-shovel bonnet with a black veil, and white slim ankles crossed about with black tape, and very wee black slippers, like a chisel, and she was leaning pensive on a tombstone on her right elbow, under a weeping willow, and her other hand hanging down her side holding a white handkerchief and a reticule, and underneath the picture it said "Shall I Never See Thee More Alas." Another one was a young lady with her hair all combed up straight to the top of her head, and knotted there in front of a comb like a chair-back, and she was crying into a handkerchief and had a dead bird laying on its back in her other hand with its heels up, and underneath the picture it said "I Shall Never Hear Thy Sweet Chirrup More Alas." There was one where a young lady was at a window looking up at the moon, and tears running down her cheeks; and she had an open letter in one hand with black sealing-wax showing on one edge of it, and she was mashing a locket with a chain to it against her mouth, and underneath the picture it said "And Art Thou Gone Yes Thou Art Gone Alas." These was all nice pictures, I reckon, but I didn't somehow seem to take to them, because if ever I was down a little, they always give me the fan-tods. Everybody was sorry she died, because she had laid out a lot more of these pictures to do, and a body could see by what she had done what they had lost. But I reckoned, that with her disposition, she was having a better time in the graveyard. She was at work on what they said was her greatest picture when she took sick, and every day and every night it was her prayer to be allowed to live till she got it done, but she never got the chance. It was a picture of a young woman in a long white gown, standing on the rail of a bridge all ready to jump off, with her hair all down her back, and looking up to the moon, with the tears running down her face, and she had two arms folded across her breast, and two arms stretched out in front, and two more reaching up towards the moon—and the idea was, to see which pair would look best and then scratch out all the other arms; but, as I was saying, she died before she got her mind made up, and now they kept this picture over the head of the bed in her room, and every time her birthday come they hung flowers on it. Other times it was hid with a little curtain. The young woman in the picture had a kind of a nice sweet face, but there was so many arms it made her look too spidery, seemed to me.

This young girl kept a scrap-book when she was alive, and used to paste obituaries and accidents and cases of patient suffering in it out of the *Presbyterian Observer,* and write poetry after them out of her own head. It was very good poetry. This is what she wrote about a boy by the name of Stephen Dowling Bots that fell down a well and was drownded:

ODE TO STEPHEN DOWLING BOTS, DEC'D.

And did young Stephen sicken,
  And did young Stephen die?
And did the sad hearts thicken,
  And did the mourners cry?

No; such was not the fate of
  Young Stephen Dowling Bots;
Though sad hearts round him thickened,
  'Twas not from sickness' shots.

No whooping-cough did rack his frame,
  Nor measles drear, with spots;
Not these impaired the sacred name
  Of Stephen Dowling Bots.

Despised love struck not with woe
   That head of curly knots,
Nor stomach troubles laid him low,
   Young Stephen Dowling Bots.

O no. Then list with tearful eye,
   Whilst I his fate do tell.
His soul did from this cold world fly,
   By falling down a well.

They got him out and emptied him;
   Alas it was too late;
His spirit was gone for to sport aloft
   In the realms of the good and great.

If Emmeline Grangerford could make poetry like that before she was fourteen, there ain't no telling what she could a done by-and-by. Buck said she could rattle off poetry like nothing. She didn't ever have to stop to think. He said she would slap down a line, and if she couldn't find anything to rhyme with it she would just scratch it out and slap down another one, and go ahead. She warn't particular, she could write about anything you choose to give her to write about, just so it was sadful. Every time a man died, or a woman died, or a child died, she would be on hand with her "tribute" before he was cold. She called them tributes. The neighbors said it was the doctor first, then Emmeline, then the undertaker—the undertaker never got in ahead of Emmeline but once, and then she hung fire on a rhyme for the dead person's name, which was Whistler. She warn't ever the same, after that; she never complained, but she kind of pined away and did not live long. Poor thing, many's the time I made myself go up to the little room that used to be hers and get out her poor old scrap-book and read in it when her pictures had been aggravating me and I had soured on her a little. I liked all that family, dead ones and all, and warn't going to let anything come between us. Poor Emmeline made poetry about all the dead people when she was alive, and it didn't seem right that there warn't nobody to make some about her, now she was gone; so I tried to sweat out a verse or two myself, but I couldn't seem to make it go, somehow.

Briefly Speaking

"Many a man that cudden't direct ye to th' dhrug store on th' corner whin he was thirty will get a respectful hearin' whin age has further impaired his mind. . . .

"Why," said Mr. Hennessy, "ye'd give annythin' to be twinty-five agin."

"I wuddn't," said Mr. Dooley. "Why shud I want to grow old agin?"

—Finley Peter Dunne

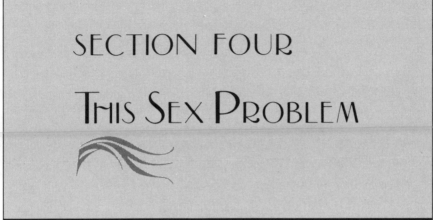

SECTION FOUR

THIS SEX PROBLEM

The sexual power struggle has been a source of comedy since at least the time of Aristophanes, who wrote a play about a female scheme to make men choose between the pleasures of war and the delights of sex. It seems a convention of this kind of humor that the women always win.

Feminists may say this is because most of the writing has been done by men who, whether out of self-pity or political guile, choose to pervert the truth. Possibly, yet even in Jane Austen, the most subtle of women writers in depicting the social ramble, arrogant Mr. Darcy succumbs to the superiority of female character.

Women certainly seem triumphant in most of the following pieces. Except for Mae West's philosophical statement, only two are by women, but in each it is the male who is trussed and skewered at the end. By confessing his taste in literature, S. J. Perelman makes it clear that Aristophanes' female schemers would have found him an easy victim. Even Abraham Lincoln, who starts by feeling nobly masculine, ends knowing that he, not Mary Owens, has been the fool.

FANNIE FLAGG

A Perplexing Question

SEPTEMBER 1, 1986

Ed Couch came home Thursday night and said that he was having trouble with a woman down at the office who was "a real ball breaker," and that none of the men wanted to work with her because of it.

The next day, Evelyn went out to the mall to shop for a bed jacket for Big Momma and while she was having lunch at the Pioneer Cafeteria, a thought popped into her head, unannounced:

What is a ball breaker?

She'd heard Ed use that term a lot, along with *She's out to get my balls* and *I had to hold on to my balls for dear life.*

Why was Ed so scared that someone was out to get his balls? What were they, anyway? Just little pouches that carried sperm; but the way men carried on about them, you'd think they were the most important thing in the world. My God, Ed had just about died when one of their son's hadn't dropped properly. The doctor said that it wouldn't affect his ability to have children, but Ed had acted like it was a tragedy and wanted to send him to a psychiatrist, so he wouldn't feel less of a man. She remembered thinking at the time, how silly . . . her breasts had never developed, and nobody ever sent her for help.

But Ed had won out, because he told her she didn't understand about being a man and what it meant. Ed had even pitched a fit when she wanted to have their cat, Valentine, who had impregnated the thoroughbred Siamese cat across the street, fixed.

He said, "If you're gonna cut his balls off, you might as well just go on and put him to sleep!"

No doubt about it, he was peculiar where balls were concerned.

She remembered how Ed had once complimented that same woman at the office when she had stood up to the boss. He had bragged on her, saying what a ballsy dame she was.

But now that she thought about it, she wondered: What did that woman's strength have to do with Ed's anatomy? He hadn't said, "Boy, she's got some ovaries"; he had definitely said what *balls* she had. Ovaries have eggs in them, she thought: Shouldn't they be as important as sperm?

And when had that woman stepped over the line of having just enough balls to having too much?

That poor woman. She would have to spend her whole life balancing imaginary balls if she wanted to get along. Balance was everything. But what about size? she wondered. She never heard Ed mention size before. It was the other thing's size they were so concerned about, so she guessed it didn't matter all that much. All that mattered in this world was the fact that you *had* balls. Then all at once, the simple and pure truth of that conclusion hit her. She felt as if someone had run a pencil up her spine and dotted an *i* on her head. She sat up straight in her chair, shocked that she, Evelyn Couch, of Birmingham, Alabama, had stumbled on the answer. She suddenly knew what Edison must have felt like when he discovered electricity. Of course! That was it . . . having balls was the most important thing in this world. No wonder she had always felt like a car in traffic without a horn.

It was true. Those two little balls opened the door to everything. They were the credit cards she needed to get ahead, to be listened to, to be taken seriously. No wonder Ed had wanted a boy.

Then another truth occurred to her. Another sad, irrevocable truth: She had no balls and never would or could have balls. She was doomed. Ball-less forever. Unless, she thought, if maybe the balls in your immediate family counted. There were four in hers . . . Ed's and Tommy's . . . No, wait . . . six, if she counted the cat. No, wait just another minute, if Ed loved her so much, why couldn't he give her one of his? A ball transplant. . . . That's right. Or, maybe she could get two from an anonymous donor. That's it, she'd buy some off a dead man and she could put them in a box and take them to important meetings and bang them on the table to get her way. Maybe she'd buy four . . .

No wonder Christianity had been such a big hit. Think of Jesus and the Apostles . . . And if you counted John the Baptist, why that was 14 pairs and 28 singles, right there!

Oh, it was all so simple to her now. How had she been so blind and not seen it before?

Yes, by heavens, she'd done it. She'd hit upon the secret that women have been searching for through the centuries . . .

THIS WAS THE ANSWER . . .

Hadn't Lucille Ball been the biggest star on television?

She banged her iced tea on the table in triumph and shouted, "YES! THAT'S IT!"

Everyone in the cafeteria turned and looked at her.

Evelyn quietly finished her lunch and thought, *Lucille Ball?* Ed might be right. I probably am going crazy.

Briefly Speaking

Give a man a free hand and he'll run it all over you.

—MAE WEST

ANITA LOOS

"Fate Keeps On Happening"

As old-movie fans may remember, Lorelei Lee was "just a little girl from Little Rock" who believed diamonds to be a girl's best friend. Under the tutelage of rich Mr. Eisman, who yearns to improve her mind, Lorelei has embarked for Europe with her pal Dorothy. Fortunately, it is the 1920s, so the transatlantic jetliner has not yet been invented.

APRIL 11TH:

Well Dorothy and I are really on the ship sailing to Europe as anyone could tell by looking at the ocean. I always love the ocean. I mean I always love a ship and I really love the *Majestic* because you would not know it was a ship because it is just like being at the Ritz, and the steward says the ocean is not so obnoxious this month as it generally is. So Mr. Eisman is going to meet us next month in Paris because he has to be there on business. I mean he always says that there is really no place to see the latest styles in buttons like Paris.

So Dorothy is out taking a walk up and down the deck with a gentleman she met on the steps, but I am not going to waste my time going around with gentlemen because if I did nothing but go around I would not finish my diary or read good books which I am always reading to improve my mind. But Dorothy really does not care about her mind and I always scold her because she does nothing but waste her time by going around with gentlemen who do not have anything, when Eddie Goldmark of the Goldmark Films is really quite wealthy and can make a girl delightful presents. But she does nothing but waste her time and yesterday, which was really the day before we sailed, she would not go to luncheon with Mr. Goldmark but she went to luncheon to meet a gentleman called Mr. Mencken from Baltimore who really only prints a green magazine which has not even got any pictures in it. But Mr. Eisman is always saying that every girl does not want to get ahead and get educated like me.

So Mr. Eisman and Lulu come down to the boat to see me off and Lulu cried quite a lot. I mean I really believe she could not care any more for me if she was light and not colored. Lulu has had a very sad life because when she was quite young a pullman porter fell madly in love with her. So she believed him and he lured her away from her home to Ashtabula and deceived her there. So she finally found out that she had been deceived and she really was broken hearted and when she tried to go back home she found out that it was to late because her best girl friend, who she had always trusted, had stolen her husband and he would not take Lulu back. So I have always said to her she could always work for me and she is going to take care of the apartment until I get back, because I would not sublet the apartment because Dorothy sublet her apartment when she went to Europe last year and the gentleman who sublet the apartment allowed girls to pay calls on him who were not nice.

Mr. Eisman has literally filled our room with flowers and the steward has had quite a hard time to find enough vases to put them into. I mean the steward said he knew as soon as he saw Dorothy and I that he would have quite a heavy run on vases. And of course Mr. Eisman has sent me quite a lot of good books as he always does, because he always knows that good books are always welcome. So he has sent me quite a large book of Etiquette as he says there is quite a lot of Etiquette in England and London and it would be a good thing for a girl to learn. So I am going to take it on the deck after luncheon and read it, because I would often like to know what a girl ought to do when a gentleman she has just met, says something to her in a taxi. Of course I always become quite vexed but I always believe in giving a gentleman another chance.

So now the steward tells me it is luncheon time, so I will go upstairs as the gentleman Dorothy met on the steps has invited us to luncheon in the Ritz, which is a special dining room on the ship where you can spend quite a lot of money because they really give away the food in the other dining room.

A PRIL 1 2 TH :

I am going to stay in bed this morning as I am quite upset as I saw a gentleman who quite upset me. I am not really sure it was the gentleman, as I saw him at quite a distants in the bar, but if it really is the gentleman it shows that when a girl has a lot of fate in her life it is sure to keep on happening. So when I thought I saw this gentleman I was with Dorothy and Major Falcon, who is the gentleman Dorothy met on the steps, and Major Falcon noticed that I became upset, so he wanted me to tell him what was the matter, but it is really so terrible that I would not want to tell anyone. So I said good night to Major Falcon and I left him with Dorothy and I went down to our room and did nothing but cry and send the steward for some champagne to cheer me up. I mean champagne always makes me feel philosophical because it makes me realize that when a girl's life is as full of fate as mine seems to be, there is nothing else to do about it. So this morning the steward brought me my coffee and quite a large pitcher of ice water so I will stay in bed and not have any more champagne until luncheon time.

Dorothy never has any fate in her life and she does nothing but waste her time and I really wonder if I did right to bring her with me and not Lulu. I mean she really gives gentlemen a bad impression as she talks quite a lot of slang. Because when I went up yesterday to meet she and Major Falcon for luncheon, I overheard her say to Major Falcon that she really liked to become intoxicated once in a "dirty" while. Only she did not say intoxicated, but she really said a slang word that means intoxicated and I am always having to tell her that "dirty" is a slang word and she really should not say "dirty."

Major Falcon is really quite a delightful gentleman for an Englishman. I mean he really spends quite a lot of money and we had quite a delightful luncheon and dinner in the Ritz until I thought I saw the gentleman who upset me and I am so upset I think I will get dressed and go up on the deck and see if it really is the one I think it is. I mean there is nothing else for me to do as I have finished writing my diary for today and I have decided not to read the book of Etiquette as I glanced through it and it does not seem to have anything in it that I would care to know because it wastes quite a lot of time telling you what to call a Lord and all the Lords I have met have told me what to call them and it is generally some quite cute name like Coocoo whose real name is really Lord Cooksleigh. So I will not waste my time on such a book. But I wish I did not feel so upset about the gentleman I think I saw.

A P R I L   1 3 T H :

It really is the gentleman I thought I saw. I mean when I found out it was the gentleman my heart really stopped. Because it all brought back things that anybody does not like to remember, no matter who they are. So yesterday when I went up on the deck to see if I could see the gentleman and see if it really was him, I met quite a delightful gentleman who I met once at a party called Mr. Ginzberg. Only his name is not Mr. Ginzberg any more because a gentleman in London called Mr. Battenburg, who is some relation to some king, changed his name to Mr. Mountbatten which Mr. Ginzberg says really means the same thing after all. So Mr. Ginzberg changed his name to Mr. Mountginz which he really thinks is more aristocratic. So we walked around the deck and we met the gentleman face to face and I really saw it was him and he really saw it was me. I mean his face became so red it was almost a picture. So I was so upset I said good-bye to Mr. Mountginz and I started to rush right down to my room and cry. But when I was going down the steps, I bumped right into Major Falcon who noticed that I was upset. So Major Falcon made me go to the Ritz and have some champagne and tell him all about it.

So then I told Major Falcon about the time in Arkansas when Papa sent me to Little Rock to study how to become a stenographer. I mean Papa and I had quite a little quarrel because Papa did not like a gentleman who used to pay calls on me in the park and Papa thought it would do me good to get away for awhile. So I was in the business colledge in Little Rock for about a week when a gentleman called Mr. Jennings paid a call on the business colledge because he wanted to have a new stenographer. So he looked over all we colledge girls and he picked me out. So he told our teacher that he would help me finish my course in his office because he was only a lawyer and I really did not have to know so much. So Mr. Jennings helped me quite a lot and I stayed in his office about a year when I found out that he was not the kind of a gentleman that a young girl is safe with. I mean one evening when I went to pay a call on him at his apartment, I found a girl there who really was famous all over Little Rock for not being nice. So when I found out that girls like that paid calls on Mr. Jennings I had quite a bad case of histerics and my mind was really a blank and when I came out of it, it seems that I had a revolver in my hand and it seems that the revolver had shot Mr. Jennings.

So this gentleman on the boat was really the District Attorney who was at the trial and he really was quite harsh at the trial and he called me names that I would not even put in my diary. Because everyone at the trial except the District Attorney was really lovely to me and all the gentlemen in the jury all cried when my lawyer pointed at me and told them that they practically all had had either a mother or a sister. So the jury was only out three minutes and then they came back and acquitted me and they were all so lovely that I really had to kiss all of them and when I kissed the judge he had tears in his eyes and he took me right home to his sister. I mean it was when Mr. Jennings became shot that I got the idea to go into the cinema, so Judge Hibbard got me a ticket to Hollywood. So it was Judge Hibbard who really gave me my name because he did not like the name I had because he said a girl ought to have a name that ought to express her personality. So he said my name ought to be Lorelei which is the name of a girl who became famous for sitting on a rock in Germany. So I was in Hollywood in the cinema when I met Mr. Eisman and he said that a girl with my brains ought not to be in the cinema but she ought to be educated, so he took me out of the cinema so he could educate me.

So Major Falcon was really quite interested in everything I talked about, because he said it was quite a co-instance because this District Attorney, who is called Mr. Bartlett, is now working for the government of America and he is on his way to a place called Vienna on some business for Uncle Sam that is quite a great secret and Mr. Falcon would like very much to know what the secret is, because the Government in London sent him to America especially to find out what it was. Only of course Mr. Bartlett does not know who Major Falcon is, because it is such a great secret, but Major Falcon can tell me, because he knows who he can trust. So Major Falcon says he thinks a girl like I ought to forgive and forget what Mr. Bartlett called me and he wants to bring us together and he says he thinks Mr. Bartlett would talk to me quite a lot when he really gets to know me and I forgive him for that time in Little Rock. Because it would be quite romantic for Mr. Bartlett and I to become friendly, and gentlemen who work for Uncle Sam generally like to become romantic with girls. So he is going to bring us together on the deck after dinner tonight and I am going to forgive him and talk with him quite a lot, because why should a girl hold a grudge against a gentleman who had to do it. So Major Falcon brought me quite a large bottle of perfume and a quite cute imitation of quite a large size dog in the little shop which is on board the boat. I mean Major Falcon really knows how to cheer a girl up quite a lot and so tonight I am going to make it all up with Mr. Bartlett.

APRIL 14TH:

Well Mr. Bartlett and I made it all up last night and we are going to be the best of friends and talk quite a lot. So when I went down to my room quite late Major Falcon came down to see if I and Mr. Bartlett were really going to be friends because he said a girl with brains like I ought to have lots to talk about with a gentleman with brains like Mr. Bartlett who knows all of Uncle Sam's secrets.

So I told Major Falcon how Mr. Bartlett thinks that he and I seem to be like a play, because all the time he was calling me all those names in Little Rock he really thought I was. So when he found out that I turned out not to be, he said he always thought that I only used my brains against gentlemen and really had quite a cold heart. But now he thinks I ought to write a play about how he called me all those names in Little Rock and then, after seven years, we became friendly.

So I told Major Falcon that I told Mr. Bartlett I would like to write the play but I really did not have time as it takes quite a lot of time to write my diary and read good books. So Mr. Bartlett did not know that I read books which is quite a co-instance because he reads them to. So he is going to bring me a book of philosophy this afternoon called "Smile, Smile, Smile" which all the brainy senators in Washington are reading which cheers you up quite a lot.

So I told Major Falcon that having a friendship with Mr. Bartlett was really quite enervating because Mr. Bartlett does not drink anything and the less anybody says about his dancing the better. But he did ask me to dine at his table, which is not in the Ritz and I told him I could not, but Major Falcon told me I ought to, but I told Major Falcon that there was a limit to almost everything. So I am going to stay in my room until luncheon and I am going to luncheon in the Ritz with Mr. Mountginz who really knows how to treat a girl.

Dorothy is up on the deck wasting quite a lot of time with a gentleman who is only a tennis champion. So I am going to ring for the steward and have some champagne which is quite good for a person on a boat. The steward is really quite a nice boy and he has had quite a sad life and he likes to tell me all about himself. I mean it seems that he was arrested in Flatbush because he promised a gentleman that he would bring him some very very good scotch and they mistook him for a bootlegger. So it seems they put him in a prison and they put him in a cell with two other gentlemen who were very, very famous burglars. I mean they really had their pictures in all the newspapers and everybody was talking about them. So my steward, whose real name is Fred, was very very proud to be in the same cell with such famous burglars. So when they asked him what he was in for, he did not like to tell them that he was only a bootlegger, so he told them that he set fire to a house and burned up quite a large family in Oklahoma. So everything would have gone alright except that the police had put a dictaphone in the cell and used it all against him and he could not get out until they had investigated all the fires in Oklahoma. So I always think that it is much more educational to talk to a boy like Fred who has been through a lot and really suffered than it is to talk to a gentleman like Mr. Bartlett. But I will have to talk to Mr. Bartlett all afternoon as Major Falcon has made an appointment for me to spend the whole afternoon with him.

A PRIL 1 5 TH :

Last night there was quite a maskerade ball on the ship which was really all for the sake of charity because most of the sailors seem to have orphans which they get from going on the ocean when the sea is very rough. So they took up quite a collection and Mr. Bartlett made quite a long speech in favor of orphans especially when their parents are sailors. Mr. Bartlett really likes to make speeches quite a lot. I mean he even likes to make speeches when he is all alone with a girl when they are walking up and down a deck. But the maskerade ball was quite cute and one gentleman really looked almost like an imitation of Mr. Chaplin. So Dorothy and I really did not want to go to the ball but Mr. Bartlett bought us two scarfs at the little store which is on the ship so we tied them around our hips and everyone said we made quite a cute Carmen. So Mr. Bartlett and Major Falcon and the tennis champion were the Judges. So Dorothy and I won the prizes. I mean I really hope I do not get any more large size imitations of a dog as I have three now and I do not see why the Captain does not ask Mr. Cartier to have a jewelry store on the ship as it is really not much fun to go shopping on a ship with gentlemen, and buy nothing but imitations of dogs.

So after we won the prizes I had an engagement to go up on the top of the deck with Mr. Bartlett as it seems he likes to look at the moonlight quite a lot. So I told him to go up and wait for me and I would be up later as I promised a dance to Mr. Mountginz. So he asked me how long I would be dancing till, but I told him to wait up there and he would find out. So Mr. Mountginz and I had quite a delightful dance and champagne until Major Falcon found us. Because he was looking for me and he said I really should not keep Mr. Bartlett waiting. So I went up on the deck and Mr. Bartlett was up there waiting for me and it seems that he really is madly in love with me because he did not sleep a wink since we became friendly. Because he never thought that I really had brains but now that he knows it, it seems that he has been looking for a girl like me for years, and he said that really the place for me when he got back home was Washington d. c. where he lives. So I told him I thought a thing like that was nearly always the result of fate. So he wanted me to get off the ship tomorrow at France and take the same trip that he is taking to Vienna as it seems that Vienna is in France and if you go on to England you go to far. But I told him that I could not because I thought that if he was really madly in love with me he would take a trip to London instead. But he told me that he had serious business in Vienna that was a very, very great secret. But I told him I did not believe it was business but that it really was some girl, because what business could be so important? So he said it was business for the United States government at Washington and he could not tell anybody what it was. So then we looked at the moonlight quite a lot. So I told him I would go to Vienna if I really knew it was business and not some girl, because I could not see how business could be so important. So then he told me all about it. So it seems that Uncle Sam wants some new aeroplanes that everybody else seems to want, especially England, and Uncle Sam has quite a clever way to get them which is to long to put in my diary. So we sat up and saw the sun rise and I became quite stiff and told him I would have to go down to my room because, after all, the ship lands at France today and I said if I got off the boat at France to go to Vienna with him I would have to pack up.

So I went down to my room and went to bed. So then Dorothy came in and she was up on the deck with the tennis champion but she did not notice the sun rise as she really does not love nature but always wastes her time and ruins her clothes even though I always tell her not to drink champagne out of a bottle on the deck of the ship as it lurches quite a lot. So I am going to have luncheon in my room and I will send a note to Mr. Bartlett to tell him I will not be able to get off the boat at France to go to Vienna with him as I have quite a headache, but I will see him sometime somewhere else. So Major Falcon is going to come down at 12 and I have got to thinking over what Mr. Bartlett called me at Little Rock and I am quite upset. I mean a gentleman never pays for those things but a girl always pays. So I think I will tell Major Falcon all about the airoplane business as he really wants to know. And, after all I do not think Mr. Bartlett is a gentleman to call me all those names in Little Rock even if it was seven years ago. I mean Major Falcon is always a gentleman and he really wants to do quite a lot for us in London. Because he knows the Prince of Wales and he thinks that Dorothy and I would like the Prince of Wales once we had really got to meet him. So I am going to stay in my room until Mr. Bartlett gets off the ship at France, because I really do not seem to care if I never see Mr. Bartlett again.

So tomorrow we will be at England bright and early. And I really feel quite thrilled because Mr. Eisman sent me a cable this morning, as he does every morning, and he says to take advantage of everybody we meet as traveling is the highest form of education. I mean Mr. Eisman is always right and Major Falcon knows all the sights in London including the Prince of Wales so it really looks like Dorothy and I would have quite a delightful time in London.

H. L. MENCKEN

"How Much Should a Woman Eat?"

The meanest man in the United States, unearthed the other day in Chicago, came into public view protesting piteously that his wife's extravagance was ruining him. Her appetite, he said, was gigantic, and on brisk, fair days she ate as much as 30 cents' worth of food. A few days afterward a Bostonian, arrested on a charge of nonsupport, admitted that he gave his wife but 8 cents a day and said that he regarded the money as sufficient for her provisioning. During the same week a Duluth man sought a divorce from his wife on the ground that she fried and consumed a peck of Bermuda onions daily, and so made his house uninhabitable, his bank account a theoretical abstraction and his dream of happiness a mere hallucination.

The world, perhaps, contemplates these men and their acts with mingled amusement and contempt, but in sober truth they have not a little justice and equity on their side. It is easy enough to laugh at them or to dismiss them with sneers, but who shall say that they are wrong? Have they violated any law or ordinance of any nation, State or municipality, or outraged any known principle of jurisprudence? Common honesty compels the admission that they have not. Our American statutes are silent upon the subject, and our courts, with their customary negligence, have never judicially determined, in any way, shape or form, the amount of food necessary to the nourishment of a wife. Failing such rules of law, every husband must solve the problem for himself, and if, in his endeavor so to solve it, his native prejudices lead him to some conclusion obnoxious to humanitarians, he is entitled, nevertheless, to the respect and tolerance due every man who essays a hazardous and difficult enterprise.

Every competent circus man knows to the fraction of an ounce how much food his various and exotic charges require in the course of 24 hours. He knows that an elephant of such-and-such tonnage needs so-and-so much hay; that a snake of such-and-such a distance from fang to rattle needs so-and-so many rabbits, rats and other snakes. And in the army, by the same token, the dietetic demands of the soldier are worked out to three places of decimals. A private carrying 80 pounds of luggage, with the temperature at 65°, can march 18⅓ miles in 16⅔ hours upon three ham sandwiches, half a pint of stuffed olives and a plug of plantation twist. A general weighing 285 pounds can ride a cayuse up four hills, each 345 feet in height on 6 ginger snaps and 12 Scotch highballs. Experiments are made to determine these things, and the results are carefully noted in official handbooks, and so attain the force of military regulations. But at the domestic hearth every young husband must figure it out for himself.

We have no doubt that much of the ill-feeling which results is due to an ignorant and romantic misinterpretation of misleading indications. When a girl is engaged in the enterprise of luring a man toward the Aisle of Sighs she affects an air of impalpable spirituality. Schooled by her elders of her own sex in the theory that a man is attracted by evidences of weakness and fragility, she pretends to an abhorrence of all the more vigorous victuals. Let her gentleman friend take her to some eating house and she orders a charlotte russe or a lettuce sandwich. Her favorite viand, judging by appearances, is celery shoots; the very thought of roast beef seems to disgust her.

The poor man marries her, and on their honeymoon she continues her deception. Her meals are made up of toast, fudge and mayonnaise. She orders half, quarter, eighth and sixteenth portions. But by the time the pair set up housekeeping in their own dear little flat the demands of hunger begin to grow irresistibly, and one morning Clarence is astounded and appalled to see his Mayme wade into five mutton chops, a rasher of bacon and half a dozen hot rolls. That night, at dinner, she eats six ears of corn, a quart of lima beans, a joint of mutton, a bowl of potato salad and two thirds of a shad. The next day, getting her true gait, she makes away with a beef-steak that would suffice for a starving commercial traveler.

Is it any wonder that the unfortunate man loses his reason and runs amuck? Is it any wonder that the sharp anguish of disillusionment carries him to fantastic extremes? Is it any wonder that a man thus deceived into believing, by deliberate chicanery, that the girl he is about to marry eats only meringues and radish tops, and led, by these deceits, to make a correspondingly low estimate of his household expenses after marriage—is it any wonder that this man, when his bride begins to consume $4 worth of food a day, should grow discontented, peevish and cruel?

JAMES THURBER

"The Secret Life of Walter Mitty"

"We're going through!" The Commander's voice was like thin ice breaking. He wore his full-dress uniform, with the heavily braided white cap pulled down rakishly over one cold gray eye. "We can't make it, sir. It's spoiling for a hurricane, if you ask me." "I'm not asking you, Lieutenant Berg," said the Commander. "Throw on the power lights! Rev her up to 8,500! We're going through!" The pounding of the cylinders increased: ta-pocketa-pocketa-pocketa-*pocketa-pocketa*. The Commander stared at the ice forming on the pilot window. He walked over and twisted a row of complicated dials. "Switch on No. 8 auxiliary!" he shouted. "Switch on No. 8 auxiliary!" repeated Lieutenant Berg. "Full strength in No. 3 turret!" shouted the Commander. "Full strength in No. 3 turret!" The crew, bending to their various tasks in the huge, hurtling eight-engined Navy hydroplane, looked at each other and grinned. "The Old Man'll get us through," they said to one another. "The Old Man ain't afraid of Hell!" . . .

"Not so fast! You're driving too fast!" said Mrs. Mitty. "What are you driving so fast for?"

"Hmm?" said Walter Mitty. He looked at his wife, in the seat beside him, with shocked astonishment. She seemed grossly unfamiliar, like a strange woman who had yelled at him in a crowd. "You were up to fifty-five," she said. "You know I don't like to go more than forty. You were up to fifty-five." Walter Mitty drove on toward Waterbury in silence, the roaring of the SN202 through the worst storm in twenty years of Navy flying fading in the remote, intimate airways of his mind. "You're tensed up again," said Mrs. Mitty. "It's one of your days. I wish you'd let Dr. Renshaw look you over."

Walter Mitty stopped the car in front of the building where his wife went to have her hair done. "Remember to get those overshoes while I'm having my hair done," she said. "I don't need overshoes," said Mitty. She put her mirror back into her bag. "We've been all through that," she said, getting out of the car. "You're not a young man any longer." He raced the engine a little.

"Why don't you wear your gloves? Have you lost your gloves?" Walter Mitty reached in a pocket and brought out the gloves. He put them on, but after she had turned and gone into the building and he had driven on to a red light, he took them off again. "Pick it up, brother!" snapped a cop as the light changed, and Mitty hastily pulled on his gloves and lurched ahead. He drove around the streets aimlessly for a time, and then he drove past the hospital on his way to the parking lot.

. . . "It's the millionaire banker, Wellington McMillan," said the pretty nurse. "Yes?" said Walter Mitty, removing his gloves slowly. "Who has the case?" "Dr. Renshaw and Dr. Benbow, but there are two specialists here, Dr. Remington from New York and Mr. Pritchard-Mitford from London. He flew over." A door opened down a long, cool corridor and Dr. Renshaw came out. He looked distraught and haggard. "Hello, Mitty," he said. "We're having the devil's own time with McMillan, the millionaire banker and close personal friend of Roosevelt. Obstreosis of the ductal tract. Tertiary. Wish you'd take a look at him." "Glad to," said Mitty.

In the operating room there were whispered introductions: "Dr. Remington, Dr. Mitty. Mr. Pritchard-Mitford, Dr. Mitty." "I've read your book on streptothricosis," said Pritchard-Mitford, shaking hands. "A brilliant performance, sir." "Thank you," said Walter Mitty. "Didn't know you were in the States, Mitty," grumbled Remington. "Coals to Newcastle, bringing Mitford and me up here for a tertiary." "You are very kind," said Mitty. A huge, complicated machine, connected to the operating table, with many tubes and wires, began at this moment to go pocketa-pocketa-pocketa. "The new anesthetizer is giving way!" shouted an interne. "There is no one in the East who knows how to fix it!" "Quiet, man!" said Mitty, in a low, cool voice. He sprang to the machine, which was now going pocketa-pocketa-queep-pocketa-queep. He began fingering delicately a row of glistening dials. "Give me a fountain pen!" he snapped. Someone handed him a fountain pen. He pulled a faulty piston out of the machine and inserted the pen in its place. "That will hold for ten minutes," he said. "Get on with the operation." A nurse hurried over and whispered to Renshaw, and Mitty saw the man turn pale. "Coreopsis has set in," said Renshaw nervously. "If you would take over, Mitty?" Mitty looked at him and at the craven figure of Benbow, who drank, and at the grave, uncertain faces of the two great specialists. "If you wish," he said. They slipped a white gown on him; he adjusted a mask and drew on thin gloves; nurses handed him shining . . .

"Back it up, Mac! Look out for that Buick!" Walter Mitty jammed on the brakes. "Wrong lane, Mac," said the parking-lot attendant, looking at Mitty closely. "Gee. Yeh," muttered Mitty. He began cautiously to back out of the lane marked "Exit Only." "Leave her sit there," said the attendant. "I'll put her away." Mitty got out of the car. "Hey, better leave the key." "Oh," said

Mitty, handing the man the ignition key. The attendant vaulted into the car, backed it up with insolent skill, and put it where it belonged.

They're so damn cocky, thought Walter Mitty, walking along Main Street; they think they know everything. Once he had tried to take his chains off, outside New Milford, and he had got them wound around the axles. A man had had to come out in a wrecking car and unwind them, a young, grinning garageman. Since then Mrs. Mitty always made him drive to a garage to have the chains taken off. The next time, he thought, I'll wear my right arm in a sling; they won't grin at me then. I'll have my right arm in a sling and they'll see I couldn't possibly take the chains off myself. He kicked at the slush on the sidewalk. "Overshoes," he said to himself, and he began looking for a shoe store.

When he came out into the street again, with the overshoes in a box under his arm, Walter Mitty began to wonder what the other thing was his wife had told him to get. She had told him twice, before they set out from their house for Waterbury. In a way he hated these weekly trips to town—he was always getting something wrong. Kleenex, he thought, Squibb's, razor blades? No. Toothpaste, toothbrush, bicarbonate, carborundum, initiative and referendum? He gave it up. But she would remember it. "Where's the what's-its-name?" she would ask. "Don't tell me you forgot the what's-its-name." A newsboy went by shouting something about the Waterbury trial.

. . . "Perhaps this will refresh your memory." The District Attorney suddenly thrust a heavy automatic at the quiet figure on the witness stand. "Have you ever seen this before?" Walter Mitty took the gun and examined it expertly. "This is my Webley-Vickers 50.80," he said calmly. An excited buzz ran around the courtroom. The judge rapped for order. "You are a crack shot with any sort of firearms, I believe?" said the District Attorney, insinuatingly. "Objection!" shouted Mitty's attorney. "We have shown that the defendant could not have fired the shot. We have shown that he wore his right arm in a sling on the night of the fourteenth of July." Walter Mitty raised his hand briefly and the bickering attorneys were stilled. "With any known make of gun," he said evenly, "I could have killed Gregory Fitzhurst at three hundred feet *with my left hand.*" Pandemonium broke loose in the courtroom. A woman's scream rose above the bedlam and suddenly a lovely, dark-haired girl was in Walter Mitty's arms. The District Attorney struck at her savagely. Without rising from his chair, Mitty let the man have it on the point of the chin. "You miserable cur!" . . .

"Puppy biscuit," said Walter Mitty. He stopped walking and the buildings of Waterbury rose up out of the misty courtroom and surrounded him again. A woman who was passing laughed. "He said 'Puppy biscuit,' " she said to her companion. "That man said 'Puppy biscuit' to himself." Walter Mitty hurried on. He went into an A. & P., not the first one he came to but a smaller one farther up the street. "I want some biscuit for small, young dogs," he said to the clerk. "Any special brand, sir?" The greatest pistol shot in the world thought a moment. "It says 'Puppies Bark for It' on the box," said Walter Mitty.

His wife would be through at the hairdresser's in fifteen minutes, Mitty saw in looking at his watch, unless they had trouble drying it; sometimes they had trouble drying it. She didn't like to get to the hotel first; she would want him to be there waiting for her as usual. He found a big leather chair in the lobby, facing a window, and he put the overshoes and the puppy biscuit on the floor beside it. He picked up an old copy of *Liberty* and sank down into the chair. "Can Germany Conquer the World Through the Air?" Walter Mitty looked at the pictures of bombing planes and of ruined streets.

. . . "The cannonading has got the wind up in young Raleigh, sir," said the sergeant. Captain Mitty looked up at him through tousled hair. "Get him to bed," he said wearily. "With the others. I'll fly alone." "But you can't, sir," said the sergeant anxiously. "It takes two men to handle that bomber and the Archies are pounding hell out of the air. Von Richtman's circus is between here and Saulier." "Somebody's got to get that ammunition dump," said Mitty. "I'm going over. Spot of brandy?" He poured a drink for the sergeant and one for himself. War thundered and whined around the dugout and battered at the door. There was a rending of wood and splinters flew through the room. "A bit of a near thing," said Captain Mitty carelessly. "The box barrage is closing in," said the sergeant. "We only live once, Sergeant," said Mitty, with his faint, fleeting smile. "Or do we?" He poured another brandy and tossed it off. "I never see a man could hold his brandy like you, sir," said the sergeant. "Begging your pardon, sir." Captain Mitty stood up and strapped on his huge Webley-Vickers automatic. "It's forty kilometers through hell, sir," said the sergeant. Mitty finished one last brandy. "After all," he said softly, "what isn't?" The pounding of the cannon increased; there was the rat-tat-tatting of machine guns, and from somewhere came the menacing pocketa-pocketa-pocketa of the new flame-throwers. Walter Mitty walked to the door of the dugout humming "Auprès de Ma Blonde." He turned and waved to the sergeant. "Cheerio!" he said. . . .

Something struck his shoulder. "I've been looking all over this hotel for you," said Mrs. Mitty. "Why do you have to hide in this old chair? How did you expect me to find you?" "Things close in," said Walter Mitty vaguely. "What?" Mrs. Mitty said. "Did you get the what's-its-name? The puppy biscuit? What's in that box?" "Overshoes," said Mitty. "Couldn't you have put them on in the store?" "I was thinking," said Walter Mitty. "Does it ever occur to you that I am sometimes thinking?" She looked at him. "I'm going to take your temperature when I get you home,'' she said.

They went out through the revolving doors that made a faintly derisive whistling sound when you pushed them. It was two blocks to the parking lot. At the drugstore on the corner she said, ''Wait here for me. I forgot something. I won't be a minute.'' She was more than a minute. Walter Mitty lighted a cigarette. It began to rain, rain with sleet in it. He stood up against the wall of the drugstore, smoking. . . . He put his shoulders back and his heels together. ''To hell with the handkerchief,'' said Walter Mitty scornfully. He took one last drag on his cigarette and snapped it away. Then, with that faint, fleeting smile playing about his lips, he faced the firing squad; erect and motionless, proud and disdainful, Walter Mitty the Undefeated, inscrutable to the last.

GARRISON KEILLOR

"What Did We Do Wrong?"

The first woman to reach the big leagues said she wanted to be treated like any other rookie, but she didn't have to worry about that. The Sparrows nicknamed her Chesty and then Big Numbers the first week of spring training, and loaded her bed at the Ramada with butterscotch pudding. Only the writers made a big thing about her being the First Woman. The Sparrows treated her like dirt.

Annie Szemanski arrived in camp fresh from the Federales League of Bolivia, the fourth second baseman on the Sparrows roster, and when Drayton stepped in a hole and broke his ankle Hemmie put her in the lineup, hoping she would break hers. ''This was the front office's bright idea,'' he told the writers. ''Off the record, I think it stinks.'' But when she got in she looked so good that by the third week of March she was a foregone conclusion. Even Hemmie had to admit it. A .346 average tells no lies. He disliked her purely because she was a woman—there was nothing personal about it. Because she was a woman, she was given the manager's dressing room, and Hemmie had to dress with the team. He was sixty-one, a heavyweight, and he had a possum tattooed on his belly alongside the name ''Georgene,'' so he was shy about taking his shirt off in front of people. He hated her for making it necessary. Other than that, he thought she was a tremendous addition to the team.

Asked how she felt being the first woman to make a major-league team, she said, "Like a pig in mud," or words to that effect, and then turned and released a squirt of tobacco juice from the wad of rum-soaked plug in her right cheek. She chewed a rare brand of plug called Stuff It, which she learned to chew when she was playing Nicaraguan summer ball. She told the writers, "They were so mean to me down there you couldn't write it in your newspaper. I took a gun everywhere I went, even to bed. *Especially* to bed. Guys were after me like you can't believe. That's when I started chewing tobacco— because no matter how bad anybody treats you, it's not as bad as this. This is the worst chew in the world. After this, everything else is peaches and cream." The writers elected Gentleman Jim, the Sparrows' P.R. guy, to bite off a chunk and tell them how it tasted, and as he sat and chewed it tears ran down his old sunburnt cheeks and he couldn't talk for a while. Then he whispered, "You've been chewing this for two years? God, I had no idea it was so hard to be a woman."

When thirty-two thousand fans came to Cold Spring Stadium on April 4th for Opening Day and saw the scrappy little freckle-faced woman with tousled black hair who they'd been reading about for almost two months, they were dizzy with devotion. They chanted her name and waved Annie flags and Annie caps ($8.95 and $4.95) and held up hand-painted bedsheets ("EVERY DAY IS LADIES' DAY," "A WOMAN'S PLACE—AT SECOND BASE," "E.R.A. & R.B.I." "THE GAME AIN'T OVER TILL THE BIG LADY BATS"), but when they saw No. 18 trot out to second with a load of chew as big as if she had the mumps it was a surprise. Then, bottom of the second, when she leaned over in the on-deck circle and dropped a stream of brown juice in the sod, the stadium experienced a moment of thoughtful silence.

One man in Section 31 said, "Hey, what's the beef? She can chew if she wants to. This is 1987. Grow up."

"I guess you're right," his next-seat neighbor said. "My first reaction was nausea, but I think you're right."

"Absolutely. She's a woman, but, more than that, she's a *person*."

Other folks said, "I'm with you on that. A woman can carry a quarter pound of chew in her cheek and spit in public, same as any man—why should there be any difference?"

And yet. Nobody wanted to say this, but the plain truth was that No. 18 was not handling her chew well at all. Juice ran down her chin and dripped onto her shirt. She's bit off more than she can chew, some people thought to themselves, but they didn't want to say that.

Arnie (the Old Gardener) Brixius mentioned it ever so gently in his "Hot Box" column the next day:

It's only this scribe's opinion, but isn't it about time baseball cleaned up its act and left the tobacco in the locker? Surely big leaguers can go two hours without nicotine. Many a fan has turned away in disgust at the sight of grown men (and now a member of the fair sex) with a faceful, spitting gobs of the stuff in full view of paying customers. Would Frank Sinatra do this onstage? Or Anne Murray? Nuff said.

End of April, Annie was batting .278, with twelve R.B.I.s, which for the miserable Sparrows was stupendous, and at second base she was surprising a number of people, including base runners who thought she'd be a pushover on the double play. A runner heading for second quickly found out that Annie had knees like ballpeen hammers and if he tried to eliminate her from the play she might eliminate him from the rest of the week. One night, up at bat against the Orioles, she took a step toward the mound after an inside pitch and yelled some things, and when the dugouts emptied she was in the thick of it with men who had never been walloped by a woman before. The home-plate ump hauled her off a guy she was pounding the cookies out of, and a moment later he threw her out of the game for saying things to him, he said, that he had never heard in his nineteen years of umpiring. ("Like what, for example?" writers asked. "Just tell us one thing." But he couldn't; he was too upset.)

The next week, the United Baseball Office Workers local passed a resolution in support of Annie, as did the League of Women Voters and the Women's Softball Caucus, which stated, "Szemanski is a model for all women who are made to suffer guilt for their aggressiveness, and we declare our solidarity with her heads-up approach to the game. While we feel she is holding the bat too high and should bring her hips into her swing more, we're behind her one hundred per cent."

Then, May 4th, at home against Oakland—seventh inning, two outs, bases loaded—she dropped an easy pop-up and three runs came across home plate. The fans sent a few light boos her way to let her know they were paying attention, nothing serious or overtly political, just some folks grumbling, but she took a few steps toward the box seats and yelled something at them that sounded like—well, like something she shouldn't have said, and after the game she said some more things to the writers that Gentleman Jim pleaded with them not to print. One of them was Monica Lamarr, of the *Press,* who just laughed. She said, "Look. I spent two years in the Lifestyles section writing about motherhood vs. career and the biological clock. Sports is my way out of the gynecology ghetto, so don't ask me to eat this story. It's a hanging curve and I'm going for it. I'm never going to write about day care again." And she wrote it:

SZEMANSKI RAPS FANS
AS "SMALL PEOPLE"

AFTER DUMB ERROR GIVES
GAME TO A'S

FIRST WOMAN ATTRIBUTES BOOS
TO SEXUAL INADEQUACY IN STANDS

Jim made some phone calls and the story was yanked and only one truck-load of papers went out with it, but word got around, and the next night, though Annie went three for four, the crowd was depressed, and even when she did great the rest of the home stand, and became the first woman to hit a major-league triple, the atmosphere at the ballpark was one of moodiness and deep hurt. Jim went to the men's room one night and found guys standing in line there, looking thoughtful and sad. One of them said, "She's a helluva ballplayer," and other guys murmured that yes, she was, and they wouldn't take anything away from her, she was great and it was wonderful that she had opened up baseball to women, and then they changed the subject to gardening, books, music, aesthetics, anything but baseball. They looked like men who had been stood up.

Gentleman Jim knocked on her door that night. She wore a blue chenille bathrobe flecked with brown tobacco-juice stains, and her black hair hung down in wet strands over her face. She spat into a Dixie cup she was carrying. "Hey! How the Fritos are you? I haven't seen your Big Mac for a while," she said, sort of. He told her she was a great person and a great ballplayer and that he loved her and wanted only the best for her, and he begged her to apologize to the fans.

"Make a gesture—*anything*. They *want* to like you. Give them a chance to like you."

She blew her nose into a towel. She said that she wasn't there to be liked, she was there to play ball.

It was a good road trip. The Sparrows won five out of ten, lifting their heads off the canvas, and Annie raised her average to .291 and hit the first major-league home run ever by a woman, up into the left-field screen at Fenway. Sox fans stood and cheered for fifteen minutes. They whistled, they stamped, they pleaded, the Sparrows pleaded, umpires pleaded, but she refused to come out and tip her hat until the public-address announcer said, "No. 18, please come out of the dugout and take a bow. No. 18, the applause is for you and is not intended as patronizing in any way," and then she stuck her head out for 1.5 seconds and did not tip but only touched the brim. Later, she told the writers that just because people had expectations didn't mean she had to fulfill them— she used other words to explain this, but her general drift was that she didn't care very much about living up to anyone else's image of her, and if anyone thought she should, they could go watch wrist wrestling.

The forty thousand who packed Cold Spring Stadium June 6th to see the Sparrows play the Yankees didn't come for a look at Ron Guidry. Banners hung from the second deck: "WHAT DID WE DO WRONG?" and "ANNIE COME HOME" and "WE LOVE YOU, WHY DO YOU TREAT US THIS WAY?" and "IF YOU WOULD LIKE TO DISCUSS THIS IN A NONCONFRONTATIONAL, MUTUALLY RE-SPECTFUL WAY, MEET US AFTER THE GAME AT GATE C." It was Snapshot Day, and all the Sparrows appeared on the field for photos with the fans except you know who. Hemmie begged her to go. "You owe it to them," he said.

"Owe?" she said. "*Owe?*"

"Sorry, wrong word," he said. "What if I put it this way: it's a sort of tradition."

"*Tradition?*" she said. "I'm supposed to worry about *tradition?*"

That day, she became the first woman to hit .300. A double in the fifth inning. The scoreboard flashed the message, and the crowd gave her a nice hand. A few people stood and cheered, but the fans around them told them to sit down. "She's not that kind of person," they said. "Cool it. Back off." The fans were trying to give her plenty of space. After the game, Guidry said, "I really have to respect her. She's got that small strike zone and she protects it well, so she makes you pitch to her." She said, "Guidry? Was that his name? I didn't know. Anyway, he didn't show me much. He throws funny, don't you think? He reminded me a little bit of a southpaw I saw down in Nicaragua, except she threw inside more."

All the writers were there, kneeling around her. One of them asked if Guidry had thrown her a lot of sliders.

She gave him a long, baleful look. "Jeez, you guys are out of shape," she said. "You're wheezing and panting and sucking air, and you just took the elevator *down* from the press box. You guys want to write about sports you ought to go into training. And then you ought to learn how to recognize a slider. Jeez, if you were writing about agriculture, would you have to ask someone if those were Holsteins?"

Tears came to the writer's eyes. "I'm trying to help," he said. "Can't you see that? Don't you know how much we care about you? Sometimes I think you put up this tough exterior to hide your own insecurity."

She laughed and brushed the wet hair back from her forehead. "It's no exterior," she said as she unbuttoned her jersey. "It's who I am." She peeled off her socks and stepped out of her cubicle a moment later, sweaty and stark naked. The towel hung from her hand. She walked slowly around them. "You guys learned all you know about women thirty years ago. That wasn't me back then, that was my mother." The writers bent over their notepads, writing down every word she said and punctuating carefully. Gentleman Jim took off his glasses. "My mother was a nice lady, but she couldn't hit the curve to save her Creamettes,'' she went on. "And now, gentlemen, if you'll excuse me, I'm going to take a shower." They pored over their notes until she was gone, and then they piled out into the hallway and hurried back to the press elevator.

Arnie stopped at the Shortstop for a load of Martinis before he went to the office to write the "Hot Box," which turned out to be about love:

> Baseball is a game but it's more than a game, baseball is people, dammit, and if you are around people you can't help but get involved in their lives and care about them and then you don't know how to talk to them or tell them how much you care and how come we know so much about pitching and we don't know squat about how to communicate? I guess that is the question.

The next afternoon, Arnie leaned against the batting cage before the game, hung over, and watched her hit line drives, fifteen straight, and each one made his head hurt. As she left the cage, he called over to her. "Later," she said. She also declined a pregame interview with Joe Garagiola, who had just told his NBC "Game of the Week" television audience, "This is a city in love with a little girl named Annie Szemanski," when he saw her in the dugout doing deep knee bends. "Annie! Annie!" he yelled over the air. "Let's see if we can't get her up here," he told the home audience. "Annie! Joe Garagiola!" She turned her back to him and went down into the dugout.

That afternoon, she became the first woman to steal two bases in one inning. She reached first on a base on balls, stole second, went to third on a sacrifice fly, and headed for home on the next pitch. The catcher came out to make the tag, she caught him with her elbow under the chin, and when the dust cleared she was grinning at the ump, the catcher was sprawled in the grass trying to inhale, and the ball was halfway to the backstop.

The TV camera zoomed in on her, head down, trotting toward the dugout steps, when suddenly she looked up. Some out-of-town fan had yelled at her from the box seats. ("A profanity which also refers to a female dog," the *News* said.) She smiled and, just before she stepped out of view beneath the dugout roof, millions observed her right hand uplifted in a familiar gesture. In bars around the country, men looked at each other and said, "Did she do what I think I saw her do? She didn't do that, did she?" In the booth, Joe Garagiola was observing that it was a clean play, that the runner has a right to the base path, but when her hand appeared on the screen he stopped. At home, it sounded as if he had been hit in the chest by a rock. The screen went blank, then went to a beer commercial. When the show resumed, it was the middle of the next inning.

On Monday, for "actions detrimental to the best interests of baseball," Annie was fined a thousand dollars by the Commissioner and suspended for two games. He deeply regretted the decision, etc. "I count myself among her most ardent fans. She is good for baseball, good for the cause of equal rights, good for America.'' He said he would be happy to suspend the suspension if she would make a public apology, which would make him the happiest man in America.

Gentleman Jim went to the bank Monday afternoon and got the money, a thousand dollars, in a cashier's check. All afternoon, he called Annie's number over and over, waiting thirty and forty rings, then trying again. He called from a pay phone at the Stop 'N' Shop, next door to the Cityview Apartments, where she lived, and between calls he sat in his car and watched the entrance, waiting for her to come out. Other men were parked there, too, in front, and some in back—men with Sparrows bumper stickers. After midnight, about eleven of them were left. ''Care to share some onion chips and clam dip?'' one guy said to another guy. Pretty soon all of them were standing around the trunk of the clam-dip guy's car, where he also had a case of beer.

''Here, let me pay you something for this beer,'' said a guy who had brought a giant box of pretzels.

''Hey, no. Really. It's just good to have other guys to talk to tonight,'' said the clam-dip owner.

''She changed a lot of very basic things about the whole way that I look at myself as a man,'' the pretzel guy said quietly.

''I'm in public relations,'' said Jim, ''but even I don't understand all that she has meant to people.''

''How can she do this to us?'' said a potato-chip man. ''All the love of the fans, how can she throw it away? Why can't she just play ball?''

Annie didn't look at it that way. ''Pall Mall! I'm not going to crawl just because some Tootsie Roll says crawl, and if they don't like it, then Ritz, they can go Pepsi their Hostess Twinkies,'' she told the writers as she cleaned out her locker on Tuesday morning. They had never seen the inside of her locker before. It was stuffed with dirty socks, half unwrapped gifts from admiring fans, a set of ankle weights, and a small silver-plated pistol. ''No way I'm going to pay a thousand dollars, and if they expect an apology—well, they better send out for lunch, because it's going to be a long wait. Gentlemen, goodbye and hang on to your valuable coupons.'' And she smiled her most winning smile and sprinted up the stairs to collect her paycheck. They waited for her outside the Sparrows office, twenty-six men, and then followed her down the ramp and out of Gate C. She broke into a run and disappeared into the lunchtime crowd on West Providence Avenue, and that was the last they saw of her—the woman of their dreams, the love of their lives, carrying a red gym bag, running easily away from them.

ABRAHAM LINCOLN

Three Letters

Young Mr. Lincoln is not striving consciously for humor in the first two of the following letters. Quite the contrary. The humor lies in the situation, which is painful indeed to a man of character, and no smiling matter to the woman in the case, Mary Owens. In the third letter he turns the incident into something to amuse his friends Eliza and Orville Browning with a laugh at his own expense.

To Mary S. Owens

Springfield, May 7. 1837

Friend Mary

I have commenced two letters to send you before this, both of which displeased me before I got half done, and so I tore them up. The first I thought wasn't serious enough, and the second was on the other extreme. I shall send this, turn out as it may.

This thing of living in Springfield is rather a dull business after all, at least it is so to me. I am quite as lonesome here as [I] ever was anywhere in my life. I have been spoken to by but one woman since I've been here, and should not have been by her, if she could have avoided it. I've never been to church yet, nor probably shall not be soon. I stay away because I am conscious I should not know how to behave myself.

I am often thinking about what we said of your coming to live at Springfield. I am afraid you would not be satisfied. There is a great deal of flourishing about in carriages here, which it would be your doom to see without shareing in it. You would have to be poor without the means of hiding your poverty. Do you believe you could bear that patiently? Whatever woman may cast her lot with mine, should any ever do so, it is my intention to do all in my power to make her happy and contented; and there is nothing I can immagine, that would make me more unhappy than to fail in the effort. I know I should be much happier with you than the way I am, provided I saw no signs of discontent in you. What you have said to me may have been in jest, or I may have misunderstood it. If so, then let it be forgotten; if otherwise, I much wish you would think seriously before you decide. For my part I have already decided. What I have said I will most positively abide by, provided you wish it. My opinion is that you had better not do it. You have not been accustomed to hardship, and it may be more severe than you now immagine. I know you are capable of thinking correctly on any subject; and if you deliberate maturely upon this, before you decide, then I am willing to abide your decision.

You must write me a good long letter after you get this. You have nothing else to do, and though it might not seem interesting to you, after you had written it, it would be a good deal of company to me in this "busy wilderness." Tell your sister I dont want to hear any more about selling out and moving. That gives me the hypo* whenever I think of it. Yours, &c.

LINCOLN.

To Mary S. Owens

Springfield Aug. 16th 1837

Friend Mary.

You will, no doubt, think it rather strange, that I should write you a letter on the same day on which we parted; and I can only account for it by supposing, that seeing you lately makes me think of you more than usual, while at our late meeting we had but few expressions of thoughts. You must know that I can not see you, or think of you, with entire indifference; and yet it may be, that you, are mistaken in regard to what my real feelings towards you are. If I knew you were not, I should not trouble you with this letter. Perhaps any other man would know enough without further information; but I consider it *my* peculiar right to plead ignorance, and your bounden duty to allow the plea. I want in all cases to do right, and most particularly so, in all cases with women. I want, at this particular time, more than any thing else, to do right with you, and if I *knew* it would be doing right, as I rather suspect it would, to let you alone, I would do it. And for the purpose of making the matter as plain as possible, I now say, that you can now drop the subject, dismiss your thoughts (if you ever had any) from me forever, and leave this letter unanswered, without calling forth one accusing murmer from me. And I will even go further, and say, that if it will add any thing to your comfort, or peace of mind, to do so, it is my sincere wish that you should. Do not

*Hypochondria.

understand by this, that I wish to cut your acquaintance. I mean no such thing. What I do wish is, that our further acquaintance shall depend upon yourself. If such further acquaintance would contribute nothing to your happiness, I am sure it would not to mine. If you feel yourself in any degree bound to me, I am now willing to release you, provided you wish it; while, on the other hand, I am willing, and even anxious to bind you faster, if I can be convinced that it will, in any considerable degree, add to your happiness. This, indeed, is the whole question with me. Nothing would make me more miserable than to believe you miserable—nothing more happy, than to know you were so.

In what I have now said, I think I can not be misunderstood; and to make myself understood, is the only object of this letter.

If it suits you best to not answer this—farewell—a long life and a merry one attend you. But if you conclude to write back, speak as plainly as I do. There can be neither harm nor danger, in saying, to me, any thing you think, just in the manner you think it.

My respects to your sister. Your friend

LINCOLN.

TO MRS. ORVILLE H. BROWNING

Springfield, April 1. 1838.

Dear Madam:

Without appologising for being egotistical, I shall make the history of so much of my own life, as has elapsed since I saw you, the subject of this letter. And by the way I now discover, that, in order to give a full and inteligible account of the things I have done and suffered *since* I saw you, I shall necessarily have to relate some that happened *before.*

It was, then, in the autumn of 1836, that a married lady of my acquaintance, and who was a great friend of mine, being about to pay a visit to her father and other relatives residing in Kentucky, proposed to me, that on her return she would bring a sister of hers with her, upon condition that I would engage to become her brother-in-law with all convenient dispach. I, of course, accepted the proposal; for you know I could not have done otherwise, had I really been averse to it; but privately between you and me, I was most confoundedly well pleased with the project. I had seen the said sister some three years before, thought her inteligent and agreeable, and saw no good objection to plodding life through hand in hand with her. Time passed on, the lady took her journey and in due time returned, sister in company sure enough. This stomached me a little; for it appeared to me, that her coming so readily showed that she was a trifle too willing; but on reflection it occured to me, that she might have been prevailed on by her married sister to come, without any thing concerning me ever having been mentioned to her; and so I concluded that if no other objection presented itself, I would consent to wave this. All this occured upon my *hearing* of her arrival in the neighbourhood; for, be it remembered, I had not yet *seen* her, except about three years previous, as before mentioned.

In a few days we had an interview, and although I had seen her before, she did not look as my immagination had pictured her. I knew she was over-size, but she now appeared a fair match for Falstaff; I knew she was called an "old maid," and I felt no doubt of the truth of at least half of the appelation; but now, when I beheld her, I could not for my life avoid thinking of my mother; and this, not from withered features, for her skin was too full of fat, to permit its contracting in to wrinkles; but from her want of teeth, weather-beaten appearance in general, and from a kind of notion that ran in my head, that *nothing* could have commenced at the size of infancy, and reached her present bulk in less than thirtyfive or forty years; and, in short, I was not all pleased with her. But what could I do? I had told her sister that I would take her for better or for worse; and I made a point of honor and conscience in all things, to stick to my word, especially if others had been induced to act on it, which in this case, I doubted not they had, for I was now fairly convinced, that no other man on earth would have her, and hence the conclusion that they were bent on holding me to my bargain. Well, thought I, I have said it, and, be consequences what they may, it shall not be my fault if I fail to do it. At once I determined to consider her my wife; and this done, all my powers of discovery were put to the rack, in search of perfections in her, which might be fairly set-off against her defects. I tried to immagine she was handsome, which, but for her unfortunate corpulency, was actually true. Exclusive of this, no woman that I have seen, has a finer face. I also tried to convince myself, that the mind was much more to be valued than the person; and in this, she was not inferior, as I could discover, to any with whom I had been acquainted.

Shortly after this, without attempting to come to any positive understanding with her, I set out for Vandalia, where and when you first saw me. During my stay there, I had letters from her, which did not change my opinion of either her intelect or intention; but on the contrary, confirmed it in both.

All this while, although I was fixed "firm as the surge repelling rock" in my resolution, I found I was continually repenting the rashness, which had led me to make it. Through life I have been in no bondage, either real or immaginary from the thraldom of which I so much desired to be free.

After my return home, I saw nothing to change my opinion of her in any particular. She was the same and so was I. I now spent my time between planing how I might get along through life after my contemplated change of circumstances should have taken place; and how I might procrastinate the evil day for a time, which I really dreaded as much—perhaps more, than an irishman does the halter.

After all my suffering upon this deeply interesting subject, here I am, wholly unexpectedly, completely out of the "scrape"; and I now want to know, if you can guess how I got out of it. Out clear in every sense of the term; no violation of word, honor or conscience. I dont believe you can guess, and so I may as well tell you at once. As the lawyers say, it was done in the manner following, towit. After I had delayed the matter as long as I thought I could in honor do, which by the way had brought me round into the last fall, I concluded I might as well bring it to a consumation without further delay; and so I mustered my resolution, and made the proposal to her direct; but, shocking to relate, she answered, No. At first I supposed she did it through an affectation of modesty, which I thought but ill-become her, under the peculiar circumstances of her case; but on my renewal of the charge, I found she repeled it with greater firmness than before. I tried it again and again, but with the same success, or rather with the same want of success. I finally was forced to give it up, at which I verry unexpectedly found myself mortified almost beyond endurance. I was mortified, it seemed to me, in a hundred different ways. My vanity was deeply wounded by the reflection, that I had so long been too stupid to discover her intentions, and at the same time never doubting that I understood them perfectly; and also, that she whom I had taught myself to believe no body else would have, had actually rejected me with all my fancied greatness; and to cap the whole, I then, for the first time, began to suspect that I was really a little in love with her. But let it all go. I'll try and out live it. Others have been made fools of by the girls; but this can never be with truth said of me. I most emphatically, in this instance, made a fool of myself. I have now come to the conclusion never again to think of marrying; and for this reason; I can never be satisfied with any one who would be block-head enough to have me.

When you receive this, write me a long yarn about something to amuse me. Give my respects to Mr. Browning. Your sincere friend

Mrs. O. H. Browning.

A. LINCOLN.

BENJAMIN FRANKLIN

"Old Mistresses Apologue"

June 25. 1745

My dear Friend,

I know of no Medicine fit to diminish the violent natural Inclinations you mention; and if I did, I think I should not communicate it to you. Marriage is the proper Remedy. It is the most natural State of Man, and therefore the State in which you are most likely to find solid Happiness. Your Reasons against entring into it at present, appear to me not well-founded. The circumstantial Advantages you have in View by postponing it, are not only uncertain, but they are small in comparison with that of the Thing itself, the being *married and settled.* It is the Man and Woman united that make the compleat human Being. Separate, she wants his Force of Body and Strength of Reason; he, her Soft-ness, Sensibility and acute Discernment. Together they are more likely to succeed in the World. A single Man has not nearly the Value he would have in that State of Union. He is an incomplete Animal. He resembles the odd Half of a Pair of Scissars. If you get a prudent healthy Wife, your Industry in your Profession, with her good Œconomy, will be a Fortune sufficient.

But if you will not take this Counsel, and persist in thinking a Commerce with the Sex inevitable, then I repeat my former Advice, that in all your Amours you should *prefer old Women to young ones.* You call this a Paradox, and demand my Reasons. They are these:

1. Because as they have more Knowledge of the World and their Minds are better stor'd with Observations, their Conversation is more improving and more lastingly agreable.
2. Because when Women cease to be handsome, they study to be good. To maintain their Influence over Men, they supply the Diminution of Beauty by an Augmentation of Utility. They learn to do a 1000 Services small and great, and are the most tender and useful of all Friends when you are sick.

Thus they continue amiable. And hence there is hardly such a thing to be found as an old Woman who is not a good Woman.

3. Because there is no hazard of Children, which irregularly produc'd may be attended with much Inconvenience.

4. Because thro' more Experience, they are more prudent and discreet in conducting an Intrigue to prevent Suspicion. The Commerce with them is therefore safer with regard to your Reputation. And with regard to theirs, if the Affair should happen to be known, considerate People might be rather inclin'd to excuse an old Woman who would kindly take care of a young Man, form his Manners by her good Counsels, and prevent his ruining his Health and Fortune among mercenary Prostitutes.

5. Because in every Animal that walks upright, the Deficiency of the Fluids that fill the Muscles appears first in the highest Part: The Face first grows lank and wrinkled; then the Neck; then the Breast and Arms; the lower Parts continuing to the last as plump as ever: So that covering all above with a Basket, and regarding only what is below the Girdle, it is impossible of two Women to know an old from a young one. And as in the dark all Cats are grey, the Pleasure of corporal Enjoyment with an old Woman is at least equal, and frequently superior, every Knack being by Practice capable of Improvement.

6. Because the Sin is less. The debauching a Virgin may be her Ruin, and make her for Life unhappy.

7. Because the Compunction is less. The having made a young Girl *miserable* may give you frequent bitter Reflections; none of which can attend the making an old Woman *happy*.

8thly and Lastly They are *so grateful*!!

Thus much for my Paradox. But still I advise you to marry directly; being sincerely Your affectionate Friend.

S. J. PERELMAN

"Somewhere a Roscoe . . ."

This is the story of a mind that found itself. About two years ago I was moody, discontented, restless, almost a character in a Russian novel. I used to lie on my bed for days drinking tea out of a glass (I was one of the first in this country to drink tea out of a glass; at that time fashionable people drank from their cupped hands). Underneath, I was still a lively, fun-loving American boy who liked nothing better than to fish with a bent pin. In short, I had become a remarkable combination of Raskolnikov and Mark Tidd.

One day I realized how introspective I had grown and decided to talk to myself like a Dutch uncle. "Luik here, Mynheer," I began (I won't give you the accent, but honestly it was a riot), "you've overtrained. You're stale. Open up a few new vistas—go out and get some fresh air!" Well, I bustled about, threw some things into a bag—orange peels, apple cores and the like—and went out for a walk. A few minutes later I picked up from a park bench a tattered pulp magazine called *Spicy Detective*. . . . Talk about your turning points!

I hope nobody minds my making love in public, but if Culture Publications, Inc., of 900 Market Street, Wilmington, Delaware, will have me, I'd like to marry them. Yes, I know—call it a school-boy crush, puppy love, the senseless infatuation of a callow youth for a middle-aged, worldly-wise publishing house; I still don't care. I love them because they are the publishers of not only *Spicy Detective* but also *Spicy Western, Spicy Mystery* and *Spicy Adventure.* And I love them most because their prose is so soft and warm.

"Arms and the man I sing," sang Vergil some twenty centuries ago, preparing to celebrate the wanderings of Aeneas. If ever a motto was tailormade for the masthead of Culture Publications, Inc., it is "Arms and the Woman," for in *Spicy Detective* they have achieved the sauciest blend of libido and murder this side of Gilles de Rais. They have juxtaposed the steely automatic and the frilly pantic and found that it pays off. Above all, they have given the world Dan Turner, the apotheosis of all private detectives. Out of Ma Barker by Dashiell Hammett's Sam Spade, let him characterize himself in the opening paragraph of "Corpse in the Closet," from the July, 1937, issue:

> I opened my bedroom closet. A half-dressed feminine corpse sagged into my arms. . . . It's a damned screwy feeling to reach for pajamas and find a cadaver instead.

Mr. Turner, you will perceive, is a man of sentiment, and it occasionally gets him into a tight corner. For example, in "Killer's Harvest" (July, 1938) he is retained to escort a young matron home from the Cocoanut Grove in Los Angeles:

> Zarah Trenwick was a wow in a gown of silver lamé that stuck to her lush curves like a coating of varnish. Her makeup was perfect; her strapless dress displayed plenty of evidence that she still owned a cargo of lure. Her bare shoulders were snowy, dimpled. The upper slopes of her breast were squeezed upward and partly overflowed the tight bodice, like whipped cream.

To put it mildly, Dan cannot resist the appeal of a pretty foot, and disposing of Zarah's drunken husband ("I clipped him on the button. His hip pockets bounced on the floor"), he takes this charlotte russe to her apartment. Alone with her, the policeman in him succumbs to the man, and "she fed me a kiss that throbbed all the way down my fallen arches," when suddenly:

> From the doorway a roscoe said "Kachow!" and a slug creased the side of my noggin. Neon lights exploded inside my think-tank . . . She was as dead as a stuffed mongoose . . . I wasn't badly hurt. But I don't like to be shot at. I don't like dames to be rubbed out when I'm flinging woo at them.

With an irritable shrug, Dan phones the homicide detail and reports Zarah's passing in this tender obituary: "Zarah Trenwick just got blasted to hellangone in her tepee at the Gayboy. Drag your underwear over here—and bring a meat-wagon." Then he goes in search of the offender:

> I drove over to Argyle; parked in front of Fane Trenwick's modest stash . . . I thumbed the bell. The door opened. A Chink house-boy gave me the slant-eyed focus. "Missa Tlenwick, him sleep. You go way, come tomollow. Too late fo' vlisito'." I said "Nerts to you, Confucius," and gave him a shove on the beezer.

Zarah's husband, wrenched out of bed without the silly formality of a search warrant, establishes an alibi depending upon one Nadine Wendell. In a trice Dan crosses the city and makes his gentle way into the lady's boudoir, only to discover again what a frail vessel he is *au fond*:

> The fragrant scent of her red hair tickled my smeller; the warmth of her slim young form set fire to my arterial system. After all, I'm as human as the next gazabo.

The next gazabo must be all too human, because Dan betrays first Nadine and then her secret; namely, that she pistolled Zarah Trenwick for reasons too numerous to mention. If you feel you must know them, they appear on page 110, cheek by jowl with some fascinating advertisements for loaded dice and wealthy sweethearts, either of which will be sent you in plain wrapper if you'll forward a dollar to the Majestic Novelty Company of Janesville, Wisconsin.

The deeper one goes into the Dan Turner saga, the more one is struck by the similarity between the case confronting Dan in the current issue and those in the past. The murders follow an exact, rigid pattern almost like the ritual of a bullfight or a classic Chinese play. Take "Veiled Lady," in the October, 1937, number of *Spicy Detective*. Dan is flinging some woo at a Mrs. Brantham in her apartment at the exclusive Gayboy Arms, which apparently excludes everybody but assassins:

> From behind me a roscoe belched "Chow-chow!" A pair of slugs buzzed past my left ear, almost nicked my cranium. Mrs. Brantham sagged back against the pillow of the lounge . . . She was as dead as an iced catfish.

Or this vignette from "Falling Star," out of the September, 1936, issue:

> The roscoe said "Chow!" and spat a streak of flame past my shoulder . . . The Filipino cutie was lying where I'd last seen her. She was as dead as a smoked herring.

And again, from "Dark Star of Death," January, 1938:

> From a bedroom a roscoe said: "Whr-r-rang!" and a lead pill split the ozone past my noggin . . . Kane Fewster was on the floor. There was a bullet hole through his think-tank. He was as dead as a fried oyster.

And still again, from "Brunette Bump-off," May, 1938:

> And then, from an open window beyond the bed, a roscoe coughed "Ka-chow!" . . . I said, "What the hell—!" and hit the floor with my smeller . . . A brunette jane was lying there, half out of the mussed covers. . . . She was as dead as vaudeville.

The next phase in each of these dramas follows with all the cold beauty and inevitability of a legal brief. The roscoe has hardly spoken, coughed, or belched before Dan is off through the canebrake, his nostrils filled with the heavy scent of Nuit de Noël. Somewhere, in some dimly lit boudoir, waits a voluptuous parcel of womanhood who knows all about the horrid deed. Even if she doesn't, Dan makes a routine check anyway. The premises are invariably guarded by an Oriental whom Dan is obliged to expunge. Compare the scene at Fane Trenwick's modest stash with this one from "Find That Corpse" (November, 1937):

> A sleepy Chink maid in pajamas answered my ring. She was a cute little slant-eyed number. I said "Is Mr. Polznak home?" She shook her head. "Him up on location in Flesno. Been gone two week." I said "Thanks. I'll have a gander for myself." I pushed past her. She started to yip . . . "Shut up!" I growled. She kept on trying to make a noise. So I popped her on the button. She dropped.

It is a fairly safe bet that Mr. Polznak has forgotten the adage that a watched pot never boils and has left behind a dewy-eyed coryphée clad in the minimum of chiffon demanded by the postal authorities. The poet in Dan ineluctably vanquishes the flatfoot ("Dark Star of Death"): "I glued my glims on her blond loveliness; couldn't help myself. The covers had skidded down from her gorgeous, dimpled shoulders; I could see plenty of delishful, shemale epidermis." The trumpets blare again; some expert capework by our *torero,* and "Brunette Bump-off"): "Then she fed me a kiss that sent a charge of steam past my gozzle . . . Well, I'm as human as the next gink."

From then on, the author's typewriter keys infallibly fuse in a lump of hot metal and it's all over but the shouting of the culprit and *"Look, Men: One Hundred Breezy Fotos!"* Back in his stash, his roscoe safely within reach, Dan Turner lays his weary noggin on a pillow, resting up for the November issue. And unless you're going to need me for something this afternoon, I intend to do the same. I'm *bushed.*

SECTION FIVE
PARODY, BURLESQUE, CRITICISM, AND PAIN

The distinction between parody and burlesque is important mainly to academics. Here it is enough to say that burlesque is parody by sophomores. Parody is subtle, even elegant; burlesque is rude, hamfisted sport. Parody stops at precisely the right point; burlesque is always charging over the cliff.

In its delicate autopsy on the silliness in James Fenimore Cooper, Bret Harte's "Muck-a-Muck" is parody. In constantly whacking potboiler-artist Harold Bell Wright with a bladder, Donald Ogden Stewart's "How Love Came to General Grant" is burlesque. You can sort out the other pieces for yourself.

Not all are parody or burlesque. S. J. Perelman, as usual, is doing something from another planet. A. J. Liebling goes after Graham Greene, a writer he obviously considers overrated, and does him in with forthright critical analysis. Deep down, all these pieces rest on foundations of malice, which is common in a great deal of humor.

Will Rogers, whose humor was popular in the 1930s, claimed he never met a man he didn't like. This invites suspicion that Rogers didn't get out of the house much. There is more than a little misanthropy in almost every humorist, and an almost irresistible compulsion to express it cruelly.

FRANK GANNON

"What He Told Me"

> People would rather think about Babe Ruth, Willie Mays, Hank Aaron, and Stan Musial. Who wants to be reminded of Attila the Hun?
> —*The Mick,* Mickey Mantle and Herb Gluck

Let's begin somewhere. I don't know what "years" are, so I guess I really couldn't tell you. Always remember that there is only one sun in the sky and there is only one of me. So don't bother me about what year it was. It was any year I felt like. And you *will* bow and taste hot steel. But only if I feel like it.

So don't bother me.

At any rate, we had just crushed the descendants of the Scythians, and we were feeling pretty good about ourselves. We were all out there on the plain, laughing, messing around, slapping each other, stabbing. If you want the truth, we were all about half bagged. We were pouring whatever it was that the descendants of the Scythians used to drink over *everybody.* We were just cracking up.

It was a long time ago, but I still remember one particular descendant of a Scythian. His name was Dnargash or something, one of those Scythian names. Anyway, this guy had the worst lisp I ever heard. I don't know about you, but if there's anything that really gets on my nerves, it's a lisp.

Anyway, this is a funny story. I'm riding along, nice day, not a care in the world. Suddenly I hear this guy behind me. He's talking just like this, I swear to God. I am not making this up.

NGASHO FLAM IK WEEDELL FURESY

Then he gets all excited:

IB FLUEW! NGASHO FLAM IK WEEDELL FURESY!

Right away I think, Cut me a break. Then I swing my horse around, bring my sword back, and his head is history. I didn't even watch the head, but I hear it went a long way. Someone told me 500 feet, but I don't know. Numbers don't mean anything to me. By that I mean numbers don't mean *anything* to me.

All I know is that I made a full, smooth swing, and I made contact. All spring I had worked on cutting down on my swing and just *meeting* the head. I had tried to stop trying to *kill* every head I saw up there.

It had paid off. It was the best year I ever had as a barbarian. I had learned patience. I was a little more mature now, and I had learned to wait on a head.

I enjoyed a great success. On top of everything else, we won the Eastern Roman Empire, which was the icing on the cake. I only wished my father could have been there to see it all, but then I remembered I had killed him a long time ago.

I slept well that winter. I had earned it.

I loved all my teammates when I was a Hun, but I guess I was closest to Thornells and Oenfig. We were an unlikely trio. Thornells's mom was one of the Kirghiz, and he talked about her often, but Oenfig's mother had been dismembered by the Kirghiz. Those two guys were as different as night and day. Me? Where did I fit in? I wouldn't know a Kirghiz from a Hungarian.

Still, the three of us hit it off almost right away. We were inseparable until Thornells got pole-axed and Oenfig got traded. I could tell a lot of stories about us three, but it's hard to think of one that you could tell in mixed company!

We were young then.

There's this one I can tell.

We had just slaughtered a lot of Teutons, I think it was. Omran, who was "one as the sun is one" at that time, told us all to take a break but be sure not to go anywhere.

That was all we needed.

We were not above bending the rules in those days, as is well known. We waited until Omran turned around. Then we hightailed it out of there and headed for the nearest town, which was some ways off. It was late, but we thought we might find an after-hours place.

We rode hard. Our horses were foaming and so was Oenfig, if I remember right.

We finally got there only to find that not only were there no private clubs, the whole place was dry!

We rode back frantically, cursing everything we could think of. It was very late and the one thing we didn't need was another fine.

We rode until we could see the campfires. Then we walked our horses up and blended into the crowd. It looked like we'd made it.

Then I heard it. That voice. I knew it instantly.

The jig was up.

It was Omran. He didn't seem real happy about our little field trip.

"Attila! I'm glad you could make it. We're not busy or anything here, so I'm glad you could find it in your schedule to drop by."

I felt like digging a hole and crawling in it, but I had tried that before. Now I knew that digging a hole and crawling into it would make Omran even crankier than he already was. And he was plenty cranky, thank you very much.

"I see you and that bum Oenfig have been gone for, oh, some long period of time."

Even though Omran was the "one as the sun is one" at that time, he was not real good with numbers. He was not a stupid man, though. He was like a lot of us back then. Born before the Depression.

Anyway, Oenfig and me were temporarily "unclean ones." We would have to ride in the back. All the way in the back. Behind the rookies, even. We would be called, by everyone, "Namd-Kark," or "without foreskin."

We looked over at Thornells and he was just smiling to himself and whistling. Like it was Sunday in the park.

Thornells, Oenfig, and me, we had a lot of laughs together. We were boys then.

When people ask me about Omran I have only one thing to say: I loved the man. We had our share of differences, but I can tell you: he was always tough but he was always fair.

Whatever else you can say about him, and it's probably plenty, he was one of a kind.

He had a very colorful way of talking. After a while we got to calling the things that he said "Omranisms." He was full of these things. Every time he opened his mouth you were liable to hear one.

"The Steppe-Land? Nobody goes there anymore. We slaughtered everyone and took their possessions. We made the strong ones slaves."

"It's not over until we have massive carnage."

"If people don't want their cities looted and burned, there's no way you're going to make them."

Whatever else he was, and it's probably plenty, he was one of a kind.

Of course one day I looked over at Omran, and he looked a little old. So I killed him.

A lot of kids ask me questions, but I guess the question I get asked the most is, "What does it take to become the leader of a vast horde of bloodthirsty, pitiless barbarians?" I always tell them the same thing: desire. You can have everything else: shortness, ugliness, a violent disposition, semi-insanity—it doesn't matter if you don't have that thing called desire. Without that, you'll never make it as a Hun. There are plenty of other things you can be. There are a lot of short, violent doctors, for instance. It's a big world and there aren't that many barbarian hordes. Find your niche and stay there.

If you think you have what it takes, leading a horde of murderous troublemakers can be one of the most rewarding lives you can have.

Just what makes a Hun? Let's see.

Mental outlook is important, but you can't overlook the physical side. You have to be in tip-top condition if you plan to spend all your spare time swarming over the plains of eastern Europe. We have a long season, and staying in shape is a number one priority. Eat right and get plenty of rest.

Go down this list and see if you measure up.

1. You have to have a strong desire to learn the toughest job there is.
2. You have to take a real sincere pleasure in mayhem and carnage.
3. You can't be squeamish.
4. You should have a good throwing arm.
5. You can't be afraid of horses.

If you measure up, you may be Hun material. Maybe. Remember, again, there are lots of jobs around and not everybody can be a Hun leader. If everybody was a Hun leader, things would be a lot different, believe me.

In closing, let me say that Hun is not an easy position. But we do have protective equipment. Remember that, and never be afraid to use it.

MICHAEL O'DONOGHUE

"Pornocopia"

THE ELEGANT ENGLISH EPISTOLARY EROTICISM

Mr. N . . . chanc'd to offer a bout of dalliance and disport. My blush serv'd but to inflame the young gentleman's ardours, and a heart-fetch'd sigh at the size of his remarkable fouling piece banish'd all reserve. Canting up my petticoats and unlacing my stays, I fell supine on the settee, my exquisite treasures at his disposal. Thus embolden'd, he took in hand the prodigious engine and, abandoning restraint, remm'd the rubid cleft where grows the wanton moss that crowns the brow of modesty, but to naught avail. Thrice again the frightful machine assail'd the region of delight which, with maidenhead's sweet mant'ling, celebrates the triumph of roses o'er the lily, but that delicious cloven spot, the fairest mark for his well-mettl'd member, quell'd and abash'd the gallant intruder. Mustering his fervour, once more didst Cupid's capt'n 'tempt to brunt the fierce prow of his formidable vessel past the shoals of luxuriant umberage which garland'd my rutt'd charms and into that uncloy'd cove where humid embars blaz'd on visitation, yet was, e'en so, repulst. Tho' toss'd 'twixt profusion and compliance, my hand crept softly to the sturdy lad's ripen'd tussle and roam'd the sprout'd tufts, whilst he my hillocks wander'd, then rekindl'd his nobly stock'd conduits, distend'd the proud steed, where'pon I near swoon'd of extasy's bright tumult as the sturdy stallion, his exhaultations fir'd, gallop'd o'er ev'ry hedge and thicket, spending the jetty sprig, won the sally, and gain'd a lodgement. Encircl'd in the pleasure-girst, ingorg'd by dissolution's tender agony, each 'fusive stroke stirr'd my in'most tendrils, devolv'd my dewy furrow of its secrets, which I, flush with straddl'd frolik, was far from disrelishing, 'til, somewhat appeas'd, his quiv'ling extremity, twin'd by unquench'd appetite, durst 'frock the fury of unflagg'd insperions, yet homeward play'd my rake the plenteous protraction, redoubl'd his endeavours that joy's thrust might soon drink deep at rapture's well, then didst, at last, sheath, to the churl'd hilt, his massy weapon, and so suffer'd me to bliss.

I am

Madam,

Yours, etc., etc., etc.

THE FIN-DE-SIECLE BRITISH BIRCHING BOOK

"And what might your name be, my child?" inquired Lord Randy Stoker, removing a tin of violet pastilles from the pocket of his tangerine-velvet waistcoat and placing one in his sensuous mouth while his flashing eyes coolly probed the buxom lass that sat trembling before him.

"My name's Miss Prissy Trapp, sir," she replied in a faint voice and working-class accent, lowered her eyes, and curtsied. "I'm the new maid."

"Welcome to Felonwart, my remote country manor house. I can assure you that your stay here will be most . . . amusing. Come into the drawing room and place yourself at the disposal of my guests."

The drawing room was that of a typical country manor house, save for the fact that the walls were padded, the windows barred, a curious array of whips and riding equipage was displayed above the fireplace, an immodest fresco graced the north wall, a number of cages hung suspended from the ceiling and, in the center of the room, towering above a bloodstained altar, loomed a moonstone-studded effigy of Kā, the nineteen-armed Babylonian Goddess of Lust.

"As you may have gathered, my tastes run somewhat toward the *outré*," Lord Stoker commented, helping himself to another violet pastille, and continued, his voice dark with menace, "a proclivity that does not limit itself to décor."

Upon seeing Prissy, a tall, gaunt man, wearing but a pair of soiled galoshes, threw himself at her feet and commenced wildly kissing her feather duster.

"Allow me to introduce Professor Schadenfreude," interposed Lord Stoker as the bewildered miss blushed crimson under the Austrian's singular attention. "His studies in aberrant behavior have taken man's sexual urges out of the Dark Ages."

"And back to the Stone Age," added Lady Wick-Burner, crawling across the carpet to gnaw on the heel of Prissy's left shoe.

"Oh . . . Oh . . . Please . . . I beseech you . . . Leave off . . . Have pity . . . Oh . . . No more . . . ," pleaded the misused maid.

Delighted by the young girl's supplications, the Duke of Pudenda discontinued reading from a slim volume of unseemly sonnets he had recently published privately in a limited edition of four copies, all of which were bound in tinted wildebeest.

"Remove her chemise!" demanded Reverend John Thomas.

Upon hearing this, Prissy, her face a mask of abasement, attempted to flee but was thwarted by two Nubian eunuchs who, despite the unfortunate's pathetic struggles, firmly secured her wrists with braided peacock tails.

"All in good time," cautioned the Sultana of Zosh. "First, allow the hapless servant to gaze upon the instrument of her chastisement." She drew back the drapes to reveal a weird machine composed of a steam engine, pistons, manacles, a glass godemiche, rubber tubing, a gilded harpsichord, a whalebone corset, asparagus tips and a vat of scented lard.

The Sultana smiled wanly and murmured, "We call it . . . 'The Blind Chicken!' "

"What does it do?" asked Prissy.

Silhouetted against the dying sunlight, the great circle of Kā's nineteen arms appeared to be a ceaseless juggernaut of shame and degradation as Lord Stoker leaned over to whisper, "You'll discover that only too soon," and stuck his purple tongue in her ear.

THE EARLY FRENCH ALGOLAGNIC NOVEL

The Comte was in the formal gardens whipping his linoleum when he was joined by the Bishop. Ceasing his exertions, he greeted the prelate, and said:

"You are undoubtedly curious why I am whipping my linoleum. And yet, on closer examination, nothing could be more natural . . . or might I say 'unnatural,' as they are the same thing. Man, it goes without saying, is intrinsically evil, bearing in mind, of course, that good and evil, vice and virtue, exist only within the confines of society. It is the laws which cause crime, for, without law, there is no crime. Nature capriciously destroys the fools who forsake their instinctual lust and hunger in the name of virtue, as Nature does us all. Man is an animal with a soul that exists only through sensations. Although man must not limit his actions, there is no free will, therefore he is not responsible for his actions. Quite obviously, the more disgusting the act, the greater the pleasure, and since pleasure, or might I say 'pain,' as pleasure is but pain diminished, remains the chief aim of all human existence, it should be enjoyed at any cost, particularly at the expense of other people, that is to say, not only is there joy in whipping my linoleum, but there is also joy in reflecting upon those who are not allowed to whip their linoleum. Hence, cruelty is nothing more than man's life force uncorrupted by civilization. As we are pawns to misery, so must we dispense misery to pawns. Since pain is the absolute, it is essential that I, as a philosopher, pursue this absolute. So it seems that the question, my dear Bishop, is not 'Why do I whip my linoleum?' but rather, 'Why doesn't everyone whip his linoleum'?''

THE RECENT FRENCH ALGOLAGNIC NOVEL*

The moon was partially obscured by a cloud.

One afternoon, a limousine had picked up E at the Buttes-Chaumont Gardens, the Bois de Vincennes, the Bassin de la Villette, or perhaps the Boulevard Haussmann, and had taken her to a *château* in southern France. The driver had departed without saying a word.

Attendants prepared E for the party that evening. She was dressed in a bird costume resembling a boat-tailed grackle. I am certain that she was forbidden to speak.

In another version, the limousine picks up E at the Bureau des Objets Trouvés.

*Ed. Note—Rumored to be the work of A. . . . M. . . . ., noted Marxist author and art critic.

E was placed on the lawn and instructed to remain there until summoned. Behind her was a row of cypress trees. Under the third tree lay a pale blue envelope. From the envelope she withdrew a photograph of three persons on an ottoman. One is blindfolded. It is difficult to determine what they are engaged in.

Her costume was perfect in every detail. The only discrepancy that might prompt the casual observer to conclude that E could be something other than an enormous boat-tailed grackle was a pair of black patent leather shoes which she is required to wear as a symbol of her absolute subjugation.

Although forbidden to speak, I believe that E was allowed to whistle.

The bird costume restricted movement and it often took E over an hour to reach places only a few feet away.

When she glances back to the third tree, she notices that the pale blue envelope and the photograph are missing.

That evening, three men, X, Y, and Z, retire from the party to chat beneath the porte-cochere. Y is her lover.

Fragments of conversation are audible from where E is standing on the lawn.

"Have you spoken to G lately?"

"It's odd you should ask. Why only last week . . ."

The three men turn toward her. X and Z appear familiar, as if she had seen them in a photograph.

"Look, there's a boat-tailed grackle," remarks Z. "An uncommonly large one, I might add."

Moments pass. The men do not move. E observes the moon clearly reflected in her black patent leather shoes. Surely her lover will recognize her, take her in his arms, and debase her in the fashion which she has grown to regard so dearly. She flaps her wings and whistles frantically.

Finally, Y speaks.

"One seldom sees them so far north this late in the season."

EXPURGATION BY LATIN

Now there once lived near Genoa a wealthy merchant named Gelfardo, who was infatuated with Bonella, a miller's daughter unsurpassed in beauty, grace, and charm.

As it happened, Bonella, spurning Gelfardo's advances, was wont to seek diversion with a certain abbot, but he, much to her displeasure, had given to *concilium loqui* swans.

One afternoon, while strolling in the forest, Gelfardo came upon the comely damsel picking flowers. With a lascivious wink, he asked the lady if she might care to unfasten her bodice and *supplicia eorum, qui in furto aut latrocinio aut aliqua noxia sint comprehensi gratiora dis immortalibus esse arbitrantur* for an hour or so.

She coyly agreed to the merchant's bold overtures, but on two conditions. The first was that he pay her 200 gold ducats; the second, that after he had *supplicia eorum, qui in furto aut latrocinio aut aliqua noxia sint comprehensi gratiora dis immortalibus esse arbitrantur,* then she, in turn could *sed cum eius generis copia defecit etiam ad innocentium supplicia descendunt.*

Suspecting nothing, Gelfardo agreed, gave her 200 gold ducats, and made ready to *tantis excitati praemiis et sua sponte multi in disciplinam conveniunt.*

As the couple began *haec poena apud eos est gravissima,* who should pass by but the abbot. Upon seeing the *consuerunt neque tributa,* he took three potatoes and a long loaf of bread from his sack and *quibus ita est interdictum, hi numero impiorum ac sceleratorum habentur his omnes decedunt, aditum eorum sermonemque defugiunt,* which he then tied to Bonella's *honos ullus communicatur.*

Waiting until the merchant had almost *hoc proprium virtutis existimant,* the abbot sprang from behind the bushes where he had been hiding and shouted, *"Expulsos agris finitimos cedere!"* Startled, Bonella *neque quemquam prope audere consistere; simul hoc se fore tutiores arbitrantur, repentinae incursionis timore sublato,* causing the string to *suumque auxilium* Gelfardo's *pollicentur atque a multitudine collaudantur* and *qui ex his secuti non sunt, in desertorum ac proditorum numero decuntur, omniumque his rerum postea fides derogatur* the three potatoes.

It was only then that she reminded him of the second condition.

Moral: Cuckolds often make merry but it is rare indeed that *omni Gallia eurum hominum qui aliquo sunt numero atque honore genera sunt duo; nam plebes paene servorum habetur loco, quae nihil audet per se, nulli adhibetur consilio.*

S. J. PERELMAN

"Cloudland Revisited: Roll On, Thou Deep and Dark Scenario, Roll"

One August morning during the third summer of the First World War, Manuel Da Costa, a Portuguese eel fisherman at Bullock's Cove, near Narragansett Bay, was calking a dory drawn up beside his shack when he witnessed a remarkable exploit. From around a nearby boathouse appeared a bumpkin named Piggy Westervelt, with a head indistinguishable from an Edam cheese, lugging a bicycle pump and a coil of rubber hose. Behind him, with dragging footsteps, because of the quantities of scrap iron stuffed into his boots, came another stripling, indistinguishable from the present writer at the age of twelve, encased in a diving helmet that was improvised from a metal lard pail. As Da Costa watched with fascinated attention, Piggy ceremoniously conducted me to the water's edge, helped me kneel, and started securing the hose to my casque.

"Can you breathe in there all right?" he called out anxiously. There was some basis for his concern, since, in the zeal of creation, we had neglected to supply a hinge for my visor, and between lack of oxygen and the reek of hot lard my eyes were beginning to extrude like muscat grapes. I signaled Piggy to hurry up and start pumping, but he became unaccountably angry. "How many hands do you think I got?" he bawled. "If you don't like the way I'm doing it, get somebody else!" Realizing my life hung on a lunatic's caprice, I adopted the only rational attitude, that of the sacrificial ox, and shallowed my breathing. Finally, just as the old mitral valve was about to close forever, a few puffs of fetid air straggled through the tube and I shakily prepared to submerge. My objective was an ancient weedy hull thirty feet offshore, where the infamous Edward Teach, popularly known as Blackbeard, was reputed to have foundered with a cargo of bullion and plate. Neither of us had the remotest idea what bullion and plate were, but they sounded eminently useful. I was also to keep a sharp lookout for ambergris, lumps of which were constantly being picked up by wide-awake boys and found to be worth forty thousand dollars. The prospects, viewed from whatever angle, were pretty rosy.

They began to dim the second I disappeared below the surface. By that time, the hose had sprung half a dozen leaks, and Piggy, in a frenzy of misdirected co-operation, had pumped my helmet full of water. Had I not been awash in the pail, I might have been able to squirm out of my boots, but as it was, I was firmly anchored in the ooze and a definite candidate for Davy Jones's locker when an unexpected savior turned up in the person of Manuel Da Costa. Quickly sculling overhead, he captured the hose with a boat hook, dragged me inboard, and pounded the water out of my lungs. The first sight I saw, as I lay gasping in the scuppers, was Manuel towering over me like the Colossus of Rhodes, arms compressed and lips akimbo. His salutation finished me forever as an undersea explorer. "Who the hell do you think you are?" he demanded, outraged. "Captain Nemo?"

That a Rhode Island fisherman should invoke anyone so recherché as the hero of Jules Verne's submarine saga may seem extraordinary, but actually there was every justification for it. All through the preceding fortnight, a movie version of *Twenty Thousand Leagues Under the Sea* had been playing to packed houses at a local peepshow, engendering almost as much excitement as the Black Tom explosion. Everyone who saw it was dumfounded—less, I suspect, by its subaqueous marvels than by its hallucinatory plot and characters—but nobody besides Piggy and me, fortunately, was barmy enough to emulate it. In general, I experienced no untoward effects from my adventure. It did, however, prejudice me unreasonably against salt water, and for years I never mentioned the ocean floor save with a sneer.

Some weeks ago, rummaging through the film library of the Museum of Modern Art, I discovered among its goodies a print of the very production of *Twenty Thousand Leagues* that had mesmerized me in 1916, and, by ceaseless nagging, bedeviled the indulgent custodians into screening it for me. Within twenty minutes, I realized that I was watching one of the really great cinema nightmares, a *cauchemar* beside which *King Kong, The Tiger Man,* and *The Cat People* were as staid as so many quilting bees. True, it did not have the sublime irrelevance of *The Sex Maniac,* a masterpiece of Krafft-Ebing symbolism I saw in Los Angeles whose laboratory monkeyshines climaxed in a scene where two Picassoesque giantesses, armed with baseball bats, beat each other to pulp in a cellar. On the other hand, it more than equaled the all-time stowage record set by D. W. Griffith's *Intolerance,* managing to combine in one picture three unrelated plots—*Twenty Thousand Leagues, The Mysterious Island,* and *Five Weeks in a Balloon*—and a sanguinary tale of betrayal and murder in a native Indian state that must have fallen into the developing fluid by mistake. To make the

whole thing even more perplexing, not one member of the cast was identified—much as if all the actors in the picture had been slain on its completion
and all references to them expunged. I daresay that if Stuart Paton, its director, were functioning today, the votaries of the Surrealist film who sibilate
around the Little Carnegie and the Fifth Avenue Playhouse would be weaving
garlands for his hair. That man could make a cryptogram out of Mother
Goose.

The premise of *Twenty Thousand Leagues,* in a series of quick nutshells, is that
the Navy, dismayed by reports of a gigantic sea serpent preying on our merchant marine, dispatches an expedition to exterminate it. Included in the party
are Professor Aronnax, a French scientist with luxuriant crêpe hair and heavy
eye makeup who looks like a phrenologist out of the funny papers; his daughter, a kittenish ingénue all corkscrew curls and maidenly simpers; and the
latter's heartbeat, a broth of a boy identified as Ned Land, Prince of Harpoon-
ers. Their quarry proves, of course, to be the submarine *Nautilus,* commanded
by the redoubtable Captain Nemo, which sinks their vessel and takes them
prisoner. Nemo is Melville's Captain Ahab with French dressing, as bizarre a
mariner as ever trod on a weevil. He has a profile like Garibaldi's, set off by a
white goatee; wears a Santa Claus suit and a turban made out of a huck towel;
and smokes a churchwarden pipe. Most submarine commanders, as a rule,
busy themselves checking gauges and twiddling the periscope, but Nemo
spends all his time smiting his forehead and vowing revenge, though on whom
it is not made clear. The décor of the *Nautilus,* obviously inspired by a Turkish
cozy corner, is pure early Matisse; Oriental rugs, hassocks, and mother-of-
pearl taborets abound, and in one shot I thought I detected a parlor floor lamp
with a fringed shade, which must have been a problem in dirty weather. In all
justice, however, Paton's conception of a submarine interior was no more
florid than Jules Verne's. Among the ship's accouterments, I find on consulting the great romancer, he lists a library containing twelve thousand volumes,
a dining room with oak sideboards, and a thirty-foot drawing room full of Old
Masters, tapestry, and sculpture.

Apparently, the front office figured that so straightforward a narrative
would never be credible, because complications now really begin piling up.
"About this time," a subtitle announces, "Lieutenant Bond and four Union
Army scouts, frustrated in an attempt to destroy their balloon, are carried out
to sea." A long and murky sequence full of lightning, falling sandbags, and
disheveled character actors occupies the next few minutes, the upshot being
that the cloud-borne quintet is stranded on a remote key called Mysterious
Island. One of its more mysterious aspects is an unchaperoned young person in
a leopard-skin sarong, who dwells in the trees and mutters gibberish to herself. The castaways find this tropical Ophelia in a pit they have dug to ward off
prowling beasts, and Lieutenant Bond, who obviously has been out of touch

with women since he was weaned, loses his heart to her. To achieve greater
obscurity, the foregoing is intercut with limitless footage of Captain Nemo and
his hostages goggling at the wonders of the deep through a window in the side
of the submarine. What they see is approximately what anybody might who
has quaffed too much sacramental wine and is peering into a home aquarium,
but, after all, tedium is a relative matter. When you come right down to it, a
closeup of scup feeding around a coral arch is no more static than one of
Robert Taylor.

At this juncture, a completely new element enters the plot to further
befuddle it, in the form of one Charles Denver, "a retired ocean trader in a
distant land." Twelve years earlier, a flashback reveals, Denver had got a
skinful of lager and tried to ravish an Indian maharani called Princess Daaker.
The lady had thereupon plunged a dagger into her thorax, and Denver, possibly finding the furniture too heavy, had stolen her eight-year-old daughter.
We see him now in a mood of remorse approaching that of Macbeth, drunk-
enly clawing his collar and reviling the phantoms who plague him—one of
them, by the way, a rather engaging Mephistopheles of the sort depicted in
advertisements for quick-drying varnish. To avoid losing his mind, the trader
boards his yacht and sets off for Mysterious Island, a very peculiar choice
indeed, for if ever there was a convocation of loonies anywhere, it is there.
Captain Nemo is fluthering around in the lagoon, wrestling with an inflated
rubber octopus; Lieutenant Bond and the leopard girl (who, it presently
emerges, is Princess Daaker's daughter, left there to die) are spooning on the
cliffs; and, just to enliven things, one of Bond's scouts is planning to supplant
him as leader and abduct the maiden.

Arriving at the island, Denver puts on a pippin of a costume, consisting of a
deerstalker cap, a Prince Albert coat, and hip boots, and goes ashore to seek
the girl he marooned. He has just vanished into the saw grass, declaiming away
like Dion Boucicault, when the screen suddenly blacks out, or at least it did
the day I saw the picture. I sprang up buoyantly, hoping that perhaps the film
had caught fire and provided a solution for everybody's dilemma, but it had
merely slipped off the sprocket. By the time it was readjusted, I, too, had
slipped off, consumed a flagon or two, and was back in my chair waiting alertly
for the payoff. I soon realized my blunder. I should have stayed in the rath-
skeller and had the projectionist phone it to me.

Denver becomes lost in the jungle very shortly, and when he fails to return
to the yacht, two of the crew go in search of him. They meet Lieutenant
Bond's scout, who has meanwhile made indecent overtures to the leopard girl
and been declared a pariah by his fellows. The trio rescue Denver, but, for
reasons that defy analysis, get plastered and plot to seize the yacht and sail
away with the girl.

During all this katzenjammer, divers from the *Nautilus* have been reconnoitering around the craft to learn the identity of its owner, which presumably is emblazoned on its keel, inasmuch as one of them hastens to Nemo at top speed to announce with a flourish, "I have the honor to report that the yacht is owned by Charles Denver." The Captain forthwith stages a display of vindictive triumph that would have left Boris Thomashefsky, the great Yiddish tragedian, sick with envy; Denver, he apprises his companions, is the man against whom he has sworn undying vengeance. In the meantime (everything in *Twenty Thousand Leagues* happens in the meantime; the characters don't even sneeze consecutively), the villains kidnap the girl, are pursued to the yacht by Bond, and engage him in a fight to the death. At the psychological moment, a torpedo from the *Nautilus* blows up the whole shebang, extraneous characters are eliminated, and, as the couple are hauled aboard the submarine, the big dramatic twist unfolds: Nemo is Prince Daaker and the girl his daughter. Any moviemaker with elementary decency would have recognized this as the saturation point and quit, but not the producer of *Twenty Thousand Leagues*. The picture bumbles on into a fantastically long-winded flashback of Nemo reviewing the whole Indian episode and relentlessly chewing the scenery to bits, and culminates with his demise and a strong suspicion in the onlooker that he has talked himself to death. His undersea burial, it must be admitted, has an authentic grisly charm. The efforts of the funeral party, clad in sober diving habit, to dig a grave in the ocean bed finally meet with defeat, and, pettishly tossing the coffin into a clump of sea anemones, they stagger off. It seemed to me a bit disrespectful not to blow "Taps" over the deceased, but I suppose nobody had a watertight bugle.

An hour after quitting the Museum, I was convalescing on a bench in Central Park when a brandy-nosed individual approached me with a remarkable tale of woe. He was, he declared, a by-blow of Prince Felix Youssoupoff, the assassin of Rasputin, and had been reared by Transylvanian gypsies. Successively a circus aerialist, a mosaic worker, a diamond cutter, and a gigolo, he had fought (or at least argued) with Wingate's Raiders, crossed Outer Mongolia on foot, spent two years in a Buddhist monastery, helped organize the Indonesian resistance, and become one of the financial titans of Lombard Street. A woman, he confided huskily, had been his undoing—a woman so illustrious that the mere mention of her name made Cabinets totter. His present financial embarrassment, however, was a purely temporary phase. Seversky had imported him to the States to design a new helicopter, and if I could advance him a dime to phone the designer that he had arrived, I would be amply reimbursed. As he vanished into oblivion cheerily jingling my two nickels, the old lady sharing my bench put down her knitting with a snort.

"Tommyrot!" she snapped. "Hunh, you must be a simpleton. That's the most preposterous balderdash I ever heard of."

"I *am* a simpleton, Madam," I returned with dignity, "but you don't know beans about balderdash. Let me tell you a movie I just saw." No sooner had I started to recapitulate it than her face turned ashen, and without a word of explanation she bolted into the shrubbery. An old screwbox, obviously. Oh, well, you can't account for anything nowadays. Some of the stuff that goes on, it's right out of a novel by Jules Verne.

A . J . LIEBLING

"A Talkative Jerk"

The traditional Englishman of Gallic fiction is a naïve chap who speaks bad French, eats tasteless food, and is only accidentally and episodically heterosexual. The sole tolerable qualities ever allowed him are to be earnest, in an obtuse way, and physically brave, through lack of imagination.

When I began reading *The Quiet American,* in its British edition, on a plane between London and New York last December (Viking has just now brought it out in this country), I discovered that Mr. Graham Greene, who is British, had contrived to make his Quiet American, Pyle, a perfect specimen of a French author's idea of an Englishman. I had bought *The Quiet American* at the waiting-room newsstand, on the assurance of the young lady attendant that it was good light reading.

Pyle is as naïve as he can be and speaks French atrociously. He dotes on bland horrors in food: "A new sandwich mixture called Vit-Health. My mother sent it from the States." (In American, I think, a thing like that is called a sandwich *spread*.) Pyle's choice of idiom convinced me that he is a thinly disguised Englishman. But I was impressed by the *toupet* of Mr. Greene, sneering down at Pyle from the gastronomic eminence of a soggy crumpet. A British author snooting American food is like the blind twitting the one-eyed. Finally, Pyle says he has never had a woman, even though he is thirty-two. He is earnest, though, in an obtuse way, and physically brave, through lack of imagination.

This exercise in national projection made me realize that Mr. Greene, the celebrated whodunist, trapped on the moving staircase of history, was registering a classical reaction to a situation familiar to me and Spengler. When

England, a French cultural colony, outstripped the homeland after Waterloo and the Industrial Revolution, all that remained for the French to say was "Nevertheless, you remain nasty, overgrown children." The Italians of the Renaissance said it to the French, and I suppose the Greeks said it to the Romans. It is part of the ritual of handing over.

When Greene undertook the composition of Pyle's sparring partner, he had more difficulty. He had already presented one basically English type as a Quiet American. Now he had to have somebody to contrast him with unfavorably—an Articulate Englishman. Such a person is a contradiction in popular-fiction terms, like a scrutable Oriental. To produce one, Greene had to defenestrate all the traits by which a whodunit reader identifies an Englishman—the tight upper lip, the understatement, the cheerful mask of unintelligence skillfully exploited to confuse the enemy. I needed a full thirty seconds in the company of the result—Fowler, the correspondent in Saigon of a London newspaper published in a grim Victorian building near Blackfriars station—to see that Greene had run out at the turn.

Fowler is a sophisticated MacTavish. He knows French writing from Pascal to Paul de Kock and speaks the language like a native, although not necessarily of France. He has brought with him from Bloomsbury, of all places, the gustatory savvy of a Prosper Montagné: "I sat hungerless over my apology for a chapon duc Charles." (He has, in fact, an edge on Montagné, who includes no such *plat* in his *Grand Livre de la Cuisine*.) He is as active sexually as a North African jack and has a taste in women unaffected by the flicks, which glorify convex Marilyns and Ginas. Fowler prefers flat women with bones like birds, and he likes them to twitter on his pillow while he smokes opium. He associates informally with foreign-language-speaking people. None of these, especially the last, is a traditional British characteristic. Yet Fowler, from the moment I laid eyes on him, which was at about the time the takeoff sign flashed FASTEN SAFETY BELTS—NO SMOKING, had a familiar air, like a stranger who resembles somebody whose name you can't remember.

Suddenly I made him. He was a mockup of a Hemingway hero—*donc* an American, *donc* One of Us. Fowler is not a Hemingway hero by Hemingway, of course. He is nearer the grade of Hemingway hero that occurs in unsolicited manuscripts. "What distant ancestors had given me this stupid conscience? Surely they were free of it when they raped and killed in their paleolithic world" is a fair example of Fowler in his jungle gym of prose. But he can also bring the beat down, quiet and sad, for contrast. Like "Ordinary life goes on—that has saved many a man's reason." Original but not gaudy. I hyphenated him Bogart-Fowler *sur le chung* (a bit of Indo-French I soaked up from Greene). There are aspects of Bogart-Fowler that lead me to think he may be an American by birth, although probably a naturalized British subject. His familiarity with the minutiae of American life that irritate him hint at a boyhood spent in a town like Barrington, Rhode Island. When he thinks that Phuong, his bird-boned baby doll, is about to marry Pyle, Fowler wonders, for example, "Would she like those bright, clean little New England grocery stores where even the celery was wrapped in cellophane?" Perhaps, when he was a child, he tried to eat the cellophane.

Maybe Fowler's father, a vicar, left Rhode Island because of a broken home, taking young Bogart with him, although he knew the boy was not his own son—a situation always rich in potential traumata. Back in Bloomsbury, he imparted to the little changeling an implacable hatred of milk shakes, deodorants, and everything else American. There—but this is again a hypothesis— Bogart-Fowler may have got a job writing readers' letters to a newspaper published in a grim Victorian building near Blackfriars station, and then fourth leaders about the wiles of chaffinches, which have bones like birds.

"Good chap, that," the old Press Lord had said, with a wintry smile, as he spread Marmite on his fried beans *maison du coin lyonnaise* and read the fourth leader. "Make a jolly good foreign correspondent." I had often wondered how some of my British newspaper friends got abroad.

I stopped there, though, because I have never been a man to let a hypothesis run away with me, and considered another possibility—that Fowler, born British, had merely been the Washington correspondent of the newspaper near Blackfriars long enough to take on a glaze of loquacity. If so, when had he got out of the Press Club bar in time to shop for celery for his wife? He had a wife; it says so in the book.

I found, as I read at Mr. Greene, that Fowler's pre-Saigon past interested me a lot more than what happened to him after he got there. Where, for instance, had he learned his distaste for reporters who asked questions at army briefings? Had he perhaps been not a reporter at all but a press-relations officer with Montgomery? In Saigon, he gets his information from a sick Eurasian assistant who comes around to his digs every evening to share a pipe. Greene leaves the newspaper part of Fowler's past a mystery, such as where he had learned what was a proper *chapon duc Charles* and what was an apology for one. Had Fowler, during this obscure period, discovered that "good little French restaurant in Soho" that is as hard to verify as the Loch Ness monster? And where is it? Yes, Fowler's past is a blank, except in one department. He tells Pyle that before coming to Saigon he had forty-odd plus four women, of whom only the four were important to him, especially one in a red kimono. On Topic A he is a Talkative Englishman, native or naturalized.

At that point, I fell into one of those short, deep airplane sleeps, ten minutes long, that you hope have been longer, and, waking, found my hand where I had left it, around half a glass of Scotch-and-soda.

The book was open at the same place: Fowler telling the Quiet American about sex.

"One starts promiscuous and ends like one's grandfather," he says. (Dead, I thought, anticipating the next word, but it wasn't.) "One starts promiscuous and ends like one's grandfather, faithful to one woman" was the complete sentence. Fowler has *had* his fun; now he is a moralist. "We are fools," he concedes, "when we love." Still, he never leaves the Quiet American in any doubt about who of the two of them is the bigger fool. Poor old Q. A. Pyle, cold-decked by Mr. Greene, never suspects that Fowler is an American, too. Greene has fixed it so Pyle doesn't read fiction, except Thomas Wolfe, and Fowler is not in Wolfe. Pyle takes Fowler for a Legit Brit., the soul of honor. That is why he trusts him.

I wandered downstairs to the lounge bar, dragging *The Quiet American* with me. It was slow, but it was all I had, because I was making the trip on short notice and the other books on the stand had looked even less promising. I had a copy of the *British Racehorse,* but I had read through that early and lent it to one of the hostesses, who said she thought the Aly Khan was cute. Between drinks and dozes, I gnawed away at the novel, as though it were a gristly piece of apology for a *chapon duc Charles,* until at an unremembered point I began to wonder when Greene himself had realized that a possible second American had infiltrated his Eastern Western, and if that was the sort of thing that made him mad at us. Reading a bad book is like watching a poor fight. Instead of being caught up in it, you try to figure out what is the matter.

I signaled to the Aly Khan's fan for a fourth drink. The book was written in imitation American, too—brutal, brusque sentences tinkling with irony, not at all like fourth leaders about chaffinches. Does Greene ever get homesick for Lewis Carroll?

"They pulled him out like a tray of ice cubes, and I looked at him." . . . "Death takes away vanity—even the vanity of the cuckold who mustn't show his pain." . . . "I was a correspondent; I thought in headlines." . . . "She was the hiss of steam, the clink of a cup, she was a certain hour of the night and the promise of rest." The last quote is a switch to the poetic, but it is an *American* style of poetry—simple, dynamic, full of homely, monosyllabic comparisons. It reminded me of a lyric I used to sing:

> You're the cream in my coffee, you're the salt in my stew,
> You're the hiss of my and the bliss of my
> Steamy dreamy of you.

Poor old Greene was in the position of the Javanese politician who told a correspondent he hated the Dutch so specially hard because he could think only in Dutch.

Mr. Greene's irritation at being a minor American author does not justify the main incident of the book, which is a messy explosion in downtown

Saigon, during the shopping hour, put on by the earnest but unimaginative Pyle in collaboration with a bandit "general" in the hope of blowing up some French officers. (The French postpone their parade, and the explosion merely tears up women and children.) When I reached that point, most of the way through, I had had breakfast and was trying to kill the two last deadly hours before Idlewild. I thought I might as well finish the book so that I could give it to the hostess, a brunette from Rye, New York.

I should perhaps explain here that the book begins with Pyle in the morgue. That is the big gag: A Quiet American. It then goes on to the events that led up to his arrival there. The trouble that starts immediately and keeps on happening is known technically as Who Cares? Near the three-eighths pole, it appears that Pyle, who is a cloak-and-dagger boy attached to the Economic side of the American Legation, is helping the bandit get plastic, which can be used in the manufacture of bombs as well as many other things. I figured the bandit was fooling naïve young Pyle. Not at all. Pyle knew all about the bombs and the contemplated explosion. So did the whole American Legation. The Minister must have O.K.'d it. The way Mr. Greene, through Fowler, tips the reader to this is Fowler is in a café and two young American Legation girls are there eating ice cream—"neat and clean in the heat," a pejorative description for Fowler, who is a great sweat-and-smell man:

> They finished their ices, and one looked at her watch. "We'd better be going," she said, "to be on the safe side." I wondered idly what appointment they had.
> "Warren said we mustn't stay later than eleven-twenty-five."

The two girls go out, and a couple of minutes later the big bomb goes off. All the Legation personnel had been warned.

At this point, I, as startled as Fowler, remembered something—a miching little introductory note in the front of the book, about how all the characters are fictitious. I turned back to it, not bothering to follow Fowler out of the café and into the horrors of the square, to which I knew he would do stark justice—brusque, brutal, ironic.

"Even the historical events have been rearranged," the part of the note I wanted to see again said. "For example, the big bomb near the Continental preceded and did not follow the bicycle bombs."

Greene was, then, writing about a real explosion, a historical event, which had produced real casualties. And he was attributing the real explosion to a fictitious organization known as the State Department. If the State Department had promoted the historical explosion, I thought, it was a terrific news story and a damned shame. We needed a new State Department.

But whether it had or hadn't, anybody who read the book would wonder whether the State Department was engaged in the business of murdering French colonels and, in their default, friendly civilians. In France, which is traversing a period of suspicion, rapidly approaching hatred, of all foreign governments, the effect would be particularly poisonous when the book was translated. I knew that Mr. Greene, like James Hadley Chase and Mickey Spillane, is a great favorite of French readers of whodunits. ("Not for a long time have Anglophobia and anti-Americanism been so much at work in Paris," Stephen Coulter of the Sunday *Times* wrote lately. "It is a rooted French political axiom: 'When in trouble blame the foreigners.' ")

Then I remembered something else. In Paris, where I had been until the day before I began my plane passage, I had noticed, without much interest, that *L'Express,* a bright new newspaper, had already begun the publication of a new serial: *Un Américain Bien Tranquille,* by Graham Greene. The serials in Paris newspapers are generally translations of fairly stale books, and they are frequently retitled to appeal to French taste. I therefore had assumed the *feuilleton* in the *Express* was a book Greene wrote years ago (but of which I had read only a review) about an American who has an affair with an Englishwoman and is punished for the sacrilege. The *Express,* a tabloid, was crowded for news space even at sixteen pages, a format it had struggled for two months to attain. It is a universal belief among French editors, however, that a newspaper must have a *feuilleton.* The readers demand it, and read it more faithfully than anything else in the paper. I could imagine the *Express*'s hundred thousand readers getting to the two-neat-girls installment and then asking their friends at lunch, *"Tu l'as vu dans l'Express? C'est les Amerloques qui ont fait sauter deux mille français sur des mines atomiques en Indochine."* People everywhere confuse what they read in newspapers with news.

L'Express is only a weekly now. *Un Américain Bien Tranquille* was an irresponsible choice for the editors, but they needed circulation desperately. They didn't get it. *L'Express* went 245 numbers before it gave up its struggle to survive as a daily, and it still annoys me to think that a sixteenth of each of at least a hundred was devoted to Mr. Greene's nasty little plastic bomb.

There is a difference, after all, between calling your oversuccessful offshoot a silly ass and accusing him of murder.

ROBERT BENCHLEY

"*The Correspondent-School Linguist*"

(Showing How a Few Words of Foreign Extraction Will Help Along a Border Story)

It was dark when we reached Chihuahua and the *cabronassos* were stretched along the dusty *cartoucheras* like so many *paneros.*

It had been a long day. We had marched from Benavides and were hot and thirsty. As El Nino, the filthy little *rurale* who carried our *balassos,* remarked in his quaint patois, *"Oyga, Senor, Quien sabe?"*

And we all agreed that he was right. It *wasn't* much like Bryant Park. And, after all, why should it be? Weren't these men fighting for their rights and their *pendicos?*

Suddenly the heavy air was rent with a sound like the rending of heavy air. We rested on the shift-keys of our typewriters, and looked at one another. There was really nothing else that we could do.

I was the first to speak. The rest had, by that time, gone to see what was the matter.

I later found out that it was a practice battle between the *Bandilleros* and the *Caballeros,* and that the noise was caused by General Ostorzo refusing to make a more picturesque fall from his horse for the moving-picture men. Considering the fact that the old general had done the fall four times already, it was hardly to be *sorolla.* (The American Public does not realize, as I do, what the "Watchful Waiting" policy of the administration has brought about in Mexico; and the end is not yet.)

As we turned the corner of the *cabecillos* I stumbled over the form of an old *carrai.* He was stretched out on the hot sand with his waistcoat entirely unbuttoned and no links in his cuffs. It was like an old clerk I had once seen when I was a very little boy, only much more terrible.

Now and then he raised his head and muttered to his press-agent, *"Quien sabe? Quien sabe?''* And when the press-agent, who was intoxicated too, did not answer, the poor wretch would fall back into his native Connecticut dialect and dig his nails into the grass.

We passed by, and on into the night. But none of us talked much after that. We had looked into the bleeding heart of a *viejos* country and it was not a pretty sight.

I was sitting on the *cabron* of the old *colorado.* The sun was setting for the first time that day. Dark faced *centavos* straggled by, crooning their peculiar *viejas.* Suddenly there was a cry of *"Viva, viva! Quien sabe?"* and out from the garage came General Ostronoco, leader of the Bonanzaists.

There was a whirring of moving-picture machines and the sharp *toscadillos* of the *bambettas,* and the man who repudiated Wilson made his way up the escalator.

He is a heavy man; not too heavy, mind you, just *todas.* In fact, the Ostronoco that I knew looked very much like his photographs. Only the photographs do not show the man's remarkable vitality, which he always carries with him.

On seeing me he leaped impulsively forward and embraced me as many times as his secretary would allow.

"Mi amigo! Mi bambino,'' he exclaimed. *"Quien sabe?''*

I told him that I was.

Then he passed on his way into the hotel bar. It was the last that I saw of him, for the next moment we were surrounded by *muyjas.*

DONALD OGDEN STEWART

"How Love Came to General Grant"

In the Manner of Harold Bell Wright

From about 1910 to 1935 Harold Bell Wright, who had started as a Baptist preacher and given it up for a writing career, was one of the country's most successful novelists. Sales of his first twelve novels totaled nearly ten million copies. His two best-known books, The Shepherd of the Hills *and* The Winning of Barbara Worth, *each sold more than two million copies.*

He could afford to be humble and was in To My Sons, *an autobiography in the form of letters.* "*I have never in my work looked toward a place in literature,*" *he wrote.* "*But I have hoped for some small part in the life of the people for whom I have written.*"

On a brisk winter evening in the winter of 1864 the palatial Fifth Avenue "palace" of Cornelius van der Griff was brilliantly lighted with many brilliant lights. Outside the imposing front entrance a small group of pedestrians had gathered to gape enviously at the invited guests of the "four hundred" who were beginning to arrive in elegant equipages, expensive ball-dresses and fashionable "swallowtails".

"Hully gee!" exclaimed little Frank, a crippled newsboy who was the only support of an aged mother, as a particularly sumptuous carriage drove up and a stylishly dressed lady of fifty-five or sixty stepped out accompanied by a haughty society girl and an elderly gentleman in clerical dress. It was Mrs. Rhinelander, a social leader, and her daughter Geraldine, together with the Rev. Dr. Gedney, pastor of an exclusive Fifth Avenue church.

"What common looking people," said Mrs. Rhinelander, surveying the crowd aristocratically with her lorgnette.

"Yes, aren't they?" replied the clergyman with a condescending glance which ill befit his clerical garb.

"I'm glad you don't have people like that *dans votre eglise,* Dr. Gedney," said young Geraldine, who thought it was "smart" to display her proficiency in the stylish French tongue. At this moment the door of the van der Griff residence was opened for them by an imposing footman in scarlet livery and they passed into the abode of the "elect".

"Hully gee!" repeated little Frank.

"What's going on to-night?" asked a newcomer.

"Gee—don't youse know?" answered the newsboy. "Dis is de van der Griffs' and to-night dey are giving a swell dinner for General Grant. Dat lady wot just went in was old Mrs. Rhinelander. I seen her pitcher in de last Harper's Weekly and dere was a story in de paper dis morning dat her daughter Geraldine was going to marry de General."

"That isn't so," broke in another. "It was just a rumor."

"Well, anyway," said Frank, "I wisht de General would hurry up and come—it's getting cold enough to freeze the tail off a brass monkey." The onlookers laughed merrily at his humorous reference to the frigid temperature, although many cast sympathetic looks at his thin threadbare garments and registered a kindly thought for this brave boy who so philosophically accepted the buffets of fate.

"I bet this is him now," cried Frank, and all waited expectantly as a vehicle drove up. The cabman jumped off his box and held the carriage door open.

"Here you are, Miss Flowers," he said, touching his hat respectfully.

A silver peal of rippling laughter sounded from the interior of the carriage.

"Why Jerry," came in velvet tones addressed to the coachman, "you mustn't be so formal just because I have come to New York to live. Call me 'Miss Ella,' of course, just like you did when we lived out in Kansas," and with these words Miss Ella Flowers, for it was she, stepped out of the carriage.

A hush fell on the crowd as they caught sight of her face—a hush of silent tribute to the clear sweet womanhood of that pure countenance. A young man on the edge of the crowd who was on the verge of becoming a drunkard burst into tears and walked rapidly away to join the nearest church. A pr-st---te, who had been plying her nefarious trade on the avenue, sank to her knees to pray for strength to go back to her aged parents on the farm. Another young man, catching sight of Ella's pure face, vowed to write home to his old mother and send her the money he had been expending in the city on drinks and dissipation.

And well might these city people be affected by the glimpse of the sweet noble virtue which shone forth so radiantly in this Kansas girl's countenance. Although born in Jersey City, Ella had moved with her parents to the West at an early age and she had grown up in the open country where a man's a man and women lead clean sweet womanly lives. Out in the pure air of God's green places and amid kindly, simple, big hearted folks, little Ella had blossomed and thrived, the pride of the whole country, and as she had grown to womanhood there was many a masculine heart beat a little faster for her presence and many a manly blush of admiration came into the features of her admirers as she whirled gracefully with them in the innocent pleasure of a simple country dance. But on her eighteenth birthday, her parents had passed on to the Great Beyond and the heartbroken Ella had come East to live with Mrs. Montgomery, her aunt in Jersey City. This lady, being socially prominent in New York's "four hundred", was of course quite ambitious that her pretty little niece from the West should also enter society. For the last three months, therefore, Ella had been fêted at all the better class homes in New York and Jersey City, and as Mrs. van der Griff, the Fifth Avenue social leader, was in the same set as Ella's aunt, it was only natural that when making out her list of guests for the dinner in honor of General Grant she should include the beautiful niece of her friend.

As Ella stepped from the carriage, her gaze fell upon little Frank, the crippled newsboy, and her eyes quickly filled with tears, for social success had not yet caused her to forget that "blessed are the weak". Taking out her purse, she gave Frank a silver dollar and a warm look of sympathy as she passed into the house.

"Gee, there went an angel," whispered the little cripple, and many who heard him silently echoed that thought in their hearts. Nor were they far from wrong.

But even an angel is not free from temptation, and by letting Ella go into society her aunt was exposing the girl to the whisperings of Satan—whisperings of things material rather than things spiritual. Many a girl just as pure as Ella has found her standards gradually lowered and her moral character slowly weakened by the contact with the so-called "refined" and "cultured" infidels one meets in fashionable society. Many a father and mother whose ambition has caused them to have their daughter go out in society have bitterly repented of that step as they watched the poor girl gradually succumbing to the temptation of the world. Let her who thinks it is "smart" to be in society consider that our brothels with their red plush curtains, their hardwood floors and their luxurious appointments, are filled largely with the worn out belles and débutantes of fashionable society.

The next minute a bugle call sounded down the street and up drove a team of prancing grays. Two soldiers sprang down from the coachman's box and stood at rigid attention while the door of the carriage opened and out stepped General Ulysses S. Grant.

A murmur of admiration swept over the crowd at the sight of his manly inspiring features, in which the clean cut virility of a life free from dissipation was accentuated by the neatly trimmed black beard. His erect military bearing—his neat, well fitting uniform—but above all his frank open face proclaimed him a man's man—a man among men. A cheer burst from the lips of the onlookers and the brave but modest general lowered his eyes and blushed as he acknowledged their greeting.

"Men and women," he said, in a voice which although low, one could see was accustomed to being obeyed, "I thank you for your cheers. It makes my heart rejoice to hear them, for I know you are not cheering me personally but only as one of the many men who are fighting for the cause of liberty and freedom, and for—" the general's voice broke a little, but he mastered his emotion and went on—"for the flag we all love."

At this he pulled from his pocket an American flag and held it up so that all could see. Cheer after cheer rent the air, and tears came to the general's eyes at this mark of devotion to the common cause.

"Wipe the d--d rebels off the face of the earth, G-d d--'em," shouted a too enthusiastic member of the crowd who, I fear, was a little the worse for drink. In an instant General Grant had stepped up to him and fixed upon him those fearless blue eyes.

"My man," said the general, "it hurts me to hear you give vent to those oaths, especially in the presence of ladies. Soldiers do not curse, and I think you would do well to follow their example."

The other lowered his head shamefacedly. "General," he said, "you're right and I apologize."

A smile lit up the general's handsome features and he extended his hand to the other.

"Shake on it," he said simply, and as the crowd roared its approval of this speech the two men "shook".

Meanwhile within the van der Griff house all were agog with excitement in expectation of the arrival of the distinguished guest. Expensively dressed ladies fluttered here and there amid the elegant appointments; servants in stylish livery passed to and fro with trays of wine and other spirituous liquors.

At the sound of the cheering outside, the haughty Mrs. Rhinelander patted her daughter Geraldine nervously, and between mother and daughter passed a glance of understanding, for both felt that to-night, if ever, was Geraldine's opportunity to win the handsome and popular general.

The doorbell rang, and a hush fell over the chattering assemblage; then came the proud announcement from the doorman—"General Ulysses S. Grant"—and all the society belles crowded forward around the guest of honor.

It had been rumored that the general, being a soldier, was ignorant of social etiquette, but such proved to be far from the case. Indeed, he handled himself with such ease of manner that he captivated all, and for each and every young miss he had an apt phrase or a pretty compliment, greatly to their delight.

"Pleased to know you"—"Glad to shake the hand of such a pretty girl"—"What a nice little hand—I wish I might hold it all evening"—with these and kindred pleasantries the general won the way into the graces of Mrs. van der Griff's fair guests, and many a female heart fluttered in her bosom as she gazed into the clear blue eyes of the soldier, and listened to his well chosen tactful words.

"And how is the dear General this evening?"—this in the affected tone of old Mrs. Rhinelander, as she forced her way through the crowd.

"Finer than silk," replied he, and he added, solicitously, "I hope you have recovered from your lumbago, Mrs. Rhinelander."

"Oh quite," answered she, "and here is Geraldine, General," and the ambitious mother pushed her daughter forward.

"*Comment vous portez vous, mon Général,*" said Geraldine in French, "I hope we can have a nice *tête-a-tête* to-night," and she fawned upon her prey in a manner that would have sickened a less artificial gathering.

Were there not some amid all that fashionable throng in whom ideals of purity and true womanhood lived—some who cared enough for the sacredness of real love to cry upon this hollow mockery that was being used to ensnare the simple, honest soldier? There was only one, and she was at that

moment entering the drawing room for the purpose of being presented to the
general. Need I name her?

Ella, for it was she, had been upstairs busying herself with her toilet when
General Grant had arrived and she now hurried forward to pay her homage to
the great soldier. And then, as she caught sight of his face, she stopped
suddenly and a deep crimson blush spread over her features. She looked again,
and then drew back behind a nearby portiere, her heart beating wildly.

Well did Ella remember where she had seen that countenance before, and
as she stood there trembling the whole scene of her folly came back to her. It
had happened in Kansas, just before her parents died, on one sunny May
morning. She had gone for a walk; her footsteps had led her to the banks of a
secluded lake where she often went when she wished to be alone. Many an
afternoon had Ella dreamed idly away on this shore, but that day, for some
reason, she had felt unusually full of life and not at all like dreaming. Obeying
a thoughtless but innocent impulse, with no intention of evil, she had taken off
her clothes and plunged thus n-k-d into the cool waters of the lake. After she
had swum around a little she began to realize the extent of her folly and was
hurriedly swimming towards the shore when a terrific cramp had seized her
lower limbs, rendering them powerless. Her first impulse, to scream for help,
was quickly checked with a deep blush, as she realized the consequences if a
man should hear her call, for nearby was an encampment of Union soldiers,
none of whom she knew. The perplexed and helpless girl was in sore straits
and was slowly sinking for the third time, when a bearded stranger in soldier's
uniform appeared on the bank and dove into the water. To her horror he
swam rapidly towards her—but her shame was soon changed to joy when she
realized that he was purposely keeping his eyes tight shut. With a few swift
powerful strokes he reached her side, and, blushing deeply, took off his blue
coat, fastened it around her, opened his eyes, and swam with her to the shore.
Carrying her to where she had left her clothes he stayed only long enough to
assure himself that she had completely recovered the use of her limbs, and
evidently to spare her further embarrassment, had vanished as quickly and as
mysteriously as he had appeared.

Many a night after that had Ella lain awake thinking of the splendid features
and the even more splendid conduct of this unknown knight who wore the
uniform of the Union army. ''How I love him,'' she would whisper to herself;
''but how he must despise me!'' she would cry, and her pillow was often wet
with tears of shame and mortification at her folly.

It was shortly after this episode that her parents had taken sick and passed
away. Ella had come East and had given up hope of ever seeing her rescuer
again. You may imagine her feelings then when, on entering the drawing room
at the van der Griffs', she discovered that the stranger who had so gallantly and

tactfully rescued her from a watery grave was none other than General Ulysses S. Grant.

The poor girl was torn by a tumult of contrary emotions. Suppose he should remember her face. She blushed at the thought. And besides what chance had she to win such a great man's heart in competition with these society girls like Geraldine Rhinelander who had been "abroad" and spoke French.

At that moment one of the liveried servants approached the general with a trayful of filled wine glasses. So engrossed was the soldier hero in talking to Geraldine—or, rather, in listening to her alluring chatter—that he did not at first notice what was being offered him.

"Will you have a drink of champagne wine, General?" said Mrs. van der Griff who stood near.

The general raised his head and frowned as if he did not understand.

"Come, *mon General*," cried Geraldine gayly, "we shall drink *à votre succès dans la guerre*," and the flighty girl raised a glass of wine on high. Several of the guests crowded around and all were about to drink to the general's health.

"Stop," cried General Grant suddenly realizing what was being done, and something in the tone of his voice made everyone pause.

"Madam," said he, turning to Mrs. van der Griff, "am I to understand that there is liquor in those glasses?"

"Why yes, General," said the hostess smiling uneasily. "It is just a little champagne wine."

"Madam," said the general, "it may be 'just champagne wine' to you, but 'just champagne wine' has ruined many a poor fellow and to me all alcoholic beverages are an abomination. I cannot consent, madam, to remain under your roof if they are to be served. I have never taken a drop—I have tried to stamp it out of the army, and I owe it to my soldiers to decline to be a guest at a house where wine and liquor are served."

An excited buzz of comment arose as the general delivered this ultimatum. A few there were who secretly approved his sentiments, but they were far too few in numbers and constant indulgence in alcohol had weakened their wills so that they dared not stand forth. An angry flush appeared on the face of the hostess, for in society, "good form" is more important than courage and ideals, and by his frank statement General Grant had violently violated the canons of correct social etiquette.

"Very well, Mr. Grant," she said, stressing the "Mr."—"if that's the way you feel about it—"

"Stop," cried an unexpected voice, and to the amazement of all Ella Flowers stepped forward, her teeth clenched, her eyes blazing.

"Stop," she repeated, "He is right—the liquor evil is one of the worst curses of modern civilization, and if General Grant leaves, so do I."

Mrs. van der Griff hesitated for an instant, and then suddenly forced a smile.

"Why Ella dear, of course General Grant is right," said she, for it was well known in financial circles that her husband, Mr. van der Griff, had recently borrowed heavily from Ella's uncle. "There will not be a drop of wine served to-night, and now General, shall we go in to dinner? Will you be so kind as to lead the way with Miss Rhinelander?" The hostess had recovered her composure, and smiling sweetly at the guest of honor, gave orders to the servants to remove the wine glasses.

But General Grant did not hear her; he was looking at Ella Flowers. And as he gazed at the sweet beauty of her countenance he seemed to feel rising within him something which he had never felt before—something which made everything else seem petty and trivial. And as he looked into her eyes and she looked into his, he read her answer—the only answer true womanhood can make to clean, worthy manhood.

"Shall we go *à la salle-à-manger?*" sounded a voice in his ears, and Geraldine's sinuous arm was thrust through his.

General Grant took the proffered talon and gently removed it from him.

"Miss Rhinelander," he said firmly, "I am taking this young lady as my partner," and suiting the action to the word, he graciously extended his arm to Ella who took it with a pretty blush.

It was General Grant's turn to blush when the other guests, with a few exceptions, applauded his choice loudly, and made way enthusiastically as the handsome couple advanced to the brilliantly lighted dining room.

But although the hostess had provided the most costly of viands, I am afraid that the brave general did not fully appreciate them, for in his soul was the joy of a strong man who has found his mate and in his heart was the singing of the eternal song, "I love her—I love her—I love her!"

It was only too apparent to the other guests what had happened and to their credit be it said that they heartily approved his choice, for Mrs. Rhinelander and her scheming daughter Geraldine had made countless enemies with their haughty manners, whereas the sweet simplicity of Ella Flowers had won her numerous friends. And all laughed merrily when General Grant, in his after dinner speech, said "flowers" instead of "flour" when speaking of provisioning the army—a slip which caused both the general and Miss Flowers to blush furiously, greatly to the delight of the good-natured guests. "All the world loves a lover"—truer words were never penned.

After dinner, while the other men, according to the usages of best society, were filling the air of the dining room with the fumes of nicotine, the general, who did not use tobacco, excused himself—amid many sly winks from the other men—and wandered out into the conservatory.

There he found Ella.

"General," she began.

"Miss Flowers," said the strong man simply, "call me Ulysses."

And there let us leave them.

ROY BLOUNT, JR.

"My Cat Book Won't Come"

"How's the big cat novel coming?" are the words I hate to hear. The average person cannot know how it feels to be under the gun as I have been—six and a half years struggling with the big one, the cat book to end them all. The longer it takes, the bigger it has to be. Every day, the question that I must live with grows: whether anything can be that big.

Get off of that!

Like a cat, I am out on a limb. And there is no calling the fire department. As I told Ted Koppel, on "Nightline," fire departments today don't get cats down out of trees. "What you are saying, if I may summarize, then, is this . . . ," said Koppel—those oddly catlike eyes never quite flicking.

"All I am saying," I snapped, "is that contemporary fire departments don't get cats down out of trees. 'You've never seen a cat skeleton in a tree, have you?' they ask." The skeletons of cat-book writers, on the other hand . . . The skeletons of true cat-book writers, I mean.

Get *off*!

To have declared openly, as I did on "The CBS Morning News," that the Garfield books are *not* cat books, because "Garfield is not only unamusing; Garfield does not convince as a cat," was to fling down a gauntlet before a consensus so entrenched, and so pleased with itself, that the issue is quite simply whose reputation will stand, mine or the literary establishment's. To have revealed in advance that my protagonist is a cat named Charles J. Guiteau was to take an enormous risk. To prove myself right about Garfield is to prove that millions of so-called cat-book lovers, and millions of professed *cat* lovers, are wrong in their love.

Get . . .

If one could extrapolate from fragments—as we do in our estimation of

Sappho—the disinterested reader (but there are not even, appearances aside, any disinterested *cats*) would have to conclude that my book is, essentially, there. The chapter in which Guiteau's "owner," the chief justice of the U.S. Supreme Court, is racked by nightmares that he is Adolf Hitler—dreams accounted for, at length, when the justice wakes to find that Guiteau, for reasons of his own, has crept into the justice's bed and placed one paw beneath the justice's nose to create the sensation of a small black moustache—is done. And, according to those who have read it in manuscript, it is fine.

But do they know? Until *I* know, I cannot move on. And my confidante Irene calls it sexist to depict the chief justice of the U.S. Supreme Court as a man. Five times that chapter has undergone anguished recasting. Each time, I have felt that something of what should be its unexampled potency has eluded my slow, stretched, pawing reach.

Get off!

My friend Leo teaches deconstructive approaches to Latin American fiction, but you wouldn't know it to look at him out somewhere. I think he only does it because it's what's happening. He calls himself the Hillbilly Cat.

"Elvis was the Hillbilly Cat," I say.

"Was," he says.

"You're from White Plains, New York," I say.

"Gimme some slack," he says.

Last night he left Lon's Miracle Mile Lounge with a woman who was . . . tawny. All of a softness well toned. *I* had her scoped out. She looked pensive, enigmatic, I thought. I was waiting until after "Twilight Time," thinking it might seem prurient to ask a stranger to slow-dance first. Then the neo-fifties combo swung into "Sixty-Minute Man," and I was counting down, "Ten . . . nine . . . ," when Leo—before he can conceivably have known it was the right thing to do—went over to her table and took the painter's cap from her head (letting her hair flow down like butterscotch over a sundae) and put it on his own. He just now called to say she turned out to be a passionate attorney from Tulsa flushed with victory in a landmark harassment case, eager for a one-night romp punctuated by warm ablutions in her equally go-with-it friend Amber's condo pool, with flume, steam, shower-massage, and bubbler attachments.

If you don't get off of that . . . !

Guiteau is an "altered" cat. A modern cat, then. But how much of his character derives from that grim erotic neutrality, and how much from catness *an sich*? Can I ever know? Can I *feel* that I know? Guiteau's look is blank. The question burns.

Cats have no moral sense. Catch a dog on the couch and he leaps as if scalded and exclaims: "I'm off! I'm off the couch now! Oh, Lord! I wasn't

. . . I was just . . . I was guarding it! *Dogs can sense when someone is about to break in and steal a couch and* . . . Oh! I can't lie to you! To *you,* after all you've done for me! I was on the couch! How could I . . . I *know* better. You *know* I know better. I just . . . ''

Catch a cat on the couch and it doesn't even shrug.

Dialogue does not flow from a cat. A cat does not even know its name. Or care. A cat has unreadable eyes.

Yet the books pour out. *Keeping Tabs* remained on the *New York Times* best-seller list for ninety-one consecutive weeks. In acquiring the film rights to *Another Man's Persian,* Avram Zorich went to eight figures. *Real Cats Don't Eat Couscous,* for all its dragged-in anti-Islamism, captivated reviewers from coast to coast. Marisha N. Puhl's *Kitten Kin,* with its sepia-tone photos of pipe-smoking, etc., kittens as archetypal "Uncle Ned," etc., struck me as too cute. Her *Kits, Cats, Sex and Wives* I found, frankly, lurid. Yet Puhl's sales, hardback and paper combined, have passed the four million mark. I happen to know that Amsler Rizell, author of *Life with a Purrpuss,* bought his first cat—*by mail*—in order to get a book out of it.

Get *off* of that!

The only writer in the field today who commands my respect is the French critic Yves Sevy-Ouiounon, who raises such questions as (my translation) "What must the cats look like who enter—as they must, else art is fraud—the world of Mickey Mouse?" Sevy-Ouiounon's thought breaks frames.

As do cats. The soft touch (with the poufy foot that seems never to *weigh* upon anything), the cherished photo toppled from the desk . . . I have paid my dues. Cats have intercepted my footsteps at the ankle for so long that my gait, both at home and on tour, has been compared to that of a man wading through low surf. And in my book it shows.

Get off!

Only someone whose domestic atmosphere has been permeated with cat hair for more than three decades could have conceived the plot-point whereby my assassin is unmasked. The mailer of the threatening note is a cat owner (cats themselves, *pace* Garfield, cannot use the postal service) who is too frugal to throw away the first two inches every time he uses Scotch tape, and who has neglected to fit his tape dispenser with a screen covering the exposed lower surface of that first strip of tape between roll and cutter, so that when he uses tape to affix the letters scissored from magazines to the sheet of paper from which the watermark has been removed, he uses—on the first two letters—tape to which adhere traceable cat hairs.

Get off of that.

I would not wish to leave the impression that my cat book is a thriller merely. That I have felt compelled to plot it so strongly—nine deaths—reflects the cultural conservatism (of which cats are part and parcel: dogs are

Democrats; cats, Republicans) pervading the arts today. The book's indwelling ambition far transcends "story." What the book would do would be as near unknowable as the animal entailed. *Intrinsically,* the book would pounce, loll, and go *m'rowr;* would present thee with felinity for a while.

Some mused-upon titles, none right:

> *Cat's Up!*
> *More Ways Than One*
> *Unkindest Cat*
> *Tabby La Raza*
> *Now I'm the King*

To enter the world of my cat book is to enter an ancient consciousness, an abysmal shallows, in whose context narrative focus, as the contemporary book-buyer knows it, is as *arriviste* a notion as foot reflexology. (Which Leo has taken up. Purely to meet women.) It will not be an easy book to read. It is not easy in the writing. There have been repeated setbacks involving my own cat and the physical manuscript. Get off of that. I'm telling you, Mieu-Mieu, *get off of that.* I swear, *I'll wring your neck!* I mean it! *Mieu . . .*

A dog book comes when summoned. A cat book, when it will.

ROY BLOUNT, JR.

"*Sitting on a Seesaw*"

*(Bringing the Month's Rejected
American Poetry into Focus)
by O. V. Wiener*

If one were constrained, under the conditions of this sort of journalism, to sketch hastily the central purport and character of the disregarded American poetry of the past few weeks, one might well postulate a sort of teeter-totter.

On the one hand—or seat, that is—there weighs the stern concentration on, almost the heady obsession with, the lack of any purport and character at all in the world about and within these poets. As Owen Frisian concludes in some of the most resonant of the recent overlooked poetry:

> I don't understand what principle is at work here
> I don't understand what principle
> I don't understand

And on the other seat, not quite strong enough to cancel or even to balance permanently this first tendency, there is the pressure of a perhaps all too ready, even factitious, arrogation, often however in a very tiny way, of an ordering grip on life—a tendency also reflected by Frisian, in a second poem.

> I've had a pit in my mouth since April—
> A material pit, that I
> Divested of an olive,
> And that would make a tree. It's mine.

Frisian, in his *Mud and Other Poems* (turned down by Knopf), tends in this way to swing back and forth from poem to poem, and therefore (a pity, since he is refreshingly in command of his means for one so young) to cancel himself out.

A poet who does not cancel herself out, at least not in this way—who adheres stoutly to the affirmation seat—is Lydia P. Messenger, whose *Lines for Then and Now* has just been sent back to her, at special fourth-class rate, by Random House. The author of "To a Youthful Friend" ("The Library lions don't really care?/ Oh, come, I think they do") and "Take Heart, Executives, Blood of the City" ("Now hop a subway pulse to the heart of town/ And spurt to work") is at bottom, one feels, and primarily, a pleasant-minded woman, who does not yield to the temptations of strident feminist trumpeting—as have so many recent poetesses manqué not considered here (because they have all yielded to the temptations of publishing themselves or each other). But Messenger doesn't stand up to scrutiny, after all.

The recently ignored poet with perhaps the most total commitment to the other—the denial—end of the board is Trini Uhl, whose unprintably titled slim volume (last seen by Menemene Press), which brings together his entire output of nearly forty years, goes on mostly in this vein:

> Oh
> Oh
> Who can even
> Know for sure
> His soul is rotten
> Oh.

In his only other mood Uhl assails everyone whom even he might be expected to value.

> Camus sold out . . . to the Leading
> Family Spray Come on Down Sartre!
> Au Go-Go Come
> On Down Sartre! Au Go-Go Come on. . . .

There is something almost appealing about Uhl; but if his tropes occasionally charm, his attitude eventually grates, and we look for a less uniform spirit, a talent willing to grapple more widely on the board.

However, one of the boldest of recent failed poetic efforts—virtually a heroic one, at first blush—seems to be an attempt to break away entirely from this seesaw oscillation. No one is likely to come along soon who handles, or finds, language as Emory Groth does. In *Closing Glories* (just returned by University of Maryland Press) he calls to mind Stevens, Lowell, Dylan Thomas, even the later Yeats (and someone else difficult to put one's finger on—Rilke?), and holds his own, in a sense, in that company. It is hard to believe that throughout a volume of twenty-eight long poems such a pitch can be maintained as in these lines from "Homeopathic I":

> Night hones no sleek charter here
> In metastatic umber: Not until
> Its plumaged hover grind
> To siftings of Susannah
> (Sheer . . . shudder . . . sheen)
> Must you chirm that heavy arpeggio
> Peggy o'mine.

But Groth's capacity for sustension is perhaps his downfall, for in the end so much robust diction rather wearies, and, further, when we look away from the language and rhythm to Groth's ideas, I fear we find his back turned; until he turns around, we must be persuaded that Groth breaks away from the prevailing up-and-down pattern only by failing to be truly contemporary—by failing to be in on, as we might say, the real pumping.

Thomas Flute has always been a difficult unsuccessful poet to classify, and on the evidence of *Flakes and Others* (lost last week by Munford Printing and Publishing Company), he still is. Flute seems a very nervous sensibility, and his susceptibility to abrupt transcendence must finally be met with some reservation by the more even-tempered. What is one to say, for instance, of this passage from the title poem?

> I am issuing note after note
> No doubt faint but at large; they remind you
> Of snowflakes: not much but they float,
> Have their shapes as they fall; there behind you
> Sweet Jesus! goes God in a boat.

There is unquestionably an immediacy here, as in many of Flute's shorter poems, that is remarkable; but one could wish it were achieved at less expense in the way of unity of tone.

A new voice, which might almost have been a truly interesting one, is heard in Grant Moon's first rejected volume, *But O! My Eyes Are Clean* (Old Directions, just folded). This sprawling stretch of verse implies some talent, but on the whole that talent is drowned in essentially arid surges perhaps typified and self-convicted by the recurrent "Oh, I'm full of it this morning." Before it can engage in any sort of significant action on our figurative board, this verse wobbles from the piquant to the banal in a single line ("Charon me back to cold Virginny, you swinging old bugger Art"), and at length dissolves— notably when Moon attempts to deal with material beyond his grasp (Logical Positivism, the sea)—into utter chaos, in which the ground for pushing up and down is completely lost and the board shakes off all riders and begins to rotate uncontrolledly into a clattering blur.

An established unpublished talent, to which we might hope to look for an effectual steadying, resolving influence, is that of Ina Tomey. Tomey has been producing poetry now, along with supportive criticism and a novel-manuscript of near permanence, for the better part of a decade; her considerable following of close friends and editorial assistants will be both rewarded and made, one suspects, increasingly impatient by her latest book. In *Bundles* ("This one's not for us either"—Valerian Press) Tomey has as usual invested considerable resources and determination in generally attractive, even at times compelling, lyrics: but, as usual as well, one finds the curious lapses from aptness that no one can ever talk her out of. The poet who can speak of "Oh,/ Those golden slippers,/ That glisten, and are gone," is also the poet who can write

> Clouds
> Were substantial as mattress-batting:
> Near at hand;
> Cows
> Seemed almost to tiptoe
> In the quiet

—the latter of which images is strained, out of nowhere, and, as anyone who has ever really attended to cattle's gait in the quiet can attest, just wrong. But try to tell her that.

Perhaps, finally, the most finished and telling of this poetry is to be found in Avram S. Mistresson's *Misgivings: 9* (personal letter from someone at Viking). His is a fine steady command of all the tools: epitomized in the nice irony, the innate tact, of the refrain (in "Song") "The behavioral sciences do not mind''; or in these lines, with their deftly calibrated, carefully modulated off-inner-rhyming and universality, from ''Reflection'':

> That I be not wasted
> I aim to write a poem
> That someone who knows
> Knows is a poem.
> How do they know?
> I can taste it.

Whatever the subject of the poems here—loss at badminton, hurt animals, an unknown Puerto Rican woman and her child—Mistresson brings to it just such imagery evenly apt, rhythm and sentiment firmly balanced, a lyricism keen if sometimes fading. Such disciplined, well-earned tension is the result, we may infer, of an acceptance, a willingness to deal with the stiff pivotry of the seesaw—down around the heart of the fulcrum, as it were. And here then may stir the potential by which the going pattern might legitimately be broken, the whole teeter-totter shunted horizontally forward—if, that is, such a poet as Mistresson can ever indeed generate the requisite torque, the heft, which are sadly lacking in these poems.

BRET HARTE

"Muck - a - Muck"

It is necessary to assume that hardly anybody reads James Fenimore Cooper anymore. Bret Harte's parody reminds us why.

CHAPTER I

It was toward the close of a bright October day. The last rays of the setting sun were reflected from one of those sylvan lakes peculiar to the Sierras of California. On the right the curling smoke of an Indian village rose between the columns of the lofty pines, while to the left the log cottage of Judge Tompkins, embowered in buckeyes, completed the enchanting picture.

Although the exterior of the cottage was humble and unpretentious, and in keeping with the wildness of the landscape, its interior gave evidence of the cultivation and refinement of its inmates. An aquarium, containing goldfishes, stood on a marble centre-table at one end of the apartment, while a magnificent grand piano occupied the other. The floor was covered with a yielding tapestry carpet, and the walls were adorned with paintings from the pencils of Van Dyke, Rubens, Tintoretto, Michael Angelo, and the productions of the more modern Turner, Kensett, Church, and Bierstadt. Although Judge Tompkins had chosen the frontiers of civilization as his home, it was impossible for him to entirely forego the habits and tastes of his former life. He was seated in a luxurious armchair, writing at a mahogany *écritoire*, while his daughter, a lovely young girl of seventeen summers, plied her crochet-needle on an ottoman beside him. A bright fire of pine logs flickered and flamed on the ample hearth.

Genevra Octavia Tompkins was Judge Tompkins' only child. Her mother had long since died on the Plains. Reared in affluence, no pains had been spared with the daughter's education. She was a graduate of one of the principal seminaries, and spoke French with a perfect Benicia accent. Peerlessly beautiful, she was dressed in a white *moire antique* robe trimmed with *tulle*. That simple rosebud, with which most heroines exclusively decorate their hair, was all she wore in her raven locks.

The Judge was the first to break the silence.

"Genevra, the logs which compose yonder fire seem to have been incautiously chosen. The sibilation produced by the sap, which exudes copiously therefrom, is not conducive to composition."

"True, father, but I thought it would be preferable to the constant crepitation which is apt to attend the combustion of more seasoned ligneous fragments."

The Judge looked admiringly at the intellectual features of the graceful girl, and half forgot the slight annoyances of the green wood in the musical accents of his daughter. He was smoothing her hair tenderly, when the shadow of a tall figure, which suddenly darkened the doorway, caused him to look up.

CHAPTER II

It needed but a glance at the new-comer to detect at once the form and features of the haughty aborigine—the untaught and untrammelled son of the forest. Over one shoulder a blanket, negligently but gracefully thrown, disclosed a bare and powerful breast, decorated with a quantity of three-cent postage-stamps which he had despoiled from an Overland Mail stage a few weeks previously. A cast-off beaver of Judge Tompkins', adorned by a simple feather, covered his erect head, from beneath which his straight locks descended. His right hand hung lightly by his side, while his left was engaged in holding on a pair of pantaloons, which the lawless grace and freedom of his lower limbs evidently could not brook.

"Why," said the Indian, in a low sweet tone,—"why does the Pale Face still follow the track of the Red Man? Why does he pursue him, even as *O-kee-chow,* the wild-cat, chases *Ka-ka,* the skunk? Why are the feet of *Sorrel-top,* the white chief, among the acorns of *Muck-a-Muck,* the mountain forest? Why," he repeated, quietly but firmly abstracting a silver spoon from the table,—"why do you seek to drive him from the wigwams of his fathers? His brothers are already gone to the happy hunting-grounds. Will the Pale Face seek him there?" And, averting his face from the Judge, he hastily slipped a silver cake-basket beneath his blanket, to conceal his emotion.

"*Muck-a-Muck* has spoken," said Genevra, softly. "Let him now listen. Are the acorns of the mountain sweeter than the esculent and nutritious bean of the Pale Face miner? Does my brother prize the edible qualities of the snail above that of the crisp and oleaginous bacon? Delicious are the grasshoppers that sport on the hillside,—are they better than the dried apples of the Pale Faces? Pleasant is the gurgle of the torrent, *Kish-Kish,* but is it better than the cluck-cluck of old Bourbon from the old stone bottle?"

"Ugh!" said the Indian,—"ugh! good. The White Rabbit is wise. Her words fall as the snow on Tootoonolo, and the rocky heart of Muck-a-Muck is hidden. What says my brother the Gray Gopher of Dutch Flat?"

"She has spoken, Muck-a-Muck," said the Judge, gazing fondly on his daughter. "It is well. Our treaty is concluded. No, thank you,—you need *not* dance the Dance of Snow Shoes, or the Moccasin Dance, the Dance of Green Corn, or the Treaty Dance. I would be alone. A strange sadness overpowers me."

"I go," said the Indian. "Tell your great chief in Washington, the Sachem Andy, that the Red Man is retiring before the footsteps of the adventurous Pioneer. Inform him, if you please, that westward the star of empire takes its way, that the chiefs of the Pi-Ute nation are for Reconstruction to a man, and that Klamath will poll a heavy Republican vote in the fall."

And folding his blanket more tightly around him, Muck-a-Muck withdrew.

Chapter III

Genevra Tompkins stood at the door of the log-cabin, looking after the retreating Overland Mail stage which conveyed her father to Virginia City. "He may never return again," sighed the young girl as she glanced at the frightfully rolling vehicle and wildly careering horses,—"at least, with unbroken bones. Should he meet with an accident! I mind me now a fearful legend, familiar to my childhood. Can it be that the drivers on this line are privately instructed to despatch all passengers maimed by accident, to prevent tedious litigation? No, no. But why this weight upon my heart?''

She seated herself at the piano and lightly passed her hand over the keys. Then, in a clear mezzo-soprano voice, she sang the first verse of one of the most popular Irish ballads:—

> ''O Arrah, my dheelish, the distant dudheen
> Lies soft in the moonlight, ma bouchal vourneen:
> The springing gossoons on the heather are still,
> And the caubeens and colleens are heard on the hills.''

But as the ravishing notes of her sweet voice died upon the air, her hands sank listlessly to her side. Music could not chase away the mysterious shadow from her heart. Again she rose. Putting on a white crape bonnet, and carefully drawing a pair of lemon-colored gloves over her taper fingers, she seized her parasol and plunged into the depths of the pine forest.

Chapter IV

Genevra had not proceeded many miles before a weariness seized upon her fragile limbs, and she would fain seat herself upon the trunk of a prostrate pine, which she previously dusted with her handkerchief. The sun was just sinking below the horizon, and the scene was one of gorgeous and sylvan beauty. ''How beautiful is Nature!'' murmured the innocent girl, as, reclining gracefully against the root of the tree, she gathered up her skirts and tied a handkerchief around her throat. But a low growl interrupted her meditation. Starting to her feet, her eyes met a sight which froze her blood with terror.

The only outlet to the forest was the narrow path, barely wide enough for a single person, hemmed in by trees and rocks, which she had just traversed. Down this path, in Indian file, came a monstrous grizzly, followed by a California lion, a wild-cat, and a buffalo, the rear being brought up by a wild Spanish bull. The mouths of the first three animals were distended with frightful significance; the horns of the last were lowered as ominously. As Genevra was preparing to faint, she heard a low voice behind her.

''Eternally dog-gone my skin ef this ain't the puttiest chance yet.''

At the same moment, a long, shining barrel dropped lightly from behind her, and rested over her shoulder.

Genevra shuddered.

''Dern ye—don't move!''

Genevra became motionless.

The crack of a rifle rang through the woods. Three frightful yells were heard, and two sullen roars. Five animals bounded into the air and five lifeless bodies lay upon the plain. The well-aimed bullet had done its work. Entering the open throat of the grizzly, it had traversed his body only to enter the throat of the California lion, and in like manner the catamount, until it passed through into the respective foreheads of the bull and the buffalo, and finally fell flattened from the rocky hillside.

Genevra turned quickly. "My preserver!" she shrieked, and fell into the arms of Natty Bumpo, the celebrated Pike Ranger of Donner Lake.

Chapter V

The moon rose cheerfully above Donner Lake. On its placid bosom a dug-out canoe glided rapidly, containing Natty Bumpo and Genevra Tompkins.

Both were silent. The same thought possessed each, and perhaps there was sweet companionship even in the unbroken quiet. Genevra bit the handle of her parasol and blushed. Natty Bumpo took a fresh chew of tobacco. At length Genevra said, as if in half-spoken revery:—

"The soft shining of the moon and the peaceful ripple of the waves seem to say to us various things of an instructive and moral tendency."

"You may bet yer pile on that, Miss," said her companion, gravely. 'It's all the preachin' and psalm-singin' I've heern since I was a boy."

"Noble being!" said Miss Tompkins to herself, glancing at the stately Pike as he bent over his paddle to conceal his emotion. "Reared in this wild seclusion, yet he has become penetrated with visible consciousness of a Great First Cause." Then, collecting herself, she said aloud: "Methinks 't were pleasant to glide ever thus down the stream of life, hand in hand with the one being whom the soul claims as its affinity. But what am I saying?"—and the delicate-minded girl hid her face in her hands.

A long silence ensued, which was at length broken by her companion.

"Ef you mean you're on the marry," he said, thoughtfully, "I ain't in no wise partikler!"

"My husband," faltered the blushing girl; and she fell into his arms.

In ten minutes more the loving couple had landed at Judge Tompkins'.

Chapter VI

A year has passed away. Natty Bumpo was returning from Gold Hill, where he had been to purchase provisions. On his way to Donner Lake, rumors of an Indian uprising met his ears. "Dern their pesky skins, ef they dare to touch my Jenny,'' he muttered between his clenched teeth.

It was dark when he reached the borders of the lake. Around a glittering fire he dimly discerned dusky figures dancing. They were in war paint. Conspicuous among them was the renowned Muck-a-Muck. But why did the fingers of Natty Bumpo tighten convulsively around his rifle?

The chief held in his hand long tufts of raven hair. The heart of the pioneer sickened as he recognized the clustering curls of Genevra. In a moment his rifle was at his shoulder, and with a sharp ''ping,'' Muck-a-Muck leaped into the air a corpse. To knock out the brains of the remaining savages, tear the tresses from the stiffening hand of Muck-a-Muck, and dash rapidly forward to the cottage of Judge Tompkins, was the work of a moment.

He burst open the door. Why did he stand transfixed with open mouth and distended eyeballs? Was the sight too horrible to be borne? On the contrary, before him, in her peerless beauty, stood Genevra Tompkins, leaning on her father's arm.

''Ye'r not scalped, then!'' gasped her lover.

''No. I have no hesitation in saying that I am not; but why this abruptness?'' responded Genevra.

Bumpo could not speak, but frantically produced the silken tresses. Genevra turned her face aside.

''Why, that's her waterfall!'' said the Judge.

Bumpo sank fainting to the floor.

The famous Pike chieftain never recovered from the deceit, and refused to marry Genevra, who died, twenty years afterwards, of a broken heart. Judge Tompkins lost his fortune in Wild Cat. The stage passes twice a week the deserted cottage at Donner Lake. Thus was the death of Muck-a-Muck avenged.

FINLEY PETER DUNNE

"A Book Review"

''Well sir,'' said Mr. Dooley, ''I jus' got hold iv a book, Hinnissy, that suits me up to th' handle, a gran' book, th' grandest iver seen. Ye know I'm not much throubled be lithrachoor, havin' manny worries iv me own, but I'm not prejudiced agin books. I am not. Whin a rale good book comes along I'm as quick as anny wan to say it isn't so bad, an' this here book is fine. I tell ye 'tis fine.''

"What is it?'' Mr. Hennessy asked languidly.

" 'Tis 'Th' Biography iv a Hero be Wan Who Knows.' 'Tis 'Th' Darin' Exploits iv a Brave Man be an Actual Eye Witness.' 'Tis 'Th' Account iv th' Destruction iv Spanish Power in th' Ant Hills,' as it fell fr'm th' lips iv Tiddy Rosenfelt an' was took down be his own hands. Ye see 'twas this way, Hinnissy, as I r-read th' book. Whin Tiddy was blowed up in th' harbor iv Havana he instantly con-cluded they must be war. He debated th' question long an' earnestly an' fin'lly passed a jint resolution declarin' war. So far so good. But there was no wan to carry it on. What shud he do? I will lave th' janial author tell th' story in his own wurruds.

" 'Th' sicrety iv war had offered me,' he says, 'th' command of a rig'mint,' he says, 'but I cud not consint to remain in Tampa while perhaps less audacious heroes was at th' front,' he says. 'Besides,' he says, 'I felt I was incompetent f'r to command a rig'mint raised be another,' he says. 'I detarmined to raise wan iv me own,' he says. 'I selected fr'm me acquaintances in th' West,' he says, 'men that had thravelled with me acrost th' desert an' th' storm-wreathed mountain,' he says, 'sharin' me burdens an' at times confrontin' perils almost as gr-reat as anny that beset me path,' he says. 'Together we had faced th' turrors iv th' large but vilent West,' he says, 'an' these brave men had seen me with me trusty rifle shootin' down th' buffalo, th' elk, th' moose, th' grizzly bear, th' mountain goat,' he says, 'th' silver man, an' other fero-cious beasts iv them parts,' he says. 'An they niver flinched,' he says. 'In a few days I had thim perfectly tamed,' he says, 'an' ready to go annywhere I led,' he says. 'On th' thransport goin' to Cubia,' he says, 'I wud stand beside wan iv these r-rough men threatin' him as an akel, which he was in ivrything but birth, education, rank, an' courage, an' together we wud look up at th' admirable stars iv that tolerable southern sky an' quote th' Bible fr'm Walt Whitman,' he says. 'Honest, loyal, thrue-hearted la-ads, how kind I was to thim,' he says.

" 'We had no sooner landed in Cubia than it become nicissry f'r me to take command iv th' ar-rmy which I did at wanst. A number of days was spint be me in reconnoitring, attinded on'y be me brave an' fluent body guard, Richard Harding Davis. I discovered that th' inimy was heavily inthrenched on th' top iv San Joon hill immejiately in front iv me. At this time it become apparent that I was handicapped by th' prisence iv th' ar-rmy,' he says. 'Wan day whin I was about to charge a block house sturdily definded by an ar-rmy corps undher Gin'ral Tamale, th' brave Castile that I afthrwards killed with a small ink-eraser that I always carry, I r-ran into th' entire military force iv th' United States lying on its stomach. 'If ye won't fight,' says I, 'let me go through,' I says. 'Who ar-re ye?' says they. 'Colonel Rosenfelt,' says I. 'Oh, excuse me,' says the gin'ral in command (if me mimry serves me thrue it was Miles) r-risin' to his knees an' salutin'. This showed me 'twud be impossible f'r to carry th' war to a successful con-clusion unless I was free, so I sint th' ar-rmy home an' attackted San Joon hill. Ar-rmed on'y with a small thirty-two which I used in th' West to shoot th' fleet prairie dog, I climbed that precipitous ascent in th' face iv th' most gallin' fire I iver knew or heerd iv. But I had a few r-rounds iv gall mesilf an' what cared I? I dashed madly on cheerin' as I wint. Th' Spanish throops was dhrawn up in a long line in th' formation known among military men as a long line. I fired at th' man nearest to me an' I knew be th' expression iv his face that th' trusty bullet wint home. It passed through his frame, he fell, an' wan little home in far-off Catalonia was made happy be th' thought that their riprisintative had been kilt be th' future governor iv New York. Th' bullet sped on its mad flight an' passed through th' intire line fin'lly imbeddin' itself in th' abdomen iv th' Ar-rch-bishop iv Santago eight miles away. This ended th' war.'

" 'They has been some discussion as to who was th' first man to r-reach th' summit iv San Joon hill. I will not attempt to dispute th' merits iv th' manny gallant sojers, statesmen, corryspondints, an' kinetoscope men who claim th' distinction. They ar-re all brave men an' if they wish to wear me laurels they may. I have so manny annyhow that it keeps me broke havin' thim blocked an' irned. But I will say f'r th' binifit iv posterity that I was th' on'y man I see. An' I had a tillyscope.'

"I have thried, Hinnissy," Mr. Dooley continued, "to give you a fair idee iv th' contints iv this remarkable book, but what I've tol' ye is on'y what Hogan calls an outline iv th' principal pints. Ye'll have to r-read th' book ye'ersilf to get a thrue conciption. I haven't time f'r to tell ye th' wurruk Tiddy did in ar-rmin' an' equippin' himsilf, how he fed himsilf, how he steadied himsilf in battle an' encouraged himsilf with a few well-chosen wur-ruds whin th' sky was darkest. Ye'll have to take a squint into th' book ye'ersilf to larn thim things."

"I won't do it," said Mr. Hennessy. "I think Tiddy Rosenfelt is all r-right an' if he wants to blow his hor-rn lave him do it."

"Thrue f'r ye," said Mr. Dooley, "an' if his valliant deeds didn't get into this book 'twud be a long time befure they appeared in Shafter's histhry iv th' war. No man that bears a gredge agin himsilf iver be governor iv a state. An' if Tiddy done it all he ought to say so an' relieve th' suspinse. But if I was him I'd call th' book 'Alone in Cubia.' "

NORA EPHRON

"The Making of Theodore H. White"

Readers over age thirty-five will be amazed by the suggestion that a younger generation may not have the vaguest notion who Theodore H. White was. For the newborn, however, let it be noted that starting in 1960, White chronicled every presidential campaign that came along until his work began to sound like the work of a man who just couldn't take it anymore. Neither could Nora Ephron.

He was alone, as always.

A man who finishes a book is always alone when he finishes it, and Theodore H. White was alone. It was a hot, muggy day in New York when he finished, or perhaps it was a cold, windy night; there is no way to be certain, although it is certain that Theodore H. White was certain of what the weather was like that day, or that night, because when Theodore H. White writes about things, he notices the weather, and he usually manages to get it into the first paragraph or first few pages of whatever he writes. "Hyannis Port sparkled in the sun that day, as did all New England" *(The Making of the President 1960).* "It was hot; the sun was blinding; there would be a moment of cool shade ahead under the overpass they were approaching" *(The Making of the President 1964).* "Thursday had been a cold day of drizzling rain in Manhattan, where Richard Nixon lived" *(The Making of the President 1968).* "I could see the fan of yellow water below shortly before the plane dipped into the overcast" *(The Making of the President 1972).* And now Theodore H. White looked at the opening line of his new book, *Breach of Faith:* "Wednesday dawned with an overcast in Washington—hot, sticky, threatening to rain—July 24th, 1974." It had worked before and it would work again.

White flicked a cigarette ash from his forty-sixth Marlboro of the day and took the last sheet of one hundred percent rag Strathmore parchment typing paper from his twenty-two-year-old IBM Executive typewriter. It was the 19,246,753rd piece of typing paper he had typed in his sixty years. He was tired. He was old and tired. He was also short. But mainly he was tired. He was tired of writing the same book over and over again. He was tired of being taken in, taken in by John F. Kennedy, Lyndon Johnson, Robert Kennedy, General Westmoreland, Richard Nixon, tired of being taken in by every major politician in the last sixteen years. He was tired of being hornswoggled by winners. He was tired of being made to look like an ass, tired of having to apologize in each successive book for the mistakes he had made in the one before. He was tired of being imitated by other journalists, and he was tired of rewriting their work, which had surpassed his own. He was tired of things going wrong, tired of being in the wrong place at the wrong time; the night of the Saturday Night Massacre, for example, he found himself not in the Oval Office but on vacation in the South of France, where he was reduced to hearing the news from his hotel maid. He was tired of describing the people he was writing about as tired.

We must understand how Theodore H. White got to be that way, how he got to be so old and so tired. We must understand how this man grew to have a respect and awe for the institutions of American government that was so overweening as to blind him to the weaknesses of the men who ran them. We must understand how he came to believe that all men in power—even base men—were essentially noble, and when they failed to be noble, it had merely to do with flaws, flaws that grew out of a massive confluence of forces, forces like PR, the burgeoning bureaucracy, television, manipulation and California. We must understand his associates, good men, tired men but good men, men he lunched with every week, men who worked at newsmagazines which had long since stopped printing run-on sentences with subordinate clauses attached to the end. And to understand what has happened to Theodore H. White, which is the story of this column, one would have to go back to earlier years, to the place where it all started.

Time magazine.

That was where it all started. At *Time* magazine. Not everything started at *Time* magazine—Theodore H. White developed his infuriating style of repeating phrases over and over again later in his life, after he had left *Time* magazine—but that is where most of it started. It was at *Time* magazine that White picked up the two overriding devices of newsmagazine writing. The first was a passion for tidbits, for small details, for color. President Kennedy liked to eat tomato soup with sour cream in it for lunch. Adlai Stevenson sunned himself in blue sneakers and blue shorts. Hubert Humphrey ate cheese sandwiches whenever he was in the midst of a crisis.

The second was omniscience, the omniscience that results when a writer has had a week, or a month, or a year to let events sift out, the kind of omniscience, in short, that owes so much to hindsight.

Until 1959, when Theodore H. White began work on the four-hundred-one-page, blue-bound *Making of the President 1960,* no reporter had written a book on a political campaign using these two devices. White did, and his book changed the way political campaigns were covered. He wrote the 1960 campaign as a national pageant, a novelistic struggle for power between two men. He wrote about what they wore and what they ate and what they said behind the scenes. He went to meetings other reporters did not even ask to attend; the participants at the meetings paid scant attention to him. And then, of course, the book was published, became a best seller, and everything began to change.

Change.

Change began slowly, as it always does, and when it began, White was slow to notice it. He covered the 1964 campaign as he had covered the one before; he did not see that all the detail and color and tidbits and dialogue made no difference in that election; the political process was not working in the neat way it had worked four years before, with hard-fought primaries and nationally televised debates and a cliff-hanger vote; the 1964 election was over before it even began. Then he came to 1968, and the change, mounting like an invisible landslide, intensified, owing to a massive confluence of factors. The first was the national press, which began to out-report him. The second was White himself. He no longer went to meetings where he was ignored; he was, after all, Theodore H. White, historian to American Presidential elections. Had he been a student of physics and the Heisenberg uncertainty principle, instead of a student of history and all the Cicero he could cram into his books, he might have understood what was happening. But he did not. The change, the invisible landslide of change, eluded him. He wrote a book about a new Nixon, an easier, more relaxed, more affable Nixon. He missed the point. He missed the point about Vietnam; he missed the point about the demonstrations. Larry O'Brien used to be important; now it was these kids; who the hell were these kids to come along and take politics away from Theodore H. White? He missed the point about the Nixon campaign too. And so, in 1969, came the first great humiliation. A young man named Joe McGinniss, a young man who had gone to low- and mid-level meetings of the Nixon campaign, where the participants had paid him scant attention, produced the campaign book of the year, *The Selling of the President,* and even knocked off Theodore H. White's title in the process. Then, before he knew it, it was 1972, another campaign, another election, and White went through it, like so many other reporters, ignoring Watergate; months later, as he was finishing the 1972 book, he was forced to deal with the escalating scandal; he stuck it in, a paragraph here, a paragraph there, a chapter to wrap it all up, all this sticking out like sore thumbs throughout the manuscript. That year, the best book on the campaign was written not by White but by Timothy Crouse, who had stayed at the fringes, reporting on the press. To make matters worse, Crouse's book, *The Boys on the Bus,* included a long, not entirely flattering section on Theodore H. White, a section in which White complained, almost bitterly, about the turn things had taken. He spoke of the night McGovern won the nomination in Miami:

"It's appalling what we've done to these guys," he told Crouse. "McGovern was like a fish in a goldfish bowl. There were three different network crews at different times. The still photographers kept coming in in groups of five. And there were at least six writers sitting in the corner—I don't even know their names. We're all sitting there watching him work on his acceptance speech, poor bastard. He tries to go into the bedroom with Fred Dutton to go over the list of Vice-Presidents, which would later turn out to be the fuck-up of the century, of course, and all of us are observing him, taking notes like mad, getting all the little details. Which I think I invented as a method of reporting and which I now sincerely regret. If you write about this, say that I sincerely regret it. Who gives a fuck if the guy had milk and Total for breakfast?"

White sat in the Harvard chair given to him by the Harvard Alumni Association and looked with irritation at his new manuscript, *Breach of Faith.* Here it was 1975 and he had a new book coming out. What in Christ was he doing with a book coming out in 1975? He wasn't supposed to have to write the next one until 1977. Theodore H. White shook his close-cropped, black-haired head. It was these damned politicians. He'd spent the best years of his life trying to train these assholes, and they couldn't even stay in office the full four years.

White stared at the title *Breach of faith.* The new book's thesis was that Richard Nixon had breached the faith of the American people in the Presidency; that was what had caused him to be driven from office. But deep down, Theodore H. White knew that the faith Nixon had breached had been his, Theodore H. White's. White was the only American left who still believed in the institution of the Presidency. Theodore H. White was depressed. Any day now, he might have to start work on the next book, on *The Making of the President 1976,* and where would he ever find a candidate who measured up to his own feelings about the United States and its institutions? The questions lay in his brain cells, growing like an invisible landslide, and suddenly Theodore H. White had the answer. He would have to run for President. That was the only way. That was the only way to be sure that the political processes would function the way he believed they ought to. That was the only way he could get all those behind-the-scenes meetings to function properly. That was the only way he could get all those other reporters out of his story. White realized that something very important was happening. And so he did what he always does when he realizes something very important is happening: he called the weather bureau.

It was forty-nine degrees and raining in Central Park.

PETER DEVRIES

"From There to Infinity"

Late Show *fans who've seen Deborah Kerr and Burt Lancaster rolling around in the* surf *in the 1953 movie "From Here to Eternity" will no doubt know that it was based on James Jones's best-selling novel of the same name.*

> We all have a guilt-edged security.
> —Moses.

"Stark romanticism" was the phrase that kept pounding through his head as he knocked on the door of Mama Paloma's, saw the slot opened and the single sloe plum that was Mama Paloma's eye scrutinizing him through the peephole. "Oh, you again," the eye grinned at him, sliding back the bolt of the door. "The girls are all pretty busy tonight but go on up." A dress of sequins that made her look like a fat mermaid with scales three-quarters instead of halfway up tightly encased the mounds of old snow that was her flesh. She glanced down at the must-be-heavy-as-lead suitcase in his hand as she closed the door. "I don't dare ast how many pages you're carting around in that by now," she grinned.

He mounted the steps with that suffocating expectation of men who are about to read their stuff, the nerves in his loins tightening like drying rawhide, the familiar knot hard in his belly. Shifting the suitcase from one hand to the other, his head swam into the densening surf of upstairs conversation, above which the tinkle of the player piano was like spray breaking all-the-time on rocks. Standing in the upper doorway, he reflected how, just as there can be damned senseless pointless want in the midst of plenty, so there can be the acutest loneliness in the midst of crowds. Fortunately, the thought passed swiftly. The whores moved, blatant as flamingos in their colored gowns, among the drinking-grinning men, and his eye ran tremulously swiftly in search of Dorine, gulpingly taking in the room for her figure moving erectly womanly through it all.

"No Princess to listen tonight," Peggy grinned toward him. "The Princess went away."

He could have slapped her. It puzzled him to find that beneath that hard, crusty exterior beat a heart of stone. What was she doing in a place like this? He turned and hurried back down the stairs.

"Come back soon, there's listeners as good as the Princess," Mama Paloma laughed jellily jollily as she let him out into the street.

With Dorine not there he couldn't bear Mama Paloma's, and he didn't know another place. Yet he had to have a woman tonight. Another woman would have to do, any woman.

Colonel Stilton's wife, he thought. Why not? She was from Boston, but there was no mistaking the look of hard insolent invitation she gave him each time she came to the Regimental Headquarters to ask if he knew where the Colonel had been since night before last. He hated Stilton's guts, or would if he, Stilton, had any. Hated that smirk and that single eyebrow always jerking sardonically skeptically up, like an anchovy that's learned to stand on end. Why not transfer out, why be a noncom under that bastard? he asked himself. I'm a noncompoop, he thought. He tried to make a joke of it but it was no good.

He knew where the Colonel lived from the time he'd taken him home stewed. He got out of the cab a block from the house. As he approached it walking, he could see Mrs. Stilton under a burning bulb on the screened terrace with her feet on a hassock, smoking a cigarette. She had on shorts and a sweater. Her slim brown legs like a pair of scissors made a clean incision in his mind. He went up the flagstone walk and rapped on the door.

"What do you want?" she said with the same insolent invitation, not stirring. He was aware of the neat, apple-hard breasts under the sweater, and of the terse, apple-hard invitation in her manner.

"I want to read this to you," he said, trying not to let his voice sound too husky.

"How much have you got in there," her voice knew all about him.

"A quarter of a million words," he said.

She came over and opened the screen door and flipped her cigarette out among the glows of the fireflies in the yard. When she turned back he caught the screen door and followed her inside. She sat down on the hassock and looked away for what seemed an eternity.

"It's a lot to ask of a woman," she said. "More than I've ever given."

He stood there shifting the suitcase to the other hand, the arm-about-to-come-out-of-its-socket ache added to that in his throat, wishing he wouldn't wish he hadn't come. She crossed her arms around her and, with that deft motion only women with their animal confidence can execute, pulled her sweater off over her head and threw it on the floor. "That's what you want, isn't it?" she said.

"You with your pair of scissors," he said. "When you can have a man who's willing to bare his soul." He gritted his teeth with impatience. "Don't you see how much we could have?"

"Come on in." She rose, and led the way inside. Nothing melts easier than ice, he thought, sad. He watched her draw the drapes across the window nook and settle herself back among the cushions. "I'm all yours," she said. "Read."

The female is a yawning chasm, he thought, glancing up from his reading at the lying listening woman. He found and read the passage explaining that, how she was the inert earth, passive potent, that waits to be beaten soft by April's fecundating rains. Rain is the male principle and there are times for it to be interminable: prosedrops into rivulets of sentences and those into streams of paragraphs, these merging into chapters flowing in turn into sectional torrents strong and hard enough to wear gullies down the flanks of mountains. After what seemed an eternity, he paused and she stirred.

"What time is it?" she sat up.

"A quarter to three."

"I never knew it could be like this," she said.

Each knew the other was thinking of Colonel Stilton.

"He never reads anything but *Quick,*" she said, rolling her head away from him.

"The sonofabitch," he said, his fist involuntarily clenching as tears scalded his eyes. "Oh, the rotten sonofabitch!"

"It's no matter. Tell me about you. How did you get like this?"

Bending his head over the manuscript again he readingly told her about that part: how when he was a kid in down-state Illinois his uncle, who had wanted to be a lawyer but had never been able to finish law school because he would get roaring drunk and burn up all his textbooks, used to tell him about his dream, and about his hero, the late Justice Oliver Wendell Holmes, who in those great early days of this country was working on a manuscript which he would never let out of his sight, carrying it with him in a sack even when he went out courting or to somebody's house to dinner, setting it on the floor beside his chair. How his uncle passed this dream on to him, and how he took it with him to the big cities, where you began to feel how you had to get it all down, had to get down everything that got you down: the singing women in the cheap bars with their mouths like shrimp cocktails, the daughters-into-wives of chicken-eating digest-reading middle-class hypocrisy that you saw riding in the purring cars on Park Avenue, and nobody anywhere loving anybody they were married to. You saw that and you saw why. You had it all figured out that we in this country marry for idealistic love, and after the honeymoon there is bound to be disillusionment. That after a week or maybe a month of honest passion you woke up to find yourself trapped with the sow Respectability, which was the chicken-eating digest-reading middle-class assurance and where it lived: the house with the, oh sure, refrigerator, oil furnace and all the other automatic contraptions that snicker when they go on—the well-lighted air-conditioned mausoleum of love. She was a better listener than Fillow, a middle-aged swell who had eight hundred jazz records and who would sit in Lincoln Park in Chicago eating marshmallow out of a can with a spoon with gloves on. Every time he tried to read Fillow a passage, Fillow would say "Cut it out." Fillow was a negative product of bourgeois society just as Stilton with his chicken-eating digest-reading complacence was a positive one, whom his wife had and knew she had cuckolded the minute she had let the suitcase cross the threshold.

"It'll never be the same again, will it?" she said fondly softly, seeing he had paused again.

He read her some more and it was the same. Except that the thing went on so long the style would change, seeming to shift gears of itself like something living a hydramatic life of its own, so that side by side with the well-spent Hemingway patrimony and the continental cry of Wolfe would be the sea-changed long tireless free-form sentences reminiscent of some but not all or maybe even much of Faulkner.

The door flew open and Stilton stood inside the room. His eyes were like two wet watermelon pips spaced close together on an otherwise almost blank plate (under the anchovies one of which had learned to stand on end).

"So," he said. The word sailed at them like a yoyo flung out horizontally by someone who can spin it that way. It sailed for what seemed an infinity and came back at him.

"So yourself," she said. "Is this how long officers' stags last?" she said.

"So he *forced his way in here,*" the Colonel cued her, at the same time talking for the benefit of a six-foot MP who hove into view behind him.

Realization went like a ball bouncing among the pegs of a pinball machine till it dropped into the proper slot in his mind and a bell rang and a little red flag went up reading "Leavenworth." He remembered what he'd heard. That an officer's wife is always safe because all she had to do was call out the single word rape and you were on your way to twenty years.

Why did he just stand there, almost detached? Why wasn't his anger rising from his guts into his head and setting his tongue into action? But what could you say to a chicken-eating digest-reading impediment like this anyhow, who with all the others of his kind had gelded contemporary literature and gelded it so good that an honest book that didn't mince words didn't stand a chance of getting even a smell of a best-seller list?

"This is my affair," he heard her say coolly, after what seemed a particularly long eternity.

The Colonel lighted a cigarette. "I suspected you were having one," they saw him smokingly smirk, "and since Klopstromer was seeing me home from the club I thought he might as well—" He stopped and looked down at the suitcase. "How long does he expect to *stay*?"

"I have something to say," he said, stepping forward.

"*Sir.*"

"I have something to say, sir," he said, picking up the suitcase to heft it for their benefit. "When Justice—"

"You'll get justice," the Colonel snapped as Klopstromer sprang alertly forward and bore down on him and wrested the suitcase from his grasp. "If you won't testify," the Colonel went on to his wife, "then Klopstromer at least will. That he assaulted a superior officer. It won't get him Leavenworth, but by God six months in the stockade will do him good."

"But why?" his wife protested. "You don't understand. He's a writer."

"Maybe," they saw the Colonel smirkingly smoke. The anchovy twitched and stood upright. "Maybe," he said, motioning to Klopstromer to march him out through the door to the waiting jeep, "but he needs discipline."

Briefly Speaking

Classical music is the kind we keep thinking will turn into a tune.

—KIN HUBBARD

SECTION SIX

FAMILY LIFE

A family is a group of people united by nature in unnatural relationships. Evidence that kinship may be a flimsy bond begins with Cain and Abel. Then Jacob stole his brother Esau's birthright. Just because she happened to be his mother, Henry Miller said, explaining why he never had much to do with her, "doesn't mean she doesn't have to earn my respect."

Why is family life such rich comic material? It's because of the obligation imposed on people who may have nothing in common except a gene pool to love or respect each other even when they detest each other. This leads to complications ranging from murderous to farcical.

There is no murder in the pieces that follow, though the urge is sometimes present. These are people struggling to control troubling emotions during the trip from love to marriage to parenthood. Alex Portnoy, perpetual son, stifles in parent prison. Parent Reinhart stifles in liberated-youth prison. Michael Arlen stifles a scream in family Thanksgiving prison.

In its crudest form, family humor became the meat and potatoes of television sitcoms in the 1950s. Though one was called "Father Knows Best," most portrayed Father as a hopeless sap. Millions of children watched them and after growing up were not so quick to marry as their parents had been.

WILLIAM GEIST

"Society Wedding: A Swinging Social Soiree"

This news report of a wedding appeared in the Chicago Tribune some fifteen years ago. The names have been changed to protect the privacy of an old married couple.

For too long, Berwyn-Cicero society has complained of receiving all too little attention vis-à-vis the North Shore, Barrington Hills, Oak Brook, Flossmoor, and other local habitats of high society. We want to do something about this.

The Berwyn-Cicero (B-C, as it is known in fashionable circles) social season opened last weekend with the celebrated nuptials of Mildred Annalee Kelton to Albert Michael Mortone at two o'clock in the afternoon on Saturday, June 2, 1979, in the First Presbyterian Church, River Forest.

Miss Kelton, the daughter of Mr. and Mrs. Peter Kelton of Berwyn, was lovely in a traditional white wedding gown. Her maid of honor, Phyllis Simmons of Cicero, wore a yellow lace gown, with her other attendants in blue lace. The groom, best man, and ushers were resplendent in powder-blue tuxedos from Henry's Formal Wear, Cicero.

Miss Kelton, eighteen, attended Wheeling High School, Wheeling, Illinois, departing prior to completion of degree requirements, and is now, hopefully, between jobs. Mr. Mortone, twenty-five, said that he is legitimately unemployed, receiving compensation from the state of Illinois.

Miss Kelton was given away in holy matrimony by her father in a traditional ceremony, highlighted by usher Frank Bascom of Cicero yelling, "Yahoo!" as the couple exchanged rings. The remaining ten minutes of the ceremony were omitted.

The couple departed the church in a shower of rice in a late-model Chevrolet and were driven to a reception at the respected Berwyn Elks Club.

About one hundred of B-C's smart set attended the reception, dancing to the toneful tunes of an unnamed guitar-accordion-drum band playing pleasurable polkas. Club manager and master of B-C soirees, George Lundgren, chose tablecloths, but no centerpieces, for simple elegance. Lundgren said whiskey, gin, and setups were available. He said the band broke for dinner at 4:30 P.M. as guests dined buffet style on roast beef, broasted chicken, mostaccioli, macaroni salad, and various Jell-O molds.

After dinner, ethnic dancing continued, and at about eight o'clock the traditional fighting commenced. While dancing with the groom's sister, Simone, Mr. Bascom observed his wife touch dancing with the groom's fifteen-year-old brother, Marty.

Mr. Bascom subjected Marty Mortone to physical abuse and threatened severe violence. A check of the social register maintained by the Berwyn Department of Public Safety indicates our Mr. Bascom is a man of his word.

The Mortones are a close, old-line Cicero family, and brother Jerome Mortone laid Mr. Bascom upside the head with a full champagne bottle, according to other prominent guests. At this point several others joined in the fisticuffs, including the groom.

So many, in fact, that the uniformed Berwyn policeman on duty at the wedding reception instructed Mr. Lundgren to call for assistance. Local authorities say it is "customary" to have a policeman at Berwyn wedding receptions, where "fights are quite common."

Two local gendarmes, respondent in dark-blue uniforms, arrived to join the festivities. "The entire place was up for grabs," said one.

Social-scene observers note that this was a truly superlative affair, attended, finally by the entire Saturday night shift of the Berwyn Police Department—the measure of any social occasion.

Brandishing dark, solid-wood nightsticks (absolutely smashing accessories with the blue uniforms), police waded into the boisterous gathering of B-C society.

"I couldn't believe what I saw," said one veteran policeman. "Glasses, champagne bottles, and beer bottles were flying. Everyone in the place was fighting—like a Western movie barroom brawl. They didn't even pay any attention to us." (For the record—the bride and groom and their parents said it was a nice reception ruined by police intervention.)

"When we stepped between people fighting, they turned on us," another policeman said. "It was frightening: a dozen of us against one hundred of them. They'd throw us to the floor, stomp us, and go back to fighting. We couldn't arrest anybody, it was all we could do to hold on to our guns and nightsticks. They threw most of us back down the stairs.

"The bride was getting in her licks, too. Her wedding gown was torn to pieces. The band members had extended their microphone stands as far as they would go and were swinging them like baseball bats to protect themselves from the guests,'' he said.

Police from a local park district, Cicero, and other surrounding communities were called in, about forty to forty-five officers in all. "We restored order, announced that the reception was over, and told the guests to disperse,'' a police spokesman said.

The crowd went outside, where fighting continued. Guns were drawn when one guest flattened two policemen with a table leg.

Passersby reportedly joined in the fighting.

The pugilism continued inside the two paddy wagons and in front of the Berwyn Police Department, where guests not yet under arrest met the police vehicles' arrival.

More than one dozen were hospitalized. Only twelve were arrested, according to authorities, "because we wanted to get out of there while we were still alive.''

A local judge, resplendent in floor-length black robes, set bonds at $5,000 to $15,000 each.

Neck braces and arm slings are the height of fashion this week at the Berwyn Police Department.

A good time was had by all, at what is being called the most exciting B-C social event since last year's Southwest Cook County Chapter 205 of the National Association of Women in Construction's candlelight bowl.

The couple is at home in Cicero following the groom's release from Cook County Jail Tuesday evening. Honeymoon plans have been postponed pending trial.

We wish the young couple all the best—in court, at future B-C welterweight wedding receptions, and in returning those armless, blood-spattered tuxedos to Henry's Formal Wear. We anxiously await the wedding photos.

GROUCHO MARX

"To Irving Hoffman"

1946

Dear Irving:

Between strokes of good fortune, I have been toying with the idea of making you my impending child's godfather. However, before doing this officially, I would like to see a notarized statement of your overall assets. I don't intend to repeat the unhappy experience that befell my parents late in the 19th century.

At that time there was an Uncle Julius in our family. He was five feet one in his socks, holes and all. He had a brown spade beard, thick glasses and a head topped off with a bald spot about the size of a buckwheat cake. My mother somehow got the notion that Uncle Julius was wealthy and she told my father, who never did quite understand my mother, that it would be a brilliant piece of strategic flattery were they to make Uncle Julius my godfather.

Well, as happens to all men, I was finally born and before I could say "Jack Robinson," I was named Julius. At the moment this historic event was taking place, Uncle Julius was in the back room of a cigar store on Third Avenue, dealing them off the bottom. When word reached him that he had been made my godfather, he dropped everything, including two aces he had up his sleeve for an emergency, and quickly rushed over to our flat.

In a speech so moist with emotion that he was blinded by his own eyeglasses, he said that he was overwhelmed by this sentimental gesture on our part and hinted that my future—a rosy one—was irrevocably linked with his. At the conclusion of his speech, still unable to see through his misty lenses, he kissed my father, handed my mother a cigar and ran back to the pinochle game.

Two weeks later he moved in, paper suitcase and all. As time went by, my mother became suspicious and one day, in discussing him with my father, she not only discovered that Uncle Julius seemed to be without funds, but what was even worse, that he owed my father $34.

Since he was only five feet one, my father volunteered to throw him out but my mother advised caution. She said that she had read of many cases where rich men, after living miserly lives, died leaving tremendous fortunes to their heirs.

Uncle Julius remained with us until I got married. By this time, he had the best room in the house and owed my father $84. Shortly after my wedding, my mother finally admitted that Uncle Julius had been a hideous mistake and ordered my father to give him the bum's rush. But Uncle Julius had grown an inch over the years while my father had shrunk proportionately, so he finally convinced my mother that violence was not the solution to the problem.

Soon after this Uncle Julius solved everything by kicking off, leaving me his sole heir. His estate, when probated, consisted of a nine ball that he had stolen from the poolroom, a box of liver pills and a celluloid dickey.

I suppose I should be more sentimental about the whole thing, but it was a severe shock to all of us, and, if I can help it, it's not going to happen again.

Well, Irving, that's the story. If you are interested, let me hear from you as soon as possible and, remember, a financial statement as of today will expedite things considerably.

Regards,
GROUCHO

Briefly Speaking

No man was iver so low as to have rayspict f'r his brother-in-law.

—FINLEY PETER DUNNE

THOMAS BERGER

Excerpt from Vital Parts

At tne end of Chapter One of Vital Parts *Carlo Reinhart has locked himself in the bathroom with binoculars, the better to spy on his next-door neighbor's sixteen-year-old daughter as she undresses. As she fails to appear, his mind wanders. Suddenly he sees "that the girl next door had not only materialized but had, bending and shifting from one leg to the other, whisked off her underpants and now stood, squarely in the frame of the window, shaking them at him and smiling shamelessly." Chapter Two follows.*

To think, Reinhart thought, that this young girl, the daughter of respectability and hard work and enlightened attitudes—both her parents were college graduates—that this young minx had turned whore. In moral outrage he lowered the glasses.

The Swedes, he had read, had evolved a theory that would encourage the natural complements to get together legally: voyeurs and exhibitionists, fags and friends, the yins and yangs of sexual peculiarities, thus satisfying one another and no longer troubling the routine society of bulls and cows who mate in bovine orthodoxy. But what of the weirdo who had once importuned Reinhart, years ago, in a public street and with a young woman on his arm— Reinhart, that is; the queer was alone but well dressed. This fellow's urge was obviously for scandal, not flesh. But why did Reinhart think of inversion while watching the body of a luscious object of heterosexual craving?

Because he understood instantaneously that he wanted only to look and in secret. He did not want her to know that he knew. And that cast of mind of course was deviate.

So he froze. He might have died from a sudden heart attack while trying to close the window against a chill draft which had threatened his old bones. But how explain the binoculars still clutched in his rigid hand? Satellite tracking. Practice for viewing a moonshot. . . . The simple fact was that no excuse would be credible. This truth made him free, and he raised the glasses again.

He now discerned that nothing was expected of him, he was still in safe hiding, the girl indeed smiled towards him but not at him, seeing nothing but the usual solipsist image of her own youth, vigor, and beauty, mirrored in the blankness of everybody else.

She pitched her pants offstage, a movement which caused her firm parts to tremble hardly at all. Reinhart's own trunk had been more tremulous when he tossed his socks aside. In all primary and secondary respects she was full grown, yet not a centimeter, a milligram beyond. She robustly straddled the apex of ripeness. By comparison even the early twenties were already the road to rot.

Reinhart thought his heart might break, but he felt no desire whatever. There was nothing this girl could have done for him but what she was doing, and of that she could not be told, not only by reason of law, social humiliation, and other ugly, essentially irrelevant possibilities, but because self-consciousness would corrupt this glorious and unreflective bestiality. A young girl who thought she knew something was unbearable. She was at her best in a silent movie, and teenlike she was moving though standing still. Life is short, but Reinhart's glasses were long enough even to characterize the dimpled navel in her golden belly. It was mauve. A dot of mole marked her left collarbone, which was no doubt usually revealed in her garb for the summertime streets, yet was the sort of thing that Reinhart saw in nudity, for he was no priapic ape with wet lips and pumping hand.

He did not dwell on the forbidden trio, the funny face of two sore eyes and Vandyke beard so often mocked by lavatory cartoonists. Rather he examined the little shadows of her nostrils, the cupids who grinned in her knees, the extraordinary hips which were at once full and flat, round but self-contained, robust yet in communication of nerve and muscle with even remote extremities, the blunt, dancing fingers, say, which had lately hurled away the wisp of undergarment and now seemed to be talking in the fluency of the deaf-and-dumb alphabet.

Versatile Time had scarcely moved a second in reality while Reinhart's inner clock, deranged, had sped on: the panties were still aloft but beyond his frame. She watched them descend on bed or dresser or floor, to her left. Then looked right, at the interior of what he saw outside as the obscure corner of the house with the darker perpendicular of the drainpipe and a black clump of something at the point where it entered the ground. This latter phenomenon stirred now and proved itself, through sinister undulations against the pale siding, as a stalking cat, and was dismissed from consideration.

The glasses climbed the wall. Another reason for running cold water into the tub was that no steam developed to befog the binoculars: one of the petty but real problems of the Peeping Tom. Sometimes the heat of the July face was enough to do it. Reinhart was a massive sweater, and kept handy a square of what the commercials termed "bathroom tissue" should the lenses need swabbing. He used it now to wipe his under-eyes.

The figment of his surveillance was moving her plump lips, and teen-agers weren't much for gum any more. Also her vision seemed more or less directed now, still into the corner, which, he quickly estimated, was large enough to hold a bed. A chum was staying over. They talked of boys, records, clothes, rot. They brazenly undressed in front of one another, having been reared to find nudity no shame. A bare-boob scene was now de rigueur in commercial movies, and Reinhart had caught a flash of pubic hair in some mannered treatment of contemporary London. Worse, bare dongs adorned the Broadway stage, according to the newsweekly to which he trial-subscribed.

A mild enough manifestation of the change in mores, when a staggering percentage of California high-school girls were pregnant. Yet Reinhart sniffed with a blue nose, by chance smelling the chemical bouquet of the Jonny Mop pads used to clean the johnny bowl. His attitudes had been fixed in another era, a lovely time of hypocrisy when it was a triumph to overwhelm the modesty of which a female was the natural exemplar. For young girls to assume the locker-room insouciance of jockstrap-doffing, crotch-scratching, nail-inspecting athletes would always to him seem heretical.

He had been made that way by wise elders masked as idiots and/or charlatans, the delightful irony of his own youth having been that one defied the established morality with the sense that he would inevitably grow up to impose it someday on another generation. If there were satisfactions in aging, paramount among them surely was restraining the young who came after. Except for the human beings who perished in childhood, this policy was as fair as life would allow and a gain over the practice of lions, say, who shoved the superannuated away from the kill and the mangy old beast, once Lord of the Jungle, chewed his yellow gums for a while and died.

Simba Reinhart shook his mane, then spat out in his hand the three-tusked bridge for which he still owed his dentist, another old schoolfellow, who owned two Cadillacs and recently had sacked his old wife for a new one met at a convention in Atlantic City, no doubt by means of a five-spot slipped to the bellboy. Reinhart knew a hooker when he saw one, or thought he did, until last week, in the city, when hustled, while buying a newspaper, by a nondescript woman attached, by a braided-leather leash, to a panting spaniel. "Would you like to come home with me and help me wash my cocker?" she asked. Of course, she could have been merely one of the cranks who, along with able-bodied panhandlers, self-righteous freaks, and winos, were taking over downtown.

As painful as were the thoughts inspired by the girl's bare body, when she with a jolly lope suddenly left his frame of vision, Reinhart was at once desolated and had his first intimations of sexual desire, typically anachronistic. He also noticed the dental bridge in his palm, and wondered how it got there. He forced it back into the break in the upper-right fence, and felt an exquisite pressure-pain, as if pumpkin seeds had been hammered through the interstices of his remaining natural teeth.

The end of the show. He was not one to linger till the scrubwomen slopped in and turned up the gum-encrusted seats. He had seen what he had come in quest of so many times, and knew the strange feeling which accompanies complete achievement of any kind: the loss of a future. The unseen roommate had probably undressed while he sat head in hands reviewing his day. Yet another ten seconds would not hurt. He had no prospects but TV. The light was still on across the way. Perhaps the guest had perched her little rump on the bed-edge to unroll her knee-high stockings, the ghosts of the teenybop-pers' wintertime boots—little Prussian martinets that they were—and lifted roseate haunches to free the weave from roughened heel and hooking toe, and before his count was done, would appear in the frame to rip off the rest of what she wore, skimpy ribbons at bosom and vee, and flex her pelt at him in turn. She might be the other kind, not the stocky, full, fruity species of the neighbor's daughter, but the tall, attenuated, languid teeny, pubesced but lemon-breasted, boyish-hipped, lean in flank, with long, pointed feet and tawny hair, tendrils of which curled into the hollow of her prominent clavi-cles. Slim, if you like, but deeper in the side view and with buttocks like twin mandolins.

Reinhart, who would gulp any wine and swallow any food he could manage to chew, was a connoisseur in these matters. Ten seconds came and went without incident, and true to the vow he left his post. For a moment the crick in his sacroiliac made him walk like a goose. As with most bathroom windows the sill was four feet above the floor; he had had to prop himself on the wrists of the hands holding the binoculars.

The tub was now three-quarters full of cold water. He turned off the faucet, and with the noise gone, heard the querulous end of a speech from the hall outside.

". . . consideration for others." He recognized it as his wife's, and supplied the missing words *You haven't any.* That she had been talking for some time he might assume. She was attracted to obscuring conditions of sound.

He immediately pulled the plug and as the water left the tub—drop by drop, owing to some obstruction in the drain—he shouted back: "One min-ute!"

The unjust feature of this situation was that another complete bathroom divided the children's bedrooms in the northwards projection of the house, a facility that was seldom used even by those for whom it had been provided and never by anyone in an emergency. As a very young child, Reinhart's daughter, inclined towards carsickness, excess weeping, and odd phobias, had professed to be upset by certain irregularities in the enamel of that tub, which indeed was a factory "second" supplied at a favorable price by the scab plumber who did the work. "It has pimples that scratch my bottom!" was the anguished assertion of Reinhart's secondborn. His son of course stated no reasons whatever for the boycott; even as a little blackguard of eight or ten he was motivated by an undifferentiated malignancy towards his dad. To get him to eat a certain food Reinhart had only to pretend a personal dislike for it, else the child would have died of malnutrition.

At puberty the boy had made a devastating change, taking up Reinhart's precise tastes and corrupting them subtly. He would watch certain of his father's television favorites with the sound turned off, if he commanded the set. If eating deep-fried chicken, the lad would peel off and discard the golden crust. He might also borrow a necktie of Reinhart's and knot it strangely, so that it would never again hang true. At sixteen, when he got his driver's license, he began to do mysterious damage to the car, some of which the keenest mechanic could not identify and correct: at the least, maddening birdlike squeaks which no tightening or greasing would eradicate; at worst, inexplicable seizures in the differential, abrasions down to metal of new brake bands, and so on. Yet not only did he drive circumspectly when under his father's surveillance, which was to be expected—Reinhart himself had so performed as a youth, but once away from Dad gunned and braked the guts out of the '38 Chevvy—but one time when Blaine could not possibly have known he was being watched, Reinhart emerged from a highwayside café to which he had been lifted by an acquaintance, to see his son tool past at a speed less than the limit and slow to a conservative stop at the nearby crossroads.

No doubt the trouble had begun two weeks after Blaine's conception when Genevieve on the first day of her missing period insisted that if it was to be a boy he must be named for her father, one of the few unmitigated scoundrels Reinhart had ever known, perhaps the only, surely the worst.

Reinhart now withdrew from behind the toilet a plumber's suction cup, the kind that, less the stick, was used in the old days of real musicianship to mute a trumpet—the time of Goodman, Basie, the Dorseys, long before the current long-locked, costumed, electronic-toned androgynes had begun the voyage down the Fallopian tubes—and plunged it into the tub water with an enormous gobble of air fleeing hyperhydration. With four or five thrusts he caused the drain to disgorge, as he suspected, an octopus of hair, the origin of which was obvious. Gen and his daughter were dark. Reinhart's own gray-blond locks were regularly clipped short at the barbershop. Blaine was very fair, in fact of so light a hue that nature furnished it only to albinos, of which company he was not a member. This pale mess was a hank from his coiffure, which was not only bleached but shoulder-length.

Very like, indeed, the lovely mane of the houseguest of the girl next door, who as luck would have it was standing in the window, her graceful back to Reinhart, when he picked up the glasses for a valedictory focus before returning the instrument to its bed of laundry. Magically enough, she confirmed his fanciful projection, exceeded it, really, because no imagination is so vivid as the actuality of young flesh: the damask of the supple skin, the pearly summit of her upthrust hip on which rested the upended tulip of her right hand as asymmetrically she stood beneath her shower of gold, slender arm akimbo, innocent of sinew or distension. Quite tall she was and of a glorious grace even in stasis. When she moved, with a subtle rearrangement of her globèd bottom and soft lavender shadows below, bisected by light's wanton yellow finger, pointing up between the slim thighs, when her hair shimmered, her slender shoulders rose and fell in some transitory teeny mirth, Reinhart discarded all control and exhorted the Devil to make her turn. It was little enough in exchange for a soul, even Reinhart's, which was something of a retread.

But the Devil replied, Wait a while, she is so beautiful—*Verweile doch, sie ist so schön,* in his native tongue—and anyway, hell, like any other public housing facility, had a long and hopeless waiting list; you would probably die before you made it. But Reinhart persisted, offering in support his forty-four years as sinner, and reluctantly an invisible but massive diabolic hand reached up from the cellar of the house next door and turned the girl as if she were a figurine. And transformed her sex as well, so that at 180 degrees she proved to be his son.

"You have hounded that boy since he was born," said Genevieve, to whom time had dealt a better hand than to Reinhart, though true enough she was his junior by several years. Short and apparently threatening to turn plump in her early twenties, she had instead acquired several inches of height—which may have been an optical illusion—and lost ten pounds of her youthful weight by the end of the first decade of their marriage. Now, twenty-two anniversaries after the fact, Gen was sharp-featured, spare-figured, and leather-skinned, to put it one way, but handsome, svelte, and flawlessly tanned, to put it the other. Which was to say she had made much the same progress as Reinhart had in the order of familial resemblance; both of them had begun as run-offs of their respective mothers (Reinhart's being muscular) and moved in middle life to favor their fathers.

Gen sat in the corner of the couch, in her usual cloud of smoke. Yet semiannual X-rays showed her lungs were clean, whereas Reinhart's chest often ached though he had given up cigarettes years since.

From his chair Reinhart said: "Look here, this is not the subject for argument, Genevieve. What I am talking about is law. That girl is underage, and Blaine was twenty-one last February." A cold bleak day, the yard spotted with clumps of dirty snow, a bucketful of which Reinhart had gathered to chill an eight-dollar bottle of champagne to salute the new manhood, but Blaine did not come home until the next morning, having had his own party with hyena friends who raved on hashish and amplified music, obscenely mutilated an effigy of the President of the United States, then buggered one another till dawn (for all Reinhart knew).

Until tonight he had never seen a jot of evidence that the boy was not queer. He still found it hard to believe that a girl would accept the sexual attentions of a male whose hair was not only longer than hers but finer, whose body was softer, and whose wardrobe at least as gaudy.

But the legal question was serious. Reinhart in his time had been a frequent law-bender but never a candid breaker of ordinances however unjust. When he himself had enjoyed the favors of an underaged girl it had been in the context of Occupation Berlin, where codes were as yet unformulated.

Gen spat smoke at him. "All right, Mr. Cop," she said through the blue stream. "Get your billyclub and pound the child's head to a bloody jelly, like the pigs did to the youngsters at Columbia who were appealing for a better life. The human body is a beautiful thing, only we have made it filthy with our stinking hypocrisy."

"Genevieve, please don't widen the scope of this discussion. I don't want to get enmired in social theories while my son is naked and in the room of the girl next door with her parents away on vacation. She is a minor person."

"Well, he isn't," said Gen. "Therefore you have no responsibility for him."

"Aw, Gen, Gen."

"I am sure," said Genevieve, as always imperfectly crushing the cigarette butt in the ashtray so that it would smolder and stink for some time to come, "I am sure there is some reasonable explanation if he is there at all, which frankly I don't place any credentials in." She had her own way with idiom. "Blaine told me definitely when he left he was heading for the Heliotrope Thing."

This discothèque occupied the disused movie house in which Reinhart had spent every Sunday afternoon as a boy, watching never-resolved serials and main features in which the cowboy did not kiss a girl, did not even, in the earliest years, sing songs. Later Reinhart had owned a piece of this theater, served as manager, helped to close its doors forever.

"Will you at least then," he asked his wife now, "go and look? Why should I tell such a vile lie?"

"Because you hate Blaine," Genevieve said flatly. "You hate all young people. Youth is hated in this country. Their idols are always shot. No, I will not go and peep through the window like a dirty pervert. I am going to bed now, as I have a job to get up and go to every morning, and if I did not, we would be on relief.''

Gen had developed the stride of a horsewoman or anyway the type used by a bygone generation of film actresses with square shoulders and jodhpured legs, a little black fox-hunting derby atop their heads and married to a man who wore a houndstooth jacket and hairline moustache. Gen's locks had got darker through the years—though Reinhart had never actually caught her dyeing them—and were pulled back into a flat doughnut at the nape. The tension served to keep her face smooth as a drumskin. She cultivated a timeless look that defied estimates of age and was relative to her companions: often she made the nearby young seem callow and those whose years matched her own, elder. And from Blaine, perhaps partly for her own uses though she doted on him, she had picked up the lie that America persecuted its youth, the country in which a teen-ager's allowance might well exceed the wages paid a European for laboring all week, not to mention the income of adult Africans and the child prostitutes of Hong Kong.

However she in no way played fast with the truth when she spoke of her job. Indeed she had one, and without it the Reinharts, at least for the moment, might have been a statistic on the roster of snouts in the public trough. Because of the reversal of roles signified by this state of affairs, Reinhart could not be too harsh with her. Breadwinner Gen deserved to come home to serenity and a hot meal, slippers, and pipe if she wanted them. Until he got going again in business he must speak softly.

Therefore he pulled in the horns which were unseemly on a parasite and blew a kiss at her departing back. He must face this crisis alone. He had a certain history of extremities, as who did not at his age; however, a precedent was lacking in this case. It takes no long deliberation to defend your life from an assailant who would destroy or mutilate it. Had Blaine and/or the neighbor's daughter jumped Reinhart in a dark alley he would instinctively have fought like a tiger. But bare-assed and in bed together they were a much more formidable enemy, and his own position was badly eroded owing on the one hand to the incessant castration of having a son like Blaine, and on the other to his own voyeuristic lech for the girl.

He who as a radiant young man had gone to fight the Nazis was now just another dirty old fascist. Reinhart had volunteered for the Army. Blaine was deferred as a college student and threatened to flee to Canada if the immunity was revoked and he was called to the colors. Reinhart half believed ''we'' should get out of S.E. Asia and with the remaining half-opinion, compounded of TV pictures of Vietcong atrocities, a historical sense of America's world mission created initially by Adolf Hitler's unopposed rise to tyrannical power, and the strident selfish objection of punks who served no cause but nihilism, favored the use of the hydrogen weapon. In less nervous moments he knew the latter of course as the expression of empty bombast, which he allowed himself since in no event was he ever consulted by White House or Pentagon.

He was wont, in heat, to tell Blaine: "Christ, I had to go to a much bigger war. The Japs held the Pacific and the Krauts all of Europe except plucky little England, who swore to fight on the beaches and in the fields until the New World came to redress—"

"Shi-i-i-t," said Blaine in his poisonous, effeminate style of drawing out one-syllabled obscenities. "Why should I be a sucker just because you were?"

And if Genevieve were in attendance, as she always tried to be lest Reinhart become physical with her darling—women and undersized, infirm, and nonviolent kinds of men tended to imply that Reinhart because of his size alone would answer reason with force; thugs like Gino on the other hand enjoyed a conviction that he would respond to their threats with pusillanimous cajolery: both in fact were right, Reinhart being a realist—if Gen were nearby she might at this juncture say. "He's got you there, Carl, ha-HA."

The cruel feature of this was that never could Reinhart have been described as a superpatriot. Indeed, in his youth he had been much more cynical than Blaine. However, if he pointed this out to his son, Blaine would suddenly turn into that flabbiest of philosophers, the young idealist.

Would swing his hair behind his right ear and squeeze his eyes into slits and then release the lids so as to flutter the long lashes while the blue irises swam in self-induced fury and pain and simulated compassion. "You still *are* a cynic about the poor and the blacks and youth and everything that represents change from the rotten system which has made you what you are."

"The system! What the hell have I ever got from it but debts? Am I a rich exploiter of the deprived? And don't tell me anything about Negroes. Before you were born I had a colored friend whom I helped out of several scrapes. For which incidentally I can't remember being thanked. I have been pro-Negro all my life, and in a time when it was not exactly popular."

Blaine wrinkled his long, skinny nose, an appendage the model for which could be found nowhere else on either side of the family. Reinhart might have been suspicious of Gen had Blaine been born so; but in fact as a baby the boy had shown a marked facial resemblance to Reinhart and his nose had actually been modest till puberty. Reinhart's own now was somewhat porcine.

"If I have ever called you fascist, I am sorry," Blaine said. "You are far worse. You are a liberal, Northern style. The Southern type wears a sheet."

Then, as Reinhart lifted his fists in chagrin, Blaine quailed as if about to be struck.

Which indeed put the thought into Reinhart's head and not for the first time that day or this life. But he had never laid a hand on Blaine in twenty-one years. Blaine was legally a man. Reinhart could not get over that. Today, when the young clamored for power as never before, they nevertheless refused to grow up. In spirit a spoiled infant, Blaine was physically far from being a child. There were black shadows under his eyes and bird-tracks in the corners. As an Olympic swimmer he would have been an old man. Without his exaggerated growth of hair he might look thirty; with it he could be seen, through wincing eyes, as a homely woman fighting middle age.

Yet there he was, over in the house next door, impugning the morals of a luscious minor. Reinhart had a dreadful thought, remembering an incident from a pornographic eight-page cartoon book of thirty years ago: a potbellied, balding dad finds young son in garage putting blocks to teen-aged girl, routs son, and climbs on maiden himself. A perfect situation for the unscrupulous, like that of the corrupt cop bursting in on a prostitute and her client. But the only way Reinhart could have managed it, and perhaps not even then, was if the initiative were taken by the girl: "If you won't tell, I'll—" Hardly likely in a shameless bitch who cared so little about publicity as not even to draw the blinds.

He lurched through the hall and into the darkened bedroom, hurting the tender instep of his bare foot on a nasty shoe Genevieve had discarded just inside the door, by blind touch found his street clothes in a chair, and climbed into shirt, trousers, and sockless brogans. Gen was at length established as a dark breathing lump in the oversized bed, bought originally so as to accommodate his large figure but from which he had since been banished on charges of snoring, striking out with brutal fists while his consciousness was lost in dreams, muttering loathsome words, and being unemployed. For some time he had taken his nightly repose upon a studio couch against the windows.

Dressed and back in the living room, his hand on the knob of the front door that projected one, in this tract house, directly into the yard, vestibules and front porches being now as obsolete as he, he hesitated. What would be the use? A rhetorical question on which his self-dialogues so often concluded. Try to borrow more money from Maw, apply for a job with Hal, make a pass at Elaine, attempt to converse with Gen, ask the bank for more time, expect the plumber to be prompt, even anticipate that a ham sandwich would be made with fresh bread and lean meat. What was the use?

You are only beaten if you think so, said Thomas Edison or George Washington or Satchel Paige, as popularly quoted. *But I think so,* said Reinhart. I can't invent a phonograph or lead armies or pitch a sinker. I am just a guy who regardless of what he thought at twenty knows at forty-four only that he will die. It is now grotesque to talk of anything else, especially suicide, which no real loser ever commits because it would deny him the years of pain he so richly deserves.

He threw the lever freeing the brass bar which sealed the door against the entry of militant Negroes bent on massacring white households who had never done them wrong, and stepped out. Too late he saw another person preparing to enter, a girl shorter than he but, in a context relative to her own height and age, quite as stout, so sturdy in fact that their collision was a standoff from which each recoiled in an equal degree.

"Sorry, Winona," he said and backstepped inside.

"Hi, Daddy," said she, from a perspiring pumpkin-face under the proscenium of high wet bangs and skimpy side curtains of her Buster Brown coiffure.

"How was the picture?"

She breathed out heavily and ran a chubby finger through the channel between temple and ear. "Not as good as *The Dead, the Maimed, and the Ravished*. But not bad."

"Isn't it funny they make those Westerns nowadays in Italy?" Reinhart observed, trying to make his mood seem light.

"Italy?" Her soft brown eyes watered. "Are you making fun of me?"

"Now there's no need to cry about that, Winona. They do it for economic reasons, I understand. Italian extras don't cost so much."

She was already in full sob. "But it's supposed to be *Texas*. Oh, that just ruins it." Winona was sixteen years old. With fallen shoulders she went to the couch and dumped herself into the corner spot earlier vacated by Gen, throwing her fat red thighs wide and clasping both chins.

Reinhart reminded her of all the trouble in the world and what was worth tears and what not and gradually she peeped waterily up at him. "You see, darling," he explained. "Even if it had been shot in present-day Texas it would be fictional, because cowboys don't carry guns any more. It's imaginary, anyway. As long as it's believable on its own terms nothing else matters." But she was not yet quite mollified, so he sat down next to her and put his heavy arm around her thick waist. She smelled of clean sweat, rather pleasantly, something like ginger in fact, but no doubt it added to her many social difficulties and he would have liked to find a way to tell her about it without reinciting a despair so hairtrigger as to be set off by disillusionment over a trashy movie.

Winona rubbed her nose. She said: "Just as you begin to like something, you find it is not what you thought it was."

Reinhart stretched his left arm along the top of the sofa, "Yes, dear," said he. "You begin to discover that at your age. And some people never get beyond it." Meaning himself, for one. But the great thing about having a sympathetic child was that by projecting oneself into him or her one could look at universal difficulties in an equilibrium between intimacy and distance. For example, Winona could be considered as himself as a pudgy female of sixteen. At the same time, she was not he but an independent entity. He did not actually bleed if she were wounded, but of course he would willingly have taken any blows directed at her.

On the other hand he could understand why people might want to abuse her: with very little effort they could elicit an expression of pain, succeeding which they naturally found her presence an unbearable reminder of the meanness they had hoped to discharge and forget about. This kept Winona in a state of imbalance. Those companions who tormented and then escaped from her today would welcome her back tomorrow for another episode of the same.

A human condition to which she no doubt referred in her latest comment on the failure of reality and appearance to jibe. This was no new observation.

"Did your friends give you the slip again?" Reinhart asked gently.

"You guessed it." However, Winona had by now returned to her usual phlegmatic state, which was the mask of pride. On her own initiative she complained only of seeing her principles mocked in the area of false animation, like movies, or gross materiality, like cheeseburgers and pizza. Until baited she would never mention her living contemporaries.

"You want to talk about it?" asked Reinhart.

She shrugged, which meant that her father felt the shifting of some seventy-five pounds of her upper body.

"It might help," he said. Or simply recall unpleasantness: one never really knows the soul of another, even one's own offspring. Perhaps in bringing up the subject he was merely joining Winona's persecutors.

She dropped her wet head on his shoulder. "When I came out of the ladies' room they were gone."

Reinhart threw his own legs out upon the carpet to match Winona's position, and looking at his sockless shoes, he said: "They've done that before, haven't they?"

"They *always* do it."

She had her tiresome side. Reinhart raised his voice. "Well, hell, Winona, then you should be prepared. Those who can't remember history are condemned to repeat it. Are you the only one who goes to the bathroom after the picture? You better train yourself to hold it."

She pulled away and said indignantly: "I always get a Coke from the machine on the way in, or a black cherry except that's usually empty I don't know why, because nobody much likes it but me. Beth has Seven-Up and Carol drinks Tab, and sometimes Dodie won't have anything, but generally they all drink as much as I do and really we all go to the ladies' afterward but they take the booths first and I have to wait and——"

"OK," said Reinhart. Somehow Winona had, in a day when other teen-aged girls had the sophistication of courtesans in the Age of Pericles, got herself into a crowd of creeps with nothing better to do postcinematically than practice toilet one-upmanship. But something good came of this in a selfish way: when he thought of Winona and her crowd he could never remember his lust for teen-agers.

"OK," he repeated. "You have a problem. The first thing to do is to identify it. Once that is done you can set about solving it. One, you don't have to give up your soft drink. Two, the john must be visited. Three, you don't want to get involved in a vulgar race for a booth, which would be undignified in a young lady." Also, with her bulk she couldn't run fast; he left that unsaid.

She writhed against his arm. "Ummm. Daddy, this is embarrassing."

"Not to me, Winona," he said quickly. "I see it as an exercise in tactics. Remember how you always beat me at checkers?" Because he let her. "You distract me by sacrificing one of your pieces, thus getting me into a position where you can jump three of mine. Now what I suggest is that before the picture is over, you get up and go to the toilet."

"What's that got to do with checkers?"

"I didn't mean literally. I meant a similar use of the unexpected."

"And miss part of the picture?" Winona wailed.

"Think of it this way," said Reinhart. "You're giving up one thing to get a better."

"You don't know *them*. No matter when it was they would say it was the best part."

Winona had managed to carry losing to a rarefied height of proficiency that Reinhart himself seldom could attain.

"What does it matter what they say?"

"Then why," howled Winona, "have them as friends?" She began to weep again, he saw from the southeast corner of his eye, looking down her cheeks which were also still running with sweat.

"A good question, dear. Friends who are not friendly are not worth much." Reinhart thought bitterly of various inert if not treacherous types for whom he had once entertained affection: few enough, actually, but he was attempting a vicarious projection into his daughter's frame of life. "You are lucky to have discovered that this early. We all die alone, Winona, though we are accompanied when we come into the world. Living is a process of developing independence."

"Easy for you to say," Winona said, settling against him like a bag of sand. "You are big and strong and popular and successful."

There were resplendent joys in having a daughter. At that moment Reinhart shook off the mortal coil: he had spent only half his years, in this era of improved medicine. He could still be anything he wanted, as at twenty. He could even realize Winona's fantastic opinion of him.

But why bother when, for no reason except that he had helped to conceive her, he already wore the crown? Reinhart loved this chubby child who, defying her epoch, refused to mature. He loved her for that, of course, and for her troubles, and for her resemblance to him, and because he had known her all her life, and because she loved him. But several of these same motives, or others of equal substance, also informed his feeling towards Blaine, and Gen too for that matter. He had enough cause to loathe his wife and son, perhaps, but he loved them. The difference was that Winona uniquely refused to confirm his self-hatred.

She deserved to hear him say: "Well, it hasn't always been easy. Daddy has had his knocks like everybody else." She made some comfortable puppy-sound. "The main thing is not to quit, dear, not to lose your hope. Something wonderful may happen at any time, and you should be ready for it." His arm was going to sleep at its broken-wing angle. For years he had worshiped the god of benevolent chance, who had repaid him in such bad fortune that the ringing of a telephone was often a knell and he could not bear to open his mail immediately.

But now he cleaned off his ancient faith for presentation to his daughter, as one might take from the attic an old Flexible Flyer sled with which one had once broken his collarbone, apply new varnish, and pass it on to a young heir. Blaine, who had from the age of twelve onwards an invincible sense of self-possession, had never given him an opportunity to do that.

Subtly disengaging his sleeping arm, Reinhart noticed that Winona was also snoozing. So secure did she feel with her old dad. Her best features were a flawless skin that, though perspiring, did not show a pore, and long, fine lashes, now stuck to her moist lower lids by the sandman. "Does he really come and sprinkle your eyes, Daddy?" Not so many years ago she still asked that, and not before her first menses would she tolerate a Christmas Eve at which Reinhart did not steal in in a Santa suit (into which the last few times there had been no room for both his natural gut and a pillow) and laugh Ho-ho-ho while stuffing her capacious stocking.

She awakened, though, as he levered himself up, freeing the couch of two hundred and sixty-five pounds—he had about a hundred on her when it came to weight—and asked, in terrified suspicion: "Where are you going, Poppy?" She had always called him that at bedtime.

No longer could he seriously consider going next door and accosting Blaine and the girl. By making him feel superior, Winona also invariably weakened his moral resolve. Were he what she thought he was, he should have a lackey do his dirty work. Failing that, forget about it. Anyway, by now Blaine had surely emptied himself, impregnating the girl, and would run off scot-free while her father shot Reinhart: in the head, quickly, was his prayer.

"I thought I might have a little snack," Reinhart said, lumbering towards the kitchen, soon followed by her amble, and the two of them with greedy efficiency transferred many comestibles from the refrigerator to Formica tabletop and proceeded to wade in. Winona polished off a quart of homogenized milk and two and a half peanut-butter-and-pickle sandwiches while Reinhart cooked for each of them a one-eyed man, an egg fried into a hole in a slice of white bread. He washed his down with two sixteen-ounce cans of beer.

Winona loyally stuck by him while he washed the skillet, going to sleep again at the table, with a milk-moustache. Looking at her sweet, guileless face, Reinhart remembered how in earlier years she would trot to meet him at the door when he came home, and he would pick her up high and swing her around and require at that moment no further justification for life. He wished he could still carry her to bed. As it stood she was burden enough merely to steer down the hall. A large rag-doll buffoon lay on her pillow. ''G'night, Poppy,'' she murmured as he kissed her forehead. ''I love you.''

L. Rust Hills

''How to Eat an Ice-Cream Cone''

Before you even get the cone, you have to do a lot of planning about it. We'll assume that you lost the argument in the car and that the family has decided to break the automobile journey and stop at an ice-cream stand for cones. Get things straight with them right from the start. Tell them that there will be an imaginary circle six feet away from the car, and that no one—man, woman, or especially child—will be allowed to cross the line and reenter the car until his ice-cream cone has been entirely consumed and he has cleaned himself up. Emphasize: Automobiles and ice-cream cones don't mix. Explain: Melted ice cream, children, is a fluid that is eternally sticky. One drop of it on a car-door handle spreads to the seat covers, to trousers, and thence to hands, and then to the steering wheel, the gear shift, the rear-view mirror, all the knobs of the dashboard—spreads everywhere and lasts forever, spreads from a nice old car like this, which might have to be abandoned because of stickiness, right into a nasty new car, in secret ways that even scientists don't understand. If necessary, even make a joke: ''The family that eats ice-cream cones together, sticks together.'' Then let their mother explain the joke and tell them you don't mean half of what you say, and no, we won't be getting a new car.

Blessed are the children who always eat the same flavor of ice cream or always know beforehand what kind they will want. Such good children should be quarantined from those who say "I want to wait and see what flavors there are." It's hard to just listen, while a beautiful young child who has always been perfectly happy with a plain vanilla ice-cream cone is subverted by a young schoolmate who has been invited along for the weekend, a pleasant and polite child, perhaps, but spoiled by permissive parents and flawed by an overactive imagination. This schoolmate has a flair for contingency planning: "Well, I'll have banana, if they have banana, but if they don't have banana, then I'll have peach, if it's fresh peach, and if they don't have banana or fresh peach, I'll see what else they have that's like that, like maybe fresh strawberry or something, and if they don't have that or anything like that that's good, I'll just have chocolate marshmallow chip or chocolate ripple or something like that." Then—turning to one's own once simple and innocent child, now already corrupt and thinking fast—the schoolmate invites a similar rigmarole: "What kind are *you* going to have?"

I'm a great believer in contingency planning. But none of this is realistic. Few adults, and even fewer children, are able to make up their mind beforehand what kind of ice-cream cone they'll want. It would be nice if they could be all lined up in front of the man who's making up the cones and just snap smartly, when their turn came, "Strawberry, please," "Vanilla, please," "Chocolate, please." But of course it never happens like that. There is always a great discussion, a great jostling and craning of necks and leaning over the counter to see down into the tubs of ice cream, and much consultation— "What kind are *you* having?"—back and forth, as if that should make any difference.

Humans are incorrigibly restless and dissatisfied, always in search of new experiences and sensations, seldom content with the familiar. It is this, I think, that accounts for others wanting to have a taste of your cone, and wanting you to have a taste of theirs. "Do have a taste of this fresh peach, it's delicious," my wife used to say to me, very much (I suppose) the way Eve wanted Adam to taste her delicious apple. An insinuating look of calculating curiosity would film my wife's eyes—the same look those beautiful, scary women in those depraved Italian films give a man they're interested in. "How's *yours?*" she would say. For this reason, I always order chocolate chip now. Down through the years, all those close enough to me to feel entitled to ask for a taste of my cone—namely wife and children—have learned what chocolate chip tastes like, so they have no legitimate reason to ask me for a taste. As for tasting other people's cones, never do it. The reasoning here is that if it tastes good, you'll wish you'd had it; if it tastes bad, you'll have had a taste of something that tastes bad; if it doesn't taste either good or bad, then you won't have missed anything. Of course no person in his right mind ever *would* want to taste anyone else's cone, but it is useful to have good, logical reasons for hating the thought of it.

Another important thing. Never let the man hand you the cones of others. Make him hand each one to each kid individually. That way you won't get disconcerting tastes of butter pecan and black raspberry on your own chocolate chip. And insist that he tell you how much it all costs and settle with him *before* he hands you your own cone. Make sure everyone has got paper napkins and everything *before* he hands you your own cone. Get *everything* straight before he hands you your own cone.

Then, when the moment finally comes, reach out and take it from him. Strange, magical, *dangerous* moment! Consider what it is that you are about to be handed: It is a huge irregular mass of ice cream, faintly domed at the top from the metal scoop that dug it out and then insecurely perched it on the uneven top edge of a hollow inverted cone made out of the most brittle and fragile of materials. Clumps of ice cream hang over the side, very loosely attached to the main body. There is always much more ice cream than the cone could hold, even if the ice cream were tamped down into the cone, which of course it isn't. And the essence of ice cream is that it melts. It doesn't just stay there teetering in this irregular, top-heavy mass, it also *melts*. And it melts fast. And it doesn't just melt, it melts into a stickiness that cannot be wiped off. The only thing one person could hand to another that might possibly be more dangerous is a live hand grenade on which the pin had been pulled five seconds earlier. And of course if anybody offered you that, you could say, "Oh. Uh, well—no thanks."

Ice-cream men handle cones routinely, and are inured. They are like professionals who are used to handling sticks of TNT, their movements quick and skillful. An ice-cream man may attempt to pass a cone to you casually, almost carelessly. Never accept a cone on this basis! Keep your hand at your side, overcoming the instinct by which everyone's hand goes out—almost automatically—whenever he is proffered something delicious and expected. The ice-cream man will look up at you, startled, questioning. Lock his eyes with your own, and *then,* slowly, calmly, and above all, deliberately, take the cone from him.

Grasp the cone firmly but gently between thumb and forefinger, two thirds of the way up. Then dart swiftly away to an open area, away from the jostling crowd at the stand. Then take up the classic ice-cream-cone-eating stance: feet from one to two feet apart, body bent forward from the waist at a twenty-five-degree angle, right elbow well up, right forearm horizontal, at a level with your collarbone and about twelve inches from it. But don't start eating yet! Check first to see what emergency repairs may be necessary.

Immediate action is sometimes needed on three fronts at once. Frequently the ice cream will be mounted on the cone in a way that is perilously lopsided. This requires immediate corrective action to move it back into balance—a slight pressure downward with the teeth and lips to seat the ice cream more firmly in and on the cone—but not so hard, of course, as to break the cone. On other occasions, gobs of ice cream will be hanging loosely from the main body, about to fall to the ground (bad) or onto one's hand (far, far worse). This requires instant action too: snapping at the gobs with the split-second timing of a frog in a swarm of flies. But sometimes trickles of ice cream will already (already!) be running down the cone toward one's fingers, and one must quickly raise the cone, tilting one's face skyward, and lick with an upward motion to push the trickles away from the fingers and (as much as possible) into the mouth.

Which to do first? Every ice-cream cone is like every other ice-cream cone in that it has the potential to present all three problems, but each ice-cream cone is paradoxically unique in that it will present the problems in a different order of emergency, and hence require a different order of solutions. And it is (thank God!) an unusual ice-cream cone that will present all three problems in *exactly* the same degree of emergency. It is necessary to make an instantaneous judgment as to which of the basic three emergencies—lopsided mount, dangling gobs, already running trickles—presents the most immediate danger and then *act!* Otherwise the whole thing will be a mess before you've even tasted it.

In trying to make wise and correct decisions about the ice-cream cone in your hand, you should always try to keep your ultimate objective in mind. The first objective is to get the cone under control. Secondarily, one will want to eat the cone calmly and with pleasure. Real pleasure, of course, lies not simply in enjoying the taste of the ice-cream cone, but in eating it *right,* which is where the ultimate objective comes in.

Let us assume that you have darted to your open space and made your necessary emergency repairs. The cone is still dangerous, of course—still, so to speak, "live." But you can now proceed with it in an orderly fashion. First revolve the cone through the full 360 degrees, turning the cone by moving the thumb away from you and the forefinger toward you, so the cone moves counterclockwise. Snap at the loose gobs of ice cream as you do this. Then, with the cone still "wound," which will require the wrist to be bent at the full right angle toward you, apply pressure with the mouth and tongue to accomplish overall realignment, straightening and settling the whole mess. Then, unwinding the cone back through the full 360 degrees, remove any trickles of ice cream. Now, have a look at the cone. Some supplementary repairs may be necessary, but the cone is now defused.

At this point, you can risk a glance around you to see how badly the others are doing with their cones. Then, shaking your head with good-natured contempt for the mess they're making, you can settle down to eating yours. This is done by eating the ice cream off the top, at each bite pressing down cautiously, so that the ice cream settles farther and farther into the cone, being very careful not to break the cone.

If these procedures are followed correctly, you should shortly arrive at the ideal, your ultimate objective, the way an ice-cream cone is always pictured as being, but never actually is when it is handed to you. The ice cream should now form a small dome whose large circumference exactly coincides with the large circumference of the cone itself: a small skullcap that fits exactly on top of a larger, inverted dunce cap.

Like the artist, who makes order out of chaos, you have taken an unnatural, abhorrent, irregular, chaotic form like this: and from it you have sculpted an ordered, ideal shape that might be envied by Praxiteles or even Euclid:

Now at last you can begin to take little nibbles of the cone itself, being very careful not to crack it. Revolve the cone so that its rim remains level as it descends, while you eat both ice cream and cone. Because it is in the geometrical nature of things, the inverted cone shape, as you keep nibbling the top off it, still remains a cone *shape*; and because you are constantly reforming with your tongue the little dome of ice cream on top, it follows in logic—and in actual practice, if you are skillful and careful—that as you eat the cone on down it continues to look exactly the same, so that at the very end you will hold between your thumb and forefinger a tiny, idealized replica of an ice-cream cone, a harmless thing perhaps an inch high.

Then, while the others are licking their sticky fingers, preparatory to wiping them on their clothes, or going back to the ice-cream stand for more paper napkins to try to clean themselves up—*then* you can hold the miniature cone up for everyone to see, and pop it gently into your mouth.

ARTEMUS WARD

"A Hard Case"

We have heard of some very hard cases since we have enlivened this world with our brilliant presence. We once saw an able-bodied man chase a party of little schoolchildren and rob them of their dinners. The man who stole the coppers from his deceased grandmother's eyes lived in our neighborhood, and we have read about the man who went to church for the sole purpose of stealing the testaments and hymn-books. But the hardest case we ever heard of lived in Arkansas. He was only fourteen years old: One night he deliberately murdered his father and mother in cold blood, with a meat-axe. He was tried and found guilty. The Judge drew on his black cap, and in a voice choked with emotion asked the young prisoner if he had anything to say before the sentence of the Court was passed on him. The court-room was densely crowded and there was not a dry eye in the vast assembly. The youth of the prisoner, his beauty and innocent looks, the mild lamblike manner in which he had conducted himself during the trial—all, all had thoroughly enlisted the sympathy of the spectators, the ladies in particular. And even the Jury, who had found it to be their stern duty to declare him guilty of the appalling crime—even the Jury now wept aloud at this awful moment. "Have you anything to say?" repeated the deeply moved Judge. "Why, no," replied the prisoner, "I think I haven't, though I hope yer Honor will show some consideration FOR THE FEELINGS OF A POOR ORPHAN!" The Judge sentenced the perfect young wretch without delay.

BARBARA EHRENREICH

"Stop Ironing the Diapers"

I was saddened to read, a few weeks ago, that a group of young women is planning a conference on that ancient question: is it possible to raise children and have a career at the same time? A group of young *men*—now that would be interesting. But I had thought that among women the issue had been put to rest long ago with the simple retort, Is it possible to raise children *without* having some dependable source of income with which to buy them food, clothing, and Nintendo?

Of course, what the young women are worried about is whether it's possible to raise children *well* while at the same time maintaining one's membership in the labor force. They have heard of "quality time." They are anxious about "missing a stage." They are afraid they won't have the time to nudge their offsprings' tiny intellects in the direction of the inevitable SATs.

And no wonder they are worried: while everything else in our lives has gotten simpler, speedier, more microwavable and user-friendly, child-raising seems to have expanded to fill the time no longer available for it. At least this is true in the trendsetting, postyuppie class, where it is not uncommon to find busy young lawyers breast-feeding until the arrival of molars, reserving entire weekdays for the company of five-year-olds, and feeling guilty about not ironing the diapers.

This is not only silly but dangerous. Except under the most adverse circumstances—such as homelessness, unsafe living conditions, or lack of spouse and child care—child-raising was not *meant* to be a full-time activity. No culture on earth outside of mid-century suburban America has ever deployed one woman per child without simultaneously assigning her such major productive activities as weaving, farming, gathering, temple maintenance, and tent building. The reason is that full-time, one-on-one child-raising is not good for women *or* children. And it is on the strength of that anthropological generalization, as well as my own two decades of motherhood, that I offer you my collected tips on *how to raise your children at home in your spare time.*

1. *Forget the "stages."* The women who are afraid to leave home because they might "miss a stage" do not realize that all "stages" last more than ten minutes. Sadly, some of them last fifteen years or more. Even the most cursory parent, who drops in only to change clothes and get the messages off the answering machine, is unlikely to miss a "stage." Once a "stage" is over—and let us assume it is a particularly charming one, involving high-pitched squeals of glee and a rich flow of spittle down the chin—the best thing you can do is *forget it* at once. The reason for this is that no self-respecting six-year-old wants to be reminded that she was once a fat little fool in a high chair; just as no thirteen-year-old wants to be reminded that she was ever, even for a moment, a six-year-old.

I cannot emphasize this point strongly enough: the parent who insists on remembering the "stages"—and worse still, bringing them up—risks turning that drool-faced little darling into a *lifelong enemy.* I mean, try to see it from the child's point of view: suppose you were condemned to being two and a half feet tall, unemployed, and incontinent for an indefinite period of time. Would you want people reminding you of this unfortunate phase for the rest of your life?

2. *Forget "quality time."* I tried it once on May 15, 1978. I know because it is still penciled into my 1978 appointment book. "Kids," I announced, "I have forty-five minutes. Let's have some quality time!" They looked at me dully in the manner of rural retirees confronting a visitor from the Census Bureau. Finally, one of them said, in a soothing tone, "Sure, Mom, but could it be after *Gilligan's Island?*"

The same thing applies to "talks," as in "Let's sit down and have a little talk." In response to that—or the equally lame "How's school?"—any self-respecting child will assume the demeanor of a prisoner of war facing interrogation. The only thing that works is *low-quality* time: time in which you—and they—are ostensibly doing something else, like housework. Even a two-year-old can dust or tidy and thereby gain an exaggerated sense of self-importance. In fact, this is the only sensible function of housework, the other being to create the erroneous impression that you do not live with children at all.

Also, do not underestimate the telephone as a means of parent-child communication. Teenagers especially recognize it as an instrument demanding full disclosure, in infinite detail, of their thoughts, ambitions, and philosophical outlook. If you want to know what's on their minds, call them from work. When you get home, they'll be calling someone else.

3. *Do not overload their intellects.* Many parents, mindful of approaching nursery-school entrance exams, PSATs, GREs, and so forth, stay up late into the night reading back issues of *Scientific American* and the *Cliff's Notes* for the *Encyclopaedia Britannica.* This is in case the child should ask a question, such as "Why do horses walk on their hands?" The *overprepared* parent answers with a

twenty-minute disquisition on evolution, animal husbandry, and DNA, during which the child slinks away in despair, determined never to ask a question again, except possibly the indispensable "Are we there yet?"

The part-time parent knows better, and responds only in vague and elusive ways, letting her voice trail off and her eyes wander to some mythical landscape, as in: "Well, they don't when they fight. . . . No, then they rear up. . . . Or when they fly . . . like Pegasus . . . mmmm." This system invariably elicits a stream of eager questions, which can then be referred to a more reliable source.

4. *Do not attempt to mold them.* First, because it takes too much time. Second, because a child is not a salmon mousse. A child is a temporarily disabled and stunted version of a larger person, whom you will someday know. Your job is to help them overcome the disabilities associated with their size and inexperience so that they get on with being that larger person, and in a form that you might *like* to know.

Hence the part-time parent encourages self-reliance in all things. For example, from the moment my children mastered Pidgin English, they were taught one simple rule: Never wake a sleeping adult. I was mysterious about the consequences, but they became adept, at age two, at getting their own cereal and hanging out until a reasonable hour. Also, contrary to widespread American myth, no self-respecting toddler enjoys having wet and clammy buns. Nor is the potty concept alien to the one-year-old mind. So do not make the common mistake of withholding the toilet facilities until the crisis of nursery-school matriculation forces the issue.

5. *Do not be afraid they will turn on you, someday, for being a lousy parent.* They *will* turn on you. They will also turn on the full-time parents, the cookie-making parents, the Little League parents, and the all-sacrificing parents. If you are at work every day when they get home from school, they will turn on you, eventually, for being a selfish, neglectful careerist. If you are at home every day, eagerly awaiting their return, they will turn on you for being a useless, unproductive layabout. This is all part of the normal process of "individuation," in which one adult ego must be trampled into the dust in order for one fully formed teenage ego to emerge. Accept it.

Besides, a part-time parent is unlikely to ever harbor that most poisonous of all parental thoughts: "What I gave up for you. . . !" No child should have to take the rap for wrecking a grown woman's brilliant career. The good part-time parent convinces her children that they are positive assets, without whose wit and insights she would never have gotten the last two promotions.

6. *Whether you work outside the home or not, never tell them that being a mommy is your "job."* Being a mommy is a relationship, not a profession. Nothing could be worse for a child's self-esteem than to think that you think that being with her is *work.* She may come to think that you are involved in some obscure

manufacturing process in which she is only the raw material. She may even come to think that her real mom was switched at birth, and that you are the baby-sitter. Which leads to my final tip:

7. Even if you are not a part-time parent, even if you haven't the slightest intention of entering the wide world of wage earning, *pretend that you are one.*

Erma Bombeck

Four Dialogues

[Dialogue between a mother who was told having a daughter drive would be a blessing and a daughter who up until now believed everything a mother did she did out of love]

MOTHER: I'm not a well woman, Debbie. You know that. After the last baby, fifteen years ago, the doctor said I would experience periods of tension and depression. I am tense and depressed now. What are you doing?

DEBBIE: Putting the key in the switch.

MOTHER: DON'T TOUCH A THING IN THIS CAR UNTIL I TELL YOU TO. First, I want you to relax. You cannot drive a car when your hands are gripped around the door handle and the whites of the knuckles are showing.

DEBBIE: You're the one clutching the door handle.

MOTHER: That's what I said. Just relax and put all the anxieties about driving out of your mind. Forget that behind the wheel of this car you are a potential killer. That you are maneuvering a ton of hard, cold steel which you can wrap around a telephone pole just by closing your eyes to sneeze. Are you relaxed?

DEBBIE: I think so.

MOTHER: All right now. Let's go over the check list. Do you have flares in your trunk for when you get a flat tire?

DEBBIE: Yes.

MOTHER: Do you have a dime so you can call AAA when the motor stops dead on you?

DEBBIE: Yes.

MOTHER: Do you have your license so you can show it to the nice officer when he stops you for violating something?

DEBBIE: Yes, Mother.

MOTHER: All right then. Just turn the key and at the same time step on the accelerator.

DEBBIE: Aren't you going to fasten your seat belt?

MOTHER: Are you crazy? I may want to leave in a hurry. Let's get on with it. Just gently touch the accelerator.

DEBBIE: Like this?

MOTHER: HOLD IT! STOP THE CAR! Let us get one thing straight. The radio has to be off. There is not room in this car for Dionne Warwick, you and me. One of us has to go. You're driving. It can't be you. I'm supervising. It can't be me. Dionne is singing. She is expendable. Now, just relax and push on the accelerator. Any idiot can drive. I do it every day. Just ease along, unwind, hang loose and don't think about the drunk over the hill waiting to slam into you. What are you doing?

DEBBIE: Stopping the car.

MOTHER: What for?

DEBBIE: There's a stop sign.

MOTHER: Why are you stopping back here? That stop sign is forty feet away, for crying out loud. Pull up. Pull up. Give it a little gas. Go ahead. NO, WAIT! Do you realize you almost sent me sailing through the windshield?

DEBBIE: I guess I'm not used to the brakes yet. I'm sorry.

MOTHER: I know. So was Sylvia's daughter. Remember I told you about her? Her MOTHER was teaching her how to drive. She took off so fast she gave her mother a whiplash. I think she's out of traction now. Her daughter is wonderful, though. Never complains when she has to drive her mother to the doctor or adjust her braces. Now then, where were we? It looks all right. Just sneak out and . . . YOU'RE TOO CLOSE TO MY SIDE OF THE ROAD. We're all tensed up. Maybe if we pulled over to the curb here and relaxed a bit. You're doing fine. It's just that you lack experience. Like, when you meet a car you have to remember that anything on his side of the line belongs to him. We can't be greedy, can we? Are you relaxed? Good. Just put your hand out and enter the stream of traffic. Not too fast now.

DEBBIE: But . . .

MOTHER: If they want to go over twenty-five miles an hour, let 'em pass. The cemeteries are full of drivers who passed.

DEBBIE: Do you suppose you could show me how to park?

MOTHER: To what?

DEBBIE: To park.

MOTHER: There's nothing to it. You just go to the shopping center and make a small right angle and there you are. When your tires bump the concrete island, stop.

DEBBIE: No, I mean parallel park between two other cars. One in front and one in back.

MOTHER: Where did you hear talk like that? You're driving ten minutes and already you want to get cute with it. It sounds like a wonderful way to get your fenders dented, missy.

DEBBIE: Our Driver's Ed teacher says that's part of the test.

MOTHER: So the Driver's Ed teacher is smarter than your mother. Then why isn't he sitting here getting stomach cramps? That's the trouble with teachers today. No guts. I think we're getting tired, Debbie. I have a headache and an acid stomach. Let's head for home. There's a pamphlet I want you to read on "Highway Statistics Compiled on a Labor Day Weekend by the New Jersey Highway Patrol."

[Dialogue between a daddy who was instructed to check out the driving ability of his wife's reckless daughter and daddy's little girl]

DEBBIE: You don't mind if I play the radio, do you, Daddy?

DADDY: Ummmmmmmmm.

DEBBIE: Want me to go over the check list?

DADDY: Neh.

DEBBIE: Could I also dispense with "Mother, may I?" every time I shift gears?

DADDY: Sure.

DEBBIE: Want to test me on the "Highway Statistics Compiled on a Labor Day Weekend by the New Jersey Highway Patrol?"

DADDY: No. You're doing fine, dear. Wake me when we get home. Szzzzzzzzzzzzz.

[Dialogue between a father who regards his car as a mistress and a son who is moving in on his territory]

FATHER: Do you know how long it took me to get a car of my own?

RALPH: You were twenty-eight years old.

FATHER: I was twenty-eight years old, boy, before I sat behind the wheel of my first car. Got my first pair of long trousers that same year. And I apprecia . . . I wish to heavens you'd stop making those noises.

RALPH: What noises?

FATHER: You sound like the sound track from the Indianapolis 500. Sitting around shifting imaginary gears and making those racing sounds. It makes your mother nervous. Now, first off, before we even start the motor I want to familiarize you with the mechanics of the car. (Lifting hood.)

RALPH: Okay.

FATHER: Here's the motor . . . this big thing over here. This gizmo is the cooling system and the big square box over there is the battery. Understand so far?

RALPH: You got a real doggie here, Dad. Boy, if it were my car I'd put a spoiler in the front and back to hold the car down, and a four-barreled carburetor . . . maybe even a super charger. Then I'd put slicks on the back wheels for a faster getaway and this old buggy would be out of sight. Incidentally, Dad, you could use some work on your points.

FATHER: Get in the car, Ralph. And pick that chewing gum wrapper off the floor. Any questions before we get on with the driving?

RALPH: I hope you're not going to get sore or anything. It's not that I'm too proud to drive a heap around but could you take out the dog in the rear window whose eyeballs light up red and green every time you touch the brakes?

FATHER: Now see here, boy, your mother bought me that for my birthday and I have no intention of taking it out of the car. It would break her heart. And what do you mean with that ''heap'' crack?

RALPH: My buddy, Steve, has a vet four-speed, tri-power with mag wheels, Fiberglas body and four-wheel disc brakes.

FATHER: Well, there's a lot of it going around these days. You'll notice over here is the glove compartment. Know your glove compartment. You'll find everything you need here for emergencies. Here's a map of the state, a cloth for wiping moisture off the inside of the windows, a box of nose tissue, a pencil, a pad and . . . YOUR GLASSES. That's the third time this month. You know it's immaturity like this that makes me doubt whether or not you are old enough to drive a car. And while I'm about it: What are you going to do about your rusty bicycle?

RALPH: Dad, could we get on with the driving lesson?

FATHER: Don't use that tone with me, boy. You probably think you got a pigeon sitting next to you. You're not fooling around with the typically square parent. What would you say if I told you I knew what ''laying a patch'' meant? Huh? I know what I'm dealing with. The insurance companies know what they're doing when they set the highest rates for young boy drivers.

RALPH: In a few months I'll have a car of my own. I've been saving for three years.

FATHER: How much do you have saved?

RALPH: $27.12.

FATHER: That dog with the traffic light eyeballs in the rear window cost more than that.

RALPH: All the guys get heaps and fix them up.

FATHER: We'll see how well you drive this one.

RALPH: Okay, Dad, hang on.

FATHER: Look, son, this isn't a test run for Platformate. Slow down. You're bruising the tires. And watch out for that car. Defensive driving, boy. That's the name of the game. It's the only way anyone can survive on the highways these days. And don't race the motor. Wait until she shifts into drive by herself.

RALPH: Well, Dad, what do you think?

FATHER (LOOKING ASHEN): Take me home. I have never seen such an abuse to a car in my life. And slow down. You're driving a lady, boy, and don't you forget it.

[Dialogue between a mother and her misunderstood driver son]

MOTHER: You remembered to open the door for your mother.

RALPH: It's nothing.

MOTHER: Remember, young man, nothing fancy.

RALPH: Don't worry. You're not nervous and high strung like Dad. Hey, look at the Daytona 500 and behind it the Duster 340.

MOTHER: Where? Where?

RALPH: Over there. Waiting for the light to change.

MOTHER: Oh.

RALPH: A fella at school has a new TT 500 and another one a GTX. Dad wouldn't understand any of this. He thinks a goat is an animal with whiskers.

MOTHER: Isn't he a scream?

RALPH: Mom, do you suppose you could get Dad to take that miserable dog that lights up out of the rear window?

MOTHER: Of course. I can't imagine where he got such a corny thing in the first place. Probably something he got with a lube job.

RALPH: You're groovy, Mom.

MOTHER: It's nothing. Drive.

MICHAEL ARLEN

"Ode to Thanksgiving"

IT IS TIME, at last, to speak the truth about Thanksgiving, and the truth is this. Thanksgiving is really not such a terrific holiday. Consider the traditional symbols of the event: Dried cornhusks hanging on the door! Terrible wine! Cranberry jelly in little bowls of extremely doubtful provenance which everyone is required to handle with the greatest of care! Consider the participants, the merrymakers: men and women (also children) who have survived passably well throughout the years, mainly as a result of living at considerable distances from their dear parents and beloved siblings, who on this feast of feasts must apparently forgather (as if beckoned by an aberrant Fairy Godmother), usually by circuitous routes, through heavy traffic, at a common meeting place, where the very moods, distempers, and obtrusive personal habits that have kept them all happily apart since adulthood are then and there encouraged to slowly ferment beneath the cornhusks, and gradually rise with the aid of the terrible wine, and finally burst forth out of control under the stimulus of the cranberry jelly! No, it is a mockery of a holiday. For instance: *Thank you, O Lord, for what we are about to receive.* This is surely not a gala concept. There are no presents, unless one counts Aunt Bertha's sweet rolls a present, which no one does. There is precious little in the way of costumery: miniature plastic turkeys and those witless Pilgrim hats. There is no sex. Indeed, Thanksgiving is the one day of the year (a fact known to everybody) when all thoughts of sex completely vanish, evaporating from apartments, houses, condominiums, and mobile homes like steam from a bathroom mirror.

Consider also the nowhereness of the time of year: the last week or so in November. It is obviously not yet winter: winter, with its death-dealing blizzards and its girls in tiny skirts pirouetting on the ice. On the other hand, it is certainly not much use to anyone as fall: no golden leaves or Oktoberfests, and so forth. Instead, it is a no-man's-land between the seasons. In the cold and sobersides northern half of the country, it is a vaguely unsettling interregnum of long, mournful walks beneath leafless trees: the long, mournful walks following the midday repast with the dread inevitability of pie following turkey, and the leafless trees looming or standing about like eyesores, and the ground either as hard as iron or slightly mushy, and the light snow always beginning to fall when one is halfway to the old green gate—flecks of cold, watery stuff plopping between neck and collar, for the reason that, it being not yet winter, one has forgotten or not chosen to bring along a muffler. It is a corollary to the long, mournful Thanksgiving walk that the absence of this muffler is quickly noticed and that four weeks or so later, at Christmastime, instead of the Sony Betamax one had secretly hoped the children might have chipped in to purchase, one receives another muffler: by then the thirty-third. Thirty-three mufflers! Some walk! Of course, things are more fun in the warm and loony southern part of the country. No snow there of any kind. No need of mufflers. Also, no long, mournful walks, because in the warm and loony southern part of the country everybody drives. So everybody drives over to Uncle Jasper's house to watch the Cougars play the Gators, a not entirely unimportant conflict which will determine whether the Gators get a Bowl bid or must take another post-season exhibition tour of North Korea. But no sooner do the Cougars kick off (an astonishing end-over-end squiggly thing that floats lazily above the arena before plummeting down toward K. C. McCoy and catching him on the helmet) than Auntie Em starts hustling turkey. Soon Cousin May is slamming around the bowls and platters, and Cousin Bernice is oohing and ahing about "all the fixin's," and Uncle Bob is making low, insincere sounds of appreciation: "Yummy, yummy, Auntie Em, I'll have me some more of these delicious yams!" Delicious yams? Uncle Bob's eyes roll wildly in his head. Billy Joe Quaglino throws his long bomb in the middle of Grandpa Morris saying grace, Grandpa Morris speaking so low nobody can hear him, which is just as well, since he is reciting what he can remember of his last union contract. And then, just as J. B. (Speedy) Snood begins his ninety-two-yard punt return, Auntie Em starts dealing everyone second helpings of her famous stuffing, as if she were pushing a controlled substance, which it well might be, since there are no easily recognizable ingredients visible to the naked eye.

Consider for a moment the Thanksgiving meal itself. It has become a sort of refuge for endangered species of starch: cauliflower, turnips, pumpkin, mince (whatever "mince" is), those blessed yams. Bowls of luridly colored yams, with no taste at all, lying torpid under a lava flow of marshmallow! And then the sacred turkey. One might as well try to construct a holiday repast around a fish—say, a nice piece of boiled haddock. After all, turkey tastes very similar to haddock: same consistency, same quite remarkable absence of flavor. But then, if the Thanksgiving *pièce de résistance* were a nice piece of boiled haddock instead of turkey, there wouldn't be all that fun for Dad when Mom hands him the sterling-silver, bone-handled carving set (a wedding present from her

parents and not sharpened since) and then everyone sits around pretending not
to watch while he saws and tears away at the bird as if he were trying to
burrow his way into or out of some grotesque, fowllike prison.

What of the good side to Thanksgiving, you ask. There is always a good side
to everything. Not to Thanksgiving. There is only a bad side and then a worse
side. For instance, Grandmother's best linen tablecloth is a bad side: the fact
that it is produced each year, in the manner of a red flag being produced before
a bull, and then is always spilled upon by whichever child is doing poorest at
school that term and so is in need of greatest reassurance. Thus: "Oh, my
God, *Veronica,* you just spilled grape juice [or plum wine or tar] on Grandmother's best linen tablecloth!" But now comes worse. For at this point
Cousin Bill, the one who lost all Cousin Edwina's money on the car dealership
three years ago and has apparently been drinking steadily since Halloween,
bizarrely chooses to say: "Seems to me those old glasses are always falling
over." To which Auntie Meg is heard to add: "Somehow I don't remember
receivin' any of those old glasses." To which Uncle Fred replies: "That's
because you and George decided to go on vacation to Hawaii the summer
Grandpa Sam was dying." Now Grandmother is sobbing, though not so un-
controllably that she can refrain from murmuring: "I think that volcano painting I threw away by mistake got sent me from Hawaii, heaven knows why."
But the gods are merciful, even the Pilgrim-hatted god of cornhusks and soggy
stuffing, and there is an end to everything, even to Thanksgiving. Indeed,
there is a grandeur to the feelings of finality and doom which usually settle on
a house after the Thanksgiving celebration is over, for with the completion of
Thanksgiving Day the year itself has been properly terminated: shot through
the cranium with a high-velocity candied yam. At this calendrical nadir, all
energy on the planet has gone, all fun has fled, all the terrible wine has been
drunk.

But then, overnight, life once again begins to stir, emerging, even by the
next morning, in the form of Japanese window displays and Taiwanese Christmas lighting, from the primeval ooze of the nation's department stores. Thus,
a new year dawns, bringing with it immediate and cheering possibilities of
extended consumer debt, office-party flirtations, good—or, at least, medio-
cre—wine, and visions of Supersaver excursion fares to Montego Bay. It is
worth noting, perhaps, that this true new year always starts with the same
mute, powerful mythic ceremony: the surreptitious tossing out, in the early
morning, of all those horrid aluminum-foil packages of yams and cauliflower
and stuffing and red, gummy cranberry substance which have been squeezed
into the refrigerator as if a reenactment of the siege of Paris were shortly
expected. Soon afterward, the phoenix of Christmas can be observed as it
slowly rises, beating its drumsticks, once again goggle-eyed with hope and
unrealistic expectations.

PHILIP ROTH

Excerpt from Portnoy's Complaint

Alexander Portnoy is Philip Roth's contribution to the world's gallery of comic-novel heroes. Afflicted with psychoanalysis, he lies on the Freudian settee forever reliving the agonies of sexual guilt and being born of woman. Having a father isn't so great either.

But back to my parents, and how it seems that by remaining in my single state I bring these people, too, nothing but grief. That I happen, Mommy and Daddy, just happen to have recently been appointed by the Mayor to be Assistant Commissioner for The City of New York Commission on Human Opportunity apparently doesn't mean shit to you in terms of accomplishment and stature—though this is not exactly the case, I know, for, to be truthful, whenever my name now appears in a news story in the *Times,* they bombard every living relative with a copy of the clipping. Half my father's retirement pay goes down the drain in postage, and my mother is on the phone for days at a stretch and has to be fed intravenously, her mouth is going at such a rate about her Alex. In fact, it is exactly as it always has been: they can't get over what a success and a genius I am, my name in the paper, an associate now of the glamorous new Mayor, on the side of Truth and Justice, enemy of slum-lords and bigots and rats ("to encourage equality of treatment, to prevent discrimination, to foster mutual understanding and respect—"my commission's humane purpose, as decreed by act of the City Council) . . . but still, if you know what I mean, still somehow not entirely perfect.

Now, can you beat that for a serpent's tooth? All they have sacrificed for me and done for me and how they boast about me and are the best public relations firm (they tell me) any child could have, and it turns out that I still won't be perfect. Did you ever hear of such a thing in your life? I just refuse to be perfect. What a pricky kid.

They come to visit: "Where did you get a rug like this?" my father asks, making a face. "Did you get this thing in a junk shop or did somebody give it to you?"

"I like this rug."

"What are you talking," my father says, "it's a worn-out rug."

Light-hearted. "It's worn, but not out. Okay? Enough?"

"Alex, please," my mother says, "it is a very worn rug."

"You'll trip on that thing," my father says, "and throw your knee out of whack, and then you'll really be in trouble."

"And with your knee," says my mother meaningfully, "that wouldn't be a picnic."

At this rate they are going to roll the thing up any minute now, the two of them, and push it out the window. *And then take me home!*

"The rug is fine. My *knee* is fine."

"It wasn't so fine," my mother is quick to remind me, "when you had the cast on, darling, up to your hip. How he *shlepped* that thing around! How miserable he was!"

"I was fourteen years old then, Mother."

"Yeah, and you came out of that thing," my father says, "you couldn't bend your leg, I thought you were going to be a cripple for the rest of your life. I told him, 'Bend it! Bend it!' I practically begged him morning, noon, and night, 'Do you want to be a cripple forever? Bend that leg!'"

"You scared the *daylights* out of us with that knee."

"But that was in nineteen hundred and forty-seven. And this is nineteen sixty-six. The cast has been off nearly twenty years!"

My mother's cogent reply? "You'll see, someday you'll be a parent, and you'll know what it's like. And then maybe you won't sneer at your family any more."

The legend engraved on the face of the Jewish nickel—on the body of every Jewish child!—not IN GOD WE TRUST, but SOMEDAY YOU'LL BE A PARENT AND YOU'LL KNOW WHAT IT'S LIKE.

"You think," my father the ironist asks, "it'll be in our lifetime, Alex? You think it'll happen before I go down into the grave? No—he'd rather take chances with a worn-out rug!" The ironist—and logician! "—And crack his head open! And let me ask you something else, my independent son—who would even know you were here if you were lying bleeding to death on the floor? Half the time you don't answer the phone, I see you lying here with God only knows what's wrong—and who is there to take care of you? Who is there even to bring you a bowl of soup, if God forbid something terrible should happen?"

"I can take care of myself! I don't go around like some people"—boy, still pretty tough with the old man, eh, Al?—"some people I know in continual anticipation of total catastrophe!"

"You'll see," he says, nodding miserably, "you'll get sick"—and suddenly a squeal of anger, a whine out of nowhere of absolute hatred *of me!*—"*you'll get old, and you won't be such an independent big shot then!*"

"Alex, Alex," begins my mother, as my father walks to my window to recover himself, and in passing, to comment contemptuously about "the neighborhood he lives in." I work *for* New York, and he still wants me to live in beautiful Newark!

"Mother, I'm thirty-three! I am the Assistant Commissioner of Human Opportunity for the City of New York! I graduated first in my law school class! Remember? I have graduated first from every class I've ever *been* in! At twenty-five I was already special counsel to a House Subcommittee—of the United States Congress, Mother! Of America! If I wanted Wall Street, Mother, I could be on Wall Street! I am a highly respected man in my profession, that should be obvious! Right this minute, Mother, I am conducting an investigation of unlawful discriminatory practices in the building trades in New York—*racial discrimination*! Trying to get the Ironworkers' Union, Mother, to tell me their little secrets! That's what I did *just today*! Look, *I* helped solve the television quiz scandal, do you *remember*—?" Oh, why go on? Why go on in my strangled high-pitched adolescent voice? Good Christ, a Jewish man with parents alive is a fifteen-year-old boy, and will remain a fifteen-year-old boy till *they die*!

Anyway, Sophie has by this time taken my hand, and with hooded eyes, waits until I sputter out the last accomplishment I can think of, the last virtuous deed I have done, then speaks: "But to us, to us you're still a baby, darling." And next comes the whisper, Sophie's famous whisper that everybody in the room can hear without even straining, she's so considerate: "Tell him you're sorry. Give him a kiss. A kiss from you would change the world."

A kiss from me *would change the world*! Doctor! Doctor! Did I say fifteen? Excuse me, I meant ten! I meant five! I meant zero! A Jewish man with his parents alive is half the time a helpless *infant*! Listen, come to my aid, will you—and quick! Spring me from this role I play of the smothered son in the Jewish joke! Because it's beginning to pall a little, at thirty-three! And also it *hoits,* you know, there is *pain* involved, a little human suffering is being felt, if I may take it upon myself to say so—only that's the part Sam Levenson leaves *out*! Sure, they sit in the casino at the Concord, the women in their minks and the men in their phosphorescent suits, and boy, do they laugh, laugh and laugh and laugh—"Help, help, my son the doctor is drowning!"—ha ha *ha,* ha ha *ha,* only what about the *pain,* Myron Cohen! What about the guy who is actually drowning! Actually sinking beneath an ocean of parental relentlessness! What about him—who happens, Myron Cohen, to be *me*! Doctor, *please,* I can't live any more in a world given its meaning and dimension by some vulgar nightclub clown. By some—some *black humorist*! Because that's who the black humorists are—of course!—the Henny Youngmans and the Milton Berles breaking them up down there in the Fountainebleau, and with what? Stories of murder and mutilation! "Help," cries the woman running along the sand at Miami Beach, "help, my son the doctor is drowning!" Ha ha ha—only it is *my son the patient,* lady! And is he drowning! Doctor, get these people off my ass, will you please? The macabre is very funny on the stage—but not to live it, thank you! So just tell me how, and I'll do it! Just tell me what, and I'll say it right to their faces! Scat, Sophie! Fuck off, Jack! Go *away* from me already!

GROUCHO MARX

"To Harry Kurnitz"

October 12, 1965

Dear Harry:

. . . Like other friends, you seem concerned about my professional inactivity. You wonder how I make the days pass. Surely (you suggest) I must be bored. And I, in reply, can only say, How little you really know me!

Let me give you a sample day. I hop out of bed at the crack of dawn. At 7 on the nose I have prune juice, whole wheat toast, a touch of marmalade and a pot of Sanka. After brushing my teeth I watch "Woody Woodpecker" and "Captain Kangaroo." At 9:00 I take a nap until noon. Then comes lunch.

I have a can of Metrecal, and a slab of apple pan dowdy. After lunch I take a nap until 2; then I watch "Huckleberry Hound" and, if my wife is out shopping, I watch "Divorce Court." After that I brush my teeth and take a nap until 5:30. Five-thirty is the hour I look forward to. We call it the cocktail hour. We each have a glass of cranberry juice, a cheese dip and a package of Sen Sen.

At six we eat our big meal, Yami Yogurt, apple jack and a sprinkling of sunflower seeds. At 6:30 we watch Soupy Sales and his madcap friends entertain each other with zany antics. At 7 we take two straight-back chairs and face to face, give each other a manicure. At 7:30 we watch "Supermarket Sweep" and "Social Security in Action." Then we play some old recordings of Lawrence Welk and his half-man, half-girl, orchestra. At 8 we take two Seconals, three aspirin and a shot of LSD and fly to slumberland, eagerly looking forward to what thrills the next day has in store for us.

And now—I'm off to the dentist.

GROUCHO

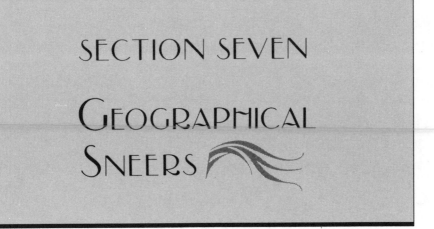

SECTION SEVEN

GEOGRAPHICAL SNEERS

Disapproving of other people's hometowns and other people's countries must be a worldwide habit. It starts many a war and many a story.

Parisian city slickers laughing at D'Artagnan's hick roots in Gascony got him into trouble with three dangerous musketeers. English travelers have tickled themselves for generations with elegant sneers at the barbarians infesting every land but England. Small-town America laughs at New York, New York jokes about Los Angeles, Dallas sneers at Fort Worth, Greenwich Village jeers at the East Side, Lake Wobegon smiles at St. Paul.

Humor often masks hostility, which often masks insecurity, and you are bound to feel insecure when you leave the good old home rut and enter new territory. One way to buck yourself up is by noting how ridiculous the new place is, compared to truly civilized places like your hometown.

Though Molly Ivins shows that humorists can sometimes also be cruel to their home earth, most of these pieces typify the cross-border fire fights caused by geographically induced unease. It is especially pleasing to have Calvin Trillin repay a little of America's debt to those generations of elegant English sneerers. Trillin's sneer, which can be as elegant as the fanciest English model, may have been honed by frequent stays in Britain.

Briefly Speaking

The town was so dull that when the tide went out it refused to come back.

—Fred Allen

Bill Vaughan

"The Hazards of Journalism . . ."

Friends, if you wish to inspire abusive mail, become a writer specializing in feature stories about states and cities. Nothing goads the outraged citizen into correspondence quite as easily as articles of this type.

An article about any locality that will please the people who live in or near it is not only difficult but impossible.

Let's make an attempt at it and see some of the pitfalls.

"Mudgeville . . ."

(Sir: If your reporter had spent more than a few hours in Clunk County, he would not have wasted your valuable space in writing about Mudgeville. We here in Fort Trimble are disappointed that material of this kind is printed when a much more worth-while article could have been prepared describing Fort Trimble, which has 123 more people than Mudgeville and two more supermarkets. Yours truly, P. J. Crouton, Mayor, Fort Trimble.)

". . . is a beautiful little town . . ."

(Sir: Copies of your filthy rag containing the gratuitous insult to Mudgeville were burned in front of City Hall last Saturday afternoon. You call Mudgeville "a . . . little town." If your reporter had taken the trouble to ascertain the facts, he would have learned that Mudgeville is, officially, a fourth-class city, and, furthermore . . .)

". . . situated in a gracious setting on the scenic banks of the murky, but lovely, Smoked Salmon river."

(SIR: I suppose you think this is smart. It is the kind of thing that gets a big laugh in the night clubs and pool halls in the so-called East. You send a so-called reporter out here to make fun of us. He must have brought a hip-flask with him, full of booze. Instead of writing it up that the Smoked Salmon river is the biggest river in this part of Clunk County and that it carries important commodities via barge and is where we get our drinking water, he writes up only that it is "murky." He must have been looking through the bottom of a glass of booze.)

"It was founded in 1857 by Colonel Elijah Mudge."

(SIR: Your unwarranted attack on my ancestor, Colonel Nathaniel Feemby, has forced me to take to my bed with a heart condition. Although many biased history books give Colonel Mudge the credit for founding Mudgeville, family letters in my possession conclusively prove that it was Colonel Feemby who commanded the expedition from Fort Trimble in 1857. Colonel Mudge was in charge of the mules, most of which died on the way. An apology, given equal prominence to this scurrilous assault on a man who is not alive to defend himself, will assuage but not erase the indignation of Yours Sincerely, Miss Bettina Feemby.)

"Mudgevillians showed great enterprise and courage in rebuilding the damage done by the tornado of 1935."

(SIR: The Mudgeville Chamber of Commerce is disappointed that your reporter saw fit to write about the tornado of 1935 without mentioning the many years during which there have been no tornadoes. An apology . . .)

"Law-abiding, hard-working citizens predominate in Mudgeville. In fact, the only crime of violence on record occurred last year when a man named Fumpf killed eighteen members of his family with a meat cleaver."

(SIR: If you can't say something nice about a person, why say anything at all?)

DAVE BARRY

"*Can New York Save Itself?*"

Here at The Miami Herald we ordinarily don't provide extensive coverage of New York City unless a major news development occurs up there, such as Sean Penn coming out of a restaurant. But lately we have become very concerned about the "Big Apple," because of a story about Miami that ran a few weeks ago in the Sunday magazine of The New York Times. Maybe you remember this story: The cover featured an upbeat photograph of suspected Miami drug dealers being handcuffed face-down in the barren dirt next to a garbage-strewed sidewalk outside a squalid shack that probably contains roaches the size of Volvo sedans. The headline asked:

CAN MIAMI SAVE ITSELF?

For those readers too stupid to figure out the answer, there also was this helpful hint:

A CITY BESET BY DRUGS AND VIOLENCE

The overall impression created by the cover was: *Sure Miami can save itself! And some day trained sheep will pilot the Concorde!*

The story itself was more balanced, discussing the pluses as well as the minuses of life in South Florida, as follows:

MINUSES

The area is rampant with violent crime and poverty and political extremism and drugs and corruption and ethnic hatred.

Voodoo is legal.

I myself thought it was pretty fair. Our local civic leaders reacted to it with their usual level of cool maturity, similar to the way Moe reacts when he is poked in the eyeballs by Larry and Curly. Our leaders held emergency break-fasts and issued official statements pointing out that much of the information in The Times story was Ancient History dating all the way back to the early 1980s, and that we haven't had a riot for, what, *months* now, and that the whole drugs-and-violence thing is overrated. Meanwhile, at newsstands all over South Florida, crowds of people were snapping up all available copies of The Sunday Times, frequently at gunpoint.

All of which got us, at The Herald, to thinking. "Gosh," we thought. "Here the world-famous New York Times, with so many other things to worry about, has gone to all this trouble to try to find out whether Miami can save itself. Wouldn't they be thrilled if we did the same thing for them?" And so it was that we decided to send a crack investigative team consisting of me and Chuck, who is a trained photographer, up there for a couple of days to see what the situation was. We took along comfortable walking shoes and plenty of major credit cards, in case it turned out that we needed to rent a helicopter, which it turned out we did. Here is our report:

Day One

We're riding in a cab from La Guardia Airport to our Manhattan hotel, and I want to interview the driver, because this is how we professional journal-ists take the Pulse of a City, only I can't, because he doesn't speak English. He is not allowed to, under the rules, which are posted right on the seat:

New York Taxi Rules

1. DRIVER SPEAKS NO ENGLISH.
2. DRIVER JUST GOT HERE TWO DAYS AGO FROM SOMEPLACE LIKE SENEGAL.
3. DRIVER HATES YOU.

Which is just as well, because if he talked to me, he might lose his concentra-tion, which would be very bad because the taxi has some kind of problem with the steering, probably dead pedestrians lodged in the mechanism, the result being that there is a delay of eight to 10 seconds between the time the driver turns the wheel and the time the taxi actually changes direction, a handicap that the driver is compensating for by going 175 miles per hour, at which velocity we are able to remain airborne almost to the far rim of some of the smaller potholes. These are of course maintained by the crack New York Department of Potholes (currently on strike), whose commissioner was recently indicted on corruption charges by the Federal Grand Jury to Indict Every Commissioner in New York. This will take some time, because New York has more commissioners than Des Moines, Iowa, has residents, including the Commissioner for Making Sure the Sidewalks Are Always Blocked by Steaming Fetid Mounds of Garbage the Size of Appalachian Foothills, and, of course, the Commissioner for Bicycle Messengers Bearing Down on You at Warp Speed with Mohawk Haircuts and Pupils Smaller Than Purely Theoretical Particles.

After several exhilarating minutes, we arrive in downtown Manhattan, where the driver slows to 125 miles so he can take better aim at wheelchair occupants. This gives us our first brief glimpse of the city we have come to investigate. It looks to us, whizzing past, as though it is beset by serious problems. We are reminded of the findings of the 40-member Mayor's Special Commission on the Future of the City of New York, which this past June, after nearly two years of intensive study of the economic, political and social problems confronting the city, issued a 2,300-page report, which reached the disturbing conclusion that New York is ''a nice place to visit'' but the commission ''wouldn't want to live there.''

Of course they probably stayed at a nicer hotel than where we're staying. We're staying at a ''medium priced'' hotel, meaning that the rooms are more than spacious enough for a family of four to stand up in if they are slightly built and hold their arms over their heads, yet the rate is just $135 per night, plus of course your state tax, your city tax, your occupancy tax, your head tax, your body tax, your soap tax, your ice bucket tax, your in-room dirty movies tax and your piece of paper that says your toilet is sanitized for your protection tax, which bring the rate to $367.90 per night, or a flat $4,000 if you use the telephone. A bellperson carries my luggage—one small gym-style bag containing primarily, a set of clean underwear—and I tip him $2, which he takes as if I am handing him a jar of warm sputum.

But never mind. We are not here to please the bellperson. We are here to see if New York can save itself. And so Chuck and I set off into the streets of Manhattan, where we immediately detect signs of a healthy economy in the form of people squatting on the sidewalk selling realistic jewelry. This is good, because a number of other businesses, such as Mobil Corp., have recently decided to pull their headquarters out of New York, much to the annoyance of Edward Koch, the feisty, cocky, outspoken, abrasive mayor who really gets on some people's nerves, yet at the same time strikes other people as a jerk. ''Why would *anybody* want to move to some dirt-bag place like the Midwest?''

Mayor Koch is always asking reporters. "What are they gonna do at *night*? Huh? *Milk the cows*? Are they gonna wear bib overalls and sit around *canning their preserves*? Huh? Are they gonna . . . Hey! come back here!"

But why *are* the corporations leaving? To answer this question, a polling firm recently took a scientific telephone survey of the heads of New York's 200 largest corporations, and found that none of them were expected to arrive at work for at least two more hours because of massive transit delays caused by a wildcat strike of the 1,200-member Wildcat Strikers Guild. So you can see the corporations' point: It *is* an inconvenience, being located in a city where taxes are ludicrously high, where you pay twice your annual income to rent an apartment that could easily be carried on a commercial airline flight, where you spend two-thirds of your work day trying to get to and from work, but as Mayor Koch philosophically points out, "Are they gonna *slop the hogs*? Are they gonna . . ."

Despite the corporate exodus, the New York economy continues to be robust, with the major industry being people from New Jersey paying $45 each to see *A Chorus Line*. Employment remains high, with most of the new jobs opening up in the fast-growing fields of:

- Person asking everybody for "spare" change.
- Person shrieking at taxis.
- Person holding animated sidewalk conversation with beings from another dimension.
- Person handing out little slips of paper entitling the bearer to one free drink at sophisticated nightclubs with names like The Bazoom Room.

As Chuck and I walk along 42nd Street, we see a person wearing an enormous frankfurter costume, handing out coupons good for discounts at Nathan's Famous hot dog stands. His name is Victor Leise, age 19, of Queens, and he has held the position of giant frankfurter for four months. He says he didn't have any connections or anything; he just put in an application and, boom, the job was his. Sheer luck. He says it's OK work, although people call him "Frank" and sometimes sneak up and whack him on the back. Also there is not a lot of room for advancement. They have no hamburger costume.

"Can New York save itself?" I ask him.

"If there are more cops on the streets, there could be a possibility," he says, through his breathing hole.

Right down the street is the world-famous Times Square. Although this area is best known as the site where many thousands of people gather each New Year's Eve for a joyous and festive night of public urination, it also serves as an important cultural center where patrons may view films such as *Sex Aliens, Wet Adulteress* and, of course, *Sperm Busters* in comfortable refrigerated theaters where everybody sits about 15 feet apart. This is also an excellent place to shop for your leisure product needs, including The Bionic Woman ("An amazingly lifelike companion") and a vast selection of latex objects, some the size of military pontoons. The local residents are very friendly, often coming right up and offering to engage in acts of leisure with you. Reluctantly, however, Chuck and I decide to tear ourselves away, for we have much more to see, plus we do not wish to spend the rest of our lives soaking in vats of penicillin.

As we leave the area, I stop briefly inside an Off-Track Betting parlor on Seventh Avenue to see if I can obtain the Pulse of the City by eavesdropping on native New Yorkers in casual conversation. Off-Track Betting parlors are the kinds of places where you never see signs that say, "Thank You For Not Smoking." The best you could hope for is, "Thank You For Not Spitting Pieces Of Your Cigar On My Neck." By listening carefully and remaining unobtrusive, I am able to overhear the following conversation:

> FIRST OFF-TRACK BETTOR: I like this *(very bad word)* horse here.
> SECOND OFF-TRACK BETTOR: That *(extremely bad word)* couldn't *(bad word)* out his own *(comical new bad word)*.
> FIRST OFF-TRACK BETTOR: *(Bad word)*.

Listening to these two men share their innermost feelings, I sense concern, yes, but also an undercurrent of hope, hope for a Brighter Tomorrow, if only the people of this great city can learn to work together, to look upon each other with respect and even, yes, love. Or at least stop shoving one another in front of moving subway trains. This happens a fair amount in New York, so Chuck and I are extremely alert as we descend into the complex of subway tunnels under Times Square, climate-controlled year-round at a comfortable 172 degrees Fahrenheit.

Although it was constructed in 1536, the New York subway system boasts an annual maintenance budget of nearly $8, currently stolen, and it does a remarkable job of getting New Yorkers from Point A to an indeterminate location somewhere in the tunnel leading to Point B. It's also very easy for the "out-of-towner" to use, thanks to the logical, easy-to-understand system of naming trains after famous letters and numbers. For directions, all you have to do is peer up through the steaming gloom at the informative signs, which look like this:

A 5 N 7 8 C 6 AA MID-DOWNTOWN 7⅜
EXPRESS LOCAL ONLY LL 67 ◆
DDD 4 ♠ 1 K ☆ AAAA 9 ONLY
EXCEPT CERTAIN DAYS BB ᴷᴷ 3

MIDWAY THROUGH TOWN 1 7 D
WALK REAL FAST AAAAAAAAA 56
LOCALIZED EXPRESS -6
"YY" ♣1,539
AAAAAAAAAAAAAAAAAAA

If for some reason you are unsure where to go, all you have to do is stand there looking lost, and within seconds a helpful New Yorker will approach to see if you have any "spare" change.

Within less than an hour, Chuck and I easily locate what could well be the correct platform, where we pass the time by perspiring freely until the train storms in, colorfully decorated, as is the tradition in New York, with the spray-painted initials of all the people it has run over. All aboard!

Here is the correct procedure for getting on a New York subway train at rush hour:

1. As the train stops, you must join the other people on the platform in pushing forward and forming the densest possible knot in front of each door. You want your knot to be so dense that, if the train were filled with water instead of people, not a single drop would escape.

2. The instant the doors open, you want to push forward as hard as possible, in an effort to get onto the train *without letting anybody get off*. This is *very important*. If anybody does get off, it is legal to tackle him and drag him back on. I once watched three German tourists—this is a true anecdote—attempt to get off the northbound No. 5 Lexington Avenue IRT train at Grand Central Station during rush hour. "Getting off please!" they said, politely, from somewhere inside a car containing approximately the population of Brazil, as if they expected people to actually *let them through*. Instead, of course, the incoming passengers propelled the Germans, like gnats in a hurricane, *away* from the door, deeper and deeper into the crowd, which quickly compressed them into dense little wads of Teutonic tissue. I never did see where they actually got off. Probably they stumbled to daylight somewhere in the South Bronx, where they were sold for parts.

Actually, though, there is reason to believe the subways are safer now. After years of being fearful and intimidated, many New Yorkers cheered in 1985 when Bernhard Goetz, in a highly controversial incident that touched off an emotion-charged nationwide debate, shot and killed the New York subway commissioner. This resulted in extensive legal proceedings, culminating recently when, after a dramatic and highly publicized trial, a jury voted not only to acquit Goetz, but also to dig up the commissioner and shoot him again.

Chuck and I emerge from the subway in Lower Manhattan. This area has been hard hit by the massive wave of immigration that has threatened to rend the very fabric of society, as the city struggles desperately to cope with the social upheaval caused by the huge and unprecedented influx of a group that has, for better or for worse, permanently altered the nature of New York: young urban professionals. They began arriving by the thousands in the 1970s, packed two and sometimes three per BMW sedan, severely straining the city's already-overcrowded gourmet-ice-cream facilities. Soon they were taking over entire neighborhoods, where longtime residents watched in despair as useful businesses such as bars were replaced by precious little restaurants with names like The Whittling Fig.

And still the urban professionals continue to come, drawn by a dream, a dream that is best expressed by the words of the song *New York, New York,* which goes:

> *Dum dum da de dum*
> *Dum dum da de dum*
> *Dum dum da de dum*
> *Dum dum da de dum dum.*

It is a powerfully seductive message, especially if you hear it at a wedding reception held in a Scranton, Pa., Moose Lodge facility and you have been drinking. And so you come to the Big Apple, and you take a peon-level position in some huge impersonal corporation, an incredibly awful, hateful job, and you spend $1,250 a month to rent an apartment so tiny that you have to shower in the kitchen, and the only furniture you have room for—not that you can afford furniture anyway—is your collection of back issues of *Metropolitan Home* magazine, but you stick it out, because this is the Big Leagues *(If I can make it there, I'll make it anywhere),* and you know that if you show them what you can do, if you really *go for it,* then, by gosh, one day you're gonna wake up, in The City That Never Sleeps, to find that the corporation has moved its headquarters to Plano, Texas.

Now Chuck and I are in Chinatown. We pass an outdoor market where there is an attractive display consisting of a tub containing I would estimate 275,000 dead baby eels. One of the great things about New York is that, if you ever need dead baby eels, you can get them. Also there is opera here. But tonight I think I'll just try to get some sleep.

At 3:14 A.M. I am awakened by a loud crashing sound, caused by workers from the city's crack Department of Making Loud Crashing Sounds During the Night, who are just outside my window, breaking in a new taxicab by dropping it repeatedly from a 75-foot crane. Lying in bed listening to them, I can hardly wait for . . .

DAY TWO

Chuck and I decide that since we pretty much covered the economic, social, political, historical and cultural aspects of New York on Day One, we'll devote Day Two to sightseeing. We decide to start with the best-known sight of all, the one that, more than any other, exemplifies what the Big Apple is all about: the Islip Garbage Barge. This is a barge of world-renowned garbage that originated on Long Island, a place where many New Yorkers go to sleep on those occasions when the Long Island Railroad is operating.

The Islip Garbage Barge is very famous. Nobody really remembers *why* it's famous; it just *is,* like Dick Cavett. It has traveled to South America. It has been on many television shows, including—I am not making this up—*Phil Donahue.* When we were in New York, the barge—I am still not making this up—was on trial. It has since been convicted and sentenced to be burned. But I am not worried. It will get out on appeal. It is the Claus von Bülow of garbage barges.

Chuck and I find out from the Director of Public Affairs at the New York Department of Sanitation, who is named Vito, that the barge is anchored off the coast of Brooklyn, so we grab a cab, which is driven by a man who of course speaks very little English and, as far as we can tell, has never heard of Brooklyn. By means of hand signals we direct him to a place near where the barge is anchored. It is some kind of garbage-collection point.

There are mounds of garbage everywhere, and if you really concentrate, you can actually see them giving off smell rays, such as you see in comic strips. Clearly no taxi has ever been here before, and none will ever come again, so we ask the driver to wait. "YOU WAIT HERE," I say, speaking in capital letters so he will understand me. He looks at me suspiciously. "WE JUST WANT TO SEE A GARBAGE BARGE," I explain.

We can see the barge way out on the water, but Chuck decides that, to get a good picture of it, we need a boat. A sanitation engineer tells us we might be able to rent one in a place called Sheepshead Bay, so we direct the driver there ("WE NEED TO RENT A BOAT"), but when we get there we realize it's too far away, so we naturally decide to rent a helicopter, which we find out is available only in New Jersey. ("NOW WE NEED TO GO TO NEW JERSEY. TO RENT A HELICOPTER.") Thus we end up at the airport in Linden, N.J., where we leave the taxi driver with enough fare money to retire for life, if he ever finds his way home.

Chuck puts the helicopter on his American Express card. Our pilot, Norman Knodt, assures me that nothing bad has ever happened to him in a helicopter excepting getting it shot up nine times, but that was in Vietnam, and he foresees no problems with the garbage-barge mission. Soon we are over the harbor, circling the barge, which turns out to be, like so many celebrities when you see them up close, not as tall as you expected. As I gaze down at it, with the soaring spires of downtown Manhattan in the background gleaming in the brilliant sky, a thought crosses my mind: I had better write at *least* 10 inches about this, to justify our expense reports.

Later that day, I stop outside Grand Central Station, where a woman is sitting in a chair on the sidewalk next to a sign that says:

TAROT CARDS

PALM READING

I ask her how much it costs for a Tarot card reading, and she says $10, which I give her. She has me select nine cards, which she arranges in a circle. "Now ask me a question," she says.

"Can New York save itself?" I ask.

She looks at me.

"That's your question?" she asks.

"Yes," I say.

"OK," she says. She looks at the cards. "Yes, New York can save itself for the future."

She looks at me. I don't say anything. She looks back at the cards.

"New York is the Big Apple," she announces. "It is big and exciting, with very many things to see and do."

After the reading I stop at a newsstand and pick up a copy of Manhattan Living magazine, featuring a guide to condominiums. I note that there are a number of one-bedrooms priced as low as $250,000.

Manhattan Living also has articles. "It is only recently," one begins, "that the word 'fashionable' has been used in conjunction with the bathroom."

DAY THREE

Just to be on the safe side, Chuck and I decide to devote Day Three to getting back to the airport. Because of a slip-up at the Department of Taxi Licensing, our driver speaks a fair amount of English. And it's a darned good thing he does, because he is kind enough to share his philosophy of life with us, in between shouting helpful instructions to other drivers. It is a philosophy of optimism and hope, not just for himself, but also for New York City, and for the world:

"The thing is, you got to look on the lighter side, because HEY WHAT THE HELL IS HE DOING! WHAT THE HELL ARE YOU DOING YOU *(very bad word)*! Because for me, the thing is, respect. If a person shows me respect, then HAH! YOU WANT TO SQUEEZE IN FRONT NOW?? YOU S.O.B.!! I SQUEEZE YOU LIKE A LEMON!! So I am happy here, but you Americans, you know, you are very, you know WHERE IS HE GOING?? You have to look behind the scenery. This damn CIA, something sticky is going on WHERE THE HELL IS THIS STUPID S.O.B. THINK HE IS GOING??? behind the scenery there, you don't think this guy, what his name, Casey, you don't LOOK AT THIS S.O.B. you don't wonder why he *really* die? You got to look behind the scenery. I don't trust *nobody*. I don't trust my own *self*. WILL YOU LOOK AT . . .''

By the time we reach La Guardia, Chuck and I have a much deeper understanding of life in general, and it is with a sense of real gratitude that we leap out of the cab and cling to the pavement. Soon we are winging our way southward, watching the Manhattan skyline disappear, reflecting upon our many experiences and pondering the question that brought us here:

Can New York save itself? Can this ultra-metropolis—crude yet sophisticated, overburdened yet wealthy, loud yet obnoxious—can this city face up to the multitude of problems besetting it and, drawing upon its vast reserves of spunk and spirit, as it has done so many times before, emerge triumphant?

And, who cares?

AMBROSE BIERCE

"The Foolish Woman"

A Married Woman, whose lover was about to reform by running away, procured a pistol and shot him dead.

"Why did you do that, madam?" inquired a Policeman, sauntering by.

"Because," replied the Married Woman, "he was a wicked man, and had purchased a ticket to Chicago."

"My sister," said an adjacent Man of God, solemnly, "you cannot stop the wicked from going to Chicago by killing them."

CALVIN TRILLIN

"A Nation of Shopkeepers Loses Three of Them through Contact with a Nation of Violence"

CYRIL CRENSHAW, STATIONER, 1905–1970

Crenshaw, a stationer of Knightsbridge, London SW2, perished in the attempt of Harvey R. ("Giveaway") Gordon, a Pontiac dealer from Indianapolis, Indiana, to purchase a ball-point pen. Gordon needed the pen in order to write his congressman that a country whose businessmen had no more initiative than British shopkeepers demonstrated should be cut off Marshall Plan aid immediately.

As the Metropolitan Police pieced the story together, Gordon's irritation at British business methods began on his first evening in London when, trying to relax from the flight over, he attempted to purchase a ticket at a Kensington cinema fourteen seconds after the final showing of the feature film had begun. The ticket seller informed Gordon that the box office was closing. When he tried to press his money upon her, she reminded him that he would not have received a fair return for it anyway, having already missed not only fourteen seconds of credits in the feature film but two trailers for coming attractions, a newsreel featuring a Manchester apprentice school's unique program for training Kenyan welders, and seven minutes of Horlicks advertisements. Gordon—who, on those occasions when he had to work on his books until three or four in the morning at Giveaway Gordon's Garden of Pontiacs, always kept all the showroom lights on just in case an insomniac station-wagon prospect wandered by—stormed into the theater, flinging a handful of coins at the ticket seller. Two police constables later agreed to remove Gordon physically from a seat in the front stalls, on the grounds not only that he entered when the box office was closing but also that he was improperly seated, having flung a total of ten shillings, the price for the loges (plus a house key), at the ticket seller and then taken a seven-shilling seat.

The following morning Gordon appeared to be less hostile. When the proprietor of a Savile Row clothing store warned him that the two-hundred-dollar cashmere sport coat he was about to buy might not wear terribly well, Gordon, who had once persuaded a mildly alcoholic machine-tool heiress to buy a Pontiac with eighty-seven thousand four hundred dollars' worth of extras, merely suggested to the clothier that he seek medical attention. But that afternoon, Gordon himself has admitted, there was another throwing incident, this time involving a greengrocer near Victoria Station. Gordon told the greengrocer that he wanted four peaches, and then began to pick them out.

"I'll get them for you, sir, thanks very much," the greengrocer said.

"That's all right, I'll get them," Gordon replied.

"But you'll take all large ones," the greengrocer said.

"Well, of course I'll take all large ones," Gordon said.

"Well, that's hardly fair to the next chap, is it?" the greengrocer said.

"Fair!" Gordon said. "If you were interested in being fair you should have gone into refereeing."

"We can't all be picking out our own peaches, sir," the greengrocer said, whereupon Gordon picked out four of his own peaches, all large ones, and threw them at the greengrocer. The greengrocer and three of the peaches were bruised.

On the same day, Gordon apparently failed to arrange the mending of a shirt, having been told by one laundry that it didn't do small holes and by the laundry next door that it was not equipped for major mending unless Gordon wanted to book three weeks in advance. Two days later, Gordon threatened violence in a shop—the Minimum Delay Cleaners on Brompton Road. Gordon, noticing that the suit he had just had pressed was about to be taken off the hanger and folded up into a paper bag by the clerk, asked to take the suit on the hanger.

"But we would have to charge you tuppence for the hanger, sir," the clerk replied.

"Sold," said Gordon, who had, within a matter of seconds, calculated that paying tuppence for the hanger would be cheaper in the long run than paying to have the suit repressed after it became wrinkled in the paper bag.

"But you could buy hangers across the road for a penny each, sir," the clerk said.

Gordon stared at the clerk. "I'll give you fourpence for your hanger," he finally said. "But not a penny more."

"Oh, tuppence will be quite all right sir," the clerk said, not quite certain that he had understood Gordon correctly. The clerk then put the suit back on the hanger and started to fold it into the paper bag again. A Mrs. Jeffrey Jowell, who was in the store at the time, has confirmed the clerk's testimony that Gordon snatched the suit from the clerk's hand in a violent motion and, as he threw open the door to leave, threatened the destruction of the shop by arson.

Gordon went directly from the Minimum Delay Cleaners to Crenshaw's stationery shop for a pen, composing the letter in his mind as he walked.

"Terribly sorry, sir," Crenshaw said. "We don't do pens."

"You mean you don't sell them?" Gordon asked.

"I'm afraid not, sir," Crenshaw replied. "Odd—ten, fifteen people a day stop off here wanting to buy pens. I suppose because we sell stationery and greeting cards and all that they expect us to sell pens as well."

"Has it ever occurred to you to begin selling pens?" Gordon said quietly, an odd tightness coming over his voice.

"Oh, no, sir," Crenshaw replied. "We don't do pens."

It was at that point that Gordon reached into his raincoat pocket, pulled out the Magnum automatic he always carried in case anyone came onto the Giveaway Gordon's Garden of Pontiacs lot looking for trouble, and finished off Crenshaw in three quick shots. He later instructed his attorney to base his defense on the claim that the shooting had been a crime of passion.

MARTIN APPLEGATE, NEWS DEALER
1911 – 1970

Applegate, a news dealer on Park Lane, was put to death by LeRoy Bean, a millionaire oilman from Ada, Oklahoma, in the normal course of business. Ironically, the killing was a direct result of Bean's making a special effort to behave courteously to the British. When he wasn't making a special effort to be courteous, Bean made a special effort to be uncouth. He prided himself on his reputation as a crude, self-made wheeler-dealer of the type common in the Southwest—although he was, in fact, a native of Chicago of Latvian descent, a graduate of the University of Illinois in musicology, and a baron of oil only through the happenstance of his wife's father having had control over two hundred and forty-seven million barrels of it.

For years, Bean had been particularly rude to the British, to the intense embarrassment of his wife, who always treated the British with the respect due one's revered ancestors, although all the British she met were live people not related to her. Once, during a reception in Tulsa given by the English Descendants of the Sooner Land Rush, Bean remarked to the British consul that he had by coincidence seen "a whole mess of little-bitty foreigners" downtown that afternoon, knowing full well that the only foreigners who had been downtown were the members of the championship Oxford rugby team who were making a special State Department goodwill tour of eastern Oklahoma. In London, whenever Bean ordered a bartender to bring plenty of ice in his drink, he always added that he realized there were only one hundred seventeen ice cubes in the greater London area at one time. In London restaurants, his orders were always something like, "Bring me one of them chicken pies of yours if you got a crane handy."

After a particularly unpleasant scene in London one night, when Bean insulted the Queen's prize corgi dogs in front of members of the British Natural Gas Association ("Why, in Oklahoma if we ever found a critter that ugly we'd put a bounty on it"), Mrs. Bean announced that if Bean did not make a special effort to be courteous to the British, there would be no more trips out of Ada, a threat she was capable of carrying out, since all of the two hundred and forty-seven million barrels of oil were still in her name.

It was Applegate's bad luck that Bean's first transaction on the morning after Mrs. Bean's dictum was to buy a *Herald-Tribune* on Park Lane. Bean had resolved to be more courteous than the British themselves; the thought of having to spend more than a few months a year in Ada, Oklahoma, surrounded by crude, self-made wheeler-dealers, filled him with dread. Walking down Park Lane, Bean had stopped in front of the Dorchester Hotel's doorman and said, "You got a real fine country here. Real fine." He had decided that at breakfast he would tell the waiter that only the British were intelligent enough to make breakfast sausages mainly out of bread, thus guarding against early-morning heartburn. When he entered Applegate's shop, he said, "A Paris *Herald-Tribune* please, if you don't mind."

"Thank you," Applegate said. He handed Bean the paper and said "Thank you" again.

"Thank *you,*" said Bean, who, after all, had been the one receiving the item in question.

"Thank you very much," Applegate said, as Bean handed him a pound note—and then added, before Bean was able to reply, "Thank you."

"Thanks a lot," Bean said.

"Thanks awfully," Applegate said, handing Bean his change.

"Thank *you.* Thank *you* awfully," Bean said, in a louder voice.

"Thank you very much indeed," Applegate said, somewhat puzzled but trying not to offend a customer.

"Thanks a lot fella—hear?" Bean said. He was almost shouting.

"Thank you, sir," Applegate said. He wondered why Bean was not leaving the store.

"Thank . . . you . . . sir . . . awfully," Bean said, very slowly.

A man in the bakery next door testified that the conversation went for approximately ten minutes before Bean pulled out a long-barreled, pearl-handled revolver—a souvenir his grandfather had come upon during a border skirmish with the Estonians in 1902—and fired at Applegate. The man in the bakery also testified that when the police constables opened the doors of the police van so that Bean could climb in, Bean said, "Thanks awfully."

Timothy Penfold, Sweetshop Proprietor, 1902–1970

Penfold, a sweetshop proprietor whose hobby was queuing, had one narrow escape from an American on the same day he eventually met his end at the hands of Myrtle Dougherty of Cleveland Heights, Ohio.

The narrow escape occurred in Penfold's sweetshop. It was a quiet Tuesday morning. Penfold was filling the order of a retired housing inspector who regularly sent a variety of candies in a gift box to the keepers working at a home for worn and misused farm animals in Sussex. It was a complicated order, since the retired housing inspector kept careful notes on the preferences of each keeper, and it often took an hour or so to complete. Penfold and the housing inspector had just spent ten minutes discussing the remarkable fondness of the Deputy Chief Keeper for Mackintosh's Quality Street Toffees when an American walked into the store, picked up a sixpence bag of mixed nuts and raisins from the rack, put a sixpence on the counter in front of Penfold, and said, "OK?"

"Won't keep you a moment, sir," Penfold said to the American, getting right down to adding an eighteen-inch column of figures.

"I'm just leaving this for the nuts and raisins," the American said. He had started out of the shop but had stopped to look at Penfold for an answer.

"I won't be long here, sir, thank you very much," Penfold said, starting to check each candy bar in the box against the numbers in the column.

"But it's the right change," the American said.

Penfold looked up from his figures. "There's a queue, sir," he said, sternly.

Penfold turned back to his figures, and the American reached into his pocket for a .45-caliber pistol he had been carrying for just such occasions. At that point, by chance, the American's wife walked in, reminded him that mixed nuts were high in cholesterol, and led him from the store.

Unaware of his narrow escape, Penfold decided to spend that evening queuing about. He often spent his evenings that way, joining first one queue then another. He had a closetful of items that he had purchased without really needing them, souvenirs of the times when he had been enjoying himself so much that he neglected to leave the queue before arriving at the counter and had to buy something or risk being accused by those behind him of having queued frivolously. Once, on Regent Street, he had been rather embarrassed when he joined what he thought was a short queue toward a shop door but turned out to be a German tourist ducking out of the wind to light a cigarette. But he continued to find queues irresistible, and he often spent an entire evening strolling from bus stops to cinemas to news dealers and back, queuing happily.

There was nothing frivolous about Penfold's presence in the fatal queue. On closing his sweetshop for the evening, he had decided to go to Hammersmith, where there was an Odeon cinema queue he had always found agreeable. He arrived at the bus stop fully intending to take a Number 74 bus to Hammersmith, although he enjoyed thinking that he was also queuing for the Number 31, which used the same stop. As it happened, there was only one person waiting at the bus stop when Penfold arrived—Mrs. Dougherty, who was returning from a beauty parlor that, according to an article on the women's page of the Cleveland *Plain Dealer,* did the hair of some close friends of Tom Jones, the singer. In Cleveland Heights, Mrs. Dougherty was vice president of her Parent-Teacher Association, recording secretary of the Housewives and Mothers Protection Society Gun Club, and a black belt in karate who had once demonstrated her murderous skill by breaking a Whirlpool washer-dryer with one chop of her bare hand. Penfold stood directly behind Mrs. Dougherty, in the proper queue position. Mrs. Dougherty, sensing someone behind her, moved slightly to the left, in better position if she decided to bring her right elbow back into the assaulter's windpipe. Penfold, not wanting to appear to be breaking the queue, dutifully moved directly behind her again. Mrs. Dougherty moved to the right, and again Penfold moved behind her, silently congratulating himself on attentive queuing. Believing her suspicions confirmed, Mrs. Dougherty faked a left elbow to the lower abdomen, spun around to a kneel-and-fire position, and shot Penfold four times with a small derringer she kept in her passport wallet. Before he expired, Penfold was heard to say, "I hope you don't think I was trying to push ahead."

H. L. MENCKEN

"The Capital of a Great Republic"

The fourth secretary of the Paraguayan legation. . . . The chief clerk to the House committee on industrial arts and expositions. . . . The secretary to the secretary to the Secretary of Labor. . . . The brother to the former Congressman from the third Idaho district. . . . The messenger to the chief of the Senate folding-room. . . . The doorkeeper outside the committee-room of the House committee on the disposition of useless executive papers. . . . The chief correspondent of the Toomsboro, Ga., *Banner* in the Senate press-gallery. . . . The stenographer to the assistant chief entomologist of the Bureau of Animal Industry. . . . The third assistant chief computor in the office of the Naval Almanac. . . . The assistant Attorney-General in charge of the investigation of postal frauds in the South Central States. . . . The former wife of the former secretary to the former member of the Interstate Commerce Commission. . . . The brother to the wife of the *chargé d'affaires* of Czecho-Slovakia. . . . The bootlegger to the ranking Democratic member of the committee on the election of President, Vice-President and representatives in Congress. . . . The acting assistant doorkeeper of the House visitors' gallery. . . . The junior Senator from Delaware. . . . The assistant to the secretary to the chief clerk of the Division of Audits and Disbursements, Bureau of Stationery and Supplies, Postoffice Department. . . . The press-agent to the chaplain of the House. . . . The commercial attaché to the American legation at Quito. . . . The chauffeur to the fourth assistant Postmaster-General. . . . The acting substitute elevator-man in the Washington monument. . . . The brother to the wife of the brother-in-law of the Vice-President. . . . The aunt to the sister of the wife of the officer in charge of ceremonials, State Department. . . . The neighbor of the cousin of the step-father of the sister-in-law of the President's pastor. . . . The superintendent of charwomen in Temporary Storehouse B7, Bureau of Navy Yards and Docks. . . . The assistant confidential clerk to the acting chief examiner of the Patent Office. . . . The valet to the Chief Justice.

P. J. O'ROURKE

"Third World Driving Hints and Tips"

During the past couple years I've had to do my share of driving in the Third World—in Mexico, Lebanon, the Philippines, Cyprus, El Salvador, Africa and Italy. (Italy is not technically part of the Third World, but no one has told the Italians.) I don't pretend to be an expert, but I have been making notes. Maybe these notes will be useful to readers who are planning to do something really stupid with their Hertz #1 Club cards.

ROAD HAZARDS

What would be a road hazard anyplace else, in the Third World is probably the road. There are two techniques for coping with this. One is to drive very fast so your wheels "get on top" of the ruts and your car sails over the ditches and gullies. Predictably, this will result in disaster. The other technique is to drive very slow. This will also result in disaster. No matter how slowly you drive into a ten-foot hole, you're still going to get hurt. You'll find the locals themselves can't make up their minds. Either they drive at 2 mph—which they do every time there's absolutely no way to get around them. Or else they drive at 100 mph—which they do coming right at you when you finally get a chance to pass the guy going 2 mph.

BASIC INFORMATION

It's important to have your facts straight before you begin piloting a car around an underdeveloped country. For instance, which side of the road do they drive on? This is easy. They drive on your side. That is, you can depend on it, any oncoming traffic will be on your side of the road. Also, how do you translate kilometers into miles? Most people don't know this, but one kilometer = ten miles, exactly. True, a kilometer is only 62 percent of a mile, but, if something is one hundred kilometers away, read that as one thousand miles because the roads are 620 percent worse than anything you've ever seen. And when you see a 50-kph speed limit, you might as well figure that means 500 *mph* because nobody cares. The Third World does not have Broderick Crawford and the Highway Patrol. Outside the cities, it doesn't have many police at all. Law enforcement is in the hands of the army. And soldiers, if they feel like it, will shoot you no matter what speed you're going.

Traffic Signs and Signals

Most developing nations use international traffic symbols. Americans may find themselves perplexed by road signs that look like Boy Scout merit badges and by such things as an iguana silhouette with a red diagonal bar across it. Don't worry, the natives don't know what they mean, either. The natives do, however, have an elaborate set of signals used to convey information to the traffic around them. For example, if you're trying to pass someone and he blinks his left turn signal, it means go ahead. Either that or it means a large truck is coming around the bend, and you'll get killed if you try. You'll find out in a moment.

Signaling is further complicated by festive decorations found on many vehicles. It can be hard to tell a hazard flasher from a string of Christmas-tree lights wrapped around the bumper, and brake lights can easily be confused with the dozen red Jesus statuettes and the ten stuffed animals with blinking eyes on the package shelf.

Dangerous Curves

Dangerous curves are marked, at least in Christian lands, by white wooden crosses positioned to make the curves even more dangerous. These crosses are memorials to people who've died in traffic accidents, and they give a rough statistical indication of how much trouble you're likely to have at that spot in the road. Thus, when you come through a curve in a full-power slide and are suddenly confronted with a veritable forest of crucifixes, you know you're dead.

LEARNING TO DRIVE LIKE A NATIVE

It's important to understand that in the Third World most driving is done with the horn, or "Egyptian Brake Pedal," as it is known. There is a precise and complicated etiquette of horn use. Honk your horn only under the following circumstances:

1. When anything blocks the road.
2. When anything doesn't.
3. When anything might.
4. At red lights.
5. At green lights.
6. At all other times.

ROADBLOCKS

One thing you can count on in Third World countries is trouble. There's always some uprising, coup or Marxist insurrection going on, and this means military roadblocks. There are two kinds of military roadblocks, the kind where you slow down so they can look you over, and the kind where you come to a full stop so they can steal your luggage. The important thing is that you must *never* stop at the slow-down kind of roadblock. If you stop, they'll think you're a terrorist about to attack them, and they'll shoot you. And you must *always* stop at the full-stop kind of roadblock. If you just slow down, they'll think you're a terrorist about to attack them, and they'll shoot you. How do you tell the difference between the two kinds of roadblocks? Here's the fun part: You can't!

(The terrorists, of course, have roadblocks of their own. They always make you stop. Sometimes with land mines.)

ANIMALS IN THE RIGHT OF WAY

As a rule of thumb, you should slow down for donkeys, speed up for goats and stop for cows. Donkeys will get out of your way eventually, and so will pedestrians. But never actually stop for either of them or they'll take advantage, especially the pedestrians. If you stop in the middle of a crowd of Third World pedestrians, you'll be there buying Chiclets and bogus antiquities for days.

Drive like hell through the goats. It's almost impossible to hit a goat. On the other hand, it's almost impossible *not* to hit a cow. Cows are immune to horn-honking, shouting, swats with sticks and taps on the hind quarters with the bumper. The only thing you can do to make a cow move is swerve to avoid it, which will make the cow move in front of you with lightning speed.

Actually, the most dangerous animals are the chickens. In the United States, when you see a ball roll into the street, you hit your brakes because you know the next thing you'll see is a kid chasing it. In the Third World, it's not balls the kids are chasing, but chickens. Are they practicing punt returns with a leghorn? Dribbling it? Playing stick-hen? I don't know. But Third Worlders are remarkably fond of their chickens and, also, their children (population problems notwithstanding). If you hit one or both, they may survive. But you will not.

ACCIDENTS

Never look where you're going—you'll only scare yourself. Nonetheless, try to avoid collisions. There are bound to be more people in that bus, truck or even on that Moped than there are in your car. At best you'll be screamed deaf. And if the police do happen to be around, standard procedure is to throw everyone in jail regardless of fault. This is done to forestall blood feuds, which are a popular hobby in many of these places. Remember the American consul is very busy fretting about that Marxist insurrection, and it may be months before he comes to visit.

If you do have an accident, the only thing to do is go on the offensive. Throw big wads of American money at everyone, and hope for the best.

SAFETY TIPS

One nice thing about the Third World, you don't have to fasten your safety belt. (Or stop smoking. Or cut down on saturated fats.) It takes a lot off your mind when average life expectancy is forty-five minutes.

Briefly Speaking

I have just returned from Boston. It is the only thing to do if you find yourself there.

—FRED ALLEN

MOLLY IVINS

"Texas Observed"

THE CLEAN CRAPPER BILL

The rest of the country is in future shock and in Texas we can't get Curtis's Clean Crapper bill through the Legislature. Curtis Graves is a state representative from Houston who introduced a bill to provide minimum standards of cleanliness for public restrooms in this state. It was defeated. Solons rose on the floor of the House to defend dirty johns. The delights of peein' against the back wall after a good whiskey drank were limned in excruciating detail. In New York City, Zero Mostel gets up on a stage and prances around singing "Tradition!" while the audience wets itself with nostalgia. In America, the rate of change shifts from arithmetic to geometric progression. In Texas, where ain't nothin' sanitized for your protection, we still peein' against the back wall.

What this country really needs, along with a new government, is a stiff dose of Texas. Things still are the way they used to be down here, and anybody who thinks that's quaint is welcome to come dip into the state's premier product. Like Johnny Winter sings, "They's so much shit in Texas/you bound to step in some."

WHY THE SKY IS BIGGER IN TEXAS

I love the state of Texas, but I regard that as a harmless perversion on my part and would not, in the name of common humanity, try to foist my pathology off on anyone else. Texas is a dandy place, in short spells, for anyone suffering from nausée de Thruway Hot Shoppe. It is resistant to Howard Johnson, plastic, interstate highways, and Standard Television American English. But the reason it's resistant to such phenomena is because it's cantankerous, ignorant, and repulsive.

The reason the sky is bigger here is because there aren't any trees. The reason folks here eat grits is because they ain't got no taste. Cowboys mostly stink and it's hot, oh God, it is hot. We gave the world Lyndon Johnson and you cowards gave him right back. There are two major cities in Texas: Houston is Los Angeles with the climate of Calcutta; to define Dallas is to add a whole new humongous dimension to bad.

Texas is a mosaic of cultures, which overlap in several parts of the state and form layers, with the darker layers on the bottom. The cultures are black, Chicano, Southern, freak, suburban, and shitkicker. (Shitkicker is dominant.) They are all rotten for women. Humanism is not alive and well in Texas. Different colors and types of Texans do not like one another, nor do they pretend to.

Shitkicker is pickup trucks with guns slung across the racks on the back and chicken-fried steaks and machismo and "D-I-V-O-R-C-E" on the radio and cheap, pink, nylon slips, and gettin' drunk on Saturday night and goin' to church on Sunday morning, and drivin' down the highway throwin' beer cans out the window, and Rastusan'-Liza jokes and high school football, and family reunions where the in-laws of your second cousins show up.

You can eat chili, barbecue, Meskin food, hush puppies, catfish, collard greens, red beans, pink grapefruit, and watermelon with Dr Pepper, Pearl, Lone Star, Carta Blanca, or Shiner's, which tastes a lot like paint thinner but don't have no preservatives in it. People who eat soul food here eat it because they can't afford hamburger. Since last year, you can buy a drink in some bars, but a lot of folks still brown-bag it 'cause it's cheaper, and Chivas and Four Roses look alike comin' out of a brown bag.

WHAT TO WATCH IN TEXAS

The frontier is what John Wayne lived on. Most Texans are Baptists. Baptists are civilized people. Beware of Church of Christers.

Once when Ronnie Dugger was being poetic he said, "To a Texan, a car is like wings to a seagull: our places are far apart and we must dip into them driving . . . the junctions in the highways and the towns are like turns in a city well known." It's true, Texans are accustomed to driving three hours to see a football game or 150 miles for a movie.

Texas is an un-self-conscious place. Nobody here is embarrassed about being who he is. Reactionaries aren't embarrassed. Rich folks aren't embarrassed. Rednecks aren't embarrassed. Liberals aren't embarrassed. And when did black folks or brown folks ever have time to worry about existential questions? Lobbyists, loan sharks, slumlords, war profiteers, chiropractors, and KKKers are all proud of their callings. Only Dallas is self-conscious; Dallas deserves it.

Texas is not a civilized place. Texans shoot one another a lot. They also knife, razor, and stomp one another to death with some frequency. And they fight in bars all the time. You can get five years for murder and 99 for pot possession in this state—watch your ass.

Environmental Advances

The only thing that smells worse than an oil refinery is a feedlot. Texas has a lot of both. Ecology in Texas started with a feedlot. So many people in Lubbock got upset with the smell of a feedlot there that they complained to the city council all the time. The city council members didn't act like yahoos; they took it serious. After a lot of hearings, it was decided to put up an Airwick bottle on every fencepost around the feedlot. Ecology in Texas has gone uphill since then.

The two newest members of the Air Pollution Control Board were up for a hearing before a state senate committee this June. E. W. Robinson of Amarillo told the committee that he was against allowin' any pollution that would prove to be very harmful to people's health. A senator asked him how harmful was very harmful. Oh, lead poisonin' and such would be unacceptable, said Robinson. What about pollution that causes allergies and asthma? Well, you don't die of it, said Robinson. While the air of Texas is entrusted to this watchdog, the water is in good hands, too. Not long ago, the director of the Texas Water Quality Board was trying to defend what the Armco Steel Company is dumping into the Houston Ship Channel. "Cyanide," he said, "is a scare word."

They Said It Was Texas Kulcher / But It Was Only Railroad Gin

Art is paintings of bluebonnets and broncos, done on velvet. Music is mariachis, blues, and country. Eddie Wilson, who used to be a beer lobbyist, started a place in Austin, in an old National Guard armory, called Armadillo World Headquarters. Willie Nelson, Freddie King, Leon Russell, Ravi Shankar, the Austin Ballet, the AFL-CIO Christmas Party, the Mahavishnu Band,

and several basketball teams have held forth in this, the southwest's largest country-western bohemian nightclub.

Kinky Friedman and the Texas Jewboys cut a single recently with "The Ballad of Charles Whitman" on the one side and "Get Your Biscuits in the Oven and Your Buns in the Bed" on the flip. Part of the lyrics of "The Ballad" go like this: "There was rumor/Of a tumor/nestled at the base of his brain . . ." Kinky lives on a ranch in Central Texas called Rio Duckworth, reportedly in a garbage can.

There is a radio station just across the border from Del Rio, Texas. It plays hymns during the day and broadcasts religious advertisements at night. They sell autographed pictures of Jesus to all you friends in radioland. Also prayer rugs as a special gift for all your travelin' salesmen friends with a picture of the face of Jesus on the prayer rug that glows in the dark. And underneath the picture is a legend that also glows in the dark; it's written, "Thou Shalt Not Commit Adultery."

Texas is not full of rich people. Texas is full of poor people. The latest count is 22 percent of the folks here under the federal poverty line—and the feds don't set the line high. The rest of the country, they tell us, has 13 percent poor folks, including such no-account states as Mississippi. Because Texas is racist, 45 percent of the black folks and the brown folks are poor.

Onliest foreign thang that approaches Texas politics is Illinois politics. We ain't never left it lyin' around in shoeboxes, elsewise, we got the jump on everybody.

Texans do not talk like other Americans. They drawl, twang, or sound like the Frito Bandito, only not jolly. *Shit* is a three-syllable word with a *y* in it.

Texans invent their own metaphors and similes, often of a scatological nature, which is kind of fun. As a group, they tell good stories well. The reason they are good at stories is because this is what anthropologists call an oral culture. That means people here don't read and write much. Neither would you if the *Dallas Morning News* was all you had to read.

Texas—I believe it has been noted elsewhere—is a big state. Someone else can tell you about the symphony orchestras and the experimental theaters and those Texans who are writing their Ph.D. theses on U.S. imperialism in Paraguay and seventeenth-century Sanskrit literature. I'm just talking about what makes Texas Texas.

SECTION EIGHT

POLITICS AND

PATRIOTS

This being a democracy, we are permitted to laugh at government and all its works and, indeed, are obliged to do so if we treasure it. The tendency of governments and governing people is to swell with pride and power. Laughter deflates this evil tendency and so impedes the rise of autocracy, not to mention insufferable arrogance.

It is a hard thing for important people to be laughed at, and they are not always grateful for the favor. During the Vietnam War President Johnson, forever fuming at the press, used to refer to the newspaper humor columnists in weary bitterness as "the funny-asses."

The American people are not always wholehearted in support of laughter either. There are always people who ascribe such nobility to a president, a party, or the government itself that they recoil from laughing at these icons as from desecration of a cathedral.

The last time it became taboo to laugh publicly at a president was during the 1950s. Not one memorable joke about President Eisenhower was told in those years. Adlai Stevenson, who contested twice for the presidency, often used humor and wit in his speeches. Afterward, political wisdom had it that his humor had offended a solemn electorate.

As the pieces in this section illustrate, such onsets of piety—luckily for democracy—have been rare in our history.

AMBROSE BIERCE

"Man and Lightning"

A man Running for Office was overtaken by Lightning.

"You see," said the Lightning, as it crept past him inch by inch, "I can travel considerably faster than you."

"Yes," the Man Running for Office replied, "but think how much longer I keep going!"

JOSEPH HELLER

Lieutenant Scheisskopf

Here is an excerpt from Chapter Eight of Catch-22. *Though the war of* Catch-22 *is World War II, it was published during the early years of the Vietnam War. Its portrayal of war as a sport among lunatics in which only the sane get killed reflects a view that became widespread during the Vietnam years but would have seemed subversive during World War II.*

Mordecai Richler reports that Heller's editor asked Evelyn Waugh, England's finest comic novelist, for prepublication comment that might help sales and that Waugh replied: "Thank you for sending Catch-22. *I am sorry that the book fascinates you so much. It has many passages quite unsuitable to a lady's reading. It suffers not only from indelicacy but from prolixity. . . . You may quote me as saying: 'This exposure of corruption, cowardice and incivility of American officers will outrage all friends of your country (such as myself) and greatly comfort your enemies.' " Waugh, of course, had just completed his own trilogy of comic war novels, which, as Richler points out, were "an exposure of corruption, cowardice and incivility" among British officers during World War II.*

Lieutenant Scheisskopf was an R.O.T.C. graduate who was rather glad that war had broken out, since it gave him an opportunity to wear an officer's uniform every day and say "Men" in a clipped, military voice to the bunches of kids who fell into his clutches every eight weeks on their way to the butcher's block. He was an ambitious and humorless Lieutenant Scheisskopf, who confronted his responsibilities soberly and smiled only when some rival officer at the Santa Ana Army Air Force Base came down with a lingering disease. He had poor eyesight and chronic sinus trouble, which made war especially exciting for him, since he was in no danger of going overseas. The best thing about him was his wife and the best thing about his wife was a girl friend named Dori Duz who did whenever she could and had a Wac uniform that Lieutenant Scheisskopf's wife put on every weekend and took off every weekend for every cadet in her husband's squadron who wanted to creep into her.

Dori Duz was a lively little tart of copper-green and gold who loved doing it best in toolsheds, phone booths, field houses and bus kiosks. There was little she hadn't tried and less she wouldn't. She was shameless, slim, nineteen and aggressive. She destroyed egos by the score and made men hate themselves in the morning for the way she found them, used them and tossed them aside. Yossarian loved her. She was a marvelous piece of ass who found him only fair. He loved the feel of springy muscle beneath her skin everywhere he touched her the only time she'd let him. Yossarian loved Dori Duz so much that he couldn't help flinging himself down passionately on top of Lieutenant Scheisskopf's wife every week to revenge himself upon Lieutenant Scheisskopf for the way Lieutenant Scheisskopf was revenging himself upon Clevinger.

Lieutenant Scheisskopf's wife was revenging herself upon Lieutenant Scheisskopf for some unforgettable crime of his she couldn't recall. She was a plump, pink, sluggish girl who read good books and kept urging Yossarian not to be so bourgeois without the r. She was never without a good book close by, not even when she was lying in bed with nothing on her but Yossarian and Dori Duz's dog tags. She bored Yossarian, but he was in love with her, too. She was a crazy mathematics major from the Wharton School of Business who could not count to twenty-eight each month without getting into trouble.

"Darling, we're going to have a baby again," she would say to Yossarian every month.

"You're out of your goddam head," he would reply.

"I mean it, baby," she insisted.

"So do I."

"Darling, we're going to have a baby again," she would say to her husband.

"I haven't the time," Lieutenant Scheisskopf would grumble petulantly. "Don't you know there's a parade going on?"

Lieutenant Scheisskopf cared very deeply about winning parades and about bringing Clevinger up on charges before the Action Board for conspiring to advocate the overthrow of the cadet officers Lieutenant Scheisskopf had appointed. Clevinger was a troublemaker and a wise guy. Lieutenant Scheisskopf knew that Clevinger might cause even more trouble if he wasn't watched. Yesterday it was the cadet officers; tomorrow it might be the world. Clevinger had a mind, and Lieutenant Scheisskopf had noticed that people with minds tended to get pretty smart at times. Such men were dangerous, and even the new cadet officers whom Clevinger had helped into office were eager to give damning testimony against him. The case against Clevinger was open and shut. The only thing missing was something to charge him with.

It could not be anything to do with parades, for Clevinger took the parades almost as seriously as Lieutenant Scheisskopf himself. The men fell out for the parades early each Sunday afternoon and groped their way into ranks of twelve outside the barracks. Groaning with hangovers, they limped in step to their station on the main paradeground, where they stood motionless in the heat for an hour or two with the men from the sixty or seventy other cadet squadrons until enough of them had collapsed to call it a day. On the edge of the field stood a row of ambulances and teams of trained stretcher bearers with walkie-talkies. On the roofs of the ambulances were spotters with binoculars. A tally clerk kept score. Supervising this entire phase of the operation was a medical officer with a flair for accounting who okayed pulses and checked the figures of the tally clerk. As soon as enough unconscious men had been collected in the ambulances, the medical officer signaled the bandmaster to strike up the band and end the parade. One behind the other, the squadrons marched up the field, executed a cumbersome turn around the reviewing stand and marched down the field and back to their barracks.

Each of the parading squadrons was graded as it marched past the reviewing stand, where a bloated colonel with a big fat mustache sat with the other officers. The best squadron in each wing won a yellow pennant on a pole that was utterly worthless. The best squadron on the base won a red pennant on a longer pole that was worth even less, since the pole was heavier and was that much more of a nuisance to lug around all week until some other squadron won it the following Sunday. To Yossarian, the idea of pennants as prizes was absurd. No money went with them, no class privileges. Like Olympic medals and tennis trophies, all they signified was that the owner had done something of no benefit to anyone more capably than everyone else.

The parades themselves seemed equally absurd. Yossarian hated a parade. Parades were so martial. He hated hearing them, hated seeing them, hated being tied up in traffic by them. He hated being made to take part in them. It was bad enough being an aviation cadet without having to act like a soldier in the blistering heat every Sunday afternoon. It was bad enough being an aviation cadet because it was obvious now that the war would not be over before he had finished his training. That was the only reason he had volunteered for cadet training in the first place. As a soldier who had qualified for aviation cadet training, he had weeks and weeks of waiting for assignment to a class, weeks and weeks more to become a bombardier-navigator, weeks and weeks more of operational training after that to prepare him for overseas duty. It seemed inconceivable then that the war could last that long, for God was on his side, he had been told, and God, he had also been told, could do whatever He wanted to. But the war was not nearly over, and his training was almost complete.

Lieutenant Scheisskopf longed desperately to win parades and sat up half the night working on it while his wife waited amorously for him in bed thumbing through Krafft-Ebing to her favorite passages. He read books on marching. He manipulated boxes of chocolate soldiers until they melted in his hands and then maneuvered in ranks of twelve a set of plastic cowboys he had bought from a mail-order house under an assumed name and kept locked away from everyone's eyes during the day. Leonardo's exercises in anatomy proved indispensable. One evening he felt the need for a live model and directed his wife to march around the room.

"Naked?" she asked hopefully.

Lieutenant Scheisskopf smacked his hands over his eyes in exasperation. It was the despair of Lieutenant Scheisskopf's life to be chained to a woman who was incapable of looking beyond her own dirty, sexual desires to the titanic struggles for the unattainable in which noble man could become heroically engaged.

"Why don't you ever whip me?" she pouted one night.

"Because I haven't the time," he snapped at her impatiently. "I haven't the time. Don't you know there's a parade going on?"

And he really did not have the time. There it was Sunday already, with only seven days left in the week to get ready for the next parade. He had no idea where the hours went. Finishing last in three successive parades had given Lieutenant Scheisskopf an unsavory reputation, and he considered every means of improvement, even nailing the twelve men in each rank to a long two-by-four beam of seasoned oak to keep them in line. The plan was not feasible, for making a ninety-degree turn would have been impossible without nickel-alloy swivels inserted in the small of every man's back, and Lieutenant Scheisskopf was not sanguine at all about obtaining that many nickel-alloy swivels from Quartermaster or enlisting the co-operation of the surgeons at the hospital.

The week after Lieutenant Scheisskopf followed Clevinger's recommendation and let the men elect their own cadet officers, the squadron won the yellow pennant. Lieutenant Scheisskopf was so elated by this unexpected achievement that he gave his wife a sharp crack over the head with the pole when she tried to drag him into bed to celebrate by showing their contempt for the sexual mores of the lower middle classes in Western civilization. The next week the squadron won the red flag, and Lieutenant Scheisskopf was beside himself with rapture. And the week after that his squadron made history by winning the red pennant two weeks in a row! Now Lieutenant Scheisskopf had confidence enough in his powers to spring his big surprise. Lieutenant Scheisskopf had discovered in his extensive research that the hands of marchers, instead of swinging freely, as was then the popular fashion, ought never to be moved more than three inches from the center of the thigh, which meant, in effect, that they were scarcely to be swung at all.

Lieutenant Scheisskopf's preparations were elaborate and clandestine. All the cadets in his squadron were sworn to secrecy and rehearsed in the dead of night on the auxiliary paradeground. They marched in darkness that was pitch and bumped into each other blindly, but they did not panic, and they were learning to march without swinging their hands. Lieutenant Scheisskopf's first thought had been to have a friend of his in the sheet metal shop sink pegs of nickel alloy into each man's thighbones and link them to the wrists by strands of copper wire with exactly three inches of play, but there wasn't time—there was never enough time—and good copper wire was hard to come by in wartime. He remembered also that the men, so hampered, would be unable to fall properly during the impressive fainting ceremony preceding the marching and that an inability to faint properly might affect the unit's rating as a whole.

And all week long he chortled with repressed delight at the officers' club. Speculation grew rampant among his closest friends.

"I wonder what that Shithead is up to," Lieutenant Engle said.

Lieutenant Scheisskopf responded with a knowing smile to the queries of his colleagues. "You'll find out Sunday," he promised. "You'll find out."

Lieutenant Scheisskopf unveiled his epochal surprise that Sunday with all the aplomb of an experienced impresario. He said nothing while the other squadrons ambled past the reviewing stand crookedly in their customary manner. He gave no sign even when the first ranks of his own squadron hove into sight with their swingless marching and the first stricken gasps of alarm were hissing from his startled fellow officers. He held back even then until the bloated colonel with the big fat mustache whirled upon him savagely with a purpling face, and then he offered the explanation that made him immortal.

"Look, Colonel," he announced. "No hands."

And to an audience stilled with awe, he distributed certified photostatic copies of the obscure regulation on which he had built his unforgettable triumph. This was Lieutenant Scheisskopf's finest hour. He won the parade, of course, hands down, obtaining permanent possession of the red pennant and ending the Sunday parades altogether, since good red pennants were as hard to come by in wartime as good copper wire. Lieutenant Scheisskopf was made First Lieutenant Scheisskopf on the spot and began his rapid rise through the ranks. There were few who did not hail him as a true military genius for his important discovery.

"That Lieutenant Scheisskopf," Lieutenant Travers remarked. "He's a military genius."

"Yes, he really is," Lieutenant Engle agreed. "It's a pity the schmuck won't whip his wife."

"I don't see what that has to do with it," Lieutenant Travers answered coolly. "Lieutenant Bemis whips Mrs. Bemis beautifully every time they have sexual intercourse, and he isn't worth a farthing at parades."

"I'm talking about flagellation," Lieutenant Engle retorted. "Who gives a damn about parades?"

Actually, no one but Lieutenant Scheisskopf really gave a damn about the parades, least of all the bloated colonel with the big fat mustache, who was chairman of the Action Board and began bellowing at Clevinger the moment Clevinger stepped gingerly into the room to plead innocent to the charges Lieutenant Scheisskopf had lodged against him. The colonel beat his fist down upon the table and hurt his hand and became so further enraged with Clevinger that he beat his fist down upon the table even harder and hurt his hand some more. Lieutenant Scheisskopf glared at Clevinger with tight lips, mortified by the poor impression Clevinger was making.

"In sixty days you'll be fighting Billy Petrolle," the colonel with the big fat mustache roared. "And you think it's a big fat joke."

"I don't think it's a joke, sir," Clevinger replied.

"Don't interrupt."

"Yes, sir."

"And say 'sir' when you do," ordered Major Metcalf.

"Yes, sir."

"Weren't you just ordered not to interrupt?" Major Metcalf inquired coldly.

"But I didn't interrupt, sir," Clevinger protested.

"No. And you didn't say 'sir,' either. Add that to the charges against him," Major Metcalf directed the corporal who could take shorthand. "Failure to say 'sir' to superior officers when not interrupting them."

"Metcalf," said the colonel, "you're a goddam fool. Do you know that?"

Major Metcalf swallowed with difficulty. "Yes, sir."

"Then keep your goddam mouth shut. You don't make sense."

There were three members of the Action Board, the bloated colonel with the big fat mustache, Lieutenant Scheisskopf and Major Metcalf, who was trying to develop a steely gaze. As a member of the Action Board, Lieutenant Scheisskopf was one of the judges who would weigh the merits of the case against Clevinger as presented by the prosecutor. Lieutenant Scheisskopf was also the prosecutor. Clevinger had an officer defending him. The officer defending him was Lieutenant Scheisskopf.

It was all very confusing to Clevinger, who began vibrating in terror as the colonel surged to his feet like a gigantic belch and threatened to rip his stinking, cowardly body apart limb from limb. One day he had stumbled while marching to class; the next day he was formally charged with "breaking ranks while in formation, felonious assault, indiscriminate behavior, mopery, high treason, provoking, being a smart guy, listening to classical music, and so on." In short, they threw the book at him, and there he was, standing in dread before the bloated colonel, who roared once more that in sixty days he would be fighting Billy Petrolle and demanded to know how the hell he would like being washed out and shipped to the Solomon Islands to bury bodies. Clevinger replied with courtesy that he would not like it; he was a dope who would rather be a corpse than bury one. The colonel sat down and settled back, calm and cagey suddenly, and ingratiatingly polite.

"What did you mean," he inquired slowly, "when you said we couldn't punish you?"

"When, sir?"

"I'm asking the questions. You're answering them."

"Yes, sir. I—"

"Did you think we brought you here to ask questions and for me to answer them?"

"No, sir. I—"

"What did we bring you here for?"

"To answer questions."

"You're goddam right," roared the colonel. "Now suppose you start answering some before I break your goddam head. Just what the hell did you mean, you bastard, when you said we couldn't punish you?"

"I don't think I ever made that statement, sir."

"Will you speak up, please? I couldn't hear you."

"Yes, sir. I—"

"Will you speak up, please? He couldn't hear you."

"Yes, sir. I—"

"Metcalf."

"Sir?"

"Didn't I tell you to keep your stupid mouth shut?"

"Yes, sir."

"Then keep your stupid mouth shut when I tell you to keep your stupid mouth shut. Do you understand? Will you speak up, please? I couldn't hear you."

"Yes, sir. I—"

"Metcalf, is that your foot I'm stepping on?"

"No, sir. It must be Lieutenant Scheisskopf's foot."

"It isn't my foot," said Lieutenant Scheisskopf.

"Then maybe it is my foot after all," said Major Metcalf.

"Move it."

"Yes, sir. You'll have to move your foot first, colonel. It's on top of mine."

"Are you telling me to move my foot?"

"No, sir. Oh, no, sir."

"Then move your foot and keep your stupid mouth shut. Will you speak up, please? I still couldn't hear you."

"Yes, sir. I said that I didn't say that you couldn't punish me."

"Just what the hell are you talking about?"

"I'm answering your question, sir."

"What question?"

" 'Just what the hell did you mean, you bastard, when you said we couldn't punish you?' " said the corporal who could take shorthand, reading from his steno pad.

"All right," said the colonel. "Just what the hell *did* you mean?"

"I didn't say you couldn't punish me, sir."

"When?" asked the colonel.

"When what, sir?"

"Now you're asking me questions again."

"I'm sorry, sir. I'm afraid I don't understand your question."

"When didn't you say we couldn't punish you? Don't you understand my question?"

"No, sir. I don't understand."

"You've just told us that. Now suppose you answer my question."

"But how can I answer it?"

"That's another question you're asking me."

"I'm sorry, sir. But I don't know how to answer it. I never said you couldn't punish me."

"Now you're telling us when you did say it. I'm asking you to tell us when you didn't say it."

Clevinger took a deep breath. "I always didn't say you couldn't punish me, sir."

"That's much better, Mr. Clevinger, even though it is a barefaced lie. Last night in the latrine. Didn't you whisper that we couldn't punish you to that other dirty son of a bitch we don't like? What's his name?"

"Yossarian, sir," Lieutenant Scheisskopf said.

"Yes, Yossarian. That's right. Yossarian. Yossarian? Is that his name? Yossarian? What the hell kind of a name is Yossarian?"

Lieutenant Scheisskopf had the facts at his finger tips. "It's Yossarian's name, sir," he explained.

"Yes, I suppose it is. Didn't you whisper to Yossarian that we couldn't punish you?"

"Oh, no, sir. I whispered to him that you couldn't find me guilty—"

"I may be stupid," interrupted the colonel, "but the distinction escapes me. I guess I *am* pretty stupid, because the distinction escapes me."

"W—"

"You're a windy son of a bitch, aren't you? Nobody asked you for clarification and you're giving me clarification. I was making a statement, not asking for clarification. You are a windy son of a bitch, aren't you?"

"No, sir."

"*No*, sir? Are you calling me a goddam liar?"

"Oh, no, sir."

"Then you're a windy son of a bitch, aren't you?"

"No, sir."

"Are you trying to pick a fight with me?"

"No, sir."

"Are you a windy son of a bitch?"

"No, sir."

"Goddammit, you *are* trying to pick a fight with me. For two stinking cents I'd jump over this big fat table and rip your stinking, cowardly body apart limb from limb."

"Do it! Do it!" cried Major Metcalf.

"Metcalf, you stinking son of a bitch. Didn't I tell you to keep your stinking, cowardly, stupid mouth shut?"

"Yes, sir. I'm sorry, sir."

"Then suppose *you* do it."

"I was only trying to learn, sir. The only way a person can learn is by trying."

"Who says so?"

"Everybody says so, sir. Even Lieutenant Scheisskopf says so."

"Do you say so?"

"Yes, sir," said Lieutenant Scheisskopf. "But everybody says so."

"Well, Metcalf, suppose you try keeping that stupid mouth of yours shut, and maybe that's the way you'll learn how. Now, where were we? Read me back the last line."

" 'Read me back the last line,' " read back the corporal who could take shorthand.

"Not *my* last line, stupid!" the colonel shouted. "Somebody else's."

" 'Read me back the last line,' " read back the corporal.

"That's *my* last line again!" shrieked the colonel, turning purple with anger.

"Oh, no, sir," corrected the corporal. "That's *my* last line. I read it to you just a moment ago. Don't you remember, sir? It was only a moment ago."

"Oh, my God! Read me back *his* last line, stupid. Say, what the hell's your name, anyway?"

"Popinjay, sir."

"Well, you're next, Popinjay. As soon as his trial ends, your trial begins. Get it?"

"Yes, sir. What will I be charged with?"

"What the hell difference does that make? Did you hear what he asked me? You're going to learn, Popinjay—the minute we finish with Clevinger you're going to learn. Cadet Clevinger, what did— You are Cadet Clevinger, aren't you, and not Popinjay?"

"Yes, sir."

"Good. What did—"

"I'm Popinjay, sir."

"Popinjay, is your father a millionaire, or a member of the Senate?"

"No, sir."

"Then you're up shit creek, Popinjay, without a paddle. He's not a general or a high-ranking member of the Administration, is he?"

"No, sir."

"That's good. What does your father do?"

"He's dead, sir."

"That's *very* good. You really are up the creek, Popinjay. Is Popinjay really your name? Just what the hell kind of a name is Popinjay, anyway? I don't like it."

"It's Popinjay's name, sir," Lieutenant Scheisskopf explained.

"Well, I don't like it, Popinjay, and I just can't wait to rip your stinking, cowardly body apart limb from limb. Cadet Clevinger, will you please repeat what the hell it was you did or didn't whisper to Yossarian late last night in the latrine?"

"Yes, sir. I said that you couldn't find me guilty—"

"We'll take it from there. Precisely what did you mean, Cadet Clevinger, when you said we couldn't find you guilty?"

"I didn't say you couldn't find me guilty, sir."

"When?"

"When what, sir?"

"Goddammit, are you going to start pumping me again?"

"No, sir. I'm sorry, sir."

"Then answer the question. When didn't you say we couldn't find you guilty?"

"Late last night in the latrine, sir."

"Is that the only time you didn't say it?"

"No, sir. I always didn't say you couldn't find me guilty, sir. What I did say to Yossarian was—"

"Nobody asked you what you did say to Yossarian. We asked you what you didn't say to him. We're not at all interested in what you did say to Yossarian. Is that clear?"

"Yes, sir."

"Then we'll go on. What did you say to Yossarian?"

"I said to him, sir, that you couldn't find me guilty of the offense with which I am charged and still be faithful to the cause of . . ."

"Of what? You're mumbling."

"Stop mumbling."

"Yes, sir."

"And mumble 'sir' when you do."

"Metcalf, you bastard!"

"Yes, sir," mumbled Clevinger. "Of justice, sir. That you couldn't find—"

"Justice?" The colonel was astounded. "What is justice?"

"Justice, sir—"

"That's not what justice is," the colonel jeered, and began pounding the table again with his big fat hand. "That's what Karl Marx is. I'll tell you what justice is. Justice is a knee in the gut from the floor on the chin at night sneaky with a knife brought up down on the magazine of a battleship sandbagged underhanded in the dark without a word of warning. Garroting. That's what justice is when we've all got to be tough enough and rough enough to fight Billy Petrolle. From the hip. Get it?"

"No, sir."

"Don't sir me!"

"Yes, sir."

"And say 'sir' when you don't," ordered Major Metcalf.

Clevinger was guilty, of course, or he would not have been accused, and since the only way to prove it was to find him guilty, it was their patriotic duty to do so. He was sentenced to walk fifty-seven punishment tours. Popinjay was locked up to be taught a lesson, and Major Metcalf was shipped to the Solomon Islands to bury bodies. A punishment tour for Clevinger was fifty minutes of a weekend hour spent pacing back and forth before the provost marshal's building with a ton of an unloaded rifle on his shoulder.

ARTEMUS WARD

"How Old Abe Received the News of His Nomination"

There are several reports afloat as to how "Honest Old Abe" received the news of his nomination, none of which are correct. We give the correct report.

The Official Committee arrived in Springfield at dewy eve, and went to Honest Old Abe's house. Honest Old Abe was not in. Mrs. Honest Old Abe said Honest Old Abe was out in the woods splitting rails. So the Official Committee went out into the woods, where sure enough they found Honest Old Abe splitting rails with his two boys. It was a grand, a magnificent spectacle. There stood Honest Old Abe in his shirt-sleeves, a pair of leather home-made suspenders holding up a pair of home-made pantaloons, the seat of which was neatly patched with substantial cloth of a different color. "Mr. Lincoln, Sir, you've been nominated, Sir, for the highest office, Sir—." "Oh, don't bother me," said Honest Old Abe, "I took a *stent* this mornin' to split three million rails afore night, and I don't want to be pestered with no stuff about no Conventions till I get my stent done. I've only got two hundred thousand rails to split before sundown. I kin do it if you'll let me alone." And the great man went right on splitting rails, paying no attention to the Committee whatever. The Committee were lost in admiration for a few moments, when they recovered, and asked one of Honest Old Abe's boys whose boy he was? "I'm my parents' boy," shouted the urchin, which burst of wit so convulsed the Committee that they came very near "gin'in eout" completely. In a few moments Honest Old Abe finished his task, and received the news with perfect self-possession. He then asked them up to the house, where he received them cordially. He said he split three million rails every day, although he was in very poor health. Mr. Lincoln is a jovial man, and has a keen sense of the ludicrous. During the evening he asked Mr. Evarts, of New York, why Chicago was like a hen crossing the street? Mr. Evarts gave it up. "Because," said Mr. Lincoln, "Old Grimes is dead, that good old man!" This exceedingly humorous thing created the most uproarious laughter.

ARTEMUS WARD

"A Romance—William Barker, the Young Patriot"

I

"No, William Barker, you cannot have my daughter's hand in marriage until you are her equal in wealth and social position."

The speaker was a haughty old man of some sixty years, and the person whom he addressed was a fine-looking young man of twenty-five.

With a sad aspect the young man withdrew from the stately mansion.

II

Six months later the young man stood in the presence of the haughty old man.

"What! *you* here again?" angrily cried the old man.

"Ay, old man," proudly exclaimed William Barker. "I am here, your daughter's equal and yours."

The old man's lips curled with scorn. A derisive smile lit up his cold features; when, casting violently upon the marble center table an enormous roll of greenbacks, William Barker cried—

"See! Look on this wealth. And I've tenfold more! Listen, old man! You spurned me from your door. But I did not despair. I secured a contract for furnishing the Army of the ———— with beef—"

"Yes, yes!" eagerly exclaimed the old man.

"—and I bought up all the disabled cavalry horses I could find—"

"I see! I see!" cried the old man. "And good beef they make, too."

"They do! they do! and the profits are immense."

"I should say so!"

"And now, sir, I claim your daughter's fair hand!"

"Boy, she is yours. But hold! Look me in the eye. Throughout all this have you been loyal?"

"To the core!" cried William Barker.

"And," continued the old man, in a voice husky with emotion, "are you in favor of a vigorous prosecution of the war?"

"I am, I am!"

"Then, boy, take her! Maria, child, come hither. Your William claims thee. Be happy, my children! and whatever our lot in life may be, *let us all support the Government!*"

ARTEMUS WARD

"The Draft in Baldinsville"

My townsmen were sort o' demoralized. There was a evident desine to ewade the Draft, as I obsarved with sorrer, and patritism was below Par—and *Mar,* too. [A jew desprit.] I hadn't no sooner sot down on the piazzy of the tavoun than I saw sixteen solitary hossmen, ridin' four abreast, wendin' their way up the street.

"What's them? Is it cavalry?"

"That," said the landlord, "is the stage. Sixteen able-bodied citizens has lately bo't the stage line 'tween here and Scotsburg. That's them. They're stage-drivers. Stage-drivers is exempt!"

I saw that each stage-driver carried a letter in his left hand.

"The mail is hevy, to-day," said the landlord. "Gin'rally they don't have more'n half a dozen letters 'tween 'em. To-day they've got one apiece! Bile my lights and liver!"

"And the passengers?"

"There ain't any, skacely, now-days," said the landlord, "and what few there is, very much prefier to walk, the roads is so rough."

"And how ist with you?" I inquired of the editor of the *Bugle-Horn of Liberty,* who sot near me.

"I can't go," he sed, shakin' his head in a wise way. "Ordinarily I should delight to wade in gore, but my bleedin' country bids me stay at home. It is imperatively necessary that I remain here for the purpuss of announcin' from week to week, that *our Gov'ment is about to take vigorous measures to put down the rebellion!*''

I strolled into the village oyster-saloon, where I found Dr. SCHWAZEY, a leadin' citizen, in a state of mind which showed that he'd bin histin' in more'n his share of pizen.

"Hello, old Beeswax," he bellered; "How's yer grandmams? When you goin' to feed your stuffed animils?''

"What's the matter with the eminent physician?'' I pleasantly inquired.

"This,'' he said; "this is what's the matter. I'm a habitooal drunkard! I'm exempt!''

* * *

This is a speciment of how things was goin' in my place of residence.

A few was true blue. The schoolmaster was among 'em. He greeted me warmly. He said I was welkim to those shores. He said I had a massiv mind. It was gratifyin', he said, to see that great intelleck stalkin' in their midst onct more. I have before had occasion to notice this schoolmaster. He is evidently a young man of far more than ord'nary talents.

The schoolmaster proposed we should git up a mass meetin'. The meetin' was largely attended. We held it in the open air, round a roarin' bonfire.

The schoolmaster was the first orator. He's pretty good on the speak. He also writes well, his composition bein' seldom marred by ingrammatticisms. He said this inactivity surprised him. "What do you expect will come of this kind of doin's? *Nihil fit*—'

"Hooray for Nihil!'' I interrupted. "Fellow-citizens, let's giv three cheers for Nihil, the man who fit!''

The schoolmaster turned a little red, but repeated—*"Nihil fit.''*

"Exactly,'' I said. "Nihil *fit*. He wasn't a strategy feller.''

"Our venerable friend,'' said the schoolmaster, smilin' pleasantly, "isn't posted in Virgil.''

"No, I don't know him. But if he's a able-bodied man he must stand his little draft.''

The schoolmaster wound up in eloquent style, and the subscriber took the stand.

I said the crisis had not only cum itself, but it had brought all its relations. It has cum, I said, with a evident intention of makin' us a good long visit. It's goin' to take off its things and stop with us. My wife says so too. This is a good war. For those who like this war, it's just such a kind of war as they like. I'll bet ye. My wife says so too. If the Federal army succeeds in takin' Washington, and they seem to be advancin' that way pretty often, I shall say it is strategy, and Washington will be safe. And that noble banner, as it were—that banner, as it were—will be a emblem, or rather, I should say, that noble banner—*as it were*. My wife says so too. [I got a little mixed up here, but they didn't notice it. Keep mum.] Feller citizens, it will be a proud day for this Republic when Washington is safe. My wife says so too.

The editor of the *Bugle-Horn of Liberty* here arose and said: "I do not wish to interrupt the gentleman, but a important despatch has just bin received at the telegraph office here. I will read it. It is as follows: *Gov'ment is about to take vigorous measures to put down the rebellion!*" [Loud applause.]

That, said I, is cheering. That's soothing. And Washington will be safe. [Sensation.] Philadelphia is safe. Gen. PATTERSON's in Philadelphia. But my heart bleeds partic'ly for Washington. My wife says so too.

There's money enough. No trouble about *money*. They've got a lot of first-class bank-note engravers at Washington (which place, I regret to say, is by no means safe) who turn out two or three cords of money a day—good money, too. Goes well. These bank-note engravers made good wages. I expect they lay up property. They are full of Union sentiment. There is considerable Union sentiment in Virginny, more specially among the honest farmers of the Shenandoah valley. My wife says so too.

Then it isn't money we want. But we do want *men,* and we must have them. We must carry a whirlwind of fire among the foe. We must crush the ungrateful rebels who are poundin' the Goddess of Liberty over the head with slungshots, and stabbin' her with stolen knives! We must lick 'em quick. We must introduce a large number of first-class funerals among the people of the South. Betsy says so, too.

This war hain't been too well managed. We all know that. What then? We are all in the same boat—if the boat goes down, we go down with her. Hence we must all fight. It ain't no use to talk now about who *caused* the war. That's played out. The war is upon us—upon us all—and we must all fight. We can't "reason" the matter with the foe. When, in the broad glare of the noonday sun, a speckled jackass boldly and maliciously kicks over a peanut-stand, do we "reason" with him? I guess not. And why "reason" with those other Southern people who are tryin' to kick over the Republic? Betsy, my wife, says so too.

The meetin' broke up with enthusiasm. We shan't draft in Baldinsville if we can help it.

David Ross Locke

"Nasby Shows Why He Should Not Be Drafted"

(August 6, 1862)

Petroleum V. Nasby was the fictional creation of David Ross Locke, owner and editor of the Toledo Blade. *Locke's aim was satirical, and he made Nasby illiterate, bigoted, and utterly loathsome. Politically, Nasby was a Copperhead, a northerner who sympathized with the South in the Civil War.*

I see in the papers last nite that the Government hez institooted a draft, and that in a few weeks sum hundreds uv thousands uv peeceable citizens will be dragged to the tented field.[1] I know not wat uthers may do, but ez for me, I cant go. Upon a rigid eggsaminashun uv my fizzleckle man, I find it wood be wus nor madnis for me to undertake a campane, to-wit:—

1. I'm bald-headid, and hev bin obliged to wear a wig these 22 years.
2. I hev dandruff in wat scanty hair still hangs around my venerable temples.
3. I hev a kronic katarr.
4. I hev lost, sence Stanton's order to draft, the use uv wun eye entirely, and hev kronic inflammashen in the other.
5. My teeth is all unsound, my palit aint eggsactly rite, and I hev hed bronkeetis 31 yeres last Joon. At present I hev a koff, the paroxisms uv wich is friteful to behold.
6. I'm holler-chestid, am short-winded, and hev alluz hed pains in my back and side.
7. I am afflictid with kronic diarrear and kostivniss. The money I hev paid (or promist to pay), for Jayneses karminnytiv balsam and pills wood astonish almost enny body.

---

[1] One of the most surprising results of the conscription was the amount of disease disclosed among men between "eighteen and forty-five," in districts where quotas could not be raised by volunteering.—Locke's note.

8. I am rupchered in nine places, and am entirely enveloped with trusses.
9. I hev verrykose vanes, hev a white-swellin on wun leg and a fever sore on the uther; also wun leg is shorter than tother, though I handle it so expert that nobody never noticed it.
10. I hev korns and bunyons on both feet, wich wood prevent me from marchin.

I don't suppose that my political opinions, wich are aginst the prossekooshn uv this unconstooshnel war, wood hev any wate, with a draftin orfiser; but the above reesons why I cant go, will, I make no doubt, be suffishent.

"Nasby Writes His Flock from a Union Jail"

(June 20, 1863)

In a Linkin Basteel,
Columbus, Ohio,

Agen I am in durence vile. Agen I am in the hands uv Linkin's hirelin minyuns, and my church is without a paster. The sheperd is smitten and the sheep may be scattered. Were it not for two barels uv whisky that we hed in the church, I doubt wether the organnizashen wood continue. My prayer is that the cohesive flooid may hold out till I return. My capcher wuz ez follows:

Wen the Diemekrats, the peece men of Homes County, declared war, I threw off the sacredotle robes and tuk up the sword. Arrivin in at Millersberg, I jined the peace forces to onst. Ability is allus recognized, and I wus immejitly made commander-in-cheef uv the forces. A full uniform uv butiful butternut cloth and a copper-heded sword wuz presented me. I immejitly commenst drillin the men, and in two days hed them perfishent in company and battalyun drill.

We fortyfide, buildin gabeyuns, faseens, and eliptiks, and neglectid no precaushen to make victry sure. Fifteen hundred strong, we pledged ourselves to hist the black flag, and never surrender.

Finally the enemy hove in site. Ez they cum up, our men trembled with anxiety to meet em. Sum two hunderd askt permishen to withdraw from the fortyfications, make a detour over the hill, and flank em wich request, bein unwillin to restrane their arder, I ackseded to. Sum 500 jined em, and I spoze are detoorin yet, ez I hev never seen em since. This movement wuz fatle, ez all went who were sober enuff to walk. Jest afterwards cum the catastrophy. Ten uv the very men who hed bin formost in advisin resistence, cum up with the Fedrals, and advised a surrender! Hopin to gain time, I askt two hours to consider. Unfortnit errer! Before the two hours wuz up, half the men wuz sober, and, instid uv histin the black flag, they capitoolatid, deliverin up the ringleeders. I wuz taken ez a hed ringleeder, and wuz ironed and taken to Columbus, wher I now am.

In hopes uv kepin my flock together, I writ em a epistle, as follows:

To the Faithful at Wingert's Corners, Greetin:

I rite yoo in bonds. I beseech yoo, deerly beloved, to be stedfast in yoor faith, holding on to sich truth ez I left you. Be viggelent in good works, patient in chasin enrollin offisers, and quick in tarrin and featherin on em. For, tho I am not with you, the tar-barl and what's left uv the feathers is in my study, jest behint the whisky barls. Be temprit. Ten or twenty nips per day is enuff fer any man in health; if weakly, the number may be indefinitly increest. I am alluz in bad health. Beware uv false teechers; let no Ablishnists pizen your minds. Keep up yure Sundy exercises; ef yoo hev wun among yoo that kin rede, let him next Sundy eddify yoo with Wood's speech. Neglect not the Sundy skool. That proper interest may be kept up in the minds uv the children, I wood sejest that Sundy afternoons you ketch a preacher and hev the darlins rotten-egg him. "Jest ez the twig is bent," et settry. Be ennergetik in tearin down meetin-houses, for they are injoorin us. In conclooshen, deerly beloved, re-member me. Send me a eucher deck, a two-gallon jug uv corn joose; also, the weekly collekshun. Ef I survive, I will be with you again. In the faith.

Ef they send wat I want, I shal be comfortable here.

In chains, but unsubdood,

PETROLEUM V. NASBY

Abraham Lincoln

Cables from the White House

Telegram to General George B. McClellan

October 24, 1862

Major-General McClellan:

I have just read your despatch about sore-tongued and fatigued horses. Will you pardon me for asking what the horses of your army have done since the battle of Antietam that fatigues anything?

A. Lincoln

Telegram to General George B. McClellan

October 27, 1862

Major-General McClellan:

Yours of yesterday received. Most certainly I intend no injustice to any, and if I have done any I deeply regret it. To be told, after more than five weeks' total inaction of the army, and during which period we sent to the army every fresh horse we possibly could, amounting in the whole to 7,918, that the cavalry horses were too much fatigued to move, presents a very cheerless, almost hopeless, prospect for the future, and it may have forced something of impatience in my dispatch. If not recruited and rested then, when could they ever be? I suppose the river is rising, and I am glad to believe you are crossing.

A. Lincoln

TELEGRAM TO GOVERNOR JOHN A. ANDREW

Please say to these gentlemen that if they do not work quickly I will make quick work with them. In the name of all that is reasonable, how long does it take to pay a couple of regiments?

A. LINCOLN

TELEGRAM TO GENERAL DANIEL TYLER

June 14, 1863

General Tyler, Martinsburg:

If you are besieged how do you despatch me? Why do you not leave before being besieged?

A. LINCOLN

TELEGRAMS TO J. K. DUBOIS AND O. M. HATCH

September 13, 1863

Hon. J. K. Dubois, Hon. O. M. Hatch:

What nation do you desire General Allen to be made quarter-master-general of? This nation already has a quarter-master-general.

A. LINCOLN

September 22, 1863

Hon. O. M. Hatch, Hon. J. K. Dubois, Springfield, Ill.:

Your letter is just received. The particular form of my despatch was jocular, which I supposed you gentlemen knew me well enough to understand. General Allen is considered here as a very faithful and capable officer and one who would be at least thought of for quarter-master-general if that office were vacant.

A. LINCOLN

E. B. WHITE

"Two Letters, Both Open"

New York, N.Y.

12 April 1951

The American Society for the Prevention of Cruelty to Animals
York Avenue and East 92nd Street
New York 28, N.Y.
Dear Sirs:

I have your letter, undated, saying that I am harboring an unlicensed dog in violation of the law. If by "harboring" you mean getting up two or three times every night to pull Minnie's blanket up over her, I am harboring a dog all right. The blanket keeps slipping off. I suppose you are wondering by now why I don't get her a sweater instead. That's a joke on you. She has a knitted sweater, but she doesn't like to wear it for sleeping; her legs are so short they work out of a sweater and her toenails get caught in the mesh, and this disturbs her rest. If Minnie doesn't get her rest, she feels it right away. I do myself, and of course with this night duty of mine, the way the blanket slips and all, I haven't had any real rest in years. Minnie is twelve.

In spite of what your inspector reported, she has a license. She is licensed in the State of Maine as an unspayed bitch, or what is more commonly called an "unspaded" bitch. She wears her metal license tag but I must say I don't particularly care for it, as it is in the shape of a hydrant, which seems to me a feeble gag, besides pointless in the case of a female. It is hard to believe that any state in the Union would circulate a gag like that and make people pay money for it, but Maine is always thinking of something. Maine puts up roadside crosses along the highways to mark the spots where people have lost their lives in motor accidents, so the highways are beginning to take on the appearance of a cemetery, and motoring in Maine has become a solemn experience, when one thinks mostly about death. I was driving along a road near Kittery the other day thinking about death and all of a sudden I heard the spring peepers. That changed me right away and I suddenly thought about life. It was the nicest feeling.

You asked about Minnie's name, sex, breed, and phone number. She doesn't answer the phone. She is a dachshund and can't reach it, but she wouldn't answer it even if she could, as she has no interest in outside calls. I did have a dachshund once, a male, who was interested in the telephone, and who got a great many calls, but Fred was an exceptional dog (his name was Fred) and I can't think of anything offhand that he *wasn't* interested in. The telephone was only one of a thousand things. He loved life—that is, he loved life if by "life" you mean "trouble," and of course the phone is almost synonymous with trouble. Minnie loves life, too, but her idea of life is a warm bed, preferably with an electric pad, and a friend in bed with her, and plenty of shut-eye, night and day. She's almost twelve. I guess I've already mentioned that. I got her from Dr. Clarence Little in 1939. He was using dachshunds in his cancer-research experiments (that was before Winchell was running the thing) and he had a couple of extra puppies, so I wheedled Minnie out of him. She later had puppies by her own father, at Dr. Little's request. What do you think about *that* for a scandal? I know what Fred thought about it. He was some put out.

Sincerely yours,
E. B. White

New York, N.Y.
12 April 1951

Collector of Internal Revenue
Divisional Office
Bangor, Maine
Dear Sir:

I have your notice about a payment of two hundred and some-odd dollars that you say is owing on my 1948 income tax. You say a warrant has been issued for the seizure and sale of my place in Maine, but I don't know as you realize how awkward that would be right at this time, because in the same mail I also received a notice from the Society for the Prevention of Cruelty to Animals here in New York taking me to task for harboring an unlicensed dog in my apartment, and I have written them saying that Minnie is licensed in Maine, but if you seize and sell my place, it is going to make me look pretty silly with the Society, isn't it? Why would I license a dog in Maine, they will say, if I don't live there? I think it is a fair question. I have written the Society, but purposely did not mention the warrant of seizure and sale. I didn't want to mix them up, and it might have sounded like just some sort of cock and bull story. I have always paid my taxes promptly, and the Society would think I was kidding, or something.

Anyway, the way the situation shapes up is this: I am being accused in New York State of dodging my dog tax, and accused in Maine of being behind in my federal tax, and I believe I'm going to have to rearrange my life somehow or other so that everything can be brought together, all in one state, maybe Delaware or some state like that, as it is too confusing for everybody this way. Minnie, who is very sensitive to my moods, knows there is something wrong and that I feel terrible. And now *she* feels terrible. The other day it was the funniest thing. I was packing a suitcase for a trip home to Maine, and the suitcase was lying open on the floor and when I wasn't looking she went and got in and lay down. Don't you think that was cute?

If you seize the place, there are a couple of things I ought to explain. At the head of the kitchen stairs you will find an awfully queer boxlike thing. I don't want you to get a false idea about it, as it looks like a coffin, only it has a partition inside, and two small doors on one side. I don't suppose there is another box like it in the entire world. I built it myself. I made it many years ago as a dormitory for two snug-haired dachshunds, both of whom suffered from night chill. Night chill is the most prevalent dachshund disorder, if you have never had one. Both these dogs, as a matter of fact, had rheumatoid tendencies, as well as a great many other tendencies, specially Fred. He's dead, damn it. I would feel a lot better this morning if I could just see Fred's face, as he would know instantly that I was in trouble with the authorities and would be all over the place, hamming it up. He was something.

About the tax money, it was an oversight, or mixup. Your notice says that the "first notice" was sent last summer. I think that is correct, but when it arrived I didn't know what it meant as I am no mind reader. It was cryptic. So I sent it to a lawyer, fool-fashion, and asked him if *he* knew what it meant. I asked him if it was a tax bill and shouldn't I pay it, and he wrote back and said, No, no, no, no, it isn't a tax bill. He advised me to wait till I got a bill, and then pay it. Well, that was all right, but I was building a small henhouse at the time, and when I get building something with my own hands I lose all sense of time and place. I don't even show up for meals. Give me some tools and some second-handed lumber and I get completely absorbed in what I am doing. The first thing I knew, the summer was gone, and the fall was gone, and it was winter. The lawyer must have been building something, too, because I never heard another word from him.

To make a long story short, I am sorry about this non-payment, but you've got to see the whole picture to understand it, got to see my side of it. Of course I will forward the money if you haven't seized and sold the place in the meantime. If you have, there are a couple of other things on my mind. In the barn, at the far end of the tieups, there is a goose sitting on eggs. She is a young goose and I hope you can manage everything so as not to disturb her until she has brought off her goslings. I'll give you one, if you want. Or would they belong to the federal government anyway, even though the eggs were laid before the notice was mailed? The cold frames are ready, and pretty soon you ought to transplant the young broccoli and tomato plants and my wife's petunias from the flats in the kitchen into the frames, to harden them. Fred's grave is down in the alder thicket beyond the dump. You have to go down there every once in a while and straighten the headstone, which is nothing but a couple of old bricks that came out of a chimney. Fred was restless, and his headstone is the same way—doesn't stay quiet. You have to keep at it.

I am sore about your note, which didn't seem friendly. I am a friendly taxpayer and do not think the government should take a threatening tone, at least until we have exchanged a couple of letters kicking the thing around. Then it might be all right to talk about selling the place, if I proved stubborn. I showed the lawyer your notice about the warrant of seizure and sale, and do you know what he said? He said, "Oh, that doesn't mean anything, it's just a form." What a crazy way to look at a piece of plain English. I honestly worry about lawyers. They never write plain English themselves, and when you give them a bit of plain English to read, they say, "Don't worry, it doesn't mean anything." They're hopeless, don't you think they are? To me a word is a word, and I wouldn't dream of writing anything like "I am going to get out a warrant to seize and sell your place" unless I meant it, and I can't believe that my government would either.

The best way to get into the house is through the woodshed, as there is an old crocus sack nailed on the bottom step and you can wipe the mud off on it. Also, when you go in through the woodshed, you land in the back kitchen right next to the cooky jar with Mrs. Freethy's cookies. Help yourself, they're wonderful.

Sincerely yours,
E. B. WHITE

FINLEY PETER DUNNE

"Woman Suffrage"

"I see be th' pa-apers that th' ladies in England have got up in their might an' demanded a vote."

"A what?" cried Mr. Hennessy.

"A vote," said Mr. Dooley.

"Th' shameless viragoes," said Mr. Hennessy. . . .

"Why," said Mr. Dooley, "they wuddn't know how to vote. They think it's an aisy job that anny wan can do, but it ain't. It's a man's wurruk, an' a sthrong man's with a sthrong stomach. I don't know annything that requires what Hogan calls th' exercise iv manly vigor more thin votin'. It's th' hardest wurruk I do in th' year. I get up befure daylight an' thramp over to th' Timple iv Freedom, which is also th' office iv a livery stable. Wan iv th' judges has a cold in his head an' closes all th' windows. Another judge has built a roarin' fire in a round stove an' is cookin' red-hots on it. Th' room is lit with candles an' karosene lamps, an' is crowded with pathrites who haven't been to bed. At th' dure are two or three polismen that maybe ye don't care to meet. Dock O'Leary says he don't know annything that'll exhaust th' air iv a room so quick as a polisman in his winter unyform. All th' pathrites an', as th' pa-apers call thim, th' high-priests iv this here sacred rite, ar-re smokin' th' best seegars that th' token money iv our counthry can buy.

"In th' pleasant warmth iv th' fire, th' harness on th' walls glows an' puts out its own peculiar aromy. Th' owner iv th' sanchooary iv Liberty comes in, shakes up a bottle iv liniment made iv carbolic acid, pours it into a cup an' goes out. Wan iv th' domestic attindants iv th' guests iv th' house walks through fr'm makin' th' beds. Afther a while th' chief judge, who knows me well, because he shaves me three times a week, gives me a contimchous stare, asks me me name an' a number iv scand'lous questions about me age.

"I'm timpted to make an angry retort, whin I see th' polisman movin' nearer, so I take me ballot an' wait me turn in th' booth. They're all occupied be writhin' freemen, callin' in sthrangled voices f'r somewan to light th' candle so they'll be sure they ain't votin' th' prohibition ticket. Th' calico sheets over th' front iv th' booths wave an' ar-re pushed out like th' curtains iv a Pullman car whin a fat man is dhressin' inside while th' thrain is goin' r-round a curve. In time a freeman bursts through, with perspyration poorin' down his nose, hurls his suffrage at th' judge an' staggers out. I plunge in, sharpen an inch iv lead pencil be rendin' it with me teeth, mutilate me ballot at th' top iv th' Dimmycratic column, an' run f'r me life.

"Cud a lady do that, I ask ye? No, sir, 'tis no job f'r th' fair. It's men's wurruk. Molly Donahue wants a vote, but though she cud bound Kamachatka as aisily as ye cud this precinct, she ain't qualified f'r it. It's meant f'r gr-reat sturdy American pathrites like Mulkowsky th' Pollacky down th' sthreet. He don't know yet that he ain't votin' f'r th' King iv Poland. He thinks he's still over there pretindin' to be a horse instead iv a free American givin' an imytation iv a steam dhredge.

"On th' first Choosday afther th' first Monday in November an' April a man goes ar-round to his house, wakes him up, leads him down th' sthreet, an' votes him th' way ye'd wather a horse. He don't mind inhalin' th' air iv liberty in a livery stable. But if Molly Donahue wint to vote in a livery stable, th' first thing she'd do wud be to get a broom, sweep up th' flure, open th' windows, disinfect th' booths, take th' harness fr'm th' walls, an' hang up a pitcher iv Niagary be moonlight, chase out th' watchers an' polis, remove th' seegars, make th' judges get a shave, an' p'raps invalydate th' iliction. It's no job f'r her, an' I told her so.

" 'We demand a vote,' says she. 'All right,' says I, 'take mine. It's old, but it's trustworthy an' durable. It may look a little th' worse f'r wear fr'm bein' hurled again a Republican majority in this counthry f'r forty years, but it's all right. Take my vote an' use it as ye please,' says I, 'an' I'll get an hour or two exthry sleep illiction day mornin',' says I. 'I've voted so often I'm tired iv it annyhow,' says I. 'But,' says I, 'why shud anny wan so young an' beautiful as ye want to do annything so foolish as to vote?' says I. 'Ain't we intilligent enough?' says she. 'Ye're too intilligent,' says I. 'But intilligence don't give ye a vote.' . . .

"I believe ye're in favor iv it ye'ersilf," said Mr. Hennessy.

"Faith," said Mr. Dooley, "I'm not wan way or th' other. I don't care. What diff'rence does it make? I wudden't mind at all havin' a little soap an' wather, a broom an' a dusther applied to polyticks. It wuddn't do anny gr-reat harm if a man cuddn't be illicited to office onless he kept his hair combed an' blacked his boots an' shaved his chin wanst a month. Annyhow, as Hogan says, I care not who casts th' votes iv me counthry so long as we can hold th' offices. An' there's on'y wan way to keep the women out iv office, an' that's to give thim a vote."

WASHINGTON IRVING

"*Salmagundi No. XI*"

Tuesday, June 2, 1807.

LETTER
From MUSTAPHA RUB-A-DUB KELI KHAN,
captain of a ketch,
to ASEM HACCHEM, principal slave-driver
to his highness the bashaw of Tripoli.

The deep shadows of midnight gather around me—the footsteps of the passenger have ceased in the streets, and nothing disturbs the holy silence of the hour, save the sound of distant drums, mingled with the shouts, the bawlings, and the discordant revelry of his majesty, the sovereign mob. Let the hour be sacred to friendship, and consecrated to thee, oh thou brother of my inmost soul!

Oh Asem! I almost shrink at the recollection of the scenes of confusion, of licentious disorganization, which I have witnessed during the last three days. I have beheld this whole city, nay this whole state, given up to the tongue and the pen, to the puffers, the bawlers, the babblers and the *slang-whangers.* I have beheld the community convulsed with a civil war, (or *civil talk*) individuals verbally massacred, families annihilated by whole sheets full, and slang-whangers coolly bathing their pens in ink, and rioting in the slaughter of their thousands. I have seen, in short, that awful despot, *the people,* in the moment of unlimited power, wielding newspapers in one hand, and with the other scattering mud and filth about, like some desperate lunatic relieved from the restraints of his strait waistcoat. I have seen beggers on horseback, ragamuffins riding in coaches, and swing seated in places of honour—I have seen liberty, I have seen equality, I have seen fraternity!—I have seen that great political puppet-show—AN ELECTION.

A few days ago the friend, whom I have mentioned in some of my former letters, called upon me to accompany him to witness this grand ceremony, and we forthwith sallied out to *the polls,* as he called them. Though for several weeks before this splendid exhibition, nothing else had been talked of, yet I do assure thee I was entirely ignorant of its nature; and when, on coming up to a church, my companion informed me we were at the poll, I supposed that an election was some great religious ceremony, like the fast of Ramazan, or the great festival of Haraphat, so celebrated in the East.

My friend, however, undeceived me at once, and entered into a long dissertation on the nature and object of an election, the substance of which was nearly to this effect: "You know," said he, "that this country is engaged in a violent internal warfare, and suffers a variety of evils from civil dissentions. An election is the grand trial of strength, the decisive battle when the Belligerents draw out their forces in martial array; when every leader burning with warlike ardour, and encouraged by the shouts and acclamations of tatterdemalians, buffoons, dependents, parasites, toad-eaters, scrubs, vagrants, mumpers, ragamuffins, bravoes and beggers, in his rear, and puffed up by his bellows-blowing slang-whangers, waves gallantly the banners of faction, and presses forward TO OFFICE AND IMMORTALITY! ,

"For a month or two previous to the critical period which is to decide this important affair, the whole community is in a ferment. Every man of whatever rank or degree, such is the wonderful patriotism of the people, disinterestedly neglects his business, to devote himself to his country—and not an insignificant fellow, but feels himself inspired on this occasion, with as much warmth in favour of the cause he has espoused, as if all the comfort of his life, or even his life itself, was dependent on the issue. . . .

"As the time for fighting the decisive battle approaches, appearances become more and more alarming—committees are appointed, who hold little encampments, from whence they send out small detachments of tatlers, to reconnoitre, harrass and skirmish with the enemy, and, if possible, ascertain their numbers; every body seems big with the mighty event that is impending—the orators they gradually swell up beyond their usual size—the little orators, they grow greater and greater—the secretaries of the ward committees strut about, looking like wooden oracles—the puffers put on the airs of mighty consequence; the slang-whangers deal out direful innuendoes, and threats of doughty import, and all is buzz, murmur, suspense and sublimity!

"At length the day arrives. The storm that has been so long gathering, and threatening in distant thunders bursts forth in terrible explosion. All business is at an end—the whole city is in a tumult—the people are running helter skelter, they know not whither, and they know not why. The hackney coaches rattle through the streets with thundering vehemence, loaded with recruiting serjeants who have been prowling in cellars and caves, to unearth some miserable minion of poverty and ignorance, who will barter his vote for a glass of beer, or a ride in a coach with such *fine gentlemen!*—The buzzards of the party scamper from poll to poll, on foot or on horseback—and they twaddle from committee to committee, and buzz, and chafe, and fume, and talk big, and— *do nothing*—like the vagabond drone, who wastes his time in the laborious idleness of *see-saw-song,* and busy nothingness.''

I know not how long my friend would have continued his detail, had he not been interrupted by a squabble which took place between two *old continentals,* as they were called. It seems they had entered into an argument on the respective merits of their cause, and not being able to make each other clearly understood, resorted to what are called *knock-down arguments,* which form the superlative degree of the *argumentum ad hominem;* but are, in my opinion, extremely inconsistent with the true spirit of a genuine logocracy. After they had beaten each other soundly, and set the whole mob together by the ears, they came to a full explanation, when it was discovered that they were both of the same way of thinking—whereupon they shook each other heartily by the hand, and laughed with great glee at their *humourous* misunderstanding.

I could not help being struck with the exceeding great number of ragged, dirty looking persons, that swaggered about the place, and seemed to think themselves the bashaws of the land. I inquired of my friend if these people were employed to drive away the hogs, dogs, and other intruders that might thrust themselves in and interrupt the ceremony? ''By no means,'' replied he; ''these are the representatives of the sovereign people, who come here to make governors, senators and members of assembly, and are the source of all power and authority in this nation.'' ''Preposterous,'' said I, ''how is it possible that such men can be capable of distinguishing between an honest man and a knave, or even if they were, will it not always happen that they are led by the nose by some intriguing demagogue, and made the mere tools of ambitious political jugglers?—Surely it would be better to trust to providence, or even chance, for governors, than resort to the discriminating powers of an ignorant mob.—I plainly perceive the consequence.—A man, who possesses superior talents, and that honest pride which ever accompanies this possession, will always be sacrificed to some creeping insect who will prostitute himself to familiarity with the lowest of mankind, and like the idolatrous egyptian, worship the wallowing tenants of filth and mire.''

''All this is true enough,'' replied my friend, ''but after all you cannot say but that this is a free country, and that the people can get drunk cheaper here, particularly at elections, than in the despotic countries of the east.'' I could not, with any degree of propriety or truth, deny this last assertion, for just at that moment a patriotic brewer arrived with a load of beer, which, for a moment, occasioned a cessation of argument.—The great crowd of buzzards, puffers, and old continentals of all *parties,* who throng to the polls, to persuade, to cheat, or to force the freeholders into the right way, and to maintain the *freedom of suffrage,* seemed for a moment to forget their antipathies, and joined, heartily, in a copious libation of this patriotic, and argumentative beverage.

These *beer barrels,* indeed seem to be most able logicians, well stored with that kind of sound argument, best suited to the comprehension, and most relished by the mob, or sovereign people, who are never so tractable as when operated upon by this convincing liquor, which, in fact, seems to be inbrued with the very spirit of logocracy. No sooner does it begin its operation, than the tongue waxes exceeding valourous, and becomes impatient for some mighty conflict. The puffer puts himself at the head of his body guard of buzzards, and his legion of ragamuffins, and woe then to every unhappy adversary who is uninspired by the deity of the beer-barrel—he is sure to be talked, and argued into complete insignificance.

While I was making these observations, I was surprised to observe a bashaw, high in office, shaking a fellow by the hand, that looked rather more ragged, than a scare-crow, and inquiring with apparent solicitude concerning the health of his family; after which he slipped a little folded paper into his hand and turned away. I could not help applauding his humility in shaking the fellow's hand, and his benevolence in relieving his distresses, for I imagined the paper contained something for the poor man's necessities; and truly he seemed verging towards the last stage of starvation. My friend, however, soon undeceived me by saying that this was an elector, and the bashaw had merely given him the list of candidates, for whom he was to vote. "Ho! ho!" said I, "then he is a particular friend of the bashaw?" "By no means," replied my friend, "the bashaw will pass him without notice, the day after the election, except, perhaps, just to drive over him with his coach."

My friend then proceeded to inform me that for some time before, and during the continuance of an election, there was a most *delectable courtship* or intrigue, carried on between the great bashaws, and *mother mob.* That *mother mob* generally preferred the attentions of the rabble, or of fellows of her own stamp, but would sometimes condescend to be treated to a feasting, or any thing of that kind, at the bashaw's expense; nay, sometimes when she was in a good humour, she would condescend to toy with them in her rough way—but woe be to the bashaw who attempted to be familiar with her, for she was the most pestilent, cross, crabbed, scolding, thieving, scratching, toping, wrong-headed, rebellious, and abominable termagant that ever was let loose in the world, to the confusion of honest gentlemen bashaws.

Just then, a fellow came round and distributed among the crowd a number of hand-bills, written by the *ghost of Washington,* the fame of whose illustrious actions, and still more illustrious virtues, has reached even the remotest regions of the east, and who is venerated by this people as the Father of his country. On reading this paltry paper, I could not restrain my indignation. "Insulted hero," cried I, "is it thus thy name is profaned, thy memory disgraced, thy spirit drawn down from heaven to administer to the brutal violence of party rage!—It is thus the necromancers of the east, by their infernal incantations, sometimes call up the shades of the just, to give their sanction to frauds, to lies, and to every species of enormity." My friend smiled at my warmth, and observed, that raising ghosts, and not only raising them but making them speak, was one of the miracles of election. "And believe me," continued he, "there is good reason for the ashes of departed heroes being disturbed on these occasions, for such is the *sandy* foundation of our government, that there never happens an election of an alderman, or a collector, or even a constable, but we are in imminent danger of losing our liberties, and becoming a province of France, or tributary to the British islands." "By the hump of Mahomet's camel," said I, "but this is only another striking example of the prodigious great scale on which every thing is transacted in this country."

By this time I had become tired of the scene; my head ached with the uproar of voices, mingling in all the discordant tones of triumphant exclamation, nonsensical argument, intemperate reproach, and drunken absurdity.—The confusion was such as no language can adequately describe, and it seemed as all the restraints of decency, and all the bands of law had been broken and given place to the wide ravages of licentious brutality. These, thought I, are the orgies of liberty, these are the manifestations of the spirit of independence, these are the symbols of man's sovereignty! Head of Mahomet! with what a fatal and inexorable despotism do empty names and ideal phantoms exercise their dominion over the human mind! The experience of ages has demonstrated, that in all nations, barbarous or enlightened, the mass of the people, the *mob,* must be slaves, or they will be tyrants—but their tyranny will not be long—some ambitious leader, having at first condescended to be their slave, will at length become their master; and in proportion to the vileness of his former servitude, will be the severity of his subsequent tyranny.—Yet, with innumerable examples staring them in the face, the people still bawl out liberty, by which they mean nothing but freedom from every species of legal restraint, and a warrant for all kinds of licentiousness: and the bashaws and leaders, in courting the mob, convince them of their power, and by administering to their passions, for the purposes of ambition, at length learn by fatal experience, that he who worships the beast that carries him on its back, will sooner or later be thrown into the dust and trampled under foot by the animal who has learnt the secret of its power, by this very adoration.

ever thine,
MUSTAPHA.

H. L. MENCKEN

"Coolidge"

The editorial writers who had the job of concocting mortuary tributes to the late Calvin Coolidge, LL.D., made heavy weather of it, and no wonder. Ordinarily, an American public man dies by inches, and there is thus plenty of time to think up beautiful nonsense about him. More often than not, indeed, he threatens to die three or four times before he actually does so, and each threat gives the elegists a chance to mellow and adorn their effusions. But Dr. Coolidge slipped out of life almost as quietly and as unexpectedly as he had originally slipped into public notice, and in consequence the brethren were caught napping and had to do their poetical embalming under desperate pressure. The common legend is that such pressure inflames and inspires a true journalist, and maketh him to sweat masterpieces, but it is not so in fact. Like any other literary man, he functions best when he is at leisure, and can turn from his tablets now and then to run down a quotation, to eat a plate of ham and eggs, or to look out of the window.

The general burden of the Coolidge memoirs was that the right hon. gentleman was a typical American, and some hinted that he was the most typical since Lincoln. As the English say, I find myself quite unable to associate myself with that thesis. He was, in truth, almost as unlike the average of his countrymen as if he had been born green. The Americano is an expansive fellow, a back-slapper, full of amiability; Coolidge was reserved and even muriatic. The Americano has a stupendous capacity for believing, and especially for believing in what is palpably not true; Coolidge was, in his fundamental metaphysics, an agnostic. The Americano dreams vast dreams, and is hag-ridden by a demon; Coolidge was not mount but rider, and his steed was a mechanical horse. The Americano, in his normal incarnation, challenges fate at every step and his whole life is a struggle; Coolidge took things as they came.

Some of the more romantic of the funeral bards tried to convert the farmhouse at Plymouth into a log-cabin, but the attempt was as vain as their effort to make a Lincoln of good Cal. His early days, in fact, were anything but pinched. His father was a man of substance, and he was well fed and well schooled. He went to a good college, had the clothes to cut a figure there, and made useful friends. There is no record that he was brilliant, but he took his degree with a respectable mark, proceeded to the law, and entered a prosperous law firm on the day of his admission to the bar. Almost at once he got into politics, and by the time he was twenty-seven he was already on the public payroll. There he remained without a break for exactly thirty years, always moving up. Not once in all those years did he lose an election. When he retired in the end, it was at his own motion, and with three or four hundred thousand dollars of tax money in his tight jeans.

In brief, a darling of the gods. No other American has ever been so fortunate, or even half so fortunate. His career first amazed observers, and then dazzled them. Well do I remember the hot Saturday in Chicago when he was nominated for the Vice-Presidency on the ticket with Harding. Half a dozen other statesmen had to commit political suicide in order to make way for him, but all of them stepped up docilely and bumped themselves off. The business completed, I left the press-stand and went to the crypt below to hunt a drink. There I found a group of colleagues listening to a Boston brother who knew Coolidge well, and had followed him from the start of his career.

To my astonishment I found that this gentleman was offering to lay a bet that Harding, if elected, would be assassinated before he had served half his term. There were murmurs, and someone protested uneasily that such talk was injudicious, for A. Mitchell Palmer was still Attorney-General and his spies were all about. But the speaker stuck to his wager.

"I am simply telling you," he roared, "what I *know*. I know Cal Coolidge inside and out. He is the luckiest goddam ———— ———— in the whole world."

It seemed plausible then, and it is certain now. No other President ever slipped into the White House so easily, and none other ever had a softer time of it while there. When, at Rapid City, S.D., on August 2, 1927, he loosed the occult words, "I do not choose to run in 1928," was it prescience or only luck? For one, I am inclined to put it down to luck. Surely there was no prescience in his utterances and maneuvers otherwise. He showed not the slightest sign that he smelt black clouds ahead; on the contrary, he talked and lived only sunshine. There was a volcano boiling under him, but he did not know it, and was not singed. When it burst forth at last, it was Hoover who got its blast, and was fried, boiled, roasted and fricasseed. How Dr. Coolidge must have chuckled in his retirement, for he was not without humor of a sad, necrotic kind. He knew Hoover well, and could fathom the full depths of the joke.

In what manner he would have performed himself if the holy angels had shoved the Depression forward a couple of years—this we can only guess, and one man's hazard is as good as another's. My own is that he would have responded to bad times precisely as he responded to good ones—that is, by pulling down the blinds, stretching his legs upon his desk, and snoozing away the lazy afternoons. Here, indeed, was his one peculiar *Fach,* his one really notable talent. He slept more than any other President, whether by day or by night. Nero fiddled, but Coolidge only snored. When the crash came at last and Hoover began to smoke and bubble, good Cal was safe in Northampton, and still in the hay.

There is sound reason for believing that this great gift of his for self-induced narcolepsy was at the bottom of such modest popularity as he enjoyed. I mean, of course, popularity among the relatively enlightened. On lower levels he was revered simply because he was so plainly just folks—because what little he said was precisely what was heard in every garage and barbershop. He gave the plain people the kind of esthetic pleasure known as recognition, and in horse-doctor's doses. But what got him customers higher up the scale of humanity was something else, and something quite different. It was the fact that he not only said little, and that little of harmless platitudes all compact, but did even less. The kind of government that he offered the country was government stripped to the buff. It was government that governed hardly at all. Thus the ideal of Jefferson was realized at last, and the Jeffersonians were delighted.

Well, there is surely something to say for that abstinence, and maybe a lot. I can find no relation of cause and effect between the Coolidge somnolence and the Coolidge prosperity, but it is nevertheless reasonable to argue that if the former had been less marked the latter might have blown up sooner. We suffer most, not when the White House is a peaceful dormitory, but when it is a jitney Mars Hill, with a tin-pot Paul bawling from the roof. Counting out Harding as a cipher only, Dr. Coolidge was preceded by one World Saver and followed by two more. What enlightened American, having to choose between any of them and another Coolidge, would hesitate for an instant? There were no thrills while he reigned, but neither were there any headaches. He had no ideas, and he was not a nuisance.

MARK TWAIN

"Call This a Govment!" Excerpt from The Adventures of Huckleberry Finn

In Chapter Six of The Adventures of Huckleberry Finn, Huck has fallen into the clutches of his father, the town drunk who keeps him imprisoned in a log hut. In this passage he gives Huck a lecture on government.

While I was cooking supper the old man took a swig or two and got sort of warmed up, and went to ripping again. He had been drunk over in town, and laid in the gutter all night, and he was a sight to look at. A body would a thought he was Adam, he was just all mud. Whenever his liquor begun to work, he most always went for the govment. This time he says:

"Call this a govment! why, just look at it and see what it's like. Here's the law a-standing ready to take a man's son away from him—a man's own son, which he has had all the trouble and all the anxiety and all the expense of raising. Yes, just as that man has got that son raised at last, and ready to go to work and begin to do suthin' for *him* and give him a rest, the law up and goes for him. And they call *that* govment! That ain't all, nuther. The law backs that old Judge Thatcher up and helps him to keep me out o' my property. Here's what the law does. The law takes a man worth six thousand dollars and upards, and jams him into an old trap of a cabin like this, and lets him go round in clothes that ain't fitten for a hog. They call that govment! A man can't get his rights in a govment like this. Sometimes I've a mighty notion to just leave the country for good and all. Yes, and I *told* 'em so; I told old Thatcher so to his face. Lots of 'em heard me, and can tell what I said. Says I, for two cents I'd leave the blamed country and never come anear it agin. Them's the very words. I says, look at my hat—if you call it a hat—but the lid raises up and the rest of it goes down till it's below my chin, and then it ain't rightly a hat at all, but more like my head was shoved up through a jint o' stove-pipe. Look at it, says I—such a hat for me to wear—one of the wealthiest men in this town, if I could git my rights.

"Oh, yes, this is a wonderful govment, wonderful. Why, looky here. There was a free nigger there, from Ohio; a mulatter, most as white as a white man. He had the whitest shirt on you ever see, too, and the shiniest hat; and there ain't a man in that town that's got as fine clothes as what he had; and he had a gold watch and chain, and a silver-headed cane—the awfulest old gray-headed nabob in the State. And what do you think? they said he was a p'fessor in a college, and could talk all kinds of languages, and knowed everything. And that ain't the wust. They said he could *vote,* when he was at home. Well, that let me out. Thinks I, what is the country a-coming to? It was 'lection day, and I was just about to go and vote, myself, if I warn't too drunk to get there; but when they told me there was a State in this country where they'd let that nigger vote, I drawed out. I says I'll never vote agin. Them's the very words I said; they all heard me; and the country may rot for all me—I'll never vote agin as long as I live. And to see the cool way of that nigger—why, he wouldn't a give me the road if I hadn't shoved him out o' the way. I says to the people, why ain't this nigger put up at auction and sold?—that's what I want to know. And what do you reckon they said? Why, they said he couldn't be sold till he'd been in the State six months, and he hadn't been there that long yet. There, now—that's a specimen. They call that a govment that can't sell a free nigger till he's been in the State six months. Here's a govment that calls itself a govment, and lets on to be a govment, and thinks it is a govment, and yet's got to set stock-still for six whole months before it can take ahold of a prowling, thieving, infernal, white-shirted free nigger, and—"

Pap was agoing on so, he never noticed where his old limber legs was taking him to, so he went head over heels over the tub of salt pork, and barked both shins, and the rest of his speech was all the hottest kind of language—mostly hove at the nigger and the govment, though he give the tub some, too, all along, here and there. He hopped around the cabin considerable, first on one leg and then on the other, holding first one shin and then the other one, and at last he let out with his left foot all of a sudden and fetched the tub a rattling kick. But it warn't good judgment, because that was the boot that had a couple of his toes leaking out of the front end of it; so now he raised a howl that fairly made a body's hair raise, and down he went in the dirt, and rolled there, and held his toes; and the cussing he done then laid over anything he had ever done previous. He said so his own self, afterwards. He had heard old Sowberry Hagan in his best days, and he said it laid over him, too; but I reckon that was sort of piling it on, maybe.

RALPH ELLISON

*"Backwacking: A Plea to the
Senator"*

Braxas, Alabama
April 4th, 1953

To the Right Honorable
Senator Sunraider
Washington, D.C.

Dear Senator Sunraider:

This evening I take my pen in hand to write you our deep appreciation for all the good things you have been doing for this pore beat down country of ours. That Cadillac speech you gave us was straight forward and to the point and much needed saying. So I thank you and my wife Marthy wants to thank you. In fact we both thank you for looking out for folks like us who firmly believe that all this WELFARE the Guv. is shoveling out to the lazy nogooders and freeloaders is something that stinks in the nostril of Heaven worse than a batch of rotten catfish that some unGodly thief has stole and scattered all over Courthouse Square at high noon on the 4th day of July. We are with you Senator because you are a good man. You have done great things for the God-fearing folks of this country and we respect you for it. And as you are one of the very *few* men in Guv. who we can depend on when the going gets real TOUGH I now take the liberty of calling something to your kind attention that is taking place down here in these parts.

I refer to this new type of sinful activity that has cropped up amongst the niggers. It is known as "BACKWACKING," which I am prepared to say under oath is probably one of the most UNGODLY and also UNATURAL activity that anybody has ever yet invented! Senator, it is no less than RADICAL! And so naturally the nigger has been going at it so HARD that he is fast getting out of hand and out of control. Here is what he is doing. HE and his woman have taken to getting undressed and standing back to back and heel to heel, shoulderblade to shoulderblade, and tale to tale with his against her's and her's against his, and then after they have horsed around and maneuvered like cats in heat and worked as tight together as a tick to a cow's tit, HE ups and starts in to HAVING AFTER HER BACKWARDS!

Now I know, Senator, that this sounds like he is taking a very roundabout and also mullet-headed path to Robin Hood's barn, but I have it on the most reliable authority that this is exactly how he is going about it. Yessir! The facts have been well established even though I have to admit that on account of he is not only defying common decency but also NATURE, I cannot explain in full detail just *how* the nigger is proceeding in this tradition busting business. Because naturally he thinks that he has him a good thing going and is trying to keep the WHITE MAN in the DARK. Even so, I want you to know that ever since it was brought to my attention I been putting a great deal of effort into trying to untangle what he is doing. I have figgered HARD and I have figgered LONG but to date nothing. I have come up with seems to fit WHAT he is doing with HOW he is going about it. Neither, I am sad to report, has anybody else. So it appears that once again and after all the trouble we have seen we are being VICTIMIZED by yet another so-called "nigger mystery." It is a crying sin and a dirty shame but once again the nigger has tossed the responsible citizenry of these parts a terrible tough nut to crack. Once again it appears that like the time when he came back from Cuba at the end of the Spanish American War and then again when he came back from Paris France after World War I, he is HELLBENT on taking advantage of our good nature. But be that as it may, I hasten to assure you that we down here are not taking it laying down. We are going after him not only with might, and main but with foresight and hindsight. And as for me personal, I am doing my level best to bring him to heel and can be counted on to KEEP on doing it! Senator, you have my word on that. I have known niggers all my life and am well acquainted with smart ones as well as dumb ones, but while heretofore this has been an advantage in many a tight place in my dealings with him, in this particular situation I am forced to admit that I have yet to come across any as backwards-acting as my most reliable information makes these here out to be. Evidently these are of a different breed, because considering that I am a GODFEARING white man in my 80th year if *I* have not heard of this "BACKWACKING" until now it has got to be something NEW! So in my considered opinion it is something that some black rascal has brought in here from somewheres else, probably from up NORTH.

But Senator, wherever this "BACKWACKING" comes from it calls for some ruthless INVESTIGATING and drastic CONTROL! Because not only is the nigger conducting himself in this UNGODLY jiggsawing fashion I have described to you, but there is OVERPOWERING evidence that he is doing it too much for his own or anybody elses good, and I say so for the following reasons. I am informed that when he and his woman reach the climax of this radical new way of sinning they get blasted by one of the *darndest* feelings that has ever been known to hit the likes of Man! My friend says it is like watching somebody being struck down by greased lightening, and he says that when it hits the nigger it is like seeing somebody being knocked down and dragged by an L & N freight train that has been doing a high-ball on a down-hill grade with its brakeshoes busted and with no red light ahead! Yes, sir! It is a mind graveler and a viscious back breaker. He says that watching it work on the black rascal is like seeing somebody get blasted to as close to dying as any normal human being can possibly come and still not die. Like he says this "BACKWACKING" is a real humdinging ripsnorter and a danger to life, limb, and social order—only you wouldn't think so if you could see how some who are practicing it are around here strutting and grinning.

Yes, sir, Senator, they are out trying to make some slick nigger propaganda to the point that they had all at once jumped way ahead of the WHITE man! But of course and as we both well know, they are badly mistaken in this regard. Because if the truth be known, all they are doing is setting back their own RACE. There is no doubt about it, because it is a "well established fact" and as I have always held No race can pull itself up by their bootstraps and bring home the bacon that dedicates itself to indulging in such UNATURAL activity as the one these here are messing with. But yet and still and as niggers will, they are going at it like old fashioned common sense has gone plum out of style! Senator, the situation he is creating is no less than critical! And it is right here that we come face to face with the most confounding detail of this "BACK-WACKING."

Now you would expect that all this powerful feeling he generates would knock the nigger out, and as I have stated it trully staggers him. It knocks the rascal as limber as a bacon rine that has been boiled in a mess of collards and turns his bones to rubber. Yes, sir! But then an absolutely CONFUSING thing takes place. Like I say, when this feeling strikes the nigger it blasts him so hard that it seems that it has knocked all such nasty notions out of his ignorant head. He goes out like a lantern in a wind storm and you would swear that he was already at the gates of hell, which is shorely where he is headed, yessir! But then it jacks him up, and the next thing you know he comes up with a quick second wind! That is the unGodly truth, Senator, and I'll swear to it. Instead of keeling over and breathing his last or at least taking him a nap, the nigger just lets out a big ole hoop-and-a-holler and leaps back to his position and commences to practicing this "BACKWACKING" again! So when you think about that and all the raw naked POWER he lets loose it is my firm opinion that this "BACKWACKING" must do no less than throw him into some new kind of TRANCE. Something about this new way of sinning he is practicing simply takes the rascal OVER. Otherwise I ask you how is it that as soon as he uses up his second-wind—which takes him a full five minutes longer by a good stop-watch—according to my friend he right away "BACKWACKS" his way into a third and then into a fourth and *fifth* wind? So it stands to reason that nothing less than a TRANCE can explain it, therefore I must stand on that. It simply has to be what happens, especially since he has been known to keep on going in this fashion until he is vibrating like a sheet-tin roof in a wind storm and his petered-out woman is wore plumb down to a slam-banging *frazzel!*

Senator, after observing this disgraceful business on several occasions, my friend holds that it is a crying pity and a down-right shame that it don't just knock the nigger out of commission the first shot out of the box, and I wholeheartedly agree. Because if this "BACKWACKING" was to kill off a few of the ornery ones who is practicing it this thing would be brought to a quick and abrupt conclusion. After that the rest of the niggers would sober up to the firmly grounded truth of the proposition which states that "No Race can prosper or long endure" that devotes itself to going against NATURE like these down here have been doing. Therefore they would go back and devote them-selves to conducting their business in the old fashion way they was taught by the WHITE man back there in slavery.

Now mind you Senator, I say that that is the proposition the nigger OUGHT to be living by, but this being a new day and age, and one in which he has lost all sense of direction, he is NOT. Instead he is coming up daily with all KINDS of new minds and new notions, most of them nasty, radical and UNGODLY. So with the nigger continuing on his "BACKWACKING" rampage it is most unfor-tunate that some of the most responsible citizens in these parts are dying off while some of the rest have given up the struggle and grown discouraged. Some are even thinking about migrating to Australia! And only the other day a friend of mine was even talking about moving to South Africa, just to get away from some of the outrages taking place down here. He's ready to cut bait and run! "Let the nigger take over, and get out while the getting is good," he says. "That's what I'm thinking. Just let him have it, lock, stock, barrel and gate-post, because that's exactly what he's out to do. One way or another, either by hook, or by crook or sinning, he means to seize control. So I'm going somewhere a WHITE man still has a chance to live in peace." That is what he says and he's from one of the finest old families in these parts. Yessir, that's just how pessimistic some folks have come to feel. But fortunately folks like my friend are in the minority and I hasten to assure you Senator that all is not lost, no, sir! Not by a long shot. Because while a few have let themselves become discouraged and intimidated by this recent rash of nigger outrages a determined VANGUARD remains on the firing line and is putting up a firm resistance. And for this I say "Praise the LORD!" as there is a growing concern that if the nigger ain't soon checked and returned to his proper balance—and I mean by any means NECESSARY—or if he don't just naturally run out of gas on his own accord, he will keep on plunging down this unatural path he is on until he is out on the street grabbing and "BACKWACKING" each and every female woman he can lay his corrupted eyes on. Such is the terrible prospect we face in a nutshell.

So it is my considered opinion that we are confronted by a crisis the likes of which we haven't had to face since back in 1918 when the nigger come home trying to talk and act like French men. Therefore I have tried to the best of my ability to give you a clear and accurate picture of our situation. What we actually have down here is not only a serious threat to our orderly society but we are in the middle of something that can best be described as a "clear and present danger"! I insist on that, Senator, and it is a danger that threatens *everybody,* including the nigger, who seems bent on no less than downright self-annihilation! And what makes our predicament so untenable is the fact that the nigger is so sly and *devious.* He knows we're watching him so he's coming up with all kinds of "diversionary tactics." But while we have yet to discover what he is sneaking around eating and drinking in order to do what he is doing and while he is keeping his hand well hid, down here in Alabama his offenses to common-decency is causing a terrible stir. Senator, our backs are against the wall and our nerves are on edge and our patience is running thin. And it is doing it so *fast* that I tell you confidential that all this "BACKWACK-ING" he is doing has got our STORM WARNINGS up. By which I mean to say that this latest of many aggravating "nigger mysteries," grievous offenses, and attacks on moral integrity and clean living has got folks so flustered and upset that they are beginning to cry out loud for some RELIEF! So Senator it is in their name as well as my own that I am calling upon you to hurry down here with a committee of your best people and INVESTIGATE! We are calling upon you because from your Cadillac speech the other day we are firmly convinced that you are the ONE for the role. You have the "intestinal fortitude" to do what needs to be done and you have the authority to SEE that it is done. So please heed our plea. Because even if what the nigger is up to wasn't against NATURE, which it simply has to be, there is no question but that he is going both against the BIBLE and against our most hallowed tradition and therefore what he is doing calls for the firm and unyielding hand of the LAW!

Senator, the above constitutes our unhappy bill of particulars, and as I appreciate that you are a busy man I beg pardon for taking up so much of your precious time. But please understand that our situation is DESPERATE and we call upon your aid because you are one of the few that trully stands for LAW AND ORDER and really looks out for the welfare of the good WHITE people, who as I have tried to make crystal clear, are once again being sorely tried and tested. So in closing both me and Marthy thank you in advance for your kind consideration and look forward to the time when we will once again be safe and at peace with our fine and honorable tradition and our straightforward way of doing things. We wish you a long life and the best of everything, and we hope and pray that you will soon find time to lay the firm hand of the law on this "BACKWACKING" and bring it to a teeth-rattling HALT! Just look into the nigger is all we ask, and GOD BLESS.

Respectfully Yrs:

NORM A. MAULER
A CONCERN CITIZEN

ROGER ANGELL

"The Great Starch Debate"

(The Author of Six Crises Begins the Long Climb Upward from 1962)

Even before becoming president, Richard Nixon seemed to see his own life as a series of dramas from which he could step aside to gaze at the action with fascination and comment on it as though he were a theater critic. This tendency showed up in pronounced form in his Six Crises, *which Roger Angell parodies here with a flawless reproduction of the Nixon writing voice.*

My experience has taught me that the first step in a crisis is the ability to recognize that the crisis does in fact exist. This requires a cool head and considerable personal background in crisis-recognition. Looking back on it now, I am certain that no one in our group but I sensed that a full-scale crisis was in the making on that warm evening, early in my campaign for the governorship of my native state, when we returned to our hotel and I discovered that my shirts had not come back from the laundry. We had enjoyed a busy and deeply satisfying day of campaigning in the upper San Fernando Valley. I had made a number of hard-hitting points in thirteen separate speeches, and from the emotional point of view I had had the always enriching experience of shaking hands with hundreds of folks who seemed decidedly pleased with the principles I had made perfectly clear to them. It had been another mountaintop experience, and after it was over, there was a distinct temptation for my campaign staff and me to relax momentarily and indulge ourselves in the luxury of retrospection and self-congratulation. My discovery, at this juncture, that my shirts had not come up from the laundry was at first only an irritation. I had exhausted my small personal stock of clean white shirts in the previous few days on the road, and the hotel laundry had made a firm commitment to me of delivery by 5 P.M. I had made it entirely clear to them that I required a clean shirt for that evening, when I was scheduled to address a Republican Peach-Pickers' Rally and then to participate in a brass-tacks public debate on the issue of water fluoridation in parochial schools. When a thorough search of my suite turned up no package of clean shirts, I knew I had to take decisive action. I got busy on the telephone, speaking in person first to the front desk, then to the laundry room. Were my shirts ready? If not, would they be ready within the next hour?

Answer: negative. No one appeared to know where my shirts were. I hung up.

My estimate of the situation sharpened. As I sat by the bedroom telephone, engaged in inner debate, Earl Mazo, Bill Key, Alvin Moscow, Don Hughes, Jim Bassett, and several other members of my team came in. They sensed that something was "up." I quickly spelled out the facts for them and asked them for their evaluations. I told them I wanted advice, not sugar-coating.

The gist of their group opinion was at first glance both sensible and attractive. They urged me to take the easy way, to ride with the punch. They pointed out that a search for the shirts and a full disclosure of the reasons for their disappearance could be time-consuming and, in the long run, frustrating. They outlined the potential political dynamite that could be touched off if some member of our press entourage got wind of any "scene" that might ensue if I determined to follow through personally and find my shirts in the hotel. Several opinions pinpointed the fact that I could still in all probability go out and buy a new shirt before the beginning of the evening schedule. At least two of my companions kindly offered to lend me one of their own clean shirts—a warm expression of personal loyalty that I still cherish. As far as content went, their advice was excellent.

Nevertheless, I asked them to leave me alone for a few minutes while I made a deeper evaluation. I explained to them that a leader must do more than count the noses of his advisers. Left alone, I realized that I would be fully pardoned if I came to the conclusion that the situation I faced lay in one of life's gray areas, where the easier decision was called for. But there were principles involved, and I knew that any man who shirked the inner struggle at a time like this was guilty of irresponsibility. I saw at once that this was a crisis of an entirely new kind. This was not simply a case of Nixon being inconvenienced by the carelessness of one hotel or one laundry. If I were to permit myself to be bluffed out at this stage, it would mean that a citizen was acquiescing to the inefficiencies that woolly-thinking apologists often declare to be an innate part of the American system. It would be a case of Nixon putting his tail between his legs and surrendering to bureaucracy. I could not in conscience take such a course and then go before the people as their candidate. My philosophy has always been to do what is right. My instinct in this case was to act, to find the shirts.

Once I saw the course I had to take, any tension I might have felt disappeared. Courage—that is, the absence of fear—comes from conviction. I had long since learned that the decision-making process—that is, thinking—is the most trying part of any crisis. Now that my mind was made up, I felt cool and ready for battle. But merely to be doubly sure, I put long-distance calls through to Herb Brownell, Tom Dewey, Allen Dulles, and Charlie Halleck. All of them concurred, in broad terms, with the wisdom of my decision, and Charlie added that I had again made him proud to be an American. Tom Dewey was most specific. "This is a matter you must decide for yourself, Dick," he stated.

I summoned my staff back into the room. Quickly I laid the program before them. We would act, I said, because we were on the right side. But we would act responsibly, after thorough preparation and with proper human respect for the workings of the hotel's administrative apparatus. I asked them to prepare the necessary background material I would require, including data on laundry operations in general in the Free World, average delivery time of shirts by non-private launderers, wages and working conditions enjoyed by union and non-union ironers and folders, and so forth. I asked them to have this material before me in fifteen minutes, which would allow me perhaps another fifteen minutes for a crash briefing and intensive homework before we swung into action. They hurried off eagerly, and then for the first time I allowed myself to relax for a moment and reflect on what curious but perennially stimulating encounters history continued to place before the man who had once, back in a plain boy's bedroom in Yorba Linda, allowed his modest daydreams to encompass only the possibility of one day making the high-school junior-varsity debating team. Now, as far as background was concerned, the stage was set for that encounter that the American press, with more enthusiasm than accuracy, was later to call the Great Starch Debate.

Accompanied by two of my aides, I stepped into the elevator, turned, and faced the front of the car. "Laundry room, please," I said in a firm voice. The operator stole a puzzled glance at me, but I looked straight ahead. As we went down, I took stock of my physical condition. I was a trifle edgy, my palms were damp, and there was an empty feeling in the pit of my stomach. I suppose some might say that I was "nervous," but by drawing on personal experience I was able to recognize and even welcome these signs for what they were—the symptoms of a normal man in descent in a fast elevator.

We alighted in the sub-basement and I strode directly through the doors of the laundry room. I was at once enveloped in clouds of steam, but my painstaking briefing had prepared me for this eventuality, and I did not hesitate. In spite of the steam and the hiss and roar of washers and pressing machines, I was able to single out my man, the laundry manager, at once. He was behind a counter, wearing a white undershirt and white trousers. I introduced myself, and we shook hands. While our aides grouped themselves around us in the manner prescribed by protocol and roughed out between them the substance of the conversations to come, I took stock of my man. He exuded an unmistakable impression of weariness and ennui. Here, I knew, was a powerful adversary—a hard-core laundry manager, steeled to complaints, magnificently trained in evasion.

I got off to a particularly good start by pointing out to him that his failure to deliver my shirts constituted a breach of contract. In effect, I told him, he had failed to live up to his end of one of those countless small but vital agreements that permit men of good will to function together in our increasingly complex world.

He feigned bewilderment. The delivery of shirts was not in his province, he stated—only their processing.

Instinctively, I knew I had to press my attack. I asked him if he ever had any difficulty sleeping at night if he knew that even one of his customers felt less than complete satisfaction with the laundry service that day. I roughed out for him a broad panoramic view of the operations of our vast mercantile system and its concomitant and essential service subdivision.

He seemed reluctant to debate the points I had raised. He pounded the counter and, with some vivid and distinctly nondiplomatic peasant adages, stated that I was adding to, rather than clarifying, our differences.

My intensive preparations allowed me to absorb and counter his attack without being thrown off balance. I knew that from the standpoint of temper control this would be the worst possible time for me to blow my stack. I decided to shift tactics. An "end run" was called for. I pointed out that while over fifty-one million American males owned white shirts the average per-capita ownership (including steelworkers) was still only 2.3 shirts each, a figure that did not allow for any slipups in the laundry-processing industry. *Time* magazine later characterized this as "a beefed-up riposte that scored heavily in the drama."

Now it was his turn to change the pace. Forcing a laugh, he asked me if I was not being guilty of obscurantism.

"That's not my way," I retorted. "I shall never be guilty of obscurantism."

He poked a pudgy finger at me. "We are capable of dialectics, too, you know," he said menacingly.

Now we were going at it hammer and tongs. I was vaguely aware that a considerable crowd of laundresses, waiters, bellboys, and house detectives had surrounded us. None of them had ever heard anything like this before behind the doors of their laundry room, and I knew that even if I failed now in my primary mission, my journey would not prove to have been entirely in vain.

At this moment, one of the manager's assistants pressed a note into his hand. We both paused, panting in the steam, while he read its contents. He hesitated. "It seems," he said at last, "that your laundry has been found. It is in this room. Our position has been entirely justified. Your shirts are washed and ironed, but they have been detained here for reprocessing, because in inadvertence the starch was omitted. You will have them tomorrow, starched."

The day was won. Without knowing it, he had played directly into my hands, but years of experience in dealing with success now warned me that this was the time for magnanimity, not crowing. Smiling, I quoted to him Abraham Lincoln's remark, made in reference to one of his generals, that he preferred "starch in the man rather than in his shirt." It was my way of telling him that I never have my own shirts ironed with starch.

The manager shrugged. He turned, received the package of shirts from an assistant, and handed them to me. We shook hands warmly. Although the one-hundred-per-cent-successful outcome of our meeting had been largely unexpected, I was not unprepared even for this eventuality. Still holding his hand, I clapped him on the shoulder and said, "Isn't it fine that two men, each trained to a peak of creative usefulness by our great system of economic and personal incentives, can meet as we have and exchange views openly and without fear, thus adding to man's centuries-long struggle for understanding and freedom?"

He nodded wordlessly, and we parted. I turned and walked toward my elevator, ignoring the confused babble of voices behind me engaged in excited interrogation, recapitulation, and speculation. I pressed the elevator button. As I stood there, it occurred to me that many American men in their middle years might be suddenly depressed to find themselves, immediately after a personal success, standing in a hotel sub-basement with a package of laundry in their arms. I knew, however, that the most dangerous part of any crisis is its aftermath, the time of letdown. This is when the human system, wearied by tension and hyperbole, is all too apt to become exhausted and to indulge itself in destructive reflection. This knowledge enabled me to put the thought aside. I watched the needle on the indicator above the elevator door. The car was moving downward, but soon, I knew, it would rise again, taking me with it.

Briefly Speaking

A fanatic is a man that does what he thinks th' Lord wud do if He knew the facts iv the' case.

—FINLEY PETER DUNNE

SECTION NINE

MEDIA

Almost all the pieces in this section are by people from the news business. A great many American humorists start out in journalism, and since writers write best about what they know, it is natural that the best humor about media will come from people who know what a city room smells like.

Public interest in the news business seems extraordinary today, but it predates the present fascination with television anchor stars. In the early twentieth century successful plays and movies about newspaper life gave the business a glamour that left young romantics eager to accept starvation salaries as the price of a ticket to glory. The memory of that age is evoked here in "The Years with Navasky" when a thoroughly modern journalist, caught in a time warp, has what will always be the writer's sweetest revenge—the last word.

A note about "media": Fifty years ago it was advertising jargon. Media (always plural) were simply devices useful for letting the world know you had something to sell. They included billboards, telephone polls, radio stations, newspapers, car bumpers, magazines, drugstore windows, subway car panels, barn walls, and, with an airplane, even the sky. Nowadays people saying "the media" almost always mean the news industry, tying together press, magazines, television, and radio in one word. With this triumph for Adspeak the advertising world at last has its own sweet revenge over the news purists of the city room.

CALVIN TRILLIN

"The Years with Navasky"

When I was approached about writing a column for *The Nation,* I asked for only one guarantee: Would I be allowed to make fun of the editor? When it comes to civil liberties, we all have our own priorities.

The editor, one Victor S. Navasky, responded to this question with what I believe the novelists call a nervous chuckle. In an editor's note introducing the first piece, he announced that I would be writing a "humor column"— apparently figuring that the readers would then assume that anything I said about him was meant as a joke. Since Navasky had once been the editor of an occasional publication called *Monocle, A Journal of Political Satire,* he presumably realized that writing a "humor column" would mean wrestling with what I have always thought of as The (Harry) Golden Rule: In modern America, anyone who attempts to write satirically about the events of the day finds it difficult to concoct a situation so bizarre that it may not actually come to pass while his article is still on the presses. The rule is named after Harry Golden because in the late fifties, when he realized that the white people in the part of North Carolina he lived in seemed to mind sitting down with black people but not standing up with them, he suggested that the schools be integrated through the simple device of removing the chairs. As I remember, he called his scheme the Harry Golden Plan for Vertical Integration. Not long after he proposed it, some libraries in the state were ordered by a federal court to desegregate, and they responded by removing their chairs.

In other words, when Jimmy Carter countered the threat of a Russian "combat brigade" in Cuba by having the Marines stage an assault landing on our own base at Guantanamo or when Ronald Reagan appointed as Deputy Secretary of State a man who could not name the Prime Minister of South Africa, some Sunday newspaper satirist somewhere in America was groaning at having his joke ruined by the legally constituted authorities. Someone who writes what has been officially labeled a "humor column" about the American scene lives in constant danger of being blindsided by the truth.

Why did I involve myself in such an unpromising enterprise? My first mistake, many years ago, was an involvement with *Monocle* and its editor, the same Victor S. Navasky. In those days, when we were all young and optimistic, I used to assure Navasky that the lack of a sense of humor was probably not an insurmountable handicap for the editor of a humor magazine. (He always responded with a nervous chuckle.) As an editor, after all, he was exacting. During the New York newspaper strike of 1963, *Monocle* published a parody edition of the *New York Post,* then as predictable in its liberalism as it was later to become in its sleaziness, and I suggested as the front-page headline "Cold Snap Hits Our Town; Jews, Negroes Suffer Most." Navasky refused to use the headline merely because there was no story inside the paper to go with it—a situation that a less precise thinker might have considered part of the parody. Even then, I must say, Navasky's hiring policies seemed erratic—particularly his appointing as advertising manager a high-minded young man who found advertising so loathsome and disgusting that, as a matter of principle, he refused to discuss the subject with anyone. What was most memorable about Victor S. Navasky at *Monocle,* though, was his system of payment to contributors—a system derived, according to my research, from a 1938 chart listing county-by-county mean weekly wages for Gray Ladies. My strongest memory of *Monocle* is receiving a bill from Navasky for a piece of mine the magazine had published—along with a note explaining that the office expenses for processing the piece exceeded what he had intended to pay me for it.

In the late sixties, *Monocle* folded. I wasn't surprised. My assurances to Navasky about his not needing a sense of humor had been quite insincere. Also, I had once observed the advertising manager's reaction to being phoned at the *Monocle* office by a prospective advertiser: "Take a message," he hissed at the secretary, as he bolted toward the door. "Tell him I'm in the bathroom. Get rid of him." Then, only about ten years later, Navasky fetched up as the new editor of *The Nation.* It was difficult for me to imagine that he would dare pay Gray Lady rates at a magazine of national reputation—even a money-losing magazine of national reputation. (Historians tell us that *The Nation* was founded many years ago in order to give a long succession of left-wing entrepreneurs the opportunity to lose money in a good cause.) *The Nation,* after all, had always railed against bosses who exploit workers. Still, it was among writers for radical journals that I most often heard the folk phrase. "There's no goniff like a left-wing goniff." I thought about Navasky's stewardship of *Monocle* for a while, and then sat down to write him a letter of congratulations on being named editor of *The Nation.* It said, in its entirety, "Does money owed writers from *Monocle* carry over?" I received no reply.

I realize that this history with Navasky is one reason for some speculation by scholars in the field about the sort of negotiations that could have led to my agreeing to do a column for *The Nation*. ("If he got caught by Navasky twice, he must be soft in the head.") The entire tale can now be told. The negotiations took place over lunch at a bar in the Village. I picked up the check. I had asked Navasky beforehand if he minded my bringing along my wife, Alice. I figured that she would be a reminder that I was no longer the carefree young bachelor who barely complained about being stiffed regularly by the *Monocle* bookkeepers, but a responsible married man with two daughters and an automatic washer-dryer combination (stack model). Navasky, the cunning beast, said Alice would be most welcome. He knew her to be a sympathetic soul who somehow saw a connection in his saving money on writers and the possibility that he might buy a new suit.

Once we had our food, Navasky made his first wily move. He suggested two very specific ideas for regular columns I might be interested in writing for *The Nation*—both of them of such surpassing dumbness that I long ago forgot precisely what they were. One of them, it seems to me, was on the practical side—a weekly gardening column, maybe, or a column of auto repair hints.

"Those are the silliest ideas I ever heard," I said, with relief. "The only column I might like to do is so far from Wobbly horticulture, or whatever you have in mind, that I don't mind mentioning it because you obviously wouldn't be interested—a thousand words every three weeks for saying whatever's on my mind, particularly if what's on my mind is marginally ignoble." As long as I was safe from an agreement, I thought I might as well take advantage of one of those rare opportunities to say "ignoble" out loud.

"It's a deal," the crafty Navasky said, putting down the hamburger I was destined to pay for and holding out his hand to shake on the agreement. Caught again.

"I hate to bring up a subject that may cause you to break out in hives," I said, "but what were you thinking of paying me for each of these columns?" I reminded him of the responsibilities of fatherhood and the number of service calls necessary to keep a stack-model washer-dryer in working order.

"We were thinking of something in the high two figures," Navasky said.

I remained calm. The sort of money we were discussing, after all, was already a step up from *Monocle* rates. The only check I ever received from *Monocle*—for presiding over a panel discussion in an early issue—was for three dollars. ("Well, it's steady," I said when Navasky later asked if I would run similar discussions as a monthly feature of *Monocle*. "A person would know that he's got his thirty-six dollars coming in every year, rain or shine, and he could build his freelance on that.") Still, I felt a responsibility to do some negotiating.

"What exactly do you mean by the high two figures?" I said.

"Sixty-five dollars," Navasky said.

"Sixty-five dollars! That sounds more like the middle two figures to me. When I hear 'high two figures,' I start thinking eighty-five, maybe ninety."

"You shook on it," Navasky said. "Are you going to go back on your word right in front of your own wife?"

I looked at Alice. She shrugged. "Maybe Victor'll buy a new suit," she said.

I called for the check.

A few weeks after I began the column, Navasky asked me if William Henry Harrison's Secretary of State had ever said what I had quoted him as saying.

"At these rates, you can't always expect real quotes, Victor," I said, preferring to leave it at that.

As it happens, the only quotation in these columns whose authenticity has been the subject of any serious controversy is H. L. Mencken's 1928 prediction that the first President from the Deep South would have, among other attributes, "a charm comparable to that of the leading undertaker of Dothan, Alabama," and I'm pleased to say that it has proved to be, in its own way, quite genuine.

Of course, we all make mistakes. After I mentioned having read that the editor of *Playboy,* one Arthur Kretchmer, made $520,734 a year, *The Nation* received a letter from a *Playboy* associate editor named Asa Baber pointing out that my source for the figure had turned out to be in error, and chastising me for not checking with Kretchmer before printing an account of his embarrassing wealth—checking with the subject being, in Baber's words, "an old tradition in journalism." Naturally, I was happy to set the record straight in the letter column of *The Nation,* and I'm happy to do so here: Despite what you may read in this book, Arthur Kretchmer makes $165 a week, plus time and a half for overtime. The annual salary of Asa Baber is $520,734.

I must admit that in these columns I haven't made a fetish of the old traditions of journalism—the tradition, for instance, of covering events only when they actually occur. In the winter of 1979, Navasky asked me why I was beginning to cover the Great Presidential Debates between Edward Kennedy and Ronald Reagan months before either party had decided on a candidate.

"I'm trying to get a jump on the other fellows," I said. "They all have expense accounts."

I have taken Navasky's handshake to mean that I am also free from whatever traditions journalism might retain in the area of fairness and civility—although I have, of course, tried to give Navasky himself every benefit of the doubt. I don't mean that I was ever a strict believer in what used to be known as objective journalism, the best definition of which I heard from a photographer in Little Rock who told me, "Before I go out to take a picture of someone, I just stop at the city desk and say, 'Do you want him gazing out toward the sunset or picking his nose?' " As a reporter, though, I have at least aspired to the standard of objectivity we used to make do with on the college paper— "We strive to be equally inaccurate about both sides."

A commentator, I learned, labors under no such restrictions. "Do you really think that's fair?" Alice said one day, after reading a manuscript in which I had made some base and underhanded statement about the Governor's girlfriend or the President's appearance or the Secretary of State's mental health.

"Not in the least," I said, putting the manuscript into an envelope for delivery to *The Nation*. "Not in the least."

RUSSELL BAKER

"The XI P.M. Report"

"Good evening. I am Gaius Fulvius. My colleague is Marcus Fluvius and this is the XI P.M. Fulvius-Fluvius Report brought to you on WSPQR Channel XVI, where the big story tonight is still that strange star hovering over the troubled Middle East. What do you make of that star, Marcus?"

"It sounds like the kind of star you see after one of those five-day orgies down at Capri, Gaius."

"Funny you should mention that, Marcus, because we also have a special film report tonight on how inflation is cutting into the orgy budget of the typical Roman family. And from faraway, fog-shrouded Britain, a new idea in how to dress for an orgy at practically no cost at all. Our cameramen have found some Englishmen up there—they call themselves Druids—who run around in the woods with nothing on but blue paint."

"When in Rome, do as the Druids do, eh, Gaius?"

"All these stories and others when the Fulvius-Fluvius Report continues, right after these messages."

Commercial interlude. The excellence of Cicero Chariot Springs illustrated. Also the superiority of Caracalla Bath Soap and Vestal Talcum Powder for relieving the itch of toga irritation. A paid plea for the election of Quintus Cunctator as quaestor of Rome. A public-service commercial urging Romans not to drop litter in the Forum, and a demonstration of a new wax that lasts twice as long on the atrium floor.

"And now, our top story tonight, that mysterious star over the oil-rich Middle East. A party of three Wise Men has been on the road for several days now, traveling eastward in the direction of the star, and they have attracted a large number of media representatives."

"Fascinating, Gaius. I saw one report that over 1,500 news people are already accredited to the Wise Men, and more applications for credentials pouring in by the hour."

"Exactly right, Marcus, and tonight that huge crowd of newsmen rioted in a small town south of Jericho when the local innkeeper was unable to put most of them up in the tiny six-room inn where the Wise Men had stopped for the night. There are rumors that King Herod, who doesn't like mysterious stars much anyhow, may crack down on the Wise Men for creating a public nuisance."

"Haven't we spent a lot of time on this story, Gaius, old pal? I want to see these blue Druids."

"One last item, Marcus. It was learned today that the Wise Men are carrying three gifts with them, and one of the gifts is frankincense."

"What are the other two?"

"We don't have time to go into detail, Marcus, but we'll be right back for a report on Emperor Augustus's reading of the chicken entrails right after these messages."

Commercial interlude promoting Mark Antony Sword Steel Razor Blades, Praetorian Guard Belt Buckles, snow rims for chariot wheels, sacrificial altars marked down 30 percent and reconditioned Greek slaves.

"Well, we seem to have lost that film we promised you of the Emperor's annual reading of the chicken entrails, Marcus. Do you have a report on what omens he found in them?"

"I do indeed, Gaius. He found a deformity in the gizzard that means there will definitely be an upswing in the economy during the second quarter of next year."

"How does that check with what your gizzard tells you, Marcus?"

"My gizzard isn't speaking to me these days, Gaius, but my corns sure are, and they tell me it's going to rain all over the Seven Hills any minute now. To find out if those corns are right, we'll hear from WSPQR's meteorologist, Cincinnatus Emptor, right after these messages."

Commercial interlude. Longer-burning torches, banquet lounges, vacations to all three parts of Gaul, Egyptian obelisks for the lawn, artificial laurel wreaths, U-Sail-It Trireme Rentals and condominiums in Sicily.

"And now, Cincinnatus, what about that rain?"

"As we look at the weather map, Gaius, we have this funny frontal pattern over the eastern Mediterranean—"

"It sure looks bad for Egypt, Cincinnatus."

"Yes, Marcus, this front is full of hail, and I wouldn't be surprised if Egypt doesn't get a pretty good onset of locusts and boils, too. But more about that after these messages."

Commercial interlude is interrupted by Goths and Huns who have seized Rome and WSPQR. Rome falls with loud bang.

"We should have had an item on these people, Marcus."

"We did, old buddy, but the film was no good. Good night for the Fulvius-Fluvius Report."

JOHN LEO

"Journalese, or Why English Is the Second Language of the Fourth Estate"

As a cub reporter, columnist Richard Cohen of *The Washington Post* trudged out one day to interview a lawyer who had been described in many newspaper reports as "ruddy-faced." The man was woozily abusive and lurched about with such abandon that young Cohen instantly realized that the real meaning of *ruddy-faced* is drunk. This was his introduction to journalese, the fascinating second tongue acquired by most reporters as effortlessly as an Iranian toddler learns Farsi or a Marin County child learns psychobabble.

Fluency in journalese means learning all about "the right stuff," "life in the fast lane," and the vexing dilemma of being caught "between a rock and a hard place," the current Scylla-Charybdis image. The Middle East is "war-torn" or "strife-torn," except during those inexplicable moments when peace briefly breaks out. Then it is simply "much-troubled." Kuwait is located just east of the adjective *oil-rich,* and the Irish Republican Army lurks right behind the word *outlawed.*

Much of the difficulty of mastering journalese stems from its slight overlap with English. *Imposing,* for instance, when used to describe a male, retains its customary English meaning, but when used in reference to a female, it means "battle-axe." In journalese the word *chilling* has the very solemn task of modifying *scenario* (in nuclear weapons stories), *reminder* (in crime stories) and *effect* (any story on AIDS or the imminent repeal of the First Amendment), whereas in English it is merely something one does with white wine.

Some English words mean exactly the opposite in journalese. *Multitalented,* for example, means untalented, and is used to identify applause-starved entertainers who prance about with amazing pep and perspiration, but do nothing particularly well. *Community* means noncommunity, as in the intelligence community, the gay community, or the journalese-speaking community. Under this usage, everyone shooting everyone else in and around Beirut, say, could be fairly described as the Lebanese community.

Feisty refers to a person whom the journalist deems too short and too easily enraged, though many in the journalese-speaking fraternity believe it is simply the adjective of choice for any male under five feet six who is not legally dead. This usage reflects the continual surprise among tall journalists that short people have any energy at all. Women are rarely feisty, although they usually meet the height restriction. No journalist in America has ever referred to a six-foot male as feisty. At that height, men are "outspoken" (i.e., abusive).

In general, adjectives in journalese are as misleading as olive sizes. Most news consumers know enough to translate *developing nations* and *disadvantaged nations* back into English, but far smaller numbers know that *militant* means "fanatic," *steadfast* means "pigheaded," and *self-made* means "crooked." *Controversial* introduces someone or something the writer finds appalling, as in "the controversial Miss Fonda," and *prestigious* heralds the imminent arrival of a noun nobody cares about, as in "the prestigious Jean Hersholt Humanitarian Award."

Journalese is rich in mystic nouns: *gentrification, quichification, greenmail, watershed elections, the sleaze factor, Japan-bashing, level playing fields,* the dread *T-word* (taxes), and the equally dread *L-word* (liberal). Though these nouns are patently glorious, students of the language agree that adjectives do most of the work, smuggling in actual information under the guise of normal journalism. Thus the use of *soft-spoken* (mousy), *loyal* (dumb), *high-minded* (inept), *ageless* (old), *hardworking* (plodding), *irrepressible* (insanely giddy), and *pragmatic* (morally appalling, felonious). A person who is truly dangerous as well as immoral can be described as a fierce competitor or gut fighter, and a meddling boss is a hands-on executive.

When strung together properly, innocuous modifiers can acquire megaton force. For instance, a journalist may write, "A private, deliberate man, Frobisher dislikes small talk, but can be charming when he wants to." In translation, this means "An antisocial and sullen plodder, Frobisher is outstandingly obnoxious and about as articulate as a cantaloupe." The familiar phrase "can be charming" is as central to good journalese as "affordable" is to automobile ads and "excellence" is to education reports. It indicates smoothly that Frobisher's charm production is the rare and meager result of mighty exertion, yet it manages to end the revelation about his dismal character on a plausibly upbeat note.

In journalese, folks are not grim but "grim-faced," not just plain upset but "visibly upset." *Spry* and *sprightly* refer to any senior citizen who is not in a wheelchair or a coma. Other useful adjectives include *crusty* (obnoxious), *unpredictable* (bonkers), *experienced* (over the hill), *earnest* (boring), and *authentic* (fake). The noun *stereotype* introduces the discussion of something entirely obvious which the writer intends to disparage, as in "the stereotype that little boys like to play with trucks and little girls like to play with dolls." *Life-style* has made the transition from psychobabble to journalese. Though often used incorrectly to indicate homosexuals, joggers, wheat-germ consumers, and other defiant minorities, it actually refers to any practice that makes the normal citizen's hair stand on end. The fellow who tortures iguanas in his basement has a life-style. The rest of us merely have lives.

The hyphenated modifier is the meat and potatoes of journalese. Who can forget "scandal-plagued Wedtech," "concession-prone Gorbachev," "the mop-top quartet" (the mandatory second reference to the Beatles), and the many "ill-fated" airliners, not to be confused with the "ill-fitting red wig" of Watergate fame. Murderers on death row are often saved by "eleventh-hour" reprieves, which would be somewhere between ten and eleven o'clock in English, but shortly before midnight in journalese.

Many sociologists have speculated (widely) about the love affair between journalese-users and their hyphens. The gist of all this cerebration seems to be that the rhythm of a hyphenated modifier is soothing, like a mother's heartbeat to a babe in arms. Besides, research shows that readers cannot stand the shock of an unmodified noun, at least on first reference, any more than viewers of TV news can bear to hear Peter Jennings or Dan Rather reveal that World War III is under way without a comforting lead-in that will enable dinner to continue, though the world may not. Thus we have "Libyan-sponsored terrorism," "earthquake-ravaged Armenia," "debt-laden Brazil," and the two most popular hyphenated modifiers of the nineteen eighties, *financially-troubled* and *financially-plagued,* which can fairly be used to describe many banks, the indoor football league, the United States of America, and the entire world economy.

Many such hyphenated constructions come and go with blinding speed. "Syrian-backed PLO," once a serious contender for the hyphenation hall of fame, had to be retired when the Syrian backers began shooting at the PLO backs. Any dictator who leaves his homeland hastily, with or without his bullion and wife's shoe collection, is not running away; he is merely traveling into that famed journalistic nirvana, "self-imposed exile." In real life nobody talks that way ("Hey, Madge, did you hear? Embattled dictator Ferdinand Marcos has fled his turmoil-ridden island nation and taken up self-imposed exile on a tree-lined street in multiracial Hawaii!"), but in journalese such hyphenated chatter is considered normal.

Many meaningless adjectives, most of them hyphenated for mesmerizing effect, are permanently welded to certain nouns: *blue-ribbon panel, fact-finding mission, devout Catholic,* and *rock-ribbed Republican.* In journalese, for some reason, there are no devout Protestants or Jews, and no Democrats with strong or stony ribs. Similarly, Republicans but not Democrats may be described as staunch, which means "stiff-necked, unbending."

Like *clinically tested* and *doctor-recommended* in headache-remedy advertising, hyphenated journalese is not weakened in the slightest by the lack of any known meaning. *Wide-ranging discussions* refers to any talks at all, and *award-winning journalist* refers to any reporter, employed three or more years, who still has his own chair in a city room. A totally disappointing report, containing nothing but yawn-inducing truisms, can always be described as a "ground-breaking new study." The most exciting news on the hyphen front is that adventurous journalese-users, like late medieval theologians, are experimenting with new forms, to wit, multihyphen modifiers. So far *actor-turned-politician,* which can be found just to the left of Clint Eastwood's name in any story about Carmel, is the most beloved two-hyphen term, while *state-of-the-art* (i.e., new) is the only approved three-hyphen entry since the memorable introduction of *dyed-in-the-wool* two generations back. It is regarded as such a successful breakthrough that it may be used several times each week without reproof from any living editor.

Unbeknownst to an unsuspecting public, Boy George's drug troubles touched off a severe crisis in hyphenated journalese. How should reporters and pundits refer to the suddenly woozy singer? *Much-troubled* seemed apropos, but that adjective, like *war-torn,* is reserved for stories about the Middle East. One tabloid, apparently eager to dismiss multiproblemed George as a wanton hussy, called him "gender-confused rock star Boy George." This was a clear violation of journalese's most cherished tenet: one must, of course, do in the rich and famous, but never appear huffy in the process. *Newsweek* settled for "cross-dressing crooner," while many newspapers daringly abandoned the hyphenated tradition to label George "flamboyant," a familiar journalese word meaning "kinky" or "a person who does not have all of his or her paddles in the water."

In general, personal attacks in journalese should be accompanied by large quantities of feigned sympathy, the more unctuous the better. Thus any journalist wishing to reveal that Representative Frobisher has not been sober for ten years, will do so by respectfully hailing the poor fellow's "decade-long battle against alcohol addiction." One imaginative magazine, dishing new dirt about wife-beating in Hollywood, sadly cited one leading man's "lonely struggle against wife abuse."

Historians of journalese will agree that the first flowering of the language occurred in the description of women by splashy tabloids during the nineteen thirties and forties. In contrast to Pentagonese, which favors oxymorons (*Peacekeeper missiles, build-down*), the tabloids relied on synecdoche (*leggy brunette, bosomy blonde, full-figured redhead*). *Full-figured,* of course, meant "fat," and *well-endowed* meant "big-breasted," a signal to all concerned that a photo must accompany the story. *Statuesque* (too large, mooselike) and *petite* (too small, mouselike) were adjectives of last resort, meaning that the woman under discussion had no bodily parts that interested the writer. The only adjective feebler than *statuesque* and *petite* was *pert,* which indicated a plain, short woman whom the writer devoutly wished would disappear from the story.

Since it is no longer considered proper to draw the reader's attention to various protuberances and organs of the female body, journalese-users have been reduced to numbingly tame references such as *an attractive woman* (any female over fifty with no obvious facial scars) and *a handsome woman* (any woman at all). *Pert* is falling out of favor, but a formerly pert woman who is overactive or too loud as well as too short can fairly be called "perky." And of course, women are no longer blond, brunette, redheaded, or gray-haired. Any reference at all to a woman's hair color will induce a blizzard of angry feminist letters asking, in effect, why President Reagan was never described as a Clairol brunette.

Like Latin, journalese is primarily a written language, prized for its incantatory powers, and is best learned early while the mind is still supple. Every cub reporter, for instance, knows that fires rage out of control, minor mischief is perpetrated by vandals (never Visigoths, Franks, or one Vandal working alone), and key labor accords are hammered out by weary negotiators in marathon, round-the-clock bargaining sessions, thus narrowly averting threatened walkouts. The discipline required for a winter storm report is awesome. The first reference to seasonal precipitation is "snow," followed by "the white stuff," then either "it" or "the flakes," but not both. The word *snow* may be used once again toward the end of the report, directly after discussion of ice-slicked roads and the grim highway toll.

One perennial challenge in journalese is the constant need to manufacture new euphemisms for *fat.* Words such as *jolly* and *Rubenesque* have long since been understood by the public and therefore discarded. One promising recent entry, "He has a heart as big as all outdoors," while not totally successful, did manage to imply that all the rest of the gentleman's organs and limbs are quite too bulky as well. A *Washington Post* writer did better by praising a prominent woman's "Wagnerian good looks," which is far more delicate than saying, "She is not bad-looking for a massive Brunhild." This is also a sturdy example of negative journalese, which works by combining a complimentary word with an apparently innocent but actually murderous modifier. "She is still pretty," for instance, means "She is amazingly long in the tooth." The favorite female companion of a recent presidential appointee was described in the *Washington Post* as having a "blushed, taut face," which means she uses too much makeup and has had at least one face-lift.

In general, detraction in journalese must be indirect. To indicate subtle distaste for the suburbs, a *New York Times* reporter once deftly called attention to the "array of carefully trimmed lawns and neat flower beds," thus artfully suggesting compulsiveness, conformity, and a high level of intolerance for life in its hearty untrimmed state.

For years the masters of this prose cast about for a nonlibelous euphemism for *mistress.* The winning entry, *great and good friend,* was invented by *Time* magazine to describe Marion Davies's relationship to William Randolph Hearst. *Constant companion* evolved later and gave way to such clunking modernisms as *roommate* and *live-in lover.* Nowadays the only sexuality about which journalese is coy tends to be homosexuality, and that is adequately covered by "He has no close female friends" or "He is not about to settle down."

Many terms in journalese come from sportswriting. *A complex, sensitive man* (lunatic) and *ebullient* (hyperactive space cadet) were developed by baseball writers confronted by a new breed of overpaid and therefore totally unpredictable jocks. *Great natural ability* is the current catchphrase for the new incompetent superstars who hit a lot of home runs but can't seem to catch a simple fly ball, throw to the right base, or correctly remember the score, the number of outs, or what day it is. Darryl Strawberry is often hailed for his great natural ability.

When ballplayers of the nineteen forties and fifties were fined for the usual excesses with women and booze, the writers dutifully reported that the penalties were for "nightclubbing." Presumably everyone knew what that meant except the nightclubbers' wives. Nowadays the vast consumption of controlled and uncontrolled substances would be covered by such time-tested circumlocutions as "He works hard and he plays hard." In sports, it is understood that all rapid declines are drug-related, and sportswriters, the original masters of journalese, are constantly casting about for nonlibelous ways of suggesting that Johnny Jumpshot is deeply in love with complex chemical compounds. The current code words are *listlessness* and *lack of concentration.* Recently, the writers have developed another unfailing indicator of drug abuse: the information that Johnny has been known to miss the team bus. This informs the astute fan that Jumpshot no longer knows where or who he is, though his body may still turn up occasionally for games. Drunken jocks, incidentally, are not listless, merely "red-eyed."

Sportswriters also taught journalese-users how to recast a boring story with exciting verbiage. Hence all the crucial issues, dramatic confrontations, and stunning breakthroughs, which stir and trigger almost daily. *Arguably* is the most useful adverb on the excitement frontier, because it introduces a sweeping factoid that no one will be able to check: "Frobisher is arguably the richest Rotarian living west of the Susquehanna." The runner-up adverb is *literally*, which always means "figuratively." Reforms and changes can only be "sweeping," and investigations are forever "widening," especially on days when the investigators have nothing to report, but would like a headline anyway. All arrays are bewildering, whereas contrasts are striking, except when the journalese-speaker is aware that his story is a crushingly dull one, in which case the contrast is allowed to be startling. Mounting is always followed by pressures, deficits, or concern. Slopes are slippery, precision is surgical, anyone tossed out of a job is "ousted unceremoniously," and nearly all references are "thinly veiled," unless, of course, they are "thinly disguised." Thickly disguised references are genuinely rare.

Television anchorpersons add interest to their monologues by accenting a few syllables chosen at random. Since print journalists cannot do this, except when reading aloud to spouse and family, they strive for a similar effect by using words like *crisis* and *revolution*. *Crisis* means any kind of trouble at all, and *revolution* means any kind of change at all, as in "the revolution in meat-packing." *Street value* lends dash to any drug-bust story without bearing any financial relationship to the actual value of the drugs being busted. In stories mentioning the street value of such contraband, it is generally wise to divide by ten or twelve to get the real, or nonstreet, value.

In political journalese, an officeholder who has no idea what is going on can best be described as one who "prefers to leave details to his staff." Or he can be described as having a hands-off or disengaged management style (i.e., his computer is down; he is out to lunch). Any Noriega-style gangster who runs a foreign country will usually be referred to as "strongman" until his death, and "dictator" thereafter. *Strongman,* unlike many terms in journalese, has no correlative. In the nineteen sixties, "Nicaraguan strongman Somoza" was never balanced with "Cambodian weakman Prince Sihanouk."

What to say about a public figure who is clearly bonkers? Since it is unsporting and possibly libelous to write, "Representative Frobisher, the well-known psychopath," journalese has evolved the helpful code words *difficult, intense,* and *driven*. If an article says, "Like most of us, Frobisher has his ups and downs," we are being told that Frobisher is manic-depressive. Any politician described as "suffering from exhaustion" has gone completely around the bend and is now having his mail opened for him at a discreet institution.

Middle America has disappeared from political journalese, for the simple reason that after eight Reagan years, America seems to be all middle with no edges. Similarly, yesterday's "radical right-winger" is today's mainstream Republican, while *unabashed* (i.e., abashed) now modifies *liberal* instead of *conservative.* Yet most political journalese is timeless. A "savvy political pro" is anyone who has lived through two or more administrations and can still get a decent table in a Washington restaurant. An elder statesman is an out-of-office politician who is senile. All seasoned reporters (old-timers) know that when two or more political appointees are fired on the same day, they need only check their calendars before tapping out "Bloody Wednesday" or "the early-Thursday-afternoon massacre." Unless, of course, *-scam* or *-gate* can be affixed to yet another noun. Each major daily has an unofficial scam-gate editor who remains ever alert for possible new coinages. A scandal involving Madison Square Garden, for instance, would be Garden-gate, and the illegal skimming of revenues could be labeled Skim-scam. *Tail-gate* has been unofficially considered for various scandals, not all of them automotive.

Political journalese also has a number of famed option plays. One man's squealer is another's whistle-blower, and Frobisher's magnificent five-point agenda can always be described as a shopping list, or worse, a wish list. My new political action group is a dedicated band of volunteers, while yours is "small but well financed" (sinister).

Political journalese, of course, requires a knowledge of sources. An unnamed analyst or observer can safely be presumed to be the writer of the article. The popular plurals *observers* and *analysts* refer to the writer and his cronies. Insiders, unlike observer-analysts, sometimes exist in the real world outside the newsroom. This, however, is never true of quotable chestnut vendors in Paris, Greenwich Village bartenders, and other colorful folk conjured up on deadline to lend a badly needed flourish to drab stories.

Almost all sources, like most trial balloonists, live in or around Washington. In order of ascending rectitude, they are: informants, usually reliable sources, informed sources, authoritative sources, sources in high places, and unimpeachable sources. Informants are low-level operatives, whose beans are normally spilled to police rather than to reporters. Informed sources, because of their informed nature, are consulted most often by sophisticated journalists. An unimpeachable source is almost always the President, with the obvious exception of Richard Nixon, who was not unimpeachable.

One of the many stressing problems in the field is writing serious articles about celebrities who recall serving in Joan of Arc's army or strolling through Iran with Jesus Christ. *Free spirit, flamboyant,* and *controversial* are not really up to the task. The journalist must avoid probing questions, such as "What does Jesus think of the Vatican's Middle East policy?" and stick to sober, respectful observations. This is best done by keeping matters vague. One *People* magazine writer, for instance, while profiling a well-known woman who has lived several times before, struck a proper tone this way: "More than most people on this earth, she has found spiritual answers."

In crime journalese, any youngster done in by a gang will turn out to be either an honor student or an altar boy. Otherwise the story will be spiked as unconventional. In any urban area, the top thug is always referred to as a "reputed mafia chieftain," or "reputed mob boss," and is generally depicted as an untutored but charismatic leader of a surprisingly efficient business operation. Except in tabloids, the chieftain's apprentice thugs are his "associates." This sort of coverage reflects the automatic respect and dignity accorded organized crime figures who know where reporters live and recognize the understandable desire of journalists everywhere to keep their kneecaps in good working order.

One inflexible rule of journalese is that American assassins must have three names: John Wilkes Booth, Lee Harvey Oswald, James Earl Ray, Mark David Chapman. This courtesy of a resonant three-part moniker is also applied to other dangerous folk. This is why the subway gunman, for the first two months of coverage, was "Bernhard Hugo Goetz" to reporters who considered him a monster. Later these same scribes stripped Goetz of his Hugo, apparently on grounds that he seemed more like a malevolent wimp than an authentic three-named villain.

One subcategory of journalese, which may yet develop into a true dialect, involves the language used to indicate a powerful or celebrated person who is about to self-destruct or walk the plank. In politics, two or more stories in the same week referring to a power person as "clever," or worse, "brilliant," indicate that the end is near. Soon Mr. Scintillation will be labeled a "loose cannon" and transmute himself into a consultant, the Washington version of self-imposed exile. In business journalism, the phrase *one of the most respected managers in his field* informs knowing readers that envy is unnecessary—the respected manager is on the way out. Before long, there will be hints that his managerial ferocity is insufficient, perhaps a profile mentioning that he drinks decaffeinated coffee, loves San Francisco, or collects porcelain miniatures. This means we are less than a week from an announcement that the executive is "leaving to pursue outside interests," just like Ferdinand Marcos.

In sum, journalese is a truly vital language, the last bulwark against libel, candor, and fresh utterance. Its prestigious, ground-breaking, state-of-the-art lingo makes it arguably the most useful of tongues, and its untimely demise would have a chilling effect, especially on us award-winning journalists.

EUGENE FIELD

"The Lowell-Hawthorne Incident"

Mr. Julian Hawthorne is finding out how it is himself. He has added interviewing to his other duties upon the New York *World,* and in last Sunday's edition of that paper he signs his name to four columns and a half of as racy gossip as we remember to have seen. It is an interview with James Russell Lowell on the phases of social and literary life in England, with a sharp running fire of comment on the principal topics of the day. Lowell spoke with remarkable freedom, and the interview bristles with satirical personalities. He denominated the Queen as "very tough," and said of the Prince of Wales that he was "very fat." "He's immensely fat, and his labors, such as they are, are chiefly physical. He delivers very good speeches, but I think there's no doubt they are written for him. They are written by a man who also used to get up the addresses delivered by the late Duke of Albany (Prince Leopold)." Further on, speaking of Leopold, Mr. Lowell says a man who knew the prince well denominated him as a "great cad." This is a sample of the personal gossip which dribbled out of Mr. Lowell when he had thrown away the spigot of his discretion. The interview appeared, and it created a great sensation. The first thing Mr. Lowell did on reading it was to write a letter denying most of the statements, and saying that he was not aware that Mr. Hawthorne was interviewing him. It is the old story, "he did n't know it was loaded." He allowed his tongue to run away with his discretion, and told the truth. Why should he regret it? Perhaps, however, the fumes of the turtle soup he consumed in England are stronger than his independence, and the smiles of royalty are dearer than his love of truth. Whether he knew his remarks were to be published or not is a matter of veracity between him and Mr. Hawthorne, for the latter prints at the first of his interview the following:

"I have come here on an errand—"

"Not of mercy," interrupted Mr. Lowell, laughing, as a brave man will, in the face of danger.

"No; to be merciful is not my privilege. I have come to learn from you what no one else can tell me—your opinion of England and the English. It is likely to be of more worth than any other American's, and I believe the American people want to know it.'

Mr. Hawthorne has written a card replying to Mr. Lowell's, but he does not seem disposed to take back anything. There is a tone of sadness that we are not surprised at. Reporters all feel that way at first. When Mr. Hawthorne has for a year or so been waking up men at two in the morning to interview them about the state of their health or as to the amount of their embezzlements he will get used to having the accuracy of his writings called to account.

October 29, 1886

The Official Explanation

One night aside the fire at hum,
Ez I wuz sittin' nappin',
Deown frum the lower hall there come
The seound of some one rappin'.
The son uv old Nat Hawthorne he—
Julian, I think his name wuz—
Uv course he feound a friend in me,
Not knowin' what his game wuz.

An' ez we visited a spell,
Our talk ranged wide an' wider,
An' if we struck dry subjects—well,
We washed 'em deown with cider.
Neow, with that cider coursin' thru
My system an' a-playin'
Upon my tongue, I hardly knew
Just what I was a-sayin'.

I kin remember that I spun
A hifalutin story
Abeout the Prince uv Wales, an' one
Abeout old Queen Victory.
But, sakes alive! I never dreamed
The cuss would get it printed—
(By that old gal I 'm much esteemed,
Ez she hez often hinted.)

Oh, if I had that critter neow,
You bet your boots I 'd l'arn him
In mighty lively fashion heow

To walk the chalk, gol darn him!
Meanwhile between his folks an' mine
The breach grows wide an' wider,
An', by the way, it's my design
To give up drinkin' cider.

November 1, 1886

BILL VAUGHAN

"Informed Opinion, the Lifeblood of Our Way of Life"

An editorial writer for the *Daily Kansan,* student newspaper of the University of Kansas, has publicly eaten one of his own compositions, with pepper and salt. There had been one of those arguments between the university and Kansas State University over the size, age, eligibility, or something of a basketball player. The journalist had offered to consume his own brain child if he were proven wrong in whatever it was he said. He was and he did.

The incident interests and saddens me, not as a basketball fan, but as an old editorial eater. The salt and pepper were particularly distressing.

To add condiments to an editorial before eating it is like soaking a steak in strong-tasting sauce. It is an admission that the food is inferior. An editorial that does not contain its own spice is not worth writing or printing, much less eating.

Had I been that hapless editorial writer I would have waved aside the salt and pepper with a disdain as lordly as that of a New Englander confronted with the suggestion that tomatoes be inserted in the clam chowder.

I would have eaten that editorial with all the enthusiasm of a gourmet tasting something served under glass at the monthly meeting of the Wine and Food society.

Bystanders would have been invited to try a morsel.

"Note, if you will," I would have said, "the delicate irony of the adjectives which seem to melt upon the tongue like the memory of a dream. Judge of the deceptive fluffiness of the rhetoric, composed as it is of the juice of sun-ripened nouns, crushed by lovely native girls treading barefoot upon a vintage edition of Webster's. Thrill to the crunchiness of the verbs. Dangle this participle upon your taste buds. Roll these sonorous sentences in your mouth."

Editorial eating has, admittedly, fallen upon evil days. Oh, there are people who will gobble down a quick paragraph now and then, but what a contrast to the easy, spacious days of our grandfathers, who thought nothing of consuming a three-column leader from the *Times* of London, topping it with a filet of Horace Greeley, and ending the meal by rolling up a copy of the editorial page of Dana's *Sun* and smoking it like a Corona Corona.

Who now revels in the delight of hitting upon a chewy "however" in the middle of a salty second paragraph or savors that delicate, indescribable taste of a properly qualified "on the other hand"?

The "whereas," a favorite of editorial eaters of another day, is not much in favor currently, as it tends to get in the teeth.

Not all editorials, of course, are equally suitable for the table. Those on foreign affairs, for example, while they highlight the festive board, may be too rich for everyday tastes.

One doesn't ordinarily eat duck curried Persian style for breakfast, and by the same token it is a mistake to include an editorial on anything so exotic as the Laotian question or Whither Ghana? on the menu for that meal.

For plain, wholesome morning fare, editorials on traffic safety, domestic politics, and public works are vitamin-packed yet not so heavy as to make the eater logy or listless. By midday a person of normal appetite should have something more solid—perhaps about a half column of analysis of the drift toward the Welfare state.

For dinner why not try a fricassee of opinion on the Congo, followed by something light and frothy about the hydrogen bomb?

A word of caution: Watch out for allergies. I have been made deathly ill by the ingestion of editorials about the Balkans. When offered this admittedly tasty dish at parties I have learned to say, "No, thank you. Never eat Balkan editorials. I like them, but they don't like me."

Some forms of editorials are, of course, completely indigestible. Among these are humorous editorials. I once heard of a man who was shipwrecked for two weeks with nothing but the Chicago newspapers. Finally, after he had eaten his way through most of the others, he was forced in desperation to consume an entire humorous editorial.

"It really wasn't so bad," he told me. "Only it tasted a little funny."

This I can hardly believe.

VERONICA GENG

"Partners"

MISS TEAS
WEDS FIANCÉ
IN BRIDAL

The marriage of Nancy Creamer Teas, daughter of Mr. and Mrs. Russell Ruckhyde Teas of Glen Frieburg, N.Y., and Point Pedro, Sri Lanka, to John Potomac Mining, son of Mr. Potomac B. Mining of Buffet Hills, Va., and the late Mrs. Mining, took place at the First Episcopal Church of the Port Authority of New York and New Jersey.

The bride attended the Bodice School, the Earl Grey Seminary, Fence Academy, Railroad Country Day School, and the Credit School, and made her début at the Alexander Hamilton's Birthday Cotillion at Lazard Frères. She is a student in the premedical program at M.I.T. and will spend her junior year at Cartier & Cie. in Paris.

The bridegroom recently graduated from Harvard College. He spent his junior year at the Pentagon, a military concern in Washington, D.C. He will join his father on the board of directors of the Municipal Choate Assistance Corporation. His previous marriage ended in divorce.

CABINET, DELOS
NUPTIALS SET

Ellen Frances Cabinet, a self-help student at Manifest Destiny Junior College, plans to be married in August to Wengdell Delos, a sculptor, of Tampa, Fla. The engagement was announced by the parents of the future bride, Mr. and Mrs. Crowe Cabinet of New York. Mr. Cabinet is a consultant to the New York Stock Exchange.

Mr. Delos's previous marriage ended in an undisclosed settlement. His sculpture is on exhibition at the New York Stock Exchange. He received a

B.F.A. degree from the Wen-El-Del Company, a real-estate-development concern with headquarters in Tampa.

Miss Burdette
Wed to Man

Pews Chapel aboard the Concorde was the setting for the marriage of Bethpage Burdette to Jean-Claude LaGuardia Case, an account executive for the Junior Assemblies. Maspeth Burdette was maid of honor for her sister, who was also attended by Massapequa Burdette, Mrs. William O. Dose, and Mrs. Hodepohl Inks.

The parents of the bride, Dr. and Mrs. Morris Plains Burdette of New York, are partners in Conspicuous Conception, an art gallery and maternity-wear cartel.

The ceremony was performed by the Rev. Erasmus Tritt, a graduate of Skidmore Finishing and Divinity School and president of Our Lady of the Lake Commuter Airlines. The Rev. Tritt was attended by the flight crew. The previous marriages he has performed all ended in divorce.

Daisy Lauderdale
Featured as Bride

Daisy Ciba Lauderdale of Boston was married at the Presbyterian Church and Trust to Gens Cosnotti, a professor of agribusiness at the Massachusetts State Legislature. There was a reception at the First Court of Appeals Club.

The bride, an alumna of the Royal Doulton School and Loot University, is the daughter of Mr. and Mrs. Cyrus Harvester Lauderdale. Her father is retired from the family consortium. She is also a descendant of Bergdorf Goodman of the Massachusetts Bay Colony. Her previous marriage ended in pharmaceuticals.

Professor Cosnotti's previous marriage ended in a subsequent marriage. His father, the late Artaud Cosnotti, was a partner in the Vietnam War. The bridegroom is also related somehow to Mrs. Bethlehem de Steel of Newport, R.I., and Vichy, Costa Rica; Brenda Frazier, who was a senior partner with Delta, Kappa & Epsilon and later general manager of marketing for the U.S. Department of State; I. G. Farben, the former King of England; and Otto von Bismarck, vice-president of the Frigidaire Division of General Motors, now a division of The Hotchkiss School.

Affiancement
for Miss Convair

Archbishop and Mrs. Marquis Convair of Citibank, N.Y., have made known the engagement of their daughter, Bulova East Hampton Convair, to the Joint Chiefs of Staff of Arlington County, Va. Miss Convair is a holding company in the Bahamas.

All four grandparents of the bride-to-be were shepherds and shepherdesses.

Art Buchwald

"Press Relations"

In December 1957, President Eisenhower and his press secretary, James Hagerty, came to Paris for a North Atlantic Treaty Organization meeting. During the course of it, I had the pleasure of writing about a mythical press briefing.

For reasons that still haven't been explained, Mr. Hagerty officially denied the spoof. The following is the article that caused all the trouble, then the news story, printed after the article appeared, giving Mr. Hagerty's side, and a follow-up conference by my press secretary.

A Late, Late Briefing

The NATO conference now going on in Paris is being covered by 1,793 top-flight, highly paid journalists from every corner of the globe. Every detail of the conference is being given careful and thorough coverage. The star of the show is President Eisenhower, and every facet of the President's stay in Paris is being reported to the public in detail. In order to keep the press up on the President's activities, briefings are held at the Hotel Crillon in the morning, at noon and in the early evening, and there is even a special one held late at night for reporters who can't sleep.

I happened to attend one of these late-night briefings with several correspondents of early-morning newspapers. To give you an idea of what takes place at one of these briefings, I took down a transcript.

The man behind the microphone arrived at 12:30 A.M.

"I'm sorry I'm late, gentlemen, but I thought the show at the Lido would end at 11:30. I have a few things to report. The President went to bed at 11:06 tonight."

Q. Jim, have Premier Gaillard and Prime Minister Macmillan also retired?

A. To my knowledge they have.

Q. Then are we to assume that they will not meet with the President until morning?

A. Yes, you could assume that.

Q. Then does that mean he's going to meet with Adenauer during the night?

A. I didn't say that. As far as I know he'll sleep until morning.

Q. Jim, whose idea was it for the President to go to sleep?

A. It was the President's idea. He was tired and decided to go to sleep.

Q. Did Sherman Adams, or Dr. Snyder, or the President's son suggest he go to sleep?

A. As far as I know, the President suggested the idea himself.

Q. Jim, did the President speak to anyone before retiring?

A. He spoke to the Secretary of State.

Q. What did he say to the Secretary of State, Jim?

A. He said: "Good night, Foster."

Q. And what did the Secretary say to the President?

A. He said: "Good night, Mr. President."

Q. The Secretary didn't say: "Pleasant dreams"?

A. Not to my knowledge. I have nothing on that.

Q. Jim, do you have any idea what the President is dreaming of this very moment?

A. No, the President has never revealed to me any of his dreams.

Q. Are we to assume from that that the President doesn't dream?

A. I'm not saying he does or he doesn't. I just said I don't know.

Q. Jim, how will the President be waked up tomorrow morning? Will it be by alarm clock, or will someone come knock on the door?

A. That hasn't been decided yet. But as soon as it has, I'll let you fellows know.

Q. Do you have any idea who the President will see first tomorrow morning?

A. I imagine he'll see the Secretary of State.

Q. What will he say to him?

A. The President plans to say: "Good morning, Foster."

Q. What will the Secretary reply?

A. "Good morning, Mr. President."

Q. That's all?

A. That's all I can tell you at this moment.

Q. Jim, when the President went to bed last night, how did he feel?

A. He was feeling chipper and in good spirits.

Q. How many blankets were on the bed?

A. I'm not sure. Maybe two or three. But certainly no more than he uses in Washington.

Q. Could we say three?

A. I better check that. I know three blankets were made available but it's possible he didn't use all of them.

Q. One could have been kicked off during the night?

A. Yes, that could be possible, but it's unlikely.

Q. Was there a glass of water by the bed?

A. There was a glass of water and a pitcher.

Q. Jim, could we have another briefing before morning?

A. I don't see what would be accomplished by that.

Q. It might tend to clarify the situation.

A. I think the best thing would be to have the briefing after the President gets up.

Q. What about breakfast, Jim?

A. I think we better have another briefing about breakfast, after it's over.

Q. Thank you, Jim.

A. Okay, see you later.

ANOTHER BRIEFING (FROM THE FRONT PAGE OF THE NEW YORK *HERALD TRIBUNE*)

White House press secretary James C. Hagerty took exception yesterday to a column in that morning's European edition of the *Herald Tribune* about an imaginary press conference—by implication one of Mr. Hagerty's.

The author was Art Buchwald, who regularly writes a column of humor from Europe. The column, which appeared on the front page, did not mention the name Hagerty nor did it contain the title "White House press secretary." It recounted in question-and-answer form a press conference by a man named "Jim"—Mr. Hagerty's nickname—in the Crillon Hotel, where Mr. Hagerty has been holding his briefings during the NATO meeting.

The column was a take-off on the endless grubbing by reporters for small details about the President's daily life—whom he talks to, what time he goes to bed, what time he arises, what he says to his aides and so forth. Mr. Hagerty considered the column an affront to himself personally and called it "unadulterated rot."

On the other hand, many American reporters in Paris for the NATO meeting took it more as a spoof at their own sometimes inconsequential questioning of the press secretary.

Mr. Hagerty called a real press conference to comment on the column about the imaginary press conference. The official transcript of that part of it relating to Mr. Buchwald's column was as follows:

MR. HAGERTY. This morning in the New York *Herald Tribune* I read what was purportedly a question-and-answer report of my press conference.

I think all of you ladies and gentlemen know that all of my press conferences since I have started this have been public and have been mimeographed and handed to you ladies and gentlemen. At no time did the reports of the New York *Herald Tribune* even remotely resemble what I ever said at a public briefing.

I would assume that the New York *Herald Tribune,* being a fair and decent paper, would give these remarks equal play on the front page in their edition tomorrow, as they did with this unadulterated rot that was printed in the paper this morning.

Q. (By Mr. Buchwald) Your name wasn't mentioned, Jim.

MR. HAGERTY. I am not going to argue the case. I am making my statement. It is up to the *Tribune* to do what they want.

Q. (Inaudible).

MR. HAGERTY. I still think it was unadulterated rot.

Q. (Inaudible).

MR. HAGERTY. Any other questions? That's all, now. I have to go out to the President's. I'm sorry.

NEWS CONFERENCE

Held in Crillon bar.

> Hotel de Crillon,
> Paris, France.
> With Jo Patrick (Mr. Buchwald's
> secretary).
> Dec. 17, 1957,
> 1:30 P.M. Paris.

MISS PATRICK. I'm sorry I'm late, gentlemen, but I was attending a very important briefing in another part of the hotel. I don't have much to report. Mr. Buchwald is having lunch with some friends in the restaurant. He will have meetings all afternoon with his editors, dinner at home, and then meet with the editors again.

Q. It was reported a few minutes ago, Jo, that one of Mr. Buchwald's readers said he wrote unadulterated rot.

MISS PATRICK. Adulterated or unadulterated?

Q. The quote was "unadulterated."

MISS PATRICK. No. That's not true. Mr. Buchwald has been known to write adulterated rot, but never to my knowledge has he written unadulterated rot. I think it might have been a misprint.

Q. It's right here. Unadulterated rot.

MISS PATRICK. That's the first I've heard of it. I think it should be cleared up, then. Let's get the record straight on that, as it could only hurt Mr. Buchwald.

Q. Has Mr. Buchwald seen the attack by the reader?

MISS PATRICK. He was there at the time.

Q. What was his reaction?

MISS PATRICK. Shock, surprise, and I think I could even say he was hurt.

Q. Someone said he cried.

MISS PATRICK. He didn't cry. He bit his lip a few times, but I was standing right next to him and he didn't cry.

Q. Did he cry later when he was alone?

MISS PATRICK. I doubt it. He did call his wife when it was over and told her to start packing just in case.

Q. Do you think Mr. Buchwald can be hurt by something like this?

MISS PATRICK. Not hurt in the sense of being hurt. Mr. Buchwald always tells Mrs. Buchwald to start packing when a reader doesn't like what he writes. In this case, which admittedly is special in nature, Mr. Buchwald also told her to pack the household goods.

Q. Did Mr. Buchwald say anything about his passport?

MISS PATRICK. He did tell his wife to hide it in a safe place.

Q. Where was that?

MISS PATRICK. I'm afraid I can't say.

Q. Is Mr. Buchwald entitled to severance pay?

MISS PATRICK. Let's jump that hurdle when we come to it.

Q. What is Mr. Buchwald eating for lunch?

MISS PATRICK. He plans to have a very light lunch. Pea soup, eggs Benedict, duck with orange, soufflé potatoes, cheese, salad, and crêpes Suzette.

Q. Did the doctor put him on this regime?

MISS PATRICK. No, several sympathetic journalists offered to take him to lunch after the briefing, on *their* expense accounts.

Q. At this point in the conference do things look all black for Mr. Buchwald?

MISS PATRICK. I would like to take issue with the pessimists in this room. We never had high hopes when Mr. Buchwald came here and we don't have them now. The most that can happen is that Mr. Buchwald will become the White Plains correspondent for the *Herald Tribune*.

Q. What's on the agenda for the rest of the week for Mr. Buchwald?

MISS PATRICK. The editors have suggested he do several pieces on Christmas shopping, Santa Claus, where birds go in the winter, walks in the woods on Sunday, fishing through ice and why American children can't read French.

Q. Does that mean Mr. Buchwald won't be in on any more of the NATO
   briefings?

MISS PATRICK. I won't go that far. If the paper thinks it's necessary they may
   send him over. But there really isn't much more he can do. The White
   House reporters can handle the detail work.

Q. Thank you, Jo.

MISS PATRICK. Thank you, gentlemen.

LARRY L. KING

"A Matter of Style"

Jim Morgan, chief articles editor at *Playboy*, called to ask me to do a
piece on "personal style." He said three other writers—William F. Buckley,
Jr., D. Keith Mano and Leonard Michaels—would also be asked; our pieces
would appear in the issue of January 1983. My problem was that I couldn't
immediately identify my "personal style." Wasn't even sure I had one. For
years, however, I had wanted to write an article about a financial misadventure
in which I had victimized myself, and others, but had no "peg" to hang it on.
So I used Morgan's invitation to write something I long had wanted to sell,
working only vaguely within his stated rules. The writer must be enterprising
in the marketplace.

My style is to get it when you can, where you can, and don't trouble to look
over your shoulder with a lot of fuddy-duddy moralizing in mind. I excuse this
by believing that should you permit yourself to grow up poorer than orphan-
shit, then you naturally will be tempted by riches early on.

Never mind I was raised a raggedy-ass yellow-dog Democrat; I wanted to
be what we in Texas called "a bidnessman." Them suckers ran thangs, I
observed, and hardly ever got caught at sweat work. A fascinating combination.

I did not, you understand, thirst to be the kind of mom 'n' pop store
bidnessman who kept dusty ledgers and faithful hours. No, I pined to be a
get-rich-quick man. I eventually discovered it was my ambition and my style
to be an entrepreneur.

It took me awhile to get the hang of it. My first venture, in the fourth grade of the Putnam public school, was to write everybody's English themes for five cents the pop. Unfortunately, I used the same handwriting, tablet paper and ink color often enough to arouse official suspicions. I didn't mind the shame so much; what hurt was having to refund all those nickels.

Next I sold autographs of the famous. Business, admittedly, was slow while I depended on the signatures of local luminaries: county commissioners, preachers and such. There was a dramatic upsurge in the summer of 1939, when I made available the autographs of Tom Mix, Tarzan and FDR. When I offered the signature of Jesus Christ at fifteen cents each or two for a quarter, I suddenly found myself back in the restitution business.

The problem, I decided as I grew and matured, was that I had not thought big. In 1957, I began to think big. Real big. Quite by accident, I stumbled onto a surefire way to make $500,000 with only a minimum of heavy lifting required.

I was then working on Capitol Hill for a Texas congressman who would just as lief I not report his name. One day, I noticed a newspaper item beckoning me to riches: lumber being used to construct the inauguration platform from which President Dwight D. Eisenhower was scheduled to take his oath for a second term would be sold after the festivities to the highest bidder. Surely, such historic wood could be put to profitable use.

I approached a friend, Dr. Glen P. Wilson, an employee of Senator Lyndon B. Johnson; we got our thinking caps on. Wilson had been selected as my potential partner because he, too, thirsted to be an entrepreneur. Never mind he had failed as the inventor of a three-dimensional gameboard that boasted several clear-glass platforms permitting players to compete simultaneously at chess, Chinese checkers, mah-jongg, dominoes and, maybe, pole vaulting. Perhaps the gameboard failed because it was bigger than an oil derrick or required too much concentration for the TV generation to handle; at any rate, his large concept qualified Dr. Wilson as an Olympian thinker. I wanted him on my side in the Eisenhower-plaque bidness.

No way the Eisenhower-plaque enterprise could fail, Ike having amassed 35,000,000 votes in his second trouncing of Adlai Stevenson and being the most beloved American since Lassie. We hired a fellow with a slide rule, who calculated we could cut 550,000 little square plaques from the historic wood. Our calculations were that by selling them for $1 each, we would easily clear a cool half million—probably more. After all, our only expenses would be the lumber itself, a couple of electric saws, a gold-stamping machine, small cardboard boxes in which to ship the historic plaques, a bit of newspaper advertising, postage and rental on P.O. Box 1956, Washington, D.C. We budgeted not a dime for labor costs, figuring we would do the dirty work ourselves until the first 100,000 plaques had been sold. Then, perhaps, we might hire disadvantaged friends and illegal aliens at hourly rates so cheap the costs would be laughable to a couple of rich swells.

We successfully bid for the lumber at a cost of only $3,200 plus the interest on our bank loan. We bought two electric saws, real beauties, for a total of $1,400, and a gold-stamping machine, which would imprint in spiffy gold letters on the wooden blocks this impressive legend:

THIS HISTORIC PLAQUE IS CERTIFIED
AS PART OF THE OFFICIAL INAUGURAL
PLATFORM OF DWIGHT D. EISENHOWER,
35TH PRESIDENT OF THE UNITED STATES,
FROM WHICH HE TOOK HIS OATH OF
OFFICE ON JANUARY 21, 1957.

The gold-stamping machine was a steal at a mere $800 and change.

Dr. Wilson approached the *New York Times,* the *Des Moines Register,* the *Chicago Tribune* and many other newspapers, as well as, cleverly, the GOP national house organ. The cost of the resulting ads—tiny, and positioned at the back near the patent-medicine and truss ads in most cases—totaled a mere $4,717.36. The dignified *New York Times,* however, insisted on official assurances that our wood blocks were pedigreed. We got a letter from the Architect of the Capitol appropriately pedigreeing them. Then we had a new inspiration: perhaps we should supply our customers with small individual certificates signed by the Architect of the Capitol. These miniature numbers, on old parchment to lend a touch of class, were fashioned for only five cents each. Unfortunately, the aggregate sum for the first 20,000—we would have the remainder delivered later, from profits—strained us an additional $1,200.

We found it necessary to return to the bankers. Our total cost had now exceeded $12,000—not counting the postage we'd need. Our original banker, faced with our burgeoning capital requirements, suddenly developed an ongoing lack of enthusiasm. Through relatives and friends, we raised another $5,000. And more lectures and horselaughs than we found seemly.

Eventually, our raw lumber was delivered to the basements of our respective homes in Alexandria, Virginia. We sighed and wrote off the resulting window breakage and wall damage to future profits.

For days, King/Wilson, their wives and a few believing friends sawed, stamped and certified historic wood around the clock. As the appearance of our first ads approached, our main worry was that the 15,000 Eisenhower plaques we had readied would not suffice to meet the initial flood of orders. We hired a lawyer. For a mere $500, he pledged to stall malcontents until income exceeded outgo and we could fill orders in a timely fashion.

Came the marvelous Sunday our ads appeared across the width and breadth of the United States. Dr. Wilson and your present hero made a midnight raid on P.O. Box 1956, Washington, D.C. Zilch. *Nada.* Nothing. That was okay. We hadn't really expected to find orders that early; our visit to the P.O. was more of a dry run, for practice, like you'd conduct just before robbing a bank.

Monday's postal run proved exactly as productive as Sunday's. Well, what the hell; the mails required awhile. Tuesday morning, we discovered nine letters ordering eleven plaques. We hugged and danced and went home on our lunch hours to produce another few dozen of our hot item before the deluge. And a deluge there would be, as our first orders proved: we had counted on only *one* plaque per order and commerce was averaging better than that. We discussed whether, once our historic wood played out, we dared send common wood and just claim it to be historic. "No," Dr. Wilson said, "that would be dishonest." I wasn't bothered by that distinction so much as I feared indictment for mail fraud.

Tuesday afternoon brought a dozen letters ordering as many historic plaques. "These are only the airmail orders," we assured each other. "Wait until the regular-postage letters and postcards start coming in!" We returned, perhaps a bit apprehensively, to our saws and stamping machine.

A week later, we had sold forty-nine Historic Eisenhower Plaques. At $1 the item. Wives began to wail; friends quit volunteering their services on our assembly line; bills began to visit P.O. Box 1956, Washington, D.C.

I telephoned Jim Hagerty, Ike's press secretary, intending to say that while I admittedly was a registered Democrat, I was big enough to rise above petty partisanship: how about Ike's plugging our entrepreneurship at his next press conference, waxing eloquent about this fine example of free enterprise, and maybe letting our P.O. box number go public, or some such? Alas, the nameless secretary to the presidential press secretary coolly proclaimed that Mr. Hagerty was far too busy to be bothered and that the White House never, but *never,* endorsed commercializations of the Highest Office in the Land. *Click.*

A month later, having sold a grand total of seventy-six plaques, we began the painful process of liquidation. You'd be surprised how many people had no use for a perfectly good gold-stamping machine. Our ads in trade journals brought a single postcard, from a man in North Carolina. We hastened to call him.

"He don't do no talkin' on the phone," a woman snapped before hanging up.

We called back to beg. The lady explained that her husband didn't do no talkin' on the phone because he was "deef and dumb." We told of her husband's interest in buying our spiffy gold-stamping machine. She laughed and laughed: "He ain't got thutty-five cents. Fact is, he's a ward of the state."

"So are we," I said glumly to my partner.

We sold our marvelous gold-stamping machine at junk weight and unloaded the twin electric saws for one-third of what we had in them.

Davis Carter, a colleague on Capitol Hill, paid $300 for the unsawed remainder of our historic Ike wood and used it to build a backyard fence. He added insult to injury by adorning it with a number of those accursed plaques.

A few nights later, I hosted a to-hell-with-it party in my own backyard. Highlight of the evening was the ceremonial public burning of 15,000 little wooden plaques, give or take a few dozen. The Alexandria Fire Department came to the party, without invitation, to douse the fire. The fire marshal handed me a $50 summons for unauthorized trash burning. He was certainly right about what I had burned.

The life-style of the entrepreneur is difficult to give up, however. I always look for the main chance. When the editors of *Playboy* asked me to write this piece, I said I would do it for $1 per word.

Per word. Per word. Per word. Per word. Per word. Per word.

FRED ALLEN

"The Cape Codder"

july
12
1950

dear editor—

you are the editor of The Cape Codder. i am a subscriber.

when a subscriber writes to an editor it is usually to complain about the paper's editorial policy, the small-sized print used in the help-wanted columns that is keeping nearsighted people, who are out of work and have no glasses, from finding jobs or to berate the editor for misspelling the name of the subscriber's wife in the news story that told how the subscriber's wife fell off a stool at a howard johnson stand and spilled 26 kinds of ice cream on her burlap ensemble.

my purpose in writing this letter is not to condemn. i have no desire to add another gray hair to your editorial cowlick. i merely want to despatch a kind word to you and to your little gazette.

to me The Cape Codder is a friend who comes to my door each week bearing tidings from the cape. the affairs of the outside world find no place in its columns. The Cape Codder chronicles only the happenings on the cape and the gossip and matters of moment to its denizens.

what other weekly gives you news and items such as these? (i quote from recent issues)

"now is the time to protect pine trees from the destructive turpentine bark beetles."

"albino woodchuck shot by frank hinckley in cummaquid."

"the striped bass struck in at pochot beach, orleans, sunday."

"cranberry clinic to be held july 12 and july 18. cranberry growers will meet to discuss bog problems."

"mildewed sails can now be prevented easily and inexpensively."

what other journal gives its readers pieces comparable to "orchard twilight," "the june woods" and "campin' on the island" by somebody who signs himself l.r.j.—colorful memories of happy yesterdays and tributes to fauna, flora and secluded nooks and crannies discovered by l.r.j. in strolls about the cape?

what other paper comes out on thursday to enable you to finish its contents and have its pages ready to wrap up a fish on friday? the answer is—no other paper.

until i subscribed to The Cape Codder i thought that a cranberry was a cherry with an acid condition. i thought that a seagull was a thyroid pigeon. i thought the mayor of cotuit was an oyster. today, thanks to The Cape Codder, i know why the pilgrim fathers, who had the entire continent available for their purposes, chose to land on cape cod.

enclosed please find check for another year's subscription. may you and The Cape Codder trudge along down through the years enjoying the success you merit for a job well done.

sincerely—

fred allen
the belmont
west harwich
massachusetts

H. L. MENCKEN

"Drill for a Rookie"

In those days a reporter who had durable legs and was reasonably sober tended to see a varied service, for it was not unusual for one of his elders to succumb to the jug and do a vanishing act. More than once during my first weeks, after turning in my own budget of assaults, fires, drownings and other such events from the Southern, I was sent out at eleven o'clock at night to find a lost colleague of the Eastern or Northeastern, and pump his news out of him, if he had any. It was by the same route, in July, that I found myself promoted to the Central, which was the premier Baltimore district, journalistically speaking, for it included the busiest of the police courts, a downtown hospital, police headquarters, the city jail, and the morgue. The regular man there had turned up at the office one noon so far gone in rum that Max relieved him of duty, and I was gazetted to his place as a means of shaming him, for I was still the youngest reporter in the office. When he continued in his cups the day following I was retained as his *locum tenens,* and when he went on to a third day he was reduced to the Northern police district, the Siberia of Baltimore, and I found myself his heir.

This man, though we eventually became good friends, resented his demotion so bitterly that for weeks he refused to speak to me, but I was too busy in my new bailiwick to pay any attention to him. Its police court was the liveliest in town, and had the smartest and most colorful magistrate, Gene Grannan by name. He was always willing to help the press by developing the dramatic content of the cases before him, and during my first week he thus watered and manured for me a couple of stories that delighted Max, and boosted my own stock. Such stories were almost a *Herald* monopoly, for *Sun* reporters were hobbled by their paper's craze for mathematical accuracy, and most *American* reporters were too stupid to recognize good stuff when they saw it. Max helped by inventing likely minor assignments for me, and one of them I still remember. It was a wedding in a shabby street given over to second-hand shops run by Polish Jews and patronized by sailors. The bride had written in demanding publicity, and I was sent to see her—partly as a means of gently hazing a freshman, but also on the chance that there might be a picturesque story in her. In the filthy shop downstairs her father directed me to the second floor, and when I climbed the stairs I found her in process of being dressed by her mother. She was standing in the middle of the floor with nothing on save a diaphanous vest and a flouncy pair of drawers. Never having seen a bride so close to the altogether before, I was somewhat upset, but she and her mother were quite calm, and loaded me with all the details of the impending cere-mony. I wrote the story at length, but Max stuck it on his "If" hook, and there it died.

But such romantic interludes were not frequent. My days, like those of any other police reporter, were given over mainly to harsher matters—murders, assaults and batteries, street accidents, robberies, suicides, and so on. I well recall my first suicide, for the victim was a lovely young gal who had trusted a preacher's son too far, and then swallowed poison: she looked almost angelic lying on her parlor floor, with a couple of cops badgering her distracted mother. I remember, too, my first autopsy at the morgue—a most trying recreation for a hot Summer day—, and my first palaver with a burglar, and my first ride with the cops in a patrol-wagon, but for some reason or other my first murder has got itself forgotten. The young doctors at the City Hospital (now the Mercy Hospital) were always productive, for they did a heavy trade in street and factory accidents, and a very fair one in attempted suicides. In those days carbolic acid was the favorite drug among persons who yearned for the grave, just as bichloride of mercury was to be the favorite of a decade later, and I saw many of its customers brought in—their lips swollen horribly, and their eyes full of astonishment that they were still alive. . . .

But a reporter chiefly remembers, not such routine themes of his art as hangings, fires and murders, which come along with dispiriting monotony, but the unprecedented novelties that occasionally inspire him, some of them gor-geous and others only odd. Perhaps the most interesting story I covered in my first six months had to do with the purloining of a cadaver from a medical college. The burglar was the head *Diener* of the dissecting-room, and he packed the body in a barrel and shipped it to a colleague in the upper Middle West, where there was a shortage of such provisions at the time. Hot weather coming on *en route,* it was discovered, and for a week we had a gaudy murder mystery. When the *Diener* shut off the uproar by confessing, it turned out that the maximum punishment he could be given, under the existing Maryland law, passed in 1730, was sixty days in the House of Correction. On his return to duty the medical students welcomed him with a beer party that lasted forty-eight hours, and he boasted that he had been stealing and shipping bodies for years. But the cops, discouraged, did nothing about it.

At a somewhat later time, after I had forsaken police reporting, the moral inadequacy of the ancient Maryland statutes was revealed again. This time the culprit was a Methodist clergyman who operated one of the vice crusades that then afflicted all the big cities of the East. The cops, of course, were violently against him, for they could see nothing wrong about honest women making honest livings according to their talents. When the pastor charged that they pooh-poohed him because they were taking bribes from the girls they determined to get him, and to that end sneaked a spy into the Y.M.C.A. One night soon afterward the pastor visited the place with a Christian young man, and the spy, concealed in a cupboard, caught the two in levantine deviltries. The former was collared at once, and the State's attorney sent for. Unhappily, he had to advise the poor cops that the acts they laid to their prisoner were not forbidden by Maryland law, which was singularly tolerant in sexual matters. The maximum penalty it then provided for adultery, however brutal and deliberate, was $10 fine, with no alternative of imprisonment, and there was no punishment at all for fornication, or for any of its non-Euclidian variations. The cops were thus stumped, but they quickly resolved their dilemma by concealing it from the scared pastor, and giving him two hours to get out of town. He departed leaving a wife and five children behind him, and has never been heard from since. The Legislature being in session, the cops then went to Annapolis and begged it to sharpen the laws. It responded by forbidding, under heavy penalties, a list of offenses so long and so bizarre that some of them are not even recorded in Krafft-Ebing.

I myself, while still assigned to the Central district, covered a case that well illustrated the humanity of the old Maryland statute. The accused was a man who had run away from Pittsburgh with another man's wife, and they had come to Baltimore in the drawing-room of a sleeper. The lady's husband, having got wind of their flight, wired ahead, asking the cops to arrest the pair on their arrival. The cops refused to collar an apparently respectable female on any such charge, but they brought in the man, and he was arraigned before Gene Grannan. As a matter of law, his guilt had to be presumed, for the Court of Appeals of Maryland had decided only a little while before that when a man and a woman went into a room together and locked the door it would be insane to give them the benefit of the doubt. Moreover, the prisoner, advised by a learned police-station lawyer, admitted the charge freely, and confined his defense to swearing that the crime had not been committed until after the train crossed the Maryland line. If he were sent back to Pennsylvania for trial he would be in serious difficulties, for the penalty for adultery there was almost as drastic as that for arson or piracy, but in Maryland, as I have said, it was a mere misdemeanor, comparable to breaking a window or spitting on the sidewalk. Grannan doubted the truth of the defense, but decided that a humane judge would have to accept it, so he fined the culprit $2, and the pair resumed their honeymoon with loud hosannas. When a Pennsylvania cop showed up the next day with extradition papers he was baffled, for the man had been tried and punished, and could not be put in jeopardy again.

Grannan held a session of his court every afternoon, and I always attended it. It was seldom, indeed, that he did not turn up something that made good copy. He had been, before his judicial days, chief of the Baltimore & Ohio's railroad police, and thus had a wide acquaintance among professional criminals, especially yeggmen, and held the professional respect of the cops. In that remote era there was no file of finger-prints at Washington, and even the Bertillon system was just coming into use. The cops, in consequence, sometimes picked up an eminent felon without knowing who he was. But if he came before Grannan he was identified at once, and started through a mill that commonly landed him in the Maryland Penitentiary. That institution, which occupied a fine new building near the city jail, then had as its warden a reformed politician named John Weyler. He had been a tough baby in his day, and was even suspected of a hand in a homicide, but when I knew him he had said goodbye to all that, and was an excellent officer. I dropped in on him two or three times a week, and usually picked up something worth printing. He had a strange peculiarity: he never came outside the prison walls save when it was raining. Then he would wander around for hours, and get himself soaked to the skin, for he never used an umbrella. Once a month his board of visitors met at the Penitentiary, and he entertained the members at dinner. These dinners gradually took on lavishness and gaiety, and during one of them a member of the board, searching for a place marked "Gents," fell down the main staircase of the place and had to be sent to hospital. After that Weyler limited the drinks to ten or twelve a head.

Another good source of the kind of news that Max Ways liked was an old fellow named Hackman, the superintendent of the morgue. The morgue was housed in an ancient building at the end of one of the city docks, and Hackman seldom left it. There was a sort of derrick overhanging the water, and on it the harbor cops would pull up the floaters that they found, and let them dry. Some of them were covered with crabs and barnacles when they were brought in, and Hackman had a long pole for knocking such ornaments off. How greatly he loved his vocation was shown when a new health commissioner fired him, and he refused to give up his keys. The health commissioner thereupon called for a squad of cops, and went down to the morgue to take possession by force, followed by a trail of reporters. But Hackman was defiant, and when firemen were sent for to aid the cops, he barricaded himself among his clients, and declared that he would never be taken alive.

The ensuing battle went on all afternoon, and was full of thrills. The cops refused to resort to firearms and the firemen refused to knock down the door with their hose, so Hackman seemed destined to hold out forever. Every now and then he would open the door for a few inches, and howl fresh defiance at the health commissioner. Finally, one of the reporters, Frank R. Kent, of the *Sun,* sneaked up along the wall, and thrust in his foot the next time the door was opened. Before Hackman could hack Kent's foot off the cops rushed him, and the morgue was taken. The poor old fellow burst into tears as he was being led away. The morgue, he wailed, was his only solace, almost his only life; he had devoted years to its upkeep and improvement, and was proud of its high standing among the morgues of Christendom. Moreover, many of the sponges, cloths and other furnishings within, including the pole he used to delouse floaters, were his personal property, and he was being robbed of them. The health commissioner promised to restore them, and so Hackman faded from the scene, a victim to a Philistine society that could not fathom his peculiar ideals.

There were press-agents in those days as in these, and though they had not reached the dizzy virtuosity now on tap they nevertheless showed a considerable ingenuity and daring. One of the best I encountered in my first years remains unhappily nameless in my memory, though I well recall some of his feats. He slaved for Frank Bostock, a big, blond, tweedy, John Bullish Englishman who had leased an old cyclorama in Baltimore and put in a wild animal show. Even before the doors were open the agent bombarded the local newspapers with bulletins worthy the best tradition of Tody Hamilton, press-agent for P. T. Barnum—battles between tigers and boa constrictors, the birth of infant giraffes and kangaroos, the sayings of a baboon who could speak Swahili, and so on. When, after the opening, business turned out to be bad, he spit on his hands, and turned off some masterpieces. The one I remember best was the hanging of a rogue elephant, for I was assigned to cover it. This elephant, we were informed, had become so onery that he could be endured no longer, and it was necessary to put him to death. Ordinarily, he would be shot, but Bostock, as a patriotic and law-abiding Englishman, preferred hanging, and would serve as executioner himself.

The butchery of the poor beast—he looked very mangey and feeble—was carried out one morning in the Bolton street railroad yards. First his legs were tied together, and then a thick hawser was passed around his neck and pulled tight, and the two ends were fastened to the hook of a railroad crane. When Bostock gave the signal the crane began to grind, and in a few minutes the elephant was in the air. He took it very quietly, and was pronounced dead in half an hour. A large crowd saw the ceremony, and after that business at the Bostock zoo picked up. The press-agent got rid of the S.P.C.A. by announcing that the elephant had been given six ounces of morphine to dull his sensations. His remains were presented to the Johns Hopkins Medical School for scientific study, but no one there was interested in proboscidean anatomy, so they finally reached a glue factory.

Six months later the Bostock zoo gave the Baltimore newspapers a good story without any effort by its press-agent. On a cold Winter night, with six inches of sleet in the streets, it took fire, and in a few minutes all its major inmates were burned to death and the small fry were at large. The pursuit of the latter went on all night and all the next day, and the cops turned up an occasional frost-bitten monkey as much as a week later. No really dangerous animal got loose, but the town was in a state of terror for weeks, and many suburban dogs, mistaken for lions or tigers, were done to death by vigilantes. I recall picking up a powerful cold by wallowing around the night of the fire in the icy slush.

But the best of all the Baltimore press-agents of that age was a volunteer who worked for the sheer love of the science. His name was Frank Thomas, and he was the son of a contractor engaged in building a new courthouse. There were to be ten or twelve huge marble pillars in the façade of the building, and they had to be brought in from a quarry at Cockeysville, fourteen miles away. The hauling was done on trucks drawn by twenty horses. One day a truck lost a wheel and the pillar aboard was broken across the middle. Frank announced at once that a fossil dog had been found in the fracture, and supported the tale by having a crude dog painted on it and the whole photographed. That photograph made both the *Herald* and the *American*, though the suspicious *Sunpaper* sniffed at it. It took the geologists at the Johns Hopkins a week to convince the town that there could be no canine fossils in sedimentary rocks. A bit later Frank made it known that the new courthouse would be fitted with a contraption that would suck up all sounds coming in from the streets, and funnel them out through the sewers. In his handout he described eloquently the comfort of judges and juries protected against the noises of traffic and trade, and the dreadful roar of the accumulated sounds as they emerged from the sewers along the waterfront. Frank indulged himself in many other inventions, and I handled most of them for the *Herald*, for the courthouse was in my parish. When the building was finished at last he published an illustrated souvenir book on it, and I wrote the 8000 words of its text. My honorarium was $25.

His days, alas, were not all beer and skittles, for putting up a large building in the heart of a busy city is a job shot through with cephalalgia. While it was under way a high board fence surrounded it, and on that fence were all the usual advertising signs, most of them hideous. The *Herald* started a violent crusade against them, arguing that they disgraced the courthouse and affronted all decent people. I was assigned by Max Ways to write some of the indignant stories we printed, and thus I met Frank in the dual rôle of friend of his fancy and enemy of his fence. So far as I could make out, the *Herald*'s crusade had no support whatsoever in public sentiment—in fact, it became more and more difficult to find anyone to endorse it—but it roared on for months. The fence came down at last at least three or four weeks later than it would have come down if there had been no hullabaloo, for Frank had iron in him as well as imagination, and held out defiantly as long as he could.

It was a crusading time, with uplifters of a hundred schools harrying every major American city, and every newspaper of any pretensions took a hand in the dismal game. I recall crusades against sweat-shops, against the shanghaiing of men for the Chesapeake oyster fleet, and against dance-halls that paid their female interns commissions on the drinks sold. I had a hand in all of them, and if they filled me with doubts they also gave me some exhilarating experiences. With the cops I toured the bastiles of the waterfront crimps, and examined the jails that they maintained for storing their poor bums, and with health department inspectors I saw all the worst sweat-shops of the town, including one in which a huge flock of hens was kept hard at work laying eggs in a filthy cellar. In the war upon bawdy dance-halls I became a witness, unwillingly, against the cops, for I was put on the stand to testify that I had seen two detectives in one of them, and that the detectives must have been aware of what was going on. The poor flatfeet were unquestionably guilty, for I had discussed the matter with them in the place, but I managed to sophisticate my testimony with so many ifs and buts that it went for nothing, and they were acquitted by the police board. That was my first and last experience as an active agent of moral endeavor. I made up my mind at once that my true and natural allegiance was to the Devil's party, and it has been my firm belief ever since that all persons who devote themselves to forcing virtue on their fellow men deserve nothing better than kicks in the pants. Years later I put that belief into a proposition which I ventured to call Mencken's Law, to wit:

Whenever A annoys or injures B on the pretense of saving or improving X, A is a scoundrel.

The moral theologians, unhappily, have paid no heed to this contribution to their science, and so Mencken's Law must wait for recognition until the dawn of a more enlightened age.

SECTION TEN

FABLE, LORE, AND FANTASY

Those who would teach a worthy lesson, as Gilbert and Sullivan advised, must "always gild the philosophic pill." This is what composers of fables do. The classic fable, like Aesop's, must be so simple that a child can grasp its lesson, yet entertaining enough to delight an adult, and resonant enough to make minds of all ages pause and ponder.

Not all the pieces that follow here qualify as fables, and those that do might more correctly be called mock fables. Edgar Allan Poe's fantasy of a man far gone in fancy wine is included mostly to prove that this giant of letters at least gave the humorous fantasy a try.

Why Stanley Elkin's fantastical account of God in Hell? For one thing, not having Elkin somewhere in a book like this would be shameful. For another, it conjures up one of the funniest ideas your editor has ever come across: the picture of a crowd of humans, given a chance to interview God, asking Him, "Where do you get your ideas?"

GEORGE ADE

"The Patient Toiler Who Got It in the Usual Place"

Once there was an Office Employee with a Copy-Book Education.

He believed it was his Duty to learn to Labor and to Wait.

He read Pamphlets and Magazine Articles on Success and how to make it a Cinch. He knew that if he made no Changes and never beefed for more Salary, but just buckled down and put in Extra Time and pulled for the House, he would Arrive in time.

The Faithful Worker wanted to be Department Manager. The Hours were short and the Salary large and the Work easy.

He plugged on for many Moons, keeping his Eye on that Roll-Top Desk, for the Manager was getting into the Has-Been Division and he knew there would be a Vacancy.

At last the House gave the old Manager the Privilege of retiring and living on whatever he had saved.

"Ah, this is where Humble Merit gets its Reward," said the Patient Toiler. "I can see myself counting Money."

That very Day the Main Gazooks led into the Office one of the handsomest Tennis Players that ever worked on Long Island and introduced him all around as the new Department Manager.

"I shall expect you to tell Archibald all about the Business," said the Main Gazooks to the Patient Toiler. "You see he has just graduated from Yale and he doesn't know a dum Thing about Managing anything except a Cat-Boat, but his Father is one of our principal Stock-Holders and he is engaged to a Young Woman whose Uncle is at the head of the Trust."

"I had been hoping to get this Job for myself," said the Faithful Worker, faintly.

"You are so valuable as a Subordinate and have shown such an Aptitude for Detail Work that it would be a Shame to waste you on a $5,000 Job," said the

Main Gazooks. "Besides you are not Equipped. You have not been to Yale. Your Father is not a Stock-Holder. You are not engaged to a Trust. Get back to your High Stool and whatever Archibald wants to know, you tell him."

Moral: *One who wishes to be a Figure-Head should not Overtrain.*

George Ade

"The Fable of How the Fool-Killer Backed Out of a Contract"

The Fool-Killer came along the Pike Road one Day and stopped to look at a Strange Sight.

Inside of a Barricade were several Thousands of Men, Women and Children. They were moving restlessly among the trampled Weeds, which were clotted with Watermelon Rinds, Chicken Bones, Straw and torn Paper Bags.

It was a very hot Day. The People could not sit down. They shuffled Wearily and were pop-eyed with Lassitude and Discouragement.

A stifling Dust enveloped them. They Gasped and Sniffled. Some tried to alleviate their Sufferings by gulping down a Pink Beverage made of Drug-Store Acid, which fed the Fires of Thirst.

Thus they wove and interwove in the smoky Oven. The Whimper or the faltering Wail of Children, the quavering Sigh of overlaced Women, and the long-drawn Profanity of Men—these were what the Fool-Killer heard as he looked upon the Suffering Throng.

"Is this a new Wrinkle on Dante's Inferno?" he asked of the Man on the Gate, who wore a green Badge marked "Marshal," and was taking Tickets.

"No, sir; this is a County Fair," was the reply.

"Why do the People congregate in the Weeds and allow the Sun to warp them?"

"Because Everybody does it."

"Do they Pay to get in?"

"You know it."

"Can they Escape?"

"They can, but they prefer to Stick."

The Fool-Killer hefted his Club and then looked at the Crowd and shook his Head doubtfully.

"I can't tackle that Outfit to-day," he said. "It's too big a Job."

So he went on into Town, and singled out a Main Street Merchant who refused to Advertise.

MORAL: *PEOPLE WHO EXPECT TO BE LUNY WILL FIND IT SAFER TO TRAVEL IN A BUNCH.*

GEORGE ADE

"The Fable of the Slim Girl Who Tried to Keep a Date That Was Never Made"

Once upon a Time there was a slim Girl with a Forehead which was Shiny and Protuberant, like a Bartlett Pear. When asked to put Something in an Autograph Album she invariably wrote the Following, in a tall, dislocated Back-Hand:

> "Life is Real; Life is Earnest,
> And the Grave is not its Goal."

That's the kind of a Girl she was.

In her own Town she had the Name of being a Cold Proposition, but that was because the Primitive Yokels of a One-Night Stand could not Attune Themselves to the Views of one who was troubled with Ideals. Her Soul Panted for the Higher life.

Alas, the Rube Town in which she Hung Forth was given over to Croquet, Mush and Milk Sociables, a lodge of Elks and two married Preachers who doctored for the Tonsilitis. So what could the Poor Girl do?

In all the Country around there was not a Man who came up to her Plans and Specifications for a Husband. Neither was there any Man who had any time for Her. So she led a lonely Life, dreaming of the One—the Ideal. He was a big and pensive Literary Man, wearing a Prince Albert coat, a neat Derby Hat and godlike Whiskers. When He came he would enfold Her in his Arms and whisper Emerson's Essays to her.

But the Party failed to show up.

Often enough she put on her Chip Hat and her Black Lisle Gloves and Sauntered down to look at the Gang sitting in front of the Occidental Hotel, hoping that the Real Thing would be there. But she always saw the same old line of Four-Flush Drummers from Chicago and St. Louis, smoking Horrid Cigars and talking about the Percentages of the League Teams.

She knew that these Gross Creatures were not prone to chase mere Intellectual Splendor, so she made no effort to Flag them.

When she was Thirty-Four years of age and was able to recite "Lucile" without looking at the Book she was Married to a Janitor of the name of Ernest. He had been kicked in the Head by a Mule when young and believed everything he read in the Sunday Papers. His pay was Twenty-Three a month, which was high, if you knew Ernest.

His Wife wore a red Mother Hubbard all during the Remainder of her Life. This is invariably a Sign of Blasted Hopes.

MORAL: *Never Live in a Jay Town.*

GEORGE ADE

"The Fable of the Copper and the Jovial Undergrads"

One Night three Well-Bred Young Men, who were entertained at the Best Houses wherever they went, started out to Wreck a College town.

They licked two Hackmen, set fire to an Awning, pulled down many Signs, and sent a Brick through the Front Window of a Tailor Shop. All the Residents of the Town went into the Houses and locked the Doors; Terror brooded over the Community.

A Copper heard the Racket, and saw Women and Children fleeing to Places of Safety, so he gripped his Club and ran Ponderously, overtaking the three Well-Bred Young Men in a dark part of the Street, where they were Engaged in tearing down a Fence.

He could not see them Distinctly, and he made the Mistake of assuming that they were Drunken Ruffians from the Iron Foundry. So he spoke harshly, and told them to Leave Off breaking the Man's Fence. His Tone and Manner irritated the University Men, who were not accustomed to Rudeness from Menials.

One Student, who wore a Sweater, and whose people butt into the Society Column with Sickening Regularity, started to Tackle Low; he had Bushy Hair and a Thick Neck, and his strong Specialty was to swing on Policemen and Cabbies.

At this, his Companion, whose Great Grandmother had been one of the eight thousand Close Relatives of John Randolph, asked him not to Kill the Policeman. He said the Fellow had made a Mistake, that was all; they were not Muckers; they were Nice Boys, intent on preserving the Traditions of dear old *Alma Mater*.

The Copper could hardly Believe it until they led him to a Street Lamp, and showed him their Engraved Cards and Junior Society Badges; then he Realized that they were All Right. The third Well-Bred Young Man, whose Male Parent got his Coin by wrecking a Building Association in Chicago, then announced that they were Gentlemen, and could Pay for everything they broke. Thus it will be seen that they were Rollicking College Boys and not Common Rowdies.

The Copper, perceiving that he had come very near getting Gay with our First Families, Apologized for Cutting In. The Well-Bred Young Men forgave him, and then took his Club away from him, just to Demonstrate that there were no Hard Feelings. On the way back to the Seat of Learning they captured a Night Watchman, and put him down a Man-Hole.

MORAL: *ALWAYS SELECT THE RIGHT SORT OF PARENTS BEFORE YOU START IN TO BE ROUGH.*

JAMES THURBER

"The Two Turkeys"

Once upon a time there were two turkeys, an old turkey and a young turkey. The old turkey had been cock of the walk for many years and the young turkey wanted to take his place. "I'll knock that old buzzard cold one of these days," the young turkey told his friends. "Sure you will, Joe, sure you will," his friends said, for Joe was treating them to some corn he had found. Then the friends went and told the old turkey what the young turkey had said. "Why, I'll have his gizzard!" said the old turkey, setting out some corn for his visitors. "Sure you will, Doc, sure you will," said the visitors.

One day the young turkey walked over to where the old turkey was telling tales of his prowess in battle. "I'll bat your teeth into your crop," said the young turkey. "You and who else?" said the old turkey. So they began to circle around each other, sparring for an opening. Just then the farmer who owned the turkeys swept up the young one and carried him off and wrung his neck.

MORAL: *YOUTH WILL BE SERVED, FREQUENTLY STUFFED WITH CHESTNUTS.*

JAMES THURBER

"The Tiger Who Understood People"

Once upon a time there was a tiger who escaped from a zoo in the United States and made his way back to the jungle. During his captivity the tiger had learned a great deal about how men do things and he thought he would apply their methods to life in the jungle. The first day he was home he met a leopard and he said, "There's no use in you and me hunting for food; we'll make the other animals bring it to us." "How will we do that?" asked the leopard. "Easy," said the tiger, "you and I will tell everybody that we are going to put on a fight and that every animal will have to bring a freshly killed boar in order to get in and see the fight. Then we will just spar around and not hurt each other. Later you can say you broke a bone in your paw during the second round and I will say I broke a bone in my paw during the first round. Then we will announce a return engagement and they'll have to bring us more wild boars." "I don't think this will work," said the leopard. "Oh, yes it will," said the tiger. "You just go around saying that you can't help winning because I am a big palooka and I will go around saying I can't lose because you are a big palooka, and everybody will want to come and see the fight."

So the leopard went around telling everybody that he couldn't help winning because the tiger was a big palooka and the tiger went around telling everybody he couldn't lose because the leopard was a big palooka. The night of the fight came and the tiger and the leopard were very hungry because they hadn't gone out and done any hunting at all; they wanted to get the fight over as soon as possible and eat some of the freshly killed wild boars which all the animals would bring to the fight. But when the hour of the combat came none of the animals at all showed up. "The way I look at it," a fox had told them, "is this: if the leopard can't help winning and the tiger can't lose, it will be a draw and a draw is a very dull thing to watch, particularly when fought by fighters who are both big palookas." The animals all saw the logic of this and stayed away from the arena. When it got to be midnight and it was obvious that none of the animals would appear and that there wouldn't be any wild-boar meat to devour, the tiger and the leopard fell upon each other in a rage. They were both injured so badly and they were both so worn out by hunger that a couple of wild boars who came wandering along attacked them and killed them easily.

MORAL: *IF YOU LIVE AS HUMANS DO, IT WILL BE THE END OF YOU.*

JAMES THURBER

"The Lion Who Wanted to Zoom"

There was once a lion who coveted an eagle's wings. So he sent a message to the eagle asking him to call, and when the eagle came to the lion's den the lion said, "I will trade you my mane for your wings." "Keep talking, brother," said the eagle. "Without my wings I could no longer fly." "So what?" said the lion. "I can't fly now, but that doesn't keep me from being king of beasts. I became king of beasts on account of my magnificent mane." "All right," said the eagle, "but give me your mane first." "Just approach a little nearer," said the lion, "so that I can hand it to you." The eagle came closer and the lion clapped a huge paw on him, pinning him to the ground. "Come across with those wings!" he snarled.

So the lion took the eagle's wings but kept his own mane. The eagle was very despondent for a while and then he had an idea. "I bet you can't fly off the top of that great rock yonder," said the eagle. "Who, me?" said the lion, and he walked to the top of the rock and took off. His weight was too great for the eagle's wings to support, and besides he did not know how to fly, never having tried it before. So he crashed at the foot of the rock and burst into flames. The eagle hastily climbed down to him and regained his wings and took off the lion's mane, which he put about his own neck and shoulders. Flying back to the rocky nest where he lived with his mate, he decided to have some fun with her. So, covered with the lion's mane, he poked his head into the nest and in a deep, awful voice said *"Harrrooo!"* His mate, who was very nervous anyway, grabbed a pistol from a bureau drawer and shot him dead, thinking he was a lion.

MORAL: *NEVER ALLOW A NERVOUS FEMALE TO HAVE ACCESS TO A PISTOL, NO MATTER WHAT YOU'RE WEARING.*

JAMES THURBER

"The Sheep in Wolf's Clothing"

Not very long ago there were two sheep who put on wolf's clothing and went among the wolves as spies, to see what was going on. They arrived on a fete day, when all the wolves were singing in the taverns or dancing in the street. The first sheep said to his companion, "Wolves are just like us, for they gambol and frisk. Every day is fete day in Wolfland." He made some notes on a piece of paper (which a spy should never do) and he headed them "My Twenty-Four Hours in Wolfland," for he had decided not to be a spy any longer but to write a book on Wolfland and also some articles for the *Sheep's Home Companion*. The other sheep guessed what he was planning to do, so he slipped away and began to write a book called "My Ten Hours in Wolfland." The first sheep suspected what was up when he found his friend had gone, so he wired a book to his publisher called "My Five Hours in Wolfland," and it was announced for publication first. The other sheep immediately sold his manuscript to a newspaper syndicate for serialization.

Both sheep gave the same message to their fellows: wolves were just like sheep, for they gambolled and frisked, and every day was fete day in Wolfland. The citizens of Sheepland were convinced by all this, so they drew in their sentinels and they let down their barriers. When the wolves descended on them one night, howling and slavering, the sheep were as easy to kill as flies on a windowpane.

MORAL: *DON'T GET IT RIGHT, JUST GET IT WRITTEN.*

JAMES THURBER

"The Tortoise and the Hare"

There was once a wise young tortoise who read in an ancient book about a tortoise who had beaten a hare in a race. He read all the other books he could find but in none of them was there any record of a hare who had beaten a tortoise. The wise young tortoise came to the natural conclusion that he could outrun a hare, so he set forth in search of one. In his wanderings he met many animals who were willing to race him: weasels, stoats, dachshunds, badger-boars, short-tailed field mice and ground squirrels. But when the tortoise asked if they could outrun a hare, they all said no, they couldn't (with the exception of a dachshund named Freddy, and nobody paid any attention to him). "Well, I can," said the tortoise, "so there's no use wasting my time on you." And he continued his search.

After many days, the tortoise finally encountered a hare and challenged him to a race. "What are you going to use for legs?" asked the hare. "Never mind that," said the tortoise. "Read this." He showed the hare the story in the ancient book, complete with moral about the swift not always being so terribly fast. "Tosh," said the hare. "You couldn't go fifty feet in an hour and a half, whereas I can go fifty feet in one and a fifth seconds." "Posh," said the tortoise. "You probably won't even finish second." "We'll see about that," said the hare. So they marked off a course fifty feet long. All the other animals gathered around. A bull-frog set them on their marks, a gun dog fired a pistol, and they were off.

When the hare crossed the finish line, the tortoise had gone approximately eight and three-quarter inches.

MORAL: *A NEW BROOM MAY SWEEP CLEAN, BUT NEVER TRUST AN OLD SAW.*

ZORA NEALE HURSTON

Talking Mule Story

The novelist and anthropologist Zora Neale Hurston wrote down these black folk tales as she heard them told by people in her hometown of Eatonville, Florida.

Ole feller one time had uh mule. His name wuz Bill. Every mornin' de man go tuh ketch 'im he say, "Come 'round, Bill!"

So one mornin' he slept late, so he decided while he wuz drinkin' some coffee he'd send his son tuh ketch Ole Bill.

Told 'im say, "Go down dere, boy, and bring me dat mule up here."

Boy, he sich a fast Aleck, he grabbed de bridle and went on down tuh de lot tuh ketch ole Bill.

He say, "Come round, Bill!"

De mule looked round at 'im. He told de mule, "Tain't no use you rollin' yo' eyes at *me*. Pa want yuh dis mawnin'. Come on round and stick yo' head in dis bridle."

Mule kept on lookin' at 'im and said, "Every mornin' it's 'Come round, Bill! Come round, Bill!' Don't hardly git no night rest befo' it's 'Come round, Bill!' "

De boy throwed down dat bridle and flew back tuh de house and told his Pa, "Dat mule is talkin'."

"Ah g'wan, boy, tellin' yo' lies! G'wan ketch dat mule."

"Naw suh, Pa, dat mule's done gone tuh talkin'. You hatta ketch dat mule yo' ownself. Ah ain't gwine."

Ole man looked at ole lady and say, "See whut uh lie dat boy is tellin'?"

So he gits out and goes on down after de mule hisself. When he got down dere he hollered, "Come round, Bill!"

Ole mule looked round and says, "Every mornin' it's come round, Bill!"

De old man had uh little fice dog useter foller 'im everywhere he go, so he lit out wid de lil fice right behind 'im. So he told de ole lady, "De boy ain't told much of uh lie. Dat mule *is* talkin'. Ah never heered uh mule talk befo'."

Lil fice say, "Me neither."

De ole man got skeered agin. Right through de woods he went wid de fice right behind 'im. He nearly run hisself tuh death. He stopped and commenced blowin' and says, "Ahm so tired Ah don't know whut tuh do."

Lil dog run and set down in front of 'im and went to hasslin and says, "Me too."

Dat man is runnin' yet.

ZORA NEALE HURSTON

Competition for a Girl

It was three mens went to court a girl, Ah told you. Dis was a real pretty girl wid shiny black hair and coal black eyes. And all dese men wanted to marry her, so they all went and ast her pa if they could have her. He looked 'em all over, but he couldn't decide which one of 'em would make de best husband and de girl, she couldn't make up her mind, so one Sunday night when he walked into de parlor where they was all sittin' and said to 'em, "Well, all y'all want to marry my daughter and youse all good men and Ah can't decide which one will make her de best husband. So y'all be here tomorrow mornin' at daybreak and we'll have a contest and de one dat can do de quickest trick kin have de girl."

Nex' mornin' de first one got up seen it wasn't no water in de bucket to cook breakfas' wid. So he tole de girl's mama to give him de water bucket and he would go to the spring and git her some.

He took de bucket in his hand and then he found out dat de spring was ten miles off. But he said he didn't mind dat. He went on and dipped up de water and hurried on back wid it. When he got to de five-mile post he looked down into de bucket and seen dat de bottom had done dropped out. Then he recollected dat he heard somethin' fall when he dipped up de water so he turned round and run back to de spring and clapped in dat bottom before de water had time to spill.

De ole man thought dat was a pretty quick trick, but de second man says, "Wait a minute. Ah want a grubbin' hoe and a axe and a plow and a harrow." So he got everything he ast for. There was ten acres of wood lot right nex' to de house. He went out dere and chopped down all de trees, grubbed up de roots, ploughed de field, harrowed it, planted it in cow-peas, and had green peas for dinner.

De ole man says "Dat's de quickest trick. Can't nobody beat dat. No use in tryin'. He done won de girl."

De last man said, "You ain't even givin' me a chance to win de girl."

So he took his high-powered rifle and went out into de woods about seben or eight miles until he spied a deer. He took aim and fired. Then he run home, run round behind de house and set his gun down and then run back out in de woods and caught de deer and held 'im till de bullet hit 'im.

So he won de girl.

ZORA NEALE HURSTON

Woman's Strength Story

"Don't you know you can't git de best of no woman in de talkin' game? Her tongue is all de weapon a woman got," George Thomas chided Gene. "She could have had mo' sense, but she told God no, she'd ruther take it out in hips. So God give her her ruthers. She got plenty hips, plenty mouf and no brains."

"Oh, yes, womens is got sense too," Mathilda Moseley jumped in. "But they got too much sense to go 'round braggin' about it like y'all do. De lady people always got de advantage of mens because God fixed it dat way."

"Whut ole black advantage is y'all got?" B. Moseley asked indignantly. "We got all de strength and all de law and all de money and you can't git a thing but whut we jes' take pity on you and give you."

"And dat's jus' de point," said Mathilda triumphantly. "You *do* give it to us, but how come you do it?" And without waiting for an answer Mathilda began to tell why women always take advantage of men.

You see in de very first days, God made a man and a woman and put 'em in a house together to live. 'Way back in them days de woman was just as strong as de man and both of 'em did de same things. They useter get to fussin' 'bout who gointer do this and that and sometime they'd fight, but they was even balanced and neither one could whip de other one.

One day de man said to hisself, "B'lieve Ah'm gointer go see God and ast Him for a li'l mo' strength so Ah kin whip dis 'oman and make her mind. Ah'm tired of de way things is." So he went on up to God.

"Good mawnin', Ole Father."

"Howdy man. Whut you doin' 'round my throne so soon dis mawnin'?"

"Ah'm troubled in mind, and nobody can't ease mah spirit 'ceptin you."

God said: "Put yo' plea in de right form and Ah'll hear and answer."

"Ole Maker, wid de mawnin' stars glitterin' in yo' shinin' crown, wid de dust from yo' footsteps makin' worlds upon worlds, wid de blazin' bird we call de sun flyin' out of yo' right hand in de mawnin' and consumin' all day de flesh and blood of stump-black darkness, and comes flyin' home every evenin' to rest on yo' left hand, and never once in all yo' eternal years, mistood de left hand for de right, Ah ast you *please* to give me mo' strength than dat woman you give me, so Ah kin make her mind. Ah know you don't want to be always comin' down way past de moon and stars to be straightenin' her out and it's got to be done. So give me a li'l mo' strength, Ole Maker and Ah'll do it."

"All right, Man, you got mo' strength than woman."

So de man run all de way down de stairs from Heben till he got home. He was so anxious to try his strength on de woman dat he couldn't take his time. Soon's he got in de house he hollered "Woman! Here's yo' boss. God done tole me to handle you in which ever way Ah please. Ah'm yo' boss."

De woman flew to fightin' 'im right off. She fought 'im frightenin' but he beat her. She got her wind and tried 'im agin but he whipped her agin. She got herself together and made de third try on him vigorous but he beat her every time. He was so proud he could whip 'er at last, dat he just crowed over her and made her do a lot of things she didn't like. He told her, "Long as you obey me, Ah'll be good to yuh, but every time yuh rear up Ah'm gointer put plenty wood on yo' back and plenty water in yo' eyes."

De woman was so mad she went straight up to Heben and stood befo' de Lawd. She didn't waste no words. She said, "Lawd, Ah come befo' you mighty mad t'day. Ah want back my strength and power Ah useter have."

"Woman, you got de same power you had since de beginnin'."

"Why is it then, dat de man kin beat me now and he useter couldn't do it?"

"He got mo' strength than he useter have. He come and ast me for it and Ah give it to 'im. Ah gives to them that ast, and you ain't never ast me for no mo' power."

"Please suh, God, Ah'm astin' you for it now. Jus' gimme de same as you give him."

God shook his head. "It's too late now, woman. Whut Ah give, Ah never take back. Ah give him mo' strength than you and no matter how much Ah give you, he'll have mo'."

De woman was so mad she wheeled around and went on off. She went straight to de devil and told him what had happened.

He said, "Don't be dis-incouraged, woman. You listen to me and you'll come out mo' than conqueror. Take dem frowns out yo' face and turn round and go right on back to Heben and ast God to give you dat bunch of keys hangin' by de mantel-piece. Then you bring 'em to me and Ah'll show you what to do wid 'em."

So de woman climbed back up to Heben agin. She was mighty tired but she was more out-done that she was tired so she climbed all night long and got back up to Heben agin. When she got befo' de throne, butter wouldn't melt in her mouf.

"O Lawd and Master of de rainbow, Ah know yo' power. You never make two mountains without you put a valley in between. Ah know you kin hit a straight lick wid a crooked stick."

"Ast for whut you want, woman."

"God, gimme dat bunch of keys hangin' by yo' mantelpiece."

"Take 'em."

So de woman took de keys and hurried on back to de devil wid 'em. There was three keys on de bunch. Devil say, "See dese three keys? They got mo' power in 'em than all de strength de man kin ever git if you handle 'em right. Now dis first big key is to de do' of de kitchen, and you know a man always favors his stomach. Dis second one is de key to de bedroom and he don't like to be shut out from dat neither and dis last key is de key to de cradle and he don't want to be cut off from his generations at all. So now you take dese keys and go lock up everything and wait till he come to you. Then don't you unlock nothin' until he use his strength for yo' benefit and yo' desires."

De woman thanked 'im and tole 'im, "If it wasn't for you, Lawd knows whut us po' women folks would do."

She started off but de devil halted her. "Jus' one mo' thing: don't go home braggin' 'bout yo' keys. Jus' lock up everything and say nothin' until you git asked. And then don't talk too much."

De woman went on home and did like de devil tole her. When de man come home from work she was settin' on de porch singin' some song 'bout "Peck on de wood make de bed go good."

When de man found de three doors fastened what useter stand wide open he swelled up like pine lumber after a rain. First thing he tried to break in cause he figgered his strength would overcome all obstacles. When he saw he couldn't do it, he ast de woman, "Who locked dis do'?"

She tole 'im, "Me."

"Where did you git de key from?"

"God give it to me."

He run up to God and said, "God, woman got me locked 'way from my vittles, my bed and my generations, and she say you give her the keys."

God said, "I did, Man, Ah give her de keys, but de devil showed her how to use 'em!"

"Well, Ole Maker, please gimme some keys jus' lak 'em so she can't git de full control."

"No, Man, what Ah give Ah give. Woman got de key."

"How kin Ah know 'bout my generations?"

"Ast de woman."

So de man come on back and submitted hisself to de woman and she opened de doors.

He wasn't satisfied but he had to give in. 'Way after while he said to de woman, "Le's us divide up. Ah'll give you half of my strength if you lemme hold de keys in my hands."

De woman thought dat over so de devil popped and tol her, "Tell 'im, naw. Let 'im keep his strength and you keep yo' keys."

So de woman wouldn't trade wid 'im and de man had to mortgage his strength to her to live. And dat's why de man makes and de woman takes. You men is still braggin' 'bout yo' strength and de women is sittin' on de keys and lettin' you blow off till she git ready to put de bridle on you.

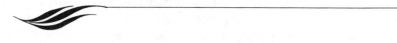

ZORA NEALE HURSTON

Squinch Owl Story

Yuh know Ole Marster had uh ole maid sister that never been married. You know how stringy white folks necks gits when dey gits ole. Well hers had done got that-a-way and more special cause she never been married.

Her name wuz Miss Pheenie and Ole Marster had uh daughter so there wuz young mens round de parlor and de porch. All in de sittin' chairs and in de hammock under de trees. So Miss Pheenie useter stand round and peer at 'em and grin lak uh possum—wishin' she could git courted and married.

So one devilish young buck, he seen de feelin' in her so he 'gin tuh make manners wid her and last thing he done, he told her says, "If you go set up on de roof uh de house all night Ah'll marry yuh in de mawnin'."

It wuz uh bitter cold night. De wind searchin' lak de police. So she clambed up dere and set straddle of de highest part cause she couldn't stick nowhere's else. And she couldn't help but shake and shiver. And everytime de clock would strike de hour she'd say, "C-o-o-o-l-d on de housetop, but uh young man in de mawnin." She kept dat up till de clock struck four, when she tumbled down, froze tuh death. But de very next night after they buried her, she took de shape of uh owl and wuz back dere shivverin' and cryin'. And dats how come us got squinch owls.*

*Screech owls [editor's note].

DON MARQUIS

"the coming of archy"

The circumstances of Archy's first appearance are narrated in the following extract from the Sun Dial column of the New York *Sun*.

Dobbs Ferry possesses a rat which slips out of his lair at night and runs a typewriting machine in a garage. Unfortunately, he has always been interrupted by the watchman before he could produce a complete story.

It was at first thought that the power which made the typewriter run was a ghost, instead of a rat. It seems likely to us that it was both a ghost and a rat. Mme. Blavatsky's ego went into a white horse after she passed over, and someone's personality has undoubtedly gone into this rat. It is an era of belief in communications from the spirit land.

And since this matter had been reported in the public prints and seriously received we are no longer afraid of being ridiculed, and we do not mind making a statement of something that happened to our own typewriter only a couple of weeks ago.

We came into our room earlier than usual in the morning, and discovered a gigantic cockroach jumping about upon the keys.

He did not see us, and we watched him. He would climb painfully upon the framework of the machine and cast himself with all his force upon a key, head downward, and his weight and the impact of the blow were just sufficient to operate the machine, one slow letter after another. He could not work the capital letters, and he had a great deal of difficulty operating the mechanism that shifts the paper so that a fresh line may be started. We never saw a cockroach work so hard or perspire so freely in all our lives before. After about an hour of this frightfully difficult literary labor he fell to the floor exhausted, and we saw him creep feebly into a nest of the poems which are always there in profusion.

Congratulating ourself that we had left a sheet of paper in the machine the night before so that all this work had not been in vain, we made an examination, and this is what we found:

expression is the need of my soul
i was once a vers libre bard
but i died and my soul went into the body of a cockroach
it has given me a new outlook upon life
i see things from the under side now
thank you for the apple peelings in the wastepaper basket
but your paste is getting so stale i cant eat it
there is a cat here called mehitabel i wish you would have
removed she nearly ate me the other night why dont she
catch rats that is what she is supposed to be for
there is a rat here she should get without delay

most of these rats here are just rats
but this rat is like me he has a human soul in him
he used to be a poet himself
night after night i have written poetry for you
on your typewriter
and this big brute of a rat who used to be a poet
comes out of his hole when it is done
and reads it and sniffs at it
he is jealous of my poetry
he used to make fun of it when we were both human
he was a punk poet himself
and after he has read it he sneers
and then he eats it

i wish you would have mehitabel kill that rat
or get a cat that is onto her job
and i will write you a series of poems showing how things look
to a cockroach
that rats name is freddy
the next time freddy dies i hope he wont be a rat
but something smaller i hope i will be a rat
in the next transmigration and freddy a cockroach
i will teach him to sneer at my poetry then

dont you ever eat any sandwiches in your office
i havent had a crumb of bread for i dont know how long
or a piece of ham or anything but apple parings
and paste leave a piece of paper in your machine
every night you can call me archy

DON MARQUIS

"*mehitabel was once cleopatra*"

boss i am disappointed in
some of your readers they
are always asking how does
archy work the shift so as to get a
new line or how does archy do
this or do that they
are always interested in technical
details when the main question is
whether the stuff is
literature or not
i wish you would leave
that book of george moores on
the floor

mehitabel the cat and i want to
read it i have discovered that
mehitabels soul formerly inhabited a
human also at least that
is what mehitabel is claiming these
days it may be she got jealous of
my prestige anyhow she and
i have been talking it over in a
friendly way who were you
mehitabel i asked her i was
cleopatra once she said well i said i

suppose you lived in a palace you bet
she said and what lovely fish dinners
we used to have and licked her chops

mehitabel would sell her soul for
a plate of fish any day i told her i thought
you were going to say you were
the favorite wife of the emperor
valerian he was some cat nip eh
mehitabel but she did not get me

                              archy

DON MARQUIS

"mehitabel and her kittens"

well boss
mehitabel the cat
has reappeared in her old
haunts with a
flock of kittens
three of them this time

archy she said to me
yesterday
the life of a female
artist is continually
hampered what in hell
have i done to deserve
all these kittens

i look back on my life
and it seems to me to be
just one damned kitten
after another

i am a dancer archy
and my only prayer
is to be allowed
to give my best to my art
but just as i feel
that i am succeeding
in my life work
along comes another batch
of these damned kittens
it is not archy
that i am shy on mother love
god knows i care for
the sweet little things
curse them
but am i never to be allowed
to live my own life
i have purposely avoided
matrimony in the interests
of the higher life
but i might just
as well have been a domestic
slave for all the freedom
i have gained
i hope none of them
gets run over by
an automobile
my heart would bleed
if anything happened
to them and i found it out
but it isn t fair archy
it isn t fair
these damned tom cats have all
the fun and freedom
if i was like some of these
green eyed feline vamps i know
i would simply walk out on the
bunch of them and
let them shift for themselves
but i am not that kind
archy i am full of mother love
my kindness has always
been my curse

a tender heart is the cross i bear
self sacrifice always and forever
is my motto damn them
i will make a home
for the sweet innocent
little things
unless of course providence
in his wisdom should remove
them they are living
just now in an abandoned
garbage can just behind
a made over stable in greenwich
village and if it rained
into the can before i could
get back and rescue them
i am afraid the little
dears might drown
it makes me shudder just
to think of it
of course if i were a family cat
they would probably
be drowned anyhow
sometimes i think
the kinder thing would be
for me to carry the
sweet little things
over to the river
and drop them in myself
but a mother s love archy
is so unreasonable
something always prevents me
these terrible
conflicts are always
presenting themselves
to the artist
the eternal struggle
between art and life archy
is something fierce
yes something fierce
my what a dramatic
life i have lived
one moment up the next

moment down again
but always gay archy always gay
and always the lady too
in spite of hell
well boss it will
be interesting to note
just how mehitabel
works out her present problem
a dark mystery still broods
over the manner
in which the former
family of three kittens
disappeared
one day she was talking to me
of the kittens
and the next day when i asked
her about them
she said innocently
what kittens
interrogation point
and that was all
i could ever get out
of her on the subject
we had a heavy rain
right after she spoke to me
but probably that garbage can
leaks and so the kittens
have not yet
been drowned

DON MARQUIS

"mehitabel dances with boreas"

well boss i saw mehitabel
last evening
she was out in the alley
dancing on the cold cobbles
while the wild december wind
blew through her frozen whiskers
and as she danced
she wailed and sang to herself
uttering the fragments
that rattled in her cold brain
in part as follows

whirl mehitabel whirl
spin mehitabel spin
thank god you re a lady still
if you have got a frozen skin

blow wind out of the north
to hell with being a pet
my left front foot is brittle
but there s life in the old dame yet

dance mehitabel dance
caper and shake a leg
what little blood is left
will fizz like wine in a keg

wind come out of the north
and pierce to the guts within

but some day mehitabel's guts
will string a violin

moon you re as cold as a frozen
skin of yellow banan
that sticks in the frost and ice
on top of a garbage can

and you throw a shadow so chilly
that it can scarcely leap
dance shadow dance
you ve got no place to sleep

whistle a tune north wind
on my hollow marrow bones
i ll dance the time with three good feet
here on the alley stones

freeze you bloody december
i never could stay a pet
but i am a lady in spite of hell
and there s life in the old dame yet

whirl mehitabel whirl
flirt your tail and spin
dance to the tune your guts will cry
when they string a violin

eight of my lives are gone
it s years since my fur was slicked
but blow north wind blow
i am damned if i am licked

girls we was all of us ladies
we was o what the hell
and once a lady always game
by crikey blood will tell

i might be somebody s pet
asleep by the fire on a rug
but me i was always romantic
i had the adventurous bug

caper mehitabel caper
leap shadow leap
you gotto dance till the sun comes up
for you got no place to sleep

i might have been many a tom cat s wife
but i got no regret
i lived my life as i liked my life
and there s pep in the old dame yet

blow wind out of the north
you cut like a piece of tin
slice my guts into fiddle strings
and we ll have a violin

spin mehitabel spin
you had a romantic past
and you re gonna cash in dancing
when you are croaked at last

i will not eat tomorrow
and i did not eat today
but wotthehell i ask you
the word is toujours gai

whirl mehitabel whirl
i once was a maltese pet
till i went and got abducted
and cripes i m a lady yet

whirl mehitabel whirl
and show your shadow how
tonight it s dance with the bloody moon
tomorrow the garbage scow

whirl mehitabel whirl
spin shadow spin
the wind will pipe on your marrow bones
your slats are a mandolin

by cripes i have danced the shimmy
in rooms as warm as a dream

and gone to sleep on a cushion
with a bellyfull of cream

it s one day up and next day down
i led a romantic life
it was being abducted so many times
as spoiled me for a wife

dance mehitabel dance
till your old bones fly apart
i ain t got any regrets
for i gave my life to my art

whirl mehitabel whirl
caper my girl and grin
and pick at your guts with your frosty feet
they re the strings of a violin

girls we was all of us ladies
until we went and fell
and oncet a thoroughbred always game
i ask you wotthehell

it s last week up and this week down
and always the devil to pay
but cripes i was always the lady
and the word is toujours gai

be a tabby tame if you want
somebody s pussy and pet
the life i led was the life i liked
and there s pep in the old dame yet

whirl mehitabel whirl
leap shadow leap
you gotta dance till the sun comes up
for you got no place to sleep

archy

RING LARDNER

"How to Tell a True Princess"

Well my little boys and gals this is the case of a prince who his father had told him he must get married but the gal he married must be a true princess. So he says to the old man how do you tell if a princess is a true princess or a phony princess. So the old man says why if she is a true princess she must be delicate.

Yes said the prince but what is the true test of delicate.

Why said the old man who was probably the king if she is delicate why she probably can't sleep over 49 eiderdown quilts and 28 mattresses provided they's a pea parked under same which might disturb her. So they made her bed this day in these regards. They put a single green pea annext the spring and then piled 28 mattresses and 49 eider quilts on top of same and says if she can sleep on this quantity of bed clothing and not feel disturbed, why she can't possibly be delicate and is therefore not a princess.

Well the princess went to bed at 10 o'clock on acct. of having called up everybody and nobody would come over and play double Canfield with her and finely she gave up and went to bed and hadn't been asleep more than 3 hrs. when she woke up and says I am very uncomfortable, they must be a pea under all these quilts. So they looked it up and sure enough they was a green pea under the quilts and mattresses. It made her miserable. She was practally helpless.

But the next day when she woke up they didn't know if she was a princess or the reverse. Because lots of people had slept under those conditions and maybe it was the mattress or the springs that had made them miserable. So finely the king suggested why not give her a modern trial.

So the next evening but one they sent her to bed under these conditions:

The counterpane was concrete and right under it was 30 layers of tin plate and then come 4 bales of cotton and beneath that 50 ft. of solid rock and under the entire layout a canary's feather.

"Now Princess," they said to her in a friendly way, "if you can tell us the name of the bird which you are sleeping on under all these condiments, why then we will know you are a true princess and worthy to marry the prince.''

''Prince!'' she said. ''Is that the name of a dog?''

They all laughed at her in a friendly way.

''Why yes,'' she said, ''I can tell you the name of that bird. His name is Dickie.''

This turned the laugh on them and at the same time proved she was a true princess.

To-morrow night I will try to tell you the story of how 6 men travelled through the wide world and the story will begin at 6:30 and I hope it won't keep nobody up.

RING LARDNER

"A Bedtime Story"

Some of the boys in the radio company has been pestering me to death to come to the broadcasting station and tell a couple bedtime stories as they received numerable request from mothers all over the country asking for something that would put their children to sleep and the rumor had got out some way another that whenever I tell a story, why whoever is within hearing distance dozes right off.

Well friends I ain't got the voice necessary to carry over the radio but will write out a fairy story like I told it to my own kiddies the other night and it acted like cloroform and parents is welcome to read it out loud to their children if they wish and the story is Little Snow-White and I can't remember how it goes in the book so am obliged to tell it in my own wds.

Well once at a time they was a Queen and she cut herself shaveing and 3 drops of blood fell in the snow and it looked so pretty that the Queen wished she could have a red and white kid and pretty soon she gave birth to a little gal that soon learned to fix herself up in the above color scheme and her mother nicknamed her Snow-White and that winter the mother died of home made gin and the King without needless delay married a chorus girl as he loved beautiful baritone voices.

The new bride had once been elected Miss America at Atlantic City and if you seen her at certain times in the day she was not ½ bad though the King gave her a mirror for a wedding present and told her to get some of that stuff out of her eyelashes.

Well the new Queen was a woman at heart and could not help from talking even when alone and one day she stood up in front of the mirror and said:

> "Mirror, mirror on the wall,
> Who is the dame for whom you'd fall?"

And the mirror replied:

> "I will half to hand it to you, O Queen,
> You are best I ever seen."

Well this kept up till little Snow-White was a 7 year old flapper and one day the Queen says to the mirror:

> "Mirror, mirror on my dresser,
> Do I still lead? No sir or yes sir?"

And the mirror replied:

> "You use to top the list, O Queen,
> Now Snow-White has got you beat, old bean."

Well this made no hit with the Queen as she could not stomach the position of runner up so she said a word that is always spelt with a capital letter and took a smash at the mirror and then gave a boy from the East Side $15.00 to take Snow-White out to the park and bump her off and he was to bring back some of the little gal's giblets to show he had not missed.

But the gun man was noble at heart and could not bear to kill Snow-White and turned her loose near the zoo and then spent a very small portion of the $15.00 on some chicken livers en brochette which he took back to the Queen as evidence.

Well Snow-White was scared at being left alone and she run until she couldn't run no more on acct. of how her dogs fret her so she finely set down on the steps of a apt. bldg. along about midnight and pretty soon the 6 Green Brothers who had a musical act come home to this bldg. in which they had a apt. and they took Snow-White in and made her their house keeper.

She told them her story and they warned her to never let nobody in the apt. unless she knew who it was as the Queen would find out sooner or later that she was still alive and would try and get her.

Mean while the Queen eat the chicken livers and then visited the mirror and says:

"Mirror, mirror upside down,
Who is the prettiest gal in town?"

And the mirror replied in a cracked voice:

"You still run second, O you Queen,
To Snow-White who is working for the Brothers Green."

Well to make it a short story the Queen tried 3 different times to get rid of Snow-White and the first time she made up like a corset salesman and Snow-White was sucker enough to let her in and the Queen sold her a corset that was too small and the poor gal was chokeing to death when the Green boys come home and released her. On another occasion the Queen sold the gal a poison comb which she stuck in her hair and the Green boys got there just in time to prevent total baldness.

On the last occasion the Queen posed as a fruit peddler and Snow-White ast her did she have any apples and the Queen says yes I have some apples today but Snow-White said she was scared to eat one as it might be poisoned so the Queen says that to prove they was no danger, she would eat the corpse of the apple herself while Snow-White eat the outside.

Well the outside was the part that was poisoned and when Snow-White eat it she fell dead.

Now the way the Queen found out that the corset gag and the poisoned comb had flopped was by consulting with her mirror, like for inst. after the poisoned comb episode she says to the mirror:

"Mirror, mirror gift of the King,
Who leads the Looks League now, old thing?"

And the mirror was obliged to answer:

"You use to be fairer than all the others,
But Snow-White is still rooming with the Six Green Brothers."

But after the apple episode the mirror said in reply to a query:

"You lead the league once more, old head,
For Snow-White seems to be practically dead."

However when the Green Brothers arrived home and found Snow-White lying on the floor with her neck kind of bulged out like it was a cyst or something they called in a Xray expert and he soon located the apple in her throat and a man from the garage got it out with a applejack, whereupon Snow-White jumped up as good as new.

To celebrate the occasion the Greens took her along that night to the Supper Club where they was employed and there she met a wealthy bond thief who liked them young and merrily rang the bells. So the same day they was married, the Queen put the usual query to her mirror and the last named replied:

> "I'd like to say you, but I've got to hand it
> To Snow-White, the wife of a well to do bandit."

This made the Queen so sore that she drunk a qt. of $55.00 Scotch which she had been saveing for company and the next day her widower married the gal who had been sent to Atlantic City that year as Miss Seattle.

STANLEY ELKIN

God Visits Hell

The Living End starts with a liquor-store holdup and murder in Minneapolis, moves quickly to Heaven, and then to Hell. There in unceasing agony dwell Ellerbee, the murder victim, and Ladlehaus, his murderer's accomplice. Outraged by the injustice, Ellerbee first denounces God, then asks Him for forgiveness and to grant one prayer: "To kill us, to end Hell, to close the camp." The reply: " 'Ha!' God scoffed and lighted up Hell's blazes like the surface of a star." There is no getting out . . . Or is there?

God came to Hell. He was very impressive, Ladlehaus thought. He'd seen Him once before, from a distance—a Being in spotless raiment who sat on a magnificent golden throne. He looked different now. He was clean-shaven and stood before Ladlehaus and the others in a carefully tailored summer suit like a pediatrician in a small town, a smart tie mounted at His throat like a dagger.

The flawless linen, light in color as an army field cot, made a quiet statement. He was hatless and seemed immensely comfortable and at ease. Ladlehaus couldn't judge His age.

"Hi," God said. "I'm the Lord. Hot enough for you?" He asked whimsically and frowned at the forced laughter of the damned. "Relax," He said, "it's not what you think. This isn't a harrowing of Hell, there'll be no gleaning or winnowing. I'm God, not Hodge. It's only an assembly. How you making out? Are there any questions?" God looked around but there were no takers. "No?" He continued, "where are My rebels and organizers. My hotshot bizarrerie, all you eggs in one basket curse-God-and-diers? Where are you? You—punks, Beelzebubs, My iambic angels in free fall, what's doing? There are no free falls, eh? Well, you're right, and it's okay if you don't have questions.

"The only reason I'm here is for ubiquitous training. I'm Himself Himself and I don't know how I do it. I don't even remember making this place. There must have been a need for it because everything fits together and I've always been a form-follows-function sort of God, but sometimes even I get confused about the details. Omniscience gives Me eyestrain. I'll let you in on something. I wear contacts. Oh yes. I grind the lenses Myself. They're very strong. Well, you can imagine. *You'd* go blind just trying them on. And omnipotence—*that* takes it out of you. I mean if you want to work up a sweat try omnipotence for a few seconds. To heck with your jogging and isometrics and crash diets. Answering prayer—that's another one. Plugged in like the only switchboard operator in the world. You should hear some of the crap I have to listen to. 'Dear God, put a wave in my hair, I'll make You novenas for a month of Sundays.' 'Do an earthquake in Paris, Lord, I'll build a thousand-bed hospital.'

"You like this? You like this sort of thing? Backstage with God? Jehovah's Hollywood? Yes? Or maybe you're archeologically inclined? Historically bent, metaphysically. Well here I am. Here I am that I am. God in a good mood. Numero Uno Mover moved. Come on, what would you *really* like to know? How I researched the Netherlands? Where I get My ideas?"

"Sir, is there Life before Death?" one of the damned near Ladlehaus called out.

"What's that," God said, "graffiti?"

"Is there Life before Death?" the fellow repeated.

"Who's that? That an old-timer? Is it? Someone here so long his memory's burned out on him, his engrams charred and gone all ashes? Can't remember whether breakfast really happened or's only part of the collective unconscious? How you doing, old-timer? Ladlehouse, right?"

Ladlehaus remained motionless, motionless, that is, as possible in his steamy circumstances, in his smoldering body like a building watched by firemen. He made imperceptible shifts, the floor of Hell like some tightrope where he juggled his weight, redistributing invisible tensions in measured increments of shuffle along his joints and nerves. All he wanted was to lie low in this place where no one could lie low, where even the disciplined reflexes of martyrs and stylites twitched like thrown dice. And all he could hope was that pain itself—which had never saved anyone—might serve him now, permitting him to appear like everyone else, swaying in place like lovers in dance halls beneath Big Bands.

"You, Ladlehaus!" the Big Band leader blared.

Throughout the Underworld the nine thousand, six hundred and forty-three Ladlehauses who had died since the beginning of time, not excepting the accomplice to Ellerbee's murder, looked up, acknowledged their presence in thirty tongues. These are my family, Ladlehaus thought, and glanced in the direction of the three or four he could actually see. Their blackened forms, lathered with smoke and fire damage, were as meaningless to him, as devoid of kinship, as the dry flinders of ancient bone in museum display cases. Meanwhile God was still out there. "Not *you,*" He said petulantly to the others, "the *old*-timer."

He means *me,* Ladlehaus thought, this shaved and showered squire God in His summer linens means *me.* He means *me,* this commissioned officer Lord with his myrrh and frankincense colognes and aromatics and His Body tingling with morning dip and agency, all the prevailing moods of fettle and immortality. He means *me,* and even though he knew there had been a mistake, that he'd not been the one who'd sounded off, Ladlehaus held his tongue. He means me, He makes mistakes.

"So you're the fellow who spouts graffiti to God, are you?" God said and Ladlehaus was kneeling beneath Him, hocus-pocus'd through Hell, terrified and clonic below God's rhetorical attention. "Go," God said. "Be off." And Ladlehaus's quiet "Yes" was as inaudible to the damned as God's under-the-breath "Oops" when He realized His mistake.

And Ladlehaus thought Well, why not? He didn't know me any better when He sent me here. He didn't know my heart. I was an accomplice, what's that? No hit man, no munitions or electronics expert sent from afar, no big deal Indy wheel-man and certainly no mastermind. Only an accomplice, a lookout, a man by the door, a sentry or a commissionaire, say, little more than an eyewitness really. Almost a mascot. And paid accordingly, his always the lowest share, sometimes nothing more than a good dinner and a night on the town. The crimes would have taken place without him. An accomplice, a redcap, a skycap, a shuffler of suitcases, of doggy bags of boodle, someone with a station wagon, seats that folded down to accommodate cartons of TV sets, stereos. What was the outrage? Even the business of his having been an accomplice to Ellerbee's murder, though true, was as much talk as anything else, something to give him cachet in his buddy's eyes, an assertion that he'd left a mark on a pal's life. And God said "Be off," and he was off.

EUGENE FIELD

Ten Primer Lessons

THE CHEWING GUM.

Here we Have a Piece of Chewing Gum. It is White and Sweet. Chew it awhile and Stick it on the Under Side of the Mantel Piece. The Hired Girl will find it There and Chew it awhile Herself and then Put it Back. In this Way one Piece of Gum will Answer for a Whole Family. When the Gum is no Good, Put it in the Rocking Chair for the Minister or your Sister's Beau to sit upon.

The Oyster.

Here we have an oyster. It is going to a Church Fair. When it Gets to the Fair, it will Swim around in a big Kettle of Warm Water. A Lady will Stir it with a Spoon, and sell the Warm Water for Forty Cents a pint. Then the Oyster will move on to the next Fair. In this Way, the Oyster will visit all the Church Fairs in Town, and Bring a great many Dollars into the Church Treasury. The Oyster goes a great Way: in a Good Cause.

The Hack-Driver.

What is the Man in a Big Coat and Broad Hat? It is a Hack-Driver. What is a Hack-Driver? He frequently is a Reformed Train-Robber. He does not Rob Trains any more, but he Robs poor Young men who are too Full to Walk

Home at Night. Does the Hack-Driver Drink? Yes, whenever he is invited. He will also smoke one of your Cigars if you Urge him. Will the Hack-Driver stop the Hack at the Corner and let you Walk the Rest of the Way to the House, so you may Tell your Wife you Walked all the Way Home? He will, by a large majority.

THE CONTRIBUTION PLATE.

This is a Contribution Plate. It has just been Handed around. What is there upon it? Now Count very Slow or you will Make a Mistake. Four Buttons, one Nickel, a Blue Chip and one Spectacle glass. Yes, that is Right. What will be Done with all these Nice things? They will be sent to foreign Countries for the good of the Poor Heathens. How the Poor Heathens will Rejoice.

THE NOSE.

Is this a Locomotive Headlight? No. Then it Must be a Drug Store Illumination? No, it is a Man's Nose. What a Funny Nose it is. It looks like a Bonfire. Half a dozen such Noses would Make a Gaudy Fourth of July Celebration. It is too Bad that such a lovely tinted Nose should have such a Homely Man behind it. The Nose has Cost the Man a great Deal of Borrowed Money.

If it were not for the Nose a Great many Breweries would Close and a great many Distilleries would Suspend. If the Man drinks too much Water, his nose will lose its Color. He must be Careful about this. How many such Noses would it take to make a Rainbow half a Mile long? Ask the man to let you Light your Cigar by his Nose.

SLEEPY KITTY.

The Cat is Asleep on the Rug. Step on her Tail and See if she will Wake up. Oh, no; She will not wake. she is a heavy Sleeper. Perhaps if you Were to saw her Tail off with the Carving knife you might Attract her attention. Suppose you try.

THE STATESMAN.

Here is a Statesman. He makes Speeches about the poor Tax-Payer and Drinks Whiskey. His Pants are too Short for him. He must Have Stood in a

Puddle of Water when he got Measured for them. He picks his Teeth with a Fork and Wipes his Nose on the Bottom of Sofas and Chairs. If you Neglect your Education and Learn to Chew plug Tobacco, maybe you will be a Statesman some time. Some Statesmen go to Congress and some go to Jail. But it is the Same Thing, after all.

THE DELICATE GIRL.

The Girl is Scratching her Back against the Door. She has been eating Buckwheat Cakes. Her Beau thinks she is Delicate, but he has Never seen her Tackle a Plate of Hot Cakes on a Frosty Morning. Cakes had better Roost High when she is Around. If we Were the Girl we Should wear Sand-Paper lining in the Dress, and not be Making a Hair-Brush out of the Poor Door.

The Baby.

Here we have a baby. It is composed of a Bald Head and a Pair of Lungs. One of the Lungs takes a Rest while the Other runs the Shop. One of them is always On Deck all of the Time. The Baby is a Bigger man than his Mother. He likes to Walk around with his Father at Night. The Father does Most of the Walking and All of the Swearing. Little Girls, you will Never Know what it is to be a Father.

The Poet.

Who is this Creature with Long Hair and a Wild Eye? He is a Poet. He writes Poems on Spring and Women's Eyes and Strange, unreal Things of that Kind. He is always Wishing he was Dead, but he wouldn't Let anybody Kill him if he could Get away. A mighty good Sausage Stuffer was Spoiled when the

Man became a Poet. He would Look well Standing under a Descending Pile-driver.

EDGAR ALLAN POE

"The Angel of the Odd"

An Extravaganza

It was a chilly November afternoon. I had just consummated an unusually hearty dinner, of which the dyspeptic *truffe* formed not the least important item, and was sitting alone in the dining-room, with my feet upon the fender, and at my elbow a small table which I had rolled up to the fire, and upon which were some apologies for dessert, with some miscellaneous bottles of wine, spirit and *liqueur*. In the morning I had been reading Glover's "Leonidas," Wilkie's "Epigoniad," Lamartine's "Pilgrimage," Barlow's "Columbiad," Tuckerman's "Sicily," and Griswold's "Curiosities;" I am willing to confess, therefore, that I now felt a little stupid. I made effort to arouse myself by aid of frequent Lafitte, and, all failing, I betook myself to a stray newspaper in despair. Having carefully perused the column of "houses to let," and the column of "dogs lost," and then the two columns of "wives and apprentices runaway," I attacked with great resolution the editorial matter, and, reading it from beginning to end without understanding a syllable, conceived the possibility of its being Chinese, and so re-read it from the end to the beginning, but with no more satisfactory result. I was about throwing away, in disgust,

> This folio of four pages, happy work
> Which not even critics criticise,

when I felt my attention somewhat aroused by the paragraph which follows:

"The avenues to death are numerous and strange. A London paper mentions the decease of a person from a singular cause. He was playing at 'puff the dart,' which is played with a long needle inserted in some worsted, and blown at a target through a tin tube. He placed the needle at the wrong end of the tube, and drawing his breath strongly to puff the dart forward with force, drew the needle into his throat. It entered the lungs, and in a few days killed him.''

Upon seeing this I fell into a great rage, without exactly knowing why. ''This thing,'' I exclaimed, ''is a contemptible falsehood—a poor hoax—the lees of the invention of some pitiable penny-a-liner—of some wretched concoctor of accidents in Cocaigne. These fellows, knowing the extravagant gullibility of the age, set their wits to work in the imagination of improbable possibilities—of odd accidents, as they term them; but to a reflecting intellect (like mine,'' I added, in parenthesis, putting my forefinger unconsciously to the side of my nose,) ''to a contemplative understanding such as I myself possess, it seems evident at once that the marvellous increase of late in these 'odd accidents' is by far the oddest accident of all. For my own part, I intend to believe nothing henceforward that has anything of the 'singular' about it.''

''Mein Gott, den, vat a vool you bees for dat!'' replied one of the most remarkable voices I ever heard. At first I took it for a rumbling in my ears—such as a man sometimes experiences when getting very drunk—but, upon second thought, I considered the sound as more nearly resembling that which proceeds from an empty barrel beaten with a big stick; and, in fact, this I should have concluded it to be, but for the articulation of the syllables and words. I am by no means naturally nervous, and the very few glasses of Lafitte which I had sipped served to embolden me no little, so that I felt nothing of trepidation, but merely uplifted my eyes with a leisurely movement, and looked carefully around the room for the intruder. I could not, however, perceive any one at all.

''Humph!'' resumed the voice, as I continued my survey, ''you mus pe so dronk as de pig, den, for not zee me as I zit here at your zide.''

Hereupon I bethought me of looking immediately before my nose, and there, sure enough, confronting me at the table sat a personage nondescript, although not altogether indescribable. His body was a wine-pipe, or a rum-puncheon, or something of that character, and had a truly Falstaffian air. In its nether extremity were inserted two kegs, which seemed to answer all the purposes of legs. For arms there dangled from the upper portion of the carcass two tolerably long bottles, with the necks outward for hands. All the head that I saw the monster possessed of was one of those Hessian canteens which resemble a large snuff-box with a hole in the middle of the lid. This canteen (with a funnel on its top, like a cavalier cap slouched over the eyes) was set on edge upon the puncheon, with the hole toward myself; and through this hole, which seemed puckered up like the mouth of a very precise old maid, the creature was emitting certain rumbling and grumbling noises which he evidently intended for intelligible talk.

''I zay,'' said he, ''you mos pe dronk as de pig, vor zit dare and not zee me zit ere; and I zay, doo, you mos pe pigger vool as de goose, vor to dispelief vat iz print in de print. 'Tiz de troof—dat it iz—eberry vord ob it.''

"Who are you, pray?" said I, with much dignity, although somewhat puzzled; "how did you get here? and what is it you are talking about?"

"As vor ow I com'd ere," replied the figure, "dat iz none of your pizziness; and as vor vat I be talking apout, I be talk apout vat I tink proper; and as vor who I be, vy dat is de very ting I com'd here for to let you zee for yourzelf.''

"You are a drunken vagabond," said I, "and I shall ring the bell and order my footman to kick you into the street."

"He! he! he!" said the fellow, "hu! hu! hu! dat you can't do."

"Can't do!" said I, "what do you mean?—I can't do what?"

"Ring de pell," he replied, attempting a grin with his little villainous mouth.

Upon this I made an effort to get up, in order to put my threat into execution; but the ruffian just reached across the table very deliberately, and hitting me a tap on the forehead with the neck of one of the long bottles, knocked me back into the arm-chair from which I had half arisen. I was utterly astounded; and, for a moment, was quite at a loss what to do. In the meantime, he continued his talk.

"You zee," said he, "it iz te bess vor zit still; and now you shall know who I pe. Look at me! zee! I am te *Angel ov te Odd.*"

"And odd enough, too," I ventured to reply; "but I was always under the impression that an angel had wings."

"Te wing!" he cried, highly incensed, "vat I pe do mit te wing? Mein Gott! do you take me vor a shicken?"

"No—oh no!" I replied, much alarmed, "you are no chicken—certainly not."

"Well, den, zit still and pehabe yourself, or I'll rap you again mid me vist. It iz te shicken ab te wing, und te owl ab te wing, und te imp ab te wing, und te head-teuffel ab te wing. Te angel ab *not* te wing, and I am te *Angel ov te Odd.*"

"And your business with me at present is—is——"

"My pizzness!" ejaculated the thing, "vy vat a low bred buppy you mos pe vor to ask a gentleman und an angel apout his pizziness!"

This language was rather more than I could bear, even from an angel; so, plucking up courage, I seized a salt-cellar which lay within reach, and hurled it at the head of the intruder. Either he dodged, however, or my aim was inaccurate; for all I accomplished was the demolition of the crystal which protected the dial of the clock upon the mantel-piece. As for the Angel, he evinced his sense of my assault by giving me two or three hard consecutive raps upon the forehead as before. These reduced me at once to submission, and I am almost ashamed to confess that either through pain or vexation, there came a few tears into my eyes.

"Mein Gott!" said the Angel of the Odd, apparently much softened at my distress; "mein Gott, te man is eder ferry dronk or ferry zorry. You mos not trink it so strong—you mos put te water in te wine. Here, trink dis, like a goot veller, und don't gry now—don't!"

Hereupon the Angel of the Odd replenished my goblet (which was about a third full of Port) with a colorless fluid that he poured from one of his hand bottles. I observed that these bottles had labels about their necks, and that these labels were inscribed "Kirschenwasser."

The considerate kindness of the Angel mollified me in no little measure; and, aided by the water with which he diluted my Port more than once, I at length regained sufficient temper to listen to his very extraordinary discourse. I cannot pretend to recount all that he told me, but I gleaned from what he said that he was the genius who presided over the *contretemps* of mankind, and whose business it was to bring about the *odd accidents* which are continually astonishing the skeptic. Once or twice, upon my venturing to express my total incredulity in respect to his pretensions, he grew very angry indeed, so that at length I considered it the wiser policy to say nothing at all, and let him have his own way. He talked on, therefore, at great length, while I merely leaned back in my chair with my eyes shut, and amused myself with munching raisins and filliping the stems about the room. But, by-and-by, the Angel suddenly construed this behavior of mine into contempt. He arose in a terrible passion, slouched his funnel down over his eyes, swore a vast oath, uttered a threat of some character which I did not precisely comprehend, and finally made me a low bow and departed, wishing me, in the language of the archbishop in Gil-Blas, *"beaucoup de bonheur et un peu plus de bon sens."*

His departure afforded me relief. The *very* few glasses of Lafitte that I had sipped had the effect of rendering me drowsy, and I felt inclined to take a nap of some fifteen or twenty minutes, as is my custom after dinner. At six I had an appointment of consequence, which it was quite indispensable that I should keep. The policy of insurance for my dwelling house had expired the day before; and, some dispute having arisen, it was agreed that, at six, I should meet the board of directors of the company and settle the terms of a renewal. Glancing upward at the clock on the mantel-piece, (for I felt too drowsy to take out my watch), I had the pleasure to find that I had still twenty-five minutes to spare. It was half past five; I could easily walk to the insurance office in five minutes; and my usual siestas had never been known to exceed five and twenty. I felt sufficiently safe, therefore, and composed myself to my slumbers forthwith.

Having completed them to my satisfaction, I again looked toward the timepiece and was half inclined to believe in the possibility of odd accidents when I found that, instead of my ordinary fifteen or twenty minutes, I had been dozing only three; for it still wanted seven and twenty of the appointed hour. I betook myself again to my nap, and at length a second time awoke, when, to my utter amazement, it *still* wanted twenty-seven minutes of six. I jumped up to examine the clock, and found that it had ceased running. My watch informed me that it was half past seven; and, of course, having slept two hours, I was too late for my appointment. "It will make no difference," I said: "I can call at the office in the morning and apologize; in the meantime what can be the matter with the clock?" Upon examining it I discovered that one of the raisin stems which I had been filliping about the room during the discourse of the Angel of the Odd, had flown through the fractured crystal, and lodging, singularly enough, in the key-hole, with an end projecting outward, had thus arrested the revolution of the minute hand.

"Ah!" said I, "I see how it is. This thing speaks for itself. A natural accident, such as *will* happen now and then!"

I gave the matter no further consideration, and at my usual hour retired to bed. Here, having placed a candle upon a reading stand at the bed head, and having made an attempt to peruse some pages of the "Omnipresence of the Deity," I unfortunately fell asleep in less than twenty seconds, leaving the light burning as it was.

My dreams were terrifically disturbed by visions of the Angel of the Odd. Methought he stood at the foot of the couch, drew aside the curtains, and, in the hollow, detestable tones of a rum puncheon, menaced me with the bitterest vengeance for the contempt with which I had treated him. He concluded a long harangue by taking off his funnel-cap, inserting the tube into my gullet, and thus deluging me with an ocean of Kirschenwasser, which he poured, in a continuous flood, from one of the long necked bottles that stood him instead of an arm. My agony was at length insufferable, and I awoke just in time to perceive that a rat had run off with the lighted candle from the stand, but *not* in season to prevent his making his escape with it through the hole. Very soon, a strong suffocating odor assailed my nostrils; the house, I clearly perceived, was on fire. In a few minutes the blaze broke forth with violence, and in an incredibly brief period the entire building was wrapped in flames. All egress from my chamber, except through a window, was cut off. The crowd, however, quickly procured and raised a long ladder. By means of this I was descending rapidly, and in apparent safety, when a huge hog, about whose rotund stomach, and indeed about whose whole air and physiognomy, there was something which reminded me of the Angel of the Odd—when this hog, I say, which hitherto had been quietly slumbering in the mud, took it suddenly into his head that his left shoulder needed scratching, and could find no more convenient rubbing-post than that afforded by the foot of the ladder. In an instant I was precipitated and had the misfortune to fracture my arm.

This accident, with the loss of my insurance, and with the more serious loss of my hair, the whole of which had been singed off by the fire, predisposed me to serious impressions, so that, finally, I made up my mind to take a wife. There was a rich widow disconsolate for the loss of her seventh husband, and to her wounded spirit I offered the balm of my vows. She yielded a reluctant consent to my prayers. I knelt at her feet in gratitude and adoration. She blushed and bowed her luxuriant tresses into close contact with those supplied me, temporarily, by Grandjean. I know not how the entanglement took place, but so it was. I arose with a shining pate, wigless; she in disdain and wrath, half buried in alien hair. Thus ended my hopes of the widow by an accident which could not have been anticipated, to be sure, but which the natural sequence of events had brought about.

Without despairing, however, I undertook the siege of a less implacable heart. The fates were again propitious for a brief period; but again a trivial incident interfered. Meeting my betrothed in an avenue thronged with the *élite* of the city, I was hastening to greet her with one of my best considered bows, when a small particle of some foreign matter, lodging in the corner of my eye, rendered me, for the moment, completely blind. Before I could recover my sight, the lady of my love had disappeared—irreparably affronted at what she chose to consider my premeditated rudeness in passing her by ungreeted. While I stood bewildered at the suddenness of this accident, (which might have happened, nevertheless, to any one under the sun), and while I still continued incapable of sight, I was accosted by the Angel of the Odd, who proffered me his aid with a civility which I had no reason to expect. He examined my disordered eye with much gentleness and skill, informed me that I had a drop in it, and (whatever a "drop" was) took it out, and afforded me relief.

I now considered it high time to die, (since fortune had so determined to persecute me), and accordingly made my way to the nearest river. Here, divesting myself of my clothes, (for there is no reason why we cannot die as we were born), I threw myself headlong into the current; the sole witness of my fate being a solitary crow that had been seduced into the eating of brandy-saturated corn, and so had staggered away from his fellows. No sooner had I entered the water than this bird took it into his head to fly away with the most indispensable portion of my apparel. Postponing, therefore, for the present, my suicidal design, I just slipped my nether extremities into the sleeves of my coat, and betook myself to a pursuit of the felon with all the nimbleness which the case required and its circumstances would admit. But my evil destiny attended me still. As I ran at full speed, with my nose up in the atmosphere, and intent only upon the purloiner of my property, I suddenly perceived that my feet rested no longer upon *terra-firma;* the fact is, I had thrown myself over a precipice, and should inevitably have been dashed to pieces but for my good fortune in grasping the end of a long guide-rope, which depended from a passing balloon.

As soon as I sufficiently recovered my senses to comprehend the terrific predicament in which I stood or rather hung, I exerted all the power of my lungs to make that predicament known to the æronaut overhead. But for a long time I exerted myself in vain. Either the fool could not, or the villain would not perceive me. Meantime the machine rapidly soared, while my strength even more rapidly failed. I was soon upon the point of resigning myself to my fate, and dropping quietly into the sea, when my spirits were suddenly revived by hearing a hollow voice from above, which seemed to be lazily humming an opera air. Looking up, I perceived the Angel of the Odd. He was leaning with his arms folded, over the rim of the car; and with a pipe in his mouth, at which he puffed leisurely, seemed to be upon excellent terms with himself and the universe. I was too much exhausted to speak, so I merely regarded him with an imploring air.

For several minutes, although he looked me full in the face, he said nothing. At length removing carefully his meerschaum from the right to the left corner of his mouth, he condescended to speak.

"Who pe you," he asked, "und what der teuffel you pe do dare?"

To this piece of impudence, cruelty and affectation, I could reply only by ejaculating the monosyllable "Help!"

"Elp!" echoed the ruffian—"not I. Dare iz te pottle—elp yourself, und pe tam'd!"

With these words he let fall a heavy bottle of Kirschenwasser which, dropping precisely upon the crown of my head, caused me to imagine that my brains were entirely knocked out. Impressed with this idea, I was about to relinquish my hold and give up the ghost with a good grace, when I was arrested by the cry of the Angel, who bade me hold on.

"Old on!" he said; "don't pe in te urry—don't! Will you pe take de odder pottle, or ave you pe got zober yet and come to your zenzes?"

I made haste, hereupon, to nod my head twice—once in the negative, meaning thereby that I would prefer not taking the other bottle at present— and once in the affirmative, intending thus to imply that I *was* sober and *had* positively come to my senses. By these means I somewhat softened the Angel.

"Und you pelief, ten," he inquired, "at te last? You pelief, ten, in te possibility of te odd?"

I again nodded my head in assent.

"Und you ave pelief in *me*, te Angel of te Odd?"

I nodded again.

"Und you acknowledge tat you pe te blind dronk und te vool?"

I nodded once more.

"Put your right hand into your left hand preeches pocket, ten, in token ov your vull zubmizzion unto te Angel ov te Odd."

This thing, for very obvious reasons, I found it quite impossible to do. In the first place, my left arm had been broken in my fall from the ladder, and, therefore, had I let go my hold with the right hand, I must have let go altogether. In the second place, I could have no breeches until I came across the crow. I was therefore obliged, much to my regret, to shake my head in the negative—intending thus to give the Angel to understand that I found it inconvenient, just at that moment, to comply with his very reasonable demand! No sooner, however, had I ceased shaking my head than—

"Go to der teuffel, ten!" roared the Angel of the Odd.

In pronouncing these words, he drew a sharp knife across the guide-rope by which I was suspended, and as we then happened to be precisely over my own house, (which, during my peregrinations, had been handsomely rebuilt), it so occurred that I tumbled headlong down the ample chimney and alit upon the dining-room hearth.

Upon coming to my senses, (for the fall had very thoroughly stunned me,) I found it about four o'clock in the morning. I lay outstretched where I had fallen from the balloon. My head grovelled in the ashes of an extinguished fire, while my feet reposed upon the wreck of a small table, overthrown, and amid the fragments of a miscellaneous dessert, intermingled with a newspaper, some broken glasses and shattered bottles, and an empty jug of the Schiedam Kirschenwasser. Thus revenged himself the Angel of the Odd.

SECTION ELEVEN

LOOKING BACK

Here is an assortment of writers at grips with their pasts. The past is the ideal subject for humorous treatment because it insists on being lightened up. The typical past contains so much pain and humiliation that only a masochist can bear to write about it honestly.

Humorists, with their skewed perspective on reality, can turn the worst of their memories into farce. Or they can exercise the humorist's prerogative and make up a past far more satisfying than the real thing. The typical past, after all, despite all its pain and embarrassment to the person who has endured it, is apt to be extremely boring to the rest of humanity, all of whom also have a typical past, so know your story all too well.

The humorist, by inventing an entertaining past for himself, can avoid putting us all to sleep with tedious honesty and tiresomely forthright detail.

Who among the memoirists assembled here is inventing his past and who is being reasonably honest about it? Let's leave that for the reader to decide. Half the fun of reading the masters when they are in this vein is trying to deduce how much truth, if any, they are telling, and how much they are inventing to prevent our becoming bored. Joseph Mitchell, for instance, says his piece about Uncle Dockery is entirely made up, but those who know Mitchell will doubt that it contains more than a grain of fiction.

JOSEPH MITCHELL

"Uncle Dockery and the Independent Bull"

I often find it comforting to think of Uncle Dockery Fitzsimmons, a serene old bright-leaf tobacco farmer who lives in Black Ankle County, about six miles from Stonewall. He is the only man I have ever known who has absolutely no respect for the mechanical genius of Western civilization. One day, when I was about fifteen, we were fishing Little Rump River for blue bream and a motorboat chugged by, scaring all the fish to the bed of the river, and Uncle Dockery said, "Son, the only inventions that make sense to me are the shotgun, the two-horse wagon, the butter churn, and the frying pan. Sooner or later such contraptions as the motorboat will drive the whole human race into Dix Hill." Dix Hill is a suburb of Raleigh, where the North Carolina State Asylum for the Insane is located.

Uncle Dockery is still opposed to the automobile. "I don't want to go nowhere," he used to say, "that a mule can't take me." His hatred of automobiles embraces people who ride in them. One summer afternoon we were sitting on his veranda, eating a watermelon, when a neighbor ran up the road and said, "There's been a terrible auto accident up on the highway, Mr. Fitzsimmons." The news pleased Uncle Dockery. He placed his rasher of watermelon on the rail of the veranda, smiled broadly, and asked, "How many killed?" "Four," said the neighbor. "Well, that's just fine," said Uncle Dockery. "Where were they going in such a rush?" "They were going to the beach for a swim," said the neighbor. Uncle Dockery nodded with satisfaction and said, "I guess they figured the Atlantic Ocean wouldn't wait."

Uncle Dockery did not often leave his farm, but once, during a series of revival meetings at the General Stonewall Jackson Baptist Church, he spent the night in Stonewall at the home of his married daughter. In the middle of the night there was a frightful uproar in his room, and his daughter and her husband ran in to rescue him. They thought someone was trying to murder him. They found he had got out of bed to get a drink of water and had pulled the electric-light cord loose from the ceiling. He said, "I tried to turn the damned thing on, but I couldn't somehow seem to make it work. I thought maybe if I grabbed hold of it and gave it a jerk, the light would come on." He was so maddened by his mistake that he wouldn't spend the balance of the night in the room. He asked his daughter to take some blankets and spread a pallet for him outside on the porch. In the morning he denounced her for having electric lights installed in her house. "A fat-pine knot or a kerosene lamp was good enough for Grandpa, and it was good enough for Pa, and it was good enough for Ma, and by God, Miss Priss, it's good enough for me," Uncle Dockery told her.

Although I always called him Uncle Dockery, we are not related. Most of the families in Black Ankle County have been there since the time of the Lords Proprietors, most of them are Scotch-Irish, and most of them *are* related. (There are, however, no aristocrats in the county; in fact, the first mint julep I ever saw was in Lundy's seafood restaurant in Sheepshead Bay in the summer of 1934.) Because almost everybody in the county is at least a cousin by marriage of everybody else, it is natural for young people to use the word "Uncle" for old men they like. People in the county seem to take it for granted that everybody is kin to them.

I remember an incident which illustrates this. There is a ragged, epileptic old Cherokee Indian in Stonewall. He wears a rooster feather in the band of his hat and his beard comes down level with his belt buckle and he looks like Henry Wadsworth Longfellow. People call him Uncle John. He goes from house to house saying, "Have you please got something for poor old Uncle John?" and housewives customarily give him a nickel. One time an aunt from South Carolina was visiting us and she went to the door when Uncle John knocked. She was rather frightened by him. The old Indian bowed and said, "I don't think you know me. I'm Uncle John." My aunt said, "Goodness gracious! Which side of the family are you on?"

I spent a lot of time at Uncle Dockery's when I was a boy. I liked him, and I liked Aunt Dolly, his wife. When I was fourteen, I was given a horse and I used to ride out in the country after school and I often stopped at his farm. Most people in Stonewall disliked him. They used to say, "That old man would just as soon shoot you as tell you howdy-do." He always went out of his way to be sarcastic, and they considered him a public nuisance. On his rare trips to Stonewall he would walk down Main Street grinning to himself, as if he had a private joke on the human race. Once he saw a display of electric fans in the show window of the Stonewall Hardware & General Merchandise Co. and commenced to laugh. He went in and said, "Sell many of them things?" The clerk said, "Selling quite a few." Uncle Dockery said, "Be damned if the whole town don't belong in Dix Hill. A man that'd pay out good money for a breeze shouldn't be allowed to run loose." One time he visited the Black Ankle County Fair and stood around in front of a game-of-skill tent until the barker yelled at him, "Why don't you try your luck, old man?" Then Uncle Dockery pointed to the shabby merchandise offered as prizes and said, "Hell, Mister, I'm afraid I might win something." Uncle Dockery was particularly disliked by Senator C. B. McAdoo, the wealthiest man in Stonewall. Uncle Dockery knew a disgraceful story about him, and told it every time he got a chance. "C.B. hasn't spoken to me in Lord knows when," Uncle Dockery used to say, "but I knew him real well when we were boys. He was raised on a farm right down the road a piece from me, and we grew up together. He was every bit as stingy then as he is now. One summer when we were boys there was a big celebration in Stonewall. They had just finished laying the tracks for the Charleston, Pee Dee, and Southern Railroad, and the first train was due to come through, and the whole town was going to take a holiday and celebrate. All the country people for miles around drove in, and the streets were crowded. A peddler came up from Charleston and set up a lemonade tent right near the depot. He brought some ice packed in sawdust in a barrel. Ice in summer was a highly unusual sight in those days, and the people stood around and watched him crack it up. And lemons were unusual, too. The peddler squeezed out his lemons and made a big tubful of lemonade, and then he hollered out, 'Made in the shade, stirred with a spade, come buy my lemonade.' Well, C.B. walked up with his girl, Sarah Ann Barnes. C.B. was a big, overgrown country boy, and he was all dressed up. He had garters around his shirtsleeves and his hair was slicked back with tallow. He and his girl went up to the lemonade tent. C.B. reached away down in his britches and drew out a nickel, and he put the nickel on the table, got a glass of lemonade, took a swallow, and smacked his lips. Then he turned to his girl and he said, 'Mighty good stuff, Sarah Ann. Better buy yourself some.'"

I learned a lot from Uncle Dockery. He taught me how to bait a hook for blue and red-breast bream, how to use a shotgun, how to tell the age of a mule by examining his teeth, how to set a hen, how to dress partridges for the skillet, how to thump a watermelon to tell if it is green or ripe, and how to chew tobacco. He was what is called a "target chewer." He would light a candle and stick it up on a stump; then he would take up a stance five yards away and extinguish the flame without upsetting the candle. I admired this trick and he tried his best to teach it to me. He advised me to practice on pigeons, saying, "It's always best to practice on a moving target." There were pigeons all over the front yard and he would point to one and make me aim at it. He told me I might get a job with a circus when I grew up if I became a good shot. If I had been blessed with perseverance, I might be travelling about the country right now with Ringling Brothers and Barnum & Bailey.

Sometimes when I rode out, Uncle Dockery would be busy, and I would turn my horse loose in the mule lot and go fishing in Briar Berry Swamp with Little Dock. When Uncle Dockery was almost sixty, he and Aunt Dolly had a son. Aunt Dolly always referred to her husband as Old Man Dock, and their son came to be known as Little Dock. Their other children had grown up, married, and left home, and the old people were extremely fond of Little Dock; Aunt Dolly used to say, "He was mighty slow getting here, but he's the best of the lot." He was a wild, strange boy. When people in the village wanted to be polite about him, they said, "The poor boy isn't quite bright." Otherwise they said, "He's crazy as a bedbug. Takes after his Pa." I was three years older, but I liked to fish with him. He was a wonderful fisherman, except that he talked all the time. He would strike up a conversation with anything, animate or inanimate. He would talk to a fence post. He would catch a fish and say, "Hello, little sun perch, quit flopping around. You're going to make a nice supper for Little Dock."

He took a great interest in religion, but Uncle Dockery wouldn't let him go to Sunday school in Stonewall because he was afraid the town boys would make fun of him. Little Dock was always asking his father about Jesus. One day the three of us were sitting under the shed of the tobacco barn, and Little Dock said, "Pa, where is Jesus located, anyhow? Is he located up in Raleigh, or in Washington, or where?" Uncle Dockery, who was, in his own way, a deeply religious man, told him Jesus was everywhere—in the air, in the sky, in the water. Little Dock smiled, as if he didn't altogether believe the explanation. Later that afternoon, however, he pointed excitedly toward the top of a wild plum tree and said, "There goes Jesus! Lord God, how he can fly!" Uncle Dockery said, "Son, you musta got Jesus confused with a jay bird. I don't see nothing up there but some old blue jays." Little Dock said, "Oh, I saw him all right. He waved to me when he flew over the plum tree." I have always admired Uncle Dockery's behavior on that occasion. He patted the boy on the shoulder and said, "Son, I'm proud of you. It ain't everybody that's got such good eyesight." Anyone who joked about Little Dock's peculiarities in Uncle Dockery's presence made an enemy for life.

Little Dock aped his father. They talked alike. Uncle Dockery often spoke of himself in the third person. He would say, "Dockery went fishing this morning and brought back a trout big as a ham." Little Dock often spoke in the same manner. Once he told me, "Little Dock tried to harness the mule and got the hell kicked out of him. Little Dock sure does hate that mule." Uncle Dockery and Little Dock got a lot of pleasure out of talking to each other. And sometimes, on autumn afternoons, they would sit on kegs in the corncrib and drink sour persimmon beer and sing together. They sang "By and By We're Going Up to See the King," "The Hell Bound Train," and "If You Don't Like My Peaches, Please Quit Shaking My Tree." Their favorite, how-

ever, was a minstrel-show song called "Just the Same." I remember two
verses of it:

> "White girl wears a high-heel shoe.
> Yellow girl does the same.
> Black girl wears no shoe at all,
> But she gets there just the same.

> "White girl lives in a big brick house.
> Yellow girl does the same.
> Black girl lives in the county jail,
> But it's a brick house just the same."

Uncle Dockery had his bad points. He was too stubborn and contrary for his
own good. One bleak January his two mules got sick and died of something
the veterinarian called vesicular stomatitis, or horsepox. Uncle Dockery was
so indignant he refused to buy new mules. He owned a big bull and he decided
he would force it to take the place of both mules. "I'll make a work bull out of
him if it kills me," he said. A few mornings later, a bitter-cold morning with
snow all over the ground, he woke up and found there was no firewood in the
house. It was so cold the water in the pigpen trough had frozen solid. Aunt
Dolly had no stovewood with which to cook breakfast. Uncle Dockery had
some firewood cut and piled in the swamp but nothing he could use to haul it
up to the house except a two-horse wagon, and he didn't think the bull could
pull it without help. He called Aunt Dolly out of her cold kitchen and said,
"Dockery is going to harness himself and the bull to that two-horse wagon and
haul some wood." Alarmed, Aunt Dolly begged him to go borrow a mule
from a neighbor to work beside the bull, but he said, "I ain't the borrowing
kind." He took the heavy mule collar off a harness, tightened it up, and put it
around his neck; then he strung some leather traces from the collar to the
whiffletree of the wagon. Then he hitched himself securely to one side of the
wagon tongue. When that was done, he ordered Aunt Dolly to harness the
bull to the other side of the tongue. He said, "Dockery and the bull make a
fine team, better than any two mules I ever saw." When everything was
ready, he reached over and gave the bull a kick and said, "Let's go, bull." The
bull, made frisky by the cold day and the unaccustomed snow, hurtled forward, pulling the wagon and Uncle Dockery with him. The driverless wagon
rattled and bounced. The bull kept circling the house with a head-long lope
and it was all Uncle Dockery could do to keep up with him. Although the
harness restricted him, Uncle Dockery took high, nimble steps, because he
knew if he stumbled once, he would fall down and the bull would drag him

across the frozen ground. Aunt Dolly stood in the front yard, moaning. Every time the bull and Uncle Dockery clattered past, she waved her apron, which frightened the bull and made matters worse. Finally the bull got tired and he and Uncle Dockery slowed down simultaneously to a walk. Aunt Dolly ran to her husband's aid. She rushed up and started to take his harness off. Uncle Dockery was frantic; he was afraid the bull would start away again. He caught his breath and said, "Dolly, don't bother with me." He pushed her away and said, "Take out the bull. Dockery will stand." That afternoon he limped into Stonewall and bought a span of mules. When he got home, he and Little Dock butchered the bull for winter meat. Uncle Dockery said, "On a farm, it's teamwork that counts, and I can't stand a bull that won't cooperate."

S. J. PERELMAN

"Reunion in Gehenna"

The envelope beside my plate the other morning, addressed in a florid feminine backhand, was tinted the particular robin's-egg blue reserved for babies' bassinets. As I slit open the flap, I stole a furtive glance at my wife across the breakfast table. Her classic features, frequently confused with Katharine Cornell's, betrayed such martyrdom that, given chain mail and a wooden sword, she could have played St. Joan in any little-theatre production in America.

"Well, go ahead and read it," she challenged. "Who is it from this time— some overblown carhop with a platinum rinse?"

"I haven't the faintest clue to what you're foompheting about," I said with hauteur.

"Fancy," she said. "Then suppose I blueprint it for you. I find this correspondence you persist in conducting with other women in abominable taste. Humiliating, in fact. Utterly and unspeakably degrading."

Rather than bandy words with a person patently corroded with jealousy, and lacking, moreover, the words to bandy, I retreated into dignified silence and made a quick scrutiny of the letter. "Well, stap my vitals!" I exclaimed. "It's an invitation from Lorna Dabchick, the secretary of my high-school class.

They're holding a forty-second reunion. And you know something?" I added reflectively. "I've got half a mind to attend."

"That's just about all you'd need," she observed. I raised one eyebrow in the manner of William Powell—ironical yet quizzical—but made no comment. "Yes," she went on. "I've felt for some time that you were aching to spend an evening with a lot of rheumatic old fogies, cackling over the pranks you used to play on your algebra teacher. It's senile dementia, dear—second childhood."

The implication that I was an imbecile wounded me in my Achilles' heel and I became quite emotional, if not altogether coherent. "Right! Right!" I bellowed, reddening with anger. "I'm a sentimental fathead, an irresponsible dotard, but let me tell *you* something, Mrs. Wisenheimer. There are still a few other values in life besides yours. There's love, and there's friendship, and—and there's loving friendship that money can't buy!" I rose and, overturning the coffee cup to underscore my words, swept from the alcove.

My passionate sincerity must have convinced the woman how futile was protest, for inside forty-eight hours I found myself aboard a crack train of the New Haven system, speeding through southern New England. Any doubts I may have entertained about my ability to recapture the past were dispelled at New London. The train butcher who embarked there was the very same one I had encountered four decades ago on my maiden journey to New York, and he still displayed the same formidable case of rhinitis. "Chickid, hab, ad peadut-butter sadwiches, folks!" he intoned, weaving his way through the steam cars. "Get your cold bilk here!" It was inconceivable that forty years had wrought no change in his status or mucous membrane, but there he was, as woebegone and infectious as ever.

The Lobster Pot, the roadhouse where the alumni of Dropsical High were congregating, housed eighty or ninety oldsters in paper hats, who, on my arrival, were noisily acquiring a skinful. Between the clash of bridgework and the drumfire crackle of arteries snapping like pipestems, the place was indistinguishable from an encampment of the G.A.R., but after a spell faces began to take on a dimly familiar look. What struck me as totally inexplicable, though, was how my contemporaries could have become so senescent while I had remained vibrant and arrowy. I noticed a good half dozen clutching to themselves phials of adrenalin, nitroglycerin, and similar restoratives, and I gave them a wide berth lest they topple onto me during a seizure and wrinkle my suit.

Within minutes, it developed that the chairman of the assemblage—the party, in fact, who had conceived and organized it—was a retired podiatrist named Dr. Harry Samovar. Harry had distinguished himself in youth, I recollected, for his forensic powers, singlehandedly vanquishing the debating team of the Lizzie Borden High School in Fall River on the proposition "Resolved, that the initiative, referendum, and recall constitute an arrant menace to the body politic." Whereas Demosthenes had improved his diction by holding a pebble in his mouth, Harry was more favored by fortune; when he spoke, the words rippled from his tongue as if strained across an entire creek bed of gravel. Tonight, plucking a microphone out of thin air, he bade us address ourselves to dinner and explained that the impetus for the reunion had come to him while he was convalescing from a stroke. Barely had he conceived the idea, however, when a second one laid him low; still, this provided him with the leisure to work out the details. After his third stroke—apoplexy hounded Samovar, apparently, much as head colds did my train butcher—he heard the swish of Father Time's scythe and hastily began rallying his classmates. Although nobody at my table appeared to be following his discourse, appetites suddenly started to flag and I felt an overwhelming urge for a cigarette. A buxom, grandmotherly lady on my left, whom I had idolized throughout the whole four-year term without disclosing my passion, scrabbled in her handbag to supply me with one and inadvertently exhumed a tin of BiSoDoL tablets. The realization that my goddess had, so to speak, feet of clay affected me keenly, and I lapsed into a reverie finally broken by the voice of Lorna Dabchick, the class secretary, beamed across the table.

"And what have you been doing all these years, Sol?" she inquired chattily.

I replied that since the death of Moriarty at the Reichenbach Fall I had travelled for two years in Tibet and amused myself by visiting Lhasa, spending some days with the head lama. I had then passed through Persia, looked in at Mecca, and paid a short but interesting visit to the khalifa at Khartoum, the results of which I had communicated to the Foreign Office. Returning to France, I had then spent some months in a research into the coal-tar derivatives, which I conducted in a laboratory at Montpellier.

Lorna listened with rapt interest. "You always had itching feet," she recalled. "Tell me, did you ever get married?"

"No," I confessed. "To me there will always be but one woman—Irene Adler."

"A lovely person," she agreed. "She was coming to the reunion, but she had an attack of gastritis—that is, she *said* it was gastritis—"

I would have loved to hear more about Irene's internal arrangements, but Dr. Samovar, occupied meanwhile in sorting a number of packages, rapped for order. "The prizes we're awarding fall into three categories," he announced. "First, for the couple here wed the longest. Is there anybody married a hundred years? . . . Ninety-five? . . . Ninety?" The search eventually produced a pair of lovebirds—regrettably, no longer on speaking terms—who had gone straight from Dropsical to the altar, and who drew a carving knife suitable for disembowelling each other. The prize for the graduate travelling the greatest distance to the banquet—a ceramic kangaroo with a pouchful of wooden matches—went to a cotton-waste dealer from Woonsocket (a singularly appropriate choice, inasmuch as he had twice been convicted of arson). As for the five-hundred-dollar award to the most distinguished retired podiatrist in the class, that posed the knottiest problem, until Samovar, over his furious protestations, was ultimately prevailed on to accept it.

These preliminaries disposed of, we were ready for the main event of the evening. A sugary-sweet matron in harlequin glasses, her nose sharpened from poking it into other people's business, rose and identified herself as our schoolmate Elise Grabhorn, currently an interviewer on a local radio station. She graciously offered to quiz volunteers on their most arresting experience after graduation, and selected as her first candidate a nearly spherical lady in dotted swiss who spoke in a penetrating, squeaky treble.

"I'm Olive Moultrie," the latter piped. "Olive Krebs when I was single. I don't know if you remember me before I put on so much flesh."

"We certainly do, my dear," said Miss Grabhorn with a vinegary smile. "I'll never forget what a kissing bug Olive was in those days, will you, gang? Now, what was your most unusual experience?"

"Well," began Olive, "Nathan, my hubby—Nathan Moultrie of Peets & Moultrie, Meats & Poultry—was always crazy about my veal birds. He used to say, 'Olive . . .' He used to say, 'Olive . . .' He used to say, 'Olive' "—Miss Grabhorn clapped her hands sharply, and Olive wrested herself from the groove she had slipped into—" 'Olive, I never can get enough of your veal birds.' "

"And did he?" asked her inquisitor.

"Did he what?" Olive repeated adenoidally.

"Get enough of your veal birds," Miss Grabhorn snapped.

"Uh-uh," said Olive. "He passed on four years ago last August."

"Well, you certainly have the sympathy of each and every one of us," said Miss Grabhorn, waving her into oblivion. "Now, who else? I think I see Everett Eubanks over there with his hand up."

"My Uncle Clint was a railroad man," declared Eubanks, a dried-up little man with watery eyes, "and the day I got my diploma he gave me a good timepiece, because, being a railroad man, he had to rely on a good timepiece—you know what I mean? Well, I carried it for nearly twelve years, and one day after I was out fishing for squeteague off Barrington I couldn't find it. Hunted high and low, but nary a trace. So about a month later I was fishing for squeteague again off Gaspee Point and I hauled in a real beauty. And what do you think was in the belly?"

"The timepiece!" several voices chorused.

"No, just a lot of grits the size of your pinky," said Eubanks. "My wife found the watch on a window sill in the attic. Must of laid it there when I put away the screens."

"Thank you, Olive Moultrie and Everett Eubanks," said Dr. Samovar, rising briskly, "and a special thanks to Elise for her brilliant job as m.c. This has been a truly memorable occasion. And now, if you will repair to the Ragtime Room adjoining, Chalky Aftertaste and his Musical Poltroons will cater to your dancing pleasure."

To the strains of "I've Got a Bimbo Down on a Bamboo Isle," "Would You Rather Be a Colonel with an Eagle on Your Shoulder, or a Private with a Chicken on Your Knee?" "Arrah, Go On, I'm Gonna Go Back to Oregon," and a host of similar favorites, I spent the next half hour impervious to aught save the worship of Terpsichore. If I say so myself, I was the cynosure of all eyes. At the behest of my powerfully muscled arms, each of them easily larger in diameter than a pencil, my partners curvetted in figure eights, whirled and skimmed like swallows; in and out of the throng we dipped and swung, shaking our bacon. And then, yielding to the entreaties of my onlookers, I consented to demonstrate the Camel Walk, my interpretation of which had electrified the Senior Prom in 1921. But in choosing Olive Moultrie to share the limelight with me I made a fatal miscalculation. As I was bending her backward in a dizzying tango glide, her weight overbalanced me, I rolled under her, and she fell solidly on my thorax, full fifteen stone. The impact must have knocked me galley-west, for when I regained consciousness I was spread out on a divan like a starfish and Dr. Samovar was distractedly canvassing the bystanders for some hint as to my next of kin.

Luckily, a bit of diathermy, a week of bed rest, and a fortnight at New York Hospital soon put me right, and my account of the train derailment near Westerly was so vivid that my wife completely forgot about the forty-second reunion. And so will I, by the time the eighty-fourth rolls around. I expect to build up quite a head of new nostalgia by then.

RUSSELL BAKER

Uncle Harold

Uncle Harold was famous for lying.

He had once been shot right between the eyes. He told me so himself. It was during World War I. An underaged boy, he had run away from home, enlisted in the Marine Corps, and been shipped to France, where one of the Kaiser's soldiers had shot him. Right between the eyes.

It was a miracle it hadn't killed him, and I said so the evening he told me about it. He explained that Marines were so tough they didn't need miracles. I was now approaching the age of skepticism, and though it was risky business challenging adults, I was tempted to say, "Swear on the Bible?" I did not dare go this far, but I did get a hint of doubt into my voice by repeating his words as a question.

"Right between the eyes?"

"Right between the eyes," he said. "See this scar?"

He placed a finger on his forehead just above the bridge of his nose. "That's all the mark it left," he said.

"I don't see any scar," I said.

"It's probably faded by now," he said. "It's been a long time ago."

I said it must have hurt a good bit.

"Hurt! You bet it hurt."

"What did you do?"

"It made me so mad I didn't do a thing but pull out my pistol and kill that German right there on the spot."

At this point Aunt Sister came in from the kitchen with cups of cocoa. "For God's sake, Harold," she said, "quit telling the boy those lies."

People were always telling Uncle Harold for God's sake quit telling those lies. His full name was Harold Sharp, and in the family, people said, "That Harold Sharp is the biggest liar God ever sent down the pike."

Aunt Sister, Ida Rebecca's only daughter, had married him shortly after my mother took Doris and me from Morrisonville. He'd spent sixteen years in the

Marines by then, but at Aunt Sister's insistence he gave up the Marine Corps and the two of them moved to Baltimore. There they had a small apartment on Hollins Street overlooking Union Square. Our place was a second-floor apartment on West Lombard Street just across the square. It was easy for my mother to stroll over to Aunt Sister's with Doris and me to play Parcheesi or Caroms or Pick-Up-Sticks with the two of them, but the real pleasure of these visits for me came from listening to Uncle Harold.

It didn't matter that my mother called him "the biggest liar God ever sent down the pike." In spite of his reputation for varnishing a fact, or maybe because of the outrageousness with which he did the varnishing, I found him irresistible. It was his intuitive refusal to spoil a good story by slavish adherence to fact that enchanted me. Though poorly educated, Uncle Harold somehow knew that the possibility of creating art lies not in reporting but in fiction.

He worked at cutting grass and digging graves for a cemetery in West Baltimore. This increased the romantic aura through which I saw him, for I had become fascinated with the Gothic aspects of death since arriving in Baltimore. In Baltimore, disposing of the dead seemed to be a major cultural activity. There were three funeral parlors within a one-block radius of our house, and a steady stream of hearses purred through the neighborhood. I had two other distant relatives from Morrisonville who had migrated to Baltimore, and both of them were also working in cemeteries. In addition, there was a fairly steady flow of corpses through our house on Lombard Street.

Our landlord there, a genial Lithuanian tailor who occupied the first floor, lent out his parlor to a young relative who was an undertaker and sometimes had an overflow at his own establishment. As a result there was often an embalmed body coffined lavishly in the first-floor parlor. Since our apartment could be reached only by passing the landlord's parlor, and since its double doors were always wide open, it seemed to me that instead of finding a home of our own, we had come to rest in a funeral home. Passing in and out of the house, I tried to avert my eyes from the garishly rouged bodies and hold my breath against inhaling the cloying odors of candle wax, tuberoses, and embalming fluid which suffused the hallway.

When Uncle Harold came over for an evening of card playing and found a corpse in the parlor, his imagination came alive. On one such evening I went down to let Aunt Sister and him in the front door. Noting the coffin in our landlord's parlor, Uncle Harold paused, strode into the room, nodded at the mourners, and examined the deceased stranger with professional scrutiny. Upstairs afterwards, playing cards at the dining-room table, Uncle Harold announced that the old gentleman in the coffin downstairs did not look dead to him.

"I could swear I saw one of his eyelids flicker," he said.

Nobody paid him any attention.

"You can't always be sure they're dead," he said.

Nobody was interested except me.

"A man I knew was almost buried alive once," he said.

"Are you going to play the jack or hold it all night?" my mother asked.

"It was during the war," Uncle Harold said. "In France. They were closing the coffin on him when I saw him blink one eye."

The cards passed silently and were shuffled.

"I came close to being buried alive myself one time," he said.

"For God's sake, Harold, quit telling those lies," Aunt Sister said.

"It's the truth, just as sure as I'm sitting here, so help me God," said Uncle Harold. "It happens every day. We dig them up out at the cemetery—to do autopsies, you know—and you can see they fought like the devil to get out after the coffin was closed on them, but it's too late by that time."

Uncle Harold was not a tall man, but the Marines had taught him to carry himself with a swaggering erect indolence and to measure people with the grave, cool arrogance of authority. Though he now shoveled dirt for a living, he was always immaculately manicured by the time he sat down to supper. In this polished man of the world—suits pressed to razor sharpness, every hair in place, eyes of icy gray self-confidence—I began to detect a hidden boy, in spirit not too different from myself, though with a love for mischief which had been subdued in me by too much melancholy striving to satisfy my mother's notions of manhood.

Admiring him so extravagantly, I was disappointed to find that he detested my hero, Franklin Roosevelt. In Uncle Harold's view, Roosevelt was a deep-dyed villain of the vilest sort. He had data about Roosevelt's shenanigans which newspapers were afraid to publish and occasionally entertained with hair-raising accounts of Rooseveltian deeds that had disgraced the Presidency.

"You know, I suppose, that Roosevelt only took the job for the money," he told me one evening.

"Does it pay a lot?"

"Not all that much," he said, "but there are plenty of ways of getting rich once you get in the White House, and Roosevelt's using all of them."

"How?"

"He collects money from everybody who wants to get in to see him."

"People have to give him money before he'll talk to them?"

"They don't give him the money face to face. He's too smart for that," Uncle Harold said.

"Then how does he get it?"

"There's a coat rack right outside his door, and he keeps an overcoat hanging on that rack. Before anybody can get in to see him, they've got to put money in the overcoat pocket.''

I was shocked, which pleased Uncle Harold. ''That's the kind of President you've got,'' he said.

''Do you know that for sure?''

''Everybody knows it.''

''How do *you* know it?''

''A fellow who works at the White House told me how it's done.''

This was such powerful stuff that as soon as I got home I passed it on to my mother. ''Who told you that stuff?'' she asked.

''Uncle Harold.''

She laughed at my gullibility. ''Harold Sharp is the biggest liar God ever sent down the pike,'' she said. ''He doesn't know any more about Roosevelt than a hog knows about holiday.''

Through Uncle Harold I first heard of H. L. Mencken. Mencken's house lay just two doors from Uncle Harold's place on Hollins Street. Uncle Harold pointed it out to me one day when we were walking around to the Arundel Ice Cream store for a treat. ''You know who lives in that house, don't you?''

Of course I didn't.

''H. L. Mencken.''

Who's H. L. Mencken?

''You mean to tell me you never heard of H. L. Mencken? He writes those pieces in the newspaper that make everybody mad,'' Uncle Harold said.

I understood from Uncle Harold's respectful tone that Mencken must be a great man, though Mencken's house did not look like the house of a great man. It looked very much like every other house in Baltimore. Red brick, white marble steps. ''I saw Mencken coming out of his house just the other day,'' Uncle Harold said.

It's doubtful Uncle Harold had ever read anything by Mencken. Uncle Harold's tastes ran to *Doc Savage* and *The Shadow*. Still, I could see he was proud of living so close to such a great man. It was a measure of how well he had done in life at a time when millions of other men had been broken by the Depression.

He had left home in 1917 for the Marines, an uneducated fifteen-year-old country boy from Taylorstown, a village not far from Morrisonville, just enough schooling to read and do arithmetic, not much to look forward to but a career of farm labor. Maybe in the Marines he even became a hero. He did fight in France and afterwards stayed on in the Marines, shipping around the Caribbean under General Smedley Butler to keep Central America subdued while Yankee corporations pumped out its wealth. For a man with negligible expectations, he had not done badly by 1937 standards. Full-time cemetery labor; a one-bedroom apartment so close to a famous writer.

My first awe of him had softened as I gradually realized his information was not really intended to be information. Gradually I came to see that Uncle Harold was not a liar but a teller of stories and a romantic, and it was Uncle Harold the teller of tales who fascinated me. Though he remained a stern figure, and I never considered sassing him, I saw now that he knew I no longer received his stories with total credulity, but that I was now listening for the pleasure of watching his imagination at play. This change in our relationship seemed to please him.

Over the Parcheesi board one evening he told a story about watching the dead in Haiti get up out of their shrouds and dance the Charleston. Aunt Sister and my mother had the usual response: "For God's sake, Harold, quit telling those lies."

His face was impassive as always when he issued the usual protest—"It's the truth, so help me God"—but I could see with absolute clarity that underneath the impassive mask he was smiling. He saw me studying him, scowled forbiddingly at me for one moment, then winked. That night we came to a silent understanding: We were two romancers whose desire for something more fanciful than the humdrum of southwest Baltimore was beyond the grasp of unimaginative people like Aunt Sister and my mother.

Still, it took me a while to understand what he was up to. He wanted life to be more interesting than it was, but his only gift for making it so lay in a small talent for homespun fictions, and he could not resist trying to make the most of it. Well, there was nothing tragic about his case. Our world in Baltimore hadn't much respect for the poetic impulse. In our world a man spinning a romance was doomed to be dismissed as nothing more than a prodigious liar.

It was common for the poorest household to contain a large dictionary, for conversation was a popular Depression pastime and Americans were passionately interested in words. Uncle Harold consulted his dictionary regularly looking for jaw-breaker vocabulary to give his tales more weight. One evening when my mother was there he made the mistake, when she spilled her cocoa, of saying that the spilled cocoa was "super-flu-us." Always the schoolmarm when it came to words, my mother chided him for ignorance. The word "superfluous," she pointed out, was ridiculously misused when talking about fluid on the tablecloth and, in any case, was not pronounced "super-flu-us."

Uncle Harold was often subjected to these small humiliations and accepted them without anger or sulkiness, at least when they came from women. Ungallant behavior toward a woman was not in his nature. This probably accounted for the happiness of his marriage, because Aunt Sister had inherited her mother's disposition to be a commander of men. Like her mother, Aunt Sister was tall, angular, tart, and forceful. Uncle Harold may have been the Marine by profession, but Aunt Sister was born and bred to be commandant of the household corps.

She had no patience for what she called Uncle Harold's "foolishness": his love of fiction, his habit of giving her romantic presents like filmy nightgowns and Evening in Paris perfume. She stored the cosmetics in a closet for use on special occasions which never arose and folded the lingerie away in chests where it lay forgotten. "Aunt Sister is too practical sometimes," said my mother, who thought Uncle Harold "a good man" despite his frailties, and therefore a man who deserved more indulgence than Aunt Sister granted him.

Without children of their own, Aunt Sister and Uncle Harold had chosen my sister, Doris, to love as dearly as the child they would never have. During our New Jersey years they had twice kept Doris with them in Baltimore during her summer vacations. These summers Uncle Harold stuffed Doris with ice cream and watermelon, rode the Ferris wheel with her at street carnivals, and entertained her with stories of gigantic serpents he'd fought in tropical jungles and cars he'd rolled over at a hundred miles an hour on the highway without denting a fender or ruffling a hair on his head.

Doris's heart belonged to Uncle Harold ever afterwards. Long after this time when he was young and she was a child, she was to discover that the ability of the true liar, which is the ability to lie to yourself, was not in him. He was to suffer a series of heart attacks so severe that only Aunt Sister and Doris were allowed at his hospital bedside. One night, trying to cheer him, Doris said, "The doctors say you're doing wonderfully. You'll be out of here and up and around in a couple of weeks now."

The true ability to lie was not in him. "You know it's no use," he said, which was the truth. He died two days later.

But that was in a time far beyond those years when he was showing me the pleasures to be had from setting imagination—even a limited imagination— free to play. To me he was the man playing Parcheesi and drinking cocoa in a two-room flat so close to H. L. Mencken, the man who infected me with the notion that there might be worse things to do with life than spend it in telling tales.

To me he was the man who could remember being born. He told me about it one night while Aunt Sister was out in the kitchen making cocoa. He could remember the very instant of birth. His mother was pleased, and the doctor who delivered him—Uncle Harold could remember this distinctly—said, "It's a boy." There were several people in the room, and they all smiled at him. He could remember their faces vividly. And he smiled back.

JEAN SHEPHERD

"My Old Man and the Lascivious Special Award"

The Depression days were the golden age of the newspaper Puzzle Contest. Most newspapers had years before given up the futile struggle to print News, since nothing much ever happened, and had turned their pages over to comic strips and endless Fifty Thousand Dollar Giant Jackpot Puzzle Contests. Dick Tracy became a national hero. Andy Gump was more widely quoted than the President. Orphan Annie's editorializing swayed voters by the million. Popeye raised the price of spinach to astronomical heights, and Wimpy spawned a chain of hamburger joints.

As for puzzles, when one ended, another began immediately and occasionally as many as three or four colossal contests ran simultaneously. NAME THE PRESIDENTS, MYSTERY MOVIE STARS, FAMOUS FIGURES IN HISTORY, MATCH THE BABY PICTURES. On and on the contests marched, all variations on the same theme, page after page of distorted and chopped-up pictures of movie stars, kings, novelists, and ballplayers, while in the great outer darkness, for the price of a two-cent newspaper, countless millions struggled nightly to Hit The Jackpot. They were all being judged for Originality, Neatness, and Aptness of Thought. All decisions, of course, were final.

Occasionally the tempo varied with a contest that featured daily a newspaper camera shot taken of a crowd at random—walking across a street, waiting for a light, standing at a bus stop. IS YOUR FACE CIRCLED? IF IT IS, CALL THE HERALD EXAMINER AND CLAIM FIVE HUNDRED DOLLARS!! The streets were full of roving bands of out-of-work contestants, hoping to have their faces circled. My father was no exception. One of his most treasured possessions was a tattered newspaper photo that he carried for years in his wallet, a photo of a crowd snapped on Huron Street that showed, not more than three inches away from the circled face, a smudged figure wearing a straw skimmer, looking the wrong way. He swore it was him. He had invented an involved story to corroborate this, which he told at every company picnic for years.

He was particularly hooked on FIND THE HIDDEN OBJECTS and HOW MANY MISTAKES ARE IN THIS PICTURE?, which consisted of three-legged dogs, ladies with eight fingers, and smokestacks with smoke blowing in three directions. He was much better at this game than the Historical Figures. No one in Hohman had ever even heard of Disraeli, but they sure knew a lot about smokestacks and how many horns a cow had, and whether birds flew upside down or not.

Contest after contest spun off into history. Doggedly my father labored on. Every night the *Chicago American* spread out on the dining-room table, paste pot handy, scissors and ruler, pen and ink, he clipped and glued; struggled and guessed. He was not the only one in that benighted country who pasted a white wig on Theodore Roosevelt and called him John Quincy Adams, or confused Charlemagne with Sitting Bull. But to the faithful and the persevering and to he who waits awards will come. The historic day that my father "won a prize" is still a common topic of conversation in Northern Indiana.

The contest dealt with GREAT FIGURES FROM THE WORLD OF SPORTS. It was sponsored by a soft-drink company that manufactured an artificial orange drink so spectacularly gassy that violent cases of The Bends were common among those who bolted it down too fast. The color of this volatile liquid was a blinding iridescent shimmering luminous orange that made *real* oranges pale to the color of elderly lemons by comparison. Taste is a difficult thing to describe, but suffice it to say that this beverage, once quaffed, remained forever in the gastronomical memory as unique and galvanic.

All popular non-alcoholic drinks were known in those days by a single generic term—''Pop.'' What this company made was called simply ''Orange pop.'' The company trademark, seen everywhere, was a silk-stockinged lady's leg, realistically flesh-colored, wearing a black spike-heeled slipper. The knee was crooked slightly and the leg was shown to the middle of the thigh. That was all. No face; no torso; no dress—just a stark, disembodied, provocative leg. The name of this pop was a play on words, involving the lady's knee. Even today in the windows of dusty, fly specked Midwestern grocery stores and poolrooms this lady's leg may yet be seen.

The first week of the contest was ridiculously easy: Babe Ruth, Bill Tilden, Man O' War, and the Fighting Irish. My Old Man was in his element. He had never been known to read anything *but* the Sport page. His lifetime subscription to the *St. Louis Sporting News* dated back to his teen-age days. His memory and knowledge of the minutia and trivia of the Sporting arenas was deadening. So naturally he whipped through the first seven weeks without once even breathing hard.

Week by week the puzzlers grew more obscure and esoteric. Third-string utility infielders of Second-Division ball clubs, substitute Purdue halfbacks, cauliflower-eared canvas-backed Welterweights, selling platers whose only distinction was a nineteen-length defeat by Man O' War. The Old Man took them all in his stride. Night after night, snorting derisively, cackling victoriously, consulting his voluminous records, he struggled on toward the Semi-Finals.

A week of nervous suspense and a letter bearing the imprint of a lady's leg informed him that he was now among the Elect. He had survived all preliminary eliminations and was now entitled to try for the Grand Award of $50,-000, plus "hundreds of additional valuable prizes."

Wild jubilation gripped the household, since no one within a thirty-mile radius had ever gotten this far in a major contest, least of all the Old Man. He usually petered out somewhere along the fourth set of FAMOUS FACES and went back to his Chinese nail puzzle and the ball scores. That night we had ice cream for supper.

The following week the first set of puzzles in the final round arrived in a sealed envelope. They were killers! Even the Old Man was visibly shaken. His face ashen, a pot of steaming black coffee at his side, the kids locked away in the bedroom so as not to disturb his massive struggle, he labored until dawn. The pop company had pulled several questionable underhanded ploys. Water Polo is not a common game in Hohman and its heroes are not on everyone's tongue. Hop Skip & Jump champions had never been lionized in Northern Indiana. No one had even *heard* of Marathon Walking! It was a tough night.

His solutions were mailed off, and again we waited. Another set of even more difficult puzzles arrived. Again the sleepless ordeal, the bitter consultations with poolroom scholars, the sense of imminent defeat, the final hopeless guesses, the sealed envelope. Then silence. Days went by with no word of any kind. Gaunt, hollow-eyed, my father watched the mailman as he went by, occasionally pausing only to drop off the gas bill or flyers offering neckties by mail. It was a nervous, restless time. Sudden flareups of temper, outbursts of unmotivated passion. At night the wind soughed emptily and prophetically through the damp clotheslines of the haunted backyards.

Three weeks to a day after the last mailing, a thin, neat, crisp envelope emblazoned with the sinister voluptuous insignia lay enigmatically on the dining-room table, awaiting my father's return from work. The minute he roared into the kitchen that night he knew.

"It's come! By God! Where is it?"

What had come? Fifty thousand dollars? Fame? A trip to the moon? The end of the rainbow? News of yet another failure?

With palsied hand and bulging eye he carefully slit the crackling envelope. A single typewritten sheet:

CONGRATULATIONS. YOU HAVE WON A MAJOR AWARD IN OUR FIFTY THOUSAND DOLLAR "GREAT HEROES FROM THE WORLD OF SPORTS" CONTEST. IT WILL

ARRIVE BY SPECIAL MESSENGER DELIVERED TO YOUR ADDRESS. YOU ARE A WIN-
NER. CONGRATULATIONS.

That night was one of the very few times my father ever actually got publicly drunk. His cronies whooped and hollered, guzzled and yelled into the early morning hours, knocking over chairs and telling dirty stories. My mother supplied endless sandwiches and constantly mopped up. Hairy Gertz, in honor of the occasion, told his famous dirty story about the three bartenders, the Franciscan monk, and the cross-eyed turtle. Three times. It was a true Victory Gala of the purest sort.

Early the next morning the first trickle of a flood of envy-tinged congratulations began to come in. Distant uncles, hazy second cousins, real estate agents, and Used-Car salesmen called to offer heartfelt felicitations and incidental suggestions for highly rewarding investments they had at their disposal. The Old Man immediately, once his head had partially cleared, began to lay plans. Perhaps a Spanish adobe-type house in Coral Gables, or maybe he'd open up his own Bowling Alley. Victory is heady stuff, and has often proved fatal to the victors.

The next afternoon a large unmarked delivery truck stopped in front of the house. Two workmen unloaded a square, sealed, waist-high cardboard carton, which was lugged into the kitchen. They left and drove off. Somehow an air of foreboding surrounded their stealthy, unexplained operation.

The Old Man, his face flushed with excitement, fumbling in supercharged haste to lay bare his hard-won symbol of Victory, struggled to open the carton. A billowing mushroom of ground excelsior surged up and out. In he plunged. And there it was.

The yellow kitchen light bulb illumined the scene starkly and yet with a touch of glowing promise. Tenderly he lifted from its nest of fragrant straw the only thing he had ever won in his life. We stood silent and in awe at the sheer shimmering, unexpected beauty of the "Major Award."

Before us in the heavy, fragrant air of our cabbage-scented kitchen stood a *life-size* lady's leg, in true blushing-pink flesh tones and wearing a modish black patent leather pump with spike heel. When I say life-size I am referring to a rather large lady who obviously had dined well and had matured nicely. It was a well filled-out leg!

It was so realistic that for a brief instant we thought that we had received in the mail the work of an artist of the type that was very active at that period— the Trunk Murderer. For some reason this spectacular form of self-expression has declined, but in those days something in the air caused many a parson's daughter to hack up her boyfriend into small segments which were then shipped separately to people chosen at random from the phone book. Upon being apprehended and tried, she was almost always acquitted, whereupon she accepted numerous offers to appear in Vaudeville as a featured headliner, recalling her days as a Trunk Murderer complete with props and a dramatized stage version of the deed.

For a split instant it seemed as though our humble family had made the headlines.

My mother was the first to recover.

"What is it?"

"A . . . leg," my father incisively shot back.

It was indeed a leg, more of a leg in fact than any leg any of us had ever seen!

"But . . . what is it?"

"Well, it's a leg. Like a statue, I guess."

"A *statue*?"

Our family had never owned a statue. A statue was always considered to be a lady wearing a wreath and concrete robes, holding aloft a torch in one hand and a book in the other. This was the only kind of statue outside of generals sitting on horses that we had ever heard about. They all had names like VICTORY or PEACE. And if this was a statue, it could only have one name:

WHOOPEE!

My mother was trying to get herself between the "statue" and the kids.

"Isn't it time for bed?"

"Holy Smokes, would you look at that!"

My father was warming up.

"Holy Smokes, would you *look* at that? Do you know what this is?"

My mother did not answer, just silently edged herself between my kid brother and the magnificient limb.

"Would you believe it, it's a LAMP!"

It was indeed a lamp, a lamp in its own way a *Definitive* lamp. A master stroke of the lightoliers' art. It was without question the most magnificent lamp that we had ever seen.

This was the age of spindly, artificially antiqued, teetery brass contrivances called "bridge lamps." These were usually of the school of design known as WPA Neo-Romanticism, a school noted for its heavy use of brass flower petals and mottled parchment shades depicting fauns and dryads inscribed in dark browns and greens. The light bulbs themselves were often formed to emulate a twisted, spiraled candle flame of a peculiar yellow-orange tint. These bulbs were unique in that they contrived somehow to make a room even dimmer when they were turned on. My mother was especially proud of her matched set, which in addition to brass tulip buds teetered shakily on bases cleverly designed to look like leopards' paws.

On the kitchen table stood the lamp that was destined to play a subtle and important role in our future. My Old Man dove back into the box, burrowing through the crackling packing.

"AHA! Here's the shade!"

A monstrous, barrel-shaped bulging tube of a shade, a striking Lingerie pink in color, topped by a glittering cut-crystal orb, was lifted reverently up and put onto the table. Never had shade so beautifully matched base. Within an instant the Old Man had screwed it atop the fulsome thigh, and there it stood, a full four feet from coquettishly pointed toe to sparkling crystal. His eyes boggled behind his Harold Lloyd glasses.

"My God! Ain't that great? Wow!!"

He was almost overcome by Art.

"What a great lamp!"

"Oh . . . I don't know."

My mother was strictly the crocheted-doily type.

"What a great lamp! Wow! This is exactly what we need for the front window. Wow!"

He swept up the plastic trophy, his symbol of Superiority, and rushed out through the dining room and into the living room. Placing the lamp squarely in the middle of the library table, he aligned it exactly at the center of the front window. We trailed behind him, applauding and yipping. He was unrolling the cord, down on all fours.

"Where's the damn plug?"

"Behind the sofa."

My mother answered quietly, in a vaguely detached tone.

"Quick! Go out in the kitchen and get me an extension!"

Our entire world was strung together with "extensions." Outlets in our house were rare and coveted, each one buried under a bakelite mound of three-way, seven-way, and ten-way plugs and screw sockets, the entire mess caught in a twisted, snarling Gordian knot of frayed and cracked lamp cords, radio cords, and God knows what. Occasionally in some houses a critical point was reached and one of these electrical bombs went off, sometimes burning down whole blocks of homes, or more often blowing out the main fuse, plunging half the town into darkness.

"Get the extension from the toaster!"

He shouted from under the sofa where he was burrowing through the electrical rat's nest.

I rushed out into the kitchen, grabbed the extension, and scurried back to the scene of action.

"Give it to me! Quick!"

His hand reached out from the darkness. For a few moments—full silence, except for clickings and scratchings. And deep breathing from beneath the sofa. The snap of a few sparks, a quick whiff of ozone, and the lamp blazed forth in unparalleled glory. From ankle to thigh the translucent flesh radiated a vibrant, sensual, luminous orange-yellow-pinkish nimbus of Pagan fire. All it needed was tom-toms and maybe a gong or two. And a tenor singing in a high, quavery, earnest voice:

"A pretty girl / Is like a melody. . . ."

It was alive!

"Hey, look."

The Old Man was reading from the instruction pamphlet which had been attached to the cord.

"It's got a two-way switch. It says here: 'In one position it's a tasteful Night Light and in the other an effective, scientifically designed Reading Lamp.' Oh boy, is this great!"

He reached up under the shade to throw the switch.

"Why can't you wait until the kids are in bed?"

My mother shoved my kid brother behind her. The shade had a narrow scallop of delicate lace circling its lower regions.

"Watch this!"

The switch clicked. Instantly the room was flooded with a wave of pink light that was pure perfume of illumination.

"Now that is a real lamp!"

The Old Man backed away in admiration.

"Hey wait. I want to see how it looks from the outside."

He rushed into the outer darkness, across the front porch and out onto the street. From a half block away he shouted:

"Move it a little to the left. Okay. That's got it. You oughta see it from out here!"

The entire neighborhood was turned on. It could be seen up and down Cleveland Street, the symbol of his victory.

The rest of that evening was spent in honest, simple Peasant admiration for a thing of transcendent beauty, very much like the awe and humility that we felt before such things as Christmas trees and used cars with fresh coats of Simoniz. The family went to bed in a restless mood of festive gaiety. That is, everyone except my mother, who somehow failed to vibrate on the same frequency as my father's spectacular Additional Major Award.

That night, for the first time, our home had a Night Light. The living room was bathed through the long, still, silent hours with the soft glow of electric Sex. The stage was set; the principal players were in the wings. The cue was about to be given for the greatest single fight that ever happened in our family.

Real-life man and wife, mother and father battles rarely even remotely resemble the Theatrical or Fictional version of the Struggle between the Sexes. Homes have been wracked by strife and dissension because of a basic difference of opinion over where to go on a vacation, or what kind of car to buy, or a toaster that made funny noises, or a sister-in-law's false teeth, not to mention who is going to take out the garbage. And why.

In all my experience I have never known homes that had the kind of fights that appear in plays by Edward Albee and Tennessee Williams. It would never have occurred to my father to bellow dramatically in the living room, after twenty-seven Scotches:

"You bitch! You're not going to emasculate *me!*"

The Old Man would not have even known what the word "emasculate" *meant,* much less figure that that's what my mother was up to.

On the other hand, my mother thought "emasculation" had something to do with women getting the vote. But, in any event, Sex is rarely argued and fought over in any household *I* ever heard of, outside of heaving novels and nervous plays. That was not the kind of fights we had at home. There was no question of Emasculation or Role Reversal. My mother was a *Mother.* She knew it. My Old Man was . . . the Old Man. *He* knew it. There was no problem of Identity, just a gigantic clash of two opposing physical presences: the Immovable Body and the Force That Is Not To Be Denied.

The lamp stood in the middle of the window for months. Every night my mother would casually, without a word, draw the curtains shut, while Bing Crosby sang from the old Gothic Crosley:

> "Hail KMH / Hail to the foe
> Onward to victory / Onward we must go. . . ."

the theme song of the Kraft Music Hall. The Old Man would get up out of his chair. Casually. He would pull the curtain back, look out—pretending to be examining the weather—and leave it that way. Ten minutes later my mother would get up out of her chair, casually, saying:

"Gee, I feel a draft coming in from somewhere."

This slowly evolving ballet spun on through the Winter months, gathering momentum imperceptibly night after night. Meanwhile, the lamp itself had attracted a considerable personal following among cruising prides of pimply-faced Adolescents who night after night could hardly wait for darkness to fall and the soft, sinuous radiation of Passion to light up the drab, dark corners of Cleveland Street.

The pop company enjoyed sales of mounting intensity, even during the normally slack Winter months. Their symbol now stood for far more than a sickeningly sweet orange drink that produced window-rattling burps and cavities in Adolescent teeth of such spectacular dimensions as to rival Mammoth Cave. Night after night kids' eyes glowed in the darkness out on the street before our house, like predatory carnivores of the jungle in full cry. Night after night the lady's leg sent out its silent message.

The breaking point came, as all crucial moments in History do, stealthily and on cats' feet, on a day that was notable for its ordinariness. We never know when lightning is about to strike, or a cornice to fall. Perhaps it is just as well.

On the fateful day I came home from school and immediately opened the refrigerator door, looking for Something To Eat. Seconds later I am knocking together a salami sandwich. My Old Man—it was his day off—is in the john. Hollering, as he always did, accompanied by the roar of running water, snatches of song, complaints about No Pressure—the usual. My mother is somewhere off in the front of the house, puttering about. Dusting.

Life is one long song. The White Sox have won a ball game, and it's only spring training. The Old Man is singing. My brother is under the daybed, whimpering. The salami is as sweet as life itself.

The first fireflies were beginning to flicker in the cottonwoods. Northern Indiana slowly was at long last emerging from the iron grip of the Midwestern Winter. A softness in the air; a quickening of the pulse. Expectations long lying dormant in the blackened rock ice of Winter sent out tentative tender green shoots and yawned toward the smoky sun. Somewhere off in the distance, ball met bat; robin called to robin, and a screen door slammed.

In the living room my mother is talking to the aphids in her fern plant. She fought aphids all of her life. The water roared. I started on a second sandwich. And then:

CAAA-RAASHH!

". . . oh!" A phony, stifled gasp in the living room.

A split second of silence while the fuse sputtered and ignited, and it began.

The Old Man *knew*. He had been fearing it since the very first day. The bathroom door slammed open. He rushed out, dripping, carrying a bar of Lifebuoy, eyes rolling wildly.

"What broke!? What happened?! WHAT BROKE!!?"

". . . the lamp." A soft, phony voice, feigning heartbreak.

For an instant the air vibrated with tension. A vast magnetic charge, a static blast of human electricity made the air sing. My kid brother stopped in mid-whimper. I took the last bite, the last bite of salami, knowing that this would be my last happy bite of salami forever.

The Old Man rushed through the dining room. He fell heavily over a footstool, sending a shower of spray and profanity toward the ceiling.

"Where is it? WHERE IS IT!?"

There it was, the shattered kneecap under the coffee table, the cracked, well-turned ankle under the radio; the calf—that voluptuous poem of feminine pulchritude—split open like a rotten watermelon, its entrails of insulated wire hanging out limply over the rug. That lovely lingerie shade, stove in, had rolled under the library table.

"Where's my glue? My glue! OH, MY LAMP!"

My mother stood silently for a moment and then said:

"I . . . don't know what happened. I was just dusting and . . . ah. . . ."

The Old Man leaped up from the floor, his towel gone, in stark nakedness. He bellowed:

"YOU ALWAYS WERE JEALOUS OF THAT LAMP!"

"Jealous? Of a *plastic leg*?"

Her scorn ripped out like a hot knife slicing through soft oleomargarine. He faced her.

"You were jealous 'cause I WON!"

"That's ridiculous. Jealous! Jealous of what? That was the ugliest lamp I ever saw!"

Now it was out, irretrievably. The Old Man turned and walked to the window. He looked out silently at the soft gathering gloom of Spring. Suddenly he turned and in a flat, iron voice:

"Get the glue."

"We're *out* of glue," my mother said.

My father always was a superb user of profanity, but now he came out with just one word, a real Father word, bitter and hard.

"DAMMIT!"

Without another word he stalked into the bedroom; slammed the door, emerged wearing a sweatshirt, pants and shoes, and his straw hat, and out he went. The door of the Oldsmobile slammed shut out in the driveway.

"K-runch. Crash!"—a tinkle of glass. He had broken the window of the one thing he loved, the car that every day he polished and honed. He slammed it in Reverse.

RRRRAAAWWWWWRRRRR!

We heard the fender drag along the side of the garage. He never paused.

RRRRAAAWWWWWRRROOOOMMMM!

And he's gone. We are alone. Quietly my mother started picking up the pieces, something she did all her life. I am hiding under the porch swing. My kid brother is now down in the coal bin.

It seemed seconds later:

BBBRRRRRRAAAAAWWWRRRR . . . eeeeeeeeh!

Up the driveway he charged in a shower of cinders and burning rubber. You could always tell the mood of the Old Man by the way he came up that driveway. Tonight there was no question.

A heavy thunder of feet roared up the back steps, the kitchen door slammed. He's carrying three cans of glue. Iron glue. The kind that garage

mechanics used for gaskets and for gluing back together exploded locomo-
tives. His voice is now quiet.

"Don't touch it. *Don't touch that lamp!*"

He spread a newspaper out over the kitchen floor and carefully, tenderly
laid out the shattered fleshy remains. He is on all fours now, and the work
began. Painfully, hopelessly he tried to glue together the silk-stockinged,
life-size symbol of his great victory.

Time and again it looked almost successful, but then he would remove his
hand carefully. . . . BOING! . . . the kneecap kept springing up and sailing
across the kitchen. The ankle didn't fit. The glue hardened into black lumps
and the Old Man was purple with frustration. He tried to fix the leg for about
two hours, stacking books on it. A Sears Roebuck catalog held the instep. The
family Bible pressed down on the thigh. But it wasn't working.

To this day I can still see my father, wearing a straw hat, swearing under his
breath, walking around a shattered plastic lady's leg, a Freudian image to make
Edward Albee's best efforts pale into insignificance.

Finally he scooped it all up. Without a word he took it out the back door
and into the ashbin. He sat down quietly at the kitchen table. My mother is
now back at her lifelong station, hanging over the sink. The sink is making the
Sink noise. Our sink forever made long, gurgling sighs, especially in the
evening, a kind of sucking, gargling, choking retch.

Aaaagggghhhh—and then a short, hissing wheeze and silence until the next
attack. Sometimes at three o'clock in the morning I'd lie in my bed and listen
to the sink—Aaaaggggghhhh.

Once in a while it would go: gaaaaagggghhhh . . . PTUI!—— and up would
come a wad of Mrs. Kissel's potato peelings from next door. She, no doubt,
got our coffee grounds. Life was real.

My mother is hanging over her sink, swabbing eternally with her Brillo pad.
If mothers had a coat of arms in the Midwest, it would consist of crossed
Plumbers' Helpers rampant on a field of golden Brillo pads.

The Old Man is sitting at the kitchen table. It was white enamel with little
chipped black marks all around the edge. They must have been made that way,
delivered with those flaws. A table that smelled like dishrags and coffee
grounds and kids urping. A kitchen-table smell, permanent and universal, that
defied all cleaning and disinfectant—the smell of Life itself.

In dead silence my father sat and read his paper. The battle had moved into
the Trench Warfare or Great Freeze stage. And continued for three full days.
For three days my father spoke not. For three days my mother spoke likewise.
There was only the sink to keep us kids company. And, of course, each other,
clinging together in the chilly subterranean icy air of a great battle. Occasionally I would try.

"Hey Ma, ah . . . you know what Flick is doing . . . uh. . . ."

Her silent back hunched over the sink. Or:

"Hey Dad, Flick says that. . . ."

"WHADDAYA WANT?"

Three long days.

Sunday was sunny and almost like a day in Midsummer. Breakfast, usually a holiday thing on Sundays, had gone by in stony silence. So had dinner. My father was sitting in the living room with the sun streaming in unobstructed through the front window, making a long, flat, golden pattern on the dusty Oriental rug. He was reading Andy Gump at the time. My mother was struggling over a frayed elbow in one of my sweaters. Suddenly he looked up and said:

"You know. . . ."

Here it comes! My mother straightened up and waited.

"You know, I like the room this way."

There was a long, rich moment. These were the first words spoken in seventy-two hours.

She looked down again at her darning, and in a soft voice:

"Uh . . . you know, I'm sorry I broke it."

"Well . . ." he grew expansive, "It was . . . it was really pretty jazzy."

"No," she answered, "I thought it was very *pretty*!"

"Nah. It was too pink for this room. We should get some kind of brass lamp for that window."

She continued her darning. He looked around for a moment, dropped the Funnies noisily to get attention, and then announced in his Now For The Big Surprise voice:

"How 'bout let's all of us going to a movie? How 'bout it? Let's all take in a movie!"

Ten minutes later we're all in the Oldsmobile, on our way to see Johnny Weissmuller.

FRANK SULLIVAN

"The Night the Old Nostalgia Burned Down"

My Own New York Childhood

When I was a boy, Fourteenth Street was where Twenty-third Street is now, and Samuel J. Tilden and I used to play marbles on the lot where the Grand Opera House still stood. Governor Lovelace brought the first marble from England to this country on August 17, 1668, and gave it to my Great-Aunt Amelia van Santvoort, of whom he was enamored. She had several copies made, and Sam Tilden and I used to amuse ourselves with them.

I remember the Sunday afternoons when Governor Lovelace would come to tea at our house, although I could not have been much more than a tad at the time. I can hear the rich clanking of the silver harness as his magnificent equipage, with its twelve ebony outriders in cerise bombazine, rolled up to our house at No. 239 East 174th Street. I was the envy of all the kids on the block because I was allowed to sit in the carriage while the Governor went in to take tea with Great-Aunt Amelia. I always chose Ada Rehan to sit beside me. She was a little golden-haired thing at the time and none of us dreamed she would one day go out from East 174th Street and shoot President Garfield.

Great-Aunt Amelia was a dowager of the old school. You don't see many of her kind around New York today, probably because the old school was torn down a good many years ago; its site is now occupied by Central Park. People used to say that the Queen, as they called Great-Aunt Amelia, looked more like my Aunt Theodosia than my Aunt Theodosia did.

But Aunt Caroline was really the great lady of our family. I can still see her descending the staircase, dressed for the opera in silk hat, satin-lined cape, immaculate shirt, white tie, and that magnificent, purple-black beard.

"Well, boy!" she would boom at me. "Well!"

"Well, Aunt Caroline!" I would say, doing my best to boom back at her.

She would chuckle and say, "Boy, I like your spirit! Tell Grimson I said to add an extra tot of brandy to your bedtime milk."

Oh, those lollipops at Preem's, just around the corner from the corner! Mm-m-m, I can still taste them! After school, we kids would rush home and shout, "Ma, gimme a penny for a lollipop at Preem's, willya, Ma? Hey, Ma, willya?" Then we would go tease Jake Astor, the second-hand-fur dealer around the corner. I shall never forget the day Minnie Maddern Fiske swiped the mink pelt from Jake's cart and stuffed it under Bishop Potter's cope.

Miss Hattie Pumplebutt was our teacher at P.S. 67. She was a demure wisp of a woman, with white hair parted in the middle, pince-nez that were forever dropping off her nose, always some lacy collar high around her throat, and paper cuffs. We adored her. Every once in a while she would climb up on her desk, flap her arms, shout "Whee-e-e! I'm a bobolink!," and start crowing. Or she would take off suddenly and go skipping about the tops of our desks with a dexterity and sure-footedness truly marvellous in one of her age. When we grew old enough, we were told about Miss Pumplebutt. She took dope. Well, she made history and geography far more interesting than a lot of nonsniffing teachers I have known.

One day, Jim Fisk and I played hooky from school and went to the old Haymarket on Sixth Avenue, which was then between Fifth and Seventh. We had two beers apiece and thought we were quite men about town. I dared Jim to go over and shoot Stanford White, never dreaming the chump would do it. I didn't know he was loaded. I got Hail Columbia from Father for that escapade.

Father was very strict about the aristocratic old New York ritual of the Saturday-night bath. Every Saturday night at eight sharp we would line up: Father, Mother, Diamond Jim Brady; Mrs. Dalrymple, the housekeeper; Absentweather, the butler; Aggie, the second girl; Aggie, the third girl; Aggie, the fourth girl; and twelve of us youngsters, each one equipped with soap and a towel. At a command from Father, we would leave our mansion on East Thirtieth Street and proceed solemnly up Fifth Avenue in single file to the old reservoir, keeping a sharp eye out for Indians. Then, at a signal from Papa, in we'd go. Everyone who was anyone in New York in those days had his Saturday-night bath in the reservoir, and it was there that I first saw and fell in love with the little girl whom I later made Duchess of Marlborough.

My Grandmamma Satterthwaite was a remarkable old lady. At the age of eighty-seven she could skip rope four hundred and twenty-two consecutive times without stopping, and every boy on the block was madly in love with her. Then her father failed in the crash of '87 and in no time she was out of pigtails, had her hair up, and was quite the young lady. I never did hear what became of her.

It rather amuses me to hear the youngsters of today enthusing about the croissants, etc., at Spodetti's and the other fashionable Fifth Avenue patisseries. Why, they aren't a patch on Horan's!

Mike Horan's place was at Minetta Lane and Washington Mews, and I clearly remember my father telling a somewhat startled Walt Whitman that old Mike Horan could bend a banana in two—with his bare hands! But I never saw him do it. We kids used to stand in front of his shop for hours after school waiting for Mike to bend a banana, but he never did. I can still hear the cheerful clang of his hammer on the anvil and the acrid smell of burning hoofs from the Loveland Dance Palace, across the way on Delancey Street, which was then Grand. Then the Civil War came and the property of the Loyalists was confiscated. I still have some old Loyalist property I confiscated on that occasion. I use it for a paperweight. Old Gammer Wilberforce was a Loyalist. We used to chase her down the street, shouting "Tory!" at her. Then she would chase us up the street, shouting:

> "Blaine, Blaine, James G. Blaine!
> Continental liar from the State of Maine!"

or:

> "Ma! Ma! Where's my Pa?"
> "Gone to the White House, ha, ha ha!"

Of course, very few white people ever went to Chinatown in those days. It was not until the Honorah Totweiler case that people became aware of Chinatown. I venture to say that few persons today would recall Honorah Totweiler, yet in 1832 the Honorah Totweiler case was the sensation of the country. In one day the circulation of the elder James Gordon Bennett jumped seventy-four thousand as a result of the Totweiler case.

One sunny afternoon in the autumn of September 23, 1832, a lovely and innocent girl, twelfth of eighteen daughters of Isaac Totweiler, a mercer, and Sapphira, his wife, set out from her home in Washington Mews to return a cup of sugar—but let the elder Bennett tell the story:

> It is high time [Bennett wrote] that the people of these United States were awakened to the menace in which the old liberties for which our forefathers fought and bled, in buff and blue, by day and night, at Lexington and Concord, in '75 and '76, have been placed as a result of the waste, the orgy of spending, the deliberate falsifications, the betrayal of public trust, and the attempt to set up a bureaucratic and unconstitutional dictatorship, of the current Administration in Washington. Murphy must go, and Tammany with him!

After dinner on Sundays, my Grandpa Bemis would take a nap, with the *Times,* or something, thrown over his face to keep out the glare. If he was in a good humor when he awoke, he would take us youngsters up to Dick Canfield's to play games, but as he was never in a good humor when he awoke, we never went to Dick Canfield's to play games.

Sometimes, when we kids came home from school, Mrs. Rossiter, the housekeeper, would meet us in the hall and place a warning finger on her lips. We knew what that meant. We must be on our good behavior. The wealthy Mrs. Murgatroyd was calling on Mother. We would be ushered into the Presence, Mother would tell us to stop using our sleeves as a handkerchief, and then Mrs. Murgatroyd would laugh and say, "Oh, Annie, let the poor children alone. Sure, you're only young once." Then she would lift up her skirt to the knee, fish out a huge wallet from under her stocking, and give us each $2,000,000. We loved her. Not only did she have a pair of d——d shapely stems for an old lady her age, but she was reputed to be able to carry six schooners of beer in each hand.

I shall never forget the night of the fire. It was about three o'clock in the morning when it started, in an old distaff factory on West Twelfth Street. I was awakened by the crackling. I shivered, for my brother, as usual, had all the bedclothes, and there I was, with fully three inches of snow (one inch powder, two inches crust) on my bare back. The next morning there were seven feet of snow on West Twenty-seventh Street alone. You don't get that sort of winter nowadays. That was the winter the elder John D. Rockefeller was frozen over solid from November to May.

On Saturdays we used to go with Great-Aunt Tib to the Eden Musee to see the wax figure of Lillian Russell. There was a woman! They don't build girls like her nowadays. You can't get the material, and even if you could, the contractors and the plumbers would gyp you and substitute shoddy.

I was six when the riots occurred. No, I was *thirty*-six. I remember because it was the year of the famous Horace Greeley hoax, and I used to hear my parents laughing about it. It was commonly believed that Mark Twain was the perpetrator of the hoax, although Charles A. Dana insisted to his dying day that it was Lawrence Godkin. At any rate, the hoax, or "sell," originated one night at the Union League Club when Horace chanced to remark to Boss Tweed that his (Horace's) wife was entertaining that night. The town was agog for days, no one having the faintest notion that the story was not on the level. Greeley even threatened Berry Wall with a libel suit.

Well, that was New York, the old New York, the New York of gaslit streets, and sparrows (and, of course, horses), and cobblestones. The newsboy rolled the *Youth's Companion* into a missile and threw it on your front stoop and the postmen wore uniforms of pink velvet and made a point of bringing everybody a letter every day.

Eheu, fugaces!——

CLARENCE DAY

"Father and His Pet Rug"

Father liked spending his summers in the country, once he had got used to it, but it introduced two major earthquakes each year into his life. One when he moved out of town in the spring, and one in the fall when he moved back. If there was one thing Father hated it was packing. It seemed a huddled, irregular affair to a man with his orderly mind. For a week or more before it was time to begin he was upset by the prospect. He had only a few drawers full of clothes to empty into a trunk, but it had to be done in a certain particular way. No one else could attend to it for him—no one else could do the thing properly. All that Mother could do was to have his trunk brought to his room. When it had been laid in a corner, gaping at him, his groaning began. He walked around, first putting his shirts in, then his clothes and his underwear, then burrowing under and taking some out again to go in the suitcase, then deciding that after all he would not take part of what he had packed. During all such perplexities he communed with himself, not in silence.

The first sounds that used to come from his room were low groans of self-pity. Later on, as the task he was struggling with became more and more complicated, he could be heard stamping about, and denouncing his garments. If we looked in his door we would see him in the middle of the room with a bathrobe, which had already been packed twice in the suitcase and once in the trunk, and which was now being put back in the trunk again because the suitcase was crowded. Later it would once more go back in the suitcase so as to be where he could get at it. His face was red and angry, and he was earnestly saying, "Damnation!"

Long before any of this began Mother had already started her end of it. Father packed only his own clothes. She packed everything else: except that she had someone to help her, of course, with the heavy things. In the fall, for instance, a man named Jerome sometimes went up to the country to do this.

He was a taciturn, preoccupied colored man, an expert at moving, who worked so well and quickly that he kept getting ahead of his schedule. It was distracting to Mother to plan out enough things to keep Jerome busy. It was also distracting to see him sit idle. He was paid by the day.

But the principal problem that Mother had to attend to was Father. He said that he didn't really mind moving but that he did object to the fuss. As to rugs, for instance, he refused to have any at all put away until after he and all his belongings had been moved from the house. This seemed unreasonable to me—I said he ought to allow them to make a beginning and put a few away, surely. He would admit, privately, that this was true perhaps, but here was the trouble: if he once let Mother get started she would go much too far. "When your mother is closing up a house," he said, "she gets too absorbed in it. She is apt to forget my comfort entirely—and also her own. I have found by experience that if I yield an inch in this matter the place is all torn up." He added that he had to insist upon absolute order, simply because the alternative was absolute chaos. Furthermore, why shouldn't the process be orderly if it were skillfully handled? If it wasn't, it was no fault of his, and he declined to be made to suffer for it.

Mother's side of it was that it was impossible to move out imperceptibly. "Things naturally get upset a little, Clare dear, when you're making a change. If they get upset too much I can't help it; and I do wish you would stop bothering me."

One result of this difference was a war about the rugs every fall. Two or three weeks before they left, Mother always had the large rug in the hall taken up—there was no need of *two* rugs in the hall, she told Father.

"I won't have it, damn it, you're making the place a barracks," he said.

"But we're *moving*," Mother expostulated; "we must get the house closed."

"Close it properly then! Do things suitably, without this cursed helter-skelter." He retreated into the library where he could sit by a fire, while Mother went in and out of cold rooms and halls with her shawl on.

The library had two large heavy pieces of furniture in it—a grand piano, and a huge desklike table piled with papers and books. This table filled the center of the room and stood square on a rug. It was hard work to lift that heavy table to get the rug out from under it. Until this was done, every year, Mother kept thinking about it at night. Strictly speaking, it wasn't necessary to have that rug put away much beforehand, but she wanted to get it over and done with so that she could sleep. But Father was particularly dependent on this rug because he liked to sit in the library; he was always determined that it shouldn't be touched till he left.

He couldn't, however, remain on guard continuously. He sometimes had to go out. In fact he was maneuvered into going out, though this he never quite learned. In the late afternoon when he supposed the day's activities over, he would come out of the library and venture to go off in the motor. Not far, just to get the evening paper, which was a very short trip. His mind was quiet: he assumed that nothing much could be done in his absence. But just as he was leaving he would be given some errand to do—some provisions to buy in the next town beyond, or a book to leave at some friend's. Or if this might make him suspicious, nothing would be said as he left, but the chauffeur would be given instructions what to say when he had bought Father's paper.

"There are some flowers in the car, sir, that Mrs. Day . . ."

Father looked up from his paper, and looked threateningly over his glasses. "What's all this?" he said. *"What?"*

The chauffeur repeated mildly "—that Mrs. Day wishes left at the church."

"Damn the church," Father answered, going back to the market reports. Not that he was down on that institution, he believed in it firmly, but he expected the church to behave itself and not interfere with his drives. However, he was looking through his paper, and he didn't say no, and the chauffeur didn't give him time to anyhow, but cranked up the car, and off they went down the Post Road, all the way into Rye.

When they got home, Father hung up his overcoat in the cold hall, and grasping his evening paper he marched back to the library fire. . . .

Meantime things had been happening. Mother had had the big table lifted, and had got up the rug; and Jerome had lugged it out to the laundry yard to beat it. After that, his orders were to roll it and wrap it and put it away. While he was doing this, which was naturally expected to take him some time, Mother thankfully went up to the china room to pack certain cups. She always felt a little more peaceful when Jerome was fully occupied. . . .

A little later, when she was in her own room and had just sat down for a minute, for the first time that day, and was sorting the linen, and humming, there was a knock at the door.

Mother sat up sharply, every bit of her alert again. "Who is that?"

She heard a deprecating little cough, then Jerome's quiet voice. "Now— er—Mrs. Day?"

"Well, what *is* it, Jerome?" Mother wailed. She had thought she had left that man enough to do for once anyhow, but here he was back on her hands again. "What is it *now?*" she said in despair. "Have you finished that work?"

"No'm," Jerome said reassuringly. "I ain't finished that yet." He paused, and coughed again, conscious that he was bringing poor news. "Mr. Day, he's hollerin' consid'able, down in the liberry."

"What about? What's the matter with him?"

Jerome knew she knew well enough. He said "Yes'm," mechanically; and added in a worried way, as if to himself, "He's a-hollerin' for that rug."

Mother didn't like Jerome to use that word, "hollerin'." It wasn't respect-ful. But it was so painfully descriptive that she couldn't think what other word he could substitute. She put down the linen. I never could see why she didn't stay quietly in her room, at such moments, and let Father keep up his hollerin' till he cooled off. But I was an outsider in these wars, and Mother of course was a combatant. She charged out into the big upper hall, and at once began an attack, launching her counter-offensive vigorously, over the banisters. She called loudly upon Father to stop right away and be still; and she told him how wicked it was of him to make trouble for her when she was working so hard. Father, from his post in the library, boomed a violent reply. It was like an artillery bombardment. Neither side could see the other. But they fired great guns with great vigor, and it all seemed in earnest.

Jerome stood respectfully waiting, wondering how it would come out. He was wholly in the dark as to which side was winning, there was so much give and take. But the combatants knew. Mother presently saw she was beaten. There was some note she detected in Father's voice, deeper than bluster; or some weariness in herself that betrayed her. At any rate, she gave in.

She turned to Jerome. He saw that she was thinking how she could fix it. Jerome felt dejected. Had that big old rug got to be toted back into the library?

"Jerome, I'll have to give Mr. Day one of those rugs from the blue room— one of the long narrow white fur pair. You know which I mean?"

"Yes'm," Jerome said with partial relief. "Put it under that desk?"

"No, between the desk and the fireplace. By Mr. Day's chair. That's all that's necessary. He just wants something under his feet."

This wasn't at all Father's idea of what he wanted, as Jerome soon discov-ered, when he took the long white fur rug down to him. Father was so completely amazed he forgot to be angry. He had supposed he had won that bombardment. He had made Mother cease firing. Yet now after he had low-ered his temperature again back to normal, and settled down to enjoy the fruits of his victory, namely his own big square rug, here was Jerome bringing him instead a long narrow hairy monstrosity.

"What's that?" he demanded.

Jerome limply exhibited the monstrosity, feeling hopeless inside, like a pessimistic salesman with no confidence in his own goods.

"What are you bringing that thing in here for?"

"Yessir, Mr. Day. Mrs. Day says put it under your feet."

Father started to turn loose his batteries all over again. But his guns had gone cold. He felt plenty of disgust and exasperation, but not quite enough fury. He fired what he had at Jerome, who stood up to it silently; and he kicked the offending white fur rug, and said he wouldn't have it. But some-thing in the air now seemed to tell him, in his turn, he had lost. Even Jerome felt this, and put the rug under his feet, "temporary," leaving Father trying to read his paper again, indignant and bitter. He particularly disliked this white rug. He remembered it now from last year.

Mother went back to the linen. The house became quiet. The only sounds were thuds in the laundry yard, where Jerome was at work, beating and sweeping his booty, concealed by the hedge.

By the library fire Father was turning over the page of his paper, and glaring at the white rug, and saying to himself loudly, "I hate it!" He kicked at the intruder. "Damn woolly thing. I want my own rug."

JAMES THURBER

"The Night the Ghost Got In"

THE GHOST that got into our house on the night of November 17, 1915, raised such a hullabaloo of misunderstandings that I am sorry I didn't just let it keep on walking, and go to bed. Its advent caused my mother to throw a shoe through a window of the house next door and ended up with my grandfather shooting a patrolman. I am sorry, therefore, as I have said, that I ever paid any attention to the footsteps.

They began about a quarter past one o'clock in the morning, a rhythmic, quick-cadenced walking around the dining-room table. My mother was asleep in one room upstairs, my brother Herman in another; grandfather was in the attic, in the old walnut bed which, as you will remember, once fell on my father. I had just stepped out of the bathtub and was busily rubbing myself with a towel when I heard the steps. They were the steps of a man walking rapidly around the dining-room table downstairs. The light from the bathroom shone down the back steps, which dropped directly into the dining-room; I could see the faint shine of plates on the plate-rail; I couldn't see the table. The steps kept going round and round the table; at regular intervals a board creaked, when it was trod upon. I supposed at first that it was my father or my brother Roy, who had gone to Indianapolis but were expected home at any time. I suspected next that it was a burglar. It did not enter my mind until later that it was a ghost.

After the walking had gone on for perhaps three minutes, I tiptoed to Herman's room. "Psst!" I hissed, in the dark, shaking him. "Awp," he said, in the low, hopeless tone of a despondent beagle—he always half suspected that something would "get him" in the night. I told him who I was. "There's something downstairs!" I said. He got up and followed me to the head of the back staircase. We listened together. There was no sound. The steps had ceased. Herman looked at me in some alarm: I had only the bath towel around my waist. He wanted to go back to bed, but I gripped his arm. "There's something down there!" I said. Instantly the steps began again, circled the dining-room table like a man running, and started up the stairs toward us, heavily, two at a time. The light still shone palely down the stairs; we saw nothing coming; we only heard the steps. Herman rushed to his room and slammed the door. I slammed shut the door at the stairs top and held my knee against it. After a long minute, I slowly opened it again. There was nothing there. There was no sound. None of us ever heard the ghost again.

The slamming of the doors had aroused mother: she peered out of her room. "What on earth are you boys doing?" she demanded. Herman ventured out of his room. "Nothing," he said, gruffly, but he was, in color, a light green. "What was all that running around downstairs?" said mother. So she had heard the steps, too! We just looked at her. "Burglars!" she shouted intuitively. I tried to quiet her by starting lightly downstairs.

"Come on, Herman," I said.

"I'll stay with mother," he said. "She's all excited."

I stepped back onto the landing.

"Don't either of you go a step," said mother. "We'll call the police." Since the phone was downstairs, I didn't see how we were going to call the police—nor did I want the police—but mother made one of her quick, incomparable decisions. She flung up a window of her bedroom which faced the bedroom windows of the house of a neighbor, picked up a shoe, and whammed it through a pane of glass across the narrow space that separated the two houses. Glass tinkled into the bedroom occupied by a retired engraver named Bodwell and his wife. Bodwell had been for some years in rather a bad way and was subject to mild "attacks." Most everybody we knew or lived near had *some* kind of attacks.

It was now about two o'clock of a moonless night; clouds hung black and low. Bodwell was at the window in a minute, shouting, frothing a little, shaking his fist. "We'll sell the house and go back to Peoria," we could hear Mrs. Bodwell saying. It was some time before mother "got through" to Bodwell. "Burglars!" she shouted. "Burglars in the house!" Herman and I hadn't dared to tell her that it was not burglars but ghosts, for she was even more afraid of ghosts than of burglars. Bodwell at first thought that she meant there were burglars in his house, but finally he quieted down and called the police for us over an extension phone by his bed. After he had disappeared from the window, mother suddenly made as if to throw another shoe, not because there was further need of it but, as she later explained, because the thrill of heaving a shoe through a window glass had enormously taken her fancy. I prevented her.

The police were on hand in a commendably short time: a Ford sedan full of them, two on motorcycles, and a patrol wagon with about eight in it and a few reporters. They began banging at our front door. Flashlights shot streaks of gleam up and down the walls, across the yard, down the walk between our house and Bodwell's. "Open up!" cried a hoarse voice. "We're men from Headquarters!" I wanted to go down and let them in, since there they were, but mother wouldn't hear of it. "You haven't a stitch on," she pointed out. "You'd catch your death." I wound the towel around me again. Finally the cops put their shoulders to our big heavy front door with its thick beveled glass and broke it in: I could hear a rending of wood and a splash of glass on the floor of the hall. Their lights played all over the living-room and crisscrossed nervously in the dining-room, stabbed into hallways, shot up the front stairs and finally up the back. They caught me standing in my towel at the top. A heavy policeman bounded up the steps. "Who are you?" he demanded. "I live here," I said. "Well, whattsa matta, ya hot?" he asked. It was, as a matter of fact, cold; I went to my room and pulled on some trousers. On my way out, a cop stuck a gun into my ribs. "Whatta you doin' here?" he demanded. "I live here," I said.

The officer in charge reported to mother. "No sign of nobody, lady," he said. "Musta got away—whatt'd he look like?" "There were two or three of them," mother said, "whooping and carrying on and slamming doors." "Funny," said the cop. "All ya windows and doors was locked on the inside tight as a tick."

Downstairs, we could hear the tromping of the other police. Police were all over the place; doors were yanked open, drawers were yanked open, windows were shot up and pulled down, furniture fell with dull thumps. A half-dozen policemen emerged out of the darkness of the front hallway upstairs. They began to ransack the floor: pulled beds away from walls, tore clothes off hooks in the closets, pulled suitcases and boxes off shelves. One of them found an old zither that Roy had won in a pool tournament. "Looky here, Joe," he said, strumming it with a big paw. The cop named Joe took it and turned it over. "What is it?" he asked me. "It's an old zither our guinea pig used to sleep on," I said. It was true that a pet guinea pig we once had would never sleep anywhere except on the zither, but I should never have said so. Joe and the other cop looked at me a long time. They put the zither back on a shelf.

"No sign o' nuthin'," said the cop who had first spoken to mother. "This guy," he explained to the others, jerking a thumb at me, "was nekked. The lady seems historical." They all nodded, but said nothing; just looked at me. In the small silence we all heard a creaking in the attic. Grandfather was turning over in bed. "What's 'at?" snapped Joe. Five or six cops sprang for the attic door before I could intervene or explain. I realized that it would be bad if they burst in on grandfather unannounced, or even announced. He was going through a phase in which he believed that General Meade's men, under steady hammering by Stonewall Jackson, were beginning to retreat and even desert.

When I got to the attic, things were pretty confused. Grandfather had evidently jumped to the conclusion that the police were deserters from Meade's army, trying to hide away in his attic. He bounded out of bed wearing a long flannel nightgown over long woolen underwear, a nightcap, and a leather jacket around his chest. The cops must have realized at once that the indignant white-haired old man belonged in the house, but they had no chance to say so. "Back, ye cowardly dogs!" roared grandfather. "Back t' the lines, ye goddam lily-livered cattle!" With that, he fetched the officer who found the zither a flat-handed smack alongside his head that sent him sprawling. The others beat a retreat, but not fast enough; grandfather grabbed Zither's gun from its holster and let fly. The report seemed to crack the rafters; smoke filled the attic. A cop cursed and shot his hand to his shoulder. Somehow, we all finally got downstairs again and locked the door against the old gentleman. He fired once or twice more in the darkness and then went back to bed. "That was grandfather," I explained to Joe, out of breath. "He thinks you're deserters." "I'll say he does," said Joe.

The cops were reluctant to leave without getting their hands on somebody besides grandfather; the night had been distinctly a defeat for them. Further-more, they obviously didn't like the "layout;" something looked—and I can see their viewpoint—phony. They began to poke into things again. A re-porter, a thin-faced, wispy man, came up to me. I had put on one of mother's blouses, not being able to find anything else. The reporter looked at me with mingled suspicion and interest. "Just what the hell is the real lowdown here, Bud?" he asked. I decided to be frank with him. "We had ghosts," I said. He gazed at me a long time as if I were a slot machine into which he had, without results, dropped a nickel. Then he walked away. The cops followed him, the one grandfather shot holding his now-bandaged arm, cursing and blaspheming. "I'm gonna get my gun back from that old bird," said the zither-cop. "Yeh," said Joe. "You—and who else?" I told them I would bring it to the station house the next day.

"What was the matter with that one policeman?" mother asked, after they had gone. "Grandfather shot him," I said. "What for?" she demanded. I told her he was a deserter. "Of all things!" said mother. "He was such a nice-looking young man."

Grandfather was fresh as a daisy and full of jokes at breakfast next morning.

We thought at first he had forgotten all about what had happened, but he hadn't. Over his third cup of coffee, he glared at Herman and me. "What was the idee of all them cops tarryhootin' round the house last night?" he demanded. He had us there.

SECTION TWELVE

A GNASHING OF HUMORISTS

This section displays the pleasures of ill humor. When most people are feeling testy, churlish, fed up, at the end of their rope, in high dudgeon, sick and tired of this, that or the other, disgusted, repelled, outraged by the insolence of life and society's insults, and, in general, so put upon that they are not going to take it anymore, what can they do? Grin and bear it, that's what.

Not the humorist. The humorist thrives on the affronts and assaults with which the world constantly bedevils common humanity. Events that leave the rest of us impotent to do anything but gnash our teeth empower the humorist to gnash his typewriter. This is getting your own back with a vengeance against an insufferable world, and what a satisfaction it must be. When hostile steam can be released with an acid smile, who could ever need psychiatry's musty comfort?

The pieces here are mostly the products of the humorous temperament at the end of its patience. Somebody is enraged by advertising that insults his intelligence, somebody else by airline pilots who never shut up, someone else by people who keep telling him it's perfectly natural for humans to fly.

S. J. PERELMAN

"Sauce for the Gander"

Every so often, when business slackens up in the bowling alley and the other pin boys are hunched over their game of bezique, I like to exchange my sweatshirt for a crisp white surgical tunic, polish up my optical mirror, and examine the corset advertisements in the New York *Herald Tribune* rotogravure section and the various women's magazines. It must be made clear at the outset that my motives are the purest and my curiosity that of the scientific research worker rather than the sex maniac. Of course, I can be broken down under cross-examination; I like a trim ankle as well as anyone, but once I start scrubbing up and adjusting the operative mask, Materia Medica comes in the door and Betty Grable flies out the window.

God knows how the convention ever got started, but if it is true that the camera never lies, a foundation garment or a girdle stimulates the fair sex to a point just this side of madness. The little ladies are always represented with their heads thrown back in an attitude of fierce desire, arms upflung to an unseen deity as though swept along in some Dionysian revel. If you hold your ear close enough to the printed page, you can almost hear the throbbing of the temple drums and the chant of the votaries. Those sultry, heavy-lidded glances, those tempestuous, Corybantic gestures of abandon—what magic property is there in an ordinary silk-and-Lastex bellyband to cause a housewife to behave like Little Egypt?

Perhaps the most curious mutation of the corset advertisement is the transformation, or clinical type, consisting of two photographs. The first shows a rather bedraggled young matron in a gaping, misshapen girdle at least half a dozen sizes too large for her, cringing under the cool inspection of a trained nurse and several friends. Judging from the flowers and the tea service, the hostess has invited her neighbors in to deride her physique, for they are exclaiming in unison, "Ugh, my dear—you've got *lordosis* [unlovely bulge and sagging backline]!'' The second photograph, naturally, depicts the miracles wrought by the proper girdle, which, in addition to the benefits promised in the text, seems to have removed the crow's feet from under the subject's eyes, marcelled her hair, reupholstered the divan, and papered the walls.

It strikes me that, by contrast, the manufacturers of dainty underthings for men have been notably colorless in their advertising. The best they are able to afford are those static scenes in which four or five grim-jawed industrialists stand about a locker room in their shorts scowling at ticker tape, testing mashie niblicks, and riffling through first editions. It may be only sexual chauvinism on my part, but I submit that the opportunities for merchandising male lingerie are limitless. I offer at least one of them in crude dramatic form to blaze a trail for future copywriters.

(Scene: The consulting room of Dr. Terence Fitch, an eminent Park Avenue specialist. The furniture consists of a few costly, unusual pieces, such as a kidney-shaped writing desk, a pancreas-shaped chair, and a spleen-shaped spittoon. As the curtain rises, Miss Mayo, the nurse, is at the telephone-shaped telephone.)

> MISS MAYO *(into phone)*— Hello, Dr. Volney? This is Miss Mayo at Dr. Fitch's office. The Doctor is forwarding you his analysis of Mr. Tichenor's under-wear problems; you should have it in the morning. . . . Not at all.
> *(As she hangs up, Dr. Fitch enters, thoughtfully stroking his Vandyke beard. He is followed by Freedley, a haggard, middle-aged patient, knotting his tie.)*
> DR. FITCH— Sit down, Freedley. . . . Oh, this is Miss Mayo. She's a niece of the Mayo brothers, out West.
> FREEDLEY *(wanly)*— How do you do, Miss Mayo? I've read grand things about your uncles.
> MISS MAYO— Not mine, you haven't. They've been in Folsom the last three years for breaking and entering. *(She exits.)*
> DR. FITCH *(seating himself)*— All right now, Freedley, suppose you tell me your symptoms.
> FREEDLEY— But I just told them to you.
> DR. FITCH— You did?
> FREEDLEY— Sure, not ten minutes ago.
> DR. FITCH— Well, repeat them. *(Angrily)* You don't suppose I have time to listen to every crackpot who comes in here bleating about his troubles, do you?
> FREEDLEY *(humbly)*— No, sir. Well, it's just that I have this stuffy, uncomfort-able sensation all the time.
> DR. FITCH— That's the way a head cold usually starts. *(Scribbling)* You're to take fifteen of these tablets forty times a day, or forty of them fifteen times a day, whichever is more convenient.

FREEDLEY— It's not my nose or throat, Doctor. I get it mostly around the hips and the small of my back.

DR. FITCH *(testily)*— Of course, of course. That's where it's localized. Now, I also want you to get hold of a tonic. I forgot the name of it, but it's about thirty dollars a bottle. The clerk'll know.

FREEDLEY— Will I feel better after I take it?

DR. FITCH *(coldly)*— I'm a physician, Freedley, not an astrologer. If you want a horoscope, there's a gypsy tearoom over on Lexington Avenue.

FREEDLEY *(plaintively)*— Gee, Dr. Fitch, this thing's got me crazy. I can't keep my mind on my work—

DR. FITCH— Work? Humph. Most of *my* patients have private incomes. What do you do?

FREEDLEY— I'm with the Bayonne Bag & String Company—assistant office manager.

DR. FITCH— Getting along pretty well there?

FREEDLEY *(pitifully)*— I was until this started. Now Mr. Borvis keeps riding me. He says I'm like a person in a fog.

DR. FITCH— That bulging, oppressive condition—notice it mostly when you're sitting down, don't you?

FREEDLEY— Why, how on earth can you tell, Doctor?

DR. FITCH— We medical men have ways of knowing these things. *(Gravely)* Well, Freedley, I can help you, but only if you face the facts.

FREEDLEY *(quavering)*— W-what is it, sir?

DR. FITCH— Your union suit is too big for you.

FREEDLEY *(burying his face in his hands)*— Oh, my God!

DR. FITCH— There, there. Buck up, old man. We mustn't give up hope.

FREEDLEY *(whimpering)*— But you might be mistaken—it's just a diagnosis.

DR. FITCH *(sternly)*— The fluoroscope never lies, Freedley. When I looked at you in there a moment ago, I saw almost five yards of excess fabric bunched around the mid-section.

FREEDLEY *(wildly)*— It's bound to shrink after I send it to the laundry! Maybe Velma can take a tuck in it!

DR. FITCH— That's only an evasion. *(Pressing a button)* It's lucky you came to me in time. If the public only knew the annual toll exacted by ponderous, loosely fitting underwear—*(Miss Mayo enters)* Miss Mayo, get me a sterile union suit, size thirty-eight, porous-knit.

FREEDLEY *(licking his lips)*— What—what are you going to do?

DR. FITCH *(soothingly)*— Now, this won't hurt a bit. We'll just slip it on for size—

FREEDLEY— I won't! *I won't!* *(He cowers into a corner, flailing at Dr. Fitch and Miss Mayo as they close in on him. They pinion his arms tightly, thrust him into an adjoining dressing room, and fling the union suit after him.)*

MISS MAYO *(in a low voice)*— Do you think he's got a chance, Doctor?

DR. FITCH— Hard to say, poor bugger. Did you feel those enlarged folds of material on his back?

MISS MAYO— He may have a blanket and some sheets hidden on him.

DR. FITCH— You can't tell. They get cunning in the later stages.

(The door-shaped door of the dressing room opens and Freedley re-enters, a changed man. He is portly, well groomed, a connoisseur of fine horseflesh and pretty women, but withal a man of keen business judgment. He wears a pearl-gray Homburg, Chesterfield overcoat, and spats, carries a gold-headed cane, a hot bird, and a cold bottle.)

FREEDLEY *(booming)*— Well, Fitch, my boy, can't waste any more time jawing with you. I've got to cut along to that board meeting. Just merged Bayonne Bag & String with Consolidated Twine, you know!

DR. FITCH— Er—that was rather sudden, wasn't it?

FREEDLEY— Can't stand beating about the bush. Think in telegrams, that's my motto. Want to know my secret, Fitch? I've worked hard and I've played hard. And I've drunk a quart of whiskey every day of my life!

DR. FITCH— Well, remember what I said. Don't overdo it.

FREEDLEY *(roaring)*— Stuff and nonsense! Why, I'm as sound as a nut. Got the appetite of a boy of twenty, sleep like a top, and I'll outdance a youngster any day! *(To demonstrate, he catches up Miss Mayo, whirls her around giddily, and, flushed with exertion, drops dead. The Doctor and his nurse exchange slow, sidelong glances.)*

MISS MAYO— Well, I guess science still has a lot to learn.

DR. FITCH *(curtly)*— None of your god-damned lip. Drag him out and show in the next patient. *(He turns back to his desk, stroking his Vandyke more thoughtfully than ever.)*

Curtain

FRED ALLEN

Letter to John J. McCarthy

march
14th
1941

mr. john j. mccarthy
fire department headquarters
municipal building
new york city
dear mr. mccarthy—

    mr. kershaw, of the texas company, has spoken to me about your kind invitation to dampen the ardor of four thousand uniformed men, who will attend the holy name communion breakfast on april 20th, through subjecting said four thousand uniformed men to an outburst of oratorical pyrotechnics using my mouth as the rocket base.

    unfortunately, my radio chores keep me going sixteen and more hours daily seven days per week. this flagrant violation of the existing labor laws not only keeps me in hot water with the wagner act officials but the many hours required for the preparation and presentation of the weekly radio programs take up the slack in my days which might otherwise be devoted to writing and memorizing talks to be given at assorted gala functions. for this reason i am compelled to forego appearances at the many festive events to which i am invited.

    I realize that it would improve my social status to be found in good company for a change. i know that the mayor's speech would be an inspiration to me in my future work. i have heard that the combination breakfast at the astor is excellent. but, even these temptations on the one hand will not shorten my days nor lighten my labors on the other. i am sure that if you were out squirting a hose sixteen and eighteen hours a day you couldn't find time to operate a sideline that involved watering lawns.

    sorry that i cannot attend but know you will appreciate my position. you can get even. if i ever have a fire you can send your regrets. i will understand. sincerely . . .

fred allen

P. J. O'Rourke

"The Fundamentals of Contemporary Courtesy"

Good breeding consists in concealing how much we think of ourselves and how little we think of the other person.

—Samuel Clemens

The purpose of old-fashioned manners was to avoid attracting attention. The reason for this was that old-fashioned manners were possessed by only a few hundred rich people. These few hundred rich people didn't want all the hundreds of millions of poor people to notice who had the money. If the rich, polite few started attracting attention, the poor, rude many might get together and commit mayhem the way they did in Russia. The heck with that, said rich people.

But nowadays there are hundreds of millions of rich people, and poor people have been pretty much rendered harmless by drugs and sleeping on sidewalks. Plus it's getting so you can't tell rich from poor anyway, what with Nigerian illegal immigrants selling Rolexes on street corners and Gloria Vanderbilt putting her name on blue jean behinds. The problem modern people have is trying to be special. Therefore, the purpose of modern manners is to attract as much attention as possible.

GREETINGS

The importance of conspicuousness in modern life has led to the phenomenon of "greeting inflation." Once, even the closest friends greeted each other with a polite bow. Today such reticence is almost extinct. A loud

"Sweetheart," a slap on the back, chuck on the arm, tousling of hair, and a cheerful "Have a nice day!" will do if you don't know a person at all. But if you have even the slightest acquaintance with someone, it is usual to embrace him physically no matter what the circumstances. If you're carrying a briefcase or package, just throw it into the gutter. This makes a dramatic gesture of good fellowship.

If you actually know someone's name, twin kisses on both cheeks are expected and should be accompanied by some highly original term of endearment. "I love you" or "You're my best friend" isn't nearly strong enough. In California, where manners are more modern than anywhere else, people say, "I'd murder my parents to have lunch with you" or even "I'm so glad to see you that I'm going to give you gross points in my new movie." (The latter statement is a lie, by the way.)

REBUFFS

At one time there was not only an etiquette of greeting people but also an etiquette of not greeting them. This ranged in degree from the coldly formal bow to the "cut direct." The cut direct was delivered by looking right at a person and not acknowledging his acquaintance or even his existence. This is no longer done. It has been replaced by the lawsuit. Opposing parties in a lawsuit (and other enemies) are expected to greet each other like lovers—especially now when it's so fashionable for hostesses to invite people who hate each other to the same dinners. If the enmity is minor or philosophical in nature, argument—or, better, tableware throwing—may resume after a drink or two. But if the hatred is deep and well occasioned, the mutual detestors are expected to chat amicably throughout the evening.

HAT, CANE, AND GLOVES

What to do with your hat and cane is a perennial awkwardness when greeting people. If the cane is necessary, it should be replaced with a crutch, which will gain you much more sympathy.

A hat should be taken off when you greet a lady and left off for the rest of your life. Nothing looks more stupid than a hat. When you put on a hat you are surrendering to the same urge that makes children wear mouse ears at Disney World or drunks wear lampshades at parties. Wearing a hat implies that you are bald if you are a man and that your hair is dirty if you are a woman. Every style of hat is identified with some form of undesirable (derby = corrupt ward heeler; fedora = male model; top hat = rich bum; pillbox

= Kennedy wife, et cetera). Furthermore, the head is symbolically identified with the sexual organs, so that when you walk down the street wearing a hat, anyone who has the least knowledge of psychology will see you as having . . . a problem. A hat should only be worn if you are employed as a baseball player or are hunting ducks in the rain.

Gloves present another problem, especially when shaking hands. Men must always remove their gloves before a handshake. There is a good reason for this. A man can be very accurately judged by his hand. A soft hand indicates a lazy, unemployed person. A hard, calloused hand shows that a person is an ignorant and dull manual laborer. A cold, clammy hand means that a person is guilty and nervous. And a warm, dry hand means a person is incapable of feeling guilt and has the nerve to pull anything on you. A woman never removes her gloves. There's a good reason for this, too. A woman can also be very accurately judged by her hand, and why would she want to be?

The Handshake

Despite the popularity of more effusive forms of greeting, the handshake is omnipresent. It is now extended to everyone—men, women, old people, young children, and, especially, pet dogs.

It's important to develop a limp and affected handshake. A firm, hearty handshake gives a good first impression, and you'll never be forgiven if you don't live up to it. Also, a firm, hearty handshake inspires confidence in others. People who go around inspiring confidence in others are probably looking to sell them something. You don't want to appear to be that sort.

Farewells

Much more important than greeting people is saying good-bye to them or getting them to say good-bye to you or getting rid of them somehow anyway. The one thing that can be safely said about the great majority of people is that we don't want them around. Be sincere and forthright about the problem. Take the person you want to get rid of aside and tell him he has to leave because the people you're with hate him. Say, ''I'm sorry, Fred, but you can't sit down with us. Molly and Bill Dinnersworth hate you because you're so much smarter and more successful than they are.''

This is nasty and flattering at the same time. And it makes life more interesting, which, if you're too sophisticated to just want attention, is the point of existence.

I n   P u b l i c

If you don't manage to get rid of everyone and end up having to go somewhere with a group of people, make sure the couples are separated and that each partner is escorted by somebody new. This will give everyone something different to fight about later.

Generally speaking, a man is supposed to walk to the left of a woman and also keep himself between her and the curb. Of course, it is frequently impossible to do both. But the great thinkers of all ages have been unanimous in their admiration of paradoxes.

Unless he is helping her into an ambulance or a paddy wagon, a man is never supposed to touch a woman in public. That is, he shouldn't if he's married to the woman. Nothing is more deleterious to the spirit of romance than watching a married couple hold hands.

If a man is walking down the street with two women, he should keep them both on his right and not appear between them like an acrobat taking a bow. Every authority on etiquette mentions this precept. But what no authority on etiquette mentions is how a man can manage to get two women in the first place. The best idea is for him to convince his wife or girlfriend to talk a friend of hers into a threesome. Most likely the result will be physically and emotionally disastrous. But everyone will get something juicy to tell the psychiatrist and something to romanticize in diary or memoirs. Again, life is made more interesting.

It's no longer *de rigueur* for a man to burden himself with anything heavy that a woman is carrying, especially not a mortgage or someone else's baby. Nor should a man necessarily hold a door for a woman, unless it is a revolving door. It's not good manners to hold a revolving door, but it is lots of fun when other people are trapped inside.

R e s t a u r a n t s ,   T a x i c a b s ,   a n d   t h e   T h e a t e r

When entering a restaurant, a man should allow the woman to precede him to their seats. This lets her find a friend whose table she can stand at and chat for half an hour while the man gets a chance to glimpse the prices on the menu and has a clear shot to bolt for the door when he sees those prices.

A wise woman allows a man to enter a taxicab ahead of her so she can slam his hand in the door if he's been acting like an ass.

At the theater, concert, or ballet, a man allows a woman to take her seat first. He then holds her coat on his lap, along with his own coat, her purse, her umbrella, both programs, and any other personal effects. Safely hidden behind this mound of belongings, he can go to sleep.

The Importance of Being on Time

Whatever type of event you're attending, it's important to be on time. Being on time should not be confused with being prompt. Being prompt means arriving at the beginning. Being on time means arriving at the most interesting moment. Excepting love affairs, that moment is rarely the beginning.

"On time" is between midnight and four A.M. in New York, even for an eight o'clock play. Between midnight and four A.M. the actors will be getting drunk in a bar, and they'll be much more fun to talk to than when they're up on the stage.

In most other urban areas, "on time" is between twenty minutes and an hour late. This gives everyone else time to be late, too, and they'll appreciate it.

In the country being on time more nearly approximates being prompt. But don't overdo it. Being early is an unpardonable sin. If you are early, you'll witness the last-minute confusion and panic that always attend making anything seem effortlessly gracious.

In California, "on time" doesn't mean anything at all. An appointment for a meeting at three o'clock on Tuesday indicates there won't be a meeting and there might not be a Tuesday. Few words and no numbers have any meaning west of the Nevada border.

At Home

One popular way to avoid the problem of being on time is to stay at home and conduct your life over the telephone. This is very chic in New York. Even New Yorkers who occasionally go outdoors have taken to telephoning every person they know once a day and twice if any of them has anything awful to say about the others.

Living over the telephone has a number of advantages. It saves on cab fare and clothing budgets, and love affairs can be conducted without the bother of contraception or hairdressers. In fact, with judicious use of answering machines, a love affair can be conducted without the bother of ever talking to the loved one.

Making Up in Public

It's bad manners to apply cosmetics in public. It reminds people that you need them.

Smoking in Public

Smoking was once subject to all sorts of polite restrictions, but now it's just illegal. Therefore, there's only one remaining rule of etiquette about smoking in public: make sure you don't smoke anywhere else. Smoking is an inexpensive and convenient means of showing fashionable contempt for middle-class rules and regulations. Smoking also looks good. People who don't smoke have a terrible time finding something polite to do with their lips. But, when no one's around to see you, it doesn't matter what you do so there's no point in smoking then.

If someone asks you not to smoke, tell him you have no intentions of living to be an embittered old person. But thank him for his concern.

Nonchalance

Nonchalance about health and well-being is what gives smoking its charm. That same nonchalance is at the heart of all really good manners. The most fundamental lesson of etiquette is ''be unconcerned.'' Proper behavior means always giving the appearance of unperturbed grace. This appearance is much easier to achieve if you really *don't* care about anything. And this is why people always seem to be on their best behavior right before they commit suicide.

AMBROSE BIERCE

Excerpts from The Devil's Dictionary

Aborigines, n. Persons of little worth found cumbering the soil of a newly discovered country. They soon cease to cumber; they fertilize.

Alone, adj. In bad company.

Ambition, n. An overmastering desire to be vilified by enemies while living and made ridiculous by friends when dead.

Applause, n. The echo of a platitude.

Architect, n. One who drafts a plan of your house, and plans a draft of your money.

Bride, n. A woman with a fine prospect of happiness behind her.

Connoisseur, n. A specialist who knows everything about something and nothing about anything else.

    An old wine-bibber having been smashed in a railway collision, some wine was poured upon his lips to revive him. "Pauillac, 1873," he murmured and died.

Egotist, n. A person of low taste, more interested in himself than in me.

Laziness, n. Unwarranted repose of manner in a person of low degree.

Liar, n. A lawyer with a roving commission.

Man, n. An animal so lost in rapturous contemplation of what he thinks he is as to overlook what he indubitably ought to be. His chief occupation is extermination of other animals and his own species, which, however, multiplies with such insistent rapidity as to infest the whole habitable earth and Canada.

Miss, n. A title with which we brand unmarried women to indicate that they are in the market. Miss, Missis, (Mrs.) and Mister (Mr.) are the three most distinctly disagreeable words in the language, in sound and sense. Two are corruptions of Mistress, the other of Master. In the general abolition of social titles in this our country they miraculously escaped to plague us. If we must have them let us be consistent and give one to the unmarried man. I venture to suggest Mush, abbreviated to Mh.

Orphan, n. A living person whom death has deprived of the power of filial ingratitude . . .

Pedigree, n. The known part of the route from an arboreal ancestor with a swim bladder to an urban descendant with a cigarette.

Piety, n. Reverence for the Supreme Being, based upon His supposed resemblance to man.

Platitude, n. The fundamental element and special glory of popular literature. A thought that snores in words that smoke. The wisdom of a million fools in the diction of a dullard. A fossil sentiment in artificial rock. A moral without the fable. All that is mortal of a departed truth. A demi-tasse of milk-and-morality. The Pope's-nose of a featherless peacock. A jelly-fish withering on the shore of the sea of thought. The cackle surviving the egg. A desiccated epigram.

Positive, adj. Mistaken at the top of one's voice.

Pray, v. To ask that the laws of the universe be annulled in behalf of a single petitioner confessedly unworthy.

Reliquary, n. A receptacle for such sacred objects as pieces of the true cross, short-ribs of saints, the ears of Balaam's ass, the lung of the cock that called Peter to repentance and so forth. Reliquaries are commonly of metal, and provided with a lock to prevent the contents from coming out and performing miracles at unseasonable times. A feather from the wing of the Angel of the Annunciation once escaped during a sermon in Saint Peter's and so tickled the noses of the congregation that they woke and sneezed with great vehemence three times each. It is related in the "Gesta Sanctorum" that a sacristan in the Canterbury cathedral surprised the head of Saint Dennis in the library. Reprimanded by its stern custodian, it explained that it was seeking a body of doctrine. This unseemly levity so enraged the diocesan that the offender was publicly anathematized, thrown into the Stour and replaced by another head of Saint Dennis, brought from Rome.

Self-esteem, n. An erroneous appraisement.

MIKE ROYKO

"Fear of Flying Isn't Groundless"

The moment I saw that *Newsweek* magazine's cover story was about phobias, I thumbed through looking for the part about mine.

I skimmed past the part about the agoraphobic (fear of spaces) lady who had come out of her apartment only three times in sixty-one years. And the gephyrophobic (bridges) man whose wife puts him in the car trunk when they cross a dreaded span. And all the other examples of phobics who fear snakes, shopping malls, strangers, eating in public, dogs, germs, vehicles or darkness.

Then I found it. Aerophobia: the fear of flying. My own, personal phobia.

As I've probably mentioned before, I have this thing about airplanes. I've been on a plane only once in the past twenty-five years. Actually, I've been on two, but I don't count the second one because I scrambled off before the stewardess closed the door.

Since I won't fly, naturally I'm interested in the subject of not flying, and I read all the articles about it—especially those that suggest a remedy.

Just once, I'd like to read something that got it right. And, I'm sorry to say, the current *Newsweek* article didn't succeed.

It said: "The fear of flying is usually experienced as the fear of being trapped inside an airplane. It is a kind of claustrophobia of the soul that has very little to do with the real dangers of air travel."

What nonsense. It has nothing to do with being trapped inside an airplane. Or any "claustrophobia of the soul," whatever that means.

I don't mind at all being trapped inside an airplane. I could get on a plane right now, sit down and be totally relaxed, comfortable, without a trace of fear. *As long as the thing stayed on the ground, where it belongs.*

That's the part that bothers me—not being inside that tin tube. But being inside of it when it is hurtling through the air at the speed of a bullet, four or five miles above the nearest rooftop.

Over the years, I've tried to explain that to those who urge me to fly or try to get to the root of my resistance.

I tried going to a shrink. He spent hours listening to me talk about all the things that can happen to an airplane. Birds flying into the jet intake. Mechanics with hangovers forgetting to tighten bolts. Guys in the control tower having nervous breakdowns or sniffing glue. Pilots with suicidal tendencies. Some passenger jumping up and saying: "Take me to Havana or we go boom!"

When I finished our last session, nothing had changed, except the psychiatrist had become so scared that he wouldn't fly either. And after all I did for him, he still sent me a bill.

Once an airline sent a public relations man over with a briefcase full of statistics that were meant to be reassuring.

He said things like: "You know, the chances of your being killed while crossing the street are much greater than of being killed in a plane."

I said: "Yeah? When I cross the street, I look both ways first. If I look both ways on an airplane, will that prevent the pilot from running into the side of a mountain?"

He said: "Do you realize that there are more dangers of being killed or injured in an accident in your own home than on an airplane?"

I said: "Yeah? Well, I've never landed my home in a swamp at two hundred miles an hour."

He said: "You are in far more danger while driving your car."

I said: "When I get ice on *my* windshield, I stop and scrape it off. Can your pilot do *that*?"

When I finished with him, he wouldn't ride an escalator.

But to get back to the *Newsweek* article. It provided possible cures, but they were the usual ones, such as the group therapy sessions run by the airlines during which they teach you how to relax and tell you how safe airplanes are.

A pilot who runs one of the programs described the fear this way: "When people go on an airplane journey, it's very similar to the journey of life."

More nonsense. I don't journey through my life at 650 miles an hour, 26,000 feet above the wilderness of Ohio, with my stomach in my mouth.

That public relations man tried to get me to join such a class. I asked him: "Do a lot of people do that?" He said: "Oh, sure. You know, there are millions of people who feel the way you do." I said: "They can't all be wrong."

I've tried all the remedies. The only one that worked was when a friend in Washington, upon hearing that I was taking a train back to Chicago, suggested that I drink martinis until I was ready to ride an airplane. It worked. After only nine large martinis, I rode the plane. The only trouble is, after nine martinis I'd also be willing to ride a bull or a python.

I even tried hypnotism once, but I don't think the hypnotist was very good. I told him that I wanted hypnotism to help me fly. When he put me under, I flapped my arms and quacked like a duck.

So I've given up. And maybe it is not a bad idea. According to the *Newsweek* article, Ronald Reagan didn't launch his political career until he overcame his dread of flying. That means that if he hadn't overcome it, he wouldn't be President today.

Who says phobias are bad?

FRAN LEBOWITZ

"Manners"

I am not a callous sort. I believe that all people should have warm clothing, sufficient food, and adequate shelter. I do feel, however, that unless they are willing to behave in an acceptable manner they should bundle up, chow down, and stay home.

I speak here not only of etiquette, for while etiquette is surely a factor, acceptable behavior is comprised of a good deal more. It demands, for instance, that the general public refrain from starting trends, overcoming inhibitions, or developing hidden talents. It further requires acceptance of the fact that the common good is usually not very and that there is indeed such a thing as getting carried away with democracy. Oppression and/or repression are not without their charms nor freedom and/or license their drawbacks. This can clearly be seen in the following chart.

| THE BY-PRODUCTS OF OPPRESSION AND/OR REPRESSION | THE BY-PRODUCTS OF FREEDOM AND/OR LICENSE |

WOMEN

1. Well-kept fingernails	1. The word *chairperson*
2. Homemade cookies	2. The acceptance of construction boots as suitable attire for members of the fair sex
3. A guarantee that at least one segment of the population could be relied upon to display a marked distaste for strenuous physical activity	3. Girl ministers
	4. The male centerfold
	5. Erica Jong
4. The distinct probability that even a small gathering would yield at least one person who knew how to respond properly to a wedding invitation	
5. Real coffee	

JEWS

1. Highly entertaining standup comedians	1. Progressive nursery schools
2. The Stage Delicatessen	2. Frozen bagels
3. A guarantee that at least one segment of the population could be relied upon to display a marked distaste for strenuous physical activity	3. The Upper West Side
	4. The notion that it is appropriate for a writer to surrender a percentage of his income to an agent
4. The development and perfection of theatrical law as a flourishing profession	5. Erica Jong
5. Interesting slang expressions, particularly those used to describe Gentiles	

BLACKS

1. Jazz
2. The provision of the southern portion of the United States with a topic of conversation
3. Tap dancing
4. The preservation in our culture of a lively interest in revenge
5. Amos 'n' Andy
6. Interesting slang expressions, particularly those used to describe white people

1. Strawberry wine
2. Negro accountants
3. Inventive forms of handshaking
4. Open admissions
5. Sammy Davis, Jr.
6. The Symbionese Liberation Army

TEEN-AGERS

1. The thrill of illicit drinking
2. Sexual denial and the resultant development of truly exciting sexual fantasies
3. The swank of juvenile delinquency
4. The glamour of alienation

1. Strawberry wine
2. Easy sexual access and the resultant premature boredom
3. Social commitment
4. People who may very well just be discovering symbolist poetry being allowed to vote

HOMOSEXUALS

1. Precision theatrical dancing
2. Sarcasm
3. Art
4. Literature
5. Real gossip
6. The amusing notion that *Who's Afraid of Virginia Woolf?* was really about two men   ·

1. *A Chorus Line*
2. Amyl nitrate
3. Leather underwear
4. Lesbian mothers
5. Heterosexual hairdressers
6. The amusing notion that *Who's Afraid of Virginia Woolf?* was really about a man and a woman

Two basic steps must be taken in order to reach the eventual goal of acceptable behavior. The first (which I assume you have already accomplished) is a careful perusal of the above chart. The second is ridding oneself of certain popular and harmful misconceptions, as follows:

It is not true that there is dignity in all work. Some jobs are definitely better than others. It is not hard to tell the good jobs from the bad. People who have good jobs are happy, rich, and well dressed. People who have bad jobs are unhappy, poor and use meat extenders. Those who seek dignity in the type of work that compels them to help hamburgers are certain to be disappointed. Also to be behaving badly.

There is no such thing as inner peace. There is only nervousness or death. Any attempt to prove otherwise constitutes unacceptable behavior.

Very few people possess true artistic ability. It is therefore both unseemly and unproductive to irritate the situation by making an effort. If you have a burning, restless urge to write or paint, simply eat something sweet and the feeling will pass. Your life story would not make a good book. Do not even try.

All God's children are not beautiful. Most of God's children are, in fact, barely presentable. The most common error made in matters of appearance is the belief that one should disdain the superficial and let the true beauty of one's soul shine through. If there are places on your body where this is a possibility, you are not attractive—you are leaking.

TOM WOLFE

"The Joggers' Prayer"

Almighty God, as we sail with pure aerobic grace and striped orthotic feet past the blind portals of our fellow citizens, past their chuck-roast lives and their necrotic cardiovascular systems and rusting hips and slipped discs and desiccated lungs, past their implacable inertia and inability to persevere and rise above the fully pensioned world they live in and to push themselves to the limits of their capacity and achieve the White Moment of slipping through the Wall, borne aloft on one's Third Wind, past their Cruisomatic cars and upholstered lawn mowers and their gummy-sweet children already at work like little fat factories producing arterial plaque, the more quickly to join their parents in their joyless bucket-seat landau ride toward the grave—help us, dear Lord, we beseech Thee, as we sail past this cold-lard desolation, to be big about it.

ARTHUR HOPPE

"The Waiting Game"

A major government commission predicted a surplus of 70,000 doctors by 1990 and warned this could mean detrimental changes to the present methods of practicing medicine.
                                                        —News item.

That doctor surplus on which the following piece is predicated—did it really occur, as predicted back in 1980? If so, the doctors have managed to conceal it, thus avoiding the patients' revenge happily anticipated here by Arthur Hoppe.

"Good afternoon. May I help you?"

"Yes, I'm Dr. Herbert Vamplew and I'm here to see a patient, Fred Frisbee, for his annual checkup."

"Oh, yes, I'm Mrs. Frisbee. Do you have an appointment, Doctor?"

"Yes, for one o'clock. I'm a few minutes early, I'm afraid."

"That's quite all right. Please have a seat in the living room and patient will be with you as soon as possible."

"Thank you. Excuse me, who are those other gentlemen in there?"

"Oh, that's Dr. Katz, Dr. Trevis and Dr. Clagenson. Patient feels you can't be too careful and he wants a second, third and fourth opinion. While you're waiting, will you please fill out this medical history form?"

"My medical history?"

"Yes, it asks where you attended medical school, what courses you took, honors, if any, and your financial assets in case of a malpractice suit. Then you might wish to browse through this copy of Liberty magazine. There's an interesting article predicting victory for Alf Landon."

"Mrs. Frisbee? Remember me, Mrs. Frisbee? I'm Dr. Vamplew and I've now been waiting an hour and a half to see the patient."

"Oh, we haven't forgotten you, Doctor. Patient is running a little late today. He got stuck in a sand trap on the 17th."

"Look here! I'm a very busy man and . . ."

"Of course, you are. But patient is with a doctor right now."

"How many doctors are ahead of me?"

"I do think maybe you're next. Why don't you follow me out here to this powder room? After I close the door, please remove your coat and put on this white medical jacket with the opening on the front and have a seat. Here's a copy of *War and Peace* to keep you occupied. I'm sure patient will be with you at any minute."

"Mrs. Frisbee, I've been in that powder room two hours and I'm not waiting another minute!"

"Oh, there you are, Dr. Vamplew. I was wondering where I put you. I'm so sorry, but patient was called away on an emergency. They needed a fourth for dominoes. But let's make another appointment, shall we? Let's see, patient can see you at 2 P.M. seven weeks from next Tuesday. How does that sound, doctor? Doctor? Doctor! Darn, now we'll need another new front door. These doctors just don't seem to understand how valuable a patient's time is these days."

Mark Twain

"Political Economy"

Political Economy is the basis of all good government.
The wisest men of all ages have brought to bear upon this
subject the—

[Here I was interrupted and informed that a stranger wished to see me down at the door. I went and confronted him, and asked to know his business, struggling all the time to keep a tight rein on my seething political-economy ideas, and not let them break away from me or get tangled in their harness. And privately I wished the stranger was in the bottom of the canal with a cargo of wheat on top of him. I was all in a fever, but he was cool. He said he was sorry to disturb me, but as he was passing he noticed that I needed some lightning-rods. I said, "Yes, yes—go on—what about it?" He said there was nothing about it, in particular—nothing except that he would like to put them up for me. I am new to housekeeping; have been used to hotels and boarding-houses all my life. Like anybody else of similar experience, I try to appear (to strangers) to be an old housekeeper; consequently I said in an offhand way that I had been intending for some time to have six or eight lightning-rods put up, but——The stranger started, and looked inquiringly at me, but I was serene. I thought that if I chanced to make any mistakes, he would not catch me by my countenance. He said he would rather have my custom than any man's in town. I said, "All right," and started off to wrestle with my great subject again, when he called me back and said it would be necessary to know exactly how many "points" I wanted to put up, what parts of the house I wanted them on, and what quality of rod I preferred. It was close quarters for a man not used to the exigencies of housekeeping; but I went through creditably, and he probably never suspected that I was a novice. I told him to put up eight "points," and put them all on the roof, and use the best quality of rod. He said he could furnish the "plain" article at 20 cents a foot; "coppered," 25 cents; "zinc-plated spiral-twist," at 30 cents, that would stop a streak of lightning any time, no matter where it was bound, and "render its errand harmless and its further progress apocryphal." I said apocryphal was no slouch of a word, emanating from the source it did, but, philology aside, I liked the spiral-twist and would take that brand. Then he said he *could* make two hundred and fifty feet answer; but to do it right, and make the best job in town of it, and attract the admiration of the just and the unjust alike, and compel all parties to say they never saw a more symmetrical and hypothetical display of lightning-rods since they were born, he supposed he really couldn't get along without four hundred, though he was not vindictive, and trusted he was willing to try. I said, go ahead and use four hundred, and make any kind of a job he pleased out of it, but let me get back to my work. So I got rid of him at last; and now, after half an hour spent in getting my train of political-economy thoughts coupled together again, I am ready to go on once more.]

> richest treasures of their genius, their experience of life, and their learning. The great lights of commercial jurisprudence, international confraternity, and bio-logical deviation, of all ages, all civilizations, and all nationalities, from Zo-roaster down to Horace Greeley, have——

[Here I was interrupted again, and required to go down and confer further with that lightning-rod man. I hurried off, boiling and surging with prodigious thoughts wombed in words of such majesty that each one of them was in itself a straggling procession of syllables that might be fifteen minutes passing a given point, and once more I confronted him——he so calm and sweet, I so hot and frenzied. He was standing in the contemplative attitude of the Colossus of Rhodes, with one foot on my infant tuberose, and the other among my pansies, his hands on his hips, his hat-brim tilted forward, one eye shut and the other gazing critically and admiringly in the direction of my principal chimney. He said now *there* was a state of things to make a man glad to be alive; and added, "I leave it to *you* if you ever saw anything more deliriously picturesque than eight lightning-rods on one chimney?" I said I had no present recollection of anything that transcended it. He said that in his opinion nothing on earth but Niagara Falls was superior to it in the way of natural scenery. All that was needed now, he verily believed, to make my house a perfect balm to the eye, was to kind of touch up the other chimneys a little, and thus "add to the generous *coup d'œil* a soothing uniformity of achievement which would allay the excitement naturally consequent upon the *coup d'état*." I asked him if he learned to talk out of a book, and if I could borrow it anywhere? He smiled pleasantly, and said that his manner of speaking was not taught in books, and that nothing but familiarity with lightning could enable a man to handle his conversational style with impunity. He then figured up an estimate, and said that about eight more rods scattered about my roof would about fix me right, and he guessed five hundred feet of stuff would do it; and added that the first eight had got a little the start of him, so to speak, and used up a mere trifle of material more than he had calculated on—a hundred feet or along there. I said I was in a dreadful hurry, and I wished we could get this business permanently mapped out, so that I could go on with my work. He said, "I *could* have put up those eight rods, and marched off about my business—some men *would* have done it. But no; I said to myself, this man is a stranger to me, and I will die before I'll wrong him; there ain't lightning-rods enough on that house, and for one I'll never stir out of my tracks till I've done as I would be done by, and told him so. Stranger, my duty is accomplished; if the recalcitrant and dephlogistic messenger of heaven strikes you—" "There, now, there," I said, "put on the other eight—add five hundred feet of spiral-twist—do anything and everything you want to do; but calm your sufferings, and try to keep your feelings where you can reach them with the dictionary. Meanwhile, if we understand each other now, I will go to work again."

I think I have been sitting here a full hour this time, trying to get back to where I was when my train of thought was broken up by the last interruption; but I believe I have accomplished it at last, and may venture to proceed again.]

wrestled with this great subject, and the greatest among them have found it a worthy adversary, and one that always comes up fresh and smiling after every throw. The great Confucius said that he would rather be a profound political economist than chief of police. Cicero frequently said that political economy was the grandest consummation that the human mind was capable of consuming; and even our own Greeley had said vaguely but forcibly that "Political—

[Here the lightning-rod man sent up another call for me. I went down in a state of mind bordering on impatience. He said he would rather have died than interrupt me, but when he was employed to do a job, and that job was expected to be done in a clean, workmanlike manner, and when it was finished and fatigue urged him to seek the rest and recreation he stood so much in need of, and he was about to do it, but looked up and saw at a glance that all the calculations had been a little out, and if a thunder-storm were to come up, and that house, which he felt a personal interest in, stood there with nothing on earth to protect it but sixteen lightning-rods—"Let us have peace!" I shrieked. "Put up a hundred and fifty! Put some on the kitchen! Put a dozen on the barn! Put a couple on the cow!—Put one on the cook!—scatter them all over the persecuted place till it looks like a zinc-plated, spiral-twisted, silver-mounted cane-brake! Move! Use up all the material you can get your hands on, and when you run out of lightning-rods put up ramrods, cam-rods, stair-rods, piston-rods—*anything* that will pander to your dismal appetite for artificial scenery, and bring respite to my raging brain and healing to my lacerated soul!" Wholly unmoved—further than to smile sweetly—this iron being simply turned back his wrist-bands daintily, and said he would now proceed to hump himself. "Well, all that was nearly three hours ago. It is questionable whether I am calm enough yet to write on the noble theme of political economy, but I cannot resist the desire to try, for it is the one subject that is nearest to my heart and dearest to my brain of all this world's philosophy.]

—"*economy is heaven's best boon to man.*" When the loose but gifted Byron lay in his Venetian exile he observed that, if it could be granted him to go back and live his misspent life over again, he would give his lucid and unintoxicated intervals to the composition, not of frivolous rhymes, but of essays upon political economy. Washington loved this exquisite science; such names as Baker, Beckwith, Judson, Smith, are imperishably linked with it; and even imperial Homer, in the ninth book of the Iliad, has said:

> Fiat justitia, ruat cœlum,
> Post mortem unum, ante bellum,
> Hic jacet hoc, ex-parte res,
> Politicum e-conomico est.

The grandeur of these conceptions of the old poet, together with the felicity of the wording which clothes them, and the sublimity of the imagery whereby they are illustrated, have singled out that stanza, and made it more celebrated than any that ever—

["Now, not a word out of you—not a single word. Just state your bill and relapse into impenetrable silence for ever and ever on these premises. Nine hundred dollars? Is that all? This check for the amount will be honored at any respectable bank in America. What is that multitude of people gathered in the street for? How?—'looking at the lightning-rods!' Bless my life, did they never see any lightning-rods before? Never saw 'such a stack of them on one establishment,' did I understand you to say? I will step down and critically observe this popular ebullition of ignorance."]

THREE DAYS LATER.—We are all about worn out. For four-and-twenty hours our bristling premises were the talk and wonder of the town. The theaters languished, for their happiest scenic inventions were tame and commonplace compared with my lightning-rods. Our street was blocked night and day with spectators, and among them were many who came from the country to see. It was a blessed relief on the second day when a thunderstorm came up and the lightning began to "go for" my house, as the historian Josephus quaintly phrases it. It cleared the galleries, so to speak. In five minutes there was not a spectator within half a mile of my place; but all the high houses about that distance away were full, windows, roof, and all. And well they might be, for all the falling stars and Fourth-of-July fireworks of a generation, put together and rained down simultaneously out of heaven in one brilliant shower upon one helpless roof, would not have any advantage of the pyrotechnic display that was making my house so magnificently conspicuous in the general gloom of the storm. By actual count, the lightning struck at my establishment seven hundred and sixty-four times in forty minutes, but tripped on one of those faithful rods every time, and slid down the spiral-twist and shot into the earth before it probably had time to be surprised at the way the thing was done. And through all that bombardment only one patch of slates was ripped up, and that was because, for a single instant, the rods in the vicinity were transporting all the lightning they could possibly accommodate. Well, nothing was ever seen like it since the world began. For one whole day and night not a member of my family stuck his head out of the window but he got the hair snatched off it as smooth as a billiard-ball; and, if the reader will believe me, not one of us ever dreamt of stirring abroad. But at last the awful siege came to an end—because there was absolutely no more electricity left in the clouds above us within grappling distance of my insatiable rods. Then I sallied forth, and gathered daring workmen together, and not a bite or a nap did we take till the premises were utterly stripped of all their terrific armament except just three rods on the house, one on the kitchen, and one on the barn—and, behold, these remain there even unto this day. And then, and not till then, the people ventured to use our street again. I will remark here, in passing, that during that fearful time I did not continue my essay upon political economy. I am not even yet settled enough in nerve and brain to resume it.

To Whom It May Concern.—Parties having need of three thousand two hundred and eleven feet of best quality zinc-plated spiral-twist lightning-rod stuff, and sixteen hundred and thirty-one silver-tipped points, all in tolerable repair (and, although much worn by use, still equal to any ordinary emergency), can hear of a bargain by addressing the publisher.

MARK TWAIN

"My Watch"

An Instructive Little Tale

My beautiful new watch had run eighteen months without losing or gaining, and without breaking any part of its machinery or stopping. I had come to believe it infallible in its judgments about the time of day, and to consider its constitution and its anatomy imperishable. But at last, one night, I let it run down. I grieved about it as if it were a recognized messenger and forerunner of calamity. But by and by I cheered up, set the watch by guess, and commanded my bodings and superstitions to depart. Next day I stepped into the chief jeweler's to set it by the exact time, and the head of the establishment took it out of my hand and proceeded to set it for me. Then he said, "She is four minutes slow—regulator wants pushing up." I tried to stop him—tried to make him understand that the watch kept perfect time. But no; all this human cabbage could see was that the watch was four minutes slow, and the regulator *must* be pushed up a little; and so, while I danced around him in anguish, and implored him to let the watch alone, he calmly and cruelly did the shameful deed. My watch began to gain. It gained faster and faster day by day. Within the week it sickened to a raging fever, and its pulse went up to a hundred and fifty in the shade. At the end of two months it had left all the timepieces of the town far in the rear, and was a fraction over thirteen days ahead of the almanac. It was away into November enjoying the snow, while the October leaves were still turning. It hurried up house rent, bills payable, and such things, in such a ruinous way that I could not abide it. I took it to the watchmaker to be regulated. He asked me if I had ever had it repaired. I said no, it had never needed any repairing. He looked a look of vicious happiness and eagerly pried the watch open, and then put a small dice-box into his eye and peered into its machinery. He said it wanted cleaning and oiling, besides regulating—come in a week. After being cleaned and oiled, and regulated, my watch slowed down to that degree that it ticked like a tolling bell. I began to be left by trains, I failed all appointments, I got to missing my dinner; my watch strung out three days' grace to four and let me go to protest; I gradually drifted back into yesterday, then day before, then into last week, and by and by the comprehension came upon me that all solitary and alone I was lingering along in week before last, and the world was out of sight. I seemed to detect in myself a sort of sneaking fellow-feeling for the mummy in the museum, and a desire to swap news with him. I went to a watchmaker again. He took the watch all to pieces while I waited, and then said the barrel was "swelled." He said he could reduce it in three days. After this the watch *averaged* well, but nothing more. For half a day it would go like the very mischief, and keep up such a barking and wheezing and whooping and sneezing and snorting, that I could not hear myself think for the disturbance; and as long as it held out there was not a watch in the land that stood any chance against it. But the rest of the day it would keep on slowing down and fooling along until all the clocks it had left behind caught up again. So at last, at the end of twenty-four hours, it would trot up to the judges' stand all right and just in time. It would show a fair and square average, and no man could say it had done more or less than its duty. But a correct average is only a mild virtue in a watch, and I took this instrument to another watchmaker. He said the king-bolt was broken. I said I was glad it was nothing more serious. To tell the plain truth, I had no idea what the king-bolt was, but I did not choose to appear ignorant to a stranger. He repaired the king-bolt, but what the watch gained in one way it lost in another. It would run awhile and then stop awhile, and then run awhile again, and so on, using its own discretion about the intervals. And every time it went off it kicked back like a musket. I padded my breast for a few days, but finally took the watch to another watchmaker. He picked it all to pieces, and turned the ruin over and over under his glass; and then he said there appeared to be something the matter with the hair-trigger. He fixed it, and gave it a fresh start. It did well now, except that always at ten minutes to ten the hands would shut together like a pair of scissors, and from that time forth they would travel together. The oldest man in the world could not make head or tail of the time of day by such a watch, and so I went again to have the thing repaired. This person said that the crystal had got bent, and that the mainspring was not straight. He also remarked that part of the works needed half-soiling. He made these things all right, and then my timepiece performed unexceptionably, save that now and then, after working along quietly for nearly eight hours, everything inside would let go all of a sudden and begin to buzz like a bee, and the hands would straightway begin to spin round and round so fast that their individuality was lost completely, and they simply seemed a delicate spider's web over the face of the watch. She would reel off the next twenty-four hours in six or seven minutes, and then stop with a bang. I went with a heavy heart to one more watchmaker, and looked on while he took her to pieces. Then I prepared to cross-question him rigidly, for this thing was getting serious. The watch had cost two hundred dollars originally, and I seemed to have paid out two or three thousand for repairs. While I waited and looked on I presently recognized in this watchmaker an old acquaintance—a steamboat engineer of other days, and not a good engineer, either. He examined all the parts carefully, just as the other watchmakers had done, and then delivered his verdict with the same confidence of manner.

He said:

"She makes too much steam—you want to hang the monkey-wrench on the safety-valve!"

I brained him on the spot, and had him buried at my own expense.

My uncle William (now deceased, alas!) used to say that a good horse was a good horse until it had run away once, and that a good watch was a good watch until the repairers got a chance at it. And he used to wonder what became of all the unsuccessful tinkers, and gunsmiths, and shoemakers, and engineers, and blacksmiths; but nobody could ever tell him.

WILLIAM K. ZINSSER

"A Little Flight Music"

Good morning, ladies and gentlemen. This is Captain Smathers welcoming you aboard your Peerless Airlines DC-80 Jetfloater flight 902 to Los Angeles. Our movie today will be the adult Biblical epic, "The Passionate Legions," in CineMagic x80, starring Charlton Lancaster and Sophia Lollobrigida and featuring Walter Brennan as the Emperor Diocletian. Your air hostess, Miss Smiley, will start the movie as soon as the aircraft is aloft and the "No Smoking" sign is off. We estimate that the picture will run four hours and eleven minutes, with an intermission after the burning of Smyrna, at which time we will land at Omaha for refueling and popcorn. Passengers disembarking at Omaha may ask Miss Smiley for a synopsis of the remainder of the film, or write directly to Epic Pictures, Aviation Division, Hollywood 33. We expect to be cruising at an altitude of 18,000 feet, but the cabin is pressurized starting at three feet, so you should experience no discomfort. Our air speed will be approximately 300 miles per hour and our ground speed will be 200 miles per hour. This discrepancy, caused by the fact that the earth is round and the air is flat, is fully explained in the informative booklet, "You and Your Flight!," which will be found in the pocket directly ahead of you, next to the airsickness bag, which you may want to use during the scene when ten Christian martyrs are mangled by tigers in the arena at Antioch. This scene should begin shortly after we cross the Mississippi River at Moline and will conclude ten minutes after Cedar Rapids. I will be pointing out to you certain interesting sights along the way. Meanwhile, Miss Smiley and the rest of your Jetfloater crew join me in hoping that you enjoy the movie. We'll be taking off in just a minute now, as soon as we get clearance from the tower. There are only twenty-three planes stacked up over the field waiting to land, and right after that we'll be off. By the way, that roaring you hear under the left wing is nothing to worry about. We had a little trouble with the automatic desludg-ifier a while ago, and that noise is simply the cleaning compound doing its job. . . . Good morning, ladies and gentlemen, this is your air hostess, Miss Smiley. I'm sorry we were so long in getting clearance. You may unfasten your seat belts now and stop observing the "No Smoking" sign. In a minute Miss Mirth and I will serve you cocktails and start the movie projector. If there is anything that you do not understand about the movie, please do not hesitate to ask us. Simply press the button next to the reading light except on seats 9, 17, 24, 36, 48, 59, 71, 86 and 101, which are the emergency escape doors. Kindly do not leave by these doors while the movie is in progress. . . . *Oh, Smartacus, thank God you've come! The Roman columns are marching toward Byblos at this very moment. What chance has a poor slave girl like me got against such Barbarian swine? . . . Never fear, my pretty little Flolita. Take these two thousand piastres and run to Damascus over the Baalbek road. Go to a man called Paul in a street called straight and tell him I will join you there as soon as the moon comes over Mountolive. Tell him . . .* Hello again, ladies and gentlemen, this is Captain Smathers. If the screen is a bit wiggly, we're encountering a little weather, but we should be out of it in another twenty minutes, I hope in time for the boiling oil scene. That girl, by the way, is Sophia Lollobrigida. You'll see when the screen is clearer. . . . *Say, you're a tasty little dish of figs, aren't you? What's a looker like you doing all alone on the road to Damascus? Notice how easily my fingers press into your pretty white flesh. . . . Leave me be, you heathen beast! When Smartacus hears about this, he'll squash you like the foul insect you are! . . . Aha! I've been trying to trap Smartacus for three long years.*

With you as bait he's sure to . . . Ladies and gentlemen, Federal regulations require that when flying over land we demonstrate this life preserver, which you will find under your seat. As you see, it is easy to operate. Simply pull the red toggle knob downward with a sharp thrust, like this, and if it fails to open, simply tug the green counterloop sideways with a revolving motion, like this, which activates the flare dispatcher, the flashlight, the whistle and the zipper. One precaution: do not effectuate these steps while you are still inside the aircraft as that will markedly hamper your escape. Thank you. . . . *But Paul, how can we warn Smartacus in time? . . . Tut, tut, my child, you must have faith. Was it not said in Galilee that the wicked would fall like wheat? Besides, I know a certain pharmacist in Aleppo who . . .* Say, folks, in just a minute you're going to get a dandy view of Sandusky, Ohio, out the left window. We don't often see it as clear. Sandusky is known for its jute mills and crampon factories. You can just see them now beyond that bend in Route 37A off to the left. . . . *Begging your pardon, Emperor, but why should we worry about a little handful of religious nuts? . . . You're young, my boy. Maybe when you get a little older you'll see that faith can be a mighty potent weapon. . . . All I know, Emperor, is if you'll give me a hundred men and ten lions I'll clean those religiosos out fast. That's what your Uncle Caligula would have done. . . . Hmmm, perhaps it's worth a try. . . .* Ladies and gentlemen, we've just heard that Omaha is closed in. They're having a bit of weather down there. Hurricane Zula: got up from Shreveport faster than anyone expected. We're going to put back to Bermuda, but don't worry, we won't interrupt the movie, and if it ends before we get down, we've got another movie aboard, Jerry Waldo's super-adult drama for adults only, "We Were Adulterers!" . . . *But Paul, how did you know the Emperor's lions wouldn't harm us? It was a miracle like how they turned on Diocletian's mercenaries instead. . . . My child, things happen that man in his vanity can never fathom. How can I make you understand? Perhaps if I recall an event that took place long ago beside a date palm in Jerusalem. I was sitting . . .* Ladies and gentlemen, this is Miss Smiley. During this flashback, which isn't very interesting, Miss Mirth and I are going to serve you your Jetfloater dinner, prepared for your eating pleasure in our Jetfloater kitchens in Pocatello Falls, Idaho. Miss Mirth and I regret that we cannot serve you your dinner and keep the movie in focus at the same time, especially during the electrical storm that we are about to pass through. But as soon as your Jetfloater dinner is over we will pick up with the siege of Ephesus, which was filmed with a cast of thousands on location outside Ephesus, Illinois, with the full cooperation of the Illinois government. Meanwhile, please fasten your seat belts again. We *do* hope you are enjoying your movie and your flight.

ROBERT BENCHLEY

"Uncle Edith's Ghost Story"

"Tell us a ghost story, Uncle Edith," cried all the children late Christmas afternoon when everyone was cross and sweaty.

"Very well, then," said Uncle Edith, "it isn't much of a ghost story, but you will take it—and like it," he added, cheerfully. "And if I hear any whispering while it is going on, I will seize the luckless offender and baste him one.

"Well, to begin, my father was a poor wood-chopper, and we lived in a charcoal-burner's hut in the middle of a large, dark forest."

"That is the beginning of a fairy story," cried little Dolly, a fat, disagreeable child who never should have been born, "and what we wanted was a *ghost* story."

"To be sure," cried Uncle Edith, "what a stupid old woopid I was. The ghost story begins as follows:

"It was late in November when my friend Warrington came up to me in the club one night and said: 'Craige, old man, I want you to come down to my place in Whoopshire for the week-end. There is greffle shooting to be done and grouse no end. What do you say?'

"I had been working hard that week, and the prospect pleased. And so it was that the 3:40 out of Charing Cross found Warrington and me on our way into Whoopshire, loaded down with guns, plenty of flints, and two of the most beautiful snootfuls every accumulated in Merrie England.

"It was getting dark when we reached Breeming Downs, where Warrington's place was, and as we drove up the shadowy path to the door, I felt Warrington's hand on my arm.

"'Cut that out!' I ordered peremptorily. 'What is this I'm getting into?'

"'Sh-h-h!' he replied, and his grip tightened. With one sock I knocked him clean across the seat. There are some things I simply will not stand for.

"He gathered himself together and spoke. 'I'm sorry,' he said. 'I was a bit unnerved. You see, there is a shadow against the pane in the guest room window.'

" 'Well, what of it?' I asked. It was my turn to look astonished.

"Warrington lowered his voice. 'Whenever there is a shadow against the windowpane as I drive up with a guest, that guest is found dead in bed the next morning—dead from fright,' he added, significantly.

"I looked up at the window toward which he was pointing. There, silhouetted against the glass, was the shadow of a gigantic man. I say 'a man,' but it was more the figure of a large weasel except for a fringe of dark-red clappers that it wore suspended from its beak."

"How do you know they were dark red," asked little Tom-Tit, "if it was the shadow you saw?"

"You shut your face," replied Uncle Edith. "I could hardly control my astonishment at the sight of this thing, it was so astonishing. 'That is in my room?' I asked Warrington.

" 'Yes,' he replied, 'I am afraid that it is.'

"I said nothing, but got out of the automobile and collected my bags. 'Come on,' I announced cheerfully, 'I'm going up and beard Mr. Ghost in his den.'

"So up the dark, winding stairway we went into the resounding corridors of the old seventeenth-century house, pausing only when we came to the door which Warrington indicated as being the door to my room. I knocked.

"There was a piercing scream from within as we pushed the door open. But when we entered, we found the room empty. We searched high and low, but could find no sign of the man with the shadow. Neither could we discover the source of the terrible scream, although the echo of it was still ringing in our ears.

" 'I guess it was nothing,' said Warrington, cheerfully. 'Perhaps the wind in the trees,' he added.

" 'But the shadow on the pane?' I asked.

"He pointed to a fancily carved piece of guest soap on the washstand. 'The light was behind that,' he said, 'and from outside it looked like a man.'

" 'To be sure,' I said, but I could see that Warrington was as white as a sheet.

" 'Is there anything that you need?' he asked. 'Breakfast is at nine—if you're lucky,' he added, jokingly.

" 'I think that I have everything,' I said. 'I will do a little reading before going to sleep, and perhaps count my laundry . . . But stay,' I called him back, 'you might leave that revolver which I see sticking out of your hip pocket. I may need it more than you will.'

"He slapped me on the back and handed me the revolver as I had asked. 'Don't blow into the barrel,' he giggled, nervously.

" 'How many people have died of fright in this room?' I asked, turning over the leaves of a copy of *Town and Country*.

" 'Seven,' he replied. 'Four men and three women.'

" 'When was the last one here?'

" 'Last night,' he said.

" 'I wonder if I might have a glass of hot water with my breakfast,' I said. 'It warms your stomach.'

" 'Doesn't it though?' he agreed, and was gone.

"Very carefully I unpacked my bag and got into bed. I placed the revolver on the table by my pillow. Then I began reading.

"Suddenly the door to the closet at the farther end of the room opened slowly. It was in the shadows and so I could not make out whether there was a figure or not. But nothing appeared. The door shut again, however, and I could hear footfalls coming across the soft carpet toward my bed. A chair which lay between me and the closet was upset as if by an unseen shin, and, simultaneously, the window was slammed shut and the shade pulled down. I looked, and there, against the shade, as if thrown from the *outside,* was the same shadow that we had seen as we came up the drive that afternoon."

"I have to go to the bathroom," said little Roger, aged six, at this point.

"Well, go ahead," said Uncle Edith. "You know where it is."

"I don't want to go alone," whined Roger.

"Go with Roger, Arthur," commanded Uncle Edith, "and bring me a glass of water when you come back."

"And whatever was this horrible thing that was in your room, Uncle Edith?" asked the rest of the children in unison when Roger and Arthur had left the room.

"I can't tell you that," replied Uncle Edith, "for I packed my bag and got the 9:40 back to town."

"That is the lousiest ghost story I have ever heard," said Peterkin.

And they all agreed with him.

NOTES ON THE CONTRIBUTORS

GEORGE ADE (1866–1944) was born in Kentland, Indiana. From 1887 to 1900 he was engaged in newspaper work, most notably as a contributor to the *Chicago Record* from 1890–1900. He wrote the books *Fables in Slang, Breaking into Society, Knocking the Neighbors, Single Blessedness,* and *The Old-Time Saloon* and the plays *The Sultan of Sulu, The Country Chairman, The College Widow,* and *Father and the Boys.*

FRED ALLEN (1894–1956) was born in Cambridge, Massachusetts. His introduction to show business came in the 1920s, when he first performed on Broadway. It was not until 1932 that he made his way to radio, quickly becoming one of the best-known radio comedians in the country. In 1935 he made his debut in film with *Thanks a Million.* He was also in the movies *Sally, Irene and Mary* and *Love Thy Neighbor.*

WOODY ALLEN (1935–) was born Allen Konigsberg in New York. Allen began his career writing television comedy for Sid Caesar and went on to great success as an actor, a filmmaker, and an author. His films include *Manhattan, Hannah and Her Sisters,* and *Annie Hall;* which won the Academy Award for Best Picture of 1977. His books include *Getting Even* and *Without Feathers.*

ROGER ANGELL (1920–) was born in New York. He worked at *Magazine X* as an editor and writer, then moved to *Holiday* magazine as a senior editor, before landing a job at *The New Yorker,* where he has served as a fiction editor and a general contributor to the present. His works include *The Stone Arbor, A*

Day in the Life of Roger Angell, The Summer Game, Five Seasons, Late Innings, and *Once More around the Park.*

MICHAEL ARLEN (1930–), a London native, moved to the United States as a child. He has worked as a reporter for *Life* magazine and a television critic for *The New Yorker.* He is the author of *Exiles, Living-Room War, Passage to Ararat, The Camera Age,* and *Say Goodbye to Sam.*

RUSSELL BAKER (1925–) was born in Virginia and grew up in Belleville, New Jersey, and Baltimore, Maryland. After graduating from Johns Hopkins University, he worked as a police reporter for the *Baltimore Sun,* then as a rewrite man and London correspondent. He has worked for the *New York Times* since 1954 and has twice won the Pulitzer Prize.

DAVE BARRY (1947–) was born in Armonk, New York. He has written many popular humorous books, including *Babies and Other Hazards of Sex, Dave Barry Talks Back,* and *Dave Barry Slept Here.* The winner of the 1988 Pulitzer Prize for commentary, he has been on the staff of the *Miami Herald* since 1983.

DONALD BARTHELME (1931–1989) was born in Philadelphia. Barthelme was best known for his short stories, collected in *Come Back, Dr. Caligari, Unspeakable Practices, Unnatural Acts, Sadness, Forty Stories,* and *Amateurs.* He was also the author of several short novels and a collection of nonfiction pieces, *Guilty Pleasures.*

ROBERT BENCHLEY (1889–1945) was born in Worcester, Massachusetts. Benchley was a versatile humorist, author, actor, playwright, columnist, critic, and radio star, and a master of literary fun. He served as associate editor of the *New York Tribune,* managing editor of *Vanity Fair,* and dramatic editor of *The New Yorker.* His works have been collected in numerous volumes, including *Benchley beside Himself, Benchley—or Else,* and *Chips off the Old Benchley.*

THOMAS BERGER (1924–) was born in Cincinnati. He is the author of many novels, some of the best known being *Crazy in Berlin, Little Big Man,* and *Vital Parts,* which is excerpted in this volume.

AMBROSE BIERCE (1842–1914?) was born in Meigs County, Ohio. After serving in the Civil War, he became a journalist for the *San Francisco News-Letter* and the *Sunday Examiner.* He also began writing his waspish, witty, and very popular *Devil's Dictionary* and short stories, often about the horrors of war and the supernatural. In 1913 he disappeared into Mexico to report on the revolution and is thought to have died there the next year.

ROY BLOUNT, JR. (1941–), was born in Indianapolis and raised in Georgia. He is a contributing editor to the *Atlantic* and *Spy* and the author of eleven books, including *One Fell Soup, Crackers, First Hubby, Soupsongs,* and *What Men Don't Tell Women.*

ERMA BOMBECK (1927–) is a Dayton, Ohio, native, and a columnist for the Universal Press Syndicate. She has been a contributing editor to *Good House-keeping* and has written many best sellers, including *If Life Is a Bowl of Cherries, What Am I Doing in the Pits?* and *When You Look Like Your Passport Photo, It's Time to Go Home.*

ART BUCHWALD (1925–), syndicated humor columnist, ran away from home at seventeen and joined the Marines. In 1949 he settled in France, where he wrote a successful trial column for the *New York Herald Tribune* called "Paris after Dark." In 1952 the *Tribune* introduced him to an American audience with a new column called "Europe's Lighter Side." Since 1950 his material has been published in a series of collections, among them *The Brave Coward, I Chose Capital Punishment, Have I Ever Lied to You?, The Buchwald Stops Here,* and *While Reagan Slept.*

CLARENCE DAY (1874–1935) was an essayist best known for his autobiographical works *God and My Father, Life with Father,* and *Father and I.* In 1939 *Life with Father* was dramatized and began the longest continuous run of any American play. His other works include *The Crow's Nest* and *Thoughts without Words.*

PETER DEVRIES (1910–) was born in Chicago. He was on the editorial staff of *The New Yorker* for over forty years and is the author of several books, among which are *Reuben, Reuben, The Vale of Laughter,* and *Peckham's Marbles.*

FINLEY PETER DUNNE (1867–1936), a Chicago native, was a reporter for the *Chicago Herald* and editor of the *New York Morning Telegram.* Dunne created the character Mr. Dooley, which appeared in a syndicated feature in several hundred papers from 1893 to 1935.

BARBARA EHRENREICH (1941–) was born in Butte, Montana. She is a writer, lecturer, contributing editor to *Mother Jones* and *Ms. Magazine,* and author of many books, including *The Worst Years of Our Lives.*

STANLEY ELKIN (1930–) was born in New York. He is an author and professor of American literature at Washington University. His work has appeared in *Best American Short Stories* and *Best American Essays.* He is also the author of several full-length books, among them *The MacGuffin* and *Pieces of Soap.*

RALPH ELLISON (1914–) was born in Oklahoma City. He is the author of the classic novel, *Invisible Man*, along with many short stories and essays.

BOB ELLIOTT (1923–) and RAY GOULDING (1922–1990) were born in Massachusetts and met while working as broadcasters for Boston's WHDH. Their humorous rapport soon earned them their own show, full of offbeat humor and gentle satire, and they remained a fixture on radio in Boston and New York for the next thirty years. Their work is collected in *Write If You Get Work* and *From Approximately Coast to Coast—It's the Bob and Ray Show*, among others.

NORA EPHRON (1941–) is a native New Yorker. She has written for the *New York Post, Esquire,* and *New York* magazine and has published several books, including *Crazy Salad, Scribble, Scribble,* and *Heartburn*. She also wrote the screenplays for *Silkwood* and *When Harry Met Sally*.

EUGENE FIELD (1850–1895), poet and journalist, was born in St. Louis. He was on the staff of the *St. Joseph Gazette,* the *St. Louis Journal,* the *Kansas City Times,* the *Denver Tribune,* and the *Chicago Morning News,* later renamed the *Record,* where most of his work appeared in the form of whimsical narratives, children's verse, wit and humor. He is perhaps best known for his children's verses *"Wynken, Blynken, and Nod"* and *"Little Boy Blue."* His other works include *A Little Book of Western Verse, A Little Book of Profitable Tales, With Trumpets and Drums,* and *A Tribune Primer 1882.*

FANNIE FLAGG (1944–) began writing and producing television specials at the age of nineteen. She has appeared in over five hundred TV shows, as well as numerous motion pictures and stage productions. She is the author of three novels, including *Fried Green Tomatoes at the Whistle Stop Cafe.*

BENJAMIN FRANKLIN (1706–1790), journalist, printer, promoter, inventor, diplomat, and statesman, was the eldest of the United States' Founding Fathers. He helped draft the Declaration of Independence and wrote, among other works, *Poor Richard's Almanack* and *The Autobiography of Benjamin Franklin.*

BRUCE JAY FRIEDMAN (1930–) is a novelist, short story writer, and playwright. His books include *About Harry Towns, A Mother's Kisses,* and *Let's Hear It for a Beautiful Guy.* He also wrote the screenplay for *Stir Crazy* and coauthored the movie *Splash!*

FRANK GANNON (1952–) was born in Camden, New Jersey. He is a regular contributor to *The New Yorker, GQ, Harper's,* and the *Atlantic* and the author of *Yo, Poe* and *Vanna Karenina.*

WILLIAM GEIST (1945–) has been a columnist for the *New York Times* and the *Chicago Tribune,* writing on life in the suburbs. He has published the books *City Slickers, Little League Confidential,* and *Toward a Safe and Sane Halloween.*

VERONICA GENG (1941–) has worked as an editor at *The New Yorker* and is the author of two books, *Partners* and *Love Trouble Is My Business.*

BRET HARTE (1836–1902), the most western of writers, was originally an easterner, from Albany, New York. At eighteen he went to California and became wealthy and famous with his short stories of California mining life. He was a friend and associate of Mark Twain.

JOSEPH HELLER (1923–) was born in Brooklyn and studied at New York University and Columbia. He has worked at several magazines, among them *Time, Look,* and *McCall's.* He is the author of many works of fiction, nonfiction, and plays, and some of his better-known works include the novels *Catch-22, Something Happened, Good as Gold,* and *God Knows,* the play *We Bombed in New Haven,* and the nonfiction books *No Laughing Matter* and *Picture This.*

O. HENRY (1862–1910) was the pseudonym for William Sydney Porter, born in North Carolina. He was indicted for embezzlement in 1896 and fled to Honduras. Upon his return to Austin, Texas, to visit his dying wife, he was arrested and jailed for three years, during which time he began to write the brief, sentimental stories which made him famous.

L. RUST HILLS (1924–) was born in Brooklyn and now lives in Key West. He has been the fiction editor for *Esquire* and the *Saturday Evening Post* and has written *How to Do Things Right* and *How to Be Good,* among other books.

CHESTER HIMES (1909–1984) was born in Missouri and began writing while in prison for jewel theft. He had published just short of twenty novels before his death, including *Cotton Comes to Harlem, The Crazy Kill,* and *The Heat's On.*

ARTHUR HOPPE (1925–) was born in Honolulu. He served as a reporter for the *San Francisco Chronicle* from 1949 to 1959 and as a columnist from 1960 to the present. He has also been a contributing editor to *The New Yorker, Harper's,* the *Nation,* and *Yachting.* His works include *The Love Everybody Crusade, Dreamboat,* and *The Perfect Solution to Absolutely Everything.*

FRANK MCKINNEY (''KIN'') HUBBARD (1868–1930) was born in Bellefontaine, Ohio. His rural philosophical character Abe Martin appeared as a syndicated feature in over three hundred papers and in numerous collections.

LANGSTON HUGHES (1902–1967), one of the leaders of the Harlem Renaissance, was born in Joplin, Missouri. Hughes was a successful humorist, writing five volumes of penetrating satirical sketches featuring Jesse B. Semple, known as Simple. He was also a poet, novelist, playwright, and historian of black lives.

ZORA NEALE HURSTON (1891–1960) was born in Florida. She graduated from Howard University in 1924, earned a Litt.D. with honors from Barnard College in 1928. Her career was spent in residence at Columbia from 1928 to 1932 and then in Haiti and the British West Indies from 1936 to 1938. She was also a scriptwriter for Paramount Pictures. Her works include *Jonah's Gourd Vine, Mules and Men, Their Eyes Were Watching God,* and *Dust Tracks on a Road.*

WASHINGTON IRVING (1783–1859) was born in New York. He studied law and was one of the leading figures in the group that published *Salmagundi*—a series of whimsical essays in which the term "Gotham" was first applied to New York City. He is best known for his works "The Legend of Sleepy Hollow" and "Rip Van Winkle," and some of his other writings include *Bracebridge Hall,* a three-volume history of Christopher Columbus, and *Life of George Washington.*

MOLLY IVINS (1944–) is a columnist with the *Fort Worth Star Telegram,* and before that worked for the now-defunct *Dallas Times Herald.* A frequent contributor to major newspapers, she is the author of *Molly Ivins Can't Say That, Can She?* and the forthcoming *Nothing but Good Times Ahead.*

NUNNALLY JOHNSON (1897–1977) was born in Columbus, Georgia, and was a journalist and short story writer before he began writing, producing, and directing movies in the early 1930s. He wrote some of Hollywood's most memorable films, including *The Grapes of Wrath, How to Marry a Millionaire,* and *The Three Faces of Eve.*

GARRISON KEILLOR (1942–) is an Anoka, Minnesota, native. Keillor has found great popularity as the creator of the radio shows "A Prairie Home Companion" and "Garrison Keillor's Radio Company." He is also the author of several books, including *Lake Wobegon Days* and *WLT: A Radio Romance,* and is a contributor to magazines such as *The New Yorker* and *Harper's.*

LARRY L. KING (1929–) was born in Putnam, Texas. He is an actor and playwright and author of many books and plays, including *The Best Little Whorehouse in Texas.*

RING LARDNER (1885–1933) was born Ringgold Wilmer Lardner in Niles, Michigan. Lardner was a newspaper columnist and sportswriter in St. Louis, Boston, and Chicago before he began writing fiction. He was the author of two successful plays and many collections, including *How to Write Short Stories,* which established his reputation as a biting satirist, and *You Know Me Al.*

FRAN LEBOWITZ (1950–) was born in Morristown, New Jersey. At eighteen she moved to New York and quickly established herself as a writer of humor, working for magazines such as *Changes, Interview,* and *Mademoiselle.* The publication of *Metropolitan Life* brought her national attention, and her book *Social Studies* earned her the title "the headmistress of wit."

JOHN LEO (1935–) joined *U.S. News & World Reports* as a senior writer in 1988 and is now a contributing editor. He was a reporter for the *New York Times* from 1967 to 1969, then worked at *Time* magazine for fourteen years, first as an associate editor and later as a senior writer. He has also held positions at the *Village Voice* and *Commonweal.*

A. J. LIEBLING (1904–1963) was born in New York City. A reporter, war correspondent, satirist, and gourmand, Liebling wrote for *The New Yorker* and wrote many books, profiles, and book reviews.

ABRAHAM LINCOLN (1809–1865), the sixteenth president of the United States, was born in Hardin County, Kentucky. Despite lack of formal schooling, he became a prominent Illinois lawyer. In 1858 he was nominated for U.S. Senate, and though he was defeated, he went on to become the Republican presidential nominee in 1860. With a poet's gift for language, he produced two of the most enduring monuments of American letters in the Gettysburg Address and the Second Inaugural. Five days after the Civil War ended in 1865 Lincoln was shot and killed by John Wilkes Booth.

DAVID ROSS LOCKE (1833–1888) was born in New York. An itinerant printer who later went into the newspaper business, he eventually became the editor and owner of the *Toledo Blade.* He was the author of a series of satirical newspaper columns written by the fictitious Petroleum V. Nasby, a character noted for his blatant bigotry.

ANITA LOOS (1893–1981), born in Sisson, California, was a prolific writer, best known for her novel *Gentlemen Prefer Blondes.* She also wrote numerous projects for stage and screen and a humor column for the *New York Evening Telegram.*

DON MARQUIS (1878–1937), journalist and humorist, was born in Walnut, Illinois. His career included editing *Uncle Remus* magazine and working at the *New York Sun*. His column at the *Sun* introduced mehitabel the cat and archy the cockroach. Marquis was also a staff member of the *New York Tribune*. His works include *The Old Soak, archy and mehitabel*, and *archy does his part*.

GROUCHO MARX (1895–1977) was born Julius Henry Marx in New York City. He performed in vaudeville and in Hollywood with his three brothers and made such classic comedies as *Animal Crackers, Duck Soup,* and *The Coconuts*. He went on to be the quizmaster for television's "You Bet Your Life" and wrote the books *Many Happy Returns, The Groucho Letters,* and *Memoirs of a Mangy Lover*.

THOMAS MEEHAN (1932–) was born in Ossining, New York. He has written for *The New Yorker, Esquire,* and the *Saturday Evening Post* and is the author of *Yma, Ava; Yma, Abba; Yma, Oona; Yma, Ida; Yma, Aga . . . and Others*. He wrote the book for the Broadway musical *Annie*.

H. L. MENCKEN (1880–1956), a Baltimore native, wrote for the *Baltimore Sun* for many years. He was a reporter, columnist, editor, and scholar of the American language. As a magazine editor and literary critic he was tremendously influential and popular during the first part of this century. Some of his best-known books are *Newspaper Days, In Defense of Women, Prejudices,* and *The American Language* in three volumes.

JOSEPH MITCHELL (1908–) was born in Fairmount, North Carolina. He was a reporter for the *New York World Telegram* and a writer for *The New Yorker*. Among his books are *My Ears Are Bent, McSorley's Wonderful Saloon, Old Mr. Flood, The Bottom of the Harbor,* and *Up in the Old Hotel*.

MICHAEL O'DONOGHUE (1940–) was a founder and editor of the *National Lampoon* magazine, and a head writer for the first three years of "Saturday Night Live." He edited the *National Lampoon Encyclopedia of Humor* and co-wrote *Socks Goes to Washington*, with J. C. Suarez.

P. J. O'ROURKE (1947–) is a Toledo, Ohio, native. He is a former editor of *National Lampoon* magazine and is presently foreign affairs desk chief of *Rolling Stone*. He has written several books, including *Modern Manners, The Bachelor Home Companion, Parliament of Whores,* and *Give War a Chance*.

S. J. PERELMAN (1904–1979), one of America's best comic writers, had a brilliant command of language and a screwball wit. He wrote for the Marx Brothers and for the Broadway theater, managed a radio show, and was a contributor to *Life, The New Yorker,* and *Holiday*.

EDGAR ALLAN POE (1809–1849) was born in Boston. He spent one term at the University of Virginia before joining the army in 1827. In 1830 and 1831 he was a student at West Point but was eventually dismissed for unruly behavior. In 1829 he published his first volume of poetry, and in 1837 he joined the staff of the *Southern Literary Messenger*. In 1839 he moved to Philadelphia, where he was an associate editor of *Burton's Gentleman's Magazine,* to which he contributed his most famous stories "The Fall of the House of Usher," "Ligeia," and "The Murders in the Rue Morgue." In 1845 *The Raven and Other Poems* was published and brought him to a period of fame. The death of his wife led to a time of despondency and poverty, during which his mental health deteriorated. His last works included "Annabel Lee," "The Bells," "Ulalume," and "For Annie."

LEO ROSTEN (1908–) was born in Lodz, now in Poland, and came to the United States at the age of eight. A humorist, a political scientist, and an economist, Rosten has written screenplays, contributed to *Harper's* and *The New Yorker,* among other magazines, and is the author of over twenty books. Some of his better-known titles include *The Joys of Yiddish, The Joys of Yinglish,* and *O K * A * P * L * A * N! My K * A * P * L * A * N!*

PHILIP ROTH (1933–), born in Newark, New Jersey, began his highly successful career with the publication of *Goodbye, Columbus, Letting Go,* and *When She Was Good.* With *Portnoy's Complaint* he received broad national fame. His later novels have included *The Breast, My Life as a Man,* and *Zuckerman Unbound.*

MIKE ROYKO (1932–) is a born-and-bred Chicago columnist. Before becoming a reporter for the *Chicago Sun Times* in 1978, he worked as a reporter for the *Chicago Northside Newspaper* and the *Chicago Daily News.* In 1984 he moved to the *Chicago Tribune.* Among his books are *Up against It, I May Be Wrong but I Doubt It,* and *Slats Grobnik and Some Other Friends.*

DAMON RUNYON (1880–1946) was a Manhattan, Kansas, native who grew up in Pueblo, Colorado. He wrote for papers in Denver and San Francisco before joining the staff of the *New York American.* He was an immensely popular short story author, writing in breezy, slangy prose ("Runyonese") about New York City, Broadway and underworld characters, and defining the idea of cynical, cool "urbanism." The Broadway musical *Guys and Dolls* was based on Runyon's short story "The Idyll of Miss Sarah Brown." His works include *Runyon à la Carte, Short Takes, Poems for Men,* and *Trials and Other Tribulations.*

JEAN SHEPHERD (1929–) was born in Chicago. He has been an actor for television and radio as well as a writer. He is the editor of *The America of George*

Ade and the author of *In God We Trust, All Others Pay Cash; Wanda Hickey's Night of Golden Memories, and Other Disasters; The Ferrari in the Bedroom*, and *The Phantom of the Open Hearth*.

DONALD OGDEN STEWART (1894–1980) was born in Columbus, Ohio, and was educated at Yale. He wrote several popular books of humor, including *A Parody Outline of History, By a Stroke of Luck, Rebound*, and *Perfect Behavior*, a send-up of Emily Post's etiquette books.

FRANK SULLIVAN (1892–1976) was born in Saratoga Springs, New York. He was a humorist and the author of *The Life and Times of Martha Hepplethwaite, Broccoli and Old Lace, In One Ear*, and *Sullivan at Bay*.

JAMES THURBER (1894–1961), born and raised in Columbus, Ohio, has been hailed as the best American humorist since Mark Twain. He joined *The New Yorker* in the late 1920s, and most of his distinctive essays, fables, and stories were created for its pages. His books include *The Years with Ross*, about the first years of *The New Yorker*, the collections *Men, Women, and Dogs* and *The Thurber Carnival*, several children's books, and a play, *The Male Animal*.

CALVIN TRILLIN (1935–) was born in Kansas City, Missouri. He is a writer for *The New Yorker*, a syndicated columnist, and the author of *Alice, Let's Eat, Uncivil Liberties, With All Disrespect, American Stories*, and *Remembering Denny*, among other books.

MARK TWAIN (1835–1910) was the pseudonym of Samuel Langhorne Clemens. Twain was a printer's apprentice, a journalist, a riverboat pilot, and, briefly, a soldier in the Civil War before making writing his primary occupation. His adventurous childhood in Hannibal, Missouri, was re-created in *The Adventures of Tom Sawyer* and *The Adventures of Huckleberry Finn*, which profoundly influenced the development of American prose style. While Twain was known as a humorist for most of his career, a series of personal losses, including bankruptcy and the deaths of his wife and two daughters, cast a permanent shadow on his later years, and his writing became somber and pessimistic.

BILL VAUGHAN (1915–1977) was born in St. Louis. He received a B.S. from Washington University and then worked for Newspapers Inc. in Springfield, Missouri, from 1936 to 1939. From 1939 to 1946 he worked as a columnist and associate editor for the *Kansas City Star*. He was also the author of *Bird Thou Never Wert* and *Sorry I Stirred It*.

ARTEMUS WARD (1834–1867) is a pseudonym for American humorist Charles Farrar Browne. Born near Waterford, Maine, Browne learned the printer's trade before working on the staff of *Vanity Fair* in New York in 1859. From 1861 to 1866 he lectured throughout the country before going on tour in England, where he died. He is the author of *Artemus Ward: His Book* and *Artemus Ward: His Travels*.

MAE WEST (1893–1980) rose to success in vaudeville and Hollywood as a mistress of sexual innuendo. She wrote much of her own material, including the Broadway play *Diamond Lil* and her autobiography, *Goodness Had Nothing to Do with It*.

E. B. WHITE (1899–1985) was born in Mount Vernon, New York. After graduating from Cornell University, he spent several years at various jobs, then joined the staff of *The New Yorker,* where he produced a steady output of satirical sketches, poems, essays, and editorials. He also wrote thirteen books of poetry and prose, including the classic children's books *Charlotte's Web, Stuart Little,* and *The Trumpet of the Swan*.

TOM WOLFE (1931–) began his career as a reporter with the *Springfield Union* in Massachusetts. From 1959 to 1962 he was the Latin American correspondent for the *Washington Post,* then went to the *New York Herald Tribune*. From 1968 to 1977 he was a contributing editor to *New York* magazine and *Esquire.* He has also been a contributing artist for *Harper's.* Among his better-known works are *The Painted Word, The Electric Kool-Aid Acid Test, The Right Stuff, The Bonfire of the Vanities,* and *The New Journalism*.

WILLIAM K. ZINSSER (1922–) was born in New York. A writer, an editor, and an educator, he earned his A.B. from Princeton, and a Litt.D. from Rollins College. He was a feature writer for the *New York Herald Tribune,* worked for *Look* and *Life* magazines and the *New York Times,* and was a faculty member at Yale University. He is the author of many books, including *Any Old Place with You, The City Dwellers, Weekend Guests, Pop Goes America, On Writing Well, Writing to Learn,* and *American Places*.

Copyright Acknowledgments

INDEX

Selection titles appearing in quotation marks are the original titles; those without quotation marks have been devised by the editor for this volume.

595

ML